the
american
democracy

the american democracy

SECOND EDITION

C. Peter Magrath
State University of New York
at Binghamton

Elmer E. Cornwell, Jr.
Brown University

Jay S. Goodman
Wheaton College

The Macmillan Company
New York

Collier-Macmillan Publishers
London

to Sandra, Caroline, and Ellen

preface

Contemporary political science and the American democracy lend themselves to a rich variety of approaches and interpretations. Although the basic pattern of this book will be familiar to users of the first edition, the revision is a fundamental one that reflects many changes. A number of new chapters have been added (and old ones either deleted or virtually rewritten), many of the case studies are new, and the entire text has been thoroughly reviewed and much of it revised and updated in response to changing events and current scholarly findings and interpretations.

Our basic objective, however, remains the same: to write an introductory-level textbook that incorporates the best of what may loosely be called the behavioral and the more traditional scholarship relevant to an understanding of government and politics in contemporary America. This book is not encyclopedic. It is intended, rather, to introduce students to the basic workings of the American democracy by presenting a blend of essential facts with analysis and interpretation. Although we have tried to stay away from editorializing and preaching, the book contains, implicitly and explicitly, judgments of value. We believe that it is meaningful to speak of "the American democracy" despite its many and often glaring imperfections. Our general assessment is favorable to the

American system of government and to the diversity and pluralism that we find manifest in American politics. Others will disagree both with some of the book's normative judgments and with certain scholarly interpretations. We believe, however, that they will find the text to be a useful and stimulating instructional tool to which teachers, no less than students, can react.

The case studies, which precede the main exposition in all but the first, second, and final chapter, require a few words of explanation. We are well aware of the limitations in the so-called case study method, and we make no claim that these case studies "tell it as it is" on the subjects, for example, of urban politics or of legislatures. What we do claim is that they will enhance the student's perception of the operation of particular aspects of American government and politics, while engaging his attention and interest in the basic subject matter covered by the chapter. Most of the cases portray the political system in action, as, for instance, in the constitutional controversy over public aid to parochial schools, the McGovern Commission reforms of the Democratic Party's presidential nominating procedures, or President Nixon's decision to intervene militarily in Cambodia. They are written with a minimum of instruction as to their meaning, and although there are references to the cases throughout the book, we have not self-consciously tried to integrate them into the more formal parts of the chapters. It is our judgment that conceptually a case study cannot serve as the illustration for the true essence, say, of the Constitution of the United States. But it can serve as a useful description of certain aspects of American constitutionalism that will engage the student's interest. At the same time, in combination with the formal exposition that follows, the case studies provide a feeling in depth for how the American democracy functions. The approach we have used leaves the instructor free to emphasize the lessons that, in his judgment, the student should derive from the case study.

There are inevitable gaps in the coverage given to certain subjects and issues; the alternative is a textbook that has the unappealing qualities of a mail-order catalog. It is our belief that instructors who wish to explore a particular problem or aspect of the political system in depth will find that the book provides a useful framework for beginning such an inquiry. A large selection of supplementary paperback books is readily available to those whose tastes and inclinations make them anxious to give special emphasis, for example, to the legislative process, the Presidency, or contemporary political issues. The suggested additional readings that follow each chapter, although necessarily selective, will also assist by providing guidance to instructor and student alike; books that are available in inexpensive paperback editions are identified with an asterisk.

As is customary and proper we assume full responsibility for the contents of this book, but we are grateful to those who have helped us in various ways. Special thanks are due to Professor Alan F. Arcuri of Stockton State College (New Jersey) for his assistance with certain parts of the second edition. We also appreciate the help of Professor Robert B. Dishman of the

University of New Hampshire. Professors Joel B. Grossman and James H. Andrews provided careful and thoughtful critiques to the original manuscript. We displayed the traditional perversity of authors by disagreeing with them at certain points, but their suggestions definitely helped us to improve the book. We have had similar constructive suggestions for the second edition from Professors Paul H. Conn, Frederick H. Hartmann, Abraham Holtzman, Duane Lockard, Michael P. Riccards, and David W. Rohde. Although these scholars bear no responsibility for the finished product, their objective professional evaluations are appreciated.

We owe a debt to Wheaton College (Massachusetts) and its former dean, Dr. Walter J. Kenworthy, for gracious assistance in the preparation of the manuscript. Mrs. Helen Durant, Mrs. Nancy Shepardson, and Mrs. Anita Teixeira typed the manuscript with professional skill. A Wheaton student, Miss Donna Garafano, helped on a number of bibliographic and research chores. In addition, Mrs. Roma Regler, a member of the executive secretarial staff of the University of Nebraska–Lincoln, provided one of the authors with special and valued help at crucial points in the work on the second edition.

The editorial and production staff of The Macmillan Company also have our thanks for their cooperation and patience. We are especially grateful to Mr. James J. Carroll, Jr., for his faith in this book and for his imaginative editorial assistance, and to Mr. George H. Carr for conscientious handling of the book's production.

Without wives, as a glance at the prefaces to most books will quickly make clear, professors could not write books; at the very least the ordeal of writing and preparation would be far worse than it is. The prefaces may exaggerate, but there is much truth in them, and this book is no different. Our wives, to whom this book is dedicated, helped in many ways, not the least of which was to live with this textbook as well as their husbands.

C. P. M.	State University of New York at Binghamton
E. E. C.	Brown University
J. S. G.	Wheaton College (Massachusetts)

contents

THE AMERICAN CONSTITUTION   67

CITIZENS AND POLITICS   103

5

PARTIES AND ELECTIONS IN A TIME OF TRANSITION 143

14 FOREIGN POLICY AND DEFENSE: THE UNITED STATES IN WORLD POLITICS 609

15 NEW ISSUES AND THE POTENTIAL OF POLITICS 651

1 the american political community

Canada and the United States:
A Tale of Two Political Cultures

It may seem strange to open a study of the American governmental system with a discussion of Canada, but that is what we propose to do. It is often said that much can be learned about a person by studying his friends and neighbors. Presumably the same is true, at least to a degree, of nations and their political systems. As a matter of fact, one of the important current trends in political-science research and writing is the study of comparative institutional systems. This interest is not merely the outgrowth of a desire to generalize and find common themes among national political systems, but stems also from a realization that the truest insights into one particular system often emerge when it is compared with others.

It is obvious that in many ways Canada is more like the United States than any other nation one might select for comparison. Both countries span a continent with all of the diversity of territory, occupation, and interest that this implies. Both are relatively "new" nations, settled by immigrants from abroad, with histories deeply rooted in the Anglo-Saxon tradition.

This range of similarity—and many other points could be added to underscore the likeness—would lead one to expect basically similar systems of government. Actually, however, Canada borrowed heavily from the British system of parliamentary and cabinet government, whereas the United States launched itself on a quite different path in 1787 and now has a presidential-congressional scheme. Accordingly, the inquiring student has available two alternative paths to pursue in any comparative study of the two countries. He can begin with surface differences in governmental systems and see whether close examination verifies the existence of the apparent differences, or whether the similarities of national context produce a degree of convergence in actual political practices. On the other hand, the student can also begin with the similarities and explore what happens when two different institutional schemes are superimposed on basically similar nations. In either case he is asking, essentially, the same sophisticated and important question: Which is more important in shaping the operation of a political system? Is it the institutional forms, or is it the context in which they operate?

If this is the basic question one wants to answer—and it is indeed basic to any comparative study of political institutions—how might one approach the task of answering it? The investigator would soon discover that it has been posed before in regard to America and Canada, directly or indirectly. General answers have been offered, based for the most part on intuitive conclusions relying on observation. But actually, a question like this cannot be answered satisfactorily, and in a sense cannot be answered at all, in general terms, for whole political systems. Apparent similarities in one area of operation may contradict impressions of decided difference in others. Thus one is soon reduced to a study of carefully chosen comparable phenomena in the two systems. How do methods for providing executive and policy leadership compare? How does the judicial role in one compare with the role courts play in the other? What can be said comparatively about the role and operation of political parties? Inquiries of this sort may well turn up similarities of actual operation reflecting similarities in the respective national communities that belie differences in institutional form. On the other hand, they may reveal that institutional differences generate differences in operation even when the contexts are similar.

Let us take, for example, the question of party operation. And let us simplify matters by looking at party operation in the one place where it is most clearly observed on a continuing basis: in the functioning of two national legislatures, those of the Congress of the United States and the Canadian Parliament. Suppose, now, that we were to assume the primacy of institutional forms—to assume, that is, that party operation will reflect above all the formal institutional setting in which it takes place. Then, based on what we know about the Mother of Parliaments in London (upon which the Canadian was modeled down to the smallest detail) and what we know about how parties operate there, we would expect to find in Ottawa parliamentary parties that are highly cohesive and disciplined, whose members almost invariably feel obliged to vote the party line.

Or suppose we take the other tack. Suppose we were to make the plausible assumption that the loose party discipline and free-wheeling behavior of members of the Congress of the United States are logically related to the kind of society they represent. Only such freedom to represent the home folks in spite of party ties, it is often said, accords with the range of diversity in a vast continental nation. Canada is also a vast continental nation with an array of divergent interests that must demand similarly flexible representation in their House of Commons. Hence, is it not likely that party cohesion will be as low in the Canadian Parliament as it is in the United States Congress?

A political scientist, Professor Allan Kornberg, interested in the comparison of Canadian with American political practices, addressed himself to precisely this question of party behavior in the respective legislatures.[1] To discover which of the above

---

[1] This discussion of the United States and Canada draws heavily on Allan Kornberg, "Caucus and Cohesion in Canadian Parliamentary Parties," *American Political Science Review,* LX (March, 1966), pp. 83–92.

hypotheses were correct, he set about the laborious task of collecting data from which he could draw firm conclusions, in the form of 165 individual interviews with members of the Canadian Parliament. The results, because the interviews were conducted on a carefully controlled basis using the same schedule of questions in each instance, could be categorized, counted, and subjected to various kinds of statistical manipulation. His analysis led to the conclusion that institutions, *not* context, seem to be the crucial variable. Canadian M.P.'s were found to support their party position to a degree far more suggestive of British than American practice.

Specifically, when asked why they supported their party's position, approximately half of the legislators replied in terms that suggested that they held the viability of their party group to be of prime importance both in general and for their own political futures. Another 14 or 15 per cent spoke in terms of the health and viability of the overall party *system*. In other words, some two thirds gave one or the other of these answers. The author comments that, if the same question had been asked of a sample of United States Congressmen, "there would have been a far smaller proportion who would have felt that the effectiveness and continued viability of their party and even the system itself required them to maintain party cohesion." [2]

We need spend time on only one of the two general reasons he advances to explain this political difference between Canada and the United States. Significantly, he does not rest his case solely on the existence in Canada of forms and institutions copied from the Mother Country. Rather, he notes that, once established, an institution tends to generate informally its own support mechanisms in the society. "These often take the form of certain norms and values which are held up as virtues and are transmitted to succeeding generations by the process of socialization." [3] That is, would be members of the Canadian Parliament, even before they are elected, have absorbed a belief that legislators ought to act "responsibly" in concert with their parties—because the survival of the system requires it.

South of the border, different values are absorbed by the fledgling Congressman. Thus, he "expects and knows others expect that he will *not* be just a party hack, that he will act independently, or else in the interest of his constituency." [4] These norms are clearly just as much a part of American political folklore as are the quite different ones of the Canadian folklore.

The foregoing discussion suggests, then, that the dichotomy with which we began —the nature of the national community versus the formal structure of the governing institutions as the key variable—is partially false. To put the point positively, these two influences on the operation of a political system blend into a closely intertwined bundle. The phrase *political folklore* used above is suggestive, although the term *political culture* is more common in contemporary political science.

The political culture of a country has slightly variant meanings, depending on the use being made of it and the taste of the user. Basically, though, it means the unique cluster of beliefs about the desirable structuring of government and the proper

[2] Ibid., p. 88.
[3] Ibid., p. 90.
[4] Ibid.

behavior of those involved in it (including its citizens); it means, too, the values shared in the national community as to what government should do and how it should do it. Thus, to refer back to the comparative discussion of party cohesion, the American and Canadian political cultures support the continued existence of the particular institutional forms through which the two countries are governed. The legislatures of both countries, through a process of socialization, instill certain values and behavior patterns in their legislators; and the legislators, as sensitive political actors, tailor their behavior to the demands of *their* political culture.

Clearly, this notion of political culture is a valuable tool for understanding both the differences between political systems and the operation of one particular system. Its overall value is that it makes us look behind the formal institutions to the patterns of belief and behavior that shape and support them. In a more basic sense, of course, these behavioral patterns are rooted in the total political community itself, which generates both the institutions and their supporting value systems. In a word, the usefulness of the notion of political culture is in explaining the uniqueness of one political system when compared with others, in spite of similarities of national context (as in our example), or in spite of similarities of institutional form, which can often be deceiving. Despite their theoretical resemblance to the British, for example, the parliamentary systems of the French Third and Fourth Republics were in practice radically different. In consequence, the primary concern of this chapter is with a portrayal of American political culture, its uniqueness, and the significance of its elements for the operation of the total political system.

Modern Governments: The Common Problems

Before considering the uniqueness of American political culture in any further detail, we must examine the broader context of modern government not only in the United States and in other democracies but also in a totalitarian system such as that of the Soviet Union. The special qualities and features of each national system must be measured against the background of the features and problems that are common to all governments in advanced industrial nations. In all such settings the political systems attempt to meet many of the same basic problems but do so within the narrower confines of each nation's peculiar way of conducting political business.

Perhaps the one overriding characteristic common to the Western democracies and shared with nondemocratic systems as well is the simple and obvious fact that all these national communities require a great deal of governing. This is so because, by definition, any technologically advanced nation is an intricate and highly interdependent socioeconomic mechanism. The various parts of such a system require a good deal of regulation and supervision if they are to intermesh in a workable manner. One need only recall descriptions of the largely self-sufficient village or individual farm of our forefathers to realize the relative simplicity of earlier periods. The pioneer farmer grew, prepared, and preserved his own food, produced his own fiber, cloth, and garments, and supplied himself with his own tools and with virtually all of the important elements of his total way of life. (It is this simple subsistence way of life that some of the current communes are attempting to recapture; the movement for organic foods and methods of gardening spring from the same desire.)

The most graphic way to pose the contrast with past days is to recall, now, the most recent power failure, transportation strike, or simple traffic jam in which one has been involved—and the intricacies and interdependencies of modern society become abundantly clear. Not only does the complex interrelatedness become evident, but the necessity of a multiplicity of governmental roles—and rules—to keep a semblance of smooth operation is equally evident. Our automotive civilization would come to an almost instant and disastrous halt if traffic regulation were suddenly to end. The regulation of transportation and communications and the governmental supervision of countless other aspects of our economic life are so essential that we take them for granted. So too is the ability of government to provide direct aid in the event of a great natural or man-made disaster, as for example, floods, droughts, economic depressions, or labor union strikes.

In all modern nations the need for such governmental intervention is automatically accepted, despite the fact that terms like *economic planning* and *socialism* are still ideological fighting words in the United States and some other countries. In fact, when policy moves in these directions, or toward the flull-fledged welfare state, the resulting further involvement of government in the life of the community is hardly more than an extension of trends already present. Similarly, the differences between the United States or the other democracies and the Soviet Union in the sheer quantity and range of government activity are differences of degree only.

All modern industrial societies, in short, have developed, along with and as a consequence of, their technological and industrial advance, a high level of dependence upon government. The institutional reflex of this obvious fact is the growth of governmental bureaucracies to their present enormous proportions. And again, the differences between the major democracies and the Soviet Union are ones of degree only.

After stressing the complex communal interdependence of modern nations, it may sound paradoxical to assert that their other outstanding common characteristic is their fragmented, pluralistic quality. Actually the paradox is more apparent than real. If one again returns in imagination to the primitive pioneer society, the very self-sufficiency of the individuals and families bespeaks a high degree of homogeneity of interest in the group at large, though not a great deal of interdependence. Or to put the point in terms the economist uses, division of labor had yet to develop to any significant degree in such a society.

In modern industrial societies, however, division of labor is the crucial organizing principle; without it such societies could not come into existence or flourish. We are interdependent, that is, because we are so far from the individual self-sufficiency of our forefathers. Most of us are in no position to supply our own needs for even the most elementary necessities. Even the drop-out or rural commune dweller of today, who is prepared to redefine his needs to eliminate most of contemporary civilization's frills, has difficulty making a total break from dependence on the greater society he has left behind. Each of us is geared to supplying one very specialized service or part of a service or commodity to a community that in turn makes available to its members tens of thousands more services and consumption items than a subsistence community could even dream about. And this situation helps to account for the pluralism. For we can assume that such a society will exhibit virtually as many different groups and interests with divergent needs and objectives as there are specialized roles in the society. In addition, of course, to these economically or functionally created diversities, there will be countless others that rest on religious, ethnic, aesthetic, class, regional, or other such lines of differentiation.

It might plausibly be assumed that this kind of pluralism is characteristic only of the great Western democracies, that a totalitarian system like the Soviet Union must be far more monolithic. In fact, and increasingly with the passing years, Soviet society has become quite diverse in its patterns of groups and interests. When the Bolsheviks won power in 1917, they inherited all of the ethnic, linguistic, cultural, and geographic diversity that had made up the polyglot empire of the Czars. Then, by their decision to turn agricultural Russia into a first-line industrial state at forced draft, they set forces in motion that inescapably increased the variegated array of groups. Industrialism *means* division of labor, an ever-multiplying division and redivision of economic and productive roles. It also means, one might note in passing, the development of classes of managerial-technical, clerical, and blue-collar workers.

From a political standpoint, pluralism means a diversity of group goals, interests, and concerns, which take the form of demands for power, position, goods, services, protection, and so on. Inevitably this cacophonous chorus of demands will be replete with overlap, conflict, and intense competition. This in turn adds a whole new dimension to the problems of governing. Not only must the political organs of a nation sort out the mounting intricacies of a technologically advanced society by manning much of its machinery, but they must also umpire the inevitable conflicts between and among its diverse groups and interests.

The role of the city manager in American local government illustrates the problem in microcosm. The manager theory when it was first advanced some half-century ago rested on the assumption that problems of city government were essentially problems of management, that they were, in brief, problems of solving the technical difficulties involved in street-paving, water supply, and garbage collection. This was a static concept. Its originators assumed that the problems changed only in degree, if at all, and never in kind. Above all, this concept ignored the essentially political aspect of government: Who, among rival claimants for limited resources, is going to get what? Managers found in practice that they had little choice but to get into the middle of the group struggle for advantage in their communities. They had to marshall support for new programs and services, negotiate compromises, mediate among rivals, all the while building and preserving their own power base. Management of things, in actual practice, often took second place to management of people and their conflicts.

By multiplying the city manager's problems a hundred or even a thousandfold, one confronts the dimensions of national political management. The government must preside over the complexities of an advanced industrial society; it must do so in a context of intense group competition and an unbelievably complicated divergence and incompatibility of interests and goals. Nor is a government always, or even often, cast in the role of an authoritative neutral arbitrator. Quite the contrary, government is typically a participant in the struggle. Like the city manager, the President or the head of an administrative agency must guard his own flanks and rear, conserve his store of power and support, and at the same time negotiate the policy agreements that alone enable the wider society to function.

Once again, the Soviet situation is apparently not unlike the American. One of the themes of Nikita Khrushchev's tenure in power (1957 to 1964) seemed to be a sharp change in policy aimed at supplying more consumer goods. Unquestionably this represented a response to felt pressures from key consumer groups that the regime felt it could no longer safely resist. Even within the planned economy, which has been progressively decentralized in recent years, the competition for raw materials in order to meet production goals has frequently led to intense conflict.

In the light of strong currents that are running, at least in American society, one must probably add a third dimension to the role of government: the responsibility many attribute to it to bring about the reforming and restructuring of society and life generally. Government, in the view of many, must take an active part in building a more just and equitable society in which power and participation are far more widely dispersed than they have been in the past. Today's radicals, of course, insist that this can be done only by revolutionary means outside the system—ultimately by smashing it and reconstructing a completely new system. The revolutionary Russian government during the 1920's and 1930's deliberately restructured social, economic, and power relations through the massive use of force, as in the liquidation of the kulaks (rich peasants) in the course of collectivizing agriculture. How much basic restructuring and reordering of priorities can be done by a government that lacks totalitarian control remains an unanswered question to which answers will have to be found in the next few years. If the revolutionary alternative is pursued, it will doubtless be painful and bloody.

Modern Governments: Differing Political Values

Our discussion of the features common to government in all modern societies has so far explicitly avoided questions of political value or ideology. Clearly, there are political problems and technical needs that transcend differences in value orientation. Just as clearly, however, value differences must be taken into account. The Western democracies share a common fund of liberal values with one another in addition to the rather striking parallels of function that they share with all advanced societies, whether democratic, authoritarian, or totalitarian.

Operationally, these shared liberal values include the freedom of expression that makes possible the direct articulation of group demands. This contrasts sharply with the situation in totalitarian systems, such as the Soviet Union, where group and individual expression is muted, and where, as a consequence, the rulers must fashion roundabout techniques for finding out what the ruled really think and want. The liberal values of democratic systems also include freedom of association, which enables groups with common objectives to organize themselves to seek explicit goals. The free existence of rival political parties, one of the significant offshoots from the principle of free association, is equally vital: it helps give meaning to the right of citizens to participate in their nation's political life, to choose among alternative sets of would-be rulers, and, ultimately therefore, to influence public policy.

Essentially, the collective impact of these core values shared by the democracies is to alter the texture of the process of public policy-making. As we have seen, the process of policy-making is hardly limited to democratic contexts, but the *way* it is carried on, the degree and openness of participation, the degree of sensitivity to group demands, and the kinds of problems the governing authorities face in maintaining their own position differ sharply. In sum, then, the political systems of all democracies reflect a sharing of common values that assert the primacy of the individual and his right to participate meaningfully in his own government. Democracies are premised on the instrumental nature of the state as servant of its citizens, and they provide an overall encouragement to the pluralistic tendencies inherent in the society. Totalitarian regimes operate in a reverse fashion. The state or party and its ideology enjoy primacy; the citizen is *its* instrument. Civic participation, though complete and universal according to theory and propaganda, is in practice muted, indirect, and inhibited.

The American Theme of Equality: The Classic Approach

Because the American political system is our primary concern, we must largely limit our study to the Western democracies as an ideological category. In looking at them as a group the same question with which the chapter opened again emerges, perhaps even more insistently. If, by definition, the democracies share common problems of political control and decision-making, and if, additionally, as a group, they approach these common problems of government on the basis of a shared fund of values, what accounts for the sharp differences of institutional structure, tone, style, and even policy outcome that are so clearly evident? What, in a word, accounts for the uniqueness of the American political system?

The answer to this question has already been anticipated in the discussion of political culture. A generation or two ago, however, the answer might have been framed in terms of a concept of a distinctive American character. But whether one looks at impressionistic writings, like those of Tocqueville, a perceptive French visitor to our shores a century or more ago, or at more recent and methodologically rigorous commentaries, there has been a surprising degree of unanimity on what the central themes of American culture are considered to be.

At the core of this cluster of themes lie the notions of equality and liberty—though perhaps above all, equality. Americans have tended to see equality as a value that characterizes the best aspirations in their own society and the goal toward which all societies should strive. Equality has also generally been seen as a fact of life as well as an aspiration. Although the current strident and often accurate critique of America enters a loud dissent, most Americans have believed, and probably still believe, that their society has indeed achieved an unprecedented degree of actual equality—at least of opportunity if not of status.

The consistency with which this theme of equality has been invoked in analyses of the American ethos is striking. Alexis de Tocqueville wrote in the 1830's:

America . . . exhibits in her social state an extraordinary phenomenon. Men are there seen on a greater equality in point of fortune and intellect, or, in other words, more equal in their strength, than in any other country of the world, or in any age of which history has preserved the remembrance.[5]

The echo of Jefferson's famous words in the Declaration of Independence, "We hold these truths to be self-evident, that all men are created equal, that they are endowed by their Creator with certain unalienable rights . . . ," is unmistakable.

It is equally evident in Lincoln's Gettysburg address, written some thirty years after Tocqueville penned his acute observations. "Our fathers," the Civil War President declared, "brought forth on this continent, a new nation, conceived in Liberty, and dedicated to the proposition that all men are created equal." Thirty years later we find another foreign commentator, Lord Bryce, observing:

The United States are deemed all the world over to be preeminently the land of equality. This was the first feature which struck Europeans . . . this has been the most constant boast of the Americans themselves, who have believed their liberty more complete than that of any other people, because equality has been more fully blended with it.[6]

Recent and somewhat more systematic students of the American ethos have repeated the same theme. David M. Potter, an historian, summarized the general point well in his thought-provoking book, *People of Plenty.* "America," he wrote, "not only practiced a full measure of mobility and social equality but also developed a creed of equality and articulated a myth to accompany the creed." [7] Equality, in other words, has been a consistent value in American life, but it has also been asserted as an actual description of the national community. Moreover, these two elements have been interwoven into a mythology best typified by Horatio Alger and his embodiment of the rags-to-riches theme. Such a myth serves as a kind of social putty, filling in for the observer the spaces and imperfections in the otherwise rather uneven surface of social reality.

Seymour Martin Lipset, an eminent political sociologist, has struck a similar note in his writings, showing that the theme has remained unvaried whatever the period in time or the discipline in social science that supplied the viewer his vantage point. Lipset's fascinating book, *The First New Nation,* which compares the United States with more recent "new nations," has as its objective the examination of the process of

---

[5] Alexis de Tocqueville, *Democracy in America,* Bradley edition, 2 vols. (New York: Vintage, 1957), I, p. 55.

[6] James Bryce, *The American Commonwealth,* 2nd ed., 2 vols. (New York: Macmillan, 1891), II, p. 615.

[7] Chicago: U. of Chicago, 1954, p. 97.

nation-building. He uses the United States as his primary illustration and relates his findings to contemporary nation-building efforts in Africa and Asia. His particular interest is in tracing the origins of the major themes in a nation's political culture to its early years and in showing the persistence of these patterns once established. "Two themes, equality and achievement," Lipset found,

emerged from the interplay between the Puritan tradition and the Revolutionary ethos in the early formation of America's institutions . . . equalitarianism was an explicit part of the revolt against the traditions of the Old World, while an emphasis upon success and hard work had long been part of the Protestant ethic.[8]

Despite the cherished place that the value of equality occupies in American political culture, some qualifications are in order. There is, to begin with, a partial tension between the ideals of equality and liberty, and indeed the value of liberty has been used to justify social and economic conditions that are distinctly nonequalitarian. The concept of liberty (like, of course, that of equality) is an abstraction, and the term is not easily defined. But traditionally, and especially in eighteenth- and nineteenth-century America, liberty has meant freedom to accumulate property and wealth without governmental interference. Significantly, both the Fifth Amendment to the Constitution (1791) and the Fourteenth (1868) forbid governmental deprivation of life, liberty, or property without due process of law; until the 1930's these amendments were often interpreted as seriously limiting the power of the federal and state governments to regulate—and thereby to correct, at least partially, social and economic inequalities—private property and business activities. In this sense, the value of liberty has primarily served the interests of the well-to-do and the aspiring middle class. The value has been used, that is, to justify the pursuit and the retention of property regardless of its consequences for those who proved unsuccessful in the competition or were unable to engage in it in the first place. It is no coincidence that modern American conservatives prefer to describe the United States as a republic, which implies liberty as its driving motive, and not as a democracy, which implies equality as the ultimate ideal.

Not only has the value of liberty served as a brake on the ideal of equality, but equality itself has never been accepted as an absolute value that should characterize the social or economic status of all individuals in the society. A provocative study of American political ideology by Robert E. Lane includes a chapter fittingly entitled, "The Fear of Equality." Drawing on lengthy and intensive interviews with fifteen lower-middle-class and working-class Americans, Lane asserts that as a nation we *do* accept the view that "America opens up opportunity to all people, if not in equal proportions, then at least enough so that a person must assume responsibility for his own status." [9] But Lane's respondents almost universally rejected a completely equalized society as a desirable goal. Life in such a society, they felt, would

[8] New York: Basic Books, 1963, p. 101.
[9] *Political Ideology: Why the American Common Man Believes What He Does* (New York: Free Press, 1962), p. 61.

lose its savor. In their view, the meaning of life turned on the achievement and monetary success around which they had structured their life goals.

The American value of equality, then, is more accurately described as equality of opportunity. This definition of equality as opportunity embodies the element of achievement that Lipset noted and that Lane also found to be so highly prized among the persons he studied. Jefferson in 1776 had given equality precisely this content when he wrote of men having been "created equal." For he followed this with the further explanation that the Creator had endowed them with the "unalienable rights to life, liberty, and the *pursuit* of happiness" (italics added). Jefferson's phrasing, moreover, implicitly suggests that liberty is instrumental to the seeking of equality. It is for this reason that the tension between equality and liberty discussed in the preceding paragraphs was described as partial instead of complete. There are subtle paradoxes in the relationship between these values of American political culture, one of the significant ones being that liberty has been idealized as a primary means for the attainment of equality. Under this view liberty serves as a guarantor of the opportunity to pursue betterment in the individual's social and economic status.

This assertion of a creed of equality of opportunity is not without its difficulties because it is bound to result in palpable and, at times, extreme inequalities. David Potter, whose comments have already been quoted, points out that the mythology accompanying our concept of equality helps convince Americans that when they see people enjoying special advantages (or handicaps), these "are not really decisive and that every man is the architect of his own destiny." [10] Another part of the prevailing mythology asserts that America is truly a nation without social and economic classes. This, too, is a useful part of the mythology. It supports the value of equality in the midst of its apparent opposite by telling the less successful that they cannot blame accidents of class birth for their lack of success.

Professor Lane's findings, however, suggest that elaborate myths and rationalizations may be less necessary than might have been thought. The American laborer, he writes, "is not so blind as to think he has equal opportunity with everyone else; but he knows that he has more opportunity than he is using, more, perhaps, than he can use." [11] Most of his respondents felt that their status in life was about what they deserved, and furthermore they saw "the status of the more eminently successful as appropriate to their talents." [12] These findings suggest that Americans accept the value of equality—but do so with an appropriate degree of subtlety.

Yet whatever the subtleties of its interpretation, equality as a belief and value has been central to American national life. It has been so consistent a theme that it has been almost universally recognized by observers; it has been, in a sense, the pivot point around which other values have been organized and integrated. Most important for our purposes, it has been the theme that has contributed most to the uniqueness

[10] Op. cit.
[11] Op. cit., p. 59
[12] Ibid., p. 69.

of the American community. It has, as we shall see, contributed significantly to the shape, operation, and tone of our political system.

The Origins of American Equality

Although the uniqueness of a nation's political culture and attendant values is the product of her history, it is rarely possible to pin down with certainty the precise trends or events that crystallized into specific cultural themes and practices. Speculation as to the origins and development of equality, as well as other American values, suggests the difficulty. Thus, the historian Frederick Jackson Turner identified the frontier as the key influence. It produced, he argued, conditions wholly different from the European background familiar to the ancestors of the Western pioneers. It produced also an enforced self-reliance; placed all men on the same equal footing; fostered antipathy to external (governmental) control; ensured the existence of limitless free land, which those unsuccessful in the East could lay claim to and use as the foundation for a fresh start in life. Above all, the frontier stimulated a social fluidity in the nation as a whole. "Among the pioneers," Turner wrote, "one man was as good as his neighbor. . . . Economic equality fostered political equality. . . . Democracy became almost the religion of the pioneer. He held with passionate devotion the idea that he was building under freedom a new society." [13] This, in Turner's eyes, was the ultimate impact of the frontier's way of life: it generated an ethos of equality which eventually permeated the political attitudes of the entire nation.

Louis Hartz, a student of American political thought, has advanced a different yet related explanation.[14] In his view, the root factors that shaped American equalitarianism were the absence of a feudal past and the timely prevalence of the ideas of John Locke. Much of the inequality in modern European society can still be traced indirectly to the rigid feudal class system of centuries ago. During the formative years of the American union, before the impact of the new kind of class system spawned by industrialization, European class structures rooted in feudal practices were even more clearly and directly evident. But in America only a few traces of feudalism took root (the plantations of the antebellum South are an example); no feudal deposit marred the impact of such equalitarian influences as the frontier.

The second part of Hartz's explanation emphasizes the idea of Locke, whose eighteenth-century writings provided the justifying theory for the English civil war that was fought against notions of divine right and absolute monarchy. If governmental authority did not derive from a single divinely anointed king, it logically could come only from the opposite end of society—all of the people. Locke theorized that prior to the coming of government there existed a state of nature in which all men enjoyed equality. Government was instituted by these free and equal individuals who covenanted with one another for their collective greater good. The thrust of

[13] *The Frontier in American History* (New York: Holt, 1920), pp. 274ff.
[14] See Louis Hartz, *The Liberal Tradition in America* (New York: Harcourt, 1955).

Locke's theory is obviously equalitarian. Because the people are all equal and share sovereignty in a state of nature, they must rightfully continue to share sovereignty on a basis of equality when government is formed. This, of course, was the prevailing theory in our formative years, and Hartz finds it profoundly significant. For, clearly, the main intellectual currents of the era in which nationhood is molded are bound to leave their political marks.

The historian David Potter, however, identifies abundance as the key variable, arguing that the continuing abundance of goods and resources accounts for the fluidity of American society. He writes:

There is no respect in which this influence has been more profound than in the forming and strengthening of the American ideal and practice of equality, with all that the ideal has implied for the individual in the way of opportunity to make his own place in society and of emanicipation from a system of status.[15]

Potter shares with Turner an emphasis on the basic causal significance of situational factors, but he broadens the focus from the free land of the frontier to the overall material resources of a "people of plenty." Hartz, on the other hand, lays greatest stress on social arrangements and ideas. In any event the precise form and direction of causation is probably less important than the virtually unanimous agreement of these scholars that equality has emerged as the dominant American theme.

Equal Opportunity:
The Case of the Black American

We cannot go any further without recognizing and dealing with the one major doubt that, especially today, is certain to greet any analysis of equality in American life. What about the black American? As Lipset bluntly puts it: "American egalitarianism is, of course, for white men only." Curiously and tragically, only in recent decades has there even begun to be recognition of the cruel paradox in the persistent contradiction between the American value of equality and the chronic treatment accorded the black man. A milestone of sorts in recognizing this paradox was perhaps finally reached in 1968. As an outgrowth of the destructive urban riots during recent summers, President Lyndon Johnson appointed a National Advisory Commission on Civil Disorders. The commission, dominated by white moderates, identified the disorders as a consequence of black privation and despair in the urban ghettos, which in turn it ascribed to a pervasive white racism. Its basic conclusion was terse and unequivocal: "Our nation is moving toward two societies, one black, one white— separate and unequal." [16]

In one sense the equalitarian creed has made the plight of the black man even worse than it might have been in, for example, a society that emphasized ascribed rather than achieved status. In such a society a niche for the black man at the bottom

---

[15] Op. cit., p. 91.
[16] Summary of the report by the National Advisory Commission on Civil Disorders. *New York Times,* March 1, 1968.

of a carefully articulated status system could—and by definition would—have been provided. This would at least have had the effect of justifying, to a degree, in terms of the values proclaimed by the society, the observable facts of systematic exclusion from equal treatment. However, in a society that advertises its commitment to equality for all men by birthright, there is no consistent and rational basis for attaching inferior worth or status to any group as a group.

In America only two avenues are available to deal with this problem. Either it is necessary, as some people have done, to assert that, in spite of the evidence of science and the ideals of the Declaration of Independence, the black man is an inferior being not entitled to share in the benefits of a general human quality. Or it is necessary that he simply be ignored, that he become, in the title words of Ralph Ellison's moving novel, an "invisible man." If the first avenue was the typical southern way, the second was typical of the North: to pretend simply that the black ghettos and all of their problems did not exist. It seems quite clear that not only has this stubborn contradiction of the ideal of equality bred a festering resentment among blacks and embarrassment among whites, but over the years it has condemned millions of black Americans to a materially and psychologically harsh way of life.

Gunnar Myrdal, the Swedish sociologist, appropriately entitled his monumental study of the black American *An American Dilemma.*[17] He, of course, had this contradiction in mind, though he ultimately drew from it more hopeful implications. His thesis was that the disjunction between the national creed and the daily treatment that whites accorded to blacks, and the whites' resulting uneasiness and embarrassment, were a promising sign. Sooner or later, he argued, Americans would be forced to make an effort to align their practice with their precepts. The national response to civil rights sit-ins and other demonstrations of rising black militancy during the 1960's has at least partially justified Myrdal's theory. He himself wrote, in a 1962 preface to the twentieth-anniversary edition of the book, regarding his prophecy of racial progress: "A student who has often been wrong in his forecasts will be excused for pointing to a case when he was right." [18] Unquestionably, the new black activism has speeded the beginnings of reform and, perhaps most significantly, has not provoked harsh repression by the dominant white majority. As a nation America has been compelled to admit that despite the occasional violence accompanying the new black militancy the civil rights cause is basically just. By contrast, in South Africa, where the value system supports unequal treatment, it can easily be made to justify harsh repression—as occurred when the white government mercilessly crushed African demonstrations in the early 1960's.

Beginning most notably with the Supreme Court's condemnation of school segregation in 1954, the United States has finally begun to correct the discrepancy between its ideals and its treatment of the black man. The first steps, as reflected in the decisions of the courts and the civil rights laws of Congress, merely removed the legal and quasi-legal forms of racial discrimination. These actions, although not

[17] *An American Dilemma: The Negro Problem and Modern Democracy,* 20th anniversary edition (New York: Harper, 1962).
[18] Op. cit., p. xxiii.

producing true equality, or even equality of opportunity, logically dictated the next step: positive use of government power to create the possibility of a real equality. In the words of Professor Lipset: "Perhaps the most important fact to recognize about the current situation of the American Negro is that [legal] *equality is not enough to insure his movement into the larger society.*" [19] Daniel P. Moynihan, one of the nation's leading urban scholars and later an aide to President Nixon, spelled out the problem in a widely publicized study that he prepared while he was Assistant Secretary of Labor. *The Moynihan Report,* as it became known, made the point in a passage that deserves full quotation:

It is increasingly demanded that the distribution of success and failure within one group be roughly comparable to that within other groups. It is not enough that all individuals start out on even terms, if the members of one group almost invariably end up well to the fore, and those of another far to the rear. This is what ethnic politics are all about in America, and in the main the Negro American demands are being put forth in this now traditional and established framework.

Here a point of semantics must be grasped. The demand for equality of opportunity has been generally perceived by white Americans as a demand for liberty, a demand not to be excluded from the competitions of life—at the polling place, in the scholarship examinations, at the personnel office, on the housing market. Liberty does, of course, demand that everyone be free to try his luck, or test his skill in such matters. But these opportunities do not necessarily produce equality: on the countrary, to the extent that winners imply losers, equality of opportunity almost insures inequality of results.

The point of semantics is that equality of opportunity now has a different meaning for Negroes than it has for whites. It is not (or at least no longer) a demand for liberty alone, but also for equality—in terms of group results. In Bayard Rustin's terms, "It is now concerned not merely with removing the barriers to full *opportunity* but with achieving the fact of *equality.*" By equality Rustin means a distribution of achievements among Negroes roughly comparable to that among whites.[20]

If the overruling of legal policies supporting segregation was the first step in the process of changing the black man's status in American society, the second step is now taking place. This positive attack is far more difficult and controversial. It includes, for example, attacks on the inferior black schools that are *de facto* segregated as a consequence of segregated housing patterns. In neither fact nor logic is there any material difference between schools segregated by law and those segregated by the long-term impact of generalized community prejudice. Unfortunately, undoing the results of deeply rooted racial prejudices takes far more than legal decrees. During the 1960's and early 1970's there have been a series of civil rights enactments aimed at affirmatively promoting true equality in employment, housing, and voting, and one of the major objectives of the War on Poverty was to equalize social and economic opportunities that have systematically, if subtly, been denied to the black American. And yet, as the report of the National Advisory Commission on Civil Disorders so fully documents, none of these steps, impressive as they are in some

[19] Op. cit., p. 331. The emphasis is Lipset's.
[20] Lee Rainwater and William L. Yancey, eds., *The Moynihan Report and the Politics of Controversy* (Cambridge: M.I.T., 1967), p. 49.

respects, has proved to be sufficient. The coming of true equality of opportunity probably depends not only on profound changes in white attitudes but also on the establishment, on a massive scale, of governmentally operated remedial programs. Such a social and economic intervention on behalf of the black minority, which the Advisory Commission recommends, would cost billions of dollars—and it may not be immediately feasible politically.

The Impact of Equality on Political Attitudes

This brief discussion of civil rights legislation and of programs, existing and proposed, to aid a disadvantaged minority emphasizes the vital relationship between such a central value—equality—in American political culture and the functioning of the political system. The legislation to aid black Americans and other racially handicapped minorities, as well as the proposals to expand such legislation, aptly suggests the impact that political values have on the substance of public policy. In other ways, too, the value of equality has made an impact on our political system, and its significance must be carefully noted.

In part this impact takes the form of certain general public attitudes and modes of approaching politics. Because Americans insist that every man is basically as good as every other man and that every man's views are as good as any other's, they tend to be relatively uninhibited and assertive once they embark upon political participation. They also accept the idea that everyone may participate, as directly as possible, in politics. At the same time, the notion of a professionally tenured civil service, though perhaps valued because of its aura of honesty and disinterest, has won relatively little favor in the United States. Professional public servants, whether elected or appointed, are viewed with suspicion and accepted grudgingly. The idea of equality makes professionalism in the public service, with its overtones of elitism, suspect. And even elected or politically appointed officials are commonly perceived as no better than anyone else.

This ambivalence in the American view of the profession of politics extends to government itself. A society that asserts the worth and potential of the individual man, that values individually achieved status, and that is jealous of the freedom to achieve will naturally view government as a necessary evil or, even worse, as meddlesome and obstructive. But the idea of positive government action, which is implicit in civil rights and general welfare legislation, rests on the assumption that government can and should provide minimal security to all members of society. It presumes, also, the ability of the government to open avenues of opportunity to individuals. In America, unlike in other industrial nations, this whole activist and interventionist way of looking at political power was only recently—and most reluctantly—accepted.

Walter Bagehot, writing in the nineteenth century, called the British a deferential people of whom "certain persons are by common consent agreed to be wiser than others . . . there are nations [like England] in which the numerous unwiser part wishes to be ruled by the less numerous wiser part." [21] Although this may be less true in Britain today than it was when Bagehot wrote, it is obviously strikingly *un*true of the United States. Neither in the past nor in this century would the aggressive equalitarian ideology of Americans permit the acceptance of any such idea that a natural political elite should govern the vast majority of their "unwise" countrymen. It is true that current critics of the American system talk of an "establishment" or a "power elite." There is, however, sharp disagreement over whether such a body or bodies exist and really dictate policy decisions. Furthermore, the very vehemence of claims that there are such elites underscores the point: there is a strong American antipathy to the idea of rule by elites.

In any event, an equalitarian value system provides little basis for the kind of deference to leadership that is also more characteristic of politics across the Atlantic. Party leaders in Britain, for instance, can hold their followers even when doubts and dissatisfactions rise, because leaders "ought" to be followed and team play is so deeply ingrained. In American politics, however, leaders must typically court or purchase their followers, either by delivering (or appearing to deliver) material betterment or by exercising special gifts of appeal and personality. Such leadership, moreover, will continue to be effective only so long as the needs of the follower are served or the leader's charisma remains untarnished. Rarely can it be claimed or held by the leader as a matter of right.

American equalitarianism is largely responsible for another paradox of our political culture, the tyranny of the majority, which is best described in Tocqueville's words:

I know no country In which there is so little true independence of mind and real freedom of discussion as in America. In any constitutional state in Europe every sort of religious and political theory may be freely preached and disseminated; for there is no country in Europe so subdued by any single authority. . . . In America the majority raises very formidable barriers to the liberty of opinion. . . .[22]

In an equalitarian society, in short, the only authoritative voice is that of the majority. Americans, of course, explicitly assert this in regard to political matters, but it applies in many other areas of life, including art and literature. Political democracy in America, with its peculiar equalitarian character, seemingly leads to a sort of cultural democracy in which those ideas and those forms of entertainment and artistic expression that command majority approval are regarded as "best."

In the mid-1950's, when Senator Joseph McCarthy's sensational investigations inspired fear of a great Communist conspiracy in the United States, a study of American attitudes on civil liberties revealed fresh evidence of the majority's tendency to tyrannize opinion. One question asked a sample of respondents was "If a person wanted to make a speech in your community favoring government ownership of all the railroads and big industries, should be allowed to speak, or not?" About three fifths (58 per cent) said Yes, but nearly a third (31 per cent) said No. (The rest

---

[21] *The English Constitution* (New York: Appleton, 1884), pp. 227 and 333.
[22] Op. cit., I, pp. 273–74.

had no opinion.) Another question that asked whether an atheist should be allowed to make a speech against churches revealed that three fifths of the sample would not permit an expression of this opinion. Similarly, 68 per cent of the respondents, more than two thirds, would ban a Communist address.[23]

Despite the official ideology in favor of freedom even for those whose ideas are generally detested—the hardest kind of freedom to tolerate in practice—Americans have been far more willing to allow freedom of activity in the economic sphere than in the intellectual. When people were asked by pollsters about their attitude toward demonstrations against the war in Vietnam, only about one quarter of a national population sample were willing to accept the dissenters as honest critics. Three fifths of the respondents viewed the demonstrators as "executing" Communist plans or as draft dodgers.[24] And yet the fact remains that such dissenters *were* allowed to march, chant, carry placards, and even obstruct traffic, often with police protection. Clearly the majority, whatever it thinks, does not often overtly prevent free expression of ideas. In that ultimate sense, freedom does exist in America, but the majority exacts a heavy psychological price from the dissenter, who is typically isolated and harassed.

One might summarize much of the impact of equalitarianism on politics and political attitudes by saying that it strongly supports the familiar assertion that American politics are consensus politics. There are no significant ideological cleavages dividing our political parties nor, for that matter, the society at large. Political discussion and campaign oratory are rarely over desirable goals, but, rather, over the means to achieve them best. Debate is normally over relatively minor adjustments in the distribution of advantages and disadvantages, of loaves and fishes, within the existing framework of policy. Only rarely are serious suggestions heard that the system itself be changed, and these are typically put forward by small and isolated minorities.

The Impact of Equality on the Political Machinery

Not only has the American concept of equality affected an entire range of political attitudes, but it has also had its impact on such specific and vital parts of the nation's political machinery as its interest or pressure groups and its political parties. The impact is indirect, but nonetheless unmistakable. Interest groups, as we will see in Chapter 6, are one of the most significant phenomena in the American political system. Indeed, many political scientists have concluded that organized interest groups are the most typical kind of political grouping in the United States. Unlike in most European nations, political groups in this country are not organized around social and economic classes. Nor have ethnic groupings, which were once highly influential, especially in the northeastern states with their heavy immigrant popula-

---

[23] Samuel A. Stouffer, *Communism, Conformity, and Civil Liberties* (New York: Doubleday, 1955).
[24] Survey by the Opinion Research Center of Princeton, New Jersey, reported in the *New York Times,* December 15, 1965.

tions (they are still of some importance), been as pervasive as interest groups. In a sense even the political party plays a less central and continuous role than the pressure group.

Actually this is not really surprising in an equalitarian and achievement-oriented society. Associations with narrow and specific economic goals, which best describe most interest groups, demand least of the individual in terms of requiring him to submerge his personality and individual aspirations in overriding collective endeavors. American-style interest groups differ from the class and clannish ethnic groups often found in other countries in that their concern extends to only one facet of a man's life. Typically, the American interest group leaves his religious, social, and even political attachments for other organizations. Furthermore, interest group memberships usually harmonize with an individual's personal striving for economic status and achievement. This is most obviously true of the typical trade association or its agricultural counterpart. An association of lingerie manufacturers or mink farmers or sesame seed raisers, for example, serves to exchange information, to agree on standards of quality and honesty, and occasionally to take common political action on matters of narrow occupational interest; ties beyond these occupational concerns are usually minimal.

American trade unions provide another excellent illustration. Historically, it took union leadership some time to attune itself to the American ethos of equality and to develop appropriate organizational strategies. During the latter years of the nineteenth century, labor leaders worked to promote political action organizations built around class interests, creating the Knights of Labor and the Industrial Workers of the World. These efforts to develop class consciousness among workers and to marshall the battalions of labor for political action were spectacularly unsuccessful. It took the shrewd cigar maker, Samuel Gompers, who led the American Federation of Labor in the late nineteenth and early twentieth centuries, to construct a truly viable and effective labor organization. Gompers' contribution was the sound insight that workers would organize and submit to leadership only for specific bread-and-butter objectives. American workers, he realized, are not easily led into broad political battles. They resist being told which party to vote for, and above all they have been notably unreceptive to being organized into a labor party, whether open or disguised. Until the 1930's, labor tactics had been ostentatiously nonpartisan and aimed solely at rewarding individual candidates who befriended labor and punishing those who were hostile. Although the poor economic conditions of the Depression combined with the prolabor policies of President Roosevelt's New Deal Administration have now given American unions a decidedly pro-Democratic orientation, they have steadfastly refused to bind themselves to any single political party. For many years, in fact, the American Federation of Labor, which is now merged with the Congress of Industrial Organizations, took a quite parochial view of its interests. In Gompers' heyday, the American Federation of Labor, along with most of the nation, resisted the idea of welfare legislation, pensions, and unemployment insurance; its sole political objective was to obtain legislative confirmation of the right to strike so that it could then pressure business for better working conditions.

In comparing the American labor movement with its European counterparts, Professor Seymour Lipset has observed that

American unions are more conservative; they are more narrowly self-interested; their tactics are more militant; they are more decentralized in their collective bargaining; and they have many more full-time salaried officials, who are on the whole much more highly paid and who exhibit a somewhat greater penchant to engage in corrupt practices.[25]

This conservatism, self-interest, aggressiveness, and decentralization relates in quite obvious ways to the American belief in equality. The unions have, in effect, acted out in group terms the American drive for achievement in a context of equal opportunity, and they rarely stray beyond the ideological consensus. Their officials have behaved similarly in their own careers. Just as many immigrants debarred from private callings found their way up a parallel ladder to status and prominence through politics, so too did many workers use the union hierarchy as a mechanism for personal advancement. This has led to a somewhat swollen and relatively highly paid union bureaucracy that is susceptible to the same temptations to achieve under pressure that characterize our society in general.

Even this brief look at American labor as an interest group and a political participant suggests sharp differences from labor's political involvement in many foreign countries. In America class and ideological objectives are essentially irrelevant. The emphasis, rather, is on specific policy goals that are carefully chosen from within the overarching national consensus. As a consequence, even the labor unions, which of all organized economic interests are the most likely to transcend the narrow interest group role in other democratic nations, have confined themselves to a highly restricted range of occupational concerns. In a sense, though, they had little choice. Wrong as Karl Marx was in assuming that the class loyalty of European labor would transcend all other claims on the individual, his error was still greater across the Atlantic. Labor has been very nearly as loyal to the creed of equality and individual achievement as business or any other segment of the community, with profoundly important results for the functioning of the political system.

One of the serious problems created by this characteristic American dependence upon interest groups as the major vehicle for political participation and representation is the premium it tends to place on the levels of education, organizing skill, and resources necessary for successful group action. It may well be that the plight of the poor and the dispossessed in the society has been exacerbated by their inability to use effectively these channels to political influence. Studies have consistently shown that group memberships are least prevalent in the poorest segments of the population.

The National Welfare Rights Organization initiated and led by Dr. George Wiley to represent the interests of welfare recipients, together with the block and neighborhood groups that have been spawned by the poverty program, suggests that the poor can make use of interest group politics. NWRO's 1971 national conference, held on the Brown University campus in Providence, Rhode Island, brought together several

[25] Op. cit., p. 172.

hundred delegates from around the country to participate in sessions conducted by LeRoi Jones; to hear speeches by Representative Bella Abzug (D—New York), Mrs. Martin Luther King, women's rights advocates, and other national figures; to listen to Pete Seeger; and to take a strong stand in opposition to President Nixon's welfare reform proposals. (See Chapter 12.) Radical as NWRO's objectives might be, it is significant to note that its organizers turned to the familiar American interest group approach in quest of their goals, rather than to the third party device so familiar in other democracies but so uniformly unsuccessful in the United States.

Actually, of course, in spite of the pervasiveness of group political tactics in America, few topics come closer to the heart of the operation of a political system than its political parties. Although subsequent chapters will examine the American party system in greater depth, the impact of the equalitarian creed on their organization and operation should be noted at the outset. In the light of the previous discussion emphasizing the broad acceptance of the concept of equality of opportunity and the basic consensus on political values, it is hardly surprising to learn that Americans are ambivalent toward parties, for the existence of political parties customarily implies sharp differences in values and objectives, usually along class and economic lines. If the people accept the idea of a governmental process dominated by parties, they will almost by the same token perceive the politics of their nation as highly competitive and ideologically divisive. Under the model of party government, policy is made through a process in which the electorate first chooses one party approach or platform, together with its candidates, and then votes them into office. The actual government policies are subsequently hammered out with the program of the majority party serving as the anvil against which the minority party strikes continuous blows. The politics of such a system are the politics of conflict—between the party leaders and their diverse ideologies and programs.

If these conclusions about American political attitudes are valid, however, this kind of political system is unlikely to have much appeal in the United States. Both because of the relative ideological unanimity and because of the nature of the values upon which Americans *already are agreed,* consensus rather than conflict tends to characterize the nation's politics. An equalitarian society sees government as less important than individual achievement and in any event finds working through disciplined party battalions highly uncongenial. Instead, Americans have often seen parties, politics, and government itself as instruments to be used for individual advancement, not as means for advancing the public weal. Party organization has provided careers for the otherwise disadvantaged, and businessmen have gone to government for special favors, grants, or protection while trumpeting loudly their aversion to government interference, welfarism, and "give-away" programs. Ideology, in short, has played little part in the activities of any of the groups involved in American politics.

It is therefore hardly surprising that the shape of the American party system has been affected by these pervasive cultural values. A society that refuses to recognize class-status lines will naturally not have class-oriented parties, and so it has been in the United States. The parties have always been broadly based, cutting across all major strata in society, and they have been almost militantly classless in their rhetoric. (Mentions of class appear only in campaign oratory as clubs to beat the opposition for committing the alleged sin of "setting class against class.") America has two bourgeois parties, large, sprawling, amorphous, nonideological, and overlapping to an extent that is the despair of those who try to identify them with consistent principles. Out of deference to the peculiar sensibilities of the electorate, they are forced to cloak their partisanship and to encourage their candidates to campaign as virtual independents. They are, moreover, highly decentralized, as might be expected in the absence of the kind of cementing group and leader loyalties found in Britain or Canada, where political parties are more dominant. The absence of any mention of political parties as such in that greatest of American treatises on political thought, *The Federalist,* often cited as a failure of foresight, is thus less out of tune with the emerging American ethos than it might appear. The nonideological pragmatism of its authors was a clear portent of the political style soon to emerge.

In the aftermath of the bitterness and even violence engendered by the Democratic National Convention of 1968, reforms were demanded to make future conventions "more representative" of their constituents' wishes. (The problems Eugene McCarthy's supporters had in securing their fair share of the delegates underlay much of the difficulty and the demand for change.) The major thrust of the subsequent McGovern Commission proposals was for delegate election rather than appointment, broader and more flexible citizen participation through presidential primaries or open caucuses, and in general a shifting of effective power from party officials and organs to the people. Buried beneath all this reform rhetoric is the same ambivalence toward parties already noted. Americans have always had the lurking suspicion that party structures inhibit and distort rather than facilitate democracy, and that the more direct the citizens' voice in political affairs the better. Current reform efforts are no exception, and produced a vastly different 1972 Democratic Convention—and McGovern's nomination.

The American Theme of Equality:
The Behavioral Evidence

Most of the preceding discussion of American political values and their influence on the governmental system has drawn heavily on careful, though unsystematic, scholarly interpretations, enhanced by brilliant flashes of insight contributed by such perceptive writers as Tocqueville or Bryce. But modern political science, as noted in the opening pages, has been greatly enriched by more systematic inquiries that apply a rigorous methodology to the subject matter. These efforts often rely on statistically manipulatable data obtained through opinion surveys. Their technique, which requires administering standardized questionnaires to scientifically chosen samples, is almost ideally suited to the study of political culture and attitudes. It enables researchers to provide the discipline of political science, over a period of time, with a growing number of verified propositions about citizen beliefs and values that supplement and sometimes confirm the intuitive insights of earlier studies. A discussion of two such studies, which are particularly revealing systematic examinations of American political culture, provides a useful conclusion to this chapter.

The first study of political culture, which we shall briefly sample, brings us full circle to the point of departure in this chapter. It, too, is based on survey interview data, but, more important, it is also comparative. This study by Professors Gabriel A. Almond and Sidney Verba is an impressive pioneer effort, unique both in its methods of research and in its broad comparative framework.[26] More than a thousand interviews, using an essentially standardized questionnaire on political beliefs and attitudes, were obtained in each of five countries: the United States, Britain, Germany, Italy, and Mexico. Primarily the results invite comparisons between Western democracies. The fact that Mexico is included provides a point of comparison that is probably outside of this basic category. Mexico's essentially one-party system and her earlier stage of modernization differentiate her from the other nations.

The title of the book, *The Civic Culture,* suggests the facet of political culture it explores: the operational viability of the respective systems as democratic polities. Are the predominant attitudes and values of the people appropriate in the light of the demands that democracy makes for belief and participation? How do these beliefs and values differ from country to country? This approach necessitated making assumptions about what beliefs, attitudes, and behavior patterns are indeed essential, and then testing to find their relative presence or absence in each of the national communities.

This brief summary of the Almond-Verba study can only illustrate the specific hypotheses posed and the results produced, and it cannot deal with all five countries. Instead, we shall note the findings on America and Britain to show differences between two otherwise similar democracies. Italy will serve to represent a marginally democratic society that displays some serious conflicts and "inadequacies" in her political culture. Mexico, which is in a category somewhere between the Western democracies and the developing nations, is also of special interest because it permits inferential comparisons with the economically poorer nations.

One of the fundamental necessities in any political system that emphasizes even a modest level of citizen participation is a minimal level of awareness and information about the national governing institutions and a positive attitude toward them. To examine this awareness, Almond and Verba asked their various national samples if they thought their national government had a great effect, some effect, or no effect on their day-to-day lives. Forty-one per cent of the American sample replied "great effect," as did 33 per cent of the British sample; but only 23 per cent of the Italian and a tiny 7 per cent of the Mexican samples felt that their government had such an effect on their daily lives.

Level of information about national politics and government was tested by asking respondents to name party leaders and government departments. More than one third of the Mexican and Italian samples could name nothing in either category; in

[26] *The Civic Culture. Political Attitudes and Democracy in Five Nations* (Princeton. Princeton University Press, 1963). The following makes use of various aspects of the analysis the authors present, selected for their appropriateness here.

America and Britain, however, only one eighth of the sample were unable to identify some party leaders or government departments. Finally, as to trust and confidence in national institutions, the samples were asked whether they felt that they would get equal treatment from their national bureaucracy and whether they would expect serious consideration of their points of view from administrative officials. The results are summarized in Table 1.1.

Clearly, America and Britain emerge in a class by themselves on all questions. They rank highest in awareness of a stake in the national government; Americans and Britons, in short, are for the most part aware of the existence of the nation and its political institutions. Their horizons are not limited by the tangible, visible local community in which they live, and their awareness is the foundation of nationhood itself—and of meaningful democratic participation.

A high level of information is only partly a matter of the extent of a person's formal education. It is also, in part, a measure of what might be called a cosmopolitan awareness of the world beyond the individual's physical experience. By contrast, if a citizen's conceptions are parochial, and he is unable to conceptualize the nation, its government, and, at least in an elementary way, its policy problems, his participation—if it can be elicited at all—will be meaningless. Even when these conditions of awareness and knowledge are met, there must be in a democratic state an ingredient of trust, loyalty, and affection before the citizen's relationship within the political process can be truly effective. The figures in the table, crude measure though they may be of this kind of relationship, differentiate the Anglo-Saxon democracies from the other two systems. In addition, the last line of the table also shows a subtle but interesting difference between British and American respondents: the former apparently have a greater confidence in the responsiveness of public officials. This seemingly confirms an earlier suggestion that the British are less ambivalent about and more deferential toward their government.

Almond and Verba's primary concern, as well as ours, centers on the mechanics or the operational characteristics of the systems they study. Some of the most im-

		US	UK	Italy	Mexico
Table 1.1 *Trust and confidence: National samples* qua *their national bureaucracies*	Equal treatment	83%	83%	53%	42%
	Serious consideration	48	59	35	14

Source: From Gabriel A. Almond and Sidney Verba, *The Civic Culture: Political Attitudes and Democracy in Five Nations* (Copyright © 1963 by Princeton University Press), pp. 108–109. Reprinted by permission of Princeton University Press.

portant of these characteristics involve the groupings into which societies organize for political purposes—specifically, interest groups and political parties. Early in the chapter, it will be recalled, the point was made that all developed societies are by definition pluralistic. And it is the organized groups that serve as one of the main operational links between this pluralism of interests and the government, with the interests pressing often competing demands upon the government, which must respond to them. Thus, the extent to which citizens hold memberships in such private organized groups will be one index of the political vitality of the national community. Almond and Verba found that 57 per cent of the American and 47 per cent of the British sample claimed one or more group memberships, a claim that was made by only 29 and 25 per cent of the Italians and Mexicans, respectively. When Almond and Verba separated those persons with more than one membership, nearly one third of the Americans and one sixth of the British still qualified. In stark contrast, only 6 per cent of the Italians and 2 per cent of the Mexicans belonged to more than one organized group.

The most important single category of grouping with political significance is of course the political party. Generally speaking, we know that America and Britain are quite similar and unique among democracies in having two-party systems. Italy shares the multipartism common on the European continent, whereas Mexico is, for all practical purposes, a modified one-party state roughly comparable to the one-party system that long prevailed in the American South and that is not wholly dead. Undoubtedly, a more important variable for measuring the political vitality of a nation than number of parties is the less tangible factor of the *kind* of partisanship its citizens exhibit. When the partisan cleavages are deep, highly charged, and therefore difficult to bridge in the making of the political compromises out of which policy must emerge, the viability of the political system is basically affected. Almond and Verba sought to measure the depth of partisan cleavage by asking such questions as this: How would the respondent feel about a marriage between a member of his family and a partisan of another party? Only negligible numbers of American and British respondents expressed any concern, but the idea of marrying, as it were, outside of one's party troubled large numbers of Italians. (Mexico's one-party system did not lend itself to this part of the analysis.)

Using this kind of information as a base, two groups of partisans were identified. The first, who described themselves as emotionally involved at election time on behalf of their chosen party, yet unconcerned about cross-party marriages, were called *open partisans*. The second group were equally involved emotionally *and* also felt strongly about cross-party alliances. These were labeled *intense partisans*. The percentages in both categories in America, Britain, and Italy are revealing, as Table 1.2 shows.

There are actually several indices of political viability and vitality in these findings. Most obviously, the higher the number of open partisans the better. Italy, by this measure, is clearly not in the same category as Britain and the United States. Another index, of course, is the number of intense partisans and the ratio between

Table 1.2		US	UK	Italy
Partisanship in	Open partisans	82%	61%	14%
three countries	Intense partisans	10	14	20

Source: Almond and Verba, op. cit., p. 155.

these figures and the number of open partisans. Finally, the totals for each column tell their own story. Ninety-two per cent in America report themselves as emotionally involved in the partisan struggle, feeling personally related to this key dimension of the political process. Seventy-five per cent gave comparable replies in Britain, the smaller figure very likely reflecting the more deferential and less aggressively activist qualities of the British culture. But only 34 per cent, or barely one third, in Italy are similarly "plugged into" the partisan political system. This, together with the fact that intense partisans outnumber open partisans, bespeaks a decidedly unhealthy state of affairs for a democratic polity.

As a result of these and other findings, Almond and Verba label Italy an *alienated political culture*. Italians were found to be low in awareness and distrustful of what they did know. They showed low levels of membership in private groups and a low potential for spontaneous group political action, and, as just noted, they had a highly unfavorable sense of political identification. (Mexico, which we have used in only a partial comparison, is in overall terms not far removed from Italy on the scale. Despite some important differences, it can also be labeled as an *alienated political culture*.)

Turning to the United States and Britain, the authors label the first a *participant civic culture* and the second a *deferential civic culture*. The *civic culture* tag describes their democratic viability as political systems when measured against the criteria of a reasonably healthy democracy. The difference between participant and deferential cultures, in turn, marks the subtler area of difference in tone and emphasis in the ways that American and British citizens tend to go about their civic business. The civic culture, briefly restated, includes the presence not of a universally attentive, aware, and informed electorate, but of an electorate that has *relatively* high scores on each of these scales. Confidence and trust are prevailing attitudes. The political game is viewed not as rigged but as one that can be played with some confidence, and it thereby invites rather than repels participation.

If relatively healthy attitudes toward the political process are present in Britain and the United States, so too are the necessary techniques and instruments to facilitate meaningful citizen involvement. There exists a vigorous private group life to foster and channel participation, making it possible to articulate and pursue real differences of goals and interests. Parties are oriented toward the gathering, sorting, and devising of policy alternatives from among the demands pressed by interest groups. They are not, for the most part, oriented toward pseudo-interests and issues born of highly charged and deeply divisive ideological differences. The result is a politics of "more or less," not of "either-or," a politics that makes up in plodding effectiveness what it lacks in color and excitement.

A second and more recent study of American attitudes highlights the flavor and texture of the system from a somewhat different perspective. The study also raises some questions about whether, in recent years, the system has in fact been as effective as we have tended, rather complacently, to assume. In a book entitled *Hopes and Fears of the American People,*[27] Albert H. Cantril and Charles W. Roll, Jr., report on research conducted through polling techniques during January and April, 1971. Their focus was not so much on the mechanics of the operation of the political system as on the quality of life, measured in the hopes and fears expressed by poll respondents, that the system has produced or allowed to develop.

The basic technique used was a series of questions asked of members of a national sample, which were to be related to a ten-point scale. Each respondent was asked to imagine his future, first in the best possible light, and then in the worst light. The former he was to equate with *10,* the top of the scale, and the latter with *0,* or the bottom. He was then asked to place himself on the scale in terms of where he thinks he stands now, where he stood five years ago, and where he thinks he will be five years hence. The same process and question routine was then repeated to measure the respondent's hopes and fears for the nation: ratings of the best and worst states of affairs for the United States, past, present, and future.

The tabulation and averaging of the scores reported by those interviewed about their own personal situations and hopes revealed rather typical American optimism and faith in an expanding future. On the average the sample placed itself at 5.8 on the 10-point scale five years ago, at 6.6 in 1971 (up 0.8), and estimated its position five years in the future at 7.5, up nearly a full point from the present. In other words, the American people, in regard to the personal destinies of individuals, seem to feel that upward trends of the past will carry on into the immediate future with little variation in the upward slope of the curve. This, of course, is the dimension over which the individual does have the greatest degree of control.

The picture changes, however, when hopes and fears for the *nation*—over which the individual feels he has less direct control—are measured in the same way. Before noting the computed scores, we might look at a tabulation of the specifically expressed hopes and fears recorded from the interviews. Here we shall use for comparison the data that Cantril and Roll introduce from a similar study done in 1964 using the same technique. On the "hopes" side, in both years 51 per cent mentioned peace—the category that received by far the greatest number of references. Next, 18 per cent cited economic stability (against only 5 per cent in 1964); followed by employment (16 per cent in 1971 versus an almost identical 15 per cent seven years earlier); then 15 per cent versus an earlier 9 per cent on national

[27] New York: Universe, 1971.

Table 1.3 *Fears of the American people for their nation (percentage)*

	1964	1971
War (especially nuclear war)	50	30
National disunity; political instability	8	26
Economic instability; inflation	13	17
Communism	29	12
Lack of law and order	5	11

Source: Adapted from Albert H. Cantril and Charles W. Roll, Jr., *Hopes and Fears of the American People* (New York: Universe Books, 1971), p. 23. Published by Universe Books for Potomac Associates.

unity; and 11 per cent versus 4 per cent on law and order. There were other categories of replies that drew progressively smaller percentages in 1971, but these five will suffice for illustration.

On the "fears" side, we might usefully present the first five categories of 1971 replies in descending percentage order, compared with 1964, in tabular form to make analysis easier (Table 1.3).

It is noteworthy that the same pattern emerges here, though in generally sharper relief than in the listing of "hopes." War and peace are at the top of both lists, though the fear of war is down sharply—nuclear war especially. The uniform yearning for peace in the hope category doubtless reflects the continuing Vietnam conflict more than it is reflected under fears.

The essentially domestic concerns that make up most of the rest of both lists are of special interest and significance. Save for the substantially lessened fear of Communism between 1964 and 1971, optimism is down and fear is up in each other instance. Inflation, fear of unemployment, law and order as an issue, and above all national unity (disunity) all engendered greater concern in 1971 than they did the year Lyndon Johnson won his overwhelming victory over Barry Goldwater. One is struck particularly by the sharp jump in concern over national unity. In the fear category, disunity has become the second most disturbing factor, a scant four points below the life-and-death issue of nuclear war. Of course, in the light of events since roughly 1968, this is hardly surprising. It is also precisely the reaction one would expect from a society that traditionally has prided itself on its homogeneity, its equalitarianism, and hence the presumed absence of causes of division. This is also precisely what one would expect of a society that believes in consensual politics and decries political strife. When division and strife *do* arise public concern is fueled by disbelief, disillusionment, and anger. How could such things as riots and bombings happen in a society that professes the values of America?

When we examine the tabulated average scores that the respondents offered to define their hopes and fears for the United States, we find that they placed the country at the 5.4 point on the scale of 10 in 1971, but, significantly, felt that it had been at 6.2 five years earlier. For the future they located it at the same 6.2 level. In other words, the sample felt that the nation had very decidedly *lost* ground in the past half decade, and at best would recoup that lost ground by 1976, thus ending up no better off than it had been ten years earlier. Clearly, the American people are worried about their country, far more worried than they have been in the recent past. The 1964 survey had resulted in scores of 6.1, 6.5, and 7.7 for the past, present (1964), and future ratings of the nation—indicating a smooth rising curve of expectation and optimism.

The Cantril and Roll study reveals, first, that a new uneasiness and pessimism has entered the thinking of Americans about their country and its performance in the recent past; second, that inferentially this reflects an increasingly negative appraisal of the performance of the American political system; and third, that the sources of concern are domestic problems, especially disunity, division, and strife. These are perceived as afflicting a society that in its perception of itself *should* be united, consensual, and geared to continuous upward progress via an ideally responsive set of political institutions. It may be that these institutions can fulfill their historic promise, but the nation clearly has more doubts than at any time in the recent past. To the details of the operation of this American political system, both in its successes and its shortcomings, we now turn.

suggested additional readings

Almond, Gabriel, and Sidney Verba.
*Civic Culture: Political Attitudes and
Democracy in Five Nations.* Princeton:
Princeton University Press, 1963.*

Bell, Daniel. *The End of Ideology: On
the Exhaustion of Political Ideas in
the Fifties.* New York: The Free
Press, 1965.*

Bryce, James. *The American
Commonwealth,* 3 vols. New York:
The Macmillan Company, 1939.

Cantril, Albert H., and Charles W.
Roll, Jr. *Hopes and Fears of the
American People.* New York:
Universe Books, 1971.*

Drukman, Mason. *Community and
Purpose in America.* New York:
McGraw-Hill Book Company, 1971.

Free, Lloyd A., and Hadley Cantril.
*The Political Beliefs of Americans:
A Study of Public Opinion.* New
York: Simon & Schuster, Inc., 1968.*

Hartz, Louis. *The Liberal Tradition in
America.* New York: Harcourt
Brace Jovanovich, Inc., 1955.*

Havens, Murray Clark. *The Challenge
to Democracy: Consensus and
Extremism in American Politics.*
Austin: University of Texas Press,
1965.

Ladd, Everett Carll, Jr. *Ideology
in America.* New York: Norton,
1972.

Lane, Robert. *Political Ideology: Why
the Common Man Believes What He
Does.* New York: The Free Press,
Inc., 1963.*

Lipset, Seymour Martin. *The First New
Nation.* New York: Basic Books,
Inc., 1963.*

Potter, David M. *People of Plenty:
Economic Abundance and the
American Character.* Chicago:
University of Chicago Press,
1958.*

Stouffer, Samuel A., et al. *Communism,
Conformity, and Civil Liberties.*
New York: John Wiley & Sons,
Inc., 1955.*

de Tocqueville, Alexis. *Democracy in
America.* New York: Harper & Row,
Publishers, 1966.

Turner, Frederick Jackson. *The
Significance of the Frontier in
American History.* Ithaca, N.Y.:
Cornell University Press, 1956.

* Available in paperback.

2 public policy and american politics

Some Analytical Perspectives

Probably the reason most people take American government courses and come to read this book is that they care about what government *does*. That concern may be self-motivated. Will I be drafted and have to fight in an Asian war? Will the government enforce antidiscrimination laws so that I will have a fair chance to get a job? Will the tax laws be changed and my inheritance cut off? If there are controls on the economy, will my family with its income from factory work or civil service come out as well as corporate executives? For others, interest in government may be altruistic. Can government be used to provide "justice" or "equality" for all citizens? Will government be turned to feed hungry children? Will individuals retain the liberty to pursue their private goals? The answers to all these questions, and thousands more, are the stuff of public policy.

There are many definitions of public policy. Professor David Easton, who developed the systems approach to politics, labeled policy the authoritative allocation of values.[1] In the 1930's, Harold Lasswell defined politics as: "Who gets what, when, how."[2] V. O. Key, Jr., observed that "politics generally comes down, over the long run, to a conflict between those who have and those who have less."[3] Another useful definition is that public policy is the *impact* government has through either acting or not acting. Through acting, for example, government can distribute benefits to some—subsidies, contracts, tax write-offs, medals, awards, status. It can also penalize by direct action. By exercising its discretion to prosecute for hundreds of potential civil, criminal, or political crimes, government can deprive individuals of their liberty, money, and status. It can intimidate political conversation by wiretapping, surveillance, or infiltration. By building a road through one route instead of another, government can legally force people from their homes.

[1] *The Political System* (New York: Knopf, 1953), pp. 125–148.
[2] *Politics: Who Gets What, When, How* (New York: McGraw-Hill, 1936).
[3] *Southern Politics* (New York: Knopf, 1949), p. 307.

Government also makes policy by not acting. The concept of policy through inaction may be difficult to comprehend, but it is crucial to understanding the strategies of those, in any system, who wish to protect a status quo they like. Because the potential power of government is so great, inactivity has the practical effect of being a form of support for things as they are. Sometimes this phenomenon is called a "pre-emptive decision," sometimes a "standing decision," and sometimes a "mobilization of bias." Whatever the phrase used to describe the nonuse of governmental power in a context where some seek change and others do not, the result is identical. That result is a conservative reinforcement of the position and power distribution as it already exists. The importance of the "standing decision" situation is that those who oppose change can pursue the relatively simpler strategy of blockage of action, always easier than the mobilization required to get something done. Blockage is made easier in the American system by the institutionalization of "overlapping powers" and "checks and balances," a set of structures with multiple access points for blockage and fewer such access points from which the momentum for extensive change can be launched. These factors, as much as characteristics of the political culture, lie behind what is often called the "incremental" nature of American policy-making. Change comes in small bits and pieces—increments—because blockage to support a "standing decision" is easier generally, and is made easier in the particular American context by the design of our institutions.

In thinking about the impact of public policy, it is useful to keep in mind that government is a factor in both economic and noneconomic rewards and deprivations. There is no doubt about the centrality of economic power in the modern world. Indeed, the key problem of democratic societies may still be, as it was in Marxian analysis, to reconcile the unequal resources available to people with greatly different amounts of wealth in a system formally committed to the concept of equality of individuals. How can the political power of the millionaire and the $15,000-a-year civil servant, the $10,000-a-year factory worker, and the $3,600-a-year welfare recipient ever be equal?

Nonetheless, the values that people seek are often nonmaterial and noneconomic: respect from others, the rights of citizenship, freedom to pursue unconventional life styles (the "counterculture"), the honors that every society bestows upon some individuals (in naming holidays and schools, in portrayals in history books), preference for one set of moral values over another. Some of the bitterest fights in American political history have been over using government to impose a set of moral values held by one segment of the society upon the whole society: prohibition and marijuana laws at the national level; abortion, Sunday closing, drugs, drunkenness, and homosexuality at the state and local levels.

Government dispenses a large proportion of the nonmaterial benefits in the United States, and *how* people are treated, the symbolic aspects of politics, may be not only an indicator of what they can expect to get in the material domain, but as important as that domain. The most certain fact of our times is the preeminent role government plays, and thus public policy plays, in the lives of every citizen. Interestingly, with all the rhetoric about decentralization, expanding government impact is as much a feature of democratic as of Communist societies.

The Elements of Public Policy

Figure 2.1 lists the six elements of any public policy: mobilizing resources, choosing priorities, distributing benefits, disbursing costs, manipulating controls, and reaction and adaptation. These are universal elements, processes that occur on every policy from fighting a war to subsidizing housing to loans for college students. On every policy, resources in favor of the policy—support in the form of ideas, numbers, campaign contributions, commitments from political leaders—have to be mobilized. Among supporters, and within government after a policy is adopted, priorities have to be set. Economic and political resources are scarce. Choices have to be made among alternative goals because no society can do everything at once, or even the most worthwhile things at once. A steady rate of economic growth sometimes blurs the need, for example, to choose between "guns and butter." But when growth slows, then the fundamental situation of relative scarcity reappears and choices have to be made, painful choices. The more painful the choices, the more likely the process of deciding will generate political conflict.

Any policy distributes benefits. Someone, or some group, or some agency, or some country gains something by the decision. A decision to use $3 to $5 billion of the American budget to provide armaments to foreign governments means that that money cannot be used to provide grants for rural development for those same countries, or that it cannot be used to build public facilities in this country, or even to aid industries in this country that are non-defense-oriented. A tax code, especially one running to thousands of pages, distributes benefits to people with certain kinds of jobs or certain kinds of income and expenses, or to some industries and not others. That is the *point* of a tax code so detailed: to provide benefits for special cases or special favored categories of cases. The other side of the coin of any policy that distributes benefits is that it disburses costs. A basic strategy of government is to provide specific benefits, but to disburse costs widely. That is, some sector gets something specific, but the costs are widely disbursed through the general public in the form of broad-based taxes collected and put into a general treasury. Thus, the one who benefits usually knows precisely what he gets, whereas the one who

Figure 2.1. Elements of public policy

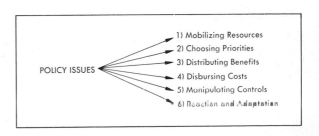

POLICY ISSUES

1) Mobilizing Resources
2) Choosing Priorities
3) Distributing Benefits
4) Disbursing Costs
5) Manipulating Controls
6) Reaction and Adaptation

pays may have only a vague notion of what the money is used for, and his taxes in particular are not transferred directly or earmarked, usually, but go into a general fund. Thus costs are hard to assess, and deliberately so, because making them so mutes resentment and political conflict.

Every policy carries with it some form of control, either the carrot or the stick, to induce compliance. Government maintains a legal monopoly on armed force in almost all countries, and in the end that legal violence could be used for compliance. Few governments prefer force to voluntary compliance. Indeed, at that point where voluntary compliance has to be replaced with systematic governmental force, the legitimacy of a governmental system may be beyond repair. But behind every government policy lies the ultimate sanction of coercion, which is what Professor Easton probably meant when he defined public policy as the *"authoritative"* allocation of values. One set of observers has noted:

Governors, administrators, dictators and even political philosophers have shown ingenious capacity for devising controls over men. Actual physical compulsion is the most obvious form, as with traditional use of military or police forces and prison systems, for example. The techniques of rendering or threatening physical violence can be quite sophisticated in the modern age. So too are medical and psychological means of compulsion. Less sinister but often equally compelling are economic and material arrangements leaving very little choice to subjects, such as providing income or job opportunities where alternatives are limited.[4]

One way to understand the elements in Figure 2.1 is to explain each in terms of an ongoing American public policy. For purposes of illustration, let us take American agricultural policy. That policy has a number of components at this time, foremost among them being a system of paying farmers cash subsidies to take land out of production. The goal is to keep market prices up by restricting output, and the program is administered by the Cabinet Department of Agriculture. As of 1970, the cost of the program was $7 billion, $3.5 billion as cash payment to farmers and the other $3.5 billion as the estimated added cost to consumers of reduced supplies.

The political resources for this bonanza for farmers, a steadily declining percentage of the total population since 1900 at least, were mobilized a long time ago. Before World War I, in order to ensure itself of a reliable base of support—a clientele—the Agriculture Department organized unorganized farmers around its county agent system. The county agents, then as now, sought out the "better farmers," meaning the more affluent, most competent farmers. Rural poverty, then as now a major problem, has always been little touched by this department. The Agriculture Department also helped into being a private group tied to government, the American Farm Bureau Federation. After World War I, the private farmers, the government officials, and the peak association, the Farm Bureau Federation, organized the "farm bloc" in the Congress, a monitored, lobbied set of congressmen from key agricultural

---

[4] Joyce M. and William C. Mitchell, *Political Analysis and Public Policy: An Introduction to Political Science* (Chicago: Rand McNally, 1969), p. 209.

Table 2.1 *Public policies: Some illustrations of the four types, with primary political institutions involved*

DISTRIBUTIVE POLICIES
The President and Congress
    Rivers and harbors acts
    Foreign Aid Bill
    Space program
    Omnibus Crime Bill, Institute
      Section
The President
    Cabinet appointments
    Judgeships
Congress
    Private immigration bills
    Special tax exemptions and
      deductions
Federal courts
    Administering bankrupt
      corporations
    Damage awards in torts cases
Federal regulatory agencies
    Which airline gets a route
    Who gets a TV license

REGULATIVE POLICIES
The President
    Wages and price controls
Congress
    Sherman Anti-Trust Act
    Law setting up rules for private
      foundations
Federal courts
    Antitrust awards and precedents
      on triple damages
Federal regulatory agencies
    Manipulation of interest rates
    Setting airline ticket prices
    Setting trucking rates
    Setting auto safety standards

SELF-REGULATIVE POLICIES
The Congress
    Absence of gun control law
    Absence of laws regulating various
      professions and trades
Federal courts
    Refusal to intervene in self-set rules
      of legislative bodies
    Refusal to intervene in foreign
      policy cases

REDISTRIBUTIVE POLICIES
The President and Congress
    Graduated income-tax amendment
      (1912)
    Wagner Act (1934, labor/
      management power)
    Social Security Act (1935)
    Selective Service Act (1947, first
      peacetime draft)
    Civil Rights Act of 1965
The President
    Setting oil import quotas
    Strong enforcement (or weak
      enforcement) of civil rights,
      antitrust, and pollution laws
    Foreign military and economic aid
    Executive order ending segregation
      in armed forces (1947)
    Executive order ending draft
      deferments (1969)
Congress
    Suffrage for eighteen-year-olds
Federal courts
    School desegregation decisions
    Reapportionment decisions
    Political trials
    Pornography decisions

or agricultural processing states. More than fifty years later this same support system still operates, through the Agriculture Department, the Farm Bureau Federation, and especially through the agriculture committees of both houses of the Congress. The strenuous mobilization that set the policy system going now requires only a constant attention to detail to enforce a "standing decision" favorable to the associated set of interests.

As for choosing priorities, every year the program goes on and passes through the executive budget, congressional authorization and appropriations committees, both houses of Congress, and the White House. There is an implicit choice of this goal—support for farmers—as opposed to some other use of the $3.5 billion of direct federal spending. The choice is not only of an overall program, but the particular priorities of distributing the money. The money goes to private farmers. It could be used to buy produce outright and feed poor children or welfare recipients. Indeed that is done in smaller separate programs. Further, numerous studies have shown that the monies go to the larger, more mechanized private farmers. These are the primary recipients of the benefits of this program. The argument is also made that the entire economy benefits indirectly through preventing a free market in agriculture, which might lead to a collapse of the farm economy.

The costs of the farm program are typically disbursed, half coming from general tax revenues and half as part of higher prices. But the higher prices are untraceable onto specific items: the average supermarket stocks over six thousand items. As for sanctions on agricultural supports, the major form of control is the positive inducements of price supports for participating farms. If farms, many of them corporations, cheat, theoretically the government will fine them or put individuals in jail, but enforcement has been minimal. The main control is that those who opt out are at the mercy of a cruel economic market. For consumers, no sanctions are needed because the low visibility of the program and the disbursement of costs into millions of tiny items makes resistance impossible. So for agricultural policy, at this stage of American politics, strong sanctions are not necessary at all.

Reaction and adaptation to the program has proceeded ever since price supports began, essentially taking their modern form in the late 1940's. Political resistance as a form of reaction is low because overall, compared to countries such as France especially, the farm sector produces great quantities of food at comparatively low prices. Poorer farmers who do not benefit as much from the support have not been able to win much help from Washington. As for adaptation, after all these years, everyone involved has learned to live with both the political and the production arrangements. For the powerful Agriculture Department, the Farm Bureau Federation, its farming beneficiaries, and their proponents in Congress, change would be vastly unsettling. It would introduce many uncertainties and possibly high costs for them. Thus, any efforts to rearrange the present pattern of adaptation to each other of government and farming would produce resistance in segments of both. With the use of the elements outlined in Figure 2.1, the main aspects of any policy can be analyzed.

A Typology of Public Policies

It is possible to characterize public policies on the basis of what the level of mobilization is, how benefits and costs are distributed, and how visible adaptation and reaction are in the political system. Four categories of public policy have been developed by political scientists: (1) distributive; (2) regulative; (3) self-regulative; and (4) redistributive.[5] Table 2.1 provides a list of illustrations of each type of policy, along with the American political institutions that play the major role in each.

Distributive policies are essentially a process of giving things to groups, case by case. These subsidies are not part of a general policy, but a series of ad hoc response to demands as they come up and as claimants on the public treasury are able to mobilize political support. Most of American domestic policies in the nineteenth century could be labeled distributive—protective tariffs for manufacturers, cheap or free land for settlers, land subsidies to railroads, canals and roads for farmers. In the twentieth century, distributive policies still include most land and resource decisions: river and harbor construction programs, oil leases in government waters or coal leases to private firms on government lands, defense contracts overall and to particular companies or regions of the country, various clientele services to labor, business, agriculture, education.

Distributive policies are not policies in the sense of a set of overall priorities being imposed, or a political response to a widely agreed upon set of goals. Rather, as case-by-case decisions, benefits are passed out on a patronage basis, unit by unit. Each unit of beneficiaries is isolated from other beneficiaries. Congressional support is obtained by logrolling, meaning that everyone votes for everyone else's pet project without compromises or the imposition of choice among scarce resources. Further, the losers are vague entities such as "the public," unorganized, and unaware of their losses. They never, therefore, mobilize to confront the winners. As units of gain and loss are small, distributive politics have a low visibility and produce minimal conflict. As long as the resource pie, or the total economy, or the supply of whatever is being distributed keeps growing, distributive policies can lead to a very stable politics. In the nineteenth century, as long as natural resources seemed inexhaustible, an emphasis on distributive policies was a calming counterbalance to the divisive (and redistributive) politics of race or section. In the twentieth century, as long as the Gross National Product appears to be growing, distributive politics is a soothing counterweight to the politics of class (redistributive).

Regulative policies apply general rules to whole categories of firms, industries, or individuals. Someone can clearly be identified as the winner or the loser, and the role of government is enlarged. Government is forced to choose among claimants— for example, whether to subsidize highways *or* mass transit. Or it has to choose whether one airline or another will get a choice vacation route authorization. Most regulatory policies are set by the so-called regulatory agencies, including the Interstate Commerce Commission, the Securities and Exchange Commission, the Federal Trade Commission, the Federal Power Commission, and the Federal Communications Commission. These agencies are described in Chapter 10. At this level of public

[5] For a seminal article on distribution, regulation, and redistribution, see Theodore J. Lowi, "American Business, Public Policy, Case-Studies, and Political Theory," *World Politics,* XVI, No. 4 (July, 1964), pp. 677–715. Robert H. Salisbury added the self-regulative category in "The Analysis of Public Policy: A Search for Theory and Roles," in Austin Ranney, *Political Science and Public Policy* (Chicago: Markham, 1968), pp. 151–178.

policy, logrolling is replaced by bargaining among interests, or by the capture of the agency by the interests it is supposed to regulate. Activists like Ralph Nader, who has led the consumer movement, have argued that these agencies, instead of protecting the public in restricting the activities of economic sectors,, customarily become the captives of the industries involved.[6] Regulatory decisions affect every American and the regulatory agencies have enormous authority. One commentator has noted:

The federal regulators today control entry into and exit from the railroad, trucking, airline and steamship businesses; the telephone, telegraph and the television and radio broadcasting industries; the business of operating natural gas pipelines, hydroelectric dams and nuclear electric generating stations; and the commercial and investment banking business. . . . No private enterprise of significant size can be started without a finding by the federal regulators that the venture is required by the "public convenience and necessity." [7]

In distributive policies, government dispenses something it possesses—land, money, control over aspects of foreign policy—to individuals and groups. In regulatory policies, government in principle sets out, on the basis of general rules, to limit, channel, and regulate the behavior of sectors of the economy and individual firms. In principle, regulation limits the autonomy that is the goal of every private group.[8] In practice, regulation has more often turned out to protect those who are supposed to be regulated from various forms of price or firm competition or to insulate the allegedly regulated from accountability to the general, unorganized mass public. The regulatory movement in American politics began in the 1890's with the Sherman Anti-Trust Act, and most of the present-day independent regulatory agencies were established during the New Deal and the 1930's.

Regulation as a form of policy does, however, establish the political right of government to intervene in the behavior of firms or economic sectors (agriculture, aviation, communications) that previously could operate in this country subject only to the restraints of the free market economy, restraints that are inoperative in conditions of monopoly (only one firm) or oligopoly (only a few firms, sometimes called *concentration*). Thus, even when regulatory agencies do not regulate, their existence represents a potential threat to those firms or sectors most directly affected. That is why business and labor (regulated by the National Labor Relations Board) make such efforts to influence appointments to these agencies, to hire expensive Washington lawyers to represent them before the agencies, and to hire former commissioners when their terms expire (for their expertise and also to lure the cooperation of those who still are commissioners).

For some segments of society, the risks of regulation are balanced by the pos-

---

[6] See the very persuasive Ralph Nader Study Group Reports: James S. Turner, *The Chemical Feast: The Food and Drug Administration* (New York: Grossman, 1970); Robert Fellmeth, *The Interstate Commerce Commission* (New York: Grossman, 1970); and John C. Esposito, *Vanishing Air* (New York: Grossman, 1971).

[7] Louis M. Kohlmeier, Jr., *The Regulators: Watchdog Agencies and the Public Interest* (New York: Harper, 1969), pp. 105–106.

[8] See Grant McConnell, *Private Power and American Democracy* (New York: Vintage, 1970), pp. 7–8.

sibility that the regulators can be captured and used to protect them from competition. For other segments, especially the trades, crafts, and professions, however, another form of policy is typically sought: *self-regulation*. It is a mark of the power of such units, particularly at the local and state levels but also at the national level, that the decisions about what the qualifications shall be for certain livelihoods, who shall be admitted, and how the practice shall be carried on are turned over to those already in the club. Thus, craft unions control who gets admitted into the union as a skilled plumber, and thus who can work on union construction. Further, this kind of policy also turns over to plumbers control over how many plumbers there will be in the whole society and, because the practice is to limit the number rigidly, reduces total supply and increases the price of those who are in. Doctors are perhaps the most successful self-regulators: through their membership on various medical school boards, in county medical societies, and on hospital boards, they have limited the production of doctors and have also decided who can and who cannot engage in private practice or practice in hospitals (even hospitals built and maintained by the public and by governments). Although they opposed the Medicare and Medicaid plans bitterly, doctors largely set the rules governing their own participation in and payment from such programs.

There are numerous other examples of self-regulation. Businessmen have trade associations that seek self-regulatory power over competition, pricing, standards, and other matters. University professors seek self-regulatory control over their performance in the classrooms and over the conditions under which they will be hired or fired (tenure). At the state level, every group from barbers to hairdressers to engineers seeks to gain control over all the conditions affecting its own situation. Nationally, the American Bar Association, through its codes of conduct, seeks to regulate lawyers' ethical behavior, just as the American Judicial Conference seeks to set the rules for financial disclosure or nondisclosure of private interests for judges. The goal of self-regulation is to keep government away, to deny, in practice, the interests of other groups or a larger public in the activities in question. Groups who manage to win the power to regulate themselves have demonstrated substantial political power.

A final kind of policy is *redistributive*. Policies of this category generate, or require, the broadest mobilization and have, at least in a psychological sense, the most visible distribution of benefits and imposition of costs. Redistributive policies force people, groups, elites, and politicians to choose among alternative goals, to list priorities. Broad categories are involved, often whole social classes. Involved here are rich and poor, or have's and have-not's, or big units versus small units, or bourgeoisie and proletariat. The impact of policy distinguishes redistributive policy because some sought-after value in life—money, power, status—is taken from one segment of the society (or in foreign relations, one nation or other subsegment of the international system) and passed on totally or in part to some different claimant.

Redistributive politics involve the greatest tension; reaction and adaptation may take a long time because the winners may be constantly insecure about their gains and the losers may constantly try to reverse the verdict. There is little doubt about who has won or lost and confrontation may be quite direct, especially if the redistribution takes place in an era where the size of the economic or status pie is fixed, not expanding. In that context, heavier taxes, for example, come directly from one group's pocket and are redistributed to another segment of society. None of the transfer can be accommodated by the gains of economic growth, which always makes it easier to avoid or to camouflage redistribution. Economic growth allows the gain to be given disproportionately to one group without directly depriving some other group.

The kinds of issues around which redistributive policies are built seem to be those that, at their extreme, underlie what we label in Chapter 5 *realigning elections*. The income tax is in theory, though much modified by practice, redistributive. The welfare system is redistributive. Suffrage for women, for blacks, for eighteen-year-olds was all potentially redistributive. For blacks and for eighteen-year-olds the vote has been translated into some redistribution of policy outputs, especially on status and symbolic issues. For women, the adoption of the Nineteenth Amendment giving them the vote in 1920 had little impact, largely because there was no distinctive group consciousness. It may be that the Women's Liberation Movement will change that past pattern. Civil rights laws, to offer another illustration, are also redistributive. They remove superior statuses and protection of the laws from whites and use the force of law to equalize those statuses and that protection for all races insofar as the laws are enforced. School busing is redistributive. In the South, it redistributes status and opportunity more equally among the races and reduces the white advantage. In the North, it reduces the advantages that wealth can provide whites in suburban schools or more affluent city neighborhoods. What is taken away is clear.

Redistributive issues may involve more than rearranging the benefits and costs among sectors of society or races or classes. They may involve the power of political institutions. If the United States Congress were to assert and achieve greater control over American foreign policy, the power of the President, his White House National Security Staff, the Defense Department, the State Department, and the CIA would be reduced. Eventually, the Cabinet agencies would regain their power by becoming responsive to individual Congressmen or congressional committees. If this process were to occur, a redistribution of institutional power will have taken place. It would be accompanied by mobilization, conflict, and a long period of reaction and adaptation. It is also certain that the substance of American policies would change in some hard-to-predict ways, with gains for some and losses for others. Another institutional redistribution has been the trend, unchecked since the turn of the century, for the federal government to increase in power vis-à-vis state and local governments. Simultaneously, national elites in industry, communications, and education have risen and local elites have declined in influence.

There is one final characteristic of redistributive policies worth noting. Most often they involve broad goals rather than conflict over details within a framework of consensus. For example, the periodic rising to the surface of American politics of the inherent contradiction of a commitment to liberty and to equality forces people to focus on choices not among means, but ends. Suffrage for eighteen-year-olds, moving to give them equal voting power with adults, is likely to be redistributive of goals in America. That is because there is evidence of group cohesiveness, some greater commitment to a moralistic style of politics, and different positions on issues that go to the heart of post-World War II American politics. Probably all redistributive issues escalate rapidly to conflict over alternative visions of society, over alternate goals, and over differing interpretations of abstractions such as "justice" or "liberty."

Contemporary Public Policy:
The Federal Budget as an Indicator

Any analysis of specific public policies for a nation represents a slice-in-time, a stopping of the clock of politics for an analytical look. One indicator of a nation's policy priorities is its budget. Nothing can be firmer than the commitment of actual dollars. The budget is a scorecard of what groups and programs have won and lost in the fight over the public purse, and, if one examines trends, what types of activities are becoming more favored or less acceptable. Our federal budget reveals what our values, filtered through governmental institutions, are. The budget is a political document, prepared by the Office of Budget and Management in the White House, reviewed overall and for very specific items by the President, and later adjusted and approved by the committees and the whole Congress.

Table 2.2 shows federal expenditures by major categories from 1960 through the 1971 fiscal year, and also the change for each of four selected time periods. The major item is defense, which jumped quite rapidly in 1967 as the costs of the Vietnam war mounted. The federal government's system of categorical budget-keeping actually underestimates the true yearly outlays for defense and war efforts. For example, the $75.3 billion spent in fiscal 1971 represents only direct Pentagon programs. Much of the space program involves military concerns. A large portion of the income maintenance consists of veterans' compensation for war injuries and pensions, and a portion of the health budget goes to maintain hospitals for veterans. In addition, the income maintenance budget now includes Social Security trust funds, paid for by the separate payroll taxes on all wages and employers and financed completely apart from other taxes. Putting these funds in the regular budget raises the overall size and thus reduces the apparent percentage share of the defense effort. Thus, although $75.3 billion is 37 per cent of $200.8 billion, others estimate the true defense share to be at least 50 per cent and perhaps as much as 60 per cent.

Next to defense, the major items are the social programs lumped under income maintenance: welfare, Medicare, Medicaid, farm supports, veterans programs, and Social Security. Other categories fall far behind, including housing and community development, development of physical resources, and space. The space program is large when considered as a single program, but less so as a category of activity. It would of course have cost much less had President John F. Kennedy not committed the United States to manned exploration of the moon, as opposed to exploration by

Table 2.2 *Trends in budget outlays, U.S., by major category, fiscal years, 1960–1971 (in billions of dollars)*

Category	Outlays					Average annual change			
	1960	1965	1967	1969	1971	1960–1965	1965–1967	1967–1969	1969–1971
National defense	46.0	49.9	70.6	81.4	75.3	0.8	10.3	5.4	−3.0
Space	0.4	5.1	5.4	4.2	3.4	0.9	0.1	−0.6	−0.4
Income maintenance *	24.5	34.2	43.9	56.8	72.7	1.9	4.9	6.5	7.9
Education, health, manpower	2.5	4.1	8.6	10.3	12.8	0.3	2.3	0.8	1.2
Housing, community development	0.7	1.5	2.6	3.3	6.8	0.2	0.6	0.4	1.7
Physical resources	6.4	10.2	10.3	10.8	13.3	0.8	0.0	0.2	1.2
Interest	6.9	8.6	10.3	12.7	13.5	0.3	0.8	1.2	0.4
Other outlays	4.9	5.9	7.8	6.2	8.3	0.2	1.0	−0.8	1.0
Sale of assets	−0.1	−1.1	−1.2	−1.1	−5.2	0.2	0.0	0.0	−2.0
Totals	92.2	118.4	158.3	184.6	200.8	5.2	20.0	13.2	8.1

Source: Charles L. Schultze, Edward K. Hamilton, and Allen Schick, *Setting National Priorities: The 1971 Budget* (Washington, D.C.: The Brookings Institution, 1970), p. 12.

* Includes welfare, Medicare, Medicaid, farm supports, veterans compensation and pensions, and Social Security.

machine alone. The rate of increase in the federal budget leveled off in the early 1970's and has remained relatively stationary.

The budget does not measure the impact of federal programs, or the important social consequences of activities such as crime control, which is lumped under the heading "Other outlays." Various types of crime control, including investigation, prosecution, research, subsidies to police departments, and prisons and correctional institutions, are in percentage terms the fastest growing items in the federal budget. Expenditures for crime control have more than doubled since 1969 and now account for over $12.4 billion. The increase in areas such as crime control indicates that even in an era when the demands on federal revenues are very extensive and efforts to economize are great, the budget still reflects the emergence of new political issues. The crime-control budget increase is a response to the growing rate of personal crime against individuals and property, to "crime in the streets," and also to a vastly stepped-up government attack on organized criminals. Because it came into office on the "social issues" of "law and order," it is not surprising that the Nixon Administration would put what discretionary funds it had in this field.

If one looks at the main outlines of the overall budget, however, it is clear that the two main priorities of the federal government are military activity and various kinds of social programs that provide direct benefits to individuals or groups. It would be a vast oversimplification to say that these are the only priorities of Washington. The budget does not measure the impact of managing the economy or prosecuting organized crime or instituting political trials or the reflected glow of "recognition" and status that groups receive when the President invites them to the White House. It does nonetheless give some quantitative answers to the question of what policies are valued most highly, and who gets what.

Contemporary Public Policy: Some Comparisons and Evaluations

Qualitative judgments are also possible. A logical place to begin is with comparisons with other industrialized Western nations. The United States spends substantially more on defense than any nation except the Soviet Union. Since the 1950's, there has been an accepted premise in Washington that a reasonable level of defense spending was 6 to 8 per cent of Gross National Product during a period when the overall federal share of the GNP was between 25 per cent and 28 per cent. No other Western nation has spent that much on defense. The Soviet Union, although comparable data are hard to obtain and the subject of considerable argument, apparently spends as much as the United States on military purposes in absolute amounts, and an even larger proportion of its total product because its economy is not as large. Students of arms races, a characteristic of the entire twentieth century, believe that the expenditures of each of the two powers are related to those of the other, at least in part. If that is right, mutual reductions might be possible, or even a sequence of steps taken separately by each side. On the other hand, no one can know for sure that reduction in American arms spending, for example, would be matched by the Russians.

Next to defense, the largest single broad category of spending in the United States is what might be called *social expenditures*. We do not have comparable data for the Soviet Union or the other Communist countries. Table 2.3 compares the United States to twenty-seven other nations, presenting these expenditures as a percentage of the GNP. The measure indicates the level of governmental commitment to these "for the general good" measures. The United States ranks well down the list of comparable industrialized nations, ranking nineteenth among the top twenty-seven countries and spending about 6 per cent of the GNP. Although the data are from the 1950's, the American ratio has not changed greatly since then. The one substantive area in which Americans do lead the Western world, expenditures for education, is not included in these calculations.

What Table 2.3 indicates, as a reflection of public policy, is the policy impact of the individualistic strain in the political culture outlined in Chapter 1. There is a smaller scope of governmental social expenditures in the United States overall, and this country has adopted certain kinds of social programs at a much later date than many Western European nations. Social Security, for example, was first utilized in Germany in the 1870's; national health care in Britain in 1948. Other Western countries came long ago to programs such as family allowances and compensation for victims of crimes. As a matter of public policy, Americans have relied less on government, more on the private use of resources to achieve goals, or, some might say, they have simply left many of the problems of social life in an industrialized society either to be solved by private means or not to be solved at all.

In still another policy dimension, manipulating controls over the economy, it is interesting that the Western nations, including the United States, have become more and more alike over the past twenty years. In the 1950's, many European nations were more willing than the United States to engage in direct, centralized controls.[9] Typical techniques included selective or across-the-board wage-and-price controls, manipulation of export subsidies and taxes on imports, and devaluation or revaluation of their currencies for international exchange. The United States, in contrast, eschewed these devices except in wartime and relied instead on manipulating the expenditure levels of the federal budget—to stimulate the economy and the money supply—to stem inflation through the availability of loan funds and through interest rates. In 1971, however, President Nixon adopted what was in effect already the standard European medicinal formula of wage-and-price controls, devaluation, and import taxes. This experience suggests that in the area of the economy, national governments perceive themselves as having very little leeway in the choice of controlling or not controlling and in what controls to choose. Even the American President most committed to unfettered free enterprise in the nation most philosophically committed to economic autonomy went the standard control route.

[9] See E. S. Kirschen et al., *Economic Policy in Our Time* (Amsterdam: North-Holland 1964), Vol. I.

Table 2.3 *Percentage of national income, 1957, spent by government on social expenditures (includes social insurance, family allowances, public employers, public health, public assistance, benefits for war victims)*

Rank	Country	Percentage expenditure/GNP
1	West Germany	20.8%
2	France	18.9%
3	Austria	17.6%
4	Belgium	16.3%
5	Italy	15.2%
6	New Zealand	13.0%
7	Sweden	12.9%
8	Netherlands	12.3%
9	Britain	12.1%
10	Denmark	12.0%
10	Finland	12.0%
11	Ireland	11.5%
12	Yugoslavia	10.3%
13	Norway	10.1%
14	Chile	9.7%
15	Australia	9.1%
16	Canada	8.7%
16	Switzerland	8.7%
17	Poland	7.7%
17	Israel	7.7%
18	Portugal	6.5%
19	United States	6.0%
		Rank 19
20	Japan	5.8%
21	Tunisia	5.7%
22	South Africa	4.5%
23	Ceylon	4.2%
24	Guatemala	3.1%
25	Turkey	1.3%
26	India	1.0%
27	Taiwan	.8%

Source: Adapted from Margaret S. Gordon, *The Economics of Welfare Policies* (New York: Columbia University Press, 1963), pp. 18–19; from *The Cost of Social Security, 1949–1957* (Geneva: International Labour Office, 1961).

There is one policy area in which American controls appear to be fewer than in many other nations: free speech. There is no question that, considering for the moment only forms of political speech, there is more freedom of political conversation, print, and electronic media in this country than in any Communist country. Although this is the roughest kind of estimate, print freedom, especially for newspapers, also appears greater in the United States than in most Western European countries. On radio and television, there is more numerical diversity in the United States than in most nations, where television, for example, is limited to one government channel or at most, as in Britain, to several government channels and one commercial channel. Whether the electronic media in the United States, all of which are licensed by the government and are thus ultimately dependent upon its acquiescence, reflect accurately the political diversity of the country is a matter of substantial controversy. What political pressures there are on the electronic media tend to be indirect, in the form of veiled threats, rather than efforts, so far, at direct censorship. Political coverage on the electronic media does not, certainly, offer the diversity and the controversial views that can be found in the range of books sold in this country. In Chapter 13 we consider this issue, usually considered under the heading of "civil liberties," in more detail. Despite conflict over the use and management of the airwaves, it seems apparent that the American values of diversity, autonomy, and individualism have had considerable impact in permitting a wider range of political free speech than there is in comparable industrialized nations.

Equality as Public Policy

We can also pursue the fate of various larger abstract values as they are translated into specific public policies in America. One such value is equality.

There are a number of paradoxes in the treatment of political equality as a goal or value in American politics. On the one hand, the push of public policy at various periods in our history has been strongly in the direction of furthering equality. The Jacksonian era before the Civil War, the Reconstruction Era after the Civil War, women's suffrage in 1920, the Civil Rights Movement in the 1960's—all have led to greater political equality in the realm of voting and have also redistributed statuses in the direction of greater equality as well. The vote for eighteen-year-olds is a logical extension of this process. The force of the movements that mobilized the support for these steps, usually against substantial resistance, indicates the appeal of equality as a value in the political culture and its appeal to individuals. There is no way to quantify a comparison with other countries. In some regards and at some times the United States has been behind other comparable Western nations and sometimes it has been ahead.

It has been behind in translating *legal equality* into practical power in voting, in the treatment of persons before the law, in hiring, and in housing. That is, the commitment in the political culture and in the law has always had to be followed by a long struggle, not yet ended by any means, to ensure that the gains had any impact. Equal voting rights, for example, are meaningless if it is impossible to register or if voters are intimidated. Yet despite stops and starts and continuous struggle, the use of government to forge a national commitment for equality has been consistent since World War II, and with none of the steps backward, so far, that followed the post-Reconstruction era of 1877 to 1900.

On the other hand, public policy in the United States has not been used as a conspicuous instrument to equalize wealth among individuals. Alexis de Tocqueville, the remarkable Frenchman who came and traveled in the United States before the Civil War, observed at that time the relative economic equality of Americans, which he took as remarkable compared to European nations. After the Civil War, however, with the coming of industrialization, the disparities in wealth among individuals began to grow. There are no comparative data for European nations. The contemporary distribution is much more equitable in the United States than it is in South American nations, where it is not uncommon for 5 per cent of the families to control half or more of the available land or industrial resources, or even the total economic product. The Communist countries, and Communist ideology in particular, have put special stress on eliminating inequities of wealth among individuals, and the evidence, inconclusive as it is, is that although special privileges do exist, great ranges in wealth and poverty have been leveled off. The Peoples Republic of China has paid special attention to standardizing and equalizing the distribution of whatever material goods the nation possesses.

Wealth allows some individuals to obtain a better standard of living for themselves, including better career opportunities for their families and better health for their children. Further, in the hands of individuals, organizations, or corporations, it gives them a strategic location in the political process. Those who contribute to campaigns are better thought of as investors than as contributors in the sense that money is given to charities. Wealth provides the possibility of strategic contributions to expensive political campaigns, which makes officeholders dependent upon the donors. Further, it provides what the political science literature gently calls *access*. People who have invested in campaigns— be they bankers or oilmen or trade union leaders—can get to see officeholders personally to plead their case. When the Democrats controlled the White House under Lyndon B. Johnson, there was a "President's Club." Anyone who contributed $1,000 got to attend special meetings and dinners with high officials and even the President. Under Richard M. Nixon, there has been a special White House liaison official to carry communications from big contributors directly to the President. Finally, in a society in which wealth is treated as a sign of achievement in itself, it brings a special kind of status.

The federal income tax, through its feature of taxing at a higher rate as incomes rise, is supposed to be "progressive" or redistributive of wealth. It is intended to operate on the principle that those who have more will pay more. A number of features of the tax laws prevent them from having this effect in practice. There is a series of special provisions that give the income or expenses of certain individuals or businesses special treatment. These deductions, exemptions, credits, and depletion allowances are called *tax expenditures* because they represent revenue the federal government would otherwise get. The government could use tax expenditure revenue to reduce the costs to all taxpayers or other categories of taxpayers, or as money to spend on new programs. The tax expenditure concept treats these funds as money the federal government has chosen to spend, through the mechanism of the tax code, on powerful and favored interests. Cumulatively it is estimated that tax expenditures amount to over $50 billion a year, or almost 25 per cent of the total federal budget.[10]

The main tax expenditure items are the 22½ per cent oil depletion allowance ($1.2 billion); tax treatment of private pension plan income ($4.0 billion); deductions for charitable and educational contributions ($3.5 billion), home mortgage interest and property taxes ($5.5 billion), consumer credit interest ($1.6 billion), and other state and local taxes ($4.1 billion); tax free interest on state and municipal bonds ($2.0 billion); and capital gains for individuals ($7.0 billion). The capital gains rule is especially beneficial to those with large incomes because it treats income from investments preferentially compared with wages or salaries. Under capital gains provisions, such income is taxed at a maximum of 35 per cent. Other tax provisions that allow large sums to go untaxed are the very generous estate and gift tax laws, and the practice of generation skipping on capital gains through trusts. These rules allow capital gains wealth to go untaxed indefinitely, or at least for several generations.[11]

The effect of all these tax features can be seen in Figure 2.2. Middle-income families benefit from family exemptions plus home and interest-based tax deductions. Upper-income taxpayers benefit from capital gains and depletion allowances. The redistributive impact of the income tax is largely negated, along with its original orientation toward the value of equality. Distribution of costs on the basis of ability to pay does not happen. Table 2.4 shows that the percentage of income paid in taxes differs very little for families earning $6,000 all the way up to families earning $50,000.

This situation has had a political impact in the "blue-collar revolt" or the alienation of "middle America." Working-class families feel aggrieved, for good reason. Approximately 68 million Americans, 60 million of them white, earned from $5,000 to $10,000 in 1968, and they paid roughly the same percentage of their incomes in taxes as those who made considerably more than they did. To add to their discontent, those with less income than $5,000 are eligible for a wide variety of benefits, including welfare, food stamps, and medical care, that working-class wage earners cannot get. (These benefits are labeled "Transfers" in Table 2.4). Additional discontent is fueled by repeated revelations that many individuals with very large incomes pay no taxes at all, or, under the 1969 Tax Reform Bill, only a minimum tax at a 10 per cent rate.[12]

The failure to use the tax laws to achieve equity is reflected in two social indicators: distribution of personal income and distribution of personal wealth (which adds to yearly income such items as stocks, bonds, and real property). There is evidence that the distribution of income has remained relatively constant since 1910. According to economist Gabriel Kolko, in 1910 the bottom 20 per cent of the

[10] See Murray L. Weidenbaum, "How to Make Decisions on Priorities," in *Changing National Priorities,* Hearings Before the Subcommittee on Economy in Government of the Joint Economic Committee, 91st Congress, 2nd Session (1970), Part 1, especially pp. 56–57.

[11] See Joseph A. Pechman, *Federal Tax Policy* (New York: Norton, 1971), pp. 186–198.

[12] See Phillip M. Stern, "How 381 Super-Rich Americans Managed Not to Pay a Cent in Taxes Last Year," the *New York Times Magazine,* April 13, 1969, pp. 30, 157–164; and Pechman, *Federal Tax Policy,* op. cit.

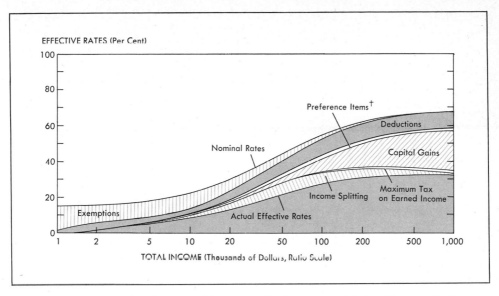

Figure 2.2 Influence of various provisions on effective rates of federal income tax, 1969 act

Source: Joseph A. Pechman, *Federal Tax Policy* (New York: W. W. Norton and Company, Inc., 1971), p. 69.

population received 8.3 per cent of national personal income; in 1959 that segment's share had actually *declined* to 4 per cent. The top 10 per cent of income receivers got 33.0 per cent in 1910; their share had dropped to 28.9 per cent in 1959, but was

Table 2.4 *Taxes and taxes less transfers as per cent of income, 1968*

Income	Taxes	Taxes less transfers *
0–2,000	40.3%	—24.7%
2,000–4,000	32.8	—5.6
4,000–6,000	30.8	14.9
6,000–8,000	30.5	23.5
8,000–10,000	29.8	25.4
10,000–15,000	30.5	27.3
15,000–25,000	30.6	28.2
25,000–50,000	33.2	31.6
50,000–and over	45.3	44.9

Source: Data from *Counterbudget, A Blueprint for Changing National Priorities 1971–1976*, edited by Robert S. Benson and Harold Wolman. © 1971 by the National Urban Coalition: Praeger Publishers, New York, 1971.

* Minus indicates that transfer payments from federal, state, and local governments exceeded amounts paid in taxes.

Table 2.5 *Percentage of aggregate income received by each fifth of the United States population*

Family segment	1947	1950	1955	1965	1968
Bottom fifth	5.0%	4.5%	4.8%	5.3%	5.7%
Second fifth	11.8	12.0	12.2	12.2	12.4
Middle fifth	17.0	17.4	17.7	17.6	17.7
Fourth fifth	23.1	23.5	23.7	23.7	23.7
Top fifth	43.0	42.6	41.6	41.3	40.6

Source: Statistical Abstract of the United States (Washington, D.C.: Government Printing Office, 1970), p. 323.

compensated for in the share received by the next two 10-per-cent segments, which obtained 22.5 per cent in 1910 and 28.5 per cent in 1959.[13] U.S. government data substantiate these findings. Despite the fantastic growth of the national economy between 1947 and 1968 (as median family income rose from $3,031 to $8,632), the share of personal income held by the lowest fifth as compared to the highest fifth changed hardly at all. Indeed, as Table 2.5 shows, in 1947 the bottom two fifths or 40 per cent of the population got 16.8 per cent of the income and in 1968 they received only 18.1 per cent. In 1947 the top 20 per cent obtained 43 per cent and in 1968 40.6 per cent.

As for distribution of wealth, one calculation is that the top 5 per cent of the population holds almost 40 per cent of the national wealth, whereas the lowest 50 per cent holds only 8 per cent.[14] Another source indicates that in 1922 the top 1 per cent held 32 per cent of the wealth and that in 1956 this segment held 26 per cent, with its share increasing at that point.[15] Through various devices, the government has stimulated economic growth, which in turn has raised the standard of living of all segments. But public policy, perhaps reflecting the influence of wealth in politics, perhaps the individualistic strain in the political culture, has not been a technique for furthering economic equality. It is a value judgment how many of America's social problems in connected fields, such as crime and pollution, one attributes to inequities. It is certain that the disparities in holdings between top and bottom have remained stationary for long periods of time, virtually since industrialization, and that the gap in life styles and perquisites remains great.

Buried in these data is a great source of potential conflict in future American politics. What will happen when the push for legal equality and suffrage, which has involved successful mass mobilization, turns, if it ever does, to the distribution of

[13] *Wealth and Power in America* (New York: Praeger, 1962).
[14] See Gerhard Lenski, *Power and Privilege* (New York: McGraw-Hill, 1966).
[15] See Robert J. Lampman, *The Share of Top Wealth-Holders in National Wealth* (Princeton: Princeton University Press, 1962).

wealth? Many of the moves toward legal equality have added to the potential power of groups at the bottom of the wealth structure: women (in terms of jobs and money of their own), blacks, Spanish-speaking Americans, and young people. To their demands must be added the visible unhappiness of working-class people who are the most notable victims of the tax system.

The conflict could turn in any one of several directions, or in all at once. Political leadership will play a key role. One possibility is an effort to turn the discontent of the workingman against newly enfranchised groups, including blacks, students, and welfare recipients. The strategy would be to imply that a gain for these elements would mean a further threat to the worker's already difficult economic and status position. Another possibility would be an effort to meld those with new legal rights with those punished most by the tax structure into a coalition for greater economic equality in the entire system. Both types of politics have occurred in the past in our political system. The coalition of the economically secure plus the workers against the new elements in the social structure characterized some of the "Know-Nothing" politics of the nineteenth century and the turn against populism in the South after 1900. A coalition of the have-not's against the have's is populism, an effort to use politics for income redistribution. Whatever the turn these conflicts take, their presence is built into the present arrangements of equality in the American system. Adaptive and reactive mechanisms are no longer functioning without conflict, and demands from some and resistance from others should not be unexpected. Patterns of public policy at any one point in time are prime sources of the future politics and future policies.

The Special Problem of Private Government

The concept of public policy implies that government will have a major influence on the allocation of various benefits and costs for the entire society. Although few would agree on the specifics of what such an interest would be, the concept also implies that there is a "public interest." Somehow the good of all 205 million citizens should be served. On the other hand, the American tradition of individualism separates a great portion of the total benefits and costs of life from the public to the private sphere. The rationale for such separation of public and private power is present in our historical national thinking about politics. In *The Federalist Number 10,* James Madison argued that strong groups with autonomy, spread widely through a heterogeneous citizenry, would protect against domination by any one group, or by government itself. Separate, nongovernment power centers become a political technique against totalitarianism. The interest group system, described in Chapter 6, is defended in these terms.

Our long practice of separation of public and private resources, especially in the economy, has many consequences for public policy. One is that a large amount of political conflict is over the proper "scope" of government—how broad should governmental activities be, how much freedom should individuals and groups and corporations have, with what safeguards? Scope-of-government conflict has swirled near the center of most electoral upheavals in this country, the realigning elections of 1896 and 1932 among them. Battles over distributive, regulative, self-regulative, and redistributive policies often come down in the end to the question of what power individuals and groups should have to decide for themselves what will be done with resources and practices and costs and what power government will have. The issue becomes what the proper province of public, that is, governmental action is.

The relationship of elected, democratic government to private spheres of power is crucial in two ways. First, private individuals and organizations could control so much of what is worthwhile in any country that what is left to government is trivial. Private decisions may dominate a large percentage of choices about jobs, resources, prestige, interesting work, technology, pollution, high prices, and privacy. In that instance, depending upon the actual situation, a few individuals, responsible to no broad electorate, might be making all the decisions that count. Second, private organizations in an increasingly complicated society of large institutions have greater and greater control over the individuals connected to them as employees and customers. Corporations, universities, unions—all have a great deal of actual or potential control over those who rely upon them. An individual's relationship with such an institution, especially through work, may be more important, especially on a day-to-day basis, than any activity of government. These two issues, the total power of private organizations and their control over individuals, are often labeled the "problem of private government."

The Power of Private Organizations in Contemporary America

There is no way to quantify the cumulative power of private organizations as a proportion of the total social power in our society. Thus, any evaluation of whether private organizations have too much power, making government a dependent pawn, or too little, leaving no sources of independent power outside government, has to be a judgment pure and simple. However, some examples may illustrate the dimensions of the problem.

There is substantial evidence that the New Deal model of the economy no longer applies because of the power of big corporations and big labor. That model held that government spending and monetary controls exerted sufficient leverage over the total economy to reduce inflation or to stimulate production when either were necessary. These stratagems were applied by the Nixon Administration between 1968 and 1971 without reducing inflation or, when the plan changed to seeking recovery, helping production very much. The problem turned out to be that large firms and large unions dominated such a large share of the economy that a system of "administered" pricing existed. The contracts these firms and unions agreed upon, and then the profit and price levels the firms set, were relatively insensitive to government manipulations. In the New Deal the free market model of a classic unrestrained economy was rejected. In the Nixon Administration the idea that indirect governmental activity could create a "managed economy" was greatly modified. The result was the first peacetime imposition of wage and price controls in American history.

There is no doubt that in the economy there has been an increasing consolidation into larger and larger corporate units. The two hundred largest manufacturing firms held 48 per cent of all assets in 1958 and over 60 per cent in 1968. The 1960–1970 decade saw over 12,000 mergers in manufacturing and mining alone. The rise of the national conglomerate, multifunction corporation has been paralleled by the rise of the international corporation. In certain industries, particularly oil, American firms have always been deeply involved in international activities, including relationships with foreign governments and international trade. One observer characterized Standard Oil of New Jersey in these terms:

With more than a hundred thousand employees around the world (it has three times as many people overseas as the U.S. State Department), a six-million-ton tanker fleet (half again bigger than Russia's), and $17 billion in assets (nearly equal to the combined assessed valuation of Chicago and Los Angeles), it can more easily be thought of as a nation-state than a commercial enterprise.[16]

A new development is the drive of nonpetroleum domestic corporations into the international realm. The ITT corporation has over 200,000 employees in fifty countries. In fields such as electronics, companies have shifted large amounts of their production and new capital investment into foreign countries, constantly shifting their plants in search of low wage rates in the underdeveloped world. Still other companies, in fields such as autos, have sought to hedge against domestic uncertainties and controls by buying into foreign companies or setting up wholly owned overseas production and marketing subsidiaries that operate in foreign markets.

The implications of these developments for American politics are very widespread. On the domestic side, domination of the economy by a declining number of firms concentrates power in fewer and fewer hands. It adds to the trend toward non-competitive, "administered" pricing and price hikes that cannot be stopped because no one has any alternative. Such price increases, approaching if not achieving monopoly pricing, are really tax increases leveled on all consumers. The consumers have no say over the process, as individuals, through a market mechanism, or through elected representatives.[17] It is also possible—experts disagree—that concentration reduces innovation and the advance of technology. Further, in this realm the corporations are increasingly politically sophisticated and involved in politics through the route of campaign contributions. Although contributions by companies as such are illegal, elaborate schemes for assessing officials and making the costs up to them have been devised.[18]

On the international side, companies with multiple overseas operations raise a

[16] Richard J. Barber, *The American Corporation* (New York: Dutton, 1970), pp. 19–20.
[17] See Morton Mintz and Jerry S. Cohen, *American Inc.: Who Owns and Operates the United States* (New York: Dial, 1971), especially pp. 34–75, 296–330.
[18] Ibid., pp. 151–178.

number of thorny questions. To what publics and governments, if any, are these companies (now common to all of the Western nations) responsible? How does the concept of public policy apply to companies that take productive facilities outside the continental range of American wage-labor relations or of pollution laws? If, as is surely likely, the investment and income of companies producing abroad and selling here or both producing and selling abroad become more and more important to domestic prosperity, in what way can any public interest be asserted over what is done?

Private Governments and Their Own Clienteles

Few would disagree that private governments exert vast influence over the lives of their employees, customers, and the general public. General Motors is a good illustration. Its annual sales produce more revenues than the state governments of the eleven northeastern states of the United States, more than the tax revenues of any foreign government except Britain or Russia, and more than the gross national product of many large countries such as Brazil. It has more than 1.3 million stockholders, 700,000 employees, and millions of customers. It is easy to specify the impact the corporation has on the lives of individuals. If its cars are safe and run well, they enhance the lives of customers. When GM decides to raise prices, the entire industry will follow, and all car buyers will pay more. In addition, if GM commits itself to pollution control, the likelihood of meeting the strict 1975 federal standards will be greater. By choosing who will be its suppliers, dealers, and banks, the company controls the prosperity and opportunities of thousands of others. Its attitude toward employees, on the production line and in the executive suites, determines what chances minority group members will have to work and what work satisfactions will be. A company decision to switch from shock-absorbing to cosmetic bumpers (a decision it has now reversed under governmental pressure), when followed by the rest of the industry, added 16 per cent to total auto insurance costs. None of this is to say that GM is without constraints. Like all corporations it has to satisfy employees, customers, unions, and various requirements of the government. But its leverage in the decisions it makes is enormous.

The problem comes when one asks: Who makes the decisions for corporations, or for large unions, or for large universities? Fifty years of serious study in sociology and political science have produced quite a clear picture. Although corporations may cling to the myth of stockholder sovereignty and unions to the concept that their members control them, every study documents the domination of large organizations by small numbers of people at the top.[19] Thus large corporations are essentially governed by self-selected and self-perpetuating directors and officers, often influenced by a few very large stockholders. Although some labor unions have a democratic

[19] The literature begins with Robert Michels's 1915 study, *Political Parties: A Sociological Study of the Oligarchical Tendencies of Modern Democracy,* reprinted by the Dover Press (New York, 1959). See also David Truman, *The Governmental Process,* 2nd ed. (New York: Borzoi Books, 1971), Part Two.

internal tradition and almost all have elaborate election procedures, the absence of membership participation and contested elections in all but a very few instances has been widely noted.[20]

Why does the phenomenon of control by the few occur? For some organizations, the answer is simply that formal legal power is hierarchically arranged. But for others, with a full panoply of formally democratic procedures, the answer is more complicated. One reason seems to be that even in democratic organizations, chosen officeholders wield a great deal of power by virtue of their position. That power— the salaries and perquisites of office, the ability to devote full time to top policy questions, the prominence necessary to articulate the goals of the organization, control over internal communications systems, and the chance to increase abilities with experience—solidifies their position. It widens the gap between leader and rank-and-file. In addition, in most organizations, including corporations, unions, and universities, top leaders want to maintain their positions. Their status becomes widely differentiated from those below them—in salary, in symbolic rewards, and in the more interesting work they have the power to perform. To stay in, they learn the manipulative techniques necessary: "office politics" in corporations, some form of mass leadership in unions, bureaucratic bargaining in universities. It becomes very difficult for a mass membership to influence a large organization even where formal democracy prevails. It is even harder for lower level workers in large corporations, not to mention for customers of such companies or the general public. These forms of institutional behavior are generally taken to be true for all large organizations, including, for that matter, governmental bureaucracies.

There is little argument about the prevalence of control by a few people in large institutions. This very prevalence is what leads us to discuss a "problem" of private government in a chapter on public policy. On the one hand, there is the perennial possibility in a society with nongovernmental sectors with real power that these sectors will eclipse public decision-making on the issues that matter most. On the other hand, there is the phenomenon that large, private institutions may be more important in the lives of their clienteles than government. In both instances, the number of people who run these powerful private organizations may be very small and subject to few controls.

There is a certain political paradox here. Few would argue that strong private institutions constitute a major counterbalance to the power of modern government. Thus the strong support in the American political tradition for a relatively autonomous economic sector, including a system of private property. Yet few can ignore the potential problems raised by private governments so powerful as to be universes in themselves.

The connection of the problem of private government with public policy-making should be evident by now. The governmental drive for regulatory control over aspects of the private sector is a response to private power. The mass politics of redistribu-

---

[20] For a classic exposition of a democratic exception and statement of the overall problem, see Seymour Martin Lipset, et al., *Union Democracy* (Garden City, N.Y.: Doubleday-Anchor, 1962).

tion is in some ways a response to private power being exercised in certain ways. The consumer movement led by Ralph Nader is an effort to give one part of the corporate clientele—the customer—some say over the quality of the product he gets. Similarly, the antipollution movement is an effort to force private governments that make polluting products to change, either by making nonpolluting products, by paying the costs of pollution themselves, or by making their customers rather than the entire public pay. To some degree the development of a "counterculture," with alternative nonbureaucratic life styles and with less rigid occupational roles for men and women represents a form of resistance to the depersonalization of individuals in large institutions. Reaction to private government, in other words, takes many forms. Private organizations and their power cannot be ignored in any discussion of public policy. Not only elected government has power in the total society. Not only elected government has power over people's lives.

How Public Policy Is Made: Three Models

The last four chapters of this textbook deal with the substance of American public policy in a variety of fields—welfare and economic policy, civil rights and liberties, policies that distribute status, military and foreign policy, pollution, housing, mass transit. The nine chapters following this one, however, discuss how policy is made and analyze political processes and institutions. We constantly confront, and try to face honestly, various questions of not only how things work, but of who holds power and how benefits and costs emerge. In the end, every student will have to decide for himself or herself how to evaluate our very complicated society and equally complex political system. At this point, however, it is appropriate to discuss three broad models, the *pluralist,* the *power elite,* and the *mass mobilization* explanations. Each purports to explain how policy actually is made, or should be made, or both. Each answers some of the questions raised in the beginning of this chapter about who governs, who benefits, who pays.

The Pluralist Model

The pluralist model has a number of distinguished academic and popular exponents.[21] Certainly until the mid-1960's it was the most widely accepted explanation of public policy-making among political scientists. To oversimplify some of the fine points, here is what most pluralists would say about how American policy is made. Public policy is the outcome of conflict among organized groups. Almost all sectors of the society are organized, or are potentially organized, and this situation causes a certain equity in public policy outcomes. No one interest can dominate any policy field, because other groups will oppose such a force and because elected politicians are also sensitive to the potential constituencies that could be organized depending upon what is done. The presence of diverse organizations with independent sources of

---

[21] For an exceptionally lucid discussion, see Robert A. Dahl, *Pluralist Democracy in the United States* (Chicago: Rand McNally, 1967).

power also acts as a check upon powerful government. In dealing with groups, government is not necessarily a neutral arbiter among them, although it may play such an umpire role. In a society characterized by multiple sources of power—pluralism—government becomes another organization. It articulates positions, wins supporters, and bargains. Some pluralists view government as a kind of supergroup in the group struggle and some view it as just another competitor.

The pluralists believe that the competition among groups guarantees fair play in the end for all Americans. In this respect, the model draws heavily upon the free enterprise market model of economists, especially the modified version put forth by John Kenneth Galbraith, who described America as possessing many powerful groups, all balancing each other by "countervailing" power.[22] Because of the competition among relatively autonomous power centers, the main technique of policy-making is bargaining. Furthermore, the pace of change is necessarily slow, because although it is easy to achieve blockage of something in this system, it is hard to put together a majority coalition. Thus policy-making is incremental; that is, there is great continuity of policy and changes are small additions or subtractions from what went before. The system is politically stable, because everyone can get something, ideology is played down for trading back and forth, and there are no abrupt or sudden changes.

The Power Elite Model

Various exponents of the power elite model argue that a small group of upper-class persons and their coopted associates run the major private sectors of the country and also the most important parts of the American government. C. Wright Mills, the famous radical sociologist, brought this thesis to renewed intellectual prominence in the 1950's with his book, *The Power Elite*.[23] G. William Domhoff has updated the thesis by describing a "governing class." [24] Many political scientists, having uncovered E. E. Schattschneider's wry comment that "The flaw in the pluralist heaven is that the heavenly chorus sings with a strong upper-class accent," [25] have also begun to explore this model.

Again in an oversimplified version, we can connect a power elite model to public policy. Members of an interlocking elite structure that consists of a tiny minority of the total population dominate most important policy issues. This class controls and, some argue, owns the important parts of the corporate sector. This elite also dominates government especially on questions of foreign, defense, and economic policy.

One elite technique is underwriting the finances of both major parties to guarantee that disagreement between the parties on the issues most likely to be of concern to the elite will be minimal. Another technique of power elite influence is placing its members in the key jobs in government, especially in the White House, the State

---

22 *The Affluent Society* (Boston: Houghton, 1958).
23 New York: Oxford University Press, 1956.
24 *Who Rules America?* (Englewood Cliffs, N.J.: Prentice-Hall, 1967).
25 *The Semisovereign People* (New York: Holt, 1960), p. 35.

Department, the CIA, the Defense Department, and the regulatory agencies. Thus, a disproportionate percentage of high executives in all these governmental posts are men with upper-class educations, corporate legal backgrounds, and often sizable personal wealth. Where members of this class do not serve themselves, the model holds, those loyal to them do. Those who have risen from poverty to speak for this establishment, such as former Rockefeller Foundation President and then Secretary of State Dean Rusk, or President Richard M. Nixon, a top corporate lawyer, do just as well as those born to the elite.

The power elitists do not argue that members of the governing class control everything, but that they set the boundaries of governmental activity and protect their interests on issues that are seen as crucial. The tax system, with its loopholes for the rich, is seen as one good indicator of elite power. Outside the key areas of foreign policy, defense, and broad economic policy, the elite may have little concern and thus many other issue domains may be run by nonelite individuals and may be subject to popular control. Cabinet agencies such as Health, Education, and Welfare or Housing and Urban Development are seen as nonelite operations. The Congress is regarded as more subject to mass opinion than the executive because its members come from a broader cross-section of the population. Furthermore, not all members of the elite will agree among themselves on some issues.

Public policy in such a model is essentially protective of the viewpoints and interests of one group. Most theorists have been clearer in outlining the existence of the elite than what the specific policy consequences are. One policy result has surely been protection of free enterprise even through the Depression. Another result would have to be the "bipartisan" policy of Cold War anti-Communism with very heavy defense spending. Policy change amounts to the minimal social progress necessary to prevent serious instabilities in a situation where the few have to cope with a mass public that is potentially mobilizable against them. Power elite theorists would probably maintain that system stability has depended, since the end of World War II, on a combination of heavy indoctrination of the mass public and on economic prosperity fueled by defense spending. Some would also add that various mass movements have undermined that stability. One social critic has argued that the Vietnam war shattered the underpinnings of the corporate-governmental elite.[26]

The Mass Mobilization Model

There is yet one more model of policy-making, the mass mobilization model. Few people think this model describes all of American policy-making, but many think it describes some aspects of it. One well-known political scientist has prescribed it as a way of overcoming the blockage in the present system.[27] Still others feel that whatever its contemporary validity, something like the mass mobilization model

[26] See Charles A. Reich, *The Greening of America* (New York: Bantam, 1971), pp. 230–232.

[27] See Theodore J. Lowi, *The Politics of Disorder* (New York: Basic Books, 1971).

would have been a good fit with the reality of nineteenth-century American politics, especially with political party activity, prior to 1890.

In the mass mobilization model, as the name implies, virtually the entire citizenry participates in politics. It can be aroused or mobilized by strong, disciplined, programmatic political parties or by charismatic leadership, or both. Partial mobilization can be managed by individual interest groups or strong social movements. In a mass mobilization context, program-oriented, goal-oriented, and often morally oriented politics replaces bargaining or behind-the-scenes manipulation. Movements aiming at mobilization often have to fight to broaden the agenda of politics so as to put their aims on the public table. They often also have to fight to achieve legitimacy for their very existence, sometimes including for their basic rights to vote. In the politics of mass mobilization, direct action techniques are not uncommon. One way to mobilize a constituency is through conflict and controversy. Thus picketing, marching, and protesting as well as neighborhood-level organizing and, in today's world, mass media are part of this kind of politics.

In a mass mobilization system, public policy is the outcome of head-to-head conflict in which someone clearly wins and someone clearly loses. Policy may be more often what we earlier called *redistributive*. Such conflict followed by victory and defeat may characterize a much less stable political system than in the other two models. Change is likely to be more rapid, and there is the probability, or at least the possibility, of wrenching alterations in how things are done and in who gets what from politics. Rapid change in policies has side effects, including greater insecurity on the part of citizens and groups accustomed to a traditional mode of politics and also on the part of those who feel that changes may take away something they do not want to give up. The entire population is likely to be more politicized.

Policy-Making in America: Which Model Applies?

Any analysis of the American political system in depth will provide some answers to the question: Which of the three models, the pluralist, the power elite, or the mass mobilization, applies? Reading through this textbook, the student will no doubt form his or her own judgment. Actually, the question itself is too simple. A preliminary listing of some opinions drawn from the text material that follows indicates that each of the models may apply to some issue areas or to some governmental agencies or to some sectors of the society. Further, in a dynamic and relatively open society, there is constant change.

Let us illustrate how this complexity in public policy operates. The available evidence shows that many aspects of public policy-making fit the pluralistic model. Certainly the politics of congressional committees and the coalition politics of the major parties involve bargaining among multiple groups. Furthermore, most domestic policy issues—housing, transportation, health, welfare, pollution—seem to be settled on this basis. On the other hand, in foreign policy, defense policy, and what might be called macroeconomic policy (especially international economic policy), a stronger case can be made that both the personnel and the policy fit the power elite model. Furthermore, some issues in American politics appear to be resolved through mass mobilization. The Civil Rights acts of the 1960's were pushed through Congress through something like a mass mobilization. Smaller mobilizations have sustained antiwar and feminist movements, and, on a different ideological basis, the Goldwater (1964) and Wallace (1968, 1972) presidential campaigns. Both political parties retain at least some potential for mass mobilization. The President, through his direct access to millions over mass media and his symbolic and moral location in the American system, is capable of considerable mobilization. In fact, the Presidency, despite the conflict of recent years, probably still remains the single most powerful office and the most usable base for mobilization politics.

To give an answer that says "on the one hand this" but "on the other hand that" is not really to beg the question of which model fits. It may not be neat and clean, but all of the models fit parts of the political system. Furthermore, there is overlap. The antiwar movement over Vietnam used a politics of mass mobilization to penetrate the Establishment position, and with partial success. The civil rights movement used protest as its first instrument to crack into the pluralist system of distributing the goodies of American life while leaving the blacks largely out. The second phase of black politics in the 1970's has adopted many pluralist strategies, including running for office, building coalitions, and bargaining. Thus, it may be that each model describes possibilities for attaining power and policy victories for different segments of a population depending upon their resources and conditions. How these choices are made, how they are shaped by the institutional and social structure of the nation, and what they mean for the participants are the subject of everything that follows in this book. In a sense, we are saying that public policies cannot be separated from structures and processes. The nature of the contest, the rules, and the referees have an impact along with the condition and the skill of the players.

suggested additional readings

Blair, John M. *Economic Concentration.* New York: Harcourt Brace Jovanovich, 1972.

Dahl, Robert A. *Pluralist Democracy in the United States.* Chicago: Rand McNally & Co., 1967.

Domhoff, G. William. *Who Rules America?* Englewood Cliffs, N.J.: Prentice-Hall, Inc., 1967.*

Easton, David. *The Political System.* New York: Alfred A. Knopf, Inc., 1953.

Kohlmeier, Louis M., Jr. *The Regulators: Watchdog Agencies and the Public Interest.* New York: Harper & Row, Publishers, 1969.*

Lasswell, Harold. *Politics: Who Gets What, When, How.* Cleveland: Meridian Books, 1958.*

Lowi, Theodore J. *The End of Liberalism.* New York: W. W. Norton & Company, Inc., 1969.*

———. *The Politics of Disorder.* New York: Basic Books, Inc., 1971.

McConnell, Grant. *Private Power and American Democracy.* New York: Vintage Books Edition, 1970.*

Mitchell, Joyce M. and William C. *Political Analysis and Public Policy.* Chicago: Rand McNally & Co., 1969.

Pechman, Joseph A. *Federal Tax Policy.* New York: W. W. Norton & Company, Inc., 1971.*

Schultze, Charles L., et al. *Setting National Priorities: The 1971 Budget.* Washington: The Brookings Institution, 1970.*

———. *Setting National Priorities: The 1973 Budget.* Washington: The Brookings Institution, 1972.*

* Available in paperback.

3 the american constitution

case study

Crumbling Walls?
Public Aid to
Parochial Schools

Each morning teenager Gregory Tomo climbs aboard a public school bus and travels eight miles to his modern, brick-and-glass high school. . . .

Once he finishes his state-financed bus ride, Greg goes to a math class taught by a teacher whose salary is, in part, paid by state funds. He does research in a library stocked with five sets of encyclopedias purchased with federal funds. He sits through an English class in which state-supplied films and projectors are used. He performs experiments in a science lab where he uses equipment supplied by both the state and federal government. And he wraps up his day by attending a state-supported driver-education course.

The one surprising fact concerned with Greg's typical school day is that his high school is Roman Catholic. This is surprising because the First Amendment states that "Congress shall make no law respecting an establishment of religion, or prohibiting the free exercise thereof." Yet, millions of Catholic students share in state- and federal-financed education programs.

There is no precise estimate of how much federal, state, and local governments aid church schools, but state aid alone could reach $100 million in 1971. New York, Louisiana, Michigan, Ohio, Connecticut, Rhode Island, and Pennsylvania have all enacted broad assistance programs to help bail out church schools—87 per cent of which are Catholic —that confront bankruptcy. In 1971, the Supreme Court handed down two landmark decisions that had potentially devastating effects for parochial education. They could spell the difference between survival and extinction of 11,351 Catholic elementary and secondary schools attended by over 4 million students.

In each of the seven states mentioned the aid programs for nonpublic schools have touched off bitter political battles. Strong opposition groups have challenged the constitutionality of all seven aid plans in the courts. The most heated opposition comes from those states that have large Catholic populations—states where church aid would cost taxpayers millions of dollars. Bipartisan support in several legislatures has favored state assistance to nonpublic schools as an economic measure. Legislators are apparently persuaded by the logic of saving tax dollars. One Pennsylvania legislator explained that "It costs up to $850 to educate a child in the public schools, but we could keep a child in the [Catholic] schools for only $37 a year in state aid."

The standard argument of Catholic educators who seek public financial assistance is that Catholic parents are taxpayers and deserve a share of the funds allotted to public education. Non-Catholic parents have responded that the public schools are always open to Catholic children. The nub of the argument from non-Catholics is that Protestants and Jews should not be compelled to subsidize parochial schools whose main function is to teach children Catholicism. Arguments of Catholic educators, in turn, are buttressed by an economic threat. Unless federal and state aid is forthcoming, Catholic elementary and secondary schools will be forced to close because of soaring costs. That would channel millions of Catholic pupils into public schools that are already overburdened. Make an unenviable but necessary choice, Catholics say: "Pay for part of our children's education in the Catholic schools—or pay for all of it in the public schools." If the public schools were flooded with over 4 million new pupils, it would add about $4.5 billion dollars a year to public school operating budgets, not including the cost of a massive school construction program that would have to be started.

Few public officials or educators dispute the severity of the financial crisis that confronts church schools. Catholic schools are economic victims of inflation and a sharp decline in the supply of nuns and priests who are available to teach at very low salaries. Today, there are over 2,000 fewer parochial educational institutions than there were in 1965, while their total enrollment slumped nearly 7 per cent in the last decade.

The problem of public aid to private and parochial schools—like many serious problems in our society—eventually found

its way to the Supreme Court. Rhode Island and Pennsylvania statutes that granted state aid to parochial schools were attacked in the lower federal courts. In both cases taxpayers claimed that the First Amendment's "free exercise" and "establishment" clauses were being violated.

Rhode Island's 1969 Salary Supplement Act provided for a 15 per cent salary increase to be paid to teachers in nonpublic schools. This salary increase would be paid only to lay teachers who earned less than their counterparts in public schools. Three hundred and seventy-five thousand dollars had been appropriated for this purpose. Of the 250 teachers who applied for state financial aid, all were employed by Roman Catholic schools. There were several statutory restrictions placed upon teachers receiving this assistance: Teachers must agree, in writing, not to teach courses in religion; they must use only those materials used in public schools; and they must teach only courses offered in public schools.

After hearing extensive testimony, a three-judge Federal District Court held—by a 2 to 1 vote—that the state law was unconstitutional for two reasons: (1) "its effect is substantially to support a religious enterprise; (2) its operations involve those reciprocal embroilments of government and religion which the First Amendment was meant to avoid." The key question that was decided by the District Court was "whether [the] degree of entanglement required by statute was likely to promote substantive evils against which the First Amendment guards."

The District Court found that the Catholic school system was an "integral part of the religious mission of the Catholic Church. Religious ideas were not (and could not be) confined to formal courses, nor were they restricted to a single area." It was unrealistic, the Court stated, to argue that nonreligious subjects taught in parochial schools could ignore the religious atmosphere of the classroom.

The Pennsylvania statute that subsidized nonpublic schools was similar to Rhode Island's except that along with financial aid for teachers' salaries, the state purchased "secular educational services," such as textbooks and instructional material. Pennsylvania had appropriated almost $20 million under this statute, the great majority of which was earmarked for Catholic schools. The statute expressly prohibited any religious instruction. A three-judge Federal District Court—by a 2 to 1 vote—declared that the Pennsylvania statute did not violate the religion clauses of the First Amendment. The state law was upheld on jurisdictional grounds. The question of "excessive entanglement" was never reached because the plaintiffs failed "to state a claim for relief."

The Rhode Island case (*Robinson* v. *DiCenso*) and the Pennsylvania case (*Lemon* v. *Kurtzman*) were appealed to the Supreme Court. Because the cases dealt with the separation of church and state, they were considered together. Both failed to pass constitutional muster; the Rhode Island decision was affirmed (8 to 1), and the Pennsylvania decision was reversed (8 to 0). The Court held that the cumulative impact of both state statutes involved "excessive entanglements" between government and religion.

Chief Justice Warren Burger, writing the opinion of the Court, acknowledged that the language of the religion clauses of the First Amendment "is at best opaque." The Amendment speaks of "no law respecting an establishment of religion." The word *respecting* is vague. Hence, it is difficult to ascertain whether the amendment means "no aid" or "some aid" to nonpublic schools. In the absence of any precise constitutional guide, the Chief Justice used three criteria in reviewing the Rhode Island and Pennsylvania school aid statutes: "sponsorship, financial support, and active involvement of the sovereign in religious activity."

Neither statute intended to advance or sponsor a religion. Both, according to the opinion of the Court, wanted to enhance the quality of education. The Chief Justice agreed with the conclusion of the majority in the Rhode Island case: the states were indeed involved in financial support of nonpublic schools, which involved "excessive entanglement between government and religion."

This "excessive entanglement" is due to to the very nature and mission of Catholic schools. The teachers, curriculum, and general atmosphere make parochial schools "a powerful vehicle for transmitting the Catholic faith to the next generation." All the checks used by both state legislatures cannot control the fundamental fact that parochial schools involve substantive religious activity. Statutory restrictions on parochial school teaching are inadequate precautions against the danger that religious instruction, however subtle, will intrude into the forbidden areas of the First Amendment. The dangers of teachers' presenting material to champion religious thought were brought out by Mr. Justice Douglas's concurring opinion. He illustrated how an arithmetic problem can be used to communicate pious thought:

If it takes forty thousand priests and a hundred forty thousand sisters to care for forty million Catholics in the United States, how many more priests and sisters will be needed to convert and care for the hundred million non-Catholics in the United States?

It would be very difficult for a dedicated teacher, inculcated with certain religious tenets, to remain religiously neutral. Unlike a book that can be periodically approved by the Commissioner of Education, a teacher's beliefs cannot be subject to the same scrutiny.

There is also a broader—and potentially more divisive—entanglement that deals with state assistance to nonpublic schools' turning into a political football. Parents of parochial school children might take strong partisan action to increase and protect state aid to church schools. The "monumental and deepening financial crisis" of the Rhode Island parochial school system would unescapably require larger and larger state appropriations. Data on the sharp increase of government expenditures for private schools are instructive. In 1960, for example, the federal government provided $500 million to private colleges and universities. State and local government contributions to private schools were negligible. In ten years the federal government's support to private institutions of higher learning has grown to $2.1 billion, and state aid to private schools has reached $100 million. With many millions of dollars at stake, candidates for office might be forced to run on an aid-to-religious-schools plank. The hazards of intense political and religious conflict would be great.

Chief Justice Burger concluded that the "cumulative impact" of the Rhode Island and Pennsylvania state aid programs fostered an "excessive" and impermissible degree of entanglement between government and religion. The degree of entanglement, therefore, was pivotal in striking down two state statutes as unconstitutional.

The *Lemon* and *DiCenso* decisions dealt a serious—and perhaps devastating—blow to the Catholic school system. If Catholic schools are forced to close their doors, public schools will face a crisis of the first magnitude. Yet these crises have been faced by the Court and by the

church before. The political struggles that inevitably surround the Court's decisions are not always "final." Indeed, powerful interests favoring parochial school aid are already seeking to find new (and to revitalize old) approaches to keep nonpublic schools open. An end run around the church-state issue, for example, is the child benefit theory. Under this plan, states provide aid to the private and parochial school pupil rather than to his school. Nearly twenty states have laws that provide for taxpayer-supported transportation of private school students. Many states provide free breakfast and hot lunch programs and visiting nurses, along with other health services. Federally funded visual aids and reference books are "loaned" to parochial school students, instead of being given as outright gifts to nonpublic schools. Generally, such student-channeled aid has been upheld by the courts. The constitutionality of free bus transportation and loaned books is currently being challenged.

No one can be certain whether the Supreme Court will declare the "child benefit" aid program unconstitutional. The only certainty is that the line of separation, far from being a wall, is often blurred and indistinct. The blurred line of demarcation between church and state was illustrated in another religious case decision handed down in 1971. In *Tilton* v. *Richardson,* the Supreme Court held in a 5 to 4 decision that federal assistance in the construction of academic buildings on campuses of private colleges—including church-affiliated colleges—is constitutional. On the college level, "entanglement" was deemed sufficiently minimal. With two new justices on the Supreme Court, the line of separation between acceptable public assistance and unconstitutional intrusion on the religion clauses may shift. No matter which way the new Supreme Court decides, aggrieved parties will seek other political avenues to achieve their goals.

SOURCES

DiCenso v. *Robinson,* 316 Federal
    Supplement 112.
Lemon v. *Kurtsman and Robinson* v.
    DiCenso, 39 Law Week 4844.
Wall Street Journal, November 10, 1970.

The American Revolution

The American Revolution brought the new nation insistent problems as well as political independence, and it completed the process of making government constitutional. The events of 1776–1783 were more than a War of Independence; they were revolutionary, and their cumulative impact was also to further democratize the relationship between the governors and the governed. Some 100,000 pro-British Loyalists, representing a sizable fraction of the colonies' upper social orders, were forced into exile, their land confiscated and redistributed. Voting rights were expanded; feudal and royal restrictions on the inheritance and acquisition of land were abolished; religious toleration was encouraged; and in some states the first steps were taken to discourage and even abolish slavery. The second half of the eighteenth century was an age of democratic revolution, and the Americans were the first successful revolutionaries. The American Revolution was not as conservative as it has seemed to some historians. As R. R. Palmer has cogently observed, "It was the weakness of conservative forces in eighteenth century America, not their strength, that made the American Revolution as moderate as it was." [1]

Besides advancing individual liberties, the Revolution compelled the former colonies to reshape their governments. Their practical need for workable governments combined naturally with their political assumptions, especially the contract and natural rights theories that had been absorbed from John Locke, the seventeenth-century English philosopher. In the colonists' view the British government had destroyed, instead of defended, their basic rights to life, liberty, and property. Accordingly, the social contract was broken and revolution justified, a conclusion boldly announced to the world in the Declaration of Independence. But John Locke, whose theories the Americans found so congenial, was no anarchist; his writings indicated that dissolving the bonds of government meant, at most, a temporary reversion into

[1] *The Age of the Democratic Revolution: A Political History of Europe and America 1700–1800* (Princeton: Princeton University Press, 1959), p. 189.

a state of nature before government was again reconstituted. In this respect, too, the Americans proved themselves faithful Lockeans. "Government is dissolved," Patrick Henry informed the First Continental Congress. "Where," he asked, "are your land-marks, your boundaries of Colonies? We are in a state of nature, Sir."

An Age of Constitution-Making

As a matter of fact, the Americans were a comfortable distance from any beastly state of nature (Patrick Henry himself was part of a cultured and polished Virginia aristocracy). Only theoretically were the old bonds of government dissolved. There was a pressing need to organize some sort of system for what the Declaration of Independence called the "Thirteen United States of America," and the governments of the "Free and Independent States" wanted revamping. In fulfilling these needs the ex-colonists were profoundly influenced by the assumptions of their political culture. Naturally, many of their institutions and practices were a direct inheritance from Britain. Most significantly, the virtually unspoken commitment to the desirability of limited, constitutional government reflected an enormous political debt to what is appropriately labeled the Mother Country. The Americans, in other words, were culturally conditioned to accept only the institutions and practices to which they had become accustomed in the countries of their origin.

But they did not simply assume their British inheritance and leave it unchanged. Quite the contrary, as a consequence of their own special situation and their political experiences vis-à-vis the British government during the colonial period and especially during the crisis years from 1760 to 1776, a distinct political culture had emerged in America by the last third of the eighteenth century. For example, the Americans had acquired a permanent and inflexible aversion to monarchy, royal pretensions, and aristocratic trappings. Similarly, they were hostile to unchecked executive power, for it reminded them of the detested George III—that "tyrant," in the words of the Declaration of Independence, "unfit to be the ruler of a free people." This particular cluster of assumptions quickly confronted them with a difficult problem as they set out to arrange their governing institutions. Although recognizing the need for some sort of an executive, they were anxious to prevent him from becoming an absolute ruler who would override the legislative assembly and ultimately the people.

The Americans' response to their need for revised governmental forms and the assumptions of their political culture resulted in one of the great ages of constitution-making. Between 1776 and 1780 fully eleven of the thirteen former colonies—now states—framed new written constitutions. Apart from differences of detail and emphasis, the early state constitutions shared many common features. They were written and they reflected the prevailing notions of social contract and of government as a trust. The idea was neatly summed up in the Massachusetts Constitution of 1780, which is still in effect. It proclaims:

The body politic is formed by a voluntary association of individuals: It is a social compact by which the whole people covenants with each citizen and each citizen with the whole people that all shall be governed by certain laws for the common good.

Here the states showed a profound debt to their recent past. The new constitutions owed their paternity to the older colonial charters, those primitive frameworks of government that, beginning with the company colonial charter of Virginia (1606), proved convenient vehicles for absorbing the idea that government should be limited.

A like indebtedness to colonial practice was reflected in the political instruments they reaffirmed: a powerful two-chamber legislature, popularly elected for short terms, and a weakened governor. The executive, suffering from its long identification as a tool of the despised monarchy, was hemmed in by restrictions. Bills of Rights, intended to secure man's "unalienable Rights," also won for the first time prominent places in the new constitutions.

Above all, the first state constitutions testified to their framers' conviction that a charter superior to ordinary legislative enactments should organize and limit government. At first the constitutions were adopted by specially empowered legislatures. By the late 1770's the conviction grew that this was not enough. A constitution was deemed to be not only law but higher law, and a special convention, whose handiwork should pass popular muster, was required. A practicable way had been found for "constituting" new governments: the people became the constituent power. "The people, having exercised sovereignty," as one scholar has written, "now came under the government. Having made law they came under law." [2] This law was divided into two levels. There was a statutory law that, subject to higher law limitations, could be made and unmade by legislators, the people's representatives. More fundamentally, there was a higher law—a constitution—that could be made or amended only by conventions specially empowered by the people. Not only had Bracton's dictum bridged the awesome gap between theory and practice, but the blending of constitutionalism (limited government) with democracy (popularly accountable rulers) was proving to be a natural development within American political culture.

Union or Disunion?

No less than the states, the Second Continental Congress felt impelled to frame a charter for governing the "United States of America." The system it produced, the "Articles of Perpetual Union and Friendship," failed to live up to the optimistic promise contained in its title. The sister states were soon one squabbling family and the plan of union turned out to be only transitory. The Articles envisioned a loose league of states allied mainly for purposes of defense and foreign affairs. As the instrument for governing the Confederation, the Articles established a unicameral Congress composed of thirteen state delegations, each casting one equal vote. Congress could declare war and field an army, make peace, sign treaties with foreign powers, regulate Indian affairs, and operate a postal service; legislation to carry out these powers, however, required approval by two thirds of the state delegations. Congress was unable to levy taxes, the first power of any effective government, and

[2] Ibid., p. 215.

it was limited to petitioning, or, to speak bluntly, to begging the states for revenue.

The Confederation, in fact, was powerless, for real sovereignty remained with the states. They continued to coin money, regulate commerce, impose tariffs, and raise armed militias. Worse yet, amendments were virtually impossible because they had to be unanimously ratified by the states. Twice Congress sought to improve the Articles by recommending an amendment allowing it to raise revenue through import duties, but the proposed reform failed. On one occasion tiny Rhode Island, a hotbed of antinationalist sentiment, rejected the amendment after its ratification by all the other states.

Institutionally, the Articles were equally defective. Congress created committees to superintend its affairs, but there was no executive and no court system. Unable to control directly the lives of its citizens, the American Confederation depended on the goodwill of the member states for the execution of its decisions. Unfortunately, goodwill, though a wholly admirable trait, is an inadequate substitute for political power. A contemporary critic put it well when he complained, "A law without a penalty is mere *advice;* a magistrate without the power of punishment is a *cypher.* Here is the *great defect* in the articles of our federal government." [3]

The wonder of it is that the United States did achieve some notable gains during the Confederation—independence, establishment of popular government, and organization for settlement of the sprawling Northwest Territory. Yet these achievements owed more to American ingenuity, geographical advantage, and luck than to the Articles. By the mid-1780's the Confederation was in danger of disintegration, and many foresaw America splitting into three sectional confederations—New England, Middle Atlantic, and Southern. Americans were generally well off in the sense of being sufficiently clothed and fed, but the Articles were a political failure, inadequate for the governing of the entire nation.

In part, the period's troubles, such as the commercial and agricultural depression, were probably inevitable consequences of America's exclusion from the protected confines of the British mercantile system. Yet, by permitting the states to coin money and to make their own locally oriented commercial regulations, the Articles encouraged business chaos and impeded postwar recovery. Perhaps most disturbing was the low international stature of the United States, which was regarded as a weak and contemptible nation unable to pay its own debts. Politically, the Confederation's great failing was its inability even to attempt solutions to these conditions.

As these weaknesses became increasingly evident, Americans active in public life divided into two broad camps without much regard to economic and social class. One camp, locally and sectionally oriented, feared the loss of its power to a central government. The other camp, nationally minded, concerned itself with America's national and international position: to use an eighteenth-century expression, it viewed political problems in terms of "continental" needs. "I do not conceive," declared George Washington, whose experience was firsthand, that "we can exist long as a

---

[3] Noah Webster, quoted in Homer G. Hockett, *The Constitutional History of the United States* (New York: Macmillan, 1939), I, pp. 185–186.

nation without having lodged somewhere a power which will pervade the whole Union in as energetic a manner as the authority of the State Governments extends over the federal States."

Framing a Constitution

An "energetic" national government—this was the object of the men who assembled at Philadelphia late in the spring of 1787. The history of the Constitutional Convention is a fascinating tale of compromises among diverse interests, of political deals, and of idealistic faith in an American union. Much can be said of the convention and its work, but four points deserve special emphasis.

1. It produced a federal system of government.

The central political authority created by the new Constitution was given all the essential powers that it had lacked under the Confederation. It was empowered to levy taxes, regulate interstate and foreign commerce, control the currency, create an army and a navy, and conduct defense and international relations. To implement these powers the national government was given what the Confederation had sorely lacked, authority to control directly the lives and affairs of its citizens. In contrast, the states were forbidden to interfere with the enumerated federal powers. No longer, for instance, were they allowed to coin money or tax imports from other states.

Unlike the weak Confederation, the new system came equipped with institutional tools for governing. It featured a bicameral Congress to legislate for the Union and a separately elected executive to command the armed forces, manage foreign affairs, and "take care that the laws be faithfully executed." It was also provided with an independent judicial system to settle disputes arising under national law and, in some cases, to declare the law and to pass on the validity of state enactments conflicting with national law.

Except for the empire-minded Alexander Hamilton, none of the framers seriously considered scrapping the states. The states, which the convention delegates had grown accustomed to as vital units of government, were retained. Their authority, however, was limited in significant respects. Article I, Section 10, prohibited them from coining money, levying export and import taxes (unless approved by Congress), and imposing tonnage duties on ships calling in their ports; state legislatures were forbidden to pass bills of attainder and laws impairing the obligation of contracts. In addition, this prohibitory section of the Constitution ordered the states to stay out of foreign affairs by forbidding them to make treaties or to engage in war. Despite these limitations, the states were nevertheless allowed to share some very important powers, such as that of taxation, with the national government. The states, moreover, retained general authority over their citizens; they had, for example, the primary responsibility for maintaining domestic peace and order, for preventing and prosecuting criminal offenses, and for making and enforcing the laws dealing with property rights and commercial relationships.

This, in brief outline, was the system devised by the framers. They called it *federal,* but that was a deliberate misnomer. In 1787 *federal* and *confederal* were interchangeable terms describing a loose union of states—the very kind of arrangement that the delegates were busily replacing. By calling their proposed government *federal* (even though its powers far exceeded those of the Confederation), they sought to disarm "federalist" states' rights critics and left their opponents in the unhappy position of being labeled as antifederalists. In reality, of course, the framers had gone a long way toward creating the "energetic" national government that Washington had so ardently commended.

2. It put together a constitution grounded in American political culture.

As with the state constitutions, the federal took its building materials from the colonial and revolutionary periods. These included a common culture and legal system, a recent but real historical tradition (the Americans had defied one of the world's great powers), and a workable set of political institutions. On the really crucial matters the framers and, more importantly, their countrymen agreed. The need for a written constitution that limited and divided governmental power and made it popularly accountable were universally accepted notions in late eighteenth-century America. When such consensus on the fundamentals of the political process is lacking, as was the case with the ill-fated constitutions of Weimar Germany (1919) and France of the Fourth Republic (1946), no words written on parchment can bring to life a working, enduring constitutional system.

Nothing better illustrates the Constitution's debt to the colonial experience than its division of national power between executive, legislative, and judicial departments (Articles I, II, and III). This division, which is commonly (though somewhat inaccurately) referred to as the "separation of powers," creates a form of government with two elected and overtly political branches, the Congress and the Presidency, having differing bases of electoral support and differing, though often overlapping, powers. Thus, only Congress can enact legislation and make financial appropriations, but the President, who is charged with executing the laws, may play a legislative role by proposing legislation and vetoing congressional enactments. The Supreme Court, too, whose primary responsibility is the ultimate adjudication of federal cases and disputes involving constitutional questions, has a distinctive governmental role. Because of the life tenure of its judges and other constitutional provisions, it is insulated to a significant degree from legislative or executive control. As a consequence of these divided powers, the American constitutional system is structurally unlike that of parliamentary systems such as the British that fuse the powers of government by concentrating all legal and political authority in a legislative body, which in turn elects the executive (the Prime Minister and the other Cabinet ministers).

What is relevant here is that the Constitution's preference for a tripartite governmental structure with separate branches able to check and balance one another grew out of the colonial *practice* of divided powers and responsibilities. It was a tribute not so much to the writings of separation-of-power theorists, such as the French thinker Montesquieu, as to a common political culture that the framers shared.

Because the King relied on his governors as agents of royal authority and the colonial assemblies had successfully asserted their right to raise and appropriate money, a mutual antagonism had developed. Representing disparate interests, the two branches had attained separate identities, though, until the final break of 1775–1776, they had been able to work together in uneasy cooperation. Similarly, the colonial courts, geographically removed from English control, had developed a partial independence from the legislatures as it had become increasingly recognized that a just legal system required judges free from political coercion. Accustomed to a division of powers, the ex-colonists retained what had become *their* system in their new state constitutions. The framers of 1787 simply incorporated the culturally familiar institutional division. Later, confronted by antifederalist charges that they had unduly concentrated power, they invoked "the celebrated Montesquieu" to defend their creation, arguing that it carefully divided political power. Some scholars have seen the Constitution as a deliberate monument to a theory, but the plea of convention delegate John Dickinson more accurately describes what took place: "Experience must be our only guide. Reason may mislead us." The practice of divided powers came first; the theory of *The Federalist* followed the institutional practices.

3. It was a masterful compromise struck by master politicians.

Merely to list the names of the most prominent delegates should be a reminder that they all had one characteristic in common: they were politicians. Such men as George Washington, James Madison, Benjamin Franklin, Gouverneur Morris, Elbridge Gerry, Luther Martin, Roger Sherman, and South Carolina's two Pinckneys (Charles and General Charles Cotesworth) were typical of the fifty-five delegates in their practical experience. Eight had signed the Declaration of Independence, twenty-one had fought in the revolutionary armies, seven had been state governors, and thirty-nine had served in Congress.

Predictably, the entire framing process was an exercise in the art of political accommodation. The prime illustration is the so-called "Great Compromise" settling the thorny problem of state representation. Though Madison, allied with the brilliant James Wilson, fought valiantly for a strongly nationalist system—the Virginia Plan was a giant step toward centralization—the convention majority favored a more moderate course. Even at this early date in the Republic's history the delegates were wisely thinking about the folks back home; they wanted a charter that could win popular ratification, not a logically satisfying system destined for a book of readings on utopianism. Madison's scheme was toned down to provide for a bicameral legislature, consisting of a lower house to be popularly elected and a senate to be chosen by the state legislatures. But what was to be the basis of representation? Representation based strictly on population favored the interests of large and populous New York, Pennsylvania, and Virginia to the detriment of states like South Carolina or New Hampshire. Large-state domination, moreover, would have endangered ratification by arousing fears of centralization and small-state subservience. The "Great Compromise," the product of skilled political practitioners, produced a satisfactory formula—popular representation in the House, state representation in the Senate.

The delegates reconciled their divergent sectional and economic interests through a similar process of mutual adjustment. Northern fears that the southern states would be overrepresented because of their potentially limitless slave population were only partially eased by the "Three Fifths Compromise"; this decreed that, for purposes of both representation in the House and direct taxation, five slaves would be counted as the equivalent of three white men. Southerners also had their fears. They were afraid that Congress might ban or unduly tax the importation of slaves and that it might heavily tax the agricultural exports on which their prosperity was based and the manufactured imports that they had to buy. The resulting agreement was a typical convention compromise. Slave importation was guaranteed until 1808 and a moderate ceiling set on its taxation. Congress was prohibited from levying export tariffs, but, contrary to southern desires for a two-thirds requirement, import tariffs could be set by a simple majority vote.

A lesser compromise foreshadowed a now-familiar *leitmotiv* in American politics: buck-passing or, less colloquially, deferral of troublesome issues. Unable to agree on whether the Constitution should assume responsibility for the state debts incurred during the war—there was some feeling against benefiting speculators who had acquired the promissory notes at bargain prices—the delegates bequeathed the problem to the future and to the driving genius of the first Secretary of the Treasury, Alexander Hamilton. In a brilliant evasion, Article VI left the debts "as valid against the United States under this constitution as under the confederation," without saying just how valid that might be.

Addressing the delegates in their last session, the aged Benjamin Franklin made his famous plea for conciliation, asking each one to "doubt a little of his own infallibility" and to sign the charter. The wise doctor pointed out that perfection was not to be expected from such a convention because its delegates were influenced by an amalgam of qualities ranging from "their joint wisdom" to "their prejudices, their passions, their errors of opinion, their local interests, and their selfish views." And certainly this was true. All these qualities were reflected in the Constitution, folly as well as wisdom. But it also reflected something more: the framers' political *savoir-faire* that elevated compromise into a major first principle. This art of political bargaining and compromise, moreover, was already as natural to Madison and his colleagues as it is to the Senators and Representatives who sit in Congress today; here, too, the framers of 1787 mirrored assumptions and patterns of behavior derived from the political culture of late eighteenth-century America. Max Farrand, a historian who devoted a lifetime to studying its formation, once commented that the Constitution "defies analysis upon a logical basis"; but then that is to be expected: the Constitution is a politician's pact, not a philosopher's treatise.

4. It established a constitutional democracy.

Like most documents written by men, the Constitution lends itself to radically conflicting interpretations. The view here is that the Constitution, both in the intent of its framers and in its scheme of government, underwrote the twin principles of constitutionalism and democracy that were clearly emergent in American political culture. Its constitutionalism is evident. Both the nation and the states are restricted in their authority. At neither level of government, for example, may the legislature pass criminal laws that, ex post facto, work to the disadvantage of the accused or inflict punishment on him without a judicial trial. In addition, the Constitution regularizes the means for reaching political decisions. Congress and President are free to pursue controversial policy goals, but their procedures are carefully prescribed by the provisions of Articles I and II.

These limits on the rulers and, ultimately, on the people themselves draw strength from the Constitution's democratic features. In the House of Representatives, with its important power of the purse, the framers created a directly elected national body —in contrast to the Confederation Congress, whose membership was elected by the state legislatures. Although the President and the Senators were to be chosen indirectly, there is little evidence that they were deliberately isolated from popular control. Quite the contrary, it was fully expected that in most elections the presidential electors would be unable to agree on a candidate, thus placing the final choice in the House of Representatives.

Indirect popular election was not regarded as a device for thwarting popular rule; in fact this was the system that nine of the thirteen states used for the selection of their governors. Ironically, some of the delegates least in sympathy with popular control (such as Gouverneur Morris) favored direct election, but the electoral college was adopted in one of the convention's typically improvised compromises. Neither was it considered undemocratic for Senators to be chosen by the popularly elected state legislatures. In deference to states' rights feeling, the Senators were to serve as quasi-ambassadors, the representatives of their state governments. It is noteworthy that the antifederalists failed to denounce this as a blow against popular rule.

Significantly, the Constitution's critics showed far less faith in a popular national government than did its framers. Too often it is overlooked that the antifederalists, many of whom were landed aristocrats, criticized the Constitution for failing adequately to check and balance political power; even more than the framers they held a pessimistic view of man's capacity for self-government. But the new Constitution was basically democratic, a point quickly proved in 1789, when many of its critics sought and won federal offices; and it was again confirmed in 1800, when the federalists, who in large part were the party for the Constitution, were driven from power.

No less democratic was the manner by which the Constitution was adopted. The convention, to be sure, exceeded the instructions of the Confederation Congress by proposing a new system instead of merely revising the old. And it violated the Articles' requirement of unanimity by deciding to make its proposals operative upon ratification by nine states. It is relevant, however, that few objected: the old Congress signed its death warrant by transmitting the charter to the states; the states cooperated by arranging for ratifying conventions. More important, for the first time in history a national government was constituted by the people. Although only about one quarter of the country's white males actually voted for delegates to the ratifying conventions, at least three quarters of them were eligible to vote had they chosen to do so. Their failure to vote proves indifference and little else; the fact remains that the suffrage was relatively open and that there was public discussion. If, as some critics have charged, the framing and adoption of the Constitution amounted to a *coup d'état,* it was in a double sense a constitutional *coup:* it set up the basic structure for a constitutional system of limited government, and it was framed and adopted by men who were preoccupied with legality. In American political culture, even a *coup d'état* had to be constitutional.

Amendments

The framers believed the Constitution could be easily amended, but experience has shown that amendment is a slow and complicated endeavor. Article V requires two distinct steps, *proposal* by some national body and *ratification* by the states. Congress proposes amendments by a two-thirds vote; alternatively, two thirds of the state legislatures may petition it to call a convention for proposing amendments. This latter method has never been used successfully, though in the late 1960's thirty-two states, two short of the required majority, petitioned Congress to call a constitutional convention that would frame an amendment modifying the Supreme Court's controversial decisions ordering the reapportionment of state legislatures. Congress, however, apparently cannot be legally compelled to pass the enabling legislation necessary to such a convention, even if a constitutional majority of the state legislatures desire it.

Ratification occurs when three fourths of the states, acting through either their legislatures or specially elected conventions (a process used only for the Twenty-first Amendment), endorse the proposed amendment. Somewhat surprisingly, the real barrier to frequent amendment seems to be the proposing instead of the ratifying requirement. In the twentieth century the states have refused ratification to only one congressionally sponsored amendment, the unsuccessful Child Labor Amendment. It has taken slightly more than an average of two years for amendments to win ratification, a process that is reasonably fast for a political system that often makes decisions slowly.

Amendments I–XXV

The Constitution has been amended twenty-six times, or about once every twelve years if the first ten amendments (customarily considered to be part of the original document) are excluded. The amendments can be loosely categorized in four ways: *declaratory,* because they reaffirm existing constitutional relationships; *procedural,* because they change or guarantee certain procedures of government; *democratic,* because they assure rights deemed essential to popular government; or *legislative,* because they attempt to commit the nation to a new policy. This classification is useful as a rough guide, but many of the amendments frequently overlap the categories. An amendment that at the time of its passage strengthens democracy may also have the legislative effect of committing the nation to a new policy. For example, the amendments adopted in the aftermath of the Civil War prohibited racial discrimination by public authorities in an effort to assure essential democratic rights to the newly freed slaves; they also attempted to legislate a changed national policy.

Two amendments are primarily declaratory: the Ninth (1791) reserves to the people rights not otherwise specified in the Constitution; the Tenth (1791) reserves to the states and to the people powers not delegated to the federal government. Both simply reaffirmed what almost every American at the time took for granted. Most of the other amendments can be classified as either procedural or democratic, particularly in their present-day effects.

The Fourth, Fifth, Sixth, Seventh, and Eighth amendments (1791) prescribe the procedures to be followed in criminal trials; persons accused of crime, for example, must be tried by a jury of their peers. All of the following amendments are also essentially procedural: Eleven (1798), immunizing the states from suits in federal courts at the hands of private citizens; Twelve (1804), changing the method of choosing Presidents and Vice-Presidents; Seventeen (1913), providing for the direct election of Senators; Twenty (1933), altering a variety of details concerning presidential succession and the terms of elected federal officials; Twenty-two (1951), limiting presidential tenure; Twenty-three (1961), allowing citizens in the District of Columbia to vote in presidential elections; and Twenty-five (1967), enabling the President to fill vacancies in the vice-presidential office and specifying the procedures to be followed in the event that the President should become seriously disabled.

A number of amendments guarantee minority rights and recognize human values essential to democratic government. These include the First (1791), protecting freedom of assembly, press, speech, and religion; the Thirteenth (1865), outlawing slavery; the Fourteenth (1868), forbidding the states from denying life, liberty, or property without due process of law or from practicing discrimination against any arbitrarily defined groups of persons by denying them the "equal protection of the laws";[4] and the Fifteenth (1870) and the Nineteenth (1920), eliminating restrictions on the right to vote that are based on race or sex. Similarly, the Twenty-fourth Amendment (1964), banning the requirement of a poll tax as a precondition for voting in federal elections, struck down a financial levy that persisted in five southern states and that had tended to discourage voting by poor Negroes (and some poor whites too); and the Twenty-sixth (1971) lowered the minimal voting age from twenty-one to eighteen.

The remaining amendments are somewhat harder to categorize. Two and Three (1791), recognizing the people's right to bear arms and forbidding the quartering of soldiers in their homes, are best described as democratic. The rights they guarantee seem less important today than they did in the revolutionary period. The leaders of the National Rifle Association, an organization of 600,000 sportsmen strongly opposed to federal legislation regulating firearms, would not, however, agree that the Second Amendment's guarantee of a right to keep and bear arms has become

---

[4] The Fourteenth Amendment, which was an outgrowth of the Civil War, also contains punitive provisions addressed to the states and persons that participated in the rebellion; these are now obsolete.

irrelevant. Sliding over the fact that the amendment was written in an age when each state depended on its male citizenry to provide militia forces for the defense of the Republic (the amendment's guarantee actually links the right to bear arms "to the security of a free State"), the NRA has armed itself with the Second Amendment in its campaign against federal firearms regulation. In the aftermath of Senator Robert F. Kennedy's assassination Congress enacted a weak law forbidding the mail-order sale of pistols and revolvers. This has not satisfied the proponents of serious firearm regulation, who seek legislation that would regulate the mail-order sale of shotguns and rifles and require the licensing and regulation of all weapons. The near-fatal shooting of Governor George C. Wallace of Alabama during his campaign for the 1972 Democratic presidential nomination again intensified the gun-control issue. Leading the opposition to such legislation, the NRA's spokesmen have contended that it would deprive Americans of "one of their most basic civil rights, the right to keep and bear arms."

The Sixteenth Amendment (1913), which authorizes federal income taxes, essentially legislates a national policy. It does by overriding the Supreme Court's constitutional interpretation in *Pollock* v. *Farmers' Loan and Trust Company* (1895) that had made it practically impossible for Congress to levy a progressive or graduated income tax. Two additional amendments that are purely legislative cancel each other out. The Eighteenth (1919), the ill-starred experiment to forbid the manufacture, sale, and consumption of liquor, was repealed by the Twenty-first (1933); the latter is notable as the only amendment ratified by specially elected conventions.

However they may be classified, all the amendments share a common characteristic: their involvement in the political process. Just as the framing and ratifying of the Constitution of the United States took place amidst the interplay of political forces, so too is its amendment an occasion for the practice of constitutional politics. The three Civil War amendments, the Thirteenth, Fourteenth, and Fifteenth, were imposed upon the southern states as part of the political settlement that the ascendant Radical Republicans dictated to the vanquished Confederacy. By freeing the blacks and guaranteeing their civil rights, they struck at the white South's most cherished beliefs and practices. Today the amendments, particularly the Fourteenth and Fifteenth, are intimately tied to a continuing political struggle over the black man's place in American society. A number of amendments passed during the second decade of this century—the Sixteenth, Seventeenth, and Nineteenth—were products of the Progressive movement, constitutional monuments to its faith in popular democracy. Politics and the Constitution, in fact, are inseparable; the one feeds the other.

The Changing Constitution: The Eighteen-Year-Old Vote

The Supreme Court sits as a "continuous constitutional convention." It has played a major role in the highly delicate task of updating and reconciling an eighteenth-century document for a twentieth-century society. Its decisions—as suggested in the

Table 3.1 *Presidential margins in 1968, new voters in the 1970's*

	Nixon plurality	Humphrey plurality	Wallace plurality	New voters 18–20	New voters total
Alabama			494,846	199,000	440,000
Alaska *	2,189			6,000	29,000
Arizona	96,207			107,000	232,000
Arkansas			50,223	104,000	230,000
California	223,346			1,169,000	2,580,000
Colorado	74,171			145,000	319,000
Connecticut		64,840		156,000	343,000
Delaware	7,520			31,000	68,000
Florida	210,010			354,000	773,000
Georgia †			155,439	—	354,000
Hawaii ‡		49,899		31,000	91,000
Idaho	76,096			42,000	90,000
Illinois	134,960			605,000	1,321,000
Indiana	261,226			303,000	662,000
Iowa	142,407			160,000	347,000
Kansas	175,678			138,000	304,000
Kentucky †	64,870			—	254,000
Louisiana			220,685	230,000	497,000
Maine		48,058		55,000	122,000
Maryland		20,315		216,000	478,000
Massachusetts		702,374		330,000	725,000
Michigan		222,417		520,000	1,127,000
Minnesota		199,095		221,000	478,000
Mississippi			264,705	136,000	297,000

* Previously allowed 19-year-olds to vote.
† Previously allowed 18-year-olds to vote.
‡ Previously allowed 20-year-olds to vote.

Source: Congressional Quarterly Weekly Report, July 2, 1971, p. 1438.

aid-to-parochial-school case study—have helped shape the turbulent course of our nation's history.

The Supreme Court, however, is not the only vehicle that fosters constitutional change. Infrequently, yet in vital political areas, constitutional amendments are added to the basic law. On June 30, 1971, the Twenty-sixth Amendment to the Constitution, which lowered the minimal voting age from twenty-one to eighteen, was ratified by the required thirty-eight states in record time. (The details and background of the amendment are explained in a case study that precedes Chapter 4.) Within three months and seven days after its passage by Congress, the amendment became law. When the Ohio legislature ratified the amendment, it became a permanent part of the Constitution. For the fourth time since the Constitution was adopted

	Nixon plurality	Humphrey plurality	Wallace plurality	New voters 18–20	New voters total
Missouri	20,488			261,000	569,000
Montana	24,718			38,000	84,000
Nebraska	150,379			88,000	191,000
Nevada	12,590			24,000	54,000
New Hampshire	24,314			44,000	95,000
New Jersey	61,261			350,000	769,000
New Mexico	39,611			58,000	129,000
New York		370,538		954,000	2,101,000
North Carolina	131,004			341,000	750,000
North Dakota	43,900			38,000	83,000
Ohio	90,428			600,000	1,313,000
Oklahoma	140,039			147,000	325,000
Oregon	49,567			119,000	259,000
Pennsylvania		169,388		626,000	1,371,000
Rhode Island		124,159		60,000	135,000
South Carolina	38,632			178,000	391,000
South Dakota	31,818			41,000	88,000
Tennessee	47,800			232,000	511,000
Texas		38,960		678,000	1,490,000
Utah	82,063			70,000	154,000
Vermont	14,887			30,000	64,000
Virginia	147,932			286,000	645,000
Washington		27,527		211,000	460,000
West Virginia		66,536		99,000	217,000
Wisconsin	61,193			263,000	565,000
Wyoming	25,754			18,000	40,000
District of Columbia		108,554		48,000	111,000
Total United States	510,314			11,159,000	25,125,000

in 1789, the electorate was enlarged: the Fifteenth Amendment gave the vote to blacks, the Nineteenth to women, and the Twenty-third permitted voting in the presidential elections in the District of Columbia.

An estimated 11 million newly enfranchised Americans between the ages of eighteen to twenty became eligible to vote in the 1972 presidential election. In addition, another 14 million persons aged twenty-one to twenty-five became eligible to vote for the first time in the 1972 elections. As a consequence, the eligible electorate in the 1970's contains 25 million potential new voters—18 per cent of the total electorate—and this percentage will continue to increase through the decade as more and more young persons from the post World War II "baby boom" join the eligible electorate.[5]

[5] *Congressional Quarterly*, July 2, 1971, p. 1438.

These new young voters can potentially become a powerful force in elections, especially in closely contested ones, at all levels of government. In the 1972 presidential election the new voters proved to be a negligible factor, in part because of the overwhelming Nixon landslide and in part because less than half of the eighteen to twenty year olds voted. By contrast, their impact could be decisive, as Table 3.1 illustrates, in close presidential elections such as the Nixon-Humphrey race in 1968 where the winning plurality was only 510,314 votes. Youthful voters, moreover, have already demonstrated their influence in many local elections where their ballots have made the difference in electing persons—some of them young candidates—to public office. In short, the potential impact of the Twenty-sixth amendment can be great—if the newly enfranchised vote.

the modern constitution

Amendment by Interpretation

Considering the vast transformation in American life since 1789, it seems remarkable that the Constitution has survived with only sixteen amendments since the adoption of the first ten. To amend the Constitution is clearly a formidable and time-consuming undertaking, as shown by the fact that it took over four years to adopt the Twenty-second Amendment. Some critics have concluded that the amending article itself should be amended. Suggestions of this kind have most often come from scholars, but occasionally practicing politicians have taken up the cry. As recently as 1962 the General Assembly of the Council of State Governments voted in favor of a proposal to amend Article V so as to simplify state initiation of amendments, and the Governor of Washington flatly declared: "The machinery for amending the Constitution is pretty much outdated. The rapid changes of our society demand that a more expeditious means be provided, with simplified machinery."

If formal amendment were the only way in which the Constitution could be kept up-to-date, the case for an easier amendment process would be beyond dispute. But the American system of government has some most effective, though informal, methods for breathing new meaning into its living Constitution. The sparse and often cryptic words of the written Constitution are continually taking on new meanings through the changing interpretation given to them by all the agencies that participate in the governmental process. President, Congress, and Supreme Court alike, and even the political parties, have made the Constitution flexible and adaptable.

It was at President Washington's insistence, for example, and not because of the specific command of the Constitution, that the Chief Executive assumed the sole right to confer, or to withdraw, diplomatic recognition of foreign governments. He took the position, at Hamilton's urging, that the President's duty to receive foreign ambassadors gave him the right to "recognize" their governments. Similarly, it was the curt refusal of the Senate to give the same President the "advise" on treaties clearly called for by the Constitution that has kept the initiation of treaties entirely in the President's hands.

The Supreme Court, as later chapters will show, plays an unusually significant part in this process of amendment by interpretation. Through its power to examine the constitutional validity of state and federal laws it is continually readjusting the Constitution to changing times and circumstances. In this century, for instance, the Supreme Court has made two major constitutional interpretations: that, under its power to raise and spend money and to regulate commerce, Congress may establish comprehensive social and economic welfare programs; and that the Constitution unequivocally forbids all public authorities from discriminating against persons because of their race.

This process of constitutional change by interpretation, which is the main focus in the remaining pages of this chapter, is an outgrowth of shifting attitudes within the American political culture, both accepting and demanding governmental assumption of new social and economic responsibilities. Because the nation has grown so much and changed from what it was in the rustic days of the eighteenth century, it is hardly surprising that the political culture has come to support a vast expansion of governmental activities along with a corresponding expansion in the federal government's constitutional powers. The constitutional changes, it should be emphasized, are ultimately traceable to changing patterns of economic and political needs, and they are frequently a direct consequence of interest-group activity. The federal government's modern commitment to programs of social and economic welfare, and the Supreme Court's constitutional interpretations endorsing this commitment, is predominantly a response to the nation's industrialization and urbanization. It is also a reaction to insistent political demands by labor unions and other groups and to the desires of middle-class Americans generally for a welfare state oriented to their interests and needs. To take another pertinent illustration, the Supreme Court's reading of the American Constitution as unequivocally forbidding all forms of public discrimination based on race is a consequence of significant, if still incomplete, shifts in the status of blacks and in white perceptions of their claims to racial justice; these shifts, moreover, have been mightily assisted by the many-sided activities of such interest groups as the National Association for the Advancement of Colored People.

It used to be a favorite theme among constitutional commentators that the American and British constitutions were distinctively different. The American, supposedly, was rigid because it was written and therefore precise. The British was contrasted as being unwritten—the sum total of gradually evolving customs and procedures, sanctioned by scattered historical charters and documents. Consequently, it was typically described as flexible. The truth, however, is that the two constitutions are much alike: neither is wholly written or unwritten; neither is entirely flexible or inflexible. In legal theory England's is certainly flexible because it can be changed by simple acts of Parliament. The British Constitution, however, is also in part written and rigid, consisting of definite and precise constitutional rules. Documents such as the Magna Carta and the Petition of Right are its written sources; they serve as declarations of the constitutional rights of Englishmen. So also are the nineteenth-century Reform

Acts that, in creating a broadly based suffrage, helped establish permanent constitutional rules. Even where the rules are unwritten they may become precise. No British monarch will today appoint a Prime Minister from among the membership of the House of Lords, for in this case custom has hardened into rigid constitutional law.

The American Constitution is similarly rigid and flexible. Although knowledge of its written provisions is essential to its understanding, this is only a starting point: the meaning of a living constitution can be only partially captured in written words, and in many respects the American, like the British, is unwritten. Of course, it has its rigid features, as in the requirement that presidential elections take place every four years. But the Constitution's most impressive quality has been its capacity, in company with American life, for continuous transformation.

A monumental constitutional study commissioned by Congress is fittingly entitled *Constitution of the United States, Annotated.*[6] Its commentary on the approximately fourteen pages of the original document and formal amendments runs to almost 1,400 pages, a graphic illustration of how the Congress, the President, the Supreme Court, and ultimately the American people have annotated—amended—their Constitution.

Evaluation of the "Amending" Process

There are, however, those who decry amendment by interpretation. According to Walter Bagehot, one of the classic writers on the British Constitution, the inflexibility of America's formal amending procedures means that "absurd fictions" must be framed to evade the plain sense of the Constitution's written clauses. The result, he thought, is that "a clumsy working and curious technicality mark the politics of a rough-and-ready people." Bagehot wrote in the nineteenth century, but some contemporary writers have continued to criticize the difficulty of formal amendment. One critic has gone so far as to charge that it gives the nation's political leaders an excuse for ignoring the popular will. Instead of submitting amendments upon which the people may then vote, Henry Hazlitt has argued that America's leaders make their own constitutional interpretation—often arrogating new powers to themselves and thereby usurping the people's sovereignty.[7]

It is hard to see the force of such objections. All men, as Plato pointed out long ago, live by myths. The myth that the changing interpretations of the Constitution were foreshadowed and sanctioned by the original document is not part of a malicious plot, but a useful fiction endorsed by succeeding generations of Americans. Furthermore, the main lines of interpretation have enjoyed majority political support. Indeed, in most instances new constitutional interpretations gain judicial sanction only *after* an extended process of open public debate. Viewed realistically, America's amending process is akin to England's, which has no formal amending procedure whatsoever, and to such political systems as that of the Fifth French Republic, where

---

[6] Edward S. Corwin, rev. ed. (Washington, D.C.: G.P.O., 1964).
[7] *A New Constitution Now* (New York: McGraw-Hill, 1942), p. 13.

amendments require both legislative and popular approval or passage by a three-fifths legislative vote, and the Federal Republic of Germany, where amendments require a two-thirds vote of the legislature.

Because the American Constitution has grown and evolved through interpretation, it is not only the original Founding Fathers who have made the law of the land, but also such later "Fathers" as Chief Justice John Marshall and Presidents Abraham Lincoln and Franklin Roosevelt:

> As the Constitution takes its unchartered course, paternity must ever assume a fresh pattern. If one has faith in the supreme law of the land, he can accord to only a few abiding places among the elect. . . . An instrument of government designed to "establish justice," "insure domestic tranquillity," and "promote the general welfare" can[not] be endowed with . . . arrested perfection. A Constitution which serves the necessities of a people is an enabling act that keeps relevant a group of living usages. New faces must appear as older ones vanish; and portraits that endure must be rehung as contributions wax and wane. The Fathers must ever be what the Sons make them.[8]

Permanent, Changeable, and Obsolete Provisions

A distinction suggested by Oliver Cromwell, whose unsuccessful *Instrument of Government* (1653) was England's sole experiment with a written constitution, may help to throw light on American constitutionalism. Cromwell distinguished between what he called "fundamental" and "circumstantial," by which he meant changeable provisions. He used this distinction in a purely normative sense—that is, certain parts of a constitution ought never be tampered with, whereas less fundamental provisions might be changed. (Cromwell's distinction, it might be noted, was made when the Lord Protector insisted that Parliament could not tamper with certain parts of the *Instrument* that *he* had framed.) But the distinction, used in an approximate fashion, has descriptive value and can be applied to the American Constitution. (See Figure 3.1.)

There is, first, the *permanent Constitution,* a core that has become precise and that is rarely changed except by formal amendment. It includes such provisions as the popular election of Representatives and Senators, the specified terms for Presidents and Congressmen, the life tenure of judges, the Supreme Court's right to pass on the constitutionality of state and federal laws, and the two-thirds vote required for congressional overriding of presidential vetoes. Viewed from another perspective, provisions of this sort form part of the government's structural machinery. For example, the limitation barring presidential third terms, now formally enshrined in the permanent Constitution by the Twenty-second Amendment, can be visualized as one of the girders in the structural framework within which the political process operates.

Second, there exists a *changeable Constitution* that is more nebulous and somewhat less stable; its provisions are (or have been and could again be) issues in the political process. In this category, for instance, are many of the provisions in the Bill of Rights and the grants of power to Congress contained in the commerce and tax clauses. At any one time a good statement of their scope and effect can be given. These clauses, however, are generally unspecific and naturally lend themselves to varying and changing interpretations. Expressions like those in the Bill of Rights prohibiting "cruel and unusual punishments" and "unreasonable searches and seizures," providing that defendants in "criminal prosecutions" shall have the "assistance of counsel," or guaranteeing to all persons "due process" and "equal protection" of the law, are standing invitations to constitutional conflicts over their meaning. These conflicts frequently embody current political issues—the status of the black man in American society or the methods to be used in arresting and convicting suspected criminals. Permanent and settled interpretations of these clauses, particularly because they may still be policy issues in the political system, are not to be found within their vague words.

Other clauses may seem specific and yet be subtly transformed in response to political changes. The working of the electoral college cannot be understood through the constitutional clauses apart from the nature of the American two-party system. Currently, the functioning of the party system is quite predictable, but profound changes could be made without formal amendment. The states, for example, could individually decide that presidential electors should be chosen by congressional districts instead of from the state as a whole. Such a change is, however, most unlikely, and the provisions for electing the President now have a fairly precise meaning; they illustrate how changeable parts of the Constitution may gradually become relatively permanent.

Figure 3.1. A view of the modern Constitution

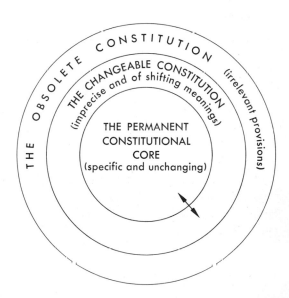

There is, finally, an *obsolete Constitution*. It consists of phrases and provisions sprinkled through the original document. Important to the framers, they are not causes of constitutional controversy in the twentieth century. Congress is not likely to award titles of nobility; nor are the state governments going to foster piracy on the high seas by granting "Letters of Marque and Reprisal" to privateers.

A Modern Constitution of Powers

Although American constitutionalism is a subject that reappears throughout this book, a few essentials deserve emphasis. They concern the truly immense federal powers and the limits that the Constitution imposes on the government at all levels. The British scholar A. V. Dicey once commented that in a federal system, unlike a unitary one such as that of England, sovereign power was "a despot hard to rouse." Writing in the late 1800's, he argued that only in times of extraordinary crisis such as the Civil War did the American national government come to life. It is not, he wrote, "like the English Parliament, an ever-wakeful legislator, but a monarch who slumbers and sleeps." Were Dicey alive today he would surely revise his conclusions, for America now has a monarch—the national government—who is wide awake and whose powers are exerted every day of every week. This, however, is hardly predictable from a reading of the Constitution; in fact, a mere handful of phrases contained in the document of 1787 provide the constitutional justification for the great power and the multitudinous activities of the modern American monarch. The most notable of these phrases appear in the supremacy clause and the clauses granting the federal government power to conduct foreign affairs, wage war, regulate commerce, and levy taxes.

1. The supremacy clause

Although the framers, for tactical reasons, dubbed their creation "federal," it is a unitary or national state with regard to the enumerated powers of Congress and the President. During the Constitutional Convention a major preoccupation was the need for securing the absolute supremacy of the national government in the execution of its functions. Madison's nationalistic Virginia Plan included a provision giving Congress, in association with the Supreme Court, power to veto state laws infringing upon national policy. This sweeping provision remained in the draft constitution until halfway through the convention. Then, in the series of compromises between the national and states' rights positions, it was replaced by a section proposed by Maryland's Luther Martin, a local-minded delegate who subsequently opposed ratification only later to become a staunch Federalist worthy of Jefferson's denunciation as an "impudent federal bull-dog." With but slight revision Martin's suggestion appeared in Article VI:

The Constitution, and the laws of the United States which shall be made in pursuance thereof, and all treaties made, or which shall be made, under the authority of the United States, shall be the supreme law of the land; and the judges in every State shall be bound thereby, any-thing in the constitution or laws of any State to the contrary notwithstanding.

Whatever the intentions of Martin and his fellow framers, the supremacy clause, combined with the Supreme Court's exercise of judicial review over state actions, has made the United States a unitary state within the scope of its enumerated powers. The Tenth Amendment's reservation of nondelegated powers to the states, once considered a limitation of federal authority, is no barrier, but merely "a truism that all is retained which has not been surrendered." [9]

To be sure, there is still scattered political dissent from this viewpoint and occasional rumblings from states' rights interests. In the recent past, usually in school desegregation disputes, there has been loud and bold talk about the eternal validity of the Tenth Amendment. Alabama Governor George C. Wallace has discovered a lively political career in the theme that the states have a constitutional duty to "interpose" their authority to block federal "usurpations." Yet the constitutional practice today, however unpalatable to some, harmonizes with the doctrine of national supremacy enunciated by John Marshall's Supreme Court in 1819. "The government of the Union," it declared, "though limited in its powers, is supreme within its sphere of action" [10]—and that sphere of action is best described as spacious and pervasive.

2. The conduct of foreign affairs

By logic and circumstance, if not by specific constitutional command, the federal government's authority to conduct foreign relations is among its most significant powers. It is, moreover, a power completely denied the states. Section 10 of Article I provides that "No State shall enter into any Treaty, Alliance, or Confederation" nor "enter into any agreement . . . with a foreign power." No limits, however, are placed on the federal power. The federal government may not violate explicit limitations, but its power over foreign relations cannot be cut down or qualified by the reservation of nondelegated powers to the states.

This federal power, which comprehends the entire range of American involvement in international relations, is formally based on a handful of constitutional grants. Article I contains clauses giving Congress power to regulate foreign commerce and to declare war. Article II, Section 2, permits the President with the consent of two thirds of the Senate to enter into treaties with other nations; and Section 3 allows him to "receive Ambassadors and other public Ministers." No less relevant than these formal provisions is one of the basic general motivations that stimulated the adoption of the Constitution: the conviction that the survival of the American union required a central authority able to marshal its military forces and competent to conduct exclusively the country's relations with foreign states. The shrinking size of the world and America's profound involvement in it are enough in themselves to account for the breadth of the foreign relations power. As the Supreme Court has explained:

[9] *U.S.* v. *Darby,* 312 U.S. 100, 124 (1941).
[10] *McCulloch* v. *Maryland,* 4 Wheat. 316, 405 (1819).

The powers to declare and wage war, to conclude peace, to make treaties, to maintain diplomatic relations with other sovereignties, if they had never been mentioned in the Constitution, would have vested in the Federal Government as necessary concomitants of nationality.[11]

3. The war power

The Court's bracketing of the powers to wage war and conduct foreign affairs was appropriate. In many respects they are of the same piece, and there has been no challenge to Alexander Hamilton's blunt assertions in *Federalist* 23 that the federal government's war powers "ought to exist without limitation, because it is impossible to foresee or define the extent and variety of national exigencies, or the correspondent extent and variety of the means which may be necessary to satisfy them." The Constitution, framed by men who directed the Revolutionary War, makes specific references to the government's capacity for war. Article I confers upon Congress power to declare war and to raise and support armed forces. Article II names the President Commander-in-Chief, thereby making him the central figure in the application of the war powers.

The war power, like that over foreign affairs, is exclusively reserved to the federal government. Its scope, as Hamilton foresaw, has included all manner of means necessary to meeting our "national exigencies"—the dictatorial actions of President Lincoln during the Civil War, the vast network of controls imposed upon the economy in World Wars I and II, and the forcible evacuation and detention of over 100,000 West Coast Japanese-Americans between 1941 and 1944. The war powers further support the President's crucially significant authority to commit America's military forces, whether to foil Communist penetrations in Korea or Vietnam, or to end race riots in Mississippi or in the urban areas of the northern states. There are, theoretically and sometimes practically, constitutional limits to the war power. But they have usually been imposed by the Supreme Court *after* a crisis or when its existence is doubtful.[12]

President Johnson's controversial actions of committing an armed force of over half a million men to Vietnam (without any formal declaration of war) similarly provoked a constitutional storm after the fact. Many critics charge that Johnson misused a 1964 congressional resolution (the Gulf of Tonkin Resolution) authorizing him to take all necessary actions to repel Communist aggression in Southeast Asia. They contend that the resolution did not provide a blank check under which the President could send the nation's military forces into an Asian land war. The important Senate Foreign Relations Committee, a leading source of criticism of our involvement in the Vietnamese war, successfully sponsored a sense-of-the-Senate resolution, asking the executive branch not to commit troops or financial resources to foreign countries unless there is specific congressional approval. Although this resolution passed the Senate by an overwhelming majority in 1969, it is purely exhortatory

---

[11] *U.S.* v. *Curtiss-Wright Export Corp.*, 229 U.S. 304, 318 (1936).

[12] In *Ex parte Milligan* (1866), decided after the cessation of Civil War hostilities, the Supreme Court ruled that President Lincoln had exceeded constitutional limitations in authorizing a military trial of a civilian suspected of treason. The Steel Seizure case (1952), discussed on page 101, came at a time when many observers doubted the reality of the emergency that the President cited to justify his actions.

and without legal effect. It is addressed, moreover, not to the Vietnam conflict that stimulated it, but to potential *future* presidential commitments. In short, the operative or de facto constitutional rules give the federal government and its chief representative, the President, extraordinary powers—powers made all the more formidable by the extraordinary nature of these years of semiwar and permanent crisis.

4. The commerce power

Sixteen words in Article I granting Congress power "to regulate commerce with foreign nations, and among the several states, and with the Indian tribes" provide a foundation upon which a huge edifice of economic regulation has been built. It was not always so. Prior to the New Deal period federal intervention in the economy, though significant, was of minor scope. And until 1937 the Supreme Court often took a decidedly narrow view of Congress's power to regulate economic and social affairs, holding that interstate "commerce" did not include production for the national market and that the states' reserved powers drastically limited what the federal government could do.

All this has now changed, largely as a result of the nationalization of the country's economic life and the demands of significant interest groups (such as labor unions). The modern interpretation, which accepts the constitutionality of national regulation, is a good example of how parts of the changeable and issue-oriented Constitution may become structural and permanent. The federal government justifies a vast array of regulations under its power to regulate commerce. Thus, it regulates the minutest details of labor-management relations, prescribes rules for the internal governance of unions, controls a vast array of commercial activities, sets minimum wages for most of the nation's workers, and controls the volume and prices of agricultural production.

The constitutional justification is as simple as it is broad in its implications: Congress can regulate any activity that is "in interstate commerce" by virtue of its relationship to two or more states. Moreover, this relationship occurs whenever Congress decides that an activity wholly within state lines has a "substantial" impact upon the national market—as, for instance, when the Supreme Court ruled that the Secretary of Agriculture (under authority of the Agricultural Adjustment Act) could penalize a farmer for planting twelve more acres of wheat than his quota allowed solely to feed his own cattle. Even this small excess production, said the Court, had a "substantial" impact on interstate commerce because it freed the farmer from the necessity of buying wheat in the national market.[13] The modern doctrine is summarized in a single sentence from a case upholding a public utility regulation: "The federal commerce power," declared the Supreme Court, "is as broad as the economic needs of the nation." [14]

5. The tax power

The constitutional twin to the commerce power is the power to tax or, more properly, to tax and spend. It too has undergone a metamorphosis that has made it

[13] *Wickard v. Fillburn*, 317 U.S. 111 (1942).
[14] *American Power Co.* v. *S.E.C.*, 329 U.S. 90, 104 (1946).

into a major instrument of national policy. Apart from certain provisions in the Bill of Rights and some clauses intended to prevent arbitrarily discriminatory exactions, there are few limitations on the use of the tax power for regulatory purposes. "The Congress," reads the first clause of Section 8 in Article I, "shall have the Power to lay and collect Taxes, Duties, Imposts and Excises, to pay the Debts and provide for the common Defense and general Welfare of the United States." The decision to tax the accumulation of income at progressively higher rates has important policy consequences because it forces a partial redistribution of wealth. The custom duties imposed on foreign imports serve the dual function of raising revenue and regulating the flow of foreign commerce. Congress left no doubt of this in its first tariff act in 1789; a schedule of custom duties, it declared, was "necessary for the support of the government, for the discharge of the debts of the United States, *and* the encouragement and protection of manufactures" (*italics added*).

The taxing power may be used in even more directly regulatory ways. By taxing certain businesses at prohibitive rates, Congress has sought to discourage the manufacture and distribution of products (such as phosphorus matches or opium) deemed to be harmful. Although these types of statutes have been ruled constitutional, the Supreme Court has recently declared that the self-incrimination clause of the Fifth Amendment prohibits federal legislation requiring gamblers and persons possessing sawed-off shotguns, machine guns, and other weapons to identify themselves as presumably engaged in criminal activities by filing tax registration forms that contain incriminating personal data.[15] This decision, which incidentally underscores the modern Supreme Court's concern with due process and individual liberties in all criminal prosecutions, does not really impair congressional discretion to combine judiciously the commerce and tax powers of Article I in order to obtain legislative ends unknown to the framers of 1787.

Bituminous coal produced for interstate commerce, for example, has been brought under federal control by the granting of tax exemptions (from a 19½ per cent tax) to producers agreeing to "cooperate" in a governmental program regulating prices and competition. In a similar vein Congress may breathe life into regulatory schemes that find no explicit sanction in the Constitution by adroit use of its spending power. Here again, as in so many matters, the Supreme Court has come to accept the Hamiltonian view that the tax clause includes, in addition to the power to raise revenue, a separate grant to Congress permitting it to spend, limited only by the requirement that the expenditure be for the *general,* rather than the local, welfare of the United States. Accordingly, the government has established national programs providing for unemployment insurance, medical-care benefits and retirement pensions for the aged, and inexpensive hot lunches for schoolchildren; these programs are made effective by the simple expedient of taxing employers and employees (as in the

---

[15] *Marchetti* v. *United States,* 390 U.S. 39; *Grosso* v. *United States,* 390 U.S. 62 (1968). The ruling will apparently also lead to the invalidation of similar tax registration provisions aimed at dealers illegally trafficking in liquor and narcotics. It does not, however, forbid congressional taxation of illegal activities, thereby leaving the criminal subject to prosecution for federal income tax evasion—*if* he is caught.

case of the Social Security system) and inducing the states to share in the benefits of federal appropriations. The states' price of admission into these federal programs is their willingness to help administer them by passing laws that conform to Congress's requirements.

More recently, the federal government has embarked on new ventures to promote the general welfare, further demonstrating the varied uses of the Constitution's fiscal clauses. President Johnson's Great Society programs providing federal financial aid to elementary and secondary schools (once regarded as a purely state and local responsibility) and making medical-care benefits available to elderly persons (the Medicare program) found their constitutional support, not in the specific enumerations of Article I, but in the more general phraseology of the taxing and spending clauses. According to an old saying, money talks. Under the modern Constitution it speaks through countless federal programs that purchase the compliance of the states and their citizens.

Doctrine of Implied Powers

Although changing domestic and international needs, ultimately reflected in attitudes manifest in the political culture, account for the development of a federal government armed with unitary powers, there is one clause, the 18th in Section 8 of Article I, that has eased this transition and made it constitutionally plausible. Commonly described as "the necessary-and-proper clause," it follows the enumeration of specific legislative powers with the declaration that Congress may "make all Laws which shall be necessary and proper for carrying into Execution the foregoing Powers, and all other Powers vested by this Constitution in the Government of the United States, or in any Department or Officer thereof."

The federal Republic's first years settled the clause's meaning and, typically, did so in the course of a political dispute. As part of his national financial policy Secretary of the Treasury Hamilton persuaded Congress to incorporate a Bank of the United States, which would stabilize the currency and provide a ready source of public credit. But the Constitution grants no such power in writing. James Madison, by then a congressional leader often opposed to his former *Federalist* co-author, and Secretary of State Jefferson represented the "Virginia school" of narrow interpretation. In challenging the bank bill as unconstitutional, they argued that Congress was confined to its enumerated powers and to those means of implementation absolutely necessary—*indispensable*—to their execution. They were answered by Hamilton, whose reply convinced President Washington that he need not veto the bill. The Treasury Secretary found the power of bank incorporation implied in the government's enumerated financial and currency powers. He urged that the necessary-and-proper clause sanctioned the use of all implied powers that were *expedient* or *convenient* means for giving effect to the specified powers—the doctrine of implied powers.

Hamilton's position received its definitive endorsement in two early constitutional incidents. The first occurred in 1803, when the presidential administration of his great protagonist, Thomas Jefferson, suddenly concluded that it had implied power to purchase and administer the enormous Louisiana Territory. Personally anxious for the sanction of an amendment (which was a practical impossibility), the strict constructionist Jefferson swallowed his constitutional doubts and approved the annexation, trusting "that the good sense of our country will correct the evil of construction when it shall produce ill effects."

The second endorsement was judicial. It came in an old Supreme Court decision authored by Chief Justice John Marshall, a judge whose constitutional principles and values were thoroughly Hamiltonian. The case, *McCulloch* v. *Maryland* (1819), tested the constitutionality of the Second Bank of the United States. Ironically, the chartering of this corporation had been recommended by President James Madison, once he was faced with the responsibility of governing the nation. In sustaining Congress's authority to charter the Bank, Marshall spoke for a flexible Constitution, one "intended to endure for ages to come, and, consequently to be adapted to the various crises of human affairs." He spoke also for a broad doctrine of implied powers:

Let the end be legitimate, let it be within the scope of the constitution, and all means which are appropriate, which are plainly adapted to that end, which are not prohibited, but consist with the letter and spirit of the constitution, are constitutional.[16]

This doctrine of implied powers, fused with the expansive interpretations of the commerce and taxing and spending powers, means that the federal government operates within the context of a permissive Constitution. The emphasis here is on the word *permissive*. The modern Constitution allows choice but does not dictate ends. The eighteenth-century document, in short, is an essentially open-ended framework for governing in the twentieth century. To be sure, the government is subject to constitutional limitations intended primarily to maintain democracy and preserve individual rights as the discussion below emphasizes. It is also true that the need to justify as constitutional innovative governmental policies in the area of social welfare and economic regulation has at times proved temporarily inhibiting. But since 1937 the courts have abandoned their earlier constitutional concern with social and economic policies, and they have instead helped fashion a charter of government whose basic quality is flexibility and permissiveness.

Constitutional Limitations and the Rule of Law

The emphasis on permissiveness should not obscure the fact that the Constitution still imposes limits on government. The states, naturally, are restricted in the scope of their functions by the provisions of Article I, Section 10, which excludes them from a number of important areas. More basically, the Constitution theoretically, and to a large extent practically, prevents all levels of American government from interfering with a whole series of individual rights deemed to be fundamental. Bills of attainder and ex post facto laws are forbidden by the original document; the Bill of

16 Wheat. 316, 416, 422 (1819).

Rights (especially the first eight amendments) is a partial listing of individual safe-guards that guarantee freedom of speech and worship, forbid the seizure of private property without just compensation, and assure the basic fairness of criminal proceedings. The Fourteenth, Fifteenth, and Nineteenth amendments prohibit governmentally sanctioned racial discrimination and forbid all official actions denying individuals the right to vote because of their race or sex.

Is, then, American government, to cite an oft-heard expression, "a government of laws and not of men"? If the thought conveys an either/or proposition—that government must be either of laws *or* of men—the answer is No. But the two elements, laws and men, are not mutually exclusive. The concept, moreover, one of the most basic in the nation's political culture, expresses an ideal. In practice it means that governmental departures from established constitutional rules and limitations are to be regarded as exceptional occurrences. This concept may be hard to formulate in precise terms, but the difference between a system such as the American or British, where public decisions are made through regular processes and applied subject to certain constitutional limitations, and one such as that of Communist China or the Soviet Union, where decisions are reached through closed processes and often applied in an arbitrary and unequal manner, is clear enough.

When, in 1952, President Truman seized the nation's steel mills and sought to compel their temporary operation under federal control, the Supreme Court decided his actions were unjustified. The seizure was nullified. The merits of the Court's decision are beside the point. What is relevant is the fact that within twenty-five minutes of its announcement President Truman was ordering his subordinates to comply with the judicial decrees. His reaction typified government by constitution—government not by law alone but government by men who feel the power of general constitutional rules.

suggested additional readings

Andrews, William G. (ed.).
Constitutions and Constitutionalism.
2nd ed. Princeton: Van Nostrand
Reinhold Company, 1963.*

Bagehot, Walter. *The English
Constitution,* 1st ed. published in
1867. New York: Doubleday &
Company, Inc.*

Beth, Loren P. *The Development of the
American Constitution 1877–1917.*
New York: Harper & Row, Publishers,
1971.

Corwin, Edward S. *The "Higher Law"
Background of American
Constitutional Law.* Ithaca, N.Y.:
Cornell University Press, 1955.*

Farrand, Max. *The Framing of the
Constitution of the United States.*
New Haven: Yale University Press,
1913.*

McCloskey, Robert G. (ed.). *Essays in
Constitutional Law.* New York:
Random House, Inc., 1957.*

McDonald, Forrest. *We the People: The
Economic Origins of the Constitution.*
Chicago: University of Chicago
Press, 1963.*

———. *The Formation of the American
Republic 1776–1790.* New York:
Penguin Books, 1967.*

McIlwain, Charles H. *Constitutionalism:
Ancient and Modern.* Ithaca, N.Y.
Cornell University Press, 1958.*

Magrath, C. Peter. *Constitutionalism and
Politics: Conflict and Consensus.*
Chicago: Scott, Foresman and
Company, 1968.*

Mason, Alpheus T., and Gerald
Garvey (eds.). *American
Constitutional History: Essays by
Edward S. Corwin.* New York:
Harper & Row, Publishers, 1964.*

Roche, John P. "The Founding Fathers:
A Reform Caucus in Action,"
American Political Science Review,
LV (December, 1961), 799–816.

Smith, James. *Constitution.* New York:
Harper & Row, Publishers, 1971.*

Wright, Benjamin F. *The Growth of
American Constitutional Law.*
Chicago: University of Chicago,
Press, 1967.*

* Available in paperback.

4 citizens and politics

case study

American Eighteen-Year-Olds Get the Vote

The 1960's saw the emergence of youth into politics in America in a variety of seemingly novel and certainly important ways. Young people, black and white, played key roles in the civil rights protest movements of the early 1960's. More young people provided the impetus to the antiwar protest against Vietnam, which reached its crescendo during 1968 and saw hundreds of thousands of youths involved in presidential campaigns. At a different level, of the over 7 million Americans to serve in Vietnam, a substantial portion were under twenty-one. In addition, the contemporary generation of eighteen- to twenty-one-year-olds was the most educated in our history. Yet oddly, when one thinks about it, these people were not full citizens. They did not have the right to vote. Furthermore, although many of the youth-led civil rights and antiwar protests drew on the tactics of the women's suffragette movement of pre-World War I days, the vote was rarely an explicit goal of young people of either activist or nonactivist persuasion. Nonetheless, when thinking about how to respond to the emergence of youth as a political force, politicians, for a variety of motives, quickly thought about extending the vote. That has been a track followed throughout American history as new groups have developed a consciousness and articulated political goals. The choice for those

in power is whether to deal the newcomers into the political game and hope that they will fit in, or to run the risk of unforeseen troubles and demands. This is the story of how these processes operated to produce the Twenty-sixth Amendment to the Constitution, enfranchising some 11 million previously voteless eighteen- to twenty-one-year-olds.

On the surface, voting age seems to be left by the Constitution to the discretion of the states. Indeed, the primacy of the states in setting their own voting rules, although challenged in the area of race, was generally accepted for length of residency and age. Thus when the political response began, it took the form of a proposed constitutional amendment, introduced in 1968 by Democratic Senate Majority Leader Mike Mansfield, with Republican Minority Leader Everett Dirksen and forty-four co-sponsors. Proponents of eighteen- to twenty-one-year-old voting realized that constitutional amendment was a long and hard route, requiring a two-thirds vote of approval in both houses of Congress and then ratification by three-fourths of the fifty state legislatures. Yet no alternative was seen at the beginning.

At early hearings of the Senate Subcommittee on Constitutional

Amendments, chaired by Senator Birch Bayh (D–Indiana), favorable testimony came from Senators Mansfield, McCarthy, Javits, and others. But the amendment did not have the necessary support to move up to the full committee, much less to the Senate floor. Public support for the concept came from President Lyndon B. Johnson, from then presidential candidate Richard M. Nixon, and from various groups, including the Republican Party (at its 1968 Miami National Convention), the NAACP, and the California Democratic Conference. A September 1968 Gallup Poll showed 66 per cent public support for lowering the voting age to eighteen. Yet the concept did not seem to be generating much political movement. The head of the Youth Franchise Coalition noted that "everybody seems to support [it], but nobody seems to think it's important enough to do something." Although President Nixon directed his Attorney General, John Mitchell, to explore the possibilities of a successful constitutional amendment in February, 1969, it was not until a year later, in February, 1970, that hearings started again in the Senate.

One amendment before the Subcommittee would have allowed eighteen-year-olds to vote in *all* elections—national, state, and local. President Nixon was supporting an amendment, however, that would have limited participation by eighteen-, nineteen-, and twenty-year-olds to federal elections —i.e., presidential and congressional elections. The administration position was that qualifications for state and local elections should be left to the states. Former Attorney General Ramsey Clark observed that "such halfway steps are one of the causes of the belief of young people that the system cannot act swiftly or meaningfully." Behind these positions were serious political calculations. The Democrats thought the youth vote would help them most, and at all electoral levels. Republicans were more uncertain, but felt confident that their best hope was nationally, where President Nixon could claim credit for reducing the Vietnam war

and reforming the draft.

Meanwhile, with the constitutional amendments under consideration, Senators Bayh and Edward Kennedy (D–Massachusetts) were thinking about a quicker way. Kennedy had a memo from an aide, Carey Parker, that suggested a legal foundation for giving eighteen-year-olds the vote by statute, a simple act of Congress. In a 1968 Supreme Court decision, *Katzenbach* v. *Morgan,* the Court had interpreted the Fourteenth Amendment as encompassing age discrimination. In Subcommittee testimony, Kennedy said the Court had acknowledged "the broader power (of Congress) to legislate in the area of equal protection and due process clauses of the Fourteenth Amendment." Kennedy therefore proposed a rider to the Voting Rights Act of 1965, which was before the Senate for extension, adding eighteen-year-old voting in all elections. He was supported by 1964 Republican presidential nominee, Senator Barry Goldwater (R–Arizona).

When the Voting Rights Act landed in the Senate, a great deal of complicated political activity developed. The version before the Senate was a Nixon Administration-backed House bill, much weakened from the original 1965 Act. Strengthening amendments were proposed by Minority Leader Hugh Scott (R–Pennsylvania). Majority Leader Mansfield, adopting the Kennedy strategy, proposed a rider giving eighteen-year-olds the vote in all elections, and providing a special mechanism to test quickly the constitutionality of such a move. First, there would be a trial in a three-judge Federal Court of Appeals, and then a direct appeal to the Supreme Court. Some opposed the Mansfield move as "an invasion of states' rights." Many civil rights leaders worried that opposition to eighteen-year-old voting, especially in the House of Representatives, would endanger the basic voting rights package—essential to the progress of blacks in the South.

Still, on March 12, 1971, the Mansfield Amendment passed 64 to 17 in the Senate, with support from a wide majority within each party. The next day the Voting Rights Act of 1970 passed in its entirety and was sent back to the House. Would the House accept the Senate version, or stick to its own original bill, or come up with something in between? Either of these last two outcomes would require still a third recourse, a House-Senate conference committee to iron out the differences.

A special problem was the attitude of the House Judiciary Committee Chairman, Emanuel Celler, over eighty years old himself and the dean of the House. Celler was a driving force behind the voting rights bill. He told Mansfield that he was "opposed to tacking on a provision as extraneous as teen-age voting. There's tremendous opposition in the House and addition of this provision might mean defeat of the conference report. I will fight like hell against the inclusion of teen-age voting." The Nixon Administration repeated its position that a separate amendment to the Constitution was necessary to enfranchise eighteen-year-olds, and asked for the separation of the eighteen-year-old provision and the rest of the voting rights bill.

A key actor in the internal legislative process was the House Rules Committee. This committee prescribes the terms of what is voted on on the floor, and it can impose limits on debate and amendments. Celler now asked the committee to report the entire bill. If it were unconstitutional, the eighteen-year-old provision could later be declared so by the courts. Richard Poff (R–Virginia) maintained that the eighteen-year-old amendment would place the Supreme Court in an "impossible dilemma." If the Court upheld such change by statute, then "bitter criticism" would come from strict constitutional constructionists; if the Court rejected the rule, then there would be the "rebuke of the frustrations and desires of eleven million young people."

In the end the Rules Committee reported out the Senate version of the voting rights bill, and with a highly restrictive rule. The bill could not be amended, and debate was limited to thirty minutes for both sides.

Although the House Republican Policy Committee was against the package, there was a drive, led by Thomas Railsback of Illinois, just back from a tour of the campuses, to round up moderate and liberal Republican support—a potential bloc of fifty votes. On June 17, 1970, the vote came. The debate was marked by a rare floor appearance by retiring House Speaker John McCormack. It was an emotional moment when that aged legislator said: ". . . nothing would make John McCormack happier, who will not be here next year, than to see this resolution adopted." With a surprisingly large vote, 272 to 132, the House accepted the Senate version of the voting rights bill, with eighteen-year-old voting attached. Democrats voted Yes by 172 to 56; Republicans did so by 100 to 76. The next move was up to the White House. Would President Nixon sign the bill?

The President faced a political dilemma, for he could not veto just part of the bill. If he vetoed the bill he would upset not only young people, but also the civil rights movement. On the other hand, he was on record as believing that eighteen-year-old voting could be granted only by the states. He resolved the issue by signing the bill while simultaneously calling for a court test:

The time has come to give the 18-year-old the vote, as I have long urged. The way to do this is by amending the Constitution. Because of the likelihood that the 18-year-old vote provisions of this law will not survive its court test, the constitutional amendment pending before the Congress should go forward to the states for ratification now.

The President signed the bill without the usual ceremony, and asked his Attorney General to precipitate an immediate court test. The Senate Judiciary Committee, in an unusual move, hired its own counsel to provide what members thought would be a more energetic constitutional defense than the Justice Department might give.

The Justice Department set August 3, 1970, as the date for compliance by the states, and waited to see in which states there might be grounds for a test suit. Several cases converged. Idaho, Oregon, Texas, New Hampshire, and North Carolina either were challenged by the federal government or challenged it. A group of five New York citizens brought separate suit claiming the age provisions of the voting rights bill were unconstitutional. The first courtroom defense came on the New Yorker's suit in a Federal Court of Appeals in Washington. The Justice Department leaned heavily, in its defense, on the arguments of Senators Kennedy and Goldwater, that denying the vote to eighteen- to twenty-year-olds violated the equal protection clause of the Fourteenth Amendment. The Chief Judge of the Court of Appeals allowed a variety of other interested parties to appear as friends of the court. Senator Kennedy argued his first case in nine years, maintaining that the Supreme Court had issued a barely camouflaged invitation to the Congress to join it as protectors of voting rights, and that the states had discriminated against eighteen- to twenty-year-olds by making them eligible for war, marriage, and taxation, but not voting. The Court of Appeals ruled unanimously that the act was constitutional. The stage was set for the Supreme Court.

The main opponents of the government's position before the Supreme Court were Texas and Oregon. The Texas brief maintained that other restrictions on state action, specifically the Fourteenth, Fifteenth, Seventeenth, Nineteenth, and Twenty-fourth Amendments, had all come about through the regular constitutional amending processes. Thus, if eighteen-year-old voting were the goal, the same process should be followed:

Impatience with the process of constitutional amendment is no justification for a shortcut that ignores both the letter and the spirit of the Constitution and that disregards both the purposes of a written Constitution and the position of the states in the Constitutional scheme.

The Oregon brief argued that there was no discrimination among persons because the "passage of time, the sole criterion upon which the classification is based, is completely impartial—and is applicable equally to all persons." The government's defense hinged upon Congress's legislative role under the Fourteenth Amendment. The Supreme Court produced an exquisite compromise. On December 21, 1970, by a 5 to 4 vote in *Oregon* v. *Mitchell,* the Court approved eighteen-year-old voting in federal elections, but said that it was unconstitutional for Congress to impose this rule for purely state and local elections.

The swing vote came from the late Justice Hugo L. Black. He voted both with the majority approving the eighteen-year-old vote for federal elections and also with the majority that did not want to extend those votes to state and local elections. His reasoning was that Congress has "ultimate supervisory power" over federal contests under Article I, Section 4 of the Constitution, which states that:

The times, places and matter of holiday elections for Senators and Representatives shall be prescribed in each State by the Legislature thereof; but the Congress may at any time by law make or alter such regulations. . . .

However, Black felt that the Fourteenth Amendment applied to discrimination by race, not by age. The practical effect of the Supreme Court's neat distinction was immediately clear. With the exception of the few states already having eighteen-year-old voting, the states would now have to set up two complete sets of registration rolls and would also, on election days, require either separate ballot boxes or special ballots. These requirements could create considerable confusion in a nation that likes its returns counted fast on election night for television. Equally distressing to many state governments, the expense of dual voting systems was likely to be considerable.

Senator Bayh's subcommittee quickly determined that the dual voting systems based on age would lead to long delays in the election process and a complicated administrative structure. The legal question of what was a federal election did not seem perfectly clear, especially where political party positions were concerned. Moreover, the cost of administering such a system were likely to be between $10 million and $20 million. The only realistic hope of untangling the situation in time for eighteen- to twenty-year-olds to vote in 1972 was a constitutional amendment. The political process was back at the beginning, except that the presence of a congressional statute—itself ruled constitutional—giving eighteen- to twenty-year-olds the vote in federal elections was an added input in favor of the approving of the youth vote in all elections.

This time around resistance was less. In February, 1971, the House Judiciary Committee by a vote of 32 to 2 overwhelmingly approved a constitutional amendment granting the vote in *all* elections. Unanimous support from the Senate Judiciary Committee quickly followed. On March 10 the full Senate approved the amendment unanimously; on March 23 the House voted Yes by the stunning tally of 401 to 19. The proposed

Twenty-sixth Amendment to the Constitution read:

SECTION 1. The right of citizens of the United States, who are eighteen to twenty-one years of age or older, to vote shall not be denied or abridged by the United States or by any state on account of age.

SECTION 2. The Congress shall have power to enforce this article by appropriate legislation.

The question now became: Would the necessary three fourths of the state legislatures ratify the amendment? And would they do so in time for eighteen-year-old voting in the 1972 election? The time problem was compounded because some state legislatures meet only every other year. Another complicating factor was that these legislatures were viewed as more conservative politically and more resistant to change than Congress. In each state, various ad hoc groups formed to push for ratification. Nationally, Common Cause, a public interest citizens' lobby, organized a campaign for ratification. Five states—Minnesota, Connecticut, Delaware, Tennessee, and Washington—immediately ratified the amendment, but resistance seemed likely in Florida, Louisiana, Mississippi, and Oklahoma.

By May, in record time, twenty-six states had ratified. Then came a minor breakthrough. The Republican-dominated New Jersey Assembly, which had previously voted No, reversed itself under the pressure of Republican Governor William Cahill. Louisiana came in with a quick surprise Yes from large majorities in both houses of its state legislature. In June, Missouri and Wisconsin became the thirty-third and thirty-fourth states to ratify. Three more states approved quickly. Only one more was needed and several legislatures wanted the honor of putting the amendment over the top. In order to beat Oklahoma, the Ohio Speaker of the House canceled all debate and called for a

Figure 4.1. Policy
views of the young

Source: Newsweek,
October 25, 1971,
p. 44.

NEW PRIORITIES: HOW THE YOUNG WOULD LIKE TO SEE TAX MONEY SPENT					
	Spend More	Spend Less		Spend More	Spend Less
Air, Water Pollution	78%	2%	Increased Social Security	38%	6%
Job Training for the Unemployed	68%	3%	Public Transportation	26%	14%
Organized Crime	56%	4%	Building Highways	15%	25%
Improved Schools	55%	4%	Military Defense	14%	33%
Street Crime	49%	3%	Economic Foreign Aid	8%	49%
Medicare	48%	4%	Space Exploration	10%	68%
Housing for the Poor	51%	11%	Military Foreign Aid	3%	64%

quick roll call. That did it. The next morning, July 1, Oklahoma approved too. The Twenty-sixth Amendment to the Constitution had been ratified with record speed, only three months and seven days after Congress had sent it to the states. A new group, young people, were now officially included in the electorate. In signing the certification of the amendment for the General Services Administration on a desk believed to have been used by Thomas Jefferson, President Nixon expressed "confidence" in America's youth. His words were witnessed by five hundred members of the well-scrubbed Young Americans in Concert in white and navy blue uniforms. The President asked the Young Americans to spread America's work as the international keeper of the peace in their forthcoming European musical tour.

The Twenty-sixth Amendment was a clear response to the emergence of a youth consciousness and the expanded military and political participation by young people. An intriguing question, naturally, was what impact it would have on the political system. Not surprisingly, the past provided conflicting clues. The Nineteenth Amendment (1920) conferring the vote on women had had little or no political effect. Indeed, for fifty years thereafter women were a largely quiescent political entity, without group consciousness and without organization. But other extensions of the franchise had made significant impacts on the political system.

Two popular theories of what youth would do emerged. One, propounded in

part by public opinion analyst Richard Scammon, held that young people would not be a significant electoral force. Eighteen- to twenty-one-year-olds, the reasoning went, would be most like twenty-one- to twenty-four-year-olds, about whom there was already considerable evidence. That is, this age range would show the lowest registration and turnout figures of any age grouping, partially because this is a highly mobile and unformed stage of life. Furthermore, the prediction was that rather than radicalizing American politics, young people would tend to vote like their parents.

A second, and somewhat different view, also circulated. Senator Edward Kennedy, a special favorite of this age group, commented that "we will have a different country tomorrow when eighteen-year-olds begin to vote because they will not be dropouts from the political process." Remembering the youth mobilizations of the 1960's and noting the high levels of educational attainment in this age category, many expected very extensive participation in general, and a much more ideological and left-oriented perspective in particular. Early polls indicated that the party affiliations of young people were different from those of their parents. They were more oriented toward the Democratic party and toward being independents, with substantial backing among noncollege youth for Alabama Governor George C. Wallace. Early polls also suggested that they were planning to register and vote at slightly lower rates than the rest of the public. As the figures in Figure 4.1 indicate, young people do bring a distinct set of

preferences on governmental priorities
to the political arena. As in every instance
when suffrage has been extended in
this country, what those with the new
franchise now do or do not do with their
potential power may turn out to be as
interesting as their struggle to be
included in the first place.

SOURCES
New York Times, 1968–1972.
Congressional Quarterly, 1968–1971.

citizenship

Being Part of the Political Community

Citizenship is a complicated concept. Fundamentally, it means that an individual or a group is part of the political community. A citizen has legal rights in relation to the state and the government. A citizen also has the opportunities and should have the abilities to use those rights. And, finally, a citizen has political power.

Within the underdeveloped world, the struggles for "independence" and "liberation" are often for citizenship in these same fundamental terms—participating, having rights, and having power. Within our own country, the struggles of black people, of immigrants, of women, of any individual and group for legal and political rights and power are really struggles over citizenship. Being a citizen provides at least the chance for other benefits in a system, such as holding office, having high status, and using government to benefit oneself or one's children or one's private livelihood. Without citizenship there is no chance. Without citizenship there is nothing for an individual. Without citizenship, the individual is an "out-law," a pariah, at the mercy of those in power. He is without dignity. The value of citizenship is so high that much political conflict is over who is to be included—and who is to be excluded—from its benefits.

One of the most attractive features of democratic ideology, which partially accounts for its worldwide appeal, is its broad definition of citizenship. There are typically three elements in the concept of citizenship within democratic political theory. First, citizenship is supposed to be a universal right of adults and is supposed to be connected to a universal right to participate in political decisions, usually through a representative system of free elections with real choices. Second, the act of participating as a citizen is supposed to have symbolic and psychological benefits for the individual as a person. Participation makes one a full human being, conferring dignity and responsibility. Third, being a citizen and participating in public life is supposed to guarantee the citizen some tangible benefits from a responsive government: material and symbolic benefits in policy pay-offs for the citizen. These three values are the ideal of democratic politics. The distance between the ideal values and their achievement is a source of tension and political conflict in any society that is committed to full citizenship but has not attained it.

The bulk of this chapter explores two crucial aspects of contemporary citizenship: how children learn about about politics, and what the actual patterns of political participation in America are in our own times. Before turning to these dynamic aspects of individual involvement in the political community, we will briefly examine the historical bases of the American conception of citizenship; trace the struggle for the extension of the right to vote over our history, because voting is the gateway to real citizenship; and analyze the experience of immigrants and black people, because the treatment of those who are different from the majority is the hard and final test of a society's seriousness about democratic ideals of citizenship.

The Historical Basis of American Citizenship

The present-day American concept of citizenship has developed through a long period of common Western political experiences as well as some distinctly native to our land. The Greeks, and primarily the Athenians, introduced the original concept of being a citizen. In Athens citizenship meant the right to participate in public life, to have a say in public decisions. As did so many subsequent societies, ancient Greece had a policy of exclusion. Slaves, women, and resident foreigners could not become citizens, and they did not have a voice in public issues.

From the ancient Greeks, too, came the concept of citizenship as a set of personal, and often legally enforceable, obligations. Greek citizens had the obligation to serve in the courts, to man the armies, and to contribute taxes. The highest right and obligation of the Greek citizen was to serve in public office. An additional aspect of the Greek concept of citizenship was pride in the community, which the citizen was supposed to feel and which, by every evidence, the Greek citizen did feel. Citizenship thus meant being an integral part of one's own community and possessing something that set one apart from those outside the community. This emotional "we-feeling" of members of a political system is clearly the psychological foundation of all modern nationalism.

Other traditions have also contributed to the American concepts. From Roman practices came the concept that citizenship brings with it a set of legal protections. The citizen of Rome enjoyed such written legal rights as the right to possess property, to be treated equally before the law, and to be given judicial trials.

From the municipalities of medieval Europe comes yet another endorsement of the principle that the privileges and burdens of citizenship are inseparable from membership in a defined political unit. The feudal system emphasized the idea that individuals owe allegiance and service to those from whom they receive protection—the philosophical basis for a military draft. From England evolved the tradition that certain basic liberties are the inheritance of all those fortunate enough to be either Englishmen or their lineal and national descendants. And, finally, the French Revolution contributed a ringing declaration of the rights of man and of the citizen.

The legal basis of American citizenship rests on two principles widely used in Europe. Under the principle of *jus sanguinis* (law of the blood) children take on the citizenship of their parents. Under the principle of *jus soli* (law of the soil) those born on American soil, American possessions, or even American vessels are also considered to be native-born citizens. Put together, these two rules mean that those born abroad of American parents, those born in America of American parents, and those born in America of foreign parentage have all been able to claim American citizenship. In addition, through a series of changing rules and regulations, America has always provided for those not covered under the *jus sanguinis* or the *jus soil* principles to become citizens through the process of *naturalization*.

Legal Citizenship: The Right to Vote

The leaders in the American colonies, including Thomas Jefferson, agreed to exclude some people from voting: children, women, and slaves. They defined the relevant electorate or the relevant citizens as those who were free adult white males. In turn, the Constitution of 1787 left largely to the states the issue of whether free adult white males would all be permitted to vote, with the proviso that the largest state electorate —that qualified to vote for representatives in a state legislature—must also be the eligible electorate for the Congress of the United States.

The states then imposed one major qualification for voting, a property requirement. Those people who paid taxes were allowed to vote. This provision has often been interpreted as restricting suffrage; in fact, however, it existed alongside a remarkably wide extension of the vote. To begin with, the requirement of taxpayer's status replaced an earlier and widely used restriction—the voter must actually own land. Because taxation was virtually universal for adult males, the suffrage was widespread. It was recognized at this time, in the late eighteenth century and the early nineteenth century, that to have only a tax-paying qualification created a suffrage system open to virtually all white males. The religious qualifications for voting of the colonial period were dropped under the new state constitutions, which followed the adoption of the federal Constitution.

In the late nineteenth century a number of states, beginning first with Wyoming, gave women the right to vote. There was also an active suffragette movement, which featured conspicuous and noisy picketing of the White House and coincided with a general early movement of women's liberation. With the ratification of the Nineteenth Amendment in 1920, women finally received the right to vote. The suffragette organization then converted itself into the League of Women Voters.

The black struggle for suffrage has been much more complicated. Two post-Civil War constitutional amendments gave blacks the theoretical right to vote. The Fourteenth Amendment made universal manhood suffrage the law of the land; the Fifteenth proscribed state or national abridgement of voting on "account of race, color, or previous condition of servitude." By a series of devices, however, black people were continually prevented from voting. Southern states particularly set up official roadblocks, including poll taxes (fees that had to be paid before one could vote) and complicated and discriminating literacy tests, which prevented blacks from registering and thus from voting. Terror and violence were also frequently applied by the Ku Klux Klan as means of intimidation.

Southern restrictions on black voting began in earnest in the 1890's when the North acquiesced in the end of the Reconstruction. The efforts of southern whites to restrict the political participation of blacks continues, in reduced form, into the present era. Some techniques, such as the white-only primary election, were struck down by the Supreme Court soon after World War II. It was federal legislative policy, however, that finally brought about black suffrage. Beginning with the Civil Rights Act of 1957, a series of laws in 1960, 1964, 1965, and 1970 (the Voting Rights Act of 1970) have cumulatively eliminated all but hard-core resistance in a few local communities. At this point, virtually two hundred years from the founding of the Republic, the goal of uniform laws that prescribe universal suffrage is finally close to attainment.

The Immigrants: Newcomers in Pursuit of the American Dream

Initially, anyone who could scrape together the cost of an ocean passage could emigrate to the United States. America, George Washington declared, "is open to receive not the Opulent and Respected Stranger, but the oppressed and persecuted of all Nations and Religions." As a developing but underpopulated new nation, the United States actively sought immigrants. The doors were open, and in the one-hundred-year period beginning in 1820, one of the great mass migrations of history occurred. Forty million people left the Old World to settle in the United States.

The rising tide of immigrants, however, was met by demands from those who were already citizens for regulation and restriction of the flow. The pressures upon Congress were intense from the late 1880's on, when the rate reached a minimum of half a million newcomers a year. In 1921, Congress placed qualitative controls on immigrants. Newcomers were barred if they fell into a list of "undesirables." The list has included at various times polygamists, convicts and criminals, lunatics and idiots, prostitutes and drug addicts, anarchists and Communists, and persons having any "dangerous and loathsome disease." Under pressure from labor interest groups, which feared wage competition from "coolie labor," the Congress first excluded all Chinese as undesirables, then, in 1924, despite voluntary restrictions by Japan, it also barred all Japanese. These acts deeply offended the proud and sensitive peoples against whom they were directed; such racial bars were not dropped until 1952.

Congress also set quantitative restrictions on immigration, beginning in the 1920's. The total number of immigrants permitted from outside the Western Hemisphere was drastically limited. Within the European quota, a total of only 156,000 during the 1950's, allotments were assigned to each nation based upon its proportionate contribution to America's white population in 1920. The point of this formula was to favor northern Europeans from the Anglo-Saxon Protestant countries over southern and eastern Europeans who were Catholic or Jewish. The formula also permitted some countries to underutilize their quotas while others had people, on forty-year waiting lists, clamoring to get in. Nevertheless, as late as 1952, when the noxious McCarran-Walter Act was passed over President Truman's veto, the United States was committed to a policy that made it impossible to transfer unused quotas to countries whose quotas were oversubscribed.

Many of the discriminatory aspects of American immigration policy were ended with the passage of the 1965 Immigration Act, ceremoniously signed by President Johnson at the Statute of Liberty. The national quota system was replaced with an overall limit of 170,000 per year for all parts of the world outside the Western Hemisphere, which now has a ceiling of 120,000 persons per year. There are still priorities on who may immigrate, with preferences given to relatives of American citizens, scientists, and refugees from Communism. The old system of national, ethnic, and religious preferences, however, is dropped entirely.

It should be added that, despite the severe and discriminatory restrictions on immigration to America after 1920, the nation did let down the barriers under certain special circumstances. It admitted 600,000 displaced persons from Europe at the end of World War II, a substantial number of the Hungarian "freedom fighters" in 1956, and over 100,000 refugees to date from Castro's Cuba.

Immigrants have the option of two legal statuses. If they remain as resident aliens, they must register with the government yearly and are excluded from many of the privileges of citizenship including voting. If they choose to become American citizens through the naturalization process, they must fulfill various residence, literacy, and character requirements and must also swear fealty to the United States. Naturalized citizens may not be elected President, and, more important, they are subject to loss of citizenship and deportation on certain political grounds such as belief in Communist doctrines or associations with Communist or totalitarian groups. Although native-born Americans may face civil penalties for such behavior, they cannot be deprived of their citizenship for it. Such threatening provisions for naturalized citizens were imposed by Congress during the 1950's, although similar practices occurred at the end of World War I.

Becoming a Citizen: An Evaluation

How does one evaluate American treatment of immigrants? There can be no argument about low points along the way: discrimination, abuse, and exploitation of various groups. Further, the motivations for the "open-door" policy were not always idealistic. America was a developing, industrializing country whose governing elites wanted manpower for various tasks, and they wanted that manpower quickly. On the other hand, the economic opportunities and political freedoms afforded the immigrants surely surpassed the wretched conditions and repressive societies from which many of them came. That is why they came. There is argument whether the melting pot of various nationality and religious groups might not better be called a boiling pot, with its tensions, pressures, and hostilities. On balance, nonetheless, the Germans, Irish, Italians, Jews, and Slavs, especially in the second and third generations, seemed to have fared well, accumulating economic and political power.

For nonwhite groups, the road to first-class citizenship in this country has been far rockier. The Constitution did not even recognize blacks as full-fledged persons for population counts, and the most recent struggle over black rights, housing, employment, and education is a familiar story in today's newspapers and on television screens. Indians have suffered brutal repression followed by stifling paternalism under the white-run Bureau of Indian Affairs in the Interior Department. Mexican-Americans, who call themselves Chicanos, have only in the 1970's come to full political consciousness and fought against voting registration laws aimed directly at disfranchising them and against discrimination in many other fields.

Any evaluation of the historical development of citizenship presents a mixed picture. In a comparative sense, America has been a more open society than many others. For some groups, however, American history has been a story of constant struggle. Black riots, Chicano riots, Indian hostility—these are symptoms of groups who feel that the system treats their citizenship differently than it does whites'. De Tocqueville's observations about suffrage are equally applicable to citizenship:

> When a nation begins to modify the elective qualification, it may easily be foreseen that, sooner or later, that qualification will be entirely abolished. There is no more invariable rule in the history of society; the further electoral rights are extended, the greater is the need of extending them; for after each concession the strength of the democracy increases, and its demands increase with its strength. The ambition of those who are below the appointed rate is irritated in exact proportion to the great number of those who are above it.[1]

Political Socialization: Creating Americans

An important aspect of citizenship is the attitudes people have about their government and society. In its broadest sense, the set of orientations people have about politics is called the *political culture*. The process of absorbing the political culture and inculcating it in new members is called *political socialization*. Political socialization is political learning and political teaching. Every system tries to teach new members, especially children, what the accepted norms, values, and behaviors are. The goal is to condition the individual to accept the system and to ease the way for his later smooth functioning within it as an adult. If political socialization is effective, new members of a society have affirmative and supportive attitudes toward officeholders, political procedures, institutions, and the way policy decisions distribute rewards and penalties. Political socialization in all societies is basically supportive.

The process of political socialization is carried out through five agents: the family, the schools, primary groups (such as friends, or cliques, or gangs), organizations, and the mass media. Totalitarian countries devote the most effort to planned political socialization. In the Soviet Union, children are carefully taught the value of group cooperation as opposed to individualistic activities. In Cuba, children are taught to hate American imperialists. In Communist China, values are inculcated through mass recitals of the thoughts of Chairman Mao. In the United States formal socialization is a haphazard and fragmented process, although our schools spend

---

[1] Alexis de Tocqueville, *Democracy in America,* Vol. I (New York: Vintage, 1958), p. 59.

more time per day on civics than do Soviet schools.[2] Schoolchildren recite the pledge of allegiance and various civics courses are required in elementary and secondary schools. The political content of public school courses in America is set not by the federal government, but by local school boards and state education agencies. The content varies considerably from district to district.

There is some disagreement about which of the five agents is the most significant in the political socialization process, or indeed on the exact way in which the dynamics of learning about politics occurs. Several propositions seem to have considerable support in the available data. The family is the main agent in younger children, and political attitudes and activities in the family unit are also the best predictors of whether college students will engage in demonstrations and other forms of expressive, activist, political behavior.[3] The great bulk of attitudes is formed in children before high school. High school civics classes have an uneven or negligible impact.[4] The details of political learning in America are worth examining, especially in the light of ever more widespread student activism.

American children begin to develop perceptions of the political world even before entering elementary school.[5] Within the family, in response to questions like, "Why can't we park here, Daddy?" or, "Who pays the policeman?" the child learns that there are laws, and that there is a mayor or a city government. In this manner, children become aware of the differentiation between the public and the private sectors of life, of the existence of public rules and regulations, and of the existence of an authority even more powerful than the family itself. These things happen even though American children do not generally add the words *politics* or *politician* to their vocabularies before the age of eleven, and even though politics is less important in a child's life than play, school, or sports.

One set of feelings about political life is definitely formed in children by age seven or the second grade. This set of attitudes consists of attachment to the United States as a political community. Children at this level express warm feelings about the United States—they do not want to leave it, they admire its natural beauty, and they like its people. As children grow older, this generalized attachment is gradually extended to specifically political objects—first toward the President, then the flag, and finally toward the abstract idea of freedom. By ages twelve and thirteen, American children have affirmative feelings extending to such abstract impersonal and political items as democracy, government, voting, and freedom of speech, press, religion, and choice of occupation. What is interesting about all of these attitudes is that they are

[2] See G. Bereday and B. Stretch, "Political Education in the USA and the USSR," *Comparative Education Review* (June, 1963), and Urie Bronfenbrenner, *Two Worlds of Childhood: US and USSR* (New York: Russell Sage, 1970).

[3] See J. Leiper Freeman, "Parents, It's Not *All* Your Fault, But . . . ," *Journal of Politics,* XXXI (August, 1969), pp. 812–817.

[4] See Kenneth P. Langdon and M. Kent Jennings, "Political Socialization and the High School Civics Curriculum in the United States," *American Political Science Review,* LXII (September, 1968), pp. 852–867.

[5] See David Easton and Jack Dennis, "The Child's Image of Government," in Roberta Sigel (ed.), "Political Socialization: Its Role in the Political Process," *The Annals of the American Academy of Political and Social Science,* CCCCXI (1965), pp. 40–57.

just that: they are feelings and reactions, largely devoid at this point of much informational content about what government is about or how it works.

Within the framework of the emotional attachments developed by the budding American citizenry, the reactions to the President occupy a special place. The President, who is viewed extremely favorably by children from grade two on, becomes a kind of idealized authority figure. He is seen as more honest, friendlier, and better than most men. Indeed, he is perceived as possessing more of these qualities than the children's own fathers. This type of unrealistic and romanticized view of the President represents an effort on the part of the child to idealize political figures as ideal authority figures.

Even young children are capable of making evaluations of their government, and these evaluations constitute a set of orientations that they retain when they become adult citizens. In Table 4.1, for example, it is possible to see the responses of a sample of one thousand Chicago area children to the statements numbered 1 to 6 down the left-hand side. The percentages are those who *agree* with each statement by grade level. Children at all grade levels roundly approve of the American government. They reject the first three statements, which imply that the government is too large in the scope of its operations. Brought up in the big government state, they are not inclined to favor something more limited. The children approve, in statements 4 and 5, the role of the government in guiding and caring for people and endorse the welfare and collectivist aspects of modern government. If adult Americans still believe in rugged individualism, it is an attitude they acquired in later life, not in school.

Table 4.1 *Children's evaluations of government in America*

Statements about government	Percentage who AGREE with the statement Grade level					
	3rd	4th	5th	6th	7th	8th
1. The government is getting too big for America.	16%	14%	10%	7%	13%	11%
2. The government meddles too much in our private lives.	28	21	17	19	19	14
3. The government has too much power.	36	19	22	10	12	15
4. The government usually knows what is best for the people.	80	77	87	84	91	84
5. The government ought to give money and food to people out of work.	70	84	80	78	71	77
6. The government should have more power over the people.	22	33	24	13	20	19

Source: David Easton and Jack Dennis, "The Child's Image of Government," *The Annals,* CCCLXI (1965), p. 52.

Statement 6, however, suggests that, in the words of Professors Easton and Dennis, the children are "conservative collectivists." They are not much in favor of extending government beyond its present limits.

The party attachments of children develop early, and preferences are formed before the children have much information about the parties they favor. Although most children do not learn what the term *political party* means until the fourth or fifth grade, many have worn campaign buttons or items of that sort as early as the second grade. By fourth grade, according to a New Haven study conducted by Professor Fred I. Greenstein,[6] six of ten children could state whether they thought of themselves as Republicans or Democrats, even though less than a third could name one public official from either party. The proportion of party identification was about the same among New Haven nine-year-olds as it is among adult Americans. New Haven fourth graders had the same frequency of party identifications as do adults in the twenty-one to twenty-four age group.

Political socialization in the United States also seems to inculcate what political scientists call a high sense of "political efficacy," an evaluation on the part of the individual that he is competent to function in the political world. Sense of political efficacy is an evaluation with a primarily psychological tint; what counts is not whether the person really can gain an audience or influence events, but whether he perceives that he can. For children the realistic probabilities associated with a sense of efficacy are especially irrelevant, because it is unlikely that most children would try to communicate with government or to influence it. Nonetheless, possession of a sense of efficacy must be an important part of the orientation children bring to the society as full-fledged citizens.

Table 4.2 contains five items utilized to measure children's senses of political efficacy for a sample of twelve thousand between the ages of seven and thirteen, along with a table reporting the results by grade level. A perfect sense of efficacy would involve rejecting all five items. The interpretation of the results is that a basic attitude, which can be labeled a sense of efficacy, is present in American school children; it is formed fairly early and maintained at least through eighth grade. This feeling of efficacy does not depend upon the child's ability to understand the government, or upon his possession of information about it. Rather, it seems to be a reflection of a general understanding of his potential role.

The sense of political efficacy increases as the child progresses from grade three to grade eight, indicating that, at the minimum, school experiences are reinforcing. Thus, only 16 per cent of the third-grade children rank "high" in political efficacy, some 54 per cent of the eighth graders have the "high" ranking. There is some evidence to indicate that successful participation in various kinds of school activities reinforces the sense of efficacy. Professors Easton and Dennis observe:

The child comes . . . both to awareness of the role of the ordinary individual in the political process and possibly even to some emergent sense of his own mastery of the political world as well. This is not to say that he sees himself as synonymous with the Leviathan of the state. Yet he begins to carve out a small piece of political authority for himself—at his own

[6] *Children and Politics* (New Haven: Yale University Press, 1965).

Table 4.2 *The development of a sense of political efficacy in American school children*

| | Grade level | | | | | |
	3rd	4th	5th	6th	7th	8th
Low efficacy	56%	55%	35%	29%	23%	17%
Medium efficacy	28	27	29	27	29	29
High efficacy	16	18	36	44	48	54

ITEMS UTILIZED:

1. "What happens in the government will happen no matter what people do. It is like the weather, there is nothing people can do about it."
2. "There are some big, powerful men in the government who are running the whole thing and they do not care about us ordinary people."
3. "My family doesn't have any say about what the government does."
4. "Citizens don't have a chance to say what they think about running the government."
5. "I don't think people in the government care much what people like my family think."

Response choices:

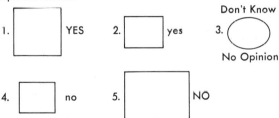

Source: David Easton and Jack Dennis, "The Child's Acquisition of Regime Norms: Political Efficacy," *American Political Science Review*, LXI (March, 1967), p. 29, 33.

level of consciousness. He is still far away from any actual role that he normally would have in the political process. Even so he begins to feel his political power when it still involves a high degree of projection to those around him and to his future role as an adult member of the system.[7]

Some Breaks in the Pattern of Supportive Socialization

The data cited so far suggest that American children are indeed socialized in such a way as to make them citizens accepting their government as it is, and at a highly affirmative level. Yet, other studies suggest that not all children conform to this pat-

[7] "The Child's Acquisition of Regime Norms: Political Efficacy," *American Political Science Review*, LXI (March, 1967), p. 33.

Figure 4.2. Levels of children's trust in government

Source: Edward S. Greenberg, "Black Children and the Political System," *Public Opinion Quarterly,* XXXIV (Fall 1970), p. 339.

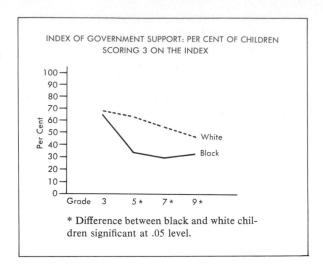

INDEX OF GOVERNMENT SUPPORT: PER CENT OF CHILDREN SCORING 3 ON THE INDEX

* Difference between black and white children significant at .05 level.

tern. These contrary findings lead to inquiry into the dynamics of socialization and the conditions under which affirmative attitudes may continue or be dissipated and replaced with cynicism or hostile behavior.

To begin with, children who are not part of the mainstream of the society do not share the attitudes of the conventionally socialized. As Figure 4.2 reveals, in two cities, Pittsburgh and Philadelphia, the percentage of black children who "trust" the government is considerably less than the rate among white children, which incidentally is not especially high. Black children, moreover, trust the President less and are absolutely hostile to policemen as authority figures. To cite another example, a study of schoolchildren in Appalachia, a rural, isolated, and white section of Kentucky, found that children there were markedly cynical about politics, did not have a high sense of efficacy, and were suspicious and hostile toward the President.[8]

In addition, not all of the children who originally support the system maintain those attitudes, even through early adulthood. Table 4.3, which shows attitudes of college and noncollege youth, is revealing on this point. Among both groups criticism of the distribution of justice within the system and its respect for human values runs deep, along with suspicion as to the true reasons behind the Vietnam war. College students, however, are more likely to support protest activities than noncollege young people, and they also put a much smaller premium on the traditional values of "national honor" and "patriotism."

How do we account for these differences in attitudes among groups? The first agent of socialization is the family. Family attitudes among those who are on the very bottom in our system are less supportive than among those on the top. But even children of privileged parents are not automatically supportive for life. The liberal, idealistic values of the parents may, in the college-age student confronting some unpleasant realities of political life, be transformed into hostile political activism. What appears

[8] See Dean Jaros, Herbert Hirsh, and Fred Fleron, "The Malevolent Leader: Political Socialization in an American Sub-Culture," *American Political Science Review,* LXII (June, 1968), pp. 564–575.

Table 4.3   *Political attitudes of college-age young people*

Statement	College students	Noncollege	Total—all youth
1. American society is characterized by injustice, insensitivity, lack of candor, and inhumanity.			
Strongly agree	15%	15%	15%
Partially agree	50%	43%	44%
2. The war in Vietnam is pure imperialism.			
Strongly agree	16%	13%	14%
Partially agree	40%	41%	
3. Can "sometimes justify" the following tactics for achieving goals:			
Sit-ins (whites)	79%	63%	
(blacks)	71%	65%	
Property destruction			
(whites)	14%	10%	
(blacks)	45%	27%	
Assaulting police			
(whites)	18%	12%	
(blacks)	51%	28%	
4. Agree that it is worth fighting a war to defend a nation's honor.	25%	59%	
5. Believe that patriotism is very important.	3%	60%	

Source: Jeremy Main, "A Special Report on Youth," *Fortune,* LXXIX (1969), pp. 73–74.

to happen is that life's experiences—the situations children and adults actually confront—affect their attitudes. Because of his dynamic process of responding to events, political learning continues through the life cycle as old attitudes are reinforced or new ones formed. Although evidence does not exist one way or the other, it is likely that the mass media play an important role in contemporary political socialization. The media, perhaps particularly television, communicate not only events, but models of authoritative and also peer-group responses to those events.

Some apparent contradictions in political socialization are resolved when it is viewed in this framework, called the *social learning model* by psychologists.[9] This experiential perspective explains why middle-class children interviewed in the placid, relatively optimistic and politically celebrative America of the early 1960's gave supportive responses, and why those left out of the rewards of this system were not as

[9] See Ira S. Rohter, "A Social-Learning Theory Approach to the Study of Political Socialization," paper presented at the 66th Annual Meeting of the American Political Science Association, Los Angeles, 1970.

supportive. A *social learning* model also explains how, in response to personal experiences with war, racism, and conflict, many young adults changed their attitudes. It may be, as some have suggested, that negative reactions can be avoided if children in elementary and secondary school are given a more candid view of the realities and conflicts of American politics than is usually done. Perhaps—in the revision of American history and government texts at the secondary level to encompass black history, Indian history, Chicano history, women's rights, and other subjects previously covered only lightly if at all—a new manner of affirmative socialization can be brought about. In any case, both recent studies and recent events suggest that the impact of experiences—the bad as well as the good—is of crucial significance in the socialization process.

participation

The Complicated Pathways of Political Involvement

Political participation includes a broad range of possible activities. Figure 4.3 lists three broad pathways: electoral/interest group politics, protest politics, and revolutionary politics. Within each pathway, the largest numbers of participants are at the bottom, because the requirements in effort, skill, and risk are always lowest for "spectators." At the top, the gladiatorial level, one finds the leaders within each pathway; these are the individuals who devote most or all of their time to leadership and political conflict. Gladiators take the largest political risks and possess the most power and the highest status. To understand who participates, how, how much, and why in American society, it is useful to examine separately each of the three political pathways.

Figure 4.3. Pathways of political participation

Source: Model adapted from Lester Milbrath, *Political Participation* (Chicago: Rand, McNally, 1956), p. 18.

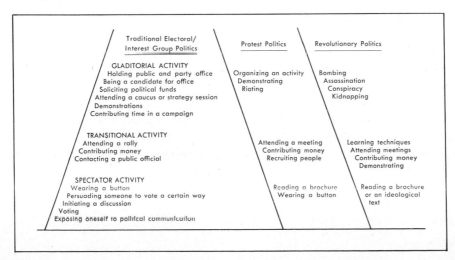

The Pathway of Electoral and Interest Group Activity

What most people, and most political scientists until recently, have in mind when they talk about political participation is the pathway of electoral and interest group politics. It encompasses by far the largest number of Americans numerically, and its leaders occupy virtually all of the governmental and private organizational offices. This pathway is "establishment" politics or the "system," as those expressions are commonly understood. Although participation in this pathway involves conflict, and often the severe warlike competition of tough national election campaigns, the conflict is carried out within commonly understood and observed rules. Among the rules, formal and informal, would be nonviolence, acceptance of the outcomes by winners and losers alike, and enough policy payoffs—even to losers—either to keep them in this procedural pathway or to maintain at least their passive acceptance.

The **apathetics,** who number approximately one third of the American population, do not engage in any of these activities. For a variety of reasons, these people are often literally unaware of the political part of the world in which they live. A second group can be identified as the **spectators,** and its ranks include about 60 per cent of the population. People in this category talk about politics, vote, wear campaign buttons, and sometimes attend rallies or contribute funds. Finally, there are the **gladiators,** who are at the top of the hierarchy in terms of participation and who comprise at the very most some 5 to 7 per cent of the population. Professor Lester Milbrath has observed:

> This division is reminiscent of the roles played at a Roman gladiatorial contest. A small band of gladiators battle fiercely to please the spectators, who have the power to decide their fate. The spectators in the stands cheer, transmit messages of advice and encouragement, and, at given periods, vote to decide who has won a particular battle (election). The apathetics do not bother to come to the stadium to watch the show.[10]

Table 4.4 divides electoral and interest group politics into five general modes of participation and lists the percentages of Americans who engage in each form.

Opinion participation is the easiest form of activity and Americans do this with a greater frequency than citizens in some other countries. Yet this tendency to hold and express an opinion when asked does not necessarily mean that Americans are well informed. The opinions of most Americans are those of the spectators, which include material picked up in a casual manner, generally as defined by the news media for capsule presentation. If being informed is a criterion for evaluating the opinion, the number of Americans who participate on this level drops to between 30 and 50 per cent of the population. Furthermore, those questions on which the citizen is well informed tend to be highly charged current issues; the war in Vietnam, civil rights, and crime are illustrations. The number who possess opinions with information content on the level of textbook knowledge of how American government actually works is even lower, ranging from 15 to 40 per cent.

[10] *Political Participation* (Chicago: Rand McNally, 1965), p. 20.

Table 4.4   *Modes of electoral and interest group participation*

Mode of participation	Estimated proportion of Americans as participants
I. Opinion participation	
Normally express political opinions when asked	70–90%
Normally express informed political opinions when asked	30–50
Possess basic "textbook" information of politics	15–40
II. Leadership participation	
Personal leadership (attempts to influence political views of others through discussion)	50–70%
Voluntary leadership in political campaigns	3–5
Partisan precinct leadership	0.25–1
III. Voter participation	
Infrequent participants (vote occasionally in elections)	30–40%
Regular participants (vote consistently in all elections— national, state, local)	25–30
Apoliticals (no voting in elections)	25–30
IV. Partisan participation	
Party identifiers (consider themselves Republicans or Democrats)	65%
Attend political meetings, rallies, dinners	5–7
Support financially campaigns of parties or candidates	4–10
Actual membership in a political club or organization	2–3
V. Voluntary organization participation	
Membership in organization of any kind	60–65%
Membership in organizations that sometimes take stands on political issues	30–35

Source: Dan Nimmo and Thomas D. Ungs, *American Political Patterns: Conflict and Consensus* (Boston: Little, Brown and Company, 1967), p. 112.

Leadership participation is most obvious at elections. Americans are inveterate talkers about politics, although largely on the level of personalities and concrete questions rather than abstractions. Seven out of ten engage in political conversations during campaigns; over 50 per cent feel they have influenced the opinions of friends in such discussions. As one moves toward leadership participation, however, which involves taking more of a public stand on politics, the numbers decline. Around 15 per cent of all Americans have written letters to public officials; only 3 per cent have written to newspapers or magazines. Campaign work—organizing volunteers, being a volunteer, passing out stickers, holding coffee hours, writing speeches—draws from 3 to 5 per cent of all Americans at one time or another. Regular precinct level party work on a year-in year-out basis apart from campaigns draws the least participation —at most 1 per cent of all Americans.

Voter participation is an especially important form of participation, and some long-term aspects of this behavior in the United States are considered later in the chapter. Approximately 25 to 30 per cent of the American citizenry vote regularly in elections at all levels, another 30 to 40 per cent vote occasionally, generally in presidential elections, and the rest of the electorate does not vote. Of the 25 to 30 per cent who do not vote, from 3 to 7 per cent of these are legally registered to vote but still do not vote. The others are not registered.

Partisan attachment consists of an "identification" or consistent affective attachment with one of the major political parties, as well as actual work on behalf of that party. Although the intensity of partisan attachments appear to be declining in our society, some 65 per cent are still party identifiers. For most people, party affiliation stops with identification or with voting. Only 4 to 10 per cent contribute money, 5 to 7 per cent ever attend rallies, and 2 to 3 per cent go so far as to take out a formal membership.

Voluntary organization participation is an important part of traditional political activity in the United States characterized by groups whose choices of political tactics are primarily litigation, lobbying, letter-writing, and elections. This organized interest group system, the collection of politically active private groups that forms the focal point of "pluralist" politics, encompasses approximately 30 to 35 per cent of all Americans at the membership level. Another 30 per cent of the population belong to private groups that are normally nonpolitical. Experience with any form of group politics, however, whether in high school or in a community organization or in corporate trade associations, increases an individual's skill and self-confidence, and provides an incentive and reinforcement for politics.

Social and Personal Correlates of Participation in the Electoral and Interest Group Pathway

In the United States participation in the electoral and interest group activity is dominated by people with certain distinctive social and personal characteristics.

Stated simply, as an individual's education, occupational status, and income increase, the likelihood of his participation increases also. Why, in contrast, do lower ranks on the variables of education, occupation, and income correlate with lower political participation? In part the cause is less leisure time available for politics among those at the lower end of the scale on these variables; in part, also, there are differing perceptions of the stakes involved and the expectations of success. People at the lower end of these scales may not perceive politics as relevant to their day-to-day concerns, or, even if they do, they may be afraid that their efforts will be unsuccessful. Middle- and upper-class citizens, in contrast, are more likely to have both the time and the awareness of what is involved in terms of their own interests. They are also more likely to possess the self-confidence and the skills for successful efforts. The overall pattern of these correlations can be seen in Table 4.5.

Education, which is a crucial variable affecting political participation in almost

Table 4.5
*Social correlates of
political involvement*

High involvement	Low involvement
Males	Females
Whites	Negroes
Over 35	Under 35
High formal education	Low formal education
High income	Low income
Urban residence	Rural residence
Membership in several organizations	No organizational memberships
OCCUPATIONS	
Professional	Farm workers
Business executives	Unskilled labor
White collar	
Skilled labor	

Source: Adapted from *Political Man,* by Seymour Martin Lipset, p. 184. Copyright © 1959, 1960 by Seymour Martin Lipset. Reprinted by permission of Doubleday & Company, Inc.

all countries, affects American citizens in a variety of ways. Increased education brings a greater consciousness of politics, a greater feeling of the obligation to participate, and a greater confidence that one *can* influence the outcomes of public life. Higher education is highly correlated with all forms of participation; the relationship is close between education and voting turnout. Occupation and income are closely tied to each other in American society. In general, those in higher status jobs and with higher pay are more likely to be campaign workers, to contribute to campaigns, and to vote.

Other social variables, such as age, sex, race, and religion, are also associated with definite patterns of political participation. In terms of age, those between thirty and fifty-five years of age tend to have higher rates of voting turnout than both younger and older persons. Participation increases as people approach their mid-forties and tapers off after the fifties. There are also clear patterns based on sex. Although outnumbered, men vote more frequently than women. Men are also more likely to engage in other forms of participation than women.

Race is also related to political participation. A variety of nationwide studies has shown that blacks participate at a lower rate than whites. To a certain degree, low levels of black participation in northern areas have been a reflection of lower education, job discrimination, and lower income. Southern nonvoting among black Americans, at least until the recent past, has also been a consequence of widespread covert and overt pressures not to register, plus the generally lower voting turnout in rural areas.

Not surprisingly, a number of studies have shown that as political interest, political information, and psychological involvement in politics go up, so too does participation. In addition, as personal sophistication and sociability go up, participation also increases. These variables, which are all highly intercorrelated with income, education, and status, paint a clear picture: the pathways of electoral and interest group participation have been dominated by persons who are white, middle class, and middle-aged. Private success, good education, self-assurance, and status move a person into politics, which in turn provides reinforcing rewards from the political system—status, material benefits, favorable policies, dignity, and the emotional satisfaction of belonging.

By contrast, those who are least active in the electoral and interest group pathway are not complete nonparticipants, and this fact is theoretically suggestive of the relationship between participating in and benefiting from the political system. Young people, students, blacks, housewives opposed to war, southern whites opposed to federal policy, policemen and hardhats—all those who feel that symbols dear to them are being denigrated—turn up as participants, but in a different path, the protest pathway.

The Pathway of Protest Politics

It is hard to define protest politics precisely. A reasonable definition would include what the President's Commission on Violence in America called "political turmoil": relatively spontaneous, unorganized strife with substantial popular participation, including political demonstrations and strikes, riots, political and ethnic clashes, and local rebellions. This category also includes organized but substantially nonviolent mass demonstrations such as the 1963 March on Washington led by Dr. Martin Luther King, the 1968 Poor Peoples' Campaign in Washington, the 1968 Vietnam Moratorium, and the 1970 Student Strike.

Table 4.6 lists the numbers of Americans involved in protest politics for the five-year period from 1963 to 1968 and the activities represented. Overall numbers nowhere approach those of such electoral and interest group activity as voting. Still, in this tumultuous five-year span over 2.1 million people protested, and the range of participants was wide. Robert Ted Gurr of the President's Commission on Violence observed:

People of all walks of life have taken part in civil strife in the United States in the last decade. Civil rights and peace demonstrations have included tens of thousands of workers, students, and professional people. Ghetto rioters have included relatively large proportions of unskilled workers, but also many of the unemployed, skilled workers, and a few members of the black bourgeoisie. "Back-lash" protest and violence have mobilized both working and middle-class whites. Only public employees have participated relatively little, aside from the tacit support some police have given to white vigilante groups and the violent response of police and soldiers to some riots and some demonstrations.[11]

[11] *The History of Violence: A Report to the National Commission on the Causes and Prevention of Violence* (New York: Bantam, 1969), p. 583.

Table 4.6 *Civil strife in the United States:*
         June, 1963–May, 1968

Type of event	Number of events	Number of participants	Reported casualties	Reported arrests
Civil rights demonstrations	369	1,117,600	389	15,379
Antiwar demonstrations	104	680,000	400	3,258
Student protests on campus issues	91	102,035	122	1,914
Anti-school integration demonstrations	24	34,720	0	164
Segregationist clashes and counter clashes	54	31,200	163	643
Black riots and disturbances	239	200,000	8,133	49,607
White terrorism against blacks and rights workers	213	2,000	112	97
Total—all turmoil		2,174,655	9,285	
Total—all conspiracy		2,040	122	
Total—all strife		2,176,695	9,407	

Source: The History of Violence: A Report to the National Commission on the Causes and Prevention of Violence (New York: Bantam Books, 1969), p. 576.

Does the political protest of Americans in the 1960's and the 1970's represent a major departure from our own past, or differentiate us from similar Western democracies? This is a fundamental question, because many Americans confronted with disorder and turmoil accuse those engaged in protest of being "un-American" for not relying upon the more sedate techniques of the ballot and the letter to one's Congressman. In fact, the historical evidence is strong that we have always been a tumultuous and frequently violent people. Aside from the well-known violence of the Revolutionary War, the Indian Wars, the draft riots of 1863, and the lynchings in the South between 1882 and 1909, the United States has experienced extensive labor-industry confrontations, anti-Catholic riots, antiblack riots, and vigilante incidents. According to one analysis, the most unsettled period in American history, in terms of strife, was the late nineteenth century.[12] It is clear that nations and their historians tend, especially in stable periods such as the 1950's and early 1960's in the United States, to forget or repress aspects of their past or to rationalize them into shapes more comfortable to contemporary feelings.

Fewer studies have been made of the social characteristics of those who protest than of those who participate in the more conventional politics of elections and inter-

---

[12] See Sheldon G. Levy, "A 150 Year Study of Political Violence in the United States," *The History of Violence* . . . , op. cit., pp. 84–100.

est groups. There are clearly wide cultural and status differences between, say, Ivy League college students and rural southern white segregationists. There are wide educational differences between suburban housewives and black ghetto youngsters. It would seem easier to identify protestors by some system other than the social determinism of background. One apparent common quality is that these are the groups who appear to participate least in the electoral and interest group pathway. Moreover, those who protest are those who are on the losing end of either policy conflicts or the distribution of benefits in the system, or—and the effect is similar— perceive themselves to be on the losing side. Historically, protest politics in America is comprised of activity by those who are the "outs," those who are low in power, status, and rewards from the system. A sizable portion of the violence associated with protest comes when those who are in power react, or overreact, to challenges to their position. Protest and violence often go together because, as Professor Charles Tilly has observed, "The oppressed have struck in the name of justice, the privileged in the name of order, those in between in the name of fear." [13]

During the period between 1961 and 1965, the United States ranked sixth in the world out of 114 countries in political turmoil. However, it ranked lower—fifty-third —in the number of casualties. As was the case in most Western countries, a large number of demonstrations, strikes, and group conflicts characterized American politics. Nevertheless, the United States saw less organized conspiracy and revolutionary activity between 1961 and 1965 than other Western countries, and considerably less conspiracy and internal war than was typical of non-Western developing countries. But even the United States is not immune from revolutionary politics.

The Pathway of Revolutionary Activities

The usual goal of protest is redress of a specific grievance or an expression of some diffuse rage. The usual goal of revolution is overthrow of the system itself and the replacement of its officeholders and political structures with different ones. Although, paradoxically, our nation was established in a revolution in 1776, and its rationale is enshrined and honored in the Declaration of Independence, the United States has regarded internal revolutionaries as mortal enemies. All established governments, of course, reflect similar attitudes—for they all have a vested interest in their survival.

Describing the extent of contemporary revolutionary politics is difficult because much of such activity is illegal and conspiratorial. Organized revolutionary thrusts are more common in underdeveloped societies, where the revolutionaries often include in their ranks members of present or past governments, such as army officers, bureaucrats, and intellectuals. In the United States today, some groups are clearly revolutionary in intent if not behavior. On the political left there are a number of Marxist groups: Students for a Democratic Society, especially its Weatherman faction; the Progressive Labor Party, and the Black Panthers. There is also the old-line Communist Party of the United States of America. On the political right there are

[13] *The History of Violence,* op. cit., p. 4.

the American Nazi Party and the Minutemen. Although there were charges in the period shortly after World War II that some federal government employees had Communist Party affiliations, present-day activities do not in any way appear to involve regime members.

We do not know the social characteristics of American revolutionaries in great detail. At least one set appear to be highly educated young people from middle- and upper-class backgrounds. There is no history of material deprivation in their lives, but their families often inculcated a set of high-minded liberal values.[14] The experience of the seeming diversion between political realities and these values apparently had profound impacts upon many of them, as did experience as oppositionists in the particular struggles for civil rights and against the Vietnam war. The contribution of traditional and Third World Marxist ideology to the behavior of these young white revolutionaries is difficult to gauge. Many see themselves as American counterparts to Third World revolutionaries and urban guerrillas in Algeria, the Tupamaras in Uruguay, and Fidel Castro and Ché Guevera in Cuba. In the cause of black American revolutionaries, the source of the motivation is usually clear-cut: exposure to racism, usually in personalized and humiliating ways.

Our understanding of the relationship between political experiences, personality structure, and political behavior is still very inadequate insofar as it concerns revolutionary politics. We do not know why some individuals turn to protest while others turn to revolution. Much of the serious violence in American politics appears to be the result of individual and isolated acts that occur without reference to any organized or systematic goals. In this category fall the assassinations of the Kennedy brothers and Dr. Martin Luther King, and the shooting of Governor George C. Wallace during his 1972 campaign. Other serious acts of violence seem to have vague revolutionary goals, but are essentially the work of local and uncoordinated guerrillas.

A considerable amount of contemporary violence, however, including bombings of political targets such as the Capitol, the Pentagon, ROTC buildings, and corporate offices, is clearly the work of organized revolutionary groups. The number of persons involved is small, and societal conditions do not really make the United States ripe for revolution. On the other hand, societal conditions are always relative—people view not their objective condition, but how they are faring in relation to others, to their hopes, to some time span. Thus relative deprivation may provide a basis for revolution in a country that is seemingly prosperous, but which contains pockets of inequalities or great perceived injustices. Further, revolutionaries, and many who are not revolutionaries, view the traditional pathways of participation and even the protest pathway as a sham, offering only the appearance of political power without any real possibility of leading to change. Finally, revolutions in many countries have been carried out by small groups that were trained and profoundly dedicated to their political visions. Revolution in the United States is extremely unlikely, but the theoretical possibility cannot be dismissed out of hand.

[14] See Kenneth Keniston, *Young Radicals: Notes on Committed Youth* (New York: Harvest, 1968).

Some Paradoxes of Political Participation in America

There are a number of paradoxes surrounding political participation in America. Today, for example, the more education, income, and status an individual has, the more likely he is to vote and participate in the electoral and interest group pathway. Yet, strangely, although the overall education and income levels in the population have been rising steadily, there has actually been a decline in the percentage of people who vote. This pattern of electoral decline occurs both in southern states, where the turnout is always markedly lower than in other regions, and also in non-southern states. The lower turnout in presidential elections, shown in Table 4.7, has also been accompanied by some additional trends in electoral disintegration. For one thing, *drop-off,* the difference between the percentage of citizens who vote in presidential elections and those who vote in off-years, has also increased. The drop-off averages 24.9 per cent for elections in the period from 1950 through 1962.

This drop-off, however, is less important than the gross trend revealed in Table 4.7; that is, the decline from the nineteenth to the twentieth century in the percentage of those voting as a percentage of those eligible. Walter Dean Burnham has analyzed this trend in these terms:

Even the crudest form of statistical analysis makes it abundantly clear that the changes which have occurred in the relative size and shape of the active electorate in this country have not only been quantitatively enormous, but have followed a directional course which seems to be unique in the contemporary universe of democratic politics. In the United States these transformations over the past century have involved devolution, a dissociation from politics as such among a growing segment of the eligible electorate and an apparent deterioration of the bonds of party linkage between electorate and government. More precisely, these trends were overwhelmingly prominent between about 1900 and 1930, were only very moderately reversed following the political realignment of 1928–1936, and now seem to be

Table 4.7   *Decline and partial resurgence: Mean levels of turnout and drop-off in national elections*

Period (presidential years)	Mean estimated turnout	Period (off-years)	Mean estimated turnout	Mean drop-off
1848–1872	75.1%	1850–1874	65.2%	7.0%
1876–1896	78.5	1878–1898	62.8	15.2
1900–1916	64.8	1902–1918	47.9	22.4
1920–1928	51.7	1922–1930	35.2	28.7
1932–1944	59.1	1934–1946	41.0	27.8
1948–1960	60.3	1950–1962	44.1	24.9

Source: Walter Dean Burnham, "The Changing Shape of the American Political Universe," *American Political Science Review,* (March, 1965), p. 10.

increasing once again along several dimensions of analysis. Such a pattern of development is pronouncedly retrograde compared with those which have obtained almost everywhere else in the Western World during the past century.[15]

Burnham's analysis shows that political participation in nineteenth-century America came much closer to fulfilling democratic standards than it does today. It was, he observes, "the most thoroughly democratized of any in the world," characterized by an effective nationwide political party machinery, party newspapers, and heavy party voting. This system, moreover, induced widespread participation apparently across class and educational lines. Despite the markedly lower general level of formal educational achievement in the population, this did not inhibit a much greater mass participation of eligible voters than exists today. Finally, one category of people who participate the least today—rural people—were among the most involved in the nineteenth century. Describing the political structure of this earlier America, Burnham remarks that, "it was quite adequate, both in partisan organization and dissemination of political information, to the task of mobilizing voters on a scale which compares favorably with recent European levels of participation."[16]

According to Burnham, the alignment that followed the election of 1896 radically depressed participation because, although preserving the forms of democratic politics, it drastically reduced the options available to citizens. With an overwhelming consensus in the North and West, an agreement with the South, and support in the federal judiciary, the Republican Party so dominated American politics until the New Deal period that a decline in participation was the outcome. Although the New Deal stimulated participation and caused some reversal of the 1900–1932 trend, it stabilized participation at a level that remained well below that of the nineteenth century. In the view of Burnham and some other scholars, the contemporary American electorate is too narrow in scope because American politics encourages or mobilizes the participation of too few of its citizens.

Other observers argue that low American voting turnout does not necessarily affect the viability of democratic institutions. Seymour Martin Lipset, for example, maintains that, "neither high nor low rates of participation and voting are in themselves good or bad for democracy; the extent and nature of that participation reflect other factors which determine far more decisively the system's chances to develop or survive."[17] Lester Milbrath has made a similar case.[18] He argues that most citizens, including those in the United States, do not live up to the classical democratic formula of being interested in, informed about, or active in politics, and yet democratic governments continue to function effectively. The continuance of democratic government depends less on high voting percentages than it does on moderate participation and a balance between the number of citizens who are activists and the number who

[15] "The Changing Shape of the American Political Universe," *American Political Science Review,* LIX (March, 1965), p. 10. See also his *Critical Elections and the Mainsprings of American Politics* (New York: Norton, 1970).

[16] Ibid., p. 22.

[17] "Elections: Who Votes and Who Doesn't," in *Political Man* (New York: Doubleday, 1960), p. 219.

[18] Op. cit., pp. 142–154.

passively support the regime. In turn, this behavior harmonizes with a basic principle of constitutional democracy: not all areas of life are political, and politics does not always touch the lives of all citizens directly.

Under these circumstances of moderate but not full participation, Milbrath points out, two other factors become particularly significant. Elites who govern must be carefully chosen and trained, and there must be open channels of political communication so that when they do choose to participate, the mass of citizens will have the information they need. Open channels of communication also make it possible, Milbrath observes, for government officials to anticipate what people want, and thus under some circumstances to keep participation low by satisfying their needs. In addition, both Lipset and Milbrath argue that if a large number of previously passive citizens who possess low information and little experience suddenly do become active in politics, there is the danger that their loyalties may be captured by a totalitarian movement. At the minimum, Lipset feels that persons from the lower social strata should be brought into participation gradually.[19]

An interesting counterpoint to this debate has been provided by a comprehensive study of the voting turnout in 104 American cities directed by Professor Stanley Kelley, Jr. Kelley and his associates focused on the question of the cause of differing turnout in terms of differing rates of registration. Examining registration seemed logical because it is an act that must precede voting. Kelley asked this question: "What factors are most strongly associated with variations in the percentage of those of voting age who do register to vote in different localities?" [20] He sought to answer this question through a multiple-correlation analysis on rates of registration and four basic variables: socioeconomic factors, interparty competition, registration requirements and systems, and residence requirements.

One set of political factors were quite significantly correlated with variation in registration rates. These rules determined the ease or difficulty in registration. One such factor, the literacy test, was, as it was intended by those who have provided for it, effective in reducing registration. More interestingly, registration rates were highly correlated with the date the registration rolls were closed. As a consequence, Kelley and his colleagues concluded that extending the closing date for registration from, for example, one month prior to the election to one week prior to the election could increase registration by the significant figure of 3.6 per cent. This finding suggests that much nonparticipation is not simply a consequence of socioeconomic deprivation; it is, rather, an outcome which has been manipulated politically. In other words, a change in the procedural rules would markedly increase registration in American communities.

A close analysis, in fact, indicates how procedural rules—such as those dealing with voter registration—are significant factors in explaining the paradoxes of American political participation. Registration rules did not exist in most states during the nineteenth century, when, as Burnham has shown, voting was much higher. Registration laws were enacted primarily between 1896 and 1924, the exact period when

[19] Op. cit., p. 219.
[20] "Registration and Voting: Putting First Things First," *American Political Science Review,* LXI (June 1967), p. 360.

participation started to decline. The enactment of these laws was no accident. The intent, often carried out under a rhetoric of "good government," was to make voting by the less educated, the immigrant, and the black more difficult. The liberalization of many registration rules since 1932 has seen a slight rise in participation. It follows from all of this that voting participation, if not other forms of participation, was reduced as part of a deliberate strategy, and thus the burden rests not on shiftless individuals, but on those elites who raised the costs to unacceptable levels for those least able to pay in time, knowledge, or energy. It also follows that making the rules still easier is an effective social strategy for increasing voting throughout the country.

There is hard evidence to support this conclusion. In American cities in which there are more than 90 per cent of those eligible already registered, actual turnout in elections compares favorably with rates in European systems. In these cities the average turnout in 1960 was 78.5 per cent compared to a postwar average of 74.3 per cent for Canada, 77.4 per cent for France, and 77.6 per cent for Great Britain. In all of the 104 cities of the Kelley study, the turnout of those already registered was 81.6 per cent, which compares favorably with any actual or abstract standard of civic interest. The problem is that fewer Americans are registered than in European systems where registration is automatic, and the responsibility for keeping people enrolled rests with the government itself, not with the individual as it does here. Additional evidence points in the same direction. The Voting Rights Act of 1965, by putting federal law enforcement on the side of blacks in the South in their efforts to register, saw some 800,000 added to the rolls. Figure 4.4 illustrates what happened.

There are still other paradoxes in the American situation. Even those groups who normally vote least turn out in astonishingly large numbers when there are candidates who are obviously representative of their point of view. In the 1967 Cleveland mayoralty race 73.4 per cent of all blacks turned out to vote for black candidate Carl Stokes, compared to a 58.4 per cent turnout among whites. Comparable phenomena have occurred wherever black candidates have run. Furthermore, and in complete contradiction to individual behavior, it has been found that on a comparative basis less well-educated communities have higher turnouts in local elections than do better educated communities.[21] The meaning of this finding is not perfectly clear, but it does seem to indicate, again, that there is nothing intrinsic, inevitable, or immutable about the patterns of higher voting participation by better-educated, middle- and upper-class people that have characterized American politics for much of this century.

Conclusions: Contemporary Turmoil
Against a Benchmark of System Support

Except for revolutionary activities, American political participation—in the electoral and interest group and also in the protest pathway—has been carried on by people who have supported the underlying organization of the society. Even exceptionally

[21] See Robert R. Alford and Eugene C. Lee, "Voting Turnout in American Cities," *The American Political Science Review*, LXII (September 1968), pp. 796–813.

Figure 4.4. What the Voting Rights Act has done

Source: New York Times, June 21, 1970. © 1970 by the New York Times Company. Reprinted by permission.

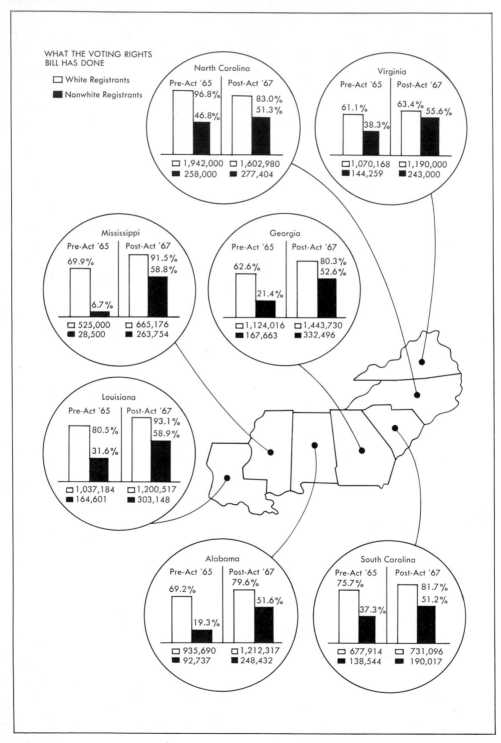

intense protest has most often been directed at particular policies and particular politicians, not at the Presidency or the Constitution.

As Chapter 1 and its examination of the concept of political culture pointed out, this conflict and turmoil took place against a starting point of diffuse system support. That is, while we can measure attitudinal shifts in the United States that show rising pessimism about national stability and political institutions, these changes occurred from a starting point, or benchmark, of high support for the system. A way of noting attitudes at one other recent point in time is to examine the seminal cross-cultural research of Gabriel Almond and Sidney Verba.[22] Between 1959 and 1961 they surveyed attitudes in five western democracies—the United States, Great Britain, West Germany, Italy, and Mexico.

American citizens were not alienated, but possessed highly affirmative reactions to the system and evaluations of their own roles in it. American responses were supportive both in an absolute and in a comparative sense.

As Table 4.8 indicates, a startling 85 per cent of the American citizens interviewed said that they took pride in the governmental and political institutions of the country, far more than the 46 per cent of the Britons or the 30 per cent of Mexican citizens who expressed pride in their political institutions. American citizens also took pride to a marked degree in their economic system and their social legislation. Interestingly, in those nations in which there is least pride in the political system, national pride is either absent or takes the form of affirmative reactions to the vague characteristics of the people (national character) and the geographical beauty of the land.

Table 4.9 should also be noted. It returns to the question of "political efficacy" previously discussed in connection with political socialization. The question here is whether *adult* citizens feel they can affect what government does. Seventy-seven per cent of all Americans said they could do something about an unjust local regulation, and 75 per cent felt they could do something about a national regulation that was unjust or harmful. This is not a picture of an alienated or separated citizenry. Quite the contrary, the Almond and Verba data portrayed a citizenry that feels that it could participate effectively and would be listened to, and that took great pride in its government.

Taking these findings from *The Civic Culture* into account, along with all the other data about pathways of participation, three conclusions seem both relevant for the present and suggestive of the future. First, the pattern that has prevailed until now—higher participation among the higher socioeconomic groups and the more educated—is not likely to continue to prevail in American politics, nor does lower participation seem to exist currently to the degree it once did among some lower-income groups. The young, the poor, the disadvantaged, the black, the white laborer, and the junior civil servant are becoming political participants in a variety of ways. Across the entire spectrum of participation, it is clear that the former nonparticipants, the "outs" of American political life have revealed their willingness, interest,

---

[22] *The Civic Culture* (Princeton: Princeton University Press, 1963).

Table 4.8 *Citizens' feelings about their political systems: Percentage in each nation who take pride in certain national characteristics*

Proud of	US	UK	W. Germany	Italy	Mexico
Governmental and political institutions	85%	46%	7%	3%	30%
Social legislation	13	18	6	1	2
Position in international affairs	5	11	5	2	3
Economic system	23	10	33	3	24
Characteristics of the people	7	18	36	11	15
Spiritual values and religion	3	1	3	6	8
Contributions to the arts	1	6	11	3	1
Contributions to science	3	7	12	3	1
Physical attributes of the country	5	10	17	25	22
Nothing or don't know	4	10	15	27	16

Source: Gabriel A. Almond and Sidney Verba, *The Civic Culture: Political Attitudes and Democracy in Five Nations,* p. 102 (copyright © 1963 by Princeton University Press). Reprinted by permission of Princeton University Press.

and intent to have a voice in American politics. The question for the future is, of course, which pathway is to receive the most emphasis. Is it to be the traditional pathway of voting, party politics, and interest groups? Or is it to be the pathway of

Table 4.9 *Citizen civic competence: Percentage who say they can do something about an unjust local or national regulation*

Nation	Can do something about local regulation	Can do something about national regulation
United States	77%	75%
United Kingdom	78	62
W. Germany	62	38
Italy	51	28
Mexico	52	38

Source: Almond and Verba, op. cit., p. 185.

protest politics, or possibly even the pathway of violent revolution? And, regardless of the path that is chosen, what goals will these newly active participants seek?

A second conclusion from the data on participation is that the American citizenry is now being expanded in much the same way as it was in the early nineteenth century. Whenever a body politic is expanded to include new groups that bring with them values and demands different from those of the established groups, instability and conflict are bound to result. The new American groups bring with their new participation a complete set of needs and demands, as well as a fully developed life style and set of values that in many instances differ from those of middle-class white America. These groups want different priorities, policies, benefits, and distributions of power. The young people, many of them college educated, have a set of demands for full acceptance of themselves as participants and a set of values on issues, such as the war in Vietnam, that often vary from the views of their elders. Blacks want symbolic values, position, benefits, and all the perquisites of full citizenship. Working-class whites want more control over their lives, as well as tax fairness, greater status and recognition. Chicanos, women, and others have still more and different demands. It is a test of the greatest magnitude for any political system to absorb large numbers of newcomers. America managed with the immigrants of the past, and it is now tested with these new citizens of the 1970's.

A third and final conclusion about participation in America is that, as the data on political socialization and the study by Almond and Verba indicate, the country, for all of its open conflict and rapid social and technological change, has possessed underneath a remarkably consensual, or at least supportive, political culture. The odds that the American democracy can adapt itself must be measured against this benchmark of affirmative nationalism supporting the established political system. The affirmative nature of these attitudes provides a firmer base for supporting policy changes and new power relationships than exists in many other societies. If any democratic nation can accommodate the expansion of participation now taking place, it should be the United States.

suggested additional readings

Almond, Gabriel, et al. *The Civic
    Culture*. Princeton: Princeton
    University Press, 1963.
Burnham, Walter Dean. *Critical
    Elections and the Mainstreams of
    American Politics*. New York:
    W. W. Norton & Company, Inc.,
    1970.
Cantril, Albert H., and Charles W. Roll,
    Jr. *Hopes and Fears of the American
    People*. New York: Universe Books,
    1971.*
Easton, David, and Jack Dennis.
    Children in the Political System.
    New York: McGraw-Hill Book
    Company, 1969.
Edelman, Murray. *The Symbolic Uses
    of Politics*. Urbana: University of
    Illinois Press, 1964.*
———. *Politics as Symbolic Action:
    Mass Arousal and Quiescence*.
    Chicago: Markham Publishing Co.,
    1971.*
Glazer, Nathan, and Daniel P. Moynihan.
    Beyond the Melting Pot. Boston:
    Massachusetts Institute of Technology
    Press, 1963.*
Gurr, Robert Ted. *Why Men Rebel*.
    Princeton: Princeton University
    Press, 1971.*
Lane, Robert E. *Political Life*. New
    York: The Free Press, 1965.*

———. *Political Ideology*. New York:
    The Free Press, 1962.*
Lipset, Seymour Martin. *Political Man*.
    New York: Doubleday & Company,
    Inc., 1960.*
Milbrath, Lester W. *Political
    Participation*. Chicago: Rand
    McNally & Co., 1965.*
Mitchell, William C. *Why Vote?*
    Chicago: Markham Publishing
    Co., 1971.*
Pranger, Robert J. *The Eclipse of
    Citizenship*. New York: Holt,
    Rinehart & Winston, Inc., 1968.*
Sigel, Roberta S. *Learning About
    Politics*. New York: Random House,
    Inc., 1970.

* Available in paperback.

142

5 parties and elections in a time of transition

case study

The Democrats Try Reform

No one who was at the 1968 Democratic National Convention in Chicago, read about it in newspapers, or watched it on television is likely to forget it. For five days, the largest national party, rent by challenges and resistance within, seemed to self-destruct in the view of the entire nation. In the Convention, the supporters of Senator Eugene McCarthy and Senator George McGovern and the remnants of the backers of the late Senator Robert Kennedy (shot two months before on the eve of the California primary) tried desperately to find an issue to break the iron lock held by Vice-President Hubert Humphrey, President Lyndon Johnson, and Mayor Richard Daley of Chicago. In the streets of Chicago, police and National Guard clashed violently with antiwar demonstrators in a holocaust of tear gas and obscenities. Behind the electrified barbed wire of the Stockyards Amphitheatre, the Democratic delegates came unhinged over the issues of public participation in the party, over the Vietnam war, and, finally, over who was in the right in the street fighting itself.

The McCarthy forces in the Convention mounted a series of legal challenges before the balloting on the main events —the peace plank and the presidential nomination. They challenged the credentials of delegates from southern states on the grounds that these units were segregated. They challenged the use of the "unit rule," a system, mainly operative in southern delegations, whereby the vote of a majority of the delegation could bind the whole delegation. Most of the credentials challenges lost in the Credentials Committee and on the Convention floor. The campaign to remove the unit rule also sank. But, on the second night of the Convention, an insurgent-supported minority report from the Rules Committee did pass, with little notice at the time.

This minority resolution said that the 1972 Convention "shall require" that all Democrats be given "full and timely opportunity to participate" in nominating candidates. The resolution also provided that the unit rule be eliminated from all stages of the delegate selection process (not only in National Convention voting, but in state caucuses and conventions as well), and that "all feasible efforts" be made to assure that delegates would be chosen—whether by open primary, state convention, or committee procedures—in the calendar year of the next Convention. This resolution, in the rage and conflict of the 1968 Convention, was all that the insurgent antiwar McCarthy-Kennedy-McGovern forces won.

145

It is hard to know why the 1968 Convention passed the minority resolution on party reform. Some delegates may have been impressed by the report of the Hughes Commission. This report, which was made available to the Convention, clearly demonstrated that charges that the party's delegates were not selected by democratic procedures had a considerable basis in fact. It revealed that about 30 per cent of the delegates had been chosen by processes that began before 1968, long before the major issues or challenging candidates had appeared in the political arena. In some states, the Democratic State Chairman personally picked all or some of the delegates. In others, delegates were picked in secret caucuses in the homes of country chairmen. In still others, victory in a primary had no relationship to the winning of delegates. Further, only 5½ per cent of the delegates were black in a party that received 20 per cent of its presidential votes from blacks; only 4 per cent were under thirty years old in a year when young people had exploded into politics with a passion; and only 13 per cent were women.

In some states, delegates were assessed heavy campaign contributions or fees to maintain "hospitality suites" at the Convention. The Hughes Report also showed that the Democratic National Chairman appointed the chairmen of all key Convention committees and offices and that the formula used for allocating the number of delegates heavily favored the smaller states. These matters might have gone unnoticed in a situation of party consensus; in the context of conflict, they became crucial. Conceivably, enough noninsurgent delegates were impressed by them to put the minority report over the top. Many Democrats surely took seriously the party's oft-stated commitment to democratic processes and its reliance on various minorities. For some too, beyond doubt, there was a secret hope that whatever was causing chaos in 1968 could somehow be avoided by 1972 if the reform were espoused. What happened to the issue of party reform between the 1968 and 1972 Conventions is the subject of this case study.

No particular outcome for reform was preordained for one simple reason. Reform is not a neutral process of modernizing a structure analogous to improving the wiring or plumbing in a house. Political reform changes the rules and opportunities for power, and thus some factions stand to gain by such change and some stand to lose. During the 1968 party struggles, reform had been the cause of the McCarthy-Kennedy-McGovern faction. Now that that fight was over, would party regulars cooperate? Would they consider reform and the integration of new elements into the party a lesser price to pay than protracted struggle and possible elimination of the party as a quasi-functioning political body? What kinds of resistance would they put up? Or, in a situation of uncertainty, would they be willing to take their chances with reform? After all, the chances that the issues and personalities of 1968 would be duplicated in 1972 seemed slim. Perhaps they could live with reform and even prosper with it. Such were the uncertainties when, on February 4, 1969, Democratic National Chairman (and Senator from Oklahoma) Fred R. Harris announced that he was going to appoint two reform commissions.

Harris appointed Senator George McGovern to head the Commission on Party Structure and Delegate Selection, and Representative James O'Hara to head the Commission on Party Rules. Before naming these two bodies, the National Chairman had cleared the procedures with the party's major presidential politicians, Senators Muskie, Humphrey, and Edward Kennedy. He apparently had not done much consulting in advance with the regional potentates who had controlled large blocs of delegates in 1968, including Mayor Daley. We will follow primarily the efforts of the McGovern Commission, but both bodies were fairly liberally sprinkled with the reformers who had been defeated at the last Convention. The Vice-chairman of the McGovern Commission was liberal Senator Harold Hughes of Iowa, who had drafted the original revealing report on party procedures. Also on the twenty-eight member McGovern Commission were Frederick Dutton, a former administrative aide to Robert Kennedy; David Mixner, a McCarthy veteran and Co-director of the Vietnam Moratorium Committee; and Dr. Aaron E. Henry, a black leader from Mississippi. At the same time, the labor wing of the party was represented by I. W. Abel, head of the United Steelworkers union, and various allies of Senators Humphrey and Muskie were selected as well.

Chairman Harris was aware that compliance with the commission's work would be a separate and difficult problem. Already within the party there was an argument as to whether whatever resulted would be binding on state parties and enforceable at the 1972 Convention, or merely advisory. An anomaly of American politics is that the national parties have very little legal control over the state parties. Yet it is at the state level that delegates are chosen in American politics, by procedures set in state law. Harris was urging all state Democratic parties to form their own "little McGovern Commissions" to work for reform.

At the first meeting of the McGovern Commission, Chairman McGovern observed that "the convention has told us that something is fundamentally wrong with our party." Vice-chairman Hughes noted that "racial minorities, the poor and the young are restlessly searching the contemporary landscape for a political movement that will measure up to their ideals and be relevant to their needs." The Commission was starting with a National Committee allocation of $75,000; McGovern was seeking an additional $200,000. On April

25, the Commission held its first hearings in Washington, D. C. Testimony came from Senators Kennedy, Muskie, and McCarthy. Both Muskie and McCarthy proposed midterm national conventions devoted solely to issues, and McCarthy thought that even annual national conventions would be a good idea. Senator Kennedy noted that what new people taking an interest in politics in 1968 found was "a system designed to discourage their participation." They were among nineteen total witnesses, some of whom denounced the party's "undemocratic" selection procedures. It was evident that the McGovern Commission was going to proceed like a cross between an administrative agency and a congressional committee. First it would hold sixteen hearings around the country; then it would issue preliminary guidelines for comment; and then it would formulate final guidelines.

From Washington, the Commission moved to New York. State Democratic Chairman John J. Burns and Theodore Sorensen, former counselor to President John F. Kennedy, urged that the party have all delegates chosen by popular election. (In 1968, about 40 per cent were chosen this way.) A Columbia University graduate student active in Students for a Democratic Society (SDS) told the Commission it was wasting its time. Only a socialist revolution could solve the country's problems.

By mid-June, 1969, the Commission had held eight hearings. It had moved its scheduled New Orleans hearing to Jackson, Mississippi, because the Louisiana Democratic National Committeeman protested its entry into the state; it had moved its Texas hearing from Austin to Houston because of complaints that the cause of party reform should not be brought too close to retired President Lyndon Johnson. At its Chicago hearings, Senator McGovern and Mayor Daley had a difficult exchange over the then-ongoing trial of the "Chicago Seven," which had grown out of the Convention riots.

McGovern said that "the harsh legal actions taken here are a cause of great concern to people all over the country." Daley replied that "if people violate the law they should accept the consequences of the law." Yet oddly, considering the role of villain ascribed to him by many critics of the 1968 Convention, Mayor Daley came forth with a strong reform proposal. He suggested that all states have binding primaries and that no candidate be eligible for the presidential nomination who had not entered at least one third of the primaries. If such a rule had been in effect in 1968, Vice-President Humphrey could not have been nominated.

The hearings in Atlanta were also lively. McGovern observed pithily that "there has never been a political party which, when confronted with the choice of reform or death, has chosen reform." Mayor Ivan Allen, Jr., declared, "The history of Democratic party politics in Georgia is a history of abuse and misuse of the very system on which our nation and our party was founded." Georgia Governor Lester Maddox was invited but did not attend. His hand-picked delegation had seen half its number unseated at the 1968 convention, and the Georgia system of having the entire delegation picked by the state chairman and the governor in consort was generally cited as the worst example of party dictatorship in the country. Maddox labeled the McGovern Commission "an arm of the Socialist part of the party."

As the hearings ended and the Commission got ready to make some decisions, Chairman McGovern was generally optimistic, noting that "within a year, most intelligent Democratic politicians are going to identify with it." About thirty state committees had appointed their own reform commissions, including such previously hard-core insider-run parties as those in Missouri and Connecticut. There were new primary laws in Rhode Island and Maryland and a strong, open, nonprimary system in Colorado that gave proportional representation to minority views. On the

debit side of the reform effort, some state chairmen were opposing the Commission's work and calling the Commission a "troublemaker." The Commission was very short on staff and had no money.

On September 22, 1969, the Commission held its first decision-making meetings in Washington and deadlocked over the crucial issue of proportional representation (PR) of minority views. Under a PR system, delegates would be present in proportion to the strength their candidate had in the electorate. Opposing this position, supported by both McGovern and Hughes, were those who favored a traditional winner-take-all rule. The final decision was postponed, and at its next meeting the Commission turned to what it could agree on. It passed on a number of guidelines: eighteen- to twenty-year-olds were to be given full membership in all party affairs, the use of proxy votes at state conventions was forbidden, and discrimination based on sex was prohibited, as was the delegates' choosing their own alternates. The Commission agreed to come back in five or six weeks to try the PR issue again.

When it did reconvene in mid-November, it voted finally to "urge" state parties to use PR rather than to require it, and to recommend to the 1972 Convention that PR be made mandatory in the future. A majority of the Commission preferred PR in principle, but, perhaps with an eye to difficulties of compliance, shied away from going all the way and requiring it for 1972. Only three votes could be mustered for a "must" vote on PR. The Commission did, by a narrow margin, approve a sweeping requirement that all delegates had to "bear a reasonable relationship" in their makeup to state populations of blacks, women, and young people.

The decisions of the Commission were over. Dr. Aaron Henry felt that the Commission had acted in the "most conservative way" on major questions, but Will Davis, a former Texas Democratic

Chairman, thought the eighteen approved guidelines were "so radical" they would never be carried out. McGovern hailed the work as a "historic breakthrough."

On April 28, 1970, the McGovern Commission issued its final report, *Mandate for Reform.* The Commission said that the only alternative to broader citizen participation was "the antipolitics of the street." McGovern predicated "broad compliance" at a press conference, but not without "some struggles." The outlines of these struggles were immediately clear. Former Vice-President Humphrey was reported opposed to some of the Commission requirements, which he called "recommendations." Humphrey's position was that the guidelines would have no effect without ratification by the full Democratic National Committee. McGovern's position was that the guidelines were mandatory, but that realistically, the DNC endorsement would help. The new National Chairman Lawrence F. O'Brien's comments about whether or not the National Committee could modify the Commission's report had been ambivalent.

O'Brien soon gave reform proponents more cause for concern. On May 22, he set up two new groups, both created by his own National Committee Executive Committee to "screen" the reforms proposed by both the McGovern Commission and the O'Hara Commission on Party Rules. Although O'Brien said his aim was "to implement the reform ideas," he also made it clear that these groups of his could recommend the acceptance of some of the commissions' proposals and the rejection of others. He thus gave his own committees the same standing as the 1972 Convention itself. The clear implication was that a group of party stalwarts was going to water down reform before it went too far. Was this to be the end of the long reform battle?

The next day McGovern responded by urging that the National Committee write the eighteen guidelines into the 1972 Convention Call (the document setting up the Convention and setting its initial conditions) "intact." Commission Member David Mixner was more direct. He called the new committees "a direct slap" at the McGovern Commission, saying that, "It's not up to Chairman O'Brien and eleven people to say, 'We'll pick the reforms we like and ignore the others.'" Thus confronted, O'Brien issued a new clarification: the two committees were "solely for the purpose of speeding implementation," and would have "no power to alter, dilute, or in any way veto" the guidelines. O'Brien's own position was difficult; he was trying to strike a balance between the several factions in the party while keeping them all as functioning Democrats. He was not, personally, insensitive to the need for reform. He later observed about 1968 that "in simplest terms, we can pledge that we will do everything we can, as a party, to see that it never happens again."

On October 16, 1970, the O'Hara Commission finished its work and voted some serious rules reforms. It voted to give the larger states a larger vote on all committees (instead of two votes for each state), a change that might well have resulted in the passage of the peace plank by the Platform Committee in 1968. It voted that all major committee meetings would be open to the public and the press, and it set up administrative procedures for the Credentials Committee, which was certain to have numerous challenges before it in 1972. The O'Hara Commission also proposed an overall apportionment formula based largely on population. The eight largest states would get 51 per cent of the total Convention vote and the voting strength of the smaller states would be reduced.

As 1971 began, the next move was up to the full National Democratic Committee. In January, Senator McGovern resigned as head of the delegate selection panel in order to campaign for the presidential nomination. He was hopeful about the impact of his Commission: thirty-four of the fifty states had already complied with at least half the guidelines. He predicted the number of black, women, and young delegates in 1972 would be double that of 1968. Despite some problems, especially in Kansas and Tennessee, he expected that the 1972 Convention would be the "least boss-ridden and the most democratic" in the party's history. Liberal Congressman Donald Fraser of Minnesota took over as head of the Commission.

In February the showdown National Committee meeting was held. The political sequence was odd. The Committee struggled for three days over the apportionment formula of the O'Hara Commission and finally modified it to give smaller states a somewhat greater strength than had been recommended (a decision that was later fought out in the federal courts by aggrieved big-state leaders). The McGovern Commission reforms sailed through without dissent. The only change was to make National Committee members themselves ex officio voting delegates to the Convention (thus violating the no ex officio and timely selection guidelines).

What was surprising was the seemingly easy approval of the other reforms and their insertion by the Committee into the 1972 Convention Call intact. Delegates had to be chosen by processes begun in the calendar year of the Convention. All Democrats had to have a fair opportunity to participate, which meant the end of closed-door meetings. The party was to be opened up to minorities. An immediate consequence was more primary laws, twenty-three in 1972 as opposed to sixteen in 1968, through which 63 per cent of the delegates could be chosen directly.

The final meeting of the Democratic National Committee before the July, 1972, Miami Beach Convention was in

Washington on October 13 and 14, 1971. There were some fireworks. With support from Chairman Lawrence F. O'Brien a black woman lawyer, former Ambassador Patricia Roberts Harris, was chosen to be Chairman of the Convention Credentials Committee. Senator Hughes was the reformers' candidate, and he was decisively beaten by the regulars and Mrs. Harris. The defeat of Hughes was interpreted as a setback for the reform movement, but Mrs. Harris strongly denied that she was uninterested or uncommitted to reform. However stung they were, the reform supporters would simply have to wait and see what Mrs. Harris did. Perhaps as a concession, the National Committee members reversed an earlier position and decided that they would not give themselves ex officio votes after all. With these steps, the stage was set for party selection politics to begin: the primaries, the bargaining, and the Convention.

In the end, the Convention saw vividly the impact of the McGovern reforms. Almost 27 per cent of the delegates were under thirty years old, 38 per cent were women, almost 15 per cent were black. Only 11 per cent had been delegates in 1968. Quite clearly, those who had lost in Chicago in 1968 won in the Democratic party in Miami in 1972. The clearest benefactor was Senator George McGovern, who rode the intense dedication of his followers through the primaries to a first ballot nomination. Yet while some elements in the party benefitted from the reforms, other elements lost. Further, many of those who felt that *they* were not represented at Miami did not support McGovern's presidential candidacy. Thus, reform had several paradoxes. Reform was the channel for the victory of one faction in the party over the other. Reform did not strengthen the electoral position of the Democrats against the Republicans. In the short run, what was heralded as strengthening the party seemed to weaken it in the quest that meant the most (by standard interpretations): the pursuit of the White House.

SOURCES

The Democratic Choice, A Report of the Commission on the Democratic Selection of Presidential Nominees, Hon. Harold Hughes, Chairman (1968).

Mandate for Reform, A Report of the Commission on Party Structure and Delegate Selection to the Democratic National Committee, Hon. George S. McGovern, Chairman (Washington, D.C.: 1970).

New York Times, 1968–1972.

parties and elections
in a time of transition

What Are Parties?

Many Americans question whether the divisions among the citizens in the United States can be healed, or whether domestic problems and international tensions can be met and reconciled. In such times, we could predict that criticism and hopes will focus on political parties. We would also predict that young people, least bound to the emotions and alignments that created existing party loyalties, would be most likely to be political "independents." Parties have been the major institutions, since the eighteenth century, for organizing political conflicts and for ordering and arranging the agendas of political life.[1] They are power-seeking structures. People use them to achieve their goals of control over government, and, sometimes but not always, as devices for systematically carrying out well-defined policies or ideologies.

It is important to remember, however, that parties are only one of many kinds of institutions that people can use to achieve power. Private issue-oriented groups may mobilize people outside of parties for goals such as ending the Vietnam war or tax reform or helping the police. Individual corporations may have more economic resources, more employees, more local branches, and better internal communications than parties, and more to say about what people will do and how they live. In many countries, the army arbitrates among private interests, defines national goals, and even organizes governmental policies and services. Parties compete with other institutions for the attention and energies of citizens who seek to use politics for personal or ideological ends.

Since the eighteenth century, political parties have been the most inclusive and probably the most important institutions as channels for political activities directed at government. The first formal parties in England and the United States evolved from legislative factions and consisted of friendly groups of notables who wanted to work together on a systematic basis. A second kind of party developed in the nineteenth century—the mass-based party with a systematic ideology.

[1] This definition draws upon the work of E. E. Schattschneider, *The Semi-Sovereign People* (New York: Holt, Rinehart and Winston, 1960), and Everett C. Ladd, Jr., *American Political Parties* (New York: Norton, 1970).

Our Republican and Democratic parties are lineal descendants of the eighteenth-century parties of notables. They are what Theodore J. Lowi has labeled *constituent* parties.[2] Constituent parties want to win elections and control the offices of government. In order to win, they cannot be choosy about who comes with them, and thus such parties often contain very unlike elements in their support. They rely upon tradition-based automatic voting support, charismatic candidates, material benefits, and changing positions on issues. Upon occasion, but only under special conditions, are they vehicles for far-reaching policy changes.

In contrast, *policy-making* parties have well-defined views of society and programs for government. Such parties have existed on the right in European Fascist parties and on the left in variations of Socialist and Communist parties around the world. Their interest in winning elections in democracies may take second place to the pursuit of homogeneous support and ideological consistency. When such parties achieve office, they are less concerned with the niceties of procedure than with establishing their ideologies in the operations of society and government. The archetypal policy-making parties are the Communist parties of the Soviet Union, Eastern Europe, and Communist China.

In all countries, parties play major roles in deciding what the scope of political conflict will be and how many of the problems of the underlying society will be put upon the agenda of politics. Constituent parties in democratic societies, with their drive toward centrist coalition-building, often try to narrow the range of subjects of politics. In so doing they frequently blur the differences between themselves and opponents. These are not, however, universal rules of party behavior; sometimes constituent parties broaden the scope of conflict because their search for votes leads them to mobilize previously excluded segments of the public, such as, in the United States, students or black people. Policy-making parties, on the other hand, often define politics to include all social issues in a system; hence the totalitarian aspects of Communist and Fascist parties. Literally all questions are defined as coming under political solutions, often without compromise and along ideological lines.

In almost all countries, too, parties care about elections. In democratic systems, elections are the only route for achieving some offices. Further, if parties are policy-making, elections may also provide a mandate for governmental action and they surely provide the opportunity for such action. In totalitarian countries, parties whose control over government is not at issue still rely upon elections to achieve popular ratification and the aura of legitimacy for whatever they have done.

The Historical Evolution of American Parties

Throughout their history, the parties in America have stood for different things at different times, have had shifting groups of supporters, and have played roles of differing significance in the total political system. During the early years of the Republic, the parties were major forces shaping the social and economic sectors of

[2] See his "Party, Policy, and Constitution in America," in William N. Chambers and Walter D. Burnham, *The American Party Systems* (New York: Oxford University Press, 1967), pp. 239–276.

American life. Since at least the Civil War, however, most scholars believe that the parties merely respond to and reflect underlying social and economic conditions. Historically, the American parties have actually evolved through five party systems.[3]

In the **experimental system, 1789–1820,** parties emphasized nation-building: creating the human and institutional symbols of a new country; defining how broadly the governing power—and thus suffrage—would be extended; and maintaining a foreign policy strong enough to fend off competing and hostile European powers active on this continent. In this period, nominations for office were made by legislative caucuses. Party support was highly sectional, with the Federalists primarily a New England party after 1800. Within the federal government, the separation of powers we now take for granted hardly existed. In the end, the moderately elitist Jeffersonian Republicans so dominated the system that competition disappeared in the "Era of Good Feelings."

The **democratizing system, 1824–1860,** is regarded by many as the most creative period in American party history. During this period the unique convention system of nominations was developed. An outsider, Andrew Jackson, won the Presidency by extending the suffrage and by mobilizing a considerable new electorate. The two-party system extended competition through the nation and had a heavy impact upon institutions and also on policy outputs. The impact was first of all to reduce elitism and increase equality. Second, a systematic policy dismantled the Hamiltonian, mercantilist enterprise of the federal government. The parties themselves developed into national coalitions of state and sectional interests, with mass followings tended by paid professional workers. Voting turnout—with straight party voting being the rule —expanded enormously and the participation of the eligible electorate was higher than it is today. This second party system fell apart over slavery, collapsing in 1860.

The **Civil War system, 1860–1893,** saw the existence of a party system that, although not institutionally innovative, was genuinely policy-making in many ways. Slavery was abolished, and federal involvement expanded in a number of economic development areas. The view of the majority party was enforced upon the minority by force. The intensity of the politics of the era set party loyalties at least until the 1890's. Indeed, the resentment of southerners toward the Republican Party was reflected in a Democratic sectionalism that has not vanished entirely to this day. Party feeling was so intense that in the years following the Civil War electoral politics kept many of the characteristics of combat: heavy mobilization, regular and undeviating party voting, and electoral urgings to "vote as you shot." As the southern states came back into the Union, the Republican hegemony declined. Between 1872 and 1896 elections ended in virtual draws and candidates with less than a majority of popular votes often won in the Electoral College.

Although immediate post-Civil War politics reflected alignment and conflicts related to that bitter conflict, American society itself was changing drastically. Large-scale industrialization fed by the war had spread across the country, bringing with it concentrations of capital, heavy industries, new technologies, the need for factory

---

[3] The following treatment draws upon Walter Dean Burnham, "Party Systems and the Political Process," in *The American Party Systems,* op. cit., pp. 285–305.

labor, and the growth of mammoth corporations. Industrialization ended the relative economic equality of Americans, and the need for labor led to massive immigration from Europe. As a reaction to the emergence of an eastern-oriented capitalism, the West, which provided the raw materials, fomented a sectional politics of "agrarian radicalism" aimed at redistributing wealth and power away from the new industrialists, their banks, their railroads, and their corporate firms. In other words, the agenda of politics changed, and the scope of political conflict altered because of changes in the underlying cleavages and forces in the society. The parties did not initiate these massive forces; they reacted to them. A severe economic depression occurred in 1893, and the Democratic Party was captured by the radical western element led by William Jennings Bryan. With Bryan at the head of their ticket, the Democrats suffered such severe losses in the presidential election of 1896 that the party went into political eclipse for thirty years.

The **industrialist system, 1896–1932,** was a period of general Republican hegemony, interrupted only by the eight years of Democratic rule under Woodrow Wilson from 1913 to 1921. Wilson won the first time because of a Republican Party split and again in 1916—by a narrow margin—because of World War I. Otherwise Republican domination was nearly complete, as the Grand Old Party controlled most state, local, and federal offices outside of the South. The Republicans were the party of the emerging national and cosmopolitan industrial system. Their primary policy was to try to divorce economic decision-making from the political arena, and to reduce the scope of political conflict by setting up a "standing decision" that the economy was beyond challenge. One symptom of Republican success was the decline of participation throughout the country. In the North, the decline was a function of one-partyism and the eclipse of the Democrats. In the South it was a deliberate strategy by upper-class white Democrats to disfranchise blacks and poor whites.

The dominant Republican Party was partially a sectional party, but it had other bases of support. Cultural conflict in America was intense at this time, and the Republicans were the party of Protestants against Catholics, nativists against immigrants, drys against wets, and rural and small-city folk against big-city dwellers. These social cleavages often overlapped: the typical Republican was a native, small-city, eastern or midwestern Protestant who favored prohibition. The Republicans in government were not unchallenged, nor were all Republicans identical in their political views. Theodore Roosevelt, for example, favored conservation of natural resources against industrial encroachment. Roosevelt also supported antitrust legislation to restrain market concentration by corporations, but his programs were primarily symbolic and rhetorical and had little impact.

One of the interesting characteristics of the Republican Party in its heyday was that in 1896 it drew heavy support from workers. Many workers, especially craftsmen, were nativists and feared competition from immigrant Catholics; many actively supported industrial expansion and the big corporations; and many were frightened by the farm-based radicalism of the Bryan Democrats. As immigrants adapted to the society, often helped along by city "machines," they entered the political system in opposition to the Republicans. This process took time, however, and became manifest first at the local level, and then, beginning around 1928, in national politics as well. Yet another political factor during this period was the third-party challenges stimulated by abuses and inequities in the industrial-dominated political system. The Socialist Party polled 900,000 votes in 1912, and in Wisconsin Senator Robert LaFollette's Progressive Party attracted 5,000,000 voters in 1924. LaFollette's program included many ideas that were later adopted by Franklin Roosevelt's New Deal Democrats.

The fifth party system was the **New Deal system,** which began with the election of 1932. In the face of widespread unemployment, voters turned to the Democratic Party. The party did not win because it had a program; it won because it was *there,* as an available channel for the expression of discontent. Once in office, the pragmatic Roosevelt cemented his new coalition based upon ethnic and racial minorities in the North, with the South included because of historical loyalties. The New Deal Democrats helped those who had previously been out of the system to make the transition into it. For example, the Democrats passed laws that gave labor unions the legal power to organize, thereby enabling the unions to move their organizational resources into the mainstream of American group politics. The Democrats generally mobilized the "out's" and "have-not's" of the country, and political participation, especially the voting turnout, rose for the first time since the term of the century. In this new party system, underlying changes in the society were translated into new political demands, primarily for government intervention in the economy through the regulation of business and guarantees of economic security for individuals.

During this period, many voters changed their party affiliations completely, and new voters entering the electorate became Democrats. Virtually overnight—between 1928 and 1934—the Democrats became the majority party and the Republicans became the minority party. These majority Democrats bore very little resemblance to their party ancestors, the Jeffersonians. They governed an urban, continental, and industrial nation, drew support from ethnic and racial minorities in big cities plus the southern section, and believed in welfare statism at home and an active military and diplomatic role for the United States in world affairs. The New Deal party system held largely intact until 1965, when new issues of race, war, and the economy emerged in American society. Since then, although both parties have been challenged on a variety of fronts, no clearly defined new party system has replaced the old one. American parties in the 1970's are in a transition phase once again.

Parties, Elections, and Political Change

As this discussion of party systems suggests, there is a cyclical quality to the fundamental questions of party fortunes—which party enjoys majority support, what the scope of political conflict is, and who holds office most of the time. At least during the twentieth century, it has been only at those transition points of cyclical change that the parties have accepted a policy-making role. In between, during the thirty- to forty-year periods, the parties have been constituent organizations that worry about winning office and using popular candidates or fleeting short-range issues of the day to win marginal advantages. The set of party identifications that makes one party the basic majority—or the *sun* to use Samuel Lubell's term—remains a basic cue to voting and does not change very much.[4] The minority party, the *moon,* has circled around the major party, probing here and there and winning office occasionally, but has been unable to achieve any permanent successes unless major changes occur in the underlying social or economic structure or unless new issues emerge.

The parties can be used either as vehicles for change or for maintaining the status quo primarily because of one fundamental reason. Ever since the nation's founding there has been a predictable and unbroken string of elections that has chosen all members of the House and one-third of the Senate every two years and the President every four. It is possible to classify types of presidential elections on the basis of the impact of existing party loyalties as compared to the impact of change-forcing movements in the larger society. Most presidential contests turn out to be **maintaining elections.** No issues are sufficiently outstanding nor any candidates sufficiently appealing to overcome the basic lead the majority party has in the electorate. There may be some switching around and some movement of voters at election time, but the net pluses or losses still leave the majority party on top and winning. Most notably, the political temperature remains low: there is no serious questioning of the existing institutional arrangements, governing elites, or outlines of major policies. Levels of participation are stable, and the majority party wins because it is the majority. Maintaining elections occurred in 1948, 1960, and 1964.

In a **deviating presidential election** short-range forces allow the minority party candidate to win office. The short-range forces may be the popularity of a particular candidate, a particular policy disagreement, or even the general feeling that it is time for a change. But because these forces are of short range and do not affect the electorate very deeply, they are only temporary. Thus, in a typical deviating election, the winning presidential candidate from the minority party will not carry the Congress with him. That is what happened to Republican Dwight Eisenhower in 1956 (he carried the Congress in 1952 but lost it in the off-year election of 1954) and Richard Nixon in 1968. Moreover, after the typical deviating election, when the special issue has gone, the majority comes back, as the Republicans came back in 1920. Or when the popular candidate retires, the old majority party comes back, as the Democrats did in 1960. Deviating elections seem to reflect discontent within a basic framework of consensus, rather than underlying social upheaval translated into politics. That last condition fits the realigning election.

In a **realigning election** everything is different.[5] Political leaders shaped in their view of issues and supporters by the previous realignment some thirty years prior now fail to respond to the buildup of new tensions. Indeed, under the new pressures they may well become more rigid and defensive. The failure of the two major parties to respond to the new problems will probably result in a strong third-party challenge some four to eight years before the actual realigning election. The third party will be strongest among new voters, will draw disproportionate support from one section of the country that feels particularly aggrieved, and will take hard stands on those very issues that the major parties want to duck. This third-party pattern has been repeated

---

[4] See *The Hidden Crisis in American Politics* (New York: Norton, 1971).

[5] The most extensive treatment of the realigning process is Walter Dean Burnham, *Critical Elections and the Mainsprings of American Politics* (New York: Norton, 1970).

with the Populists in 1892, the Progressives in 1924, and the strong George Wallace American Independent insurgency in 1968.

With widespread social tension, caused most often in the past by economic dislocations and affecting almost everyone, and with a lack of response by the majority party, the former minority party may seize upon the new issues and become the channel for political change. In the process it becomes the majority party, as millions of voters switch parties and new voters coming into the electorate identify with it. Realigning elections are not politics as usual or the politics of consensus. They signal heavy conflict, rising demands for participation by excluded groups, and, in the end, fundamental policy changes in government. Thus, the realigning election of 1896 established the Republicans as the majority party, decided that the new capitalist-corporate economic order could operate largely unchallenged, and depressed participation by challenging groups, including poor whites and all blacks in the South and labor and immigrants in the North. The realigning election of 1932 signaled Democratic dominance, the establishment of a broadened role for government in regulating the economy and in guaranteeing individual economic security, and the elevation of workers, organized labor, ethnic minorities, Catholics, blacks, and Jews to positions of influence and power previously denied them.

What kind of election was Mr. Nixon's 1972 victory? Were the Republican issues of law and order (as opposed to greater permissiveness), social stability (as opposed to economic redistribution), and orderly change (as opposed to faster change) operative only in the short-run? If so, then 1972 was a replay of 1964, after which the losing party, at that time the Republicans, bounced back. If 1972's issues were primarily short-run in their impact, then we saw a *deviating* election and the Democrats would be expected to come back strong in 1976. On the other hand, the issues that favored the Republicans could turn out to cut very deeply, building, for the first time, a *realignment* on essentially cultural more than economic issues. If that were so, then Mr. Nixon will have created a new majority. His party could then be expected to win at the 1974 congressional elections and capture the presidency again in 1976. The true dimensions of the 1972 election will become clearer, as is always the case, with the passage of time and the succeeding set of contests.

The American party systems and the electoral system are inextricably connected. In the maintaining elections, the electorate ratifies the status quo; in the deviating elections, it signals a desire for temporary changes of people or policies; and in the realigning elections it forces change that cuts through the entire society. Parties are the vehicle because they are collections of politicians, groups, and individual activists who seek power and want to govern. Elections are the channel, rather than coups or seizures, because they are available and predictable and have worked in the past.

The Organization of American Parties: Form Follows Function

The aim of American parties is to win elections, and the parties are organized for that task at the national, state, and local levels. In terms of organization, political scientists classify parties as *mass parties* and *cadre parties*. Mass parties have large memberships that are clearly identified by party leaders, and the organizational structure reaches deep into these memberships, to the block or factory level. Cadre parties, in contrast, are composed of professional party leaders, elected public officials affiliated with the party and volunteer activists recruited for campaigns. Theoretically, in mass parties many individuals contribute to the day-to-day decisions and tasks, working on election drives, considering issues, and developing the party's position on governmental questions. In cadre parties, the work is carried on by a much smaller number. The professionals, aided by associated interest group leaders or highly motivated amateurs, interact with each other on party matters and assign much of the routine work to paid technicians responsible only to them. Despite their lack of interest in ideology during the nineteenth century, in the urban machines as well as at the national level, American parties often approached the mass party model. During the twentieth century, American parties have been of the cadre type.

Each party has four levels of full-time cadres: the President and his aides (if the party controls the White House), the members of the party in the Congress and their staffs, the National Committee, and the party and the elected officials from the fifty states. These activists communicate among themselves on an informal basis all the time.

The National Committee

If the national convention serves as the party's quadrennial representative body, the national committee serves as its governing body when the delegates are not in session. Each state party, again in a number of different ways, chooses representatives whose selection is then ratified by the convention. These national committeemen and -women meet only infrequently and do not make party policy. Instead, they are charged with certain formal responsibilities, which occasionally may prove to be significant: they choose the convention site, prepare a temporary roll of convention delegates, and, if the party national chairman resigns, choose his successor.

The National Chairman

In recent years both national committees have become increasingly active, but the expanded activities center almost exclusively around the chairmen and the permanent staffs they supervise. Unlike the national committeemen, the chairman is a full-time executive officer who directs the party's daily activities on a national scale. He owes his selection to the party's presidential nominee, although nominally it must be approved by the national committee.

Understandably, the chairman's role will depend upon the outcome of the presidential election. If his party holds the Presidency, the chairman's role is passive and subordinate. The President himself acts as party leader, and the chairman concentrates on strengthening the national party's organizational ties with the state parties. If, however, his party was defeated, the chairman's role is more visible. He then becomes a leading party spokesman, but at the same time his position is made more difficult. He must speak for the party and yet, because of the coalition nature, there are relatively few issues on which he can speak candidly. In fact, the best way for him to unite the party's disparate following is to emphasize the sins of the opposition, which explains why the political dueling between the two national chairmen is usually so hackneyed and sterile.

There are a number of recent trends in the national committee operations of both parties. With the national chairmen leading the way, each party is driving toward a more efficient and managerial approach to politics. The national chairmen, themselves technically oriented, have increasingly organized information about people rather than the people themselves. The committee staff have become professional, with special training in campaign techniques and fund-raising; they have also become specialized, with separate sections on research, fund-raising, and data-processing. As a result, special party committees work on policy issues, minority-group relations, and voter registration.

Perhaps most important, the chairmen have incorporated modern electronic techniques into daily political operations. Fund-raising using computerized letters has broadened the base of small contributors, and both parties conduct door-to-door and telephone polling on a regular basis. Both chairmen project themselves into national issues by appearing regularly on television. Most interestingly, each party has developed special relationships with some of the three hundred professional campaign firms now operating in American politics.[6] These firms are political technicians for hire, tied to no one community, shifting among party units (although usually not between parties). The campaign consultants provide specialized services in producing TV ads, buying TV time, registering voters, mobilizing the vote, devising strategy, and raising funds. They are, in a sense, "instant parties," available to anyone with money. Because the national committees have had extensive and close relationships with these firms, they now possess a specialized knowledge of electoral information and campaign techniques.

The actual organization of parties beneath the national committee level is prescribed not by the Constitution or by federal statute, but by state laws. State laws regulating party organization were a post-Civil War response to corruption and boss rule. In every state, constitutional provisions, statutory enactments, and judicial rules regulate the organization of parties, prescribing in detail the structure and functions of party bodies and the manner by which they select their officials. Other laws regulate party financing and party nominating procedures, whether nominations are made by conventions or in primaries.

In a federal system of fifty states, these legal regulations vary enormously, most noticeably in the allocation of responsibilities for staffing the party committee and for nominating candidates. A fairly common scheme of pyramidal organization does nevertheless exist. Its logic, as Figure 5.1 demonstrates, is a simple electoral one: the party units generally correspond to the governmental units that they hope to capture. In other words, the individual party organizations are oriented toward those specific

---

[6] See Dan Nimmo, *The Political Persuaders: The Techniques of Modern Election Campaigns* (Englewood Cliffs, N.J.: Prentice-Hall, Inc., 1970) and John S. Saloma III and Frederick H. Sontag, "Developments in American Party Structure; Recent Trends and Consequences for the 1970's," paper presented at the 66th Annual Meeting of the American Political Science Association, Los Angeles, September 8–12, 1970.

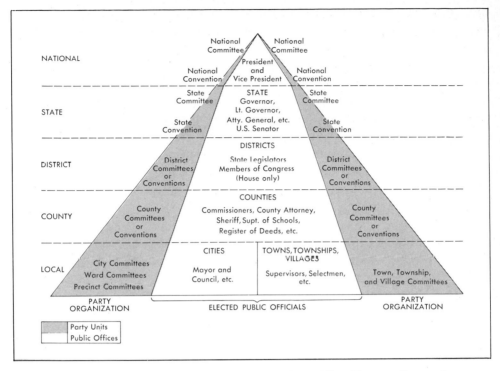

Figure 5.1. Units of party structure correspond to the public offices parties seek

governmental organizations for which they nominate candidates. The base begins with a voting precinct that contains between two hundred and two thousand voters. In the larger cities the precinct committeeman, and in small towns the town chairman, acts as the most local party chief. He is normally selected in a direct primary open to registered party voters. In most cities, however, the basic unit is the ward, composed of a number of precincts. The ward typically sends a representative to the city council, and the party leader is a ward committeeman, also elected in a direct primary. If the party is well organized, as it is not in many cities, ward committeemen themselves appoint subordinate precinct captains whose duty is to turn out the party vote on election days. In many cities a city committee whose concern is the mayoralty election stands above the ward committees.

Organizationally superior to the precinct, town, and ward is the county committee, a good-sized group that most commonly consists of all the elected committeemen within the county. This committee selects its leader, and, though real party power very often is not parallel with the formal table of organization, the Republican and Democratic county chairmen are the mainstays of their party organizations. Whereas the county committee (or convention) focuses on the election of county officials, some states also have a district committee, which is geared to the election of state and federal legislators. Situated at the top of the pyramid is the state central committee, chosen in a number of ways but most frequently by direct primary. Its main responsibilities are to nominate candidates for statewide office, to run the party primaries, and to select the state chairman, who is always a leading figure, though he is not necessarily the state party leader.

Impressive as this formal scheme may seem, it is, to use a favorite epithet of the Chinese Communists, a "paper tiger." Without dues-paying members, lacking centralized power, and dependent upon the cooperation of independent local leaders, the state parties are actually caucuslike miniatures of their national counterparts. Only at the local level does one find strong organizations. These can be of the courthouse variety in areas where a monotonous one-party dominance is sustained by a homogeneous pattern of economic interest. The party structure is skeletal, and an essentially feudal political leader, a rural boss, dictates his party's local nominations and manages the community's public affairs.

A second variety of local party structure, with much greater organizational flesh and blood, exists in many medium- and large-sized cities. Typically, a majority Democratic organization dominates the city's political life, but even the minority, whose cause is never totally hopeless, may be organizationally alive. Party workers and leaders, particularly the precinct captains and ward committeemen, man the organizational machinery, and they do so for any number of individual motives. Most obviously, however, they do so because politics is a rewarding profession, with the rewards being the hope of material gain and the desire for sociability with like-minded and generally gregarious persons.

In blunt fact, the spoils of office are these workers' main sustenance. The spoils can be—according to the tolerant and perhaps honestly realistic standards of politicians—licit: providing government jobs to party workers, purchasing insurance or surety bonds through political leaders who act as special agents, and awarding public work contracts to favored contractors. (There is no Republican or Democratic way to pave streets, but there are Republican and Democratic contractors and some who, in the best nonpartisan tradition, make campaign contributions to both parties.) Or it can be the illicit spoils that flow from crime. Racketeers need the protection of policemen and public officials whose indulgence, in one way or another, has been purchased. A study of Philadelphia politics in the 1950's provides an illustration. Sam Dash, a crusading young lawyer, became, briefly, city district attorney to fill out an unexpired term:

> Eight of the most prosperous numbers banks were raided, and their proprietors were placed under arrest. Almost immediately, Dash began to receive phone calls, advising him to lay off, from councilmen, ward leaders, members of the state legislature, and high-ranking officials in the Democratic party. One of the last group assured him that the arrests would mean the loss of $50,000 in direct campaign contributions to the party. Dash stuck by his guns . . . but his time in the district attorney's office was too short to bring any of the arrested men actually to trial. In January of 1956, Victor Blanc came into office and the cases against the numbers bankers were allowed to fade away, not a single conviction ever having been obtained.[7]

[7] James Reichley, *The Art of Government: Reform and Organizational Politics in Philadelphia* (New York: The Fund for the Republic, Inc., 1959), pp. 91–92.

electoral politics

Nominations and Campaigns

Because the main impact of contemporary parties comes through elections, the party organization is an apparatus oriented toward elections. Not surprisingly, the major preoccupation of parties is electoral; to understand them it is essential to know how nominations are won, how campaigns are managed, and what impact is made by these election activities. There are contests for nominations on all levels of American politics, but the major office is the Presidency.

Presidential nominations are the most ardently sought of all nominations because the Presidency is the most important single office in our government. Presidential aspirants are chosen through a bruising ordeal of private negotiations with state political leaders, campaigns in various state presidential primary elections, and struggles at the quadrennial national party conventions. The competition for presidential nominations embodies *all* facets of the process of seeking a nomination for office in American public life. A good point to begin our examination of this process is with the national conventions.

Evolution of the Presidential Nominating Convention System

The present convention system, roughly familiar to all who watch summer television every four years, has developed in uneven stages since the nation's founding. As an institution, it is *sui generis,* unique to American politics. Furthermore, the conventions, like the parties that run them, are nowhere mentioned in the Constitution. Yet, in a formal sense, the conventions nominate our presidential candidates. How and why did presidential nominating conventions come into being?

In the Federalist period (1789–1801) presidential nominations were made in haphazard ways. Nominations resulted from informal agreements between leaders within each of the two competing parties, the Federalists and the Republicans. Both presidential nominees for 1800 were named by the parties' congressional caucuses, which were closed meetings of congressional party members. The caucus remained the major means of nominating presidential candidates through 1824. The only variations on caucus nominations were private, and by invitation—the conventions held by the declining Federalist Party in 1808 and 1812. Between 1800 and 1825, however, many candidates for state offices were nominated in conventions held by the state parties. When the national parties finally switched to the convention method, they were simply adapting institutions already commonplace at the state level.

In 1824, the caucus system broke down when the one remaining major party, the Republican, split over five would-be candidates. Seventy-five per cent of the Republican Congressmen boycotted the caucus that nominated William H. Crawford of Georgia. A Pennsylvania state convention nominated Andrew Jackson, while state legislatures put forth three additional candidates. When no candidate was able to gain a majority of votes in the Electoral College meeting that followed the presidential election, the House of Representatives elected John Quincy Adams. In 1828, each of the two contenders, Adams and Jackson, was nominated by a variety of state legislatures and state conventions acting independently. This method resulted in a further dilution of party strength, an undesirable feature in a political environment where party structures were already loose and communications were still primitive. What was clearly needed was a mechanism for nominating presidential candidates that would provide recognition to all important elements in the party and, at the same time, maximize the party's chances of winning the election. Whatever evolved would have to reflect the then-changing face of American politics—the passing of power from the nationally oriented Virginia dynasty of presidents and the Congress to powerful *state* political magnates. Out of these profound political needs, the national party conventions were born.

The first national party convention was held by a minor party, the Anti-Masons, in Baltimore in 1831. This was not to be the last time a minor party provided the model for major party behavior. One hundred and sixteen delegates came to the 1831 gathering. They set four precedents later followed by the major parties: 1) the delegations came from each state and were chosen in a manner determined by the individual state; 2) each delegation received as many votes as the state's representation in Congress; 3) a two-thirds vote was required to nominate (a rule never adopted by the modern Republican party but utilized by the Democrats until 1936); 4) a national committee was appointed to carry on for the party between elections. In 1831 the National Republicans also met in convention to nominate Henry Clay, and in 1832 the Democratic-Republicans similarly endorsed Jackson. Thus, all three candidates for the Presidency in 1832 were nominated by national conventions.

The party system itself was in great flux between 1832 and the Civil War, and, as a consequence, it took some years before the convention system developed to its present institutionalized and authoritative status. The Democrats held a second convention in 1835 and a third in 1840, when they adopted the first party platform, consisting of nine short resolutions. Prior to 1852, candidates were nominated before platforms were written, but mounting tensions over the slavery issue led to adoption of a procedure that is still followed, the composition of platform planks prior to the nomination of candidates.

Presidential Nominating Conventions Today

The thought of presidential nominating conventions probably brings to mind the picture of a television scene such as this, described by Theodore White:

Down from the rafters cascaded flakes of inch-square gold foil; up from the pit boomed the bass drum that beat in rhythm . . . from behind the rostrum a band blared, "When the Saints Come Marching In." Onto the floor poured the demonstrators: The Californians in golden bibs, the Nevadans in red silk shirts, Texans carrying longhorn insignia. Gold balloons rose from the floor. . . . Signs were brandished.[8]

Typically, however, the demonstrations—carefully stage-managed and timed—are aimed not at the delegates in the hall but at the vast audience outside watching on television. One factor that has altered the shape and substance of modern conventions is technology, the accelerating American revolution in mass communications. Convention results were first transmitted rapidly to a national audience when the telegraph covered the sessions in 1844; radio broadened the coverage and the audience when it appeared in 1924. But television has revolutionized conventions, beginning with its presence in 1948 and expanding in importance ever since. Millions of Americans watch the action from better seats than those accorded the delegates, many of whom have to watch on TV themselves because their chairs are located behind camera booms! In the earliest days of TV convention telecasting, the cameras were trained relentlessly on the podium of the hall; now, mobile units range through hotel rooms and backstage studios in search of local color and dramatic incidents. Media representatives often outnumber delegates: at the 1972 presidential conventions accredited newspaper, radio, and television personnel outnumbered delegates almost four to one. The politicians have responded to the presence of the media and the opportunity for publicity by gearing their movements more and more to the audience outside. Even the great convention set-pieces—the keynote, nominating, and acceptance speeches—are directed to the home viewers and not to the delegates crowded onto the floor below the rostrum.

The modern presidential convention also differs from those of the past in that a successful preconvention campaign by a delegate can strip the actual convention of all but the power of formal ratification. To understand how preconvention strategies operate and have increased their significance, one must turn to the various ways of selecting the delegates. The selection rules, which are set by the states, will not please those who like order in life, for they represent an overlay of two different political objectives. One objective is delegate selection and thus eventual nomination by party leaders. Before 1900, all delegates were selected at state conventions of party professionals, and they were usually sent uncommitted to the national meetings. This

---

[8] *The Making of the President 1964* (New York: Atheneum, 1965), pp. 202–203.

method gave maximum power to state party leaders, who might pledge themselves in advance to a powerful contender or who might keep their delegations on the fence until the last moment and the best bargain came along. Whatever they did, they followed their own inclinations without legally binding directives from anyone, including the public. In 1905, however, Wisconsin became the first state to adopt the direct presidential primary. The objective of the Wisconsin law, inspired by reform-minded progressives, was to take the choice of delegates, and thus of the eventual nominee, away from the professional politicians and to place it in the hands of the people. Such has been the intent, if not the outcome, of all subsequent primary laws.

Today, partially as a result of the party reform described in the case study of this chapter, potentially as many as 50 per cent of all delegates can be selected in primary elections. There are several types of primaries. They vary, depending on whether or not the delegates are listed on the ballot as supporters of a particular candidate, whether or not candidates have any option about the presence of their own names on the ballot, and whether or not the voters commit or merely choose or "instruct" delegates. This crazy-quilt pattern is further confused by the often concomitant presence of so-called preference polls alongside the primaries to tell uninstructed delegates whom the people prefer. In Oregon, for example, the preference poll itself is a binding instruction; in Pennsylvania it is a gratuitous piece of information. Finally, in many states, slates of delegates who are unidentified on the ballot declare themselves informally and receive support and endorsements from candidates and interest groups.

The most important primaries in recent years have been those of New Hampshire, West Virginia, Nebraska, Oregon, California, Ohio, and Wisconsin. Primaries in general are important because they force would-be nominees to test their vote-getting appeal in open political combat. Particular primaries have had special significance for individual candidates: General Eisenhower's popularity was dramatically revealed in 1952 when he received over one hundred thousand *write-in* votes in a Minnesota primary; John F. Kennedy proved to the professional politicians that, although a Catholic, he could carry a Protestant state when he beat Hubert Humphrey in the 1960 West Virginia primary. John F. Kennedy's nomination was a direct result of his sequence of primary victories.

Nonetheless, one can draw no general rule about the relationship of winning primaries to winning a nomination. When Taft and Eisenhower fought to a standstill in 1952 Republican primaries, the nomination was won at the convention itself. In 1952, Democrat Estes Kefauver did better than Adlai Stevenson in the primaries, but Stevenson won the nomination anyway. Barry Goldwater's 1964 primary record was undistinguished, but he won the nomination with ease on the first ballot at San Francisco. Hubert Humphrey was not entered directly in any 1968 primaries, and slates leaning to him unofficially did poorly, yet he was nominated easily. Richard M. Nixon's 1968 and 1972 nominations included a string of unchallenged primary races. For him the primaries served, first, to reestablish his prominence, and, later, to cement and testify to his preeminence in the Republican party. Senator

George McGovern's 1972 Democratic nomination depended in large part on a string of hard-fought primary wins, but also upon victory in a number of state conventions and caucuses.

Where delegates are not chosen by primaries, the conventions and caucuses of state leaders and party activists are the medium. Although the McGovern reforms described in the case study of this chapter were aimed at the Democratic party, wherever changes in state selection laws were made, they would apply to Republican delegate selection as well. Thus, if there is an intraparty contest for the nomination in 1976, the Republicans might very well have a conflictual, primary-oriented selection process of their own.

Strategies for Winning Presidential Nominations

All would-be presidential candidates have strategies—plans that they hope will enable them to capture their party's nomination. Strategies, of course, involve choices. Should the candidate enter primaries? Which ones? What personal qualities should he stress in bargaining with state leaders? Should he emphasize other qualities in appealing to the public? What should his position be on the established issues of national politics? What new programs should he advocate? Winning a nomination is not exactly like winning a general election, but it is always a first and indispensable step.

The nomination process takes place in one of two settings. Sometimes the party already *has* a national leader. The leader may be an incumbent President who has been elected or who has succeeded to the office. Or the leader may be a defeated former presidential candidate. In this setting, the choice is whether or not the party is going to *confirm the existing leadership*. In the nineteenth century, four presidents-by-succession were dropped by their parties—John Tyler, Millard Fillmore, Andrew Johnson, and Chester Arthur. All twentieth-century chief executives who have sought renomination have received it, including presidents-by-succession Theodore Roosevelt, Calvin Coolidge, Harry Truman (in 1948), and Lyndon Johnson (in 1964). The incumbent has potent advantages in seeking party endorsement. He has the publicity and majesty of the presidential office as well as control over the machinery of the party itself. Still, two recent incumbent Presidents, Harry Truman in 1952 and Lyndon Johnson in 1968, have chosen not to seek renomination at least in part because they perceived the possibility of serious challenge and even defeat within their own party.

The nomination prospects of once-defeated candidates, the titular leaders, are also complex. Such candidates are burdened by the onus of past defeat, but have the advantages of national reputations and campaign experience. Parties seem to embrace such leaders most enthusiastically if it appears that the nominee will either certainly win or certainly lose. Some titular leaders have been renominated: Bryan (Dem.—1896, 1900, 1908), Dewey (Rep.—1944, 1948), Stevenson (Dem.—1952, 1956), and Nixon (Rep.—1960, 1968). Others have failed: Smith (Dem.—1928, but not 1932) and Willkie (Rep.—1940, but not 1944). Such leaders seeking renomination must work diligently to maintain their public and party appeal between elections, and they must prove themselves by running in presidential primaries.

The second setting exists when the party must *choose new leadership*. There are four historical patterns in this type of selection process (see Table 5.1): inheritance, inner group selection, compromise, and factional victory. A contender can be said to be nominated by inheritance if he makes himself the chosen heir of a retiring president (Nixon in 1960) or the clear choice of *all* the important elements of the party (Hoover—Rep.—1928). A candidate emerges as a result of inner group selection when an important inner party cabal arranges his nomination even though he is unknown to many party activists or has less support than other aspirants (Landon—Rep.—1936).

Compromise candidates are popularly called "dark horses." Their strategy is to make themselves acceptable to all of the major contenders, to avoid primaries, and to wait until deadlock occurs on the convention floor. In the frustration of stalemate, the dark horse hopes, the party will turn to him as one who displeases none and around whom all can unite. Warren Harding's clever manager, Harry Daugherty, outlined the classic dark-horse maneuver, which worked at the 1920 Chicago Republican Convention, in this way:

Well, there will be no nomination on the early ballots. After the other candidates have failed, after they have gone their limit, the leaders, worn out and wishing to do the very best thing, will get together in some hotel room about 2:11 in the morning. Some fifteen men, bleary-eyed with lack of sleep and perspiring profusely with the excessive heat will sit down around a big table. I will be with them and will present the name of Senator Harding. When the time comes, Harding will be selected, because he fits in perfectly with every need of the party and nation. He is the logical choice, and the leaders will determine to throw their support to him.[9]

Individuals still try the dark-horse approach: Senator Stuart Symington (Dem.) in 1960 and Governor Ronald Reagan (Rep.) in 1968. Nonetheless, there have been no successful compromise candidates since 1924, when the Democrats nominated John W. Davis. The presidency has become too great a prize, the preconvention campaigns have become too expensive and too exhaustively organized, and the public has become involved too thoroughly for front-runners to allow a Johnny-come-lately to be chosen. Modern nominations of new leaders in both parties are almost always the consequence of a *factional victory*.

A party faction is a coalition of leaders, states, interests, and outlooks supporting one contender for the nomination. There seem to be consistent factions within each party based both on region and on liberal-conservative ideological differences. Patterns of state delegation voting within these factions have been relatively consistent since 1940 at least. When several factions contest and one wins, a factional victory is the outcome. The difference between competing factions may be serious, involving basic disagreements on philosophy or the total direction of the party. The

---

[9] Cited in Gerald M. Pomper, *Nominating the President* (New York: Norton, 1966), pp. 191–192.

Table 5.1 *Patterns of new leadership selection for presidential nominations, 1832–1972*

Inheritance	Inner group selection	Compromise	Factional victory
DEMOCRATS			
Van Buren, 1836	Cass, 1848	Polk, 1844	Buchanan, 1856
Smith, 1928	McClellan, 1864	Pierce, 1852	Douglas, 1860
Humphrey, 1968	Greeley, 1872	Seymour, 1886	Tilden, 1876
	Hancock, 1880	Davis, 1924	Bryan, 1896
	Cleveland, 1884		Wilson, 1912
	Parker, 1904		Cox, 1920
			Roosevelt, 1932
			Stevenson, 1952
			Kennedy, 1960
			McGovern, 1972
REPUBLICANS			
H. Clay, 1831	Frémont, 1856	Hayes, 1876	Harrison, 1840
Taft, 1908	Grant, 1886	Garfield, 1880	Taylor, 1848
Hoover, 1928	Hughes, 1916	Harding, 1920	Scott, 1852
Nixon, 1960	Landon, 1936		Lincoln, 1860
			Blaine, 1884
			Harrison, 1888
			McKinley, 1896
			Willkie, 1940
			Dewey, 1944
			Eisenhower, 1952
			Goldwater, 1964
			Nixon, 1968

Adapted from Paul T. David, Ralph M. Goldman, and Richard C. Bain, *The Politics of National Party Conventions* (Washington, D.C.: Brookings Institution, 1960), p. 117.

Republician splits between Taft and Eisenhower factions in 1952 and between Goldwater and the northeastern liberal group in 1964 were of such a fundamental sort. Sometimes, however, the factions are separated simply by loyalties to competing individuals whose outlooks and qualifications are similar.

The Value of Conventions

The American primary system is unique in the world and collecting delegates through state party conventions and primary elections has largely pre-empted the choice of nominees. There have been no multiballot conventions in either party, for example, since 1952. Contemporary conventions ratify and legitimize nominees, but do not choose them. If that is so, what purposes do conventions really serve, or should they be abolished and replaced with national primaries as some have urged?

Contemporary conventions seem to serve several major functions both for the parties and for the citizens. The reader will have to decide for himself how well or how badly he thinks these functions are carried out in each particular instance. To begin with, the predictable existence of the conventions provides an institutional opportunity for those groups wishing to bring about change, as well as for those who want to protect the status quo. The former have the primaries and the national organizations of would-be candidates as their vehicles for challenge; the latter cannot avoid a defense. As the history of the McGovern Reform Commission recounted in the case study to this chapter indicates, even if a change-seeking faction loses one year, the continuing existence of the convention system opens the possibility for a response in future years. When one set of winners assess the costs of their victory, they may agree that compromise and change are better. The same response may come from a set of former losers, and from these experiences the parties are sometimes put back together after severe conflict.

In addition, the conventions are mechanisms for important kinds of political communications among the parties, their followers, and the independent voters. Americans pay attention to politics only in certain kinds of situations. They pay attention when political decisions interrupt their private lives—in wars, economic dislocations, or racial conflicts. And they watch the regular institutionalized political spectaculars—the conventions and the campaigns. The conventions give the parties nationwide television audiences encompassing almost the entire electorate. Before this electorate they have the chance to sell their candidates and their programs, their style, and their overall image, and to make broadside appeals or deal in nuances aimed at special publics. What they say and how they conduct themselves as well as what they intend to convey—all are part of the communications opportunity that comes only every four years.

It is obvious that the convention provides a communications opportunity for the would-be nominees and the eventual candidate. It may be less obvious how the platform, that often derided collection of policy-positions that politicians are supposed to be so cynical about, serves the same function. Yet the platforms represent significant efforts to communicate, to reinforce the affections of supporters, and to sway those who are uncommitted. Professor Gerald Pomper has demonstrated, in a seminal study, that:

In choosing their issues, parties act rationally, emphasizing the policy areas of their strength and neglecting the strong points of their opponents. They tend to be specific on these issues of direct, distributive benefit to the voters and to resort to vagueness where the voters are unclear, uninterested, or divided. Policies favored by a majority of the voters are endorsed by the parties, as are those supported by an unopposed minority. Where opposing minorities exist, the party rationally evades a policy choice.[10]

In other words, the platforms are clear in what will be given to those who are their supporters, but vague on great policy issues—such as school busing—where division exists at the leadership and the mass level. The vagueness may aggravate some people, but as a strategy it has a rational basis.

The platform also has an impact upon future government policy. As Table 5.2

[10] *Elections in America* (New York: Dodd, Mead, 1968), p. 177.

Table 5.2 *Governmental fulfillment of party convention platform pledges 1944–1964 (in percentages)*

Subject	Democratic pledge	Republican pledge	Both parties' pledge	In-party pledge	Out-party pledge	Total fulfillment record
Foreign policy						
Some affirmative action	76	47	96	76	53	79
No action or defeated	24	53	4	24	47	21
Defense policy						
Some affirmative action	86	62	86	91	53	74
No action or defeated	14	38	14	9	47	26
Economic policy						
Some affirmative action	68	66	95	84	53	73
No action or defeated	32	35	5	16	47	27
Labor policy						
Some affirmative action	39	50	64	54	26	50
No action or defeated	61	50	36	46	74	50
Welfare policy						
Some affirmative action	66	56	97	73	54	72
No action or defeated	34	44	3	27	46	28
Civil rights						
Some affirmative action	50	62	63	67	50	60
No action or defeated	50	38	37	33	50	40

Source: Gerald M. Pomper, *Elections in America* (New York: Dodd, Mead & Company, 1968), pp. 188–189. Reprinted by permission of Dodd, Mead & Company, Inc. Copyright © 1968 by Dodd, Mead & Company, Inc.

shows, if both parties endorse a pledge in their platforms on foreign policy, defense, economic, or welfare policy, the odds are overwhelming that there will be affirmative government action. Similarly, when the party in power makes a commitment in these policy areas, it is very likely that the commitment will be honored. The record is less clear in the fields of labor and civil rights policy, probably because in these areas the southern wing of the Democratic Party separates from the other parts and votes more with the Republicans in the Congress. The Republican record on fulfilling commitments is not as high as the Democratic record primarily because the GOP was out of power twelve of the twenty years covered by the data. As the total record shows, although parties may dodge some issues and individual candidates may back down on some pledges, the platforms are not idly conceived documents. Over a period of time, what their platforms promise, the parties enact.

There is one final function served by the conventions. For those activists who are chosen as delegates, the conventions are a reward for party service, an opportunity to meet and talk with the top leaders and with each other. The convention process reinforces their commitment to their party and probably also to the larger political system. It sends them off invigorated to do political battle once again.

The Road to The White House: The Big Campaign

Presidential campaigns are the most elaborate, hectic, exciting, and expensive. They attract the greatest public interest. Traditionally, the formal campaign starts with the candidate's acceptance speech before a roaring horde of partisans at the national convention. In reality, the campaign has begun long before. Incumbent Presidents are always in the public eye, and they try, with the help of a trained press staff, to utilize their natural advantages and cast their actions in the best possible light. Challengers too, while seeking party nomination, cast their nets for a larger public, search for appealing issues, and work at building a national image.

Nineteenth-century presidential campaigns were sleepy affairs. William McKinley never left his home town of Canton, Ohio, before his 1896 victory. Warren G. Harding, in 1920, was the last stay-at-home candidate. (His promoters perhaps wisely felt that the best thing he could do was remain silent.) More recent campaigns contain a dazzling blitz of tightly scheduled personal handshaking tours run by a staff of advance men and press secretaries. They also rely on heavy doses of professionally produced propaganda disseminated through the mass media. Nor is this all: the modern presidential campaign requires many sophisticated decisions about strategy and operations. *Strategic* decisions are basic. What will the candidate do about his image? What positions will he take on particular issues—and what does he think the new issues should be? What states will he concentrate on to piece together an electoral majority? *Operating* decisions involve choices on tactical tools he will use: How large is the candidate's staff to be, and who will have what roles on it? How much money is needed and how is it to be raised and spent? Should emphasis be on regular party units in each state or should national volunteer committees be organized? How should the candidate's time on the road be allocated? Should he advertise in back-country weeklies or on "spots" over national TV?

In one form or another, personality has been a force in American presidential competition at least since the days of Andrew Jackson. A good image affects the election outcome even when it is not the sole determinant. According to the Michigan Survey Research Center, the image variable has been responsible for a full 13-percent fluctuation in presidential elections. Candidates strive to stress good points and correct or mitigate their liabilities. On issues, if his party last occupied the White House, a candidate is obligated to stand within the administration's general framework, not always a pleasant or easy task—as Hubert Humphrey learned during the 1968 campaign. Challengers are not so bound.

Most candidates try to make their positions accord with those of the vast majority of Americans who sit firmly in the ideological center. Optimal behavior couples a moderate stance and an appropriately vague slogan: Kennedy's 1960 promise to "get America moving again" is a good illustration of the genre. Johnson gained support in 1964 by characterizing Barry Goldwater's "trigger-happy" policy. One kind of foreign policy issue is especially good for electoral mileage. Unpopular wars such as the Korean War during the Truman Administration and the war in Vietnam during the Johnson Administration can be profitably exploited by the opposition party.

The candidate's staffs consist of speech writers, pollsters, fund raisers, advance men, bargainers, and publicity experts, all performing complicated political tasks. Sometimes these entourages, such as John F. Kennedy's "Irish Mafia," are developed years in advance of the formal presidential campaigns. Richard Nixon's 1972 staff was a different group from that of the 1960 campaign. In 1952, the Eisenhower team was put together as the campaign proceeded. But however accumulated, the staff is ever-present: the modern presidential candidate, like an executive in any major endeavor, is a plural man.

In the scheduling of the candidate's own appearances, the rule-of-thumb is to go where the outcome is in doubt. Thus, in 1960, Kennedy and Nixon spent an identical 74 per cent of their time in the twenty-four most closely contested states. Beyond this, however, the consequences of barnstorming are largely unknown. Sometimes it does help to stump a state. Harry Truman's 1948 "whistle-stop" railroad tour activated partisan support for his upset win. What does the handshaking tour do? Nelson Polsby and Aaron Wildavsky write:

No one really knows how much value in changed votes or turnout is gained by personal visits to a particular state. Most voters have made up their minds. Opponents of the candidate are unlikely to go to see him anyway and one wonders what a glimpse in a motorcade will do to influence a potential voter. Yet no one is certain that whistlestop methods produce no useful results. Visiting localities may serve to increase publicity because many of the media of communications are geared to "local" events. It also provides an opportunity to stress issues like public power or race relations which may be of special significance to citizens in a given region. Party activists may be energized by a glimpse at, or a handshake with, the candidate. . . . And so rather than let the opportunity pass, the candidates usually decide to take no chances and get out on the hustings. They hedge against uncertainty by doing all they can.[11]

Three Controversial Campaign Problems: Media, Money, and Impact

The presidential candidate relies heavily upon the media—radio, television, news-papers, and direct mail—to project his image and his positions on issues. A number of controversial questions are raised by contemporary media usage. For one thing, decisions about media are often made for the candidate by paid managers who view the problem of political communication as directly analogous to selling soap or cars.[12] And, for complicated reasons, the same methods often are effective. Television offers the best example. Television commercials, especially thirty- and sixty-second spots, are designed to project carefully crafted impressions that put the product in the best possible setting, without defining its qualities very clearly.[13] The viewer then reads into the product those qualities he most values or would like to have himself. Voting for X-brand politician brings determination, or sincerity, or what-ever quality the viewer cares most about. Those who make the ads *know* what the viewer cares about because they have carefully polled him in advance and have tailored their product to fit.

Managers prefer paid-for time. The second choice is seemingly spontaneous settings that are in reality easily manipulated—such as the question panel with amateurs or the orchestrated rally. Despite the heavy drive to get free time and the legitimacy that comes with being seen on the news programs, most managers choose control above all, and often choose no exposure over uncontrolled exposure.

Such uses of the media raise serious questions for democratic politics. What about the enormous amounts that have to be raised to mount such media-oriented campaigns? Both the physical production of advertisements and the purchase of air time are enormously expensive. Presidential campaign costs have risen from $17.2 million in 1956 to $35 million in 1968 and $70 million in 1972. Cost for all political contests in the country went from $155 million in 1956 to over $400 million in 1972.

The 1971 Federal Election Campaign Act limited media spending for the first time to about 10 cents per voter, of which no more than 60 per cent could be for broadcast advertising. Thus for the 1972 presidential campaign, postconvention spending for TV and radio was limited to $8.5 million by law, with another $5.8 for print media. The effect of this act was to reduce electronic media spending from 1968 levels. But no limits were placed on the production costs of ads, or on the use of direct mail and other techniques.

Both parties have made strenuous and systematic efforts to broaden the base of their contributors. The Republicans now collect most of the money to run their

---

[11] *Presidential Elections* (New York: Scribner's, 1968), p. 132.
[12] See Joe McGinniss, *The Selling of the President 1968* (New York: Trident, 1969).
[13] See Nimmo, op. cit., pp. 163–199.

regular National Committee operations from their list of over 650,000 $10 to $100 contributors. But in the heat of the national campaigns, both parties become heavily dependent upon bigger givers, especially as money is desperately sought for the last two weeks of "blitz." What big contributors extract from these investments in return can never be specified precisely. Surely the pattern of giving is such that although some givers hedge their bets with both sides, the interests generally associated with each party give the most to that party, through fund drives and individual gifts. At a minimum, big givers get access to top leaders, including the President, that ordinary folk do not have. Such access gives them a special opportunity to plead their case and ask for favors from government. Should money be the criterion for such special privilege? As long as the present system of campaigning through the media and free-enterprise fund-raising goes on, this questionable situation is certain to continue.

What is the impact of campaigns and what difference do they make? The traditional view is that they matter little, but this interpretation might logically be expected to change. In an era of almost universal party loyalty and little switch-ticket voting—the end of the nineteenth century, for example—the function of campaigns was to mobilize supporters. Today that is still a major goal, but the number of certain partisans is declining in both parties. With more independents, who make up their minds as campaigns proceed, campaigns can be expected to be more important in the future, not less. In order to explore more closely the how and why of the relationship between campaigns and individual voters, we must turn to the general phenomenon of voting behavior.

Voting Behavior: Choices and Loyalties for Parties

Few Americans now belong to political parties in the sense that they hold membership cards or perform cadre roles. But a surprising number acknowledge an emotional attachment to one party or the other, which makes them vote for that party with predictable regularity. These attachments are set in realigning elections and then passed on primarily within the family. Seventy-five per cent of all Americans vote as their parents did. The party loyalty of the parents themselves is partially conditioned by how strongly they identify with their party. Table 5.3 shows that the strongest party identifiers on both sides are the most reliable partisan voters; the weakest party identifiers and the independents are the most unpredictable voters. Therefore, when the electorate enters into a period of transition and the number of independents rises, we can expect a greater volatility and "swing" in presidential elections, with a greater impact for the short-term forces of personalities and issues.

A realigning election not only sets loyalties that are then passed on, but it also affects the total electorate in differing ways. Because of the appeals the parties make during this crucial loyalty-setting phenomenon, some economic and social groups become supporters of one party virtually en masse, whereas others stay with their original party. For example, the entire South became Democratic during the Civil War and stayed that way until the early 1950's. The Catholic immigrants of the

Table 5.3 *Effects of intensity of party identification on voting choices*

| Year/vote | Individual party identifications | | | | |
| | Democratic | | Independent | Republican | |
	Strong	Weak		Weak	Strong
1952					
Eisenhower	16%	38%	67%	94%	99%
Stevenson	84	62	33	6	1
1956					
Eisenhower	15%	37%	73%	93%	99%
Stevenson	85	63	27	7	1
1960					
Nixon	9%	29%	54%	87%	98%
Kennedy	91	71	46	13	2
1964					
Goldwater	5%	18%	34%	57%	90%
Johnson	95	82	66	43	10
1968					
Humphrey	85%	57%	26%	10%	3%
Nixon	7	26	55	81	96
Wallace	7	14	20	8	1

Source: Michigan Survey Research Center. Reprinted by permission.

nineteenth and early twentieth centuries in the big cities started voting Democratic because the urban machines of that party welcomed them and the Republicans did not. The New Deal solidified their attachment. In contrast, prior to the New Deal, Jews and blacks voted almost solidly Republican. Since then, however, they have been the most loyal Democrats.

Because of the group impact of realigning elections and the resulting social "set" of loyalties, we can talk about the demographic characteristics of each party's support. As Table 5.4 indicates, Democrats *tend* to draw their supporters from the less educated, the black, Catholic and Jewish ethnic groups, the working class, and the urban sectors of the American population. The Republicans tend to draw their supporters from the better educated, whites, Protestants, professional classes, and rural and suburban folk. These trends in social group loyalty to party are by no means absolute: some workers are Republicans and some bankers are Democrats. Nonetheless, the trends are decisive, and when one finds a workingman Republican, he is likely to be a Protestant, small-town worker. The Democratic banker is likely to be Jewish or Catholic. Younger citizens tend to be Democrats, although the proportion of independents is highest in this social category. Figure 5.2 portrays these alignments graphically.

Table 5.4 *Social group characteristics of support for political parties*

	Republican	Democrat	Independent
National	28%	42%	30%
Sex			
Men	28%	39%	33%
Women	28	44	28
Race			
White	30%	39%	31%
Nonwhite *	4	77	20
Education			
College	35%	28%	37%
High school	27	42	31
Grade school	24	52	24
Occupation			
Professional and business	31%	32%	37%
White collar	30	38	32
Farmers	35	40	25
Manual	35	46	31
Age			
21–29 years	23%	35%	42%
30–49 years	28	41	31
50 and over	31	45	24
Religion			
Protestant	33%	39%	28%
Catholic	20	50	30
Jewish †	7	61	32
Region			
East	29%	43%	28%
Midwest	33	37	30
South	19	47	34
West	33	39	28
Income			
$10,000 and over	31%	34%	35%
7,000 and over	30	36	34
5,000–6,999	23	44	33
3,000–4,999	30	45	25
Under $3,000	26	53	21
Community size			
1,000,000 and over	26%	42%	32%
500,000 and over	25	42	33
50,000–499,999	19	48	33
2,500–49,999	33	40	27
Under 2,500, rural	34	36	30

Source: Gallup Opinion Index, August, 1969. Reprinted by permission.

* 1968 Gallup Data, cities over 100,000.

† 1968 Gallup Data.

Figure 5.2. Political x-ray: As each party sees the other

Source: Carl Rose, *New York Times Magazine,* November 4, 1962. © 1962 by The New York Times Company. Reprinted by permission.

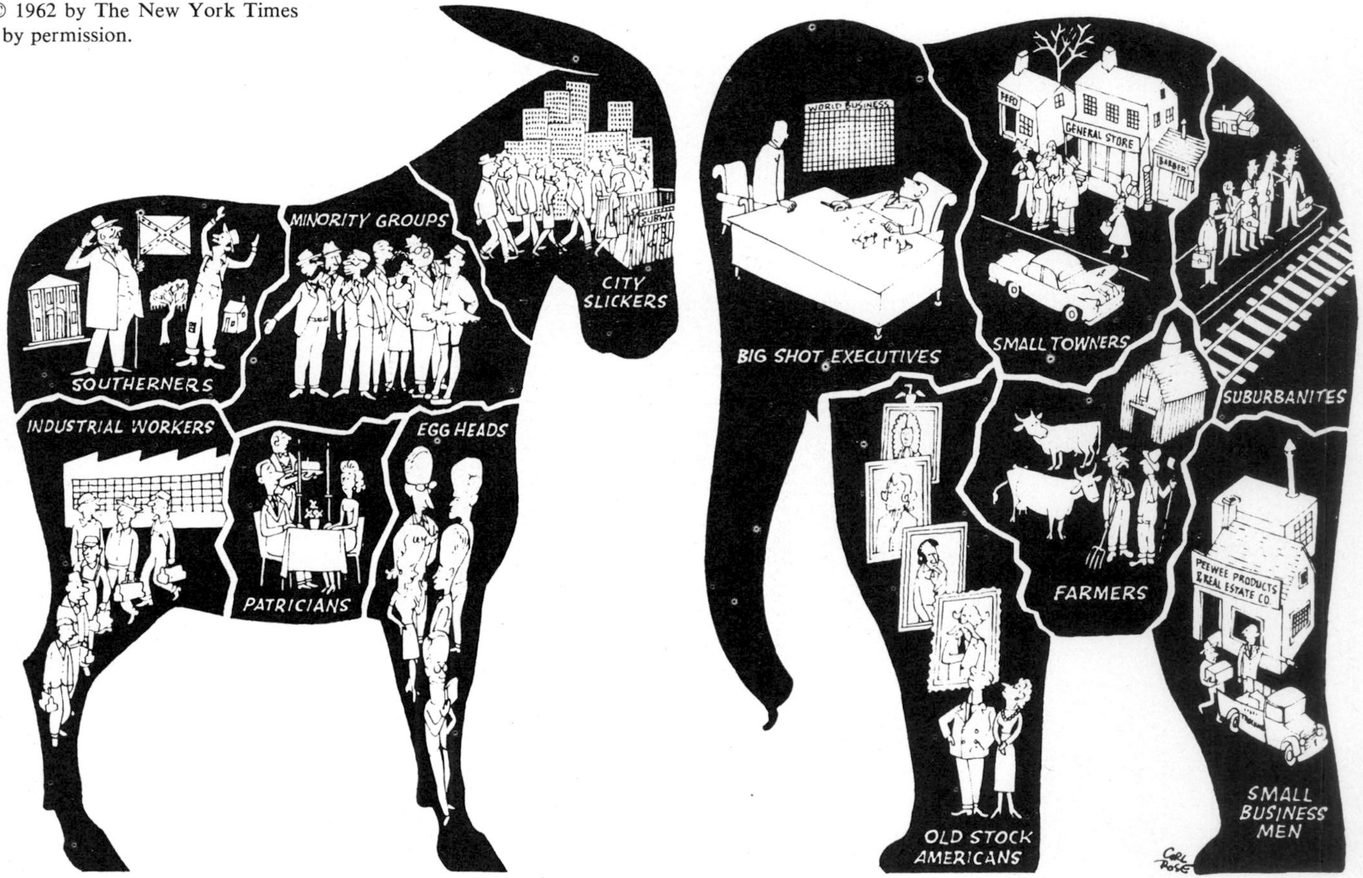

Labels within illustration:

SMALL BUSINESS MEN

SUBURBANITES

FARMERS

SMALL TOWNERS

OLD STOCK AMERICANS

BIG SHOT EXECUTIVES

CITY SLICKERS

MINORITY GROUPS

EGG HEADS

PATRICIANS

SOUTHERNERS

INDUSTRIAL WORKERS

"This year I'm not getting involved in any complicated issues. I'm just voting my straight ethnic prejudices."

Figure 5.3

Source: Drawing by Whitney Darrow, Jr., © 1970
The New Yorker Magazine, Inc.

Once possessing a stable body of supporters, each party tries to keep those it has and to appeal to the *least* loyal supporters of the other party. This syndrome accounts for certain predictable aspects of party strategy—it explains why Democrats always favor economic policies supported by organized labor and Republicans favor those preferred by big business. This pattern of party behavior rewards and reinforces the loyalists. Similarly, the parties' divide-and-conquer strategy sends Democrats after newly successful businessmen who have benefited from their inflationary and expansionist economic policies. And it sends Republicans after white southerners, who have grown restive with the emphasis given to blacks within the national Democratic Party since World War II. Interestingly, however, deliberate strategy by the opposition does not seem to be the major factor, over the long haul, that leads to disintegration or disaggregation of hard-core party support. Time and the emergence of new issues are far more significant factors than anything deliberately contrived by one side or the other.

Time erodes loyalties simply because the event or the set of policies that originally drew a group to a party recedes. The memory is less intense for those who experienced the original experience; it is a secondary attachment anyway for those who are young and did not live through it themselves. The natural effects of time explain why younger people have the fewest ties to parties. Time also explains why, as the New Deal fades more and more into the past, split-ticket voting has risen in all sections of the country. The overall rise in independents can be seen in Figure 5.4.

One way to mitigate the increasing remoteness of any historical experience is to evoke constantly the symbols and rhetoric of that experience. It is for this reason that professional politicians, especially those from the majority party, always run in ways aimed at recreating the aura of the original realignment. In our own times, Democrats always campaign using economic issues as if it were 1932 and the opponent was Herbert Hoover. And, whenever the economy does slip, the old symbols regain their cogency and the appeals work, as they did in the off-year elections of 1970. This strategy of invoking the past to counteract the natural erosion of loyalty due to the effects of time probably keeps economic and ethnic cleavages alive well after the point when they might otherwise have faded.[14]

This strategy also makes American party politicians seem out of touch when new issues that agitate the electorate arise. Partially from uncertainty about how to act and partially because the old appeals, the old cleavages and the old ways of organizing political conflict are what they have based careers on and what they know, regular party politicians stick to the familiar old issues. This phenomenon is yet another manifestation of the situation described at the beginning of the chapter—that parties respond to changes in the society, rather than provide leadership in initiating social changes.

Such behavior, which focuses on vote-seeking in the issues of the past, runs

---

[14] See Raymond E. Wolfinger, "The Development and Persistence of Ethnic Voting," *The American Political Science Review*, LIX, No. 4 (December 1965), pp. 896–908, for a brilliant demonstration of this point.

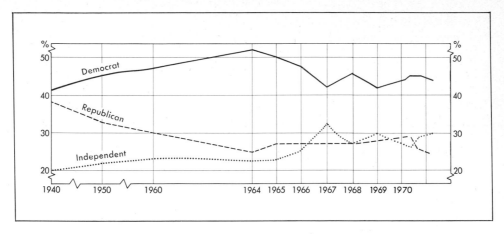

Figure 5.4. Party affiliation, 1940–1972: The growth of the independents

Source: Gallup Opinion Index, October 1971, p. 23.

head-on into another factor that is increasingly undermining the reliable group support of the parties. New issues have emerged in contemporary America, because society is changing in ways that directly affect many persons and that lead them to demand political action. Several such new issues first emerged in the last decade. One was "law and order," which surfaced in the 1964 campaign and has become more important in the 1970's. By *law and order,* many Americans sought political action that would halt the rise of crime, particularly street crime against persons and property, as well as racial conflict and rioting. Another new issue was the Vietnam war. It developed as a challenge to that specific war, but later shifted to the entire shape of foreign and defense policy and the constitutional role of the executive branch of the federal government. A third new issue is labeled the *environment,* a topic containing many subcauses but related to many significant issues involving the role of technology in society, the quality of life, and the question of priorities.

The parties did not generate any of these issues. On law and order and, to a much lesser degree, on environment, they quickly took positions. More significantly, the emergence of these new issues means that the old ways of organizing politics no longer fit the concerns and divisions among many Americans. It has become harder and harder, for example, for the Democratic Party to hold its white ethnic groups (many of whom are of Catholic Eastern European origin) in a viable coalition with blacks, students, and highly educated suburbanities.

The 1970's, in summary, appear to be characterized by a rising number of independents because the last realigning election, the New Deal, is more remote, and by an accelerating challenge to the old group coalitions because new issues have emerged. In the face of this situation, what will happen to the traditional two-party system? And what impact is there likely to be on the nature and style of American politics?

The Two-Party System and
the Future of American Politics

Most democratic societies have multiparty instead of two-party systems. Although America has almost always had minor parties, none has had consistent staying power or significant electoral success. Why, in fact, has the American political system been so thoroughly dominated by the two major parties? There seem to be a number of reasons. For one thing, there exists a powerful historical tradition of support for two parties. Political leaders have traditionally organized political conflict around dualistic positions: agrarianism versus industrialism, slavery versus abolition, or governmental economic interventionism versus laissez-faire. Beyond these rather basic issue cleavages, the two parties have assembled broad coalitions and have not worried about the internal consistency of their supporters on other issues. This easygoing acceptance of supporters has been facilitated by the willingness of the political parties to define certain issues as being outside of competitive politics. Bipartisanship on foreign policy is a perfect illustration. Both parties entered into a cadre agreement at the highest levels that there would be no competition on our Cold War position, thereby foreclosing debate on that crucial subject from 1946 until 1965 when Vietnam brought the consensus to an end. Excluding a subject, like excluding some people, reduces the difficulty in organizing politics for parties; conversely, adding issues, like adding voters, adds problems.

In addition to the drive to organize issues in a dualistic way, the two-party system has been reinforced by the electoral laws. These laws are, of course, made by the two parties at the national and state levels. The most significant procedure is the practice of electing candidates by plurality vote in single member districts. The votes cast for losing candidates are wasted at both the local and the state level in the Electoral College vote for President. In other electoral systems, with multimember districts or proportional representation vote-counting rules, losing parties get at least *some* legislative seats if they have some popular support. American electoral rules make it possible to appeal to voters to vote for a major party candidate on the grounds that to do otherwise is to "waste your vote."

Perhaps the most powerful support of the two-party system is the way party identifications are set in realigning elections and then passed on in the family without much regular or rational reexamination. Americans place considerable faith in the process of elections as a way of articulating demands and resolving controversies.[15] As long as one of the traditional parties is present at a realigning stage, ready and willing to respond to the new crisis, it is used as a vehicle. Once the crisis point is past, support is relatively automatic or at least can be generated through a low level of political intensity based on personalities and short-range issues typical of maintaining and deviating elections. There is no need to shift to third or fourth parties.

How firm are these foundations? We have already seen that the emergence of new issues and new divisions in society has broken down the arrangements of the

---

[15] See Jack Dennis, "Support for the Institution of Elections by the Mass Public," *The American Political Science Review*, LXIV, No. 3 (September 1970), pp. 819–835.

New Deal coalitions. Will the parties be able to rearrange the new conflicts into new patterns of support? Their task is complicated by the fact that some of the new issues will no longer simply be excludable, such as the conduct of American foreign policy or the primacy of the executive branch of the federal government. Nor will some groups be excludable. Black Americans are better organized and voting in growing numbers, and their successes provide a strong stimulus to the Mexican-American (Chicano) movement in the western and southwestern states. The suffrage now extends to all eighteen-year-olds, making millions of new young voters eligible to participate in the electoral politics of the 1970's. Simultaneously, group identities and demands are rising from working-class Americans. Various social changes are pushing an expansion of the agenda of politics, but the parties have not yet met the challenge of these forces in such a way as to make their own futures clear.

The existing electoral rules permitting the winner to take all seem safe for the moment. But the move *within* the national Democratic Party to select convention delegates on a proportional basis provides the potential for extension to general election procedures. Finally, one may wonder about the loyalty of individual Americans to the two-party system as such. Americans apparently regard the party system itself with considerable ambivalence, for the parties do not generate the citizen loyalty that other institutions do.[16] Support for the party system is apparently tied to performance, especially in times of stress or transition.

Thus, the fate of the two-party system as we know it is no more certain than the solution of the problems agitating Americans. In reaching for solutions to the problems, parties have to compete with a variety of nonparty groups such as interest groups and social movements. Party politicians have to compete with nonparty leaders or leaders who might bolt the regular parties to form new ones. The inescapable conclusion is that fate of the present parties rests in the hands of their present-day leaders. It depends on their adaptability to new problems, their ability to mobilize support in a competitive political market, and their skill in either solving problems or persuading people that they are trying to solve problems.

A continuation of two-party politics would give America a political system not unlike the one it knows so well, although faces might change, issues would change, and the underlying social coalitions of the parties would change. But multiparty politics, or one-party politics, or no-party politics would mean that the United States, as it began its third century as a nation, was moving into a completely new political environment. Each alternative would be better for some people and worse for others. A multiparty system might improve the representation of minority interests at the expense of currently organized sectors of society. Such a system would surely raise the conflict level of American politics and result in less stability of politics, if not of policy. A one-party system could be dominated by the right or the left, and could be communist, socialist, or fascist. The party would probably be activist and an initiator, and the entire country would be different. A no-party system would mean rule by

---

[16] See Jack Dennis, "Support for the Party System by the Mass Public," *The American Political Science Review*, LX, No. 3 (September 1966), pp. 600–615.

corporations or by the military, or, indeed, the total breakdown of government and society into anarchy.

This mere sketch of the alternatives reveals how different America would be without the two-party system. Whatever one's positions on any issue or feelings about any political leader, it is obvious that the certainty and predictability of everyone's life is tied intimately to this system. People have different stakes in stability, of course, but no one should underestimate the dislocations, costs, and unpredictable outcomes if the stable two-party system that has served our entire national existence should collapse at this point in American history.

suggested additional readings

Burnham, Walter Dean. *Critical
Elections and the Mainsprings of
American Politics*. New York:
W. W. Norton & Company Inc.,
1970.

Campbell, Angus, et al. *The American
Voter*. New York: John Wiley &
Sons, Inc., 1960.

Chambers, William N., and Walter Dean
Burnham (eds.). *The American
Party Systems*. New York: Oxford
University Press, 1967.*

Crotty, William J., et al. (eds.).
*Political Parties and Political
Behavior*, 2nd ed. Boston: Allyn &
Bacon, Inc., 1971.*

Key, V. O., Jr. *Politics, Parties and
Pressure Groups*, 4th ed. New York:
Thomas Y. Crowell Company, 1958.
———. *The Responsible Electorate*.
Cambridge, Mass.: Belknap Press,
1966.*

Ladd, Everett C., Jr. *American
Political Parties*. New York:
W. W. Norton & Company, Inc.,
1970.*

Lubell, Samuell. *The Hidden Crisis in
American Politics*. New York:
W. W. Norton & Company, Inc.,
1970.*

Nimmo, Dan. *The Political Persuaders:
The Techniques of Modern Election
Campaigns*. Englewood Cliffs, N.J.:
Prentice-Hall, Inc., 1970.*

Phillips, Kevin P. *The Emerging
Republican Majority*. Garden City,
N.Y.: Doubleday-Anchor, 1970.*

Pomper, Gerald M. *Elections in
America*. Boston: Little, Brown
& Co., 1968.*

Scammon, Richard M., and Ben J.
Wattenberg. *The Real Majority*.
New York: Coward-McCann,
Inc., 1970.*

Schattschneider, E. E. *The Semi-Sovereign
People*. New York: Holt, Rinehart &
Winston, Inc., 1960.*

Sorauf, Frank J. *Party Politics in
America*. Boston: Little, Brown
and Company, 1968, 1972.

* Available in paperback.

6 interest groups

case study

A New Department for a Restless Nation

On October 15, 1966, President Johnson, before an audience of several hundred in the White House East Room, signed the legislation establishing the Department of Transportation as the twelfth Cabinet-level department. Thus ended, for the time being, and more or less successfully, an effort that the President had launched the previous year. In August, 1965, he had written to Congressman F. Bradford Morse of Massachusetts, in response to the latter's plea that something be done to coordinate the activities of some thirty federal agencies engaged in making transportation policy, that he planned to set up a National Transportation Council to prepare legislation on the subject for consideration in Congress.

How long the White House had been thinking along these lines before Representative Morse raised the matter is hard to say. The idea of a Department of Transportation was by 1965 of truly ancient lineage. As the Director of the Budget noted in his testimony before the House Committee considering the President's bill, a proposal for a Bureau of Transportation had been introduced into Congress as early as 1874. Many subsequent suggestions had been made to bring together in one agency the growing number of federal activities relating to transportation. A task force of

the first Hoover Commission on Reorganization of the Federal Government of 1949 recommended the creation of such a department. President Eisenhower did the same in his last budget message as President in 1961, and that same year a special study group of the Senate Committee on Commerce came to the same conclusion.

Why, then, did an idea with such a long history, such a plausible basis, and such distinguished proponents take until October, 1966, to fight its way into the statute books? In a word, the answer is to be found in the resistance that administrative reorganization always encounters. Existing patterns and relationships are invariably defended both by the personnel of agencies, who feel knowledgeable and secure in them, and by outside interest groups. The latter have learned to accommodate themselves to an existing arrangement; change threatens to disadvantage these interests by disrupting the established relationships. We might begin, somewhat arbitrarily, in 1933. It was a rare problem of public policy that did not come up for fresh and often creative consideration in the restless minds of Franklin Roosevelt and his New Deal cohorts. This was no less true of transportation policy. In a campaign speech in September, 1932, Mr. Roosevelt had called for a basic reorganization of our transportation structure and the coordination of all carrier services.

After his election, during the interregnum, he conferred with people knowledgeable about the ailing transportation industries. Among the transportation experts was Joseph B. Eastman, a long-time member of the Interstate Commerce Commission (ICC) and recognized as one of the nation's leading authorities on transportation policy. After March 4, a working committee was set up, including Eastman, that produced draft legislation that later became the Emergency Transportation Act of 1933. One of the key provisions of this legislation was the creation of an office called the Coordinator of Transportation, with a vaguely worded mandate to work toward railroad consolidation, but also enjoined to study and recommend other proposals for coordination. Eastman was appointed to the position.

This was a notable event because it was the first concrete step in the direction of meshing the various federal policies relating to transportation (centering in the 1930's on the railroads, including waterborne commerce, and soon to embrace various forms of motor and air travel). Even more interesting and instructive was Eastman's experience as Coordinator, which lasted until 1936. When he testified before a Senate committee on the proposed legislation, he summed up the theoretical need for coordination:

The proper place for each of these [new transportation] agencies must be found, and in some way they must be coordinated and welded into a well-knit whole, into a transportation system operating more nearly as a unit, without cross purposes and all manner of lost motion.

A major part of his duties as Coordinator related to the thankless effort to bring some order out of the chaos of railroad lines and corporate structures, either through merger or other means. To this he gave much attention. On broader fronts, however, he pushed hard to bring motor and water carriers under ICC regulation; he saw the former objective carried to implementation via the Motor Carrier Act of 1935. His vision of integrated federal policy-making for transportation also included control of air traffic and pipe lines and appropriate restructuring of the ICC to handle these new burdens. He proposed that the Commission be divided into four sections dealing with railroads, motor and air carriers, water and pipe lines, and finance.

The year 1936 turned out to be one of mounting crisis in the uncertain career of the federal Coordinator of Transportation. In January, in his fourth report, he chastised the railroads for their laggard tendencies and again called for ICC reorganization. Eastman's long-time friend, Commission Chairman Mahaffie, again rejected the reorganization plan, and, one suspects in retaliation, questioned the wisdom of continuing the office of Coordinator.

The railroad executives were even more nettled, denying Eastman's charge that they had failed to meet their public responsibility. Railway labor had other reasons for being lukewarm toward the continuance of the Coordinator's role, although they were not as determined as the executives. The latter, according to Eastman's biographer, "were leaving nothing undone to have the office of Coordinator abolished and its incumbent returned summarily to the Interstate Commerce Commission."

Some minor support for the office was felt at the White House, but no one in Congress undertook to sponsor the continuation of the Emergency Act under which it had been established, and which was due to expire at midnight June 16, 1936. Expire it did, and Eastman, "wiser than he had been, somewhat bruised and battered, but by no means disheartened," returned to his ICC duties after three years' service in the cause of a coordinated transportation policy.

Coordination is demanded when someone or some group concludes that too many authorities exist in a given policy area, which overlap too much, mesh too little, and conflict too often. In a general way, we can assume that this is what both Representative Morse and the White House had in mind when on January 13, 1966, the President said in his State of the Union message:

A new Department of Transportation is needed to bring together our transportation activities. The present structure—35 government agencies, spending $5 billion yearly—makes it almost impossible to serve either the growing demands of this great nation, or the needs of the industry, or the right of the taxpayer to full efficiency and real frugality.

This was followed by the introduction of the actual legislation proposed by the White House early in March, and a lengthy message from the President to the Congress setting forth in detail his proposals and the reasons behind them.

Some of the tactical considerations that went into the draft bill were related in a *New York Times* story appearing on March 13, doubtless the result of a background session in the White House with people who had been involved in drafting it. In general, it seems that the effort had been to take a solid first step, rather than to try to accomplish all that might be desirable at once and fail. A proposal to write into the legislation authority for the new Department to establish uniform standards for the setting of rates, fares, route awards, and subsidies was rejected as too controversial. The uninitiated might feel that this is the very essence of coordination, without which

the bill would be pretty innocuous. But as any good sailor knows, there are many objectives that must be approached by a series of zig-zag tacking maneuvers when winds are adverse.

The White House strategists, it was reported, anticipated some of their strongest opposition from the aviation industry. They proposed to bring the Federal Aviation Agency (which establishes safety regulations, operates air navigation facilities, manages air traffic, and performs similar services) into the Department. But they were sure the Agency would be unhappy with this suggestion. Their airline clients would not want the FAA to have to give up its existing autonomy and become lost in the new conglomerate Department. Furthermore, there would be the aviation industry's knowledge that it would have far less influence over one agency in a large department than over one free from such ties. But the President's advisers apparently decided they were prepared to fight this battle. If they catered to every desire to preserve cherished bureaucratic autonomy, they would literally have had no bill at all!

Clearly, then, the process of policy-making and interest-group influence on that process begins long before the legislation comes up for floor debate, and indeed long before it even gets to the committee-hearing stage. This latter stage is nevertheless a key part of the process because hearings are published, and the pattern of forces at work behind the scenes frequently emerges clearly on the record.

Hearings were held before the Senate Committee on Government Operations on bill S. 3010 on March 29 and 30, May 3, 4, 5, 18, and 19, and again on June 28 and 29. The record of these hearings covers 743 printed pages. On the House side, the President's bill carried the number H.R. 13200; it was considered by a subcommittee of the House Committee on Government Operations four days in April, six days in May, and one in June, producing a total of 856 pages of printed record.

A sampling from the April hearings before the House Committee reveals that the initial appearances before the group were made by heads of existing federal departments and agencies that would be somehow affected or had been involved in preparing the bill. The first of these, introduced by Congressman Dawson, who presided, was Charles L. Schultze, Director of the Bureau of the Budget. He appeared essentially as spokesman for the President, as did the second man to appear, Secretary of Commerce John T. Connor, and the third, Alan Boyd, Undersecretary of Commerce for Transportation. (Boyd later became the first head of the new Department of Transportation, appropriately enough.)

On April 7, 1966, the cast of characters began to change. Though the Commerce Department had a considerable stake in the proposed changes (it would lose to the new Department a segment of its current responsibility and the personnel attached thereto), April 7 saw the appearance of a range of institutional interest groups whose stake was, in a sense, considerably higher. First, there was the Chief of Engineers, U.S. Army. Some might find his presence surprising until it was discovered that certain civilian Engineer Corps functions relative to inland water transportation would now be shared with the new Department if the bill became law. General Cassidy was questioned closely and given every opportunity to express his dissent from the relevant provisions by Committee members who, like many of their congressional colleagues, have a highly developed and cordial community of interest with the Engineer Corps. It is the latter who carry out local rivers-and-harbors projects and similar improvements that fill annual "pork-barrel" bills, from which juicy tidbits are gratefully received in dozens of congressional districts. One surmises from the testimony that the General was not wildly enthusiastic about

the bill, but he was satisfied with its terms, doubtless because the White House drafters had taken carefully into account the powerful vested interests in and out of Congress that center on the Corps' work.

There next appeared representatives of two agencies very closely affected by the proposed bill: the Civil Aeronautics Board and the Federal Aviation Agency. The former was to lose some of its functions to the new Department though retain its identity and much of its role; the latter was to be absorbed in toto. The FAA's representative concluded his statement by noting that "The integrity of its [FAA's] functions and operations are emphasized by the provisions of section 4 (b) of the bill." In other words, a measure of autonomy satisfactory to the FAA was guaranteed.

By far the most venerable set of preexisting agency relationships that would be disrupted by the bill involved the transfer of the Coast Guard from its 175-year association with the Treasury Department. As Admiral Shields, Assistant Commandant, said quite frankly to the Committee:

When we were first consulted . . . our reaction was one of regret in leaving the Treasury Department. . . . A close association has evolved with various Treasury Bureaus as we have worked in supporting their missions. [But] we favor the establishment of the new Department. . . . In the drafting of the bill now before this committee, we stressed the necessity of continuing the Coast Guard's integral status because it is an armed force. . . . Section 6(b) continues this necessary and important status. . . .

Thus did "Hooligan's Navy" (as men of the "real" Navy derisively call it) also seek and win protection for a special degree of autonomy in the new Department.

The next meeting of the Committee to consider the Transportation Department bill was on April 25. The first of a parade of private interests appeared in the form of representatives of the American Waterways Operators, Inc. Some insight into both the clientele of this group and its internal functioning emerged when Mr. Mechling, one of its spokesmen, discussed the resolution, requesting changes in the bill, passed by the association's thirty-seven-man board of directors "made up of executives of towboat and tugboat operating companies, shipyards, terminals, and fleeting companies from throughout the United States." The directors' action followed consideration of the matter by the association's legislative committee under Mechling's chairmanship. Undersecretary of Commerce Boyd had appeared before this committee to discuss the provisions of the legislation with them.

Briefly, the association sought amendments to provide: 1) an Assistant Secretary in the Department for each mode of transportation; 2) provisions leaving with Congress decisions on water resource improvement projects (pork-barrel projects, in other words); and 3) assurances that their Industry's interests would be protected against decisions of the new Secretary. In summary, Mechling emphasized that his people would accept a department that did research, promoted expansion, and dealt with transportation accidents, but did *not* want one with power to "control or allocate what mode should carry the traffic" or "make decisions as to what facilities should or should not be built." In a word, as Representative Holifield, chief protagonist for the bill, noted, this group wanted a weak, decentralized department that would have little, if any, genuine coordinating power and would preserve much of the status quo. The fight, as usual, was for autonomy.

The next witness was Frederick B. Lee, the Director of the National Pilots Association. Interestingly enough, he was a Washington lawyer who had been associated for a number of years with the Civil Aeronautics Administration (which had been merged into the FAA in a 1958 reorganization), serving as Administrator from 1953 to 1955. His appearance as chief witness for an aviation pressure group illustrates a general pattern of the flow of personnel back and forth between government agencies and their organized clienteles outside of government.

Lee's main point was that, while his old agency, the CAA, was in the Department of Commerce, it had had great difficulty securing adequate funds to do its job, that things were much better when it became part of the FAA—an agency set up specifically to work with the aviation industry—and that merger of the FAA into the new Department would revive the old problem. He insisted that coordination of surface and water transportation programs was essential, but that air transport was different: ". . . aviation with its unique problems of growth and rapid technological change should be a separate agency with the Administrator reporting directly to the President of the United States." Coordination in the abstract is fine, and even in practice when applied to someone else, but when an agency's own status is affected it will demand autonomy for unique reasons.

Following Mr. Lee, there appeared representatives of the Air Traffic Control Association, the National Business Aircraft Association, and at another day's hearings, the Common Carrier Conference of Domestic Water Carriers, the Aircraft Owners and Pilots Association, the Grocery Manufacturers of America, Inc., the Air Line Pilots Association, the National Association of State Aviation Officials, the Air Transport Association, and many others.

The last named deserves a further word. This group, as its representative before the Committee noted, includes in its membership most of the nation's scheduled certified air carriers. Much of Mr. Tipton's testimony was a quite sophisticated plea that the FAA be transferred "intact" to the new Department, again with the objective of preserving its autonomy. When pressed by Representative Holifield as to just what he meant, the legal ramifications of his Association's recommendation emerge:

Mr. Holifield: Now, is it your thinking that if the FAA is transferred intact into the new Department very much as the Coast Guard is, that the Administrator would have all his present powers and duties directly and independently of the Secretary of Transportation? Or would they be transferred to the Secretary and delegated to the FAA Administrator?

Mr. Tipton: . . . that the functions of the Administrator . . . would not be transferred to the Secretary of Transportation but would be retained by the Administrator. . . .

Mr. Holifield: . . . then the Secretary of Transportation and his Undersecretaries become, in effect, an advisory board with only the power to advise and recommend. Is this what you seek? And I would assume that the railroad people would come forward with the same type of a recommendation and that the shipping people would . . .

The Coast Guard's successful assertion of a right to autonomy bade fair to become a precedent eagerly seized upon by all other affected parties, each of which could make the same case (to its own satisfaction) for uniqueness and special treatment.

Holifield's mention of the "shipping people" turned out to be oddly prophetic. The major battle over the terms of the bill —in which victory went to a cluster of institutional and associated private interests—involved the "shipping people." Opposition had obviously been building up behind the scenes to the inclusion of the Maritime Administration, then part of the Department of Commerce, in the new Department of Transportation. A series of maritime industry witnesses had appeared before the House Committee (whose

hearings are used here for illustration), including the Director of the Department of Legislation, AFL-CIO, and representatives of the Committee of American Steamship Lines, the Seafarers International Union (whose President, Paul Hall, said he spoke for all maritime labor), and the American Merchant Marine Institute, each of whom insisted that the problems of his industry were unique and that an independent Maritime Administration was essential. At an executive session of the Committee on Government Operations, Representative Edward A. Garmatz, Chairman of the House Committee on Merchant Marine and Fisheries, read a letter transmitting two resolutions passed by his Committee with reference to H.R. 13200. The first called for the establishment of an independent Maritime Administration, and the second requested that the Coast Guard be left in the Treasury. This, obviously, was a flanking maneuver: the maritime industry was using its friends on Representative Garmatz's Committee to bring pressure on the Government Operations Committee, and, eventually, on Congress and the White House.

One month later, on July 21, 1966, *The New York Times* reported:

American shipping executives carefully watched the Washington scene yesterday as organized labor played a major role in a legislative drama that will shape the future of the nation's maritime industry.

They gave "rave reviews" after the American Federation of Labor and Congress of Industrial Organizations had put its political muscle behind bills that would create an independent Federal Maritime Administration.

The account went on to note that labor spokesman Paul Hall, addressing his remarks to Representative Garmatz's sympathetic Committee, had reiterated all of the standard arguments about the uniqueness of the industry and the danger that its vital interests would be neglected by a new Transportation Department. Far more important than anything he said was the ploy that his appearance, and the Merchant Marine Committee hearings themselves, represented. They were bound to, and probably calculated to, embarrass the Johnson Administration. Clearly they were being used by an industrywide coalition of steamship companies and maritime labor as a weapon in what observers predicted would be a nip-and-tuck fight between the two Committees.

The Government Operations Committee, sensing the danger, had hurriedly reported out its bill for a Transportation Department a few days before, hoping, no doubt, to secure floor action before this new threat gained momentum. The Committee did win the next round: a Rules Committee clearance for floor consideration, over the opposition of the Maritime Committee people, who wanted Rules to wait until they were ready to report the separate Maritime Administration proposal. About a week later Representative Garmatz's Committee reported its bill and the race was on, with the industry lustily cheering its team from the sidelines. The Rules Committee obligingly cleared the way for the independent Maritime Administration bill to be given floor consideration also, opening the way for a bitter fight. Meanwhile, the Republican Policy Committee endorsed it and denounced the Johnson Administration for "scuttling" the merchant fleet.

These developments provoked a *Times* reporter to write on August 21:

An Administration proposal to create a Cabinet-level Department of Transportation, which once seemed headed for easy Congressional approval, has been caught in a squeeze being applied by the nation's maritime interests.

On August 24, debate opened on the bill, with aviation, rail, and highway interests generally in support, but likely to reconsider and demand new concessions

if ocean transport won its fight for autonomy. As debate waxed hot on the floor, charges and countercharges flew back and forth via the press. Hall charged that the President had tried to buy off the industry and the unions with a promise to build twenty-five new cargo ships if they dropped their separate commission demand. Representative Holifield, sponsor of the White House bill, claimed that he and other bill supporters had been threatened by Hall with reprisal at the polls for their stand.

On August 30, the House voted 260 to 117 to strip the bill of its provisions covering the maritime industry, and then passed it and sent it to the Senate, 336 to 42. By this time the Senate Committee on Government Operations had virtually completed hearings on the bill as introduced in that branch, but, in an apparent effort to meet the situation that had boiled up at the other end of the capitol, reported out a compromise version. This kept the maritime functions in the Department, but provided these and other divisions with greater autonomy than originally contemplated by making their respective administrators presidential appointees. Despite these efforts, however, the bill as it finally emerged from the conference committee that met to reconcile differences between the House and Senate versions had been shorn of its ocean transport provisions. The maritime coalition had won. On October 14, both houses approved the conference report, and thereby placed their official seal on the results of this bitter interest-group struggle. Two days later, the President participated in the signing ceremony with which this case study opened.

This had been a fight not so much over the shape of public policy (the assumed objective of interest groups), but was, rather, an effort by an array of organized interests, private and governmental, to control and shape the apparatus of government to suit their special objectives. The shape of the bureaucratic apparatus is, of course, inseparable from the policy outcomes it generates. Interests seek to control both. When, for example, an agency enjoys maximum autonomy, it has maximum leeway to shape policy as it sees fit, and its clients have the most flexible possible instrument available to serve their ends. But the same agency integrated into a tight departmental structure will be forced to adapt its decisions to the competing demands of its associates in the department—at the expense, often, of its own clients. In any event, it will be forced to balance client desires against the imperatives of coordination. As a consequence, if an established agency enjoying autonomy confronts a proposed reorganization that will serve high-level government desires for improved coordination and policy integration, the agency and its associated interests almost invariably will resist—fighting to retain their independence. In short, who the policy-makers are and how they relate to each other and to their clients help determine the policy output of government. Groups strive not only to win the game, but also to write the rules.

In 1970 there was an interesting indication that the new Department might well realize at least some of the hopes of those who had urged such an agency over the years. On October 14, 1970 (one day before the fourth anniversary of the approval of the bill that created the Department), President Nixon signed legislation setting up the National Railroad Passenger Corporation. This semipublic body was designed to take over rail passenger service and operate a reorganized set of routes designated by the Department of Transportation. The new policy stopped just short of nationalization of the ailing railroads. Some thirty-five years after Joseph Eastman had served his frustrating stint as Coordinator, it seemed possible that genuine coordination might be on the way. Perhaps a serious effort would now be made to fit a rationalized rail passenger scheme into the overall transportation

system of the nation under the auspices of the Department.

SOURCES

Fuess, Claude M. *Joseph B. Eastman: Servant of the People* (New York: Columbia University Press, 1952).

Latham, Earl G., *The Politics of Railroad Coordination, 1933–1936* (Cambridge: Harvard University Press, 1959).

New York Times, various issues, August, 1965, through October, 1966.

U.S. Congress, House, Committee on Government Operations, *Creating a Department of Transportation,* Hearings, 89th Congress, 2nd session, on H.R. 13200, Parts 1 and 2.

U.S. Congress, Senate, Committee on Government Operations, *Establishing a Department of Transportation,* Hearings, 89th Congress, 2nd session, on S. 3010, Parts 1–4.

interests and government

Interest Groups and Representative Democracy

How do people as citizens relate to a political system? Put more simply, how do they exercise their popular sovereignty, and how do they tell the government what they want and whether they agree or disagree with what their rulers are doing? The chapters in this part of the book are, of course, all designed to answer this question. Obviously the citizen relates to his governors as a voter. Theoretically this is the essence of his "sovereignty." Logically, then, the electoral apparatus in all its complex American forms provides the means for the exercise of voter sovereignty. Political parties perform a similar function by structuring the pattern of choices for the citizen, both as to candidates and as to general policies.

In perhaps less obvious ways, those organized and unorganized groupings called *interest groups* also provide opportunities for the citizen to relate to his government. This kind of popular participation in the political process is less familiar and apparent —and certainly less official—than voting, but it is nonetheless just as real and important. It is, in fact, one of the most obvious forms of influence people attempt to use on public officials, so obvious that it may go quite unnoticed as a form of political action. When a group of neighbors becomes exercised about the need for a stop sign at the corner or annoyed at a zoning change to allow use of a nearby house as a beauty shop, and circulates a petition for presentation at City Hall, they are an interest group taking political action. Moreover, their effort to influence the local government is considerably more direct, and likely to be considerably more effective for their immediate objectives, than reliance on the electoral machinery would be.

As a practical matter, all that the public can ordinarily do to influence government through the machinery of parties and elections is to alter the tone and broad emphases of general policies and programs. Specific influence on policy-making to achieve a specific end must often come through less formal and extralegal approaches, such as those of the neighborhood concerned with the proposed zoning change, or a poor peoples' sit-in to demand more assistance. In light of the countless ways that government does touch the lives of the citizenry, it is usually these specific implementations of policies that citizens are most anxious to influence. To do so they must approach not just legislators or political executives—councilmen, assemblymen, mayors, or governors—but the countless appointive officials staffing the agencies and bureaus that tax, license, regulate, and subsidize so much of their daily lives. In an era of increasingly pervasive government, techniques more subtle and flexible than those represented by the ballot box and party responsibility are required. The interest group has become the focal point for many, if not most, of these extralegal and informal techniques. At the local level, at least in smaller communities, the individual citizen can perhaps approach public officials with his demand or complaint and have some hope of success. Almost invariably, however, successful exertion of influence demands numbers concerted in pursuit of a common end, and some application of the resources of organization, money, know-how, access, public relations, and the other ingredients often disdainfully lumped together as pressure politics.

Despite the failure of classic democratic theory to recognize methods of citizen influence other than those of the ballot box, pressure-group politics are of vast importance both to the ruled and to the rulers. Without the opportunity of using their freedom of association to organize around their interests, the citizens of a democracy would be without effective political influence; and without the information gleaned from group activity, public officials would be far more insecure and frustrated in their efforts to govern than they are. The legitimacy and utility of pressure groups will be reconsidered later in the chapter, after we have examined more closely what they are and how they operate in practice within the American political system.

Interest Groups and American Society

Every textbook on American government provides some definition of an interest or pressure group. Although this book is no exception, its primary objective is not so much the framing of a neat definition for readers to memorize as it is simply to stress the comprehensiveness that should be attached to the term *interest group*. In broadest terms, it covers that whole range of political activity and potential that lies between the involvement of the individual citizen *as* an individual, and the elaborate role played by the political party. Thus defined, the concept of interest group serves to fill much of the void in democratic theory left by the characteristic emphasis of John Stuart Mill and others on the individual citizen-voter as the only political unit worthy of consideration. The development in recent decades of a positive theory of the vital role played by political parties has also helped to fill the void left by classic democratic theory.

More specifically, one can usefully include in the interest-group category entities ranging from the small, ad hoc neighborhood cluster of concerned householders; through the organized association, local or national, with dues-paying members, paid officials, and, of course, objectives that are at least partially political; and on to such vast and amorphous clusters of people with shared, if not wholly self-conscious, interests, such as all consumers of natural gas, all parents of draftable sons, all the isolated elderly, all black people, or even all whites who share concern about the race problem. In other words, the term encompasses political entities almost as small and as casual as two neighbors who agree in conversation over the back fence "that there ought to be a law," the countless organized, articulate, and highly self-conscious groups normally encompassed by the term, and also potential groups with little self-consciousness but possessed of political potential either that they come to realize, or that politicians anticipate in formulating their policy decisions.

To a degree, this pattern of group life mirrors the community that spawns it. This does not mean that the pattern of organized groups replicates with mathematical accuracy every conceivable category of political concern, realized or not, in the society. It does mean, however, that the general pattern of interests in the population will be reflected. The major economic and occupational categories will have their counterparts in organized groups and these counterparts will reflect in their size and strength the prestige as well as the importance of the segments of the society they represent. America's devotion to free enterprise, her achievement ethic, and, therefore, business orientation are reflected in the special prestige and high level of organization of business interest groups. Perhaps even more striking is the power and prestige of the organized representatives of agriculture, particularly when one recalls that a relatively small proportion of the national community is today engaged in farming. Yet our national heritage as a pioneer agrarian society and the central role played by rural values in our scheme of things (even after we became a highly industrialized nation) lend special prestige to the farmers' group representatives.

Labor, on the other hand, numerically superior as a population segment to either agriculture or industry, enjoys far less status in the organizational life of the nation. In fact, it has succeeded in mobilizing considerably less of its organizational potential than the businessman or the farmer. (Some of the reasons for the stepchildlike position occupied by organized labor in the United States were considered in Chapter 1.) As a consequence, although the broad pattern of economic life is bound to reflect itself in the pattern of interest groups, there are differences in the influence and status of the diverse groups that are rooted in the more subtle characteristics of the national community.

Ethnic, religious, and nationality patterns will also, inevitably, find themselves reflected in associational life. Perhaps nowhere does the uniqueness of America's history manifest itself more clearly in the pattern of interest groups than here. A people compounded of as many ethnic and national strains as Americans are inevitably includes in its group life associations spawned by these diversities. And so it has certainly been. The groups themselves—the Irish, the Germans, the French Canadians, the Polish, the Jews, and the Italians—have been among the major entities taken into account by politicians and parties, as have the formal organizations that came forth ostensibly to represent them and preserve their special cultures. Only rarely, however, have these groups bred the kind of separatist and disruptive activity so characteristic elsewhere. Even in Canada, a nation of immigrants like the United

States, Quebec separatism has become a disturbing political force in recent years. *Racial* groups, on the other hand, have posed and are posing formidable problems.

If America has successfully blended ethnic politics into her general interest-group amalgam—with the important exception that will be explored specially—so her unique experiment in religious pluralism has its counterpart in the group life of the country. As with most other interest categories, American religious groupings have not sought political party channels of articulation, but have relied again on associational vehicles. In consequence, they too have added to the richness and variety of the group life of the community rather than fostering the kind of intercreedal warfare that has been characteristic in Europe.[1]

A final, but in recent years increasingly important, category of interest group comprises associational representatives of governmental units, office holders, and employees. These, obviously, exist in order to attempt to influence other political institutions and/or officials. In this category fall groups like the U. S. Conference of Mayors, the National League of Cities, the National Association of Counties, and the growing number of labor unions made up of public employees (see Chapter 10). As we shall note later, specific governmental units such as the city of New York maintain Washington lobby representation.[2]

Group and Public Policy-Making: A Classification

The group life that flourishes in America is, of course, politically significant because of its contributions to the making of public policy. But precisely what kinds of inputs flow from the various categories of groups into the overall process of policy-making? Not surprisingly, the character of the inputs produced by a group is in part a function of its inclusiveness or narrowness of focus. In each of the major areas of economic life—business, labor, and agriculture, for example—there are a few very broadly representative groups that purport to speak for the whole range of activity they seek to cover. The National Association of Manufacturers tries to speak for all manufacturing and related enterprise, while the United States Chamber of Commerce represents itself as the spokesman for an even wider range of commercial and industrial activity. In the area of labor organization, there is a similar umbrella group, the American Federation of Labor and Congress of Industrial Organizations (AFL-CIO), which encompasses many labor unions in a loose federation. Some unions have been traditionally aloof from the AFL-CIO, such as the railroad brotherhoods, and a few, such as the giant Teamsters Union, have been expelled. The huge United Auto Workers broke away in 1968. Finally, there are three major and inclusive farm groups. The largest is the American Farm Bureau Federation, but it faces competi-

---

[1] See James L. Adams, *The Growing Church Lobby in Washington* (Grand Rapids, Mich.: Eerdmans, 1970). Adams notes, among other things, that the churches were heavily involved in lobbying regarding civil rights legislation, the Poverty Program, federal aid to education, and the Vietnam war.

[2] See Suzanne G. Farkas, *Urban Lobbying, Mayors in the Federal Arena.* New York University Press, 1971.

tion from the old-fashioned National Grange and the liberal Farmers' Union. Perhaps all three will in time be challenged by the new National Farmers' Organization.

Groups of this kind tend to lose in concentrated punch what they gain in the breadth of their constituencies. That is, because they try to encompass so much of the spectrum in their sector of the economy, they tend to be relatively loose and amorphous as organizational entities. Furthermore, they must avoid divisive issues when making pronouncements and stick to broad general questions on which their members will not be divided. The Chamber of Commerce, for instance, traditionally has used an elaborate referendum system with its membership to identify issues on which there is enough agreement for the parent organization to take a stand. These business organizations must, for the most part, deal broadly with general issues such as the size of the federal budget or labor policy, while carefully avoiding questions of import quotas, upon which members will certainly have divergent views. The same imperatives govern the other umbrella organizations. It is, of course, true that leaders of such broad groups have some leeway to take specific stands, since the membership is unlikely to be informed in detail on everything said in the group's name.

One level lower in degree of specificity or generality appears the trade association type of group. This, in business, is the organization made up of one particular type of enterprise, e.g., the Iron and Steel Institute representing steel manufacture, or the Association of American Railroads, or any of thousands of similar single-industry groups.[3] Unlike the broader based groups, they usually have more concrete objectives and hence a much greater political punch on a narrower range of issues. Between the level of the trade association and the broad general groups, there are examples of trade association federations—the National Retail Federation is one illustration —that bring together for objectives connected with their common interests a cluster of trade groups that find added strength in such an alliance. Labor organizations have a counterpart to the trade association in their national (or "international") unions such as the Automobile Workers, the Steel Workers, or the Rubber Workers. As with the trade associations, these groups are related to the concerns of a single industry and gain considerable homogeneity of view because of their specific focus. (Unions, especially, also take positions on broad public issues.) In the farm sector, the commodity organization is the analogous category. Associations of all dairymen, apple growers, tobacco growers, and so on can address themselves to the government with more or less united voices. In addition, they often have specific bureaus in the Department of Agriculture set up to deal with the problems encountered in their particular form of agricultural production.

At the most specific level of interest-group activity exists the individual corporation.[4] It is harder to find counterparts in labor or agriculture for this type of interest-group unit. In the business sector, however, the fact that much of the activity of the country is carried on by a few giant corporate entities—many of them controlling far

[3] Louis Galambos in *Competition and Cooperation: The Emergence of a National Trade Association* (Baltimore: Johns Hopkins U.P., 1966) examines the Cotton Textile Institute.
[4] See Edwin M. Epstein, *The Corporation in American Politics* (Englewood Cliffs, N.J.: Prentice-Hall, 1969).

more in assets than all the members of many individual trade associations combined —has fostered a pattern of individual firm representation. Such economic giants as American Telephone and Telegraph, the oil companies, and General Motors are directly affected by government policies relating to antitrust enforcement, offshore oil, oil imports, auto safety standards, labor relations, and other matters. In their view representation through trade associations is not enough, and they maintain their own lobbying establishments. These can be activated on short notice when a particular challenge to their industry or corporate interests arises by, for example, sending in company executives to testify before legislative committees or investigating bodies. Regarding the response of the oil industry to the challenge of the tidelands oil controversy in 1953 (in which the companies were trying to shift the control of these resources from the federal to the state governments), one student has written:

Deployed in full force were the various echelons of respectable law firms, ex-government and congressional personnel, public relations consultants, former and practicing newsmen also serving as advisors and agents, trade association representatives, sales officers, company vice presidents in charge of governmental relations, company legal counsels and public relations executives, specially mobilized "grass roots" organization spokesmen and even men of lesser social status who called themselves and registered as lobbyists.[5]

As the quotation suggests, the persons who actually do the lobbying perform a vital role in interest-group politics. A significant study by Professor Lester W. Milbrath examines their part in the political process, while making a valuable addition to our knowledge of interest groups.[6] Milbrath's study is the first one to use the lobbyist himself, and not the group, as its primary focus: its data are drawn from a carefully selected sample of people who responded to an elaborate schedule of interviews. Milbrath drew his sample from the lists of lobby registrants compiled by the Clerk of the House of Representatives and the Secretary of the Senate. To be sure, the registration in compliance with the Regulation of Lobbying Act of 1946 is of somewhat uncertain coverage. Some register out of an excess of caution, feeling their role *might* be construed as paid lobbying—that is, attempting to influence the passage of legislation before Congress. Others, who probably should, do not register because they claim that they are not really trying to influence the passage or defeat of legislation. Furthermore, anyone who lobbys just the executive establishment is exempt under the registration act. Nevertheless, Milbrath, taking these lists as the best available, drew a scientific sample of 114 (101 of which he actually interviewed) from the 614 names he found on registers for the first half of 1956.

There is particular interest in the breakdown of the various types of interest groups his sample encompassed. The figures, in somewhat abbreviated form, are presented in Table 6.1.

The leading role played by trade associations and by business groups in general is notable. There are fifty-two trade associations, nearly half of the total; if the seventeen corporations are added, well over half of the sample is composed of this cate-

[5] Robert Engler, *The Politics of Oil* (New York: Macmillan, 1961), p. 373.
[6] *The Washington Lobbyists* (Chicago: Rand McNally, 1963).

Table 6.1	Labor organizations	18
Interest groups in Washington	Farm organizations	5
	Trade associations	52
Source: Lester W. Milbrath, *The Washington Lobbyists* (Chicago: Rand, McNally & Company, 1963), p. 31.	Corporations	17
	Citizen groups	6
	Service or veterans groups	2
	Church/humanitarian groups	5
	Foreign governments or firms	2
	More than one type	7
	Total	114

gory. The table also shows that, although most of the groups are directly or indirectly economic in base, several noneconomic types are represented.

Among the more interesting entries on the table is that for foreign governments or firms. Foreign governments presumably have always been interested in attempting to influence the policies of the United States through something that might be described as lobbying, but this has obviously grown enormously in an era of massive foreign aid, intense competition by other nations for the support of the United States against potential enemies, and elaborate arrangements for the management of international trade and monetary policies. In 1962, to cite an example, data on foreign lobbying emerged on the front pages because of publicity given to efforts to win import quotas under newly passed legislation to regulate sales of foreign sugar in the United States. Most of these efforts were directed at the chairman of the House Committee on Agriculture, Representative Harold D. Cooley of North Carolina. No less than twenty-three countries were represented by lobbyists, most of them Washington lawyers retained for the purpose.[7]

The Unorganized and the Underrepresented

The "fit" between the pattern of the organized groups just described and the full panorama of interests within the community (actual and potential) is by no means a perfect one. Quite the contrary—organized and articulate groups speak for only a portion of the American society. The oil industry, for instance, which involves but a tiny portion of the nation's population even when all its employees and stockholders are included, has such an intimate and potent relationship with government that it has been called "the fourth branch of government."[8] At the other extreme, as noted in Chapter 1, well over half of the population belongs to one or more groups, but the remainder, some 43 per cent, belong to and hence are represented by none.

[7] *New York Times,* July 15, 1962.
[8] Erwin Knoll, "The Oil Lobby Is Not Depleted," *New York Times Magazine,* March 8, 1970, p. 26.

Clearly, these and other data that could be cited indicate that a substantial part of the population is not directly represented by any interest group. The data also show that this tends to be the poorer and more disadvantaged in the community.

Vast numbers of blacks and whites who are below the poverty line play no part in interest-group politics, and their needs and desires are therefore at best indirectly represented in this important aspect of the democratic political process. To some extent, established political leaders are anxious and able to speak for these segments of the population. The NAACP, a middle-class organization, has for many years vigorously represented the cause of Negro rights in the courts and the Congress. The Southern Christian Leadership Conference organized the 1968 Poor Peoples' Campaign, which culminated in the construction of Resurrection City in a Washington, D.C., park. Self-appointed representatives of the poor in Congress and the executive branch spurred the original passage of antipoverty legislation. This in turn has spawned organizational activity in poverty and ghetto areas by providing for the election of neighborhood members of various advisory and administrative boards and councils. Spotty as the record of these groups has been, they provide something new in representation for the poor.

Nevertheless, the lack of direct representation, through either political parties or interest groups, for a substantial portion of the national community, constitutes a potential danger to the stability of the political system. Members of organized interests by virtue of their organization and the self-consciousness about their needs that is thus engendered are able to make specific requests and introduce carefully worked-out new policy proposals. The unorganized lack a means of articulating their discontents and frustrations, or even of developing an understanding of how government might be persuaded to meet their needs. The government, lacking both incentives and cues to action, may allow situations to smolder until they explode.

The black ghetto riots that have become an almost expected part of urban life graphically depict the problem. Such savage outbursts of anger and resentment are, of course, one kind of process through which group demands can be articulated. But orgies of arson, looting, and sniping demonstrate only that remedial action is imperatively required. They provide little guidance as to the kind of action the government should take. Even worse, they harden attitudes of hostility on the part of both blacks and whites toward each other, and thus make peaceful reform more difficult.

It remains to be seen how the black power movement will fit into this picture. Its angry rhetoric of outrage and hostility makes many whites very uncomfortable. Yet many black power groups show signs of constructively fostering racial pride. The seemingly systematic attacks by police and local prosecutors against one such group, the Black Panthers, may, however, have the effect of driving other groups toward more overt violence. Few would dare predict what will ultimately happen.

It is a momentous challenge to American attitudes, which emphasize government by consensus, to cope with growing alienation in a part of the citizenry. One thing is certain. No system of interest-group politics, democratic or not, can survive when too large a portion of its constituents denies its validity and rejects its rules.

The Accessible Structure of American Governments

As might be expected, the network of relationships that links the interest groups with government and the policy-making process generally, and through which they seek to exert influence, is a highly complex one. The point has already been made that the ballot box is by no means the only channel of access the citizen has to his government, and that the mass of activity that falls under the heading of interest-group politics supplements election politics in important ways. Even a sampling of the avenues of access available to interest groups amply confirms the assertion that in sheer bulk, as well as in flexibility, these rival the legal franchise as guarantors of popular sovereignty. In fact, one of the important reasons why interest politics have loomed so large in the American political system is the number and variety of points of access to the policy-making process that our constitutional scheme provides.

By contrast, in Britain, though something may be gained by approaching local authorities or Parliament in quest of influence on policy-making, it is essentially the national executive that is the most important point of contact. Unless the Cabinet— or the responsible Minister—can be persuaded, the chances of influencing major policy decisions are minimal. What this means, in short, is that the key to policy-making lies with the leadership of the current majority party. For the countless more routine policy matters in which British interests seek access to policy-makers, the civil servants in the departments must be seen. Relations between administrative personnel and interest-group representatives in London are very close indeed. Often the two will be from the same exclusive social group from which Britain traditionally draws her top permanent civil servants. The formal incorporation of group representatives into the machinery of government, as well as numerous informal contacts, links the departments with their clientele. In turn, because the organized interests have easy entree to the departments, they are inhibited from seeking access in Parliament; it is simply an unnecessary supplement to a successfully functioning departmental tie. All of this takes place in what Professor Abraham Holtzman refers to as a "cultural milieu that approves the articulation of claims by interest groups and the consideration of such claims in the making of public policy." [9] We tend to view interest-group politics less favorably, appropriate as they may be in our system.

American pressure groups not only have a choice of three branches of the national government to approach—the President, Congress, and the courts—and the administrative "fourth branch," but also the partially sovereign state governments with their own tripartite structures. At the national level, we normally think of lobbying as taking place in the halls (literally, and this is probably the derivation of the term) of Congress. Yet the advantages that accrue to a group that enlists

---

[9] *Interest Groups and Lobbying* (New York: Macmillan, 1966), p. 40.

the President on its side are obvious. Even in the era of Calvin Coolidge, as the Vermonter often made clear in his press conferences, he was pressured to make favorable mention of this or that pending measure on which some group sought congressional action.

The usefulness of the courts, and especially of the Supreme Court, need hardly be underscored for those who have been even casual readers of the press since the landmark school desegregation decision of 1954. As a matter of carefully calculated long-term strategy, the NAACP's Legal Defense and Educational Fund, in full realization of the fact that southern control of Congress made the legislative avenue to civil rights progress unpromising, moved forward on first one and then another judicial front. It chose and fought test cases, prepared *amicus curiae* briefs, and even went so far as to foster a spate of law review articles regarding the law affecting restrictive covenants on real estate. Their purpose was to change subtly the climate of legal thinking and thereby provide a more conducive atmosphere for a new ruling.

When Professor Milbrath questioned his lobbyist respondents he found that only 18 in his sample of 114 dealt only with Congress when advocating their group's point of view, whereas 85 dealt with both Congress and the executive branch. Interestingly, when the sample is examined more closely, it turns out that of the 52 trade association lobbyists, 42 mentioned both branches, but of the large labor organizations, only half cited the executive as well as Congress. Labor is more likely to be concerned with broad welfare and policy questions, whereas trade associations apparently often find themselves dealing with administrative personnel regarding more narrow matters of concern for their industries.[10] These figures must be read against the fact that lobbyists who deal only with the executive establishment are not required by law to register at all. If one assumes there are a substantial number with this sole preoccupation, in addition to the major concern the registered lobbyists have with the departments and the bureaus, then the true importance of these executive contacts becomes evident. The fact that the incentive to deal with both branches is much greater here than in Britain hardly detracts from the major importance of the departments as points of access and concern for American interest groups.

What about interest groups and political parties? Again, one would expect the contrast with Britain to be marked. Our parties are simply not as central to the policy-making process as their counterparts abroad, and Professor Milbrath's figures bear out this assumption. In fact, he finds even less contact than one might expect. It is often suggested that interest groups appear before party convention platform committees to state their case and seek party support. Actually, he found that 62 per cent of his sample said they never presented their views before the platform committee of a major party, and 58 per cent said they never have contact with party officials at all in the conduct of their business. Approximately three quarters of the lobbyists did indicate having made contributions at campaign time, though to in-

---

[10] Op. cit., p. 163 and passim.

dividual candidates rather than to the party organizations.[11] Labor organizations are a partial exception to this tendency in that they at times become involved in party-like activity on behalf of candidates they favor at the grass roots level.[12]

In short, the American national government does offer the lobbyist a variety of tactical opportunities for access by virtue of its tripartite—one could even say, quadripartite—structure. Moreover, the federal system multiplies the opportunities open to an interest group with skillful leadership. What cannot be accomplished by approaching one level of government can often be secured from another. During the nineteenth century, when only the states were presumed likely or competent to tamper with the freedom of the entrepreneur, business used the courts, whenever possible, to nullify state regulatory efforts. Later, as business expanded and its activities became national in scope, those bent on securing regulation turned to the national government as the only authority capable of dealing on equal terms with the corporate giants. At this point a familiar cry—states' rights—was again heard. The attorneys and publicists for the large enterprises argued that business regulation was exclusively a state, not a federal, prerogative, a rather cynical argument made with the knowledge that most regulation was beyond the ability of individual states to implement.

A more recent example of the same kind of group maneuver occurred during the tidelands oil controversy in the mid-twentieth century. At issue was the control of the rich oil reserves under the ocean floor off the coasts of the United States, especially those off California and Louisiana. Under the leadership of President Truman the federal government established its superior rights to these oil lands by obtaining a judicial decision in favor of federal control. The oil companies counter-attacked by arguing that the lands were properly a state responsibility and that federal control threatened the rights of the states. But, as one scholar observed:

> the solicitude of the oil companies for states' rights is hardly based on convictions derived from political theory, but rather on fears that federal ownership may result in the cancellation or modification of state leases favorable to their interests, their knowledge that they can successfully cope with state oil regulatory agencies, and uncertainty concerning their ability to control a federal agency.[13]

The companies secured enactment of legislation by Congress confirming state control, but it was vetoed by the President. Then, following the 1952 election of General Eisenhower, they tried again. This time they found a sympathetic ear in the White House, and a bill was passed and signed that effectively reversed the judicial decision and established state control. These events have a double significance. Not only were the oil interests using opportunities provided by the federal system to by-pass distasteful governmental control, but they played one branch of the federal government—the Congress—off against the other two, and later secured one of these—

---

[11] Ibid., pp. 270ff.

[12] See J. David Greenstone, *Labor in American Politics* (New York: Random House, 1969).

[13] Quoted in Harmon Zeigler, *Interest Groups in American Society* (Englewood Cliffs, N.J.: Prentice-Hall, 1964), p. 48.

the Presidency—as an ally after an election changed the occupants of the White House. The structure of the American system of government does indeed reward the skillful interest-group tactician!

Resources and History

Although the structural framework of government provides the lobbyist with many advantages, he can usually draw on other resources too. A reasonably complete list of resource categories includes organization, membership, legitimacy and prestige, money, information, entree, and allies. Organization refers to the group's degree of centralization and cohesiveness, the kind of staff employed, and similar considerations. The number of members and their loyalty and capacity for mobilization behind a group stand are obviously most important. The question of a group's legitimacy and prestige has already been noted. Money as a source of power and influence needs little explanation, though the resources of entree and information are less obvious. Entree includes the personal contacts and other means of securing the ear of the policy-maker; information is shorthand for the data—not wholly unbiased—that a group supplies to government officials to aid them in their making of policy decisions.

Each of these is a resource to an interest group because in the last analysis it represents either a presumed ability to mobilize votes in support of a demand, or a carefully nurtured reservoir of goodwill and understanding that can be used to win concessions. The stock in trade of the interest group in dealing with government is, in short, votes and favors. In this respect the lobbyist is in very much the same position as any other politician. The legislator, for instance, secures his position by mobilizing a majority of the votes in his state or district, and he holds it by maintaining the support of as many voting blocs and individual voters as he can. This he accomplishes, in turn, partly by doing favors for constituents and group leaders in exchange for which they provide continued support. The appointive official, or even the civil servant, finds himself in a more or less similar position. He may not be directly dependent upon votes, but he is dependent on others who are! The growth and even the survival of his agency may depend on his ability to show key members of Congress that its services are worth votes *to them*. And the mutual exchange of favors and services between administrators and legislators also plays its role in smoothing what otherwise might well be an antagonistic relationship.

The lobbyist, though technically outside this interlocking system of executive and legislative officials, relates to it on very much the same terms that its various actors relate to each other. He can act as broker of votes back home that he is able to deliver, or claims to be able to influence for or against the legislator. Actually, of course, he will rarely reach the point of threatening to withhold electoral support. If he has the votes to deliver or divert, his legislator target will know it as well as he does and will shape his action accordingly. In the favors category fall information that the lobbyist is able to provide and the money he may donate for campaign war chests, in exchange for which he is more likely to want entree than a specific vote on a specific measure. His most valuable asset is a friendly relationship with an administrator or legislator, which will gain him an ear when he needs it, provide him with a sympathetic hearing, and, in the best of all possible worlds, provide a more or less automatic guarantee of support for whatever his group wants.

Before we take a closer look at this contemporary pattern of interest-group politics, it should be pointed out that things were not always so complex. The elaboration and refinement of interest-group tactics paralleled, naturally, the growth in the needs felt by private groups for access to the policy-making process, and this in turn came with the broadening scope of activity engaged in by the federal government and the state governments. Yet at the same time, there probably never was a period in American history—nor in the history of any free government—during which there were not some activities carried on with the aim of influencing policy that, however primitive, could be identified as interest-group activities. The record of the first Congress, for example, indicates that it was subjected to great pressures on behalf of the controversial fiscal policies proposed by Secretary of the Treasury Alexander Hamilton. As the eighteenth century gave way to the nineteenth, certain lines of policy emerged that became fruitful and continuing targets for pressure activity: tariffs, patent renewals, land grants, and internal improvements. The range was not broad, yet the stakes for those concerned were high. No student of American history need be reminded of the key role played by the periodic orgies of tariff revision, not only in the activity of Congress, but in national political struggles generally.

In an era of economic transformation from agricultural to industrial pursuits, certain inventions played key roles, and lobbyists were often hired to secure the necessary legislation for renewal when the statutory period of protection threatened to expire. The princely grants to the railroads and the growing role of the national government in financing internal improvements, eventually known as the annual "pork-barrel" raids on the Treasury, were stimulated by persistent efforts to create favorable climates of congressional opinion. Although a few of the national associations active today had their origins in the last century, most of the efforts to cultivate Congress were carried on by lobbyists available to any prospective client for a fee.

Their approach by and large was *ad hominem* and quite nonideological. The structure of Congress has always lent itself to tactics whereby influence over a small number of key members could produce favorable results. Such lobbyists of the last century as Samuel Ward acted on this awareness. Ward, often called king of the lobbyists in his day, offered his services for a fee. During the Civil War he was much involved in war contracts; after the war his clients included the major railroad and telegraph interests. In promoting legislation for such employers, he and others like him wined and dined legislators, who, in those days, were more inclined to come to the seat of the government without the sobering influence of their families and live the unsatisfactory existence of boardinghouse dwellers. Apparently the lobbyists also catered to other needs of the Congressmen by helping to pay off gambling debts, and bribery was probably much more prevalent then than in recent decades.

The pay-offs today now seem to take the more subtle form of campaign contributions or the purchase of $100 tickets to fund-raising and testimonial dinners. How common these practices are, for which the late Senator Thomas J. Dodd of Connecticut was censured in 1967, no one seems to know—or at least no one is willing to say. (Dodd was accused of collecting twice for air fares and using money raised at dinners held in his honor for personal expenses.) But during the nineteenth century the lobbyists' tactics could be relatively simple. Transportation and communication were slow, and the Congressman was far less intimately in touch with the people back home than he is today. As a result, the "folks back home" very probably were far more habituated to ignoring the Washington scene and concentrating their attention on the state capitals, where most of the governing that affected their lives took place. Because the federal government rarely touched the ordinary citizen in his daily life, a lobbyist able to persuade the key legislators with personal contacts seasoned with a bit of discreet bribery could often accomplish a great deal.

The year 1890 is perhaps as convenient as any to take as signaling a change in lobbyist tactics. Actually, of course, the new patterns took shape gradually. But in that year popular concern with the "trusts" communicated itself to Congress sufficiently that the Sherman Anti-Trust Act was passed. Little was done to enforce it for some years, and even Theodore Roosevelt's tirades against these restrictive business combinations were accompanied by relatively little action. Nonetheless, for the first time business was seriously put on the defensive. Furthermore, the passage of the Sherman Act, along with the Interstate Commerce Act, which three years earlier established the Interstate Commerce Commission to regulate railroad rates, marked the start of a growing involvement in economic affairs by the national government. The response of the newly threatened business community was, naturally, organization. The National Association of Manufacturers, for example, was established in 1895. In 1912 the Chamber of Commerce appeared as a national organization. With the coming of World War I and America's first experience with near-total war mobilization, the government, in order to make dealing with major segments of industry easier, fostered and encouraged the development of trade associations. The same result flowed from the ill-starred National Recovery Administration (NRA) of the early New Deal. A scheme for self-government in industry, it also involved government sponsorship for industrywide organization so that the resulting trade associations could negotiate the codes of fair practice that were the basis of the NRA policy.

The impact of World War I and of the NRA in encouraging the growth of trade associations raises the broader question of what, generally speaking, causes the multiplication of organized interest groups. One theory is the simple notion that an increasingly complex community and economy will naturally generate organized groups that can speak for its proliferating interests. Doubtless this is part of the answer. Others have advanced the disequilibrium theory: a segment of the community that finds itself placed at a disadvantage because of some new development or change in the balance of power among groups will organize to protect itself and restore its previous position. Yet if this is the case, why does union membership, for example, decline in periods of unemployment?

Professor Robert Salisbury advances a third theory based on a benefit exchange notion.[14] His basic idea is that people join organized interest groups because they expect to receive in benefits from their membership at least as much as they put in by way of time or membership fees. Accordingly, memberships are more likely to climb in periods of relative prosperity, when there are surplus resources available in the hands of prospective members; memberships are likely to fall when a period of belt-tightening sets in. Salisbury's explanation emphasizes the group "entre-preneur." Just as in more orthodox business ventures, so with interest groups, an entrepreneur must invest "capital" in forming a group and must "sell" advantages or services to members sufficient to attract them as "customers" (members) and to hold their "patronage." If the members do not feel they are getting value for value invested, or can no longer afford their membership, they will drop out and the group will decline. This essentially economically derived model of group development explains much about the dynamics of the overall process.

In America, a massive campaign mounted by the associated private power companies during the twenties to head off government involvement in power generation and transmission was the prototype of a major change in modern interest-group politics; it adapted the highly successful mass propaganda campaign mounted by the federal government's Committee on Public Information during World War I. With the coming of the New Deal, American politics polarized along ideological lines to a degree unlike anything in the past. This coincided with the launching of the Social Security system as a first modest installment in the welfare state and new federal incursions into economic regulation that were typified by controversial labor relations and public utilities legislation. At the same time many businessmen and citizens in the upper income groups came increasingly to fear and hate the leading sponsor of this New Deal legislation, President Franklin D. Roosevelt.

These developments gave birth to a new type of interest group, whose primary concern was to undertake research and propaganda aimed at ideological tendencies it thought dangerous or misguided. On the right wing of the political spectrum, for example, there emerged the Committee for Constitutional Government, and on the left various groups affiliated with labor unions. Organizations of this sort, aided by public figures in and out of politics, conducted a vigorous dialogue replete with mutual accusations that the other side was "socialistic" or "reactionary," which lasted from the mid-1930's until roughly the early 1960's. During the 1964 presidential campaign there was a new rapprochement between labor and the Democratic Party on the one hand, and the business community on the other, leaving the articulation of right-wing views to the John Birch Society and similar groups. After that, the traditional left splintered badly because of the divisive impact of the war in Vietnam and the growth of black nationalism as a new force in race relations.

What seems to be happening now, besides a sharp decline in concern with ideological issues on the part of the major economic groups in the nation, is an increasing preoccupation with these issues by extremist groups, right and left, who

[14] "An Exchange Theory of Interest Groups," in *Interest Group Politics in America,* ed. by Robert H. Salisbury (New York: Harper, 1970), pp. 32–67.

are at least partially alienated from the political system itself. The strident utterances and conspiratorial notions of the John Birch Society have at least a partial counterpart in the theories propounded by the so-called "New Left," such as the Students for a Democratic Society (SDS) and other similar groups. In turn, both share some of the frustration with the "power structure" that is the hallmark of the black nationalist groups. Although individual observers may disagree in their evaluations, all of these groups appear to share a common rejection of the normal assumptions governing interest-group politics and a desire to change the game itself—not merely to win a larger share of its rewards.

To conclude this brief tour of group history, it is clear that several developments caused the supplanting of the simple lobbying tactics of the last century with the much more complex pattern we know today: the revolution in transportation and communication that put the Congressman in much closer touch with his district and rendered him less of a free agent than he had been, the growth of business organization, and the rapid movement of the federal government into areas of regulation that had been left to the states or not touched at all earlier and that induced economic groups to organize. The responses to these changed conditions included the emergence of more elaborate Washington lobbying offices that replaced the single lobbyist who worked for a fee, an increased emphasis on contacting the folks back home as a means of swaying their representatives in Washington, and the introduction of public relations campaigns and what is now known as institutional advertising.

the politics of interest groups

Group Resources

At the very heart of interest-group politics lies the notion that collective rather than individual action can more effectively influence public policy. Accordingly, a group's organizational strength is a crucial factor. If it is a loose confederation of relatively dissimilar entities with partially divergent interests—the classic example is the AFL-CIO—then its punch will be drastically diminished. If, like the Anti-Saloon League in its heyday, it is a highly centralized power structure, it can pack a tremendous wallop. The Anti-Saloon League was ostensibly a union of various state leagues, but actual power was concentrated in the national organization. Care was taken to ensure that the more populous states like New York, which at the same time seemed less dependable than the more thinly populated agricultural states of the Bible Belt, were limited in their representation on the national board of directors. Key officials at the state level were appointed by the national officials, and throughout, control was effectively in the hands of a full-time, salaried bureaucracy.[15]

Common Cause, a "citizen's lobby," formed in September, 1970, by former Secretary of Health, Education and Welfare John Gardner, represents a direct and obvious effort to implement the theory that only collective action is likely to be effective. It already claims credit for helping to bring about the January, 1971, reforms in Congress mentioned in Chapter 8. Its thousands of individual members are organized from the grass roots upward in a manner that is designed to make the taking of concerted action, such as bringing pressure on Congress, rapid and unified. The success of such an interest-group venture will depend in large part, in the long run, on the success Gardner has in playing the group entrepreneurial role already described, and on the ability of the group to maintain its unity on policy. Its Policy

---

[15] See Peter H. Odegard, *Pressure Politics: The Story of the Anti-Saloon League* (Boulder: U. of Colorado, 1928).

Council has chosen its "causes" thus far, though it aims at broadly based member participation in the future.

It is axiomatic in the life of groups that in practice most of them are run by a small, active minority. The bulk of the members of union locals, clubs, or similar groups often do not even attend meetings, retaining but a nominal affiliation and rarely taking an active part in the affairs of the association. In consequence, the small number that are interested, often because they derive some particular material or psychic advantages from their leadership roles, effectively run things. This has been labeled in a famous monograph "the iron law of oligarchy." [16] Contrary to what might be thought, the passivity of most members is not a sign of organizational weakness. If the leaders act more or less responsibly in concert with the apparent views of the members, and if their rise to prominence was the result of a natural selection process that pushed the most talented to the top, the bureaucratization of an interest group's leadership can actually be a source of strength. For example, in the case of the Anti-Saloon League the transfer of effective control to a corps of professional career employees meant, as bureaucratization often means, the maximization of effectiveness. An oligarchical leadership group, after all, has a strong vested interest in the survival and growth of the organization, and it will presumably promote its development with all of its ingenuity. There are indeed cases in which an individual or a small group actually creates a pressure group that they can head and that supplies them with a career and income! During the New Deal, a conservation law was passed providing for government grants to farmers to be used in applying lime to their fields. The program encountered annual resistance in Congress until a Department of Agriculture employee named Robert Koch left the government and organized the National Agricultural Limestone Institute to sell the program. Quite naturally he went to the limestone industry for aid and eventually put together a hard-hitting lobby whose backbone was some four hundred manufacturers and distributors of agricultural limestone.[17]

The relations of an interest group to other interest groups can also be a source of either strength or weakness, for very frequently the organization of one interest group breeds a counterorganization. Any group can almost automatically assume that those who oppose its objectives will organize, thereby providing the basis for a long-term rivalry and mutual harassment as both camps try to influence the making of public policy. According to the findings of Lester Milbrath, however, this situation does not always develop. In reply to a question as to the kinds of opposition groups that they faced, his sample turned up twenty-seven cases of little or no organized opposition. Only a fifth of the lobbyists offered replies that clearly fitted the expectation that they had to contend with a directly competitive organized group. The remaining respondents listed their opposition as consisting of competing economic forces or political philosophies.[18]

In the other direction, ad hoc alliances among friendly groups may provide a

---

[16] Robert Michels, *Political Parties* (New York: Dover, 1959).

[17] Wesley McCune, *Who's Behind Our Farm Policy?* (New York: Praeger, 1956).

[18] Op. cit., p. 50.

major source of strength to the component groups when faced with a challenge that directly or indirectly affects all.[19] Thus, in the 1930's a conflict between the chain stores and the independent merchants, who were on the defensive and sought laws to limit the chains, moved into the nation's legislatures. At the state level, the independents had the upper hand because of their ties in the local communities and their ability to tag their opponents as "foreign big business." The locale then shifted to Congress, where efforts were made in 1938 to curb chains through the device of a special tax. But here the chains turned out to have the upper hand, successfully putting together a formidable coalition of supporters. Although the National Association of Retail Druggists allied itself with the independents, other organizations such as the Farm Bureau Federation, the National Association of Real Estate Boards, many large food manufacturers, some labor unions, and the Departments of Agriculture and Commerce joined the chains in keeping the tax bill bottled up in a congressional committee.[20]

A more recent illustration of such intergroup alliances—this one related to an issue of much broader national importance—involved the effort by Senator Everett M. Dirksen, the Senate's Republican Minority Leader, in the mid-1960's to reverse the Supreme Court ruling on equal apportionment of legislative seats. In January, 1966, a new group calling itself the Committee for Government of the People was organized under the backstage auspices of a famous California public relations firm specializing in political campaigns, Whitaker and Baxter. Supporting this Committee were some familiar faces in American interest-group politics: the Farm Bureau, the Chamber of Commerce, the National Association of Manufacturers, the National Association of Real Estate Boards, the National Grange, and, interestingly, the politically liberal National Farmers' Union.[21] All, apparently, perceived the equalizing of urban with rural legislative representation as a threat, and their alliance was a broad one that spanned the economic spectrum. Despite its strength, the congressional supporters of the Supreme Court decision, who were themselves allied with a powerful coalition of civil rights, church, and labor groups (the Leadership Conference on Civil Rights), were able to block the Dirksen amendment.

The second major resource of interest groups is their membership. The range of possibilities is, of course, almost limitless. Groups may have a mass of individual members, as do the veterans' groups, or be very small and highly specialized—such as a recently organized association of state lieutenant governors! Membership figures for the various veterans' organizations show the American Legion with 2.6 million members, the Veterans of Foreign Wars with 1.3 million, and the three smaller groups listing a total of 665,000, an impressive combined total of over 4.5 million. On the other hand, the members of an interest group may not be individuals at all, but rather corporations (as in the NAM), component unions (as in the AFL-CIO), or individual firms, as in the case of virtually any trade association. The significance

---

[19] See Donald R. Hall, *Cooperative Lobbying, The Power of Pressure* (Tucson: U. of Arizona, 1969).

[20] Zeigler, op. cit., p. 46.

[21] *New York Times,* January 19, 1966.

of the membership naturally varies according to its loyalty and the completeness of its absorption in the group, and hence, the corresponding likelihood that it will follow the activities of the group carefully and respond to leadership calls for united support. The American Medical Association has often illustrated the power that can be wielded by a mass membership organization whose members are absorbed in the group and responsive to it. Yet it was revealed at the time of the 1971 annual convention of the AMA that membership growth had so far failed to keep pace with the growth in the medical profession that, for the first time in half a century, less than 50 per cent of the nation's doctors belonged. This development reflects rising discontent among young doctors with their national association, and it will certainly weaken the political impact of the AMA.

One of the key characteristics of the interest group, and one of the things, as noted in Chapter 1, that makes this form of political grouping congenial to Americans, is that it does not usually attempt to envelop the member completely. Instead, most such groups attempt to represent only one facet of the member's life or daily activity: his occupation or profession, his hobby (the National Rifle Association, the Isaak Walton League), his religious affiliation, or his concern with civic issues (the American Civil Liberties Union, the League of Women Voters, or Common Cause). Many people—about a third of those sampled in America by Professors Almond and Verba—belong to more than one group.[22] Others will feel an affinity for additional groups, even though they may not actually hold formal membership. Thus, numerous individuals with no church ties nevertheless call themselves Protestants.

This matter of multiple or overlapping membership, as students of group theory have called it, is important because it is one of the key factors in determining the relation an individual will have to any particular group. If his union pulls him one way, but his church group, or neighborhood association, or veterans' organization is pulling him another way, neither is likely to end up with his total loyalty. In fact, the cross-pressured member may resolve the dilemma by withdrawing entirely from the dispute. Even such groups as churches that make something approaching total claims on their members receive in practice no more than a partial loyalty. The most devout American church member, though granting to his minister or priest complete authority in matters of faith and morals, will often decline to follow urgings from the pulpit that he vote a certain way. Politics, he will feel, is outside the legitimate scope of a religious body's authority. This feeling has prompted membership revolts in more than one Protestant denomination whose national leadership voted appropriations to one or another militant black cause. In one such instance, the issue was a contribution to the defense fund for Angela Davis; Miss Davis, a former University of California faculty member, is a self-avowed Communist who was accused of complicity in the spectacular killing of a California judge in a shootout at the Marin County Hall of Justice. (She was ultimately tried and acquitted.)

[22] See Chapter 1.

This aspect of an interest group's claim to the loyalty of its members, which raises the question of its ability to make good on threats to withhold the electoral support, or, conversely, on promises to deliver votes to a favored candidate, is both crucial and unanswerable. It is crucial because, as noted earlier, the votes of the membership are theoretically the ultimate weapon any group possesses. Much of what the lobbyist says and does in his efforts to exert influence carries weight because these threats or promises loom, perhaps unspoken, in the background. Yet it is virtually impossible to prove with any remote degree of certainty that group efforts to deliver their membership at the ballot box either do or do not succeed.

The late Professor V. O. Key, Jr., a careful and painstaking analyst of political behavior, cites two major problems faced by the student of interest-group impact on voting (and, it should be added, by the group leader as well). Most people most of the time vote in response to long-term, even inherited, party loyalties. The leader who would activate his followers along lines that parallel their natural tendencies may well appear to have considerable impact. But when John L. Lewis, the legendary and seemingly all-powerful head of the United Mine Workers, tried to get his devoted followers (who customarily voted Democratic) to vote for Wendell Willkie in 1940, their devotion stopped short of accepting his demand that they abandon Franklin D. Roosevelt.

Key cites figures to illustrate the second problem (it is relevant to the first as well): that when electoral tides are running in a certain direction, voters of all categories and classes tend to respond. Table 6.2 shows the Republican presidential vote in percentages cast by members of union families, and by all manual-worker families. Throughout this period, it is true, union voters were more Democratic than nonunion, and this suggests that the members responded to some degree to the exhortations of their leaders. Yet the broad trends among manual workers in general (many of whom are not union members) were in the same direction, and this would indicate that the Democratic votes cast by the union members were essentially a reflection of fundamental political currents. Moreover, in the two Eisenhower elections of 1952 and 1956, both groups shifted heavily in the Republican direction against their leaders' will, maintaining then as in other years, a quite uniform differential between the two groups.

Any effort to study systematically the voting behavior of members of trade associations, veterans groups, or other groups, which presumably have even less of a hold on their members than labor unions, would encounter even more serious problems. It would be virtually impossible to isolate the impact of group leadership factors from the host of other influences that play on the voter. Key sums up the problem well:

Clearly the model of the lobbyist who speaks for a united following, determined in its aims and prepared to reward its friends and punish its enemies at the polls, does not often fit reality. . . . Yet legislators listen respectfully to the representations of the spokesmen of private groups. . . . All this activity must have some functional significance in the political system.[23]

[23] *Public Opinion and American Democracy* (New York: Knopf, 1961), p. 525.

Table 6.2
Republican percentage of union and manual-worker families' vote

Source: V. O. Key, Jr., *Public Opinion and American Democracy* (New York: Alfred A. Knopf, Inc., 1961). Copyright 1961 by V. O. Key, Jr. Reprinted by permission of Alfred A. Knopf, Inc., p. 523.

	Union families	Manual-worker families
1936	20%	26%
1940	28	34
1944	28	38
1948	27	34
1952	39	45
1956	43	50
1960	35	40

The third major resource potentially available to an interest group, which has already been touched on, is the influence generated by its legitimacy and prestige. Business groups typically enjoy high public prestige, as do the associations of such professional people as doctors, lawyers, or professors, whereas labor unions carry lower prestige with many people. To be sure, high prestige, even that of religious organizations in a nation noted for its religiosity, may not be automatically transferable into political influence. Prestige and legitimacy are important, *but* the group must be viewed as *properly* the source of political demands or influence.

By the same token, nonmembers may be influenced by the stand a group takes. To put the point somewhat more technically, an organization may play the role of reference group for large numbers of people who have never had anything directly to do with it at all. Many will support or look favorably upon a proposal put forth by a labor union, because of its source and their general sympathies with the liberal stand that unions generally take. Alternatively, those with a more conservative bent may be moved to supporting a position endorsed by a prominent business group in a particular controversy. (Of course, the reference-group influence can work in reverse; many persons think that anything favored by labor unions is automatically bad.) Such groups as the Americans for Democratic Action, the American Civil Liberties Union, the League of Women Voters, and many research and ideologically oriented organizations spread across the political spectrum undoubtedly have a considerable part of their influence as reference groups. If they were to rely on the power they could wield by virtue of the size of their memberships alone, they would be of little consequence in the political process.

How, one might well ask, does such a phenomenon as Ralph Nader, the consumer crusader, fit into this kind of analysis? He certainly does not qualify as an "interest group" even when his fellow researchers are taken into account! And yet he has had the kind of impact on public policy that countless interest groups with hundreds or even thousands of members only dream about. Why? The question is not easily answered. Information is an ingredient in pressure-group power, and Nader's careful research has turned up potent information of unquestioned accuracy. The eager willingness of legislators to latch onto a new issue, as in the case of Nader's carefully documented arguments for auto safety, that might enhance their legislative record and prestige probably accounts in part for Nader's success. Unquestionably, too, his earnest, unselfish, and unbiased approach has brought him prestige that is of enormous value in the political struggle. Historically he fits into a group of crusaders and muckrakers, such as Upton Sinclair, whose exposure of the filthy conditions in slaughterhouses hastened corrective legislation just after the turn of the century. It could even be that individuals such as Nader or Sinclair are the exceptions who prove the rule that the individual citizen must join an organization to be effective.

Group Tactics

Each of the resource categories discussed so far derives its significance from the electoral weight that interest groups, either directly or indirectly, can muster, but the remaining categories have a different basis. They correspond with the favor doing tactics that the politician uses to build up credit balances of gratitude to be drawn upon at some future date. Through the shrewd use of these tactics, even groups that are far too weak numerically to threaten anyone with ballot-box punishment can exert considerable influence. The first of these categories refers to the capacity of a group to make or place friends where they can provide assistance when it is needed. Entree may be no more than the simple matter of cultivating individuals in Congress, on congressional staffs, or in the agencies, who out of sheer friendship and trust will make themselves useful at some later time. Or it may take the form of actually placing personnel in key agency positions where they can aid the interest group, or conversely, of securing the services on lobbying staffs of former office-holders or government employees who can turn their past experience to advantage on behalf of their new employers.

The flow of personnel to government from private groups, and from government employ to interest-group staffs, is the easiest to document of these various tactics for gaining entree. When the Johnson Administration left office and the Nixon Administration came in, a familiar pattern was reenacted. For instance, the Department of the Interior gained as its new Secretary Walter Hickel, known to have interests in resource development in his state of Alaska. Interior, of course, is the chief custodian of the portion of the public domain under direct federal control and plays an important role in regulating industries like the oil industry. An even clearer case of the placing of an interest-group man in a corresponding government position was the appointment of James G. Watt, former lobbyist and secretary of the National Resources Committee of the U.S. Chamber of Commerce, as Deputy Assistant Secretary of the Interior for water and power development.[24] Moving in the other direction were five former Johnson Administration officials who registered as lobbyists, respectively, for Procter and Gamble Manufacturing Co. (a former White House assistant); for the A.F.L.-C.I.O. (a former official of the Department of

[24] *Providence* (Rhode Island) *Journal,* May 31, 1969.

Table 6.3

Lobbyists' prior careers

Source: Lester W. Milbrath, *The Washington Lobbyists* (Chicago: Rand McNally & Company, 1963), p. 68.

Nothing else prior	2
Lawyer	9
Journalist	1
Elective public office	3
Businessman	18
Government job—exec.	41
Government job—legis.	16
Other professional	4
Labor union employee	5
Other	7
No response	8
Total	114

Health, Education and Welfare); for the Communications Satellite Corp. (a former Assistant Secretary of State); for the American Association of Retired Persons and the National Retired Teachers Association (a former Veterans Administration official); and for the Emergency Committee for Gun Control and the National Music Publishers Association (!) (another former State Department and HEW employee).[25]

Professor Milbrath asked his sample of lobbyists what their occupation had been immediately prior to their shift to a career of lobbying. The results are instructive as developed by Milbrath in Table 6.3. By far the biggest clustering is in the category of former government personnel, almost entirely former staff people rather than elective officeholders. And of these, the great bulk came from the executive branch. All together, those who indicated government work as their former occupation accounted for more than half of the sample. (The only other large category is former businessmen, many of whom, doubtless, found their way into lobbying through connections with trade associations to whose staffs they may well have been sent by their companies.) This preeminence of former government personnel among the lobbyists clearly underscores the usefulness tc interest groups of this type of entree.

The defense establishment and the vast number of businesses that work for the military under contract or supply products that the armed forces require represent, especially in periods like the Korean or Vietnamese wars, an enormously important realm of interaction between government and private groups. The stake that aircraft companies, missile manufacturers, and potential suppliers of other major weapons systems have in the allocation of defense contracts would be hard indeed to over-estimate. But at the same time, the countless suppliers of clothing, small hardware, petroleum and food products, though individually their stakes may seem small, cumulatively also play a very important role. All of these imperatively need access

[25] *New York Times,* April 20, 1969.

Table 6.4		
Whom the lobbyist sees	Members of Congress	26
	Staff assistants to members	7
Source: Lester W. Milbrath, *The*	Congressional committee staffs	28
Washington Lobbyists (Chicago: Rand	Executive agency staffs	27
McNally & Company, 1963), p. 266.	Miscellaneous and no response	26
	Total	114

to the officials who distribute the vital largesse—the defense procurement contracts. It is hardly surprising, then, that one student of interest groups has written, "A recent check indicated that nearly 1500 retired military officers were on the staffs of companies holding 80 per cent of outstanding contracts." [26]

An interesting final question on the subject of entree has to do with precisely whom the lobbyist most often sees. What kinds of officials does he cultivate and develop as his contacts? Granted that only lobbyists that have occasion to deal with Congress have to register, Professor Milbrath's sample replied to this question as shown in Table 6.4. The next to last entry would very probably be larger if lobbyists dealing only with the executive departments also had to register. Perhaps the most interesting finding in the data is that the group representative is considerably more likely to seek out staff people, and in dealing with Congress, committee staff people, than the members themselves. The Congressman's time is limited, and, though the lobbyist may occasionally need to see him, often business can be transacted as effectively with a staff person. The special usefulness of committee staff personnel is clear. It is the committee unit, rather than the individual member (or Congress as a whole), that is the crucial entity for the interest group. And it is the staffer, rather than the Congressman (with many other demands on his time), who is likely to have the work of the committee and the desires of interested outsiders most continually in mind.

A graphic illustration of the tactical utility of having entree with a friendly member of a legislative body emerges in the following statement by one of the lobbyists whom Milbrath interviewed:

Once in a while, in order to convince someone that they ought to go along on a compromise measure, we will completely block a thing. We will get some friend of ours to just nail up something tight in committee. Then when the fellow realizes what has hit him he will come around and say, "All right, let's talk, I understand now what you mean, so let's go to work on this thing." [27]

Having that friendly committee member who is willing to do the "nailing" and thereby provide a group with the tactical advantage it needs can be exceedingly use-

[26] Zeigler, op. cit., p. 125.
[27] Op. cit., p. 51.

ful. The comment also underscores the obvious point that the lobbyist does not always ask legislators for their votes; some less-direct form of aid may actually be more important.

Take another example of really high-powered entree:

On Thursday evening, Nov. 6, 1969, the Governors of three states met over a quiet dinner at the Tavern Club in Washington with Frank N. Ikard, a former Texas Congressman who is now president of the American Petroleum Institute, the trade association of the nation's largest oil companies. . . . [B]y coincidence or otherwise—the same three Governors and a fourth were at the White House early the next morning to urge the Nixon Administration to retain the 11-year-old system of import quotas, which costs consumers more than $5-billion a year in higher prices for petroleum products.[28]

To be sure, their meeting was not with the President himself, but rather with a presidential assistant who served as the staff expert on oil. The four governors brought with them telegrams of support from thirteen other state chief executives. Any interest group that can mobilize a third of the state governors as its emissaries, and has ready access to presidential assistants, has entree indeed! The quota system is yet to be significantly modified despite the anguished cries of consumers in the Northeast—though the Administration made a small concession in 1972.

When entree is not secured by the planting or hiring of personnel, there are ways of securing a cooperative relationship through the exchange of favors. To a very substantial degree a lobbyist is a broker in information, and information is a major form of the currency of exchange in politics generally and in interest-group politics particularly. Often the lobbyist is hired by his parent organization primarily to supply them with information, rather than, as is popularly supposed, to sway legislators. The organization and its clientele need to know what bills have been introduced that might affect their business, and thus one of their agent's tasks is constantly to monitor the flow of legislative proposals and to provide advice on which are dangerous possibilities and how to deal with them. Equally vital, in this era of the regulatory state, is monitoring the flow of administrative orders and decisions that affect the parent organization and its interests.

The importance of these services, plus the role the lobbyist plays in supplying information to legislators and executive officials, suggests that he must spend less time than is commonly supposed in patrolling the legislative corridors and more at his desk doing research. Professor Milbrath's interviews reveal that this is indeed the case. Most of his respondents reported spending 10 per cent or less of their time calling on Congressmen or executive branch officials. There are, of course, other reasons besides the competing demands on the lobbyist's time for this low figure. For one thing, a visit to the office of a legislator may well take far more time in research and prior preparation than will be consumed in the actual call. For another, the old political adage, "Do not carry your pitcher to the well too often," applies here as elsewhere in the system. If you cash all your claims on favors and wear out your

[28] Knoll, op. cit., pp. 26 and 104.

welcome unnecessarily, you may be at a disadvantage when a major crisis arises later. As for just loitering around the corridors, most respondents reported spending little if any time in this presumably traditional pursuit. Seventy per cent of all the lobbyists reported that at least half their time was consumed working in their own offices: phoning (at times a more efficient way of making contacts than personal visits), doing research, preparing testimony for a committee hearing, and reading official documents to keep abreast of developments of importance to the interest group. Some reported spending as much as 90 per cent of their time in these office-bound ways.[29]

The relation of these activities to the central business of contriving the means for influence exertion emerges from a listing Professor Donald R. Matthews has compiled in the course of interviewing Senators for his study of that body.[30] In the first place, the lobbyist can perform much of the research and many of the speech-writing chores that otherwise would have to be done in the Senator's office. Senators who are especially eager for publicity, and those in the party that does not control the White House, are particularly pleased to get this kind of help. The latter do not have access to the information resources of the departments that their majority party colleagues do, and without lobbyists they would have to allocate much staff time to digging out needed facts and figures. The fact that Senators (and members of the House, too) must specialize in one or a few areas of policy, which leaves little time for other areas politically relevant to their careers, offers the lobbyist yet another opportunity to be of service. Friendly legislators can be supplied with information and warned of impending developments that they should know about. In addition, lobbyists may draft bills, advise on legislative tactics, and help build support for bills both in and out of Congress. As a rule these forms of aid are not pressed upon the Senator and his staff. Quite the contrary, the legislator requests them, though the lobbyist tries to develop this kind of relationship. "We try to get them habitually to draw upon our services," said one. Another noted, "If you make a Congressman or Senator look good, he'll come to *you* for help." [31]

More familiar perhaps is the information that the interest group supplies through its representative in the course of committee hearings. Here, too, legislators can readily become dependent on outside groups for the data and ideas upon which to make legislative decisions. This is, of course, hardly less true of the administrative branch. A familiar form of interest-group assistance to the departments and agencies is that of reviewing on request draft rules and specifications before they are to go into effect. For the agency charged with implementing a broad congressional policy by issuing detailed administrative orders, this prior solicitation of comment both provides needed expert information and criticism and helps create a cooperative atmosphere. From the standpoint of the private interests, it gives them a chance to win back some of what they may have lost in the original passage of the legislation. If they can

[29] Milbrath, p. 117 and passim.
[30] *U.S. Senators and Their World* (New York. Vintage, 1960), pp. 183ff.
[31] Ibid.

show that a certain requirement cannot be met for technical reasons, their position will be improved. When Congress recently required safety features on automobiles, the actual details were hammered out with the industry in just this fashion.

Money as a resource available to interest groups can be overrated, though its indirect importance is, of course, considerable. To take the oil and gas industry once more as an example, although no one knows how much of its money pours into politics, there is common agreement that it outspends all other industries. Much of this money flows into presidential campaigns (on the Republican side usually). Congress, however, is not neglected. Oilmen were prominent contributors to the Nixon personal expense fund that became a cause célèbre during his 1952 campaign for Vice President. The investigations of the affairs of former Senate Majority Secretary Bobby Baker revealed that he was both the collector and the distributor of oil largesse, rewarding through the Democratic Senate Campaign Committee those members of the body who could be counted on to vote the way the industry preferred.[32]

Money is by no means the entire story in interest-group politics. Arguments to the effect that certain groups have much more to spend in securing influence than others, thereby creating a dangerous disparity, may often be countered with the assertion that financially poorer groups like labor do at least have far larger mass membership bases. Potential votes, however problematical their full mobilization, certainly are also a valuable asset. The real questions are what kinds of things can money buy for the interest group, and how important are these in the overall picture of interest-group politics?

Professor Matthews tells the story of two women watching a Senator and a lobbyist in conversation, whereupon one said to the other: "Is he bribing him now?" [33] Actually, of course, as a lobbyist put it, "The green stuff doesn't change hands much any more." [34] What, then, can money buy if not votes sold on the auction block? Staff, expertise, the talents of prestige law firms, and, above all in this image-conscious era, public relations talents—these are likely to come at a high price. Most commonly the interest group uses a public relations campaign, not to head off a particular measure, but to create a favorable impression of the group or industry in the public mind. True, the American Medical Association did spend vast sums in a concentrated campaign to defeat President Truman's national health insurance scheme, and it may well have affected the result through its efforts, but campaigns of this kind are the exception rather than the rule. General Motors used some of its corporate funds to investigate the private life of Ralph Nader at the height of his campaign against the auto industry, only to have Nader win a large cash court judgment against them, and put the proceeds into supporting further investigations!

More typical are the continuing advertising campaigns that are conducted in the mass-circulation magazines on behalf of the private power companies. Their objective is to demonstrate to the public that the government should not take tax dollars in order to build competing public generating facilities. A similar effort was mounted

[32] Knoll, op. cit., pp. 108ff.
[33] Op. cit., p. 176.
[34] Ibid., p. 178.

on behalf of the oil industry after World War II. In 1946 it received the report of an elaborate opinion survey showing that in general the public was poorly informed about the oil industry, and harbored some dark suspicions about price-fixing, the holding back of new developments that might cut sales, and monopoly tendencies. The survey organization urged its clients that the basic lack of information provided an opportunity to fill the vacuum with favorable content. For instance, when the sample had been asked how retail prices were determined, 56 per cent did not know, and 13 per cent said, "They get together." Because of these consultations it was decided to mount a public relations campaign emphasizing the industry's progressiveness. The PR consultants argued that "the progressive character of the industry is its best defense against regulation. A public impressed with that characterization . . . is likely to think: 'Let it alone—there's no need to nationalize a progressive!' " [35] Specific pitches were also aimed at specific information gaps. It was found, for example, that the more companies people thought there were in the industry, the less monopolistic it seemed and the more favorable was their attitude. The advertising therefore called attention to the fact that there were 42,000 independent competing companies in addition to some 200,000 gas station operators. Eventually this campaign was put into the hands of an industry-created body, the Oil Information Committee, which grew to a staff of more than one hundred employees and an annual budget of over $3 million.

As with other forms of interest-group activity, it is well nigh impossible to assess precisely the effectiveness of this kind of institutional advertising. Unquestionably, however, the great corporations were well advised to give up their "public be damned" attitudes of years gone by. Moreover, in a society that is basically favorable to the institutions of free enterprise, especially in times of prosperity, yet that harbors populistic suspicions of bigness and monopoly, image-building may help keep a balance favorable to industry.

The Rules of the Game

Any survey of interest-group tactics and techniques of the sort just traversed implies the existence of norms and rules of the game within which such activity is normally conducted. These, in turn, are functions both of the liberal ideology and the particular cultural values of the society in question. As noted earlier, the American political culture is less hospitable to overt interest-group activity than the British, but it does at least grudgingly condone most of the practices discussed in the preceding pages. Needless to say, the limits set by the rules of the game on group activity are not fixed for all time. The only more or less immutable recognition accorded to interest-group politics in classical democratic theory is freedom of association and the right to petition, both of which are constitutionally guaranteed in the Bill of Rights. And yet, as our sketch of the history of lobbying suggested, changing circumstances, needs, and technology have brought an ever-widening array of techniques within the bounds of

[35] Engler, op. cit., p. 434 and passim.

legitimate group activity. For example, in recent decades the Supreme Court has taken the position that peaceful picketing by union representatives is a form of communication protected by the free speech clause of the First Amendment.

Until recently, violence and quasi-violence were ostensibly proscribed by the rules of the game that Americans generally applied to group tactics. This may have been true on the surface, but recent scholarship makes a persuasive case that, as one commentator put it: "violence [is] deeply ingrained in the American tradition and . . . virtually every group in our history [has] used it for protection or to gain an end." [36] This proposition was massively documented in the collection of studies entitled *Violence in America: Historical and Comparative Perspective* prepared for the Commission on the Causes and Prevention of Violence in 1969.[37] This volent tradition is clearly seen in the settling of the West (as we are reminded interminably on television) and in the early efforts of workingmen to organize unions—for example, the bloody Homestead, Pennsylvania, steel strike of 1892.

In recent years there have been accelerating changes taking place in American practices regarding group tactics, some of which are gradually incorporating tactics reminiscent of this violent past into the realm of the legitimate and acceptable. Perhaps the early black lunch-counter and restaurant sit-ins marked the beginning of this trend. These have since been upheld by the Supreme Court as legal means of protest. These were followed by "wade-ins" at public swimming pools and similar efforts, all of which unquestionably helped the spread of integration of community facilities.[38]

Mass demonstrations and direct action have since become standard tactics for civil rights groups, for citizens protesting the war in Vietnam, even for students who object to the way universities are governed.[39] The lines separating some of these activities from the city race riots are not wholly clear. All are forms of articulating demands and grievances and pressuring authorities into taking remedial action. But what is legitimate and what is not? The contemporary rules of the game are obviously in a state of flux, out of which will have to emerge a set of new boundaries. The trend toward militancy is well represented in the tart comment of black leader H. Rap Brown that "Violence is as American as cherry pie." No one can deny the presence of violence in American history. Violence has marked group struggles between labor and management and scarred racial relations. Individual assassins have cut down in just a few years a President, a Senator, a Nobel Peace Prize-winning civil rights leader, and seriously wounded a Governor running for the 1972 Presidential nomination. The consequences of continued physical violence are alarming to contemplate. No democratic system can survive if such means become a standard resource for its interest groups or its citizens.

[36] John Herbers, "It *Is* as American as Cherry Pie," *New York Times,* June 8, 1969.

[37] Edited by Ted Robert Gurr and Hugh Davis Graham (Washington, D.C.: U.S. G. P. O., 1969).

[38] See John Herbers, "Nonviolence Making Quiet Gains in U.S. Despite Disorders," *New York Times,* April 5, 1970.

[39] See Richard Rogin, "Now It's Welfare Lib," *New York Times Magazine,* September 27, 1970; and Michael Lipsky, "Protest as a Political Resource," *American Political Science Review,* December, 1968.

"Would you believe that the streets are full of rioting farmers . . . ?"

Figure 6.1.

Interest Groups
at the State and Local Level

Aside from differences of size and scale, there is little that sharply differentiates interest-group tactics at the state and local levels from those used with the national government. In fact, everything known about democratic political systems leads to the expectation that group activity flourishes at any level of government at which decisions are made, unless the scale is so small that face-to-face influence by individuals is normally possible.

At the state level, the similarities with the national scene are most striking. Some states like California, New York, or Texas are such large political entities that the profusion, range and variety, level of organization, and other characteristics of the array of interests active at the state capital will compare very closely with those in Washington.[40] Even in the territorially smallest state (tiny Rhode Island), there is widespread group activity. In the course of the 1970 session of the Rhode Island General Assembly, seventy-seven individuals registered under the lobby registration provisions as "legislative counsel before committees"; another thirty-two signed in as "legislative agents." The distinction is between lawyers retained to lobby on behalf of a client (counsel), and nonlawyers such as union representatives (agents).

Lobbying in Albany is big business, befitting the size and complexity of the Empire State. Many of the lobbyists, as in Rhode Island and elsewhere, are lawyers, some of whom represent the New York Stock Exchange, Consolidated Edison, the

[40] Lewis A. Froman, Jr., "Some Effects of Interest Group Strength in State Politics," *American Political Science Review,* December, 1966.

AFL-CIO, Mobil Oil, Columbia University, farmers, liquor dealers, and policemen's unions.[41] There are instances, known to insiders, in which in good entrepreneurial fashion, lobbyists have sought to have bills introduced inimical to a particular interest, so that they could then seek a retainer from the threatened industry to get the bill sidetracked. In the 1969 legislative session, the records of itemized expenses in the custody of the Secretary of State show over a million dollars expended in lobby activity. The most expensive effort was put on by the United Federation of Teachers, which reported spending $629,198.42. They were concerned about the urban school decentralization issue. The Sperry and Hutchinson Company mounted a much more modest effort, costing $13,000, to block a series of measures that would hurt the trading-stamp business, including one that would force stores that give stamps to provide cash instead to customers who refused the stamps.

Illustrating again the links between government and lobbying in personnel terms, David K. Shipler of the *New York Times* has written: "Probably the best paid lobbyist here is Mr. Carlino, the Long Beach, L.I., Republican who served as Speaker of the Assembly from 1959 to 1964. To some observers, Mr. Carlino's power in the Legislature seems to have diminished only slightly since his defeat by the voters in 1964." [42] Shipler goes on to note that Carlino earned a fee of $25,000 from the New York Racing Association to push a bill legalizing pari-mutuel betting. (Newsmen saw a Democratic Assemblyman passing out free passes to the tracks to his colleagues during the vote on this bill.) Three men who were aides of the former speaker while he was in office are currently acting as lobbyists.

Despite a remarkable similarity to the Washington scene, some characteristics of the state level do differentiate it from national lobbying. Leadership in the state legislature tends to be more concentrated in the hands of the House Speaker, the party leaders, and similar functionaries. In contrast, the power structure in Washington is much more dispersed. At the state level, moreover, whole ranges of federal policy questions are absent. Thus, national defense procurement or regulation of interstate and foreign commerce are of no particular concern to interest groups operating in the state capitals.

Though state governmental structures differ somewhat, the overall constitutional arrangement of three branches, each susceptible to group influence, is found at the state level as well as the national. State court systems may be somewhat less useful to the lobbyist because their subservience to the federal Supreme Court is quite immediate on any matter that has national constitutional implications, but the same possibilities for approaching chief executives, administrators, and agencies exist.

Professor Andrew Hacker has illustrated this point vividly in a case study of a struggle in Pennsylvania between the trucking industry and the railroads over weight limits imposed on trucks using the public highways.[43] Each side in this fiercely fought

[41] David K. Shipler, "Lobbyists Play Big Role in Albany Law Making," *New York Times,* February 1, 1970.

[42] Ibid.

[43] "Pressure Politics in Pennsylvania: The Truckers vs. The Railroads," in Alan F. Westin, *The Uses of Power* (New York: Harcourt, 1962), pp. 323–376.

battle used a basically different strategy, which was an outgrowth of its particular strength as an interest group, and sought to use a different pressure point in the state government to exert its influence. The Pennsylvania Motor Truck Association (PMTA), a trade association made up of the trucking firms doing business in the state, made a concentrated effort to win over a majority of the legislators to its cause. "An association composed of small businessmen situated in local communities has," Professor Hacker noted, "for that very reason, a potential array of ground troops for a political battle." [44] Using this base and an elaborate lobby setup in Harrisburg, the PMTA demonstrated great strength in the state.

Its primary adversary was the Eastern Railroad Presidents Conference and the Pennsylvania Railroad, one of the largest in the country (the now-bankrupt Penn Central). Structurally, the railroads differed sharply from the truckers as an interest group. As large corporations, many of which were located out of the state, they had to synthesize, as it were, the kind of grass-roots base their opponents already had. This they sought to do by retaining a public relations firm to launch an elaborate campaign in the mass media. When a trucker-sponsored bill relaxing rate limits did pass the legislature, it was vetoed by the Governor. The public relations firm later insisted that it had created a prorailroad climate of opinion to which the Governor responded. In Pennsylvania, then, the legislative and executive branches, along with the public itself, all became targets for influence in an interest-group campaign virtually identical with many conducted at the national level.

In a recent and very good study of lobbying at the state legislative level, L. Harmon Zeigler and G. Wayne Peak compared patterns in four states: Massachusetts, North Carolina, Utah, and Oregon. They found, as one might imagine, substantial differences in style and effectiveness. Lobbyists in the two western states, for example, turned out to be more influential than those in the two chosen from the eastern seaboard. To some extent this seems to be true because party competition is more highly developed in the latter pair of states than in the former. Furthermore, lobbyists in Utah and Oregon appear to be responding to situations in which the stakes of politics are higher than in Massachusetts and North Carolina. Yet, the authors also note, "in comparison with other sources of influence within the state legislatures, lobbyists, even in Utah and Oregon, do not appear to be very effective." [45]

As might be expected, at the local government level, although there are many striking similarities, the differences in degree are somewhat more pronounced. At this level there are significant differences in the structure of government. If there is a strong mayoralty system in a city, it may well be that the mayor alone represents *the* important pressure point, with the council or municipal legislative body in a decidedly secondary role. But the opposite may also be the case. Professor Edward C. Banfield's description of the government of the Chicago/Cook County metropoli-

---

[44] Ibid., p. 333.
[45] *Lobbying: Interaction and Influence in American State Legislatures* (Belmont, Calif.: Wadsworth, 1969), p. 199 and passim.

tan area reveals a system of unbelievably complicated decentralization.[46] The would-be influencer of policy is faced, not just with the problem of selecting the proper pressure point, but of identifying the half dozen or more individuals or bodies whose agreement must be sought, or veto avoided, if a program is to become a reality. Mayor Richard Daley has power that to a degree transcends this fantastic pattern of political pluralism, but it is power based, not on constitutional grants, but on extralegal cohesion imposed by the last of the big-city political machines.

The first job of the interest group at the local level is, therefore, to identify which of several governmental units needs to be persuaded. The second is to discover whether local government can do what is wanted at all, without either authorization from the state capital or funds and approval from Washington. The route of the local lobbyist may be circuitous indeed before he reaches his policy goal. So important is the role of the state government in city affairs that many cities maintain full-time lobbyists in the state capital. In Providence, for example, a top assistant to the Mayor patrols the State House corridors regularly during legislative sessions. In recent years the federal government has become even more vital to the cities' interests, and they have responded by stepping into the ranks of the Washington lobbyists. Federal programs for combating poverty, constructing public housing, improving water resource and sewage disposal facilities, and renewing urban areas—to name only a few—have brought mayors and their representatives hat in hand to various departments of the federal government.

New York City has had a full-time lobbyist in Washington for some time. In April, 1970, a new lobbyist, Neel H. Klores, was appointed. At the time of his appointment, Klores was a federal antipoverty official who had spent the previous five years administering aid programs for Indians, migrant farm workers, and people in Puerto Rico, Guam, and American Samoa. Klores is a lawyer whose position pays $28,000 a year and includes a staff of three and an annual budget of $100,000. The job consists of "protecting the city's interests in legislation going through Congress and of guiding applications for Federal aid grants through the Federal departments and agencies." [47] Presumably, Klores worked to support Mayor Lindsay's interest in the enactment of President Nixon's plan for sharing federal revenues with states and cities.

Professors Wallace S. Sayre and Herbert Kaufman, who made a major study of the government and politics of New York City, have prepared a diagram (see Figure 6.2) that usefully illustrates the workings of interest-group politics in the city.[48] Civic groups and the communications media fall into the second (northeast) quadrant; they have wide-ranging interests and, at the same time, display a high level of activity. This type of group, however, tends to be rare. In the first (northwest) quadrant are to be found equally active groups, but ones with quite narrow and restricted con-

---

[46] See Edward C. Banfield, *Political Influence* (New York: Free Press, 1961).

[47] Richard L. Madden, "City's Lobbyist Sets Forth Aims," *New York Times,* April 5, 1970.

[48] *Governing New York City: Politics in the Metropolis* (New York: Norton, 1965). Much of the following is drawn from Ch. 13, "Non-governmental Groups and Governmental Action."

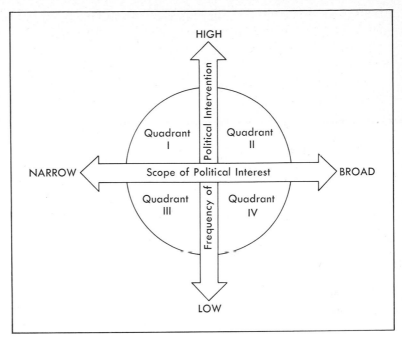

Figure 6.2. Classification of nongovernmental groups by scope of political interest and frequency of political intervention in governmental decision-making.

Source: Wallace S. Sayre and Herbert Kaufman, *Governing New York City: Politics in the Metropolis* (New York: Russell Sage Foundation, 1965), p. 79.

cerns—in health, in the enforcement of the building code, or in some other specific program. They, like the first set of groups, are highly active and quite successful, but far more numerous. In the third (southwest) quadrant fall either groups of the neighborhood sort that spring up in response to a particular problem, or citywide ad hoc organizations that are formed in order to fight fluoridation or to undertake some other specific battle. These groups, therefore, are infrequent or limited political participants moved to action by a particular provocation. The fourth quadrant (southeast) is virtually vacant because its occupants would have to have the unlikely attributes of a low level of activity but wide-ranging interests!

The various groups identified by Sayre and Kaufman have open to them numerous modes of exerting influence that the authors divided into two obvious categories, direct and indirect. The direct influences comprise, first of all, the giving of testimony at public hearings held by the Board of Estimate (the "upper house" of the city legislature), the City Planning Commission, and the committees of the City Council. In five selected years between 1927 and 1955, there were more than nineteen hundred appearances before, or communications to, the Board of Estimate. In contrast to these highly formal approaches, there are manifold opportunities for informal liaison and influence, as for instance, between the Fire Department and the fire insurance companies or between the Department of Health and the food-processing industry.

Contacts at social functions are always of considerable importance and rank as significant ingredients in the total pattern of group-government interaction. The formal incorporation of groups or their views into the governing process through the mechanism of advisory bodies and formal consultation are also features of interest-group politics in New York and other cities, as they are at the national level.

Indirect modes of influence include attempts to manipulate the selection of office-holders with an eye to securing a "friend at court" who may be of future assistance. Such attempts are commonly made when parties nominate their candidates and when administrative offices have appointments to make. At times groups have a long-recognized, if not actually a statutory, right to the selection of particular officials from the ranks of their group or profession. Appeals for public support, public relations campaigns, and other tactics involving the mass media can bring potent indirect influence to bear. Ethnic, racial, and religious groups frequently approach the parties and seek their mediation in a dispute with a city department or agency. Resorting to a higher (and presumably more sympathetic) official to bring pressure on a lesser and more reluctant functionary is another effective tactic; sometimes it is even possible to persuade a federal official to bring his influence to bear on a city department. Finally, there is always the possibility of coalescing with other like-minded groups and using the cumulative strength of such an ad hoc alliance to win a struggle.

Sayre and Kaufman sum up their discussion of New York City interest-group politics with conclusions that are certainly applicable to the impact of private groups wherever they are found:

. . . [Any] group can fight City Hall, almost every group does, and many are remarkably effective. . . . [But] this process is not without its costs. . . . Every positive policy, every new idea, must run a gauntlet fatal to many. Originality and innovation always face a hostile reception; the odds at the start favor the obstructors. . . . The balance between the need for community leadership and the desire for group influence on governmental decisions is always delicate. However the New York City adjustment may be evaluated, one feature of it will probably gain widespread agreement: this is indeed an open political system.[49]

Interest Groups in a Democratic Political System

It is a significant commentary on American political culture that the role and even the very existence of interest groups as major parts of the system have come under almost continual questioning.[50] Some of the reasons for this were discussed in the first chapter. The theme of the criticism in the past has normally been that somehow the public interest is submerged, distorted, or abandoned entirely in the face of the special pleadings of the "pressure boys." Government, therefore, must be insulated from or learn to cope with these insidious influences.

[49] Ibid., p. 515.

[50] One of the most comprehensive current critiques of the role of interest groups and the pluralist interpretation of the American political system is to be found in Theodore J. Lowi, *The End of Liberalism* (New York: Norton, 1969).

Laws intended to compel the registration of interest groups who seek to influence legislation have been the most prevalent political solution to this problem. If only, it is thought, the lobbyists can be made to emerge into the bright light of publicity so that legislators can see their true interests, the lawmakers will be able to gird themselves and hold out for the public interest. Little more need be said to indicate the limited success of this approach. Not only do questions about the constitutionality of such registration and penalty provisions follow hard on the heels of the more obvious queries as to who is supposed to register, but who is going to bother reading the resulting list once registration has been accomplished, and what, precisely, is the legislator to do if he does read it?

A more realistic approach to the evaluation of the impact of organized interests on the political system might well begin with a rephrasing of this very sentence. It is not a question, at bottom, of impact *on* the system, but rather of role *in* the system. If a democratic political system, such as the American one, is as pluralistic as has been argued earlier, and if its policy-making organs and potentials are as multiform as the chapters of this volume seem to insist, then organized interests are no less a part of the system than are the formal institutional mechanisms.

Actually, the dilemma that Sayre and Kaufman pose in the quotation concluding the last section constitutes the real problem. Let it be granted that in the political system of the United States, or for that matter in the City of New York or in any democratic political system, the process of policy-making is, usually, a fragmented affair characteristic of pluralistic political systems. (Put theoretically, it is in this same fragmentation that there is to be found the democratic responsiveness to popular wishes that must be the hallmark of popular government.) Yet fragmented policymaking in which inaction may be easier for a minority to bring about than action can mean dangerously ineffective government. The corrective must be found in the skills of political leadership, or in the coordinating potential of institutional or bureaucratic centralization. But what is the resulting loss in governmental responsiveness to the subleties of group needs and demands, and how much such loss can a democratic system tolerate? This is the problem of balance posed by Sayre and Kaufman.

There is no magic formula for locating the ideal point of equipoise. The times and the circumstances, as well as the demands of groups themselves, will determine how much responsiveness balanced against how much leadership, coordination, and rationalization is demanded. In short, here as in so many other questions that intrigue and confound the student of democratic politics, there are no final answers. And such interim answers as may from time to time be contrived are themselves the product of the same group and interest forces whose existence causes the difficulty in the first place!

Contemporary critics of American pluralism mount a broader based attack than traditional reformers. The "New Left" view may accept rather grudgingly the existence of a plurality of political groups but raises in more sweeping terms the problem of the representativeness of the group pattern, and hence the legitimacy of the vote that highly organized interests can wield. Moreover, exponents of this position decry the notion that however descriptive of reality the pluralistic policy-making model may be, it is not defensible in terms of its outputs and certainly cannot be viewed normatively as the best system possible. In place of pluralism, these critics would put a combination of participatory democracy and planning. Theoretically the first part of the prescription would shift power from organized minorities to a kind of "one man, one vote" decisional process. Planning, in their view, would replace haphazard incrementalism and permit the devising of policy in a much broader, more rational, and longer term context than at present (see last chapter). Whether such a theoretical approach can be translated into reality is far from clear.

suggested additional readings

Bailey, Harry A., Jr. (ed.). *Negro Politics in America*. Columbus, Ohio: Charles E. Merrill Books, Inc., 1967.*

Bauer, Raymond A., et al. *American Business and Public Policy: The Politics of Foreign Trade*. New York: Atherton Press, Inc., 1963.

Bentley, Arthur F. *The Process of Government*. Cambridge: Harvard University Press, 1967.

Dexter, Lewis A. *How Organizations Are Represented in Washington*. New York: Bobbs-Merrill Co., Inc., 1969.*

Engler, Robert. *The Politics of Oil*. New York: The Macmillan Company, 1961.*

Greenstone, J. David. *Labor in America*. New York: Random House, Inc., 1970.*

Holtzman, Abraham. *Interest Groups and Lobbying*. New York: The Macmillan Company, 1966.*

Matthews, Donald R., and James W. Prothro. *Negroes and the New Southern Politics*. New York: Harcourt Brace Jovanovich, Inc., 1966.*

Milbrath, Lester. *The Washington Lobbyists*. Chicago: Rand McNally & Co., 1963.

Mintz, Morton, and Jerry S. Cohen. *America: Who Owns and Operates the United States*. New York: The Dial Press, 1971.

National Advisory Commission on Civil Disorders. *Report*. New York: Bantam Books, 1968.

Salisbury, Robert H. *Interest Groups in America*. New York: Harper & Row, Publishers, 1970.

Truman, David B. *The Governmental Process*. New York: Alfred A. Knopf, Inc., 1951.

Wooton, G. *Interest Groups*. Englewood Cliffs, N.J.: Prentice-Hall, Inc., 1969.*

Zeigler, Harmon, and G. Wayne Peak. *Interest Groups in American Society*. Englewood Cliffs, N.J.: Prentice-Hall, Inc., 2nd ed., 1972.

* Available in paperback.

7 leading the nation: the executive

case study

Cambodia

"The action I have announced tonight puts the leaders of North Vietnam on notice that . . . we will not be humiliated. We will not be defeated." The President of the United States is speaking. The date is Thursday, April 30, 1970. The occasion is a nationwide television address to the American people about certain decisions the President has taken regarding the situation in Vietnam and specifically in its small neighbor, Cambodia. He has just been detailing the reasons that prompted the basic decision: to send American and South Vietnamese troops into Cambodia to clean out North Vietnamese "privileged sanctuaries."

Four days later, in Kent, Ohio, on the campus of Kent State University there was a milling crowd, one of hundreds of similar student crowds across the land, a product of the anger that welled up in the wake of the President's announcement. A detachment of the National Guard, which had arrived on campus two days earlier, moved against the crowd. There were confused accounts afterward of what provoked them to fire, or whether, indeed, they were really provoked, but, "There was a single shot—some people heard it as two almost simultaneous shots—then a period of silence lasting about two seconds, then a prolonged but thin fusillade . . .

then silence, and two final shots. The shooting had covered thirteen seconds." Four students lay dead.

We all know that what the President said on Thursday in Washington about events happening half a world away in Cambodia and what happened in Kent, Ohio, the following Monday were very closely linked. Yet, it would be hard to convince the fabled man from Mars, who had not lived through those five days, that there could possibly be any connection. Such is the tangled skein of interwoven events and consequences and destinies and motives in which any governmental decision has its effect. A decision may unwind a few tangles, or it may add new snarls that were not present before. But the skein itself will remain, with no beginning, and no ending, like a mass of kite string that has become hopelessly snarled and knotted.

A process of decision can be made to look deceptively precise and isolated. Several reporters who pieced together the scraps of information on the decision to intervene in Cambodia insist that the President made it himself, alone, on the evening of April 27, at just about 9 p.m. Perhaps that *was* the hour or the minute at which Mr. Nixon said to himself, "This is it." But the skein of deliberations and conclusions that make up a decision, like the skein of events it is designed to affect, has no real beginning—and no real ending. An arbitrary beginning point can, however, be selected.

On March 18, 1970, Prince Sihanouk, long-time ruler of Cambodia, was deposed by his erstwhile Premier, Lon Nol, while the former was in France. Control of Cambodia thus passed from the essentially neutralist prince, who had (with increasing reluctance) allowed the North Vietnamese to use territory along the South Vietnamese borders for bases, to an avowedly anti-North Vietnam and decidedly shaky regime. From the point of view of American policy-makers, this was a shift fraught with considerable significance. If the Lon Nol government survived, the North's base and supply complex might well suffer considerably, to the clear advantage of the South and its ally. On the other hand, should the North move successfully against the new leadership in Phnom Penh, the whole of Cambodia, instead of a small border area, could be turned into a North Vietnamese stronghold.

It takes just such a change in circumstances as this to set the government's elaborate policy-making machinery in motion. All of the relevant agencies in Washington drafted proposals for coping with or exploiting the new situation, as did the American command in Saigon at Secretary of Defense Melvin Laird's invitation. Reduced to their simplest terms there were two problems: the first was how to keep the Lon Nol regime afloat, and the second was to decide what to do about the border area sanctuaries. On April 1 the American commander on the scene, General Creighton Abrams, offered the Pentagon several options:

Free the South Vietnamese to harass the North Vietnamese across the border; Help the South mount larger attacks over a period of time aimed at disrupting the North's bases; Link American forces with those of the South for a swift, full-scale assault designed to eliminate the bases.

While the Washington policy-makers were receiving proposals and beginning to digest them, the situation in Cambodia was not static. Lon Nol tried to work out some kind of live-and-let-live arrangement with Hanoi roughly similar to the sort Sihanouk had had. The United States hinted that it would respect such a deal. Meanwhile, the South, against American advice, was already staging some sporadic raids across the border. And U.S. Air Force bombing raids against Cambodian bases increased.

General Abrams' alternatives were examined by the Joint Chiefs of Staff and sent on to the White House. There was no sign of likely action on them, and, in fact, Secretary Laird, in discussing the situation with the President during the second week in April, opposed the idea of an American assault on the grounds that heavy casualties might well result—as many as four hundred to eight hundred dead in the first week of such a thrust—and that there would be a public outcry against such a policy.

Again, events advanced apace. It became known in Saigon to American officials that the forces of the North Vietnamese in the border areas had begun to move westward, toward Phnom Penh and the heart of Cambodia, cutting communications and harassing military outposts as they went. The threat to Lon Nol seemed to be mounting. Accordingly, General Abrams and Ambassador Ellsworth Bunker, the ranking American civilian official in Saigon, jointly recommended to Washington that the time had come to mount an attack on the border areas. At this point, however, the White House was still more concerned with keeping the war from spreading into Cambodia.

As the pressure on the shaky Phnom Penh

regime increased, the President attempted indirect avenues of assistance. He let South Vietnamese forces step up their attacks across the border, and on April 17 he approved a shipment of several thousand captured Soviet-designed rifles to the Cambodian army. Because the time the President can devote to any one problem is of necessity limited, it is probably significant that Mr. Nixon was concurrently embroiled in the battle over one of his controversial Supreme Court nominations and the return to earth of the trouble-plagued Apollo 13 moon mission.

On April 20, Mr. Nixon, in the course of making a previously planned television speech to announce the next phase in the withdrawal of troops from Vietnam, took the occasion to note with concern, "the enemy's escalation in Laos and Cambodia" and to warn that he would take whatever action was necessary to protect the American troops remaining in Vietnam. That same day also brought the further disturbing news of Cambodian defeats, and Lon Nol submitted a request to the United States for $500 million in military aid.

Not only is the limited time that the American one-man executive can devote to a particular problem a key factor in the development of policy decisions, but so too is the question of which problem is really uppermost in his mind. The April 20 speech had been made from the Western White House, in San Clemente, California. Reports indicated that "Mr. Nixon was restless that night—'wound up,' his wife said—and after his speech, abruptly flew back to Washington." Hedrick Smith of the *New York Times* writes that "By morning, intelligence reports had built up a picture of steady deterioration in Cambodia, but the problem hit Mr. Nixon with sudden force." Cambodia had finally risen to the top of the President's pile of clamoring problems and from now on it would engage his attention fully. He began receiving daily briefings from Central

Intelligence Agency Director Richard Helms on the situation.

Now that the President was engaged, the pace accelerated rapidly. He called a National Security Council meeting on April 22, and for the first time the NSC discussed the contingency plans General Abrams had submitted earlier. Most of the discussion centered on an attack by the South Vietnamese on one of the sanctuary areas called the Parrot's Beak. There was some talk also about a possible American attack on another such area, dubbed the Fishhook. By the next morning, the President seemed clearly bent on some kind of action. He called for operational plans for the proposed Parrot's Beak move and put the Washington Special Action Group (WASAG) on a crisis footing.

WASAG was a body headed by Special Assistant to the President for Security Affairs Henry Kissinger, and it had been created as a kind of super staff group in April, 1969, when an American intelligence-gathering plane had been shot down by North Korea. Its members, besides Kissinger, were David Packard, Deputy Secretary of Defense; U. Alexis Johnson, Under Secretary of State for Political Affairs; General Earle Wheeler, Chairman of the Joint Chiefs of Staff; Marshall Greene, Assistant Secretary of State for East Asian Affairs; and Helms of the CIA. The group met twice on April 23 and again the next day. As it developed, this group of essentially second-echelon officials became the primary vehicle used by the President, and it provided him with two or three of his closest advisors as the Cambodia plan matured.

The President continued to push the pace faster. He was apparently nettled by the fact that the North Vietnamese in Cambodia were moving ahead in spite of his warnings and were clearly discounting any risk of an attack at their rear (on the sanctuary areas). On Friday morning, April 24, Mr. Nixon called for plans for the Fishhook operation to be delivered from

Saigon within twenty-four hours. He also called a secret meeting of the NSC for Sunday night, with the implication that the final decisions would be made then—or by then—thereby allowing the generals in Saigon the seventy-two hours they would need to get the attack rolling by dawn, April 30.

On Friday afternoon, the President flew to Camp David, where he and Kissinger studied the developing plans on Saturday, before returning and conferring with Secretary Laird and Attorney General John Mitchell. This little group met on board the presidential yacht *Sequoia* on the Potomac. Later they attended a private showing of the motion picture *Patton,* a biography of that colorful and defiant World War II general, which Mr. Nixon had seen once before and was apparently eager to see again. This bit of information is cited without comment by those who pieced together the story of these late April days. It is hard to escape the thought, however, that the viewing of the film was not without significance at that point. Could it be that the President, frustrated by the intractable problem of the Vietnam war, was encouraged to make the invasion decision by a kind of secret yearning to emulate the impetuous general?

Secretary of State William Rogers, having returned from New York on Sunday morning, April 26, in time to be brought abreast of developments, then joined the President, Laird, Mitchell, General Wheeler, Helms, and Kissinger for the previously scheduled meeting of the NSC at the White House. Two statutory members of the group were absent, Vice President Agnew and the Director of the Office of Emergency Preparedness. The President opened the discussion by making it clear that he had decided "to do something," that the South Vietnamese operation in the Parrot's Beak area had his tentative approval, and that a possible move of American forces into the Fishhook was an open question.

Not surprisingly, the Pentagon point of view as expressed in the following discussion was highly favorable to a major military effort. It was argued that the North Vietnamese operating in Cambodia were bent either on eliminating the Lon Nol regime or reopening the supply corridor they had formerly enjoyed to Cambodia's major seaport. If they succeeded in either objective, both the future defense of South Vietnam and the American troop withdrawal would be jeopardized. The Pentagon point of view also insisted that the South Vietnamese thrust into the Parrot's Beak would be insufficient, serving as no more than a warning. The Fishhook area, it was argued, must also be attacked, and there were compelling reasons why American troops should do that job. The rainy season would begin in a month. Lon Nol was unlikely to survive that long without the planned action to relieve pressure on him—and therefore it was now or never.

Secretary Rogers seems to have been the chief spokesman for the opposition. He made the case that the use of American troops would mean widening the war; that there was grave risk of becoming trapped in a pattern of expanding hostilities just as the Johnson Administration had been; that the President had won wide popular support for his policy of gradual troop withdrawal and should not risk losing that; and finally, that the objectives being discussed could be achieved by the use of South Vietnamese troops alone. The debate lasted for three hours and left the President with the conclusion that his choices were either to do nothing or to involve American troops. The arguments against using only Saigon's troops seemed persuasive, especially because American air support would be essential anyway. And, as Smith of the *Times* wrote, "Besides, the President was determined to prove that he could meet force with force."

At a subsequent press conference on May 8, the President was to say that the decision to send American troops into Cambodia was his alone: "I made the decision, I take the responsibility for it." The record of events following the Sunday NSC meeting bear him out. After it was concluded he retired to his hideaway office in the Executive Office Building across the street from the White House and ordered a tray of dinner. On one of his favorite pads of yellow legal paper he jotted a summary of the pros and cons. His notes show clearly the importance he had come to attach to the survival of the Lon Nol government and the extent to which it had become linked in his mind with American success in Vietnam. In summarizing whether the Cambodian incursion should be undertaken, Mr. Nixon listed only arguments in favor: " 'Time running out' was followed by 'military aid' to Lon Nol could be 'only symbolic.' Then came a scribble saying inaction might tempt Hanoi to install a puppet regime in Phnom Penh and a final entry saying that inaction by both sides would leave an 'ambiguous situation' with time favoring the Communists." In a similar manner the President went over the pros and cons for American troop involvement in the action, and recognized that it "would bring a 'deep division' of the American people."

Secretary Rogers' opposition apparently had left lingering doubts in the President's mind, though he was determined to attack. As a result, he called another meeting on Monday morning, April 27, consisting of Rogers, Laird, Kissinger, and H. R. Haldeman, his chief of staff, but not the military or intelligence chiefs. Perhaps it was Rogers who suggested at that meeting that the military might be telling their chief only what he wanted to hear. (One account has the first three all arguing against invasion, earlier, if not at this particular meeting.) In any event, the suggestion about the military caused a disturbed President to place a direct call to General Abrams and demand that he give him the "unvarnished truth" man to

man. Abrams replied that an American assault was necessary.

With this reply in hand, and other last-minute memos, the President retired again to make his final decision alone. He placed several calls while thus closeted to Kissinger, to Haldeman, and also to John D. Ehrlichman, the White House staff's domestic affairs chief, and to William Timmons, his assistant for Congressional liaison. At 9:15 p.m. he left his office and went back to his living quarters in the White House. President Nixon had made up his mind.

A final difference of opinion that the President resolved personally had to do with the method of presentation to the American people. Some in the White House called for low-key treatment. Mr. Nixon, however, decided on the Thursday evening televised announcement and report. He personally prepared the text, working late into the night through eight long hand drafts on Tuesday and Wednesday evenings. Unlike his predecessors, Kennedy and Johnson, he did not submit the final draft for editing by his principal Cabinet advisors. Later, several in his entourage took exception to some of the President's rhetoric, to the accuracy of certain factual assertions, and to the wisdom of the promised capture of the North Vietnamese command group.

It is strikingly obvious that no one had begun to assess adequately in advance the public outcry that the decision would evoke, especially on the nation's college campuses; Kent State and the killings at Jackson State were only the most excruciating examples of the volcanic upheaval produced by the President's policy. Was this monumental miscalculation perhaps the fault of the decision-making process itself?

Governmental critics of the way the decision was made noted the narrow group that was ultimately involved and the fact that many high officials who presumably might have been or should have been consulted or informed had no inkling until the die was cast. "The problem, as seen by the bureaucrats, [was] that the President, Kissinger, Laird, and Rogers reached their decision without any detailed staff work being done." Instead, the President relied on people like Mitchell, Haldeman, Ehrlichman, and the officials who made up WASAG. But, on the other hand, would reliance on the bureaucratic experts have saved the President from the deep political difficulties into which the decision led him? Presumably, the people he did consult were the ones best suited to give him precisely this kind of advice. Mitchell, after all, had managed his 1968 campaign.

The answer may lie in the very nature of the Presidency as an office, rather than in the pattern of consultation in which the Chief Executive engages—important as this pattern is. The American President, in the sphere of foreign and military policy, has enormous autonomous power, and, if he chooses, he can exercise this power without consulting anyone. Presidents rarely do this, but they can if they choose. Furthermore, the President can make any decision, domestic or foreign, by himself and without staff assistance. No matter how much the Presidency as an institution made up of hundreds of staff aids may grow, it can never diminish this fundamental presidential autonomy any more than the man who holds the office is prepared to allow it to be diminished or shared. This case underscores the point dramatically. Cambodia was Nixon's decision, ultimately, and his alone. Possibly the ghost of General Patton had as much to do with it as any one of his White House associates!

SOURCES

Loory, Stuart H., "In the End, the President Alone Decided," *Providence Journal*, May 10, 1970 (Los Angeles Times News Service).

Martin, James A., Jr., "The Presidential Decision-Making Process: The Cuban Missile Crisis v. The Cambodian Invasion," unpublished seminar paper, Brown University, 1971.

Michener, James A., *Kent State: What Happened and Why* (New York: Random House, Inc., 1971).

Smith, Hedrick, "Cambodian Decision: Why the President Acted," *New York Times,* June 30, 1970.

the offices
and their powers

The Executive in Government

"The executive power," asserts the opening sentence in Article II of the Constitution, "shall be vested in a President of the United States." The innocent reader might assume from this terse statement that there must be little doubt as to what the executive power is and who has it in the American system. The President clearly has it, and reading on, the inquiring student could easily conclude that essentially it consists of taking care "that the laws be faithfully executed." On both scores, however, he would in part be wrong.

It may well have been true that the framers intended the President to have all of the executive power, and it is probably also true that they conceived of this as "executing"—carrying out, as it were—the will of Congress, in whose hands they had placed the authority to make laws. Actually, in light of what has happened to the President's role since 1789, it now seems clear that the framers, too, were in part wrong. In the first place, the executive power in the American system (or, for that matter, in any other governmental system) consists not only of the chief executive, but also of a host of top-level assistants with executive responsibilities. In addition, there are tens of thousands of civil servants who in fact do most of the executing of the laws. The President, by contrast, spends most of *his* time formulating policy and attempting to meet the broad problems, foreign and domestic, that beset the nation. His top-level political associates spend a part of their time assisting him in these tasks, and another part supervising the execution of those policies falling under the jurisdiction of the various departments and agencies they head.

Accordingly, if the Constitution's framers could somehow rewrite the opening sentence of Article II today in light of how things actually have developed, they might well put it this way:

The executive power, which consists of policy formulation and leadership, as well as the carrying out of policy once made, is vested in a President of the United States; it is further vested in the top-level presidential associates, many of whom head the departments and agencies of the executive branch of government, and in the more than two million bureaucrats who staff these departments and their field offices.

Moreover, for the statement to be a fully realistic description of the executive power, it should contain a footnote that at least some of this sprawling establishment escapes the effective superintendence of either the President or his appointed officials; certain agencies have been granted quasi-independent status by Congress, and others have won de facto independence by playing other power sources off against the President.

Even the foregoing is but a rough and simplified sketch of the executive power in the American system of government. It might be just as accurate to use the circular statement that the American executive is what it does, and leave it at that. In this chapter, the focus will be primarily upon the policy-making and leadership functions of the President as chief executive (and on his counterparts at the state level, the Governors); in a later chapter (10) some of the bureaucratic elements in the system will be considered.

Presidential Government

The American executive is the command post of our political system. Despite the great negative power of Congress, the Presidency is now predominant. In the 1880's Woodrow Wilson described the national government as "congressional," and even today this term is not wholly without meaning. Nevertheless, the modern American system is most accurately referred to as presidential, a tribute to the central position of the President in the federal government and of the Governors in the state governments.

As forms of presidential government the American national and state systems contrast with the other main type of democratic government, the parliamentary. Ironically, the British system, which so influenced the development of American political institutions, is the model parliamentary type; and ours is the model presidential type. The fundamental constitutional difference between the two systems lies in the position of the executive. In Britain the working or political executive—the Prime Minister and his Cabinet—is located in Parliament, elected by and responsible to its membership. In America the chief executives—the President or the state Governors —are independent of the legislature. They need its support for their policies, but they are free of its control. Their accountability is to the people who elect them.[1]

The British executive system, moreover, is far more collegial than the American. Its Prime Minister leads a Cabinet knit together by a feeling of common purpose and collective responsibility for major decisions. In contrast, there are no cabinets in

---

[1] In practice the British executive-legislative relationship is more complicated than this. The Prime Minister actually controls Parliament because he is the leader of the party with a parliamentary majority. His ability to control a party majority, however, depends on his ability to win and to hold popular support in the nation at large. In this respect the Prime Minister's position is not much different from that of the American President. Still, he is part of Parliament, and his power flows from it: the system is parliamentary.

the American state governments, and the President's Cabinet is one in name only.[2] National policy is not made in the U.S. Cabinet. Its sense of collective responsibility is typified by the reply of President Franklin Roosevelt's Secretary of the Treasury to a request made by his Cabinet colleague, Secretary of Agriculture Henry Wallace, for financial aid to his department: "Henry, that's your cross, you bear it." [3]

Constitutional Sources of Power: The President

Not all Governors and Presidents are politically adept in exploiting the authority of the executive office, but those who are have at their disposal a vast and assorted arsenal of powers. Even in the states where the chief executive is politically weak he plays a key role that in the last century most Governors knew of only in their dreams. The origins of these powers are as diverse as their uses: in part they are constitutional, in part they are statutory, and in part they are derived from the very nature of the executive office as it reacts to modern political conditions.

When one turns to the actual grants of power in the written constitutions, they hardly appear earthshaking. Those assigned to the President in the federal Constitution are only twelve in number, and three are distinctly petty. This is true of his powers to grant pardons and reprieves to criminals convicted of federal offenses, to issue the formal commission of office to all officers of the United States, and to request written opinions from the heads of the executive departments on subjects relating to their duties.

The remaining nine powers, described in a handful of short phrases, seem inconsequential enough on the surface, yet they are nothing less than the constitutional foundation of the modern Presidency. They may be conveniently divided into three broad sets of powers: executive, legislative, and over foreign affairs.

1. The executive power

The opening words of Article II declare that "The executive Power shall be vested in a President of the United States." Another short clause near the end of the Article tells the President to "take care that the Laws be faithfully executed." To President Theodore Roosevelt and many of his equally strong-minded successors these clauses vest in the President a general commission to act as a roving minister in the public interest. This is the famous "Stewardship Theory" of the Presidency discussed later in this chapter.

To manage the executive branch the President must be able to choose his immediate subordinates, especially the one thousand or so political executives who

---

[2] In a few states Governors meet more or less regularly with the heads of the executive departments; by courtesy these can be called *cabinet meetings*. Florida, however, has a unique Cabinet system in which the Governor can actually be outvoted on policy decisions. See Coleman B. Ransone, Jr., *The Office of Governor in the United States* (University, Ala.: University of Alabama Press, 1956), pp. 259–280.

[3] Richard F. Fenno, Jr., *The President's Cabinet* (New York: Vintage, 1959), p. 133.

explicitly make policy decisions. The Constitution provides that, subject to the Senate's concurrence, he shall appoint the major public officers of the United States. Throughout America's entire history only eight Cabinet appointments have been voted down on the Senate floor, though before submitting a name the President takes account of possible repercussions. Occasionally, Presidents withdraw controversial names that seem headed for defeat. Eisenhower, for example, did so six times in eight years. Johnson withdrew his nomination of Abe Fortas as Chief Justice in 1968.

An additional check on the President's power of appointment is the old custom of "senatorial courtesy." Except for his Cabinet and his diplomatic nominations, the President is expected to clear his lesser appointments with the Senators of his own party who come from the state in which the prospective nominee resides. Should the President fail to do this, the Senator whose advice has been ignored is likely to declare the nominee is "personally obnoxious" to him. His fellow Senators will then usually do him the courtesy of rejecting the presidential nomination. In practice the custom means that Senators can often dictate certain appointments, especially those that involve positions that are located within their states, for example, federal judgeships and postmasterships. If there is no Senator from the party representing a particular state, the President's discretion is naturally greater. But even in such cases he is likely to be guided by the recommendations of the dominant politicians from his party within the state.

It is important to the President's ability to manage the executive departments that he have the power to remove his principal executive subordinates. A series of executive precedents extending back to Washington's Administration, which have been confirmed by the Supreme Court, establish the constitutional rule that the President's power to appoint carries with it the power to remove his political assistants.[4] The power to remove need not be used for its effect to be felt. Occasionally, however, a President will oust a major associate. President Nixon did precisely this in firing Interior Secretary Walter J. Hickel, who flamboyantly challenged administration policies while developing his own base of political power. In short, there is a Damoclean sword hanging over the heads of the political executives, a reminder that subordinates who contradict presidential policies risk, if not their heads, their jobs.

2. The legislative power

Three constitutional provisions underwrite the President's position as the central influence in the national legislative process. One of these is his power to adjourn Congress if the two houses cannot agree on an adjournment date and to convene

---

[4] *Myers* v. *United States,* 272 U.S. 52, 122 (1926). The removal power does not affect civil service employees, who can only be removed through special administrative proceedings. It also does not extend to the commissioners of independent regulatory agencies: the Supreme Court has ruled that their quasi-judicial positions are deliberately isolated from presidential control. *Humphrey's Executor* v. *United States,* 295 U.S. 602 (1935); *Wiener* v. *United States,* 357 U.S. 349 (1958).

Congress "on extraordinary occasions." The other two powers are far more significant. Because the President can veto bills, which can only be repassed by a two-thirds vote of both houses, he is, in effect, a superlegislator. All legislation requires his vote of approval—and he casts a negative vote that is the political equivalent to 67 votes in the Senate and 290 in the House. Unlike many state Governors, however, Presidents cannot veto specific items in a bill. Bills come to them on a take-it-or-leave-it basis, and Presidents are sometimes forced to approve needed legislation despite its inclusion of provisions that they oppose. Even then they may achieve the effect of an item veto over appropriation bills by refusing to spend undesired funds. At other times they may sign a bill but declare their intention to disregard one of its "unconstitutional" provisions. On one occasion, for example, President Lyndon B. Johnson signed a Public Works Appropriation Act, but issued the following statement:

I have today approved the Public Works Appropriation Act. This does not mean approval of that provision in the Act which precludes the Panama Canal Company from disposing of any real property without first obtaining the approval of the appropriate legislative committees of the House and Senate. Four Attorneys General of the United States have held provisions of this nature unconstitutional. . . .[5]

"From time to time" the President is directed to send messages to Congress on the state of the Union and to recommend to it measures that he believes are "necessary and expedient." This power too has taken on broad dimensions. The success of presidential sponsorship varies, depending on the nature and number of the President's requests, the skill with which he advocates them, the party lineup in Congress, and the political mood of the nation. The growing tendency to bombard Congress with presidential requests makes the evaluation of an administration's legislative success difficult. Not all bills are of equal weight: the passage of Medicare is more significant than the failure to enact scores of less important presidential proposals. Moreover, a President's legislative batting average is less noteworthy than the fact that the initiative is in his hands. There was grumbling among Congressmen of both parties when, in 1953, the newly installed Eisenhower Administration did not present Congress with a legislative program because it had lacked the time to prepare one. "Don't expect us to start from scratch on what you people want," a committee chairman informed an Administration aide. "That's not the way we do things here— *you* draft the bills and *we* work them over." [6] But in 1954 and every year thereafter Eisenhower sent a detailed legislative program to Congress. As he remarked to a news conference, "The Constitution put the President right square into the legislative business." The Nixon Administration was similarly criticized in 1969 for not sending its legislative agenda to Congress. Eventually, in mid-April, a ten-point domestic program was submitted.

[5] *Congressional Quarterly,* January 3, 1964.
[6] Richard E. Neustadt, "Presidency and Legislation: Planning the President's Program," *American Political Science Review,* XLIX (December, 1955), 1015.

3. The power over foreign affairs

The remaining presidential powers are those that, in their modern usage, commission the President to be the nation's leader in international relations and national defense. He is given the power to receive foreign ambassadors, which is the basis of his discretionary power to either recognize or terminate the recognition of foreign governments. He is also given the authority to negotiate treaties, but this last power is shared with the Senate, which must approve the treaties by a two-thirds majority.

Today Presidents usually rely on the formal treaty only for such great national decisions as to enter the United Nations, to support the NATO defense alliances, or to join with the Soviet Union in suspending nuclear testing. For their more routine conduct of foreign affairs they rely on executive agreements. These are simply agreements entered into by the President with foreign governments; he carries them out by drawing on his existing constitutional and statutory powers. In a classic illustration of their use, President Franklin Roosevelt in the early stages of World War II agreed to aid the British government by giving it fifty destroyers in return for American use of British bases in the Western Hemisphere. Roosevelt's action was strengthened by his constitutional position as "Commander-in-Chief of the Army and Navy of the United States."

The "Destroyer Deal" neatly illustrates the intimate tie between the President's powers in matters of foreign and defense policy. Naturally the "war powers," whose enormous potentialities were first dramatized by Lincoln, are most significant in time of war. But even in time of peace they are formidable. This is especially true when, as during the late 1930's or as today, the peace may be but an uneasy prelude to war.

Constitutional Sources of Power: The Governor

The constitutional powers of the state Governors are broadly similar to those of the President in certain respects but different in others. To begin with, the Governors are excluded from both foreign affairs and national defense. Most state constitutions, it is true, name the Governor, as the commander-in-chief of the state's military forces. This residual vestige from the days when revolutionary state militiamen fought redcoats does, however, confirm his power as head of the state National Guard.

Governors have frequently called out the Guard to maintain public order in times of rioting or serious disasters like earthquakes or floods. Their discretion to mobilize Guard units and to impose a temporary dictatorship over a disturbed locality by declaring martial law is great, but it is not without limit. In 1959, for example, federal courts ruled that a Minnesota Governor had exceeded his powers when he ordered the State Guard to close down a meat-packing house that was the scene of a union-management dispute.[7] A Governor also faces the possibility that

---

[7] *Wilson and Company* v. *Freeman,* 179 F. Supp. 520 (1959).

he may have to relinquish command of the Guard to the President, the nation's supreme military commander, if he misuses his authority or if a national emergency arises. A presidential proclamation may federalize a state's National Guard and literally take it out of a Governor's hands. President Eisenhower, for instance, did this to Arkansas Governor Faubus in a bitter dispute over the desegregation of the Little Rock schools.

1. The executive power

The Governors, like the President, exercise a reservoir of discretionary executive powers. They too possess discretion in deciding which law to use when, as often is the case, alternative laws can be invoked. They have options in deciding how vigorously to enforce existing legislation. Moreover, they derive strength from a popular expectation that they will use all powers available to them when a public emergency, such as a destructive drought, a crippling strike of a key public utility, or a pattern of racial violence threatens the well-being of their state. But, unlike the President, to whom is given "*the* executive power . . . of the United States," almost all state chief executives are handicapped: the executive power is not theirs alone. They must share it. The wording of the Oklahoma Constitution suggests the problem. It reads:

The Executive authority of the State shall be vested in a Governor, Lieutenant Governor, Secretary of State, Attorney General, State Treasurer, Superintendent of Public Instruction, State Examiner and Inspector, Chief Mine Inspector, Commissioner of Labor, Commissioner of Charities and Corrections, Commissioner of Insurance, and other officers provided by law and this Constitution.

Not all state executive branches, of course, are so fragmented, and even in Oklahoma "the *supreme* executive authority" is vested in the Governor.

Despite his "supreme executive power," the Governor in most states cannot *constitutionally* control many of the leading officials in the executive branch. His power to appoint and to remove subordinates is generally weak. In many of the states the Governor appoints less than half of the major executive officials. Conversely, only in Alaska, Missouri, and New Jersey does the Governor have removal powers similar to those of the President. In other states the Governor cannot remove officials unless he can prove in court that they have been dishonest, incompetent, or obstructive, and this is no easy matter. In addition, in only ten states does the Governor share the executive authority with as few as four officials whose election is independent of his. Most Governors are weak in three important components of executive strength—term of office (its length and possibility of succession), appointive powers, and removal powers. In only a few states, such as Alaska, Hawaii, Illinois, New Jersey, and New York, do the Governors match the President in these measurements of executive strength.

2. The legislative power

State Governors compare much more favorably to the President in their constitutional allotment of legislative powers. They are granted the power to deliver "state of the State" messages to the legislature and to recommend legislative measures. Most Governors can call special sessions of the legislature, and many of them can prescribe the agenda for such sessions, thereby forcing the legislature at least to confront an issue.

Governors in forty-nine states can veto legislation (the maverick is North Carolina), and in forty-one states they can item-veto objectionable parts of otherwise acceptable bills. Moreover, in twenty-four states the requirement for overriding vetoes (two thirds of the total elected membership) is more stringent than the one in the federal government (two thirds of those voting). In fact, the gubernatorial veto is virtually irreversible. But the Governor's veto power is much more than a great negative force. The ever-present threat to use it enables a Governor to shape positively the content of legislation. It also leads department heads to seek his approval for their legislative proposals, giving the Governor one of his few sanctions over the rest of the executive branch.

These constitutional powers, when added to the political resources available to the Governor, frequently make him the master of the state legislative process. He has the advantage of being the leading representative of the people, of being expected by the people and the legislators alike to provide a legislative program, and of being a full-time chief executive confronting a part-time legislature whose powers and prestige are limited. It is not surprising that Governors regularly obtain the legislature's approval for between 50 to 90 per cent of their programs; in recent years their batting averages appear to be more often nearer the top rather than the bottom of the scale.[8]

Professor Joseph A. Schlesinger has developed a useful method of measuring the relative power of Governors in the fifty states, based on four variables.[9] The first column in Table 7.1 contains an index figure for each state measuring the extent to which the Governor controls the budget process, ranging from a score of five points for those states in which he has exclusive responsibility, to one point in those where he is only one of a group of elected officials participating jointly in budget-making. In the second column, if a Governor appoints all the major department heads, he scores five points; at the other end of the scale he receives zero points if the officials are elective and beyond his control. In the third column, Governors enjoying four-year terms with unlimited reeligibility get five points, whereas Governors with two-year terms, reeligible only once, are rated at one point. The fourth column rates the Governor's veto power: very strong (four points), strong (three points), medium (two points), and weak (one point). The last column totals the four scores into an overall index of gubernatorial power.

Legislative Sources of Power

Nothing, an old adage goes, succeeds like success. In their relationships with the legislature, Governors and Presidents alike have exploited their constitutional powers so as to bring them added powers. At the executive's request legislatures now

[8] Ransone, op. cit., pp. 176–180.
[9] "The Politics of the Executive," in Herbert Jacob and Kenneth N. Vines, *Politics in the American States* (Boston: Little, Brown, 1965), pp. 217–232.

routinely enact the general outlines of laws that delegate legislative rule-making powers to those charged with their execution.

For instance, the Trade Expansion Act of 1962 delegates to the President *discretionary* power to reduce import duties by 50 per cent, to raise them by 50 per cent of 1934 levels, or to eliminate completely the duties on certain goods. It also allows him to enter negotiations for an international system of quotas on the importation of goods. Finally, at his discretion, he can provide relief and assistance to workers and industries suffering from the consequences of increased international trade. Thousands of similar federal laws allow executives and administrators to act under mandates that do little more than tell them to serve "the public interest" and to be "just, fair, and reasonable."

Nothing, however, better illustrates the legislature's contribution to the growth of the executive power than the voluntary transfer of its budgetary and fiscal powers to the chief executive. The Presidency especially has benefited, thanks to the Budget and Accounting Act of 1921. This law marked the beginning of a centralized executive budget and of a systematic means of presidential control over legislation. The very fact that it was passed while Warren G. Harding sat in the White House suggests that the strong Presidency is at least partially an inevitable consequence of a changed political environment. Gradually, the Bureau of the Budget grew into one of the key legislative and management tools of the modern Presidency. Franklin D. Roosevelt had the Bureau shifted from the Treasury Department to a newly established Executive Office as part of the President's personal staff.

Today it not only scrutinizes all matters relating to appropriations, which naturally include a large area of legislation, but it also concerns itself with *all* proposed laws. Its functions and scope—all, remember, under the authority of an act of Congress—span the full range of the legislative process. All bills introduced in Congress by the executive departments and agencies must first clear the Bureau of the Budget—the Office of Management and Budget (OMB) as it was renamed under a Nixon reorganization in 1970—so that there can be interagency coordination and approval on the President's behalf. Moreover, when any bills are introduced in Congress, congressional committees customarily solicit the views of the interested agencies; the agency responses are then channeled through the Office of Management and Budget in order to get its advice on how the proposed bills relate to the President's program. Finally, before bills that have passed Congress come to the President for his signature or veto, the OMB as his representative coordinates and summarizes the opinions of the agencies on the merits of the legislation. In every case it prepares a dossier for the President and recommends that he either sign or veto the bill.

Presidents still find it difficult to manage and coordinate the administrative bureaucracy and to sponsor legislative programs, for some administrators have special relationships with congressional committees that enable them to appeal covertly over the President's head for funds and legislation. Moreover, most expenditures in the annual budget are predetermined by earlier legislative commitments, and Congress is always free to reject presidential legislation. But without the OMB these problems would be incomparably more difficult.

Table 7.1 *A combined index of the formal powers of the governors*

	Budget powers	Appointive powers	Tenure potential	Veto powers	Total index
New York	5	5	5	4	19
Illinois	5	5	5	3	18
New Jersey	5	5	4	4	18
Pennsylvania	5	5	3	4	17
Virginia	5	5	3	4	17
Washington	5	4	5	3	17
California	5	3	5	4	17
Maryland	5	5	4	2	16
Missouri	5	4	3	4	16
Oregon	5	4	4	3	16
Utah	5	3	5	3	16
Wyoming	5	3	5	3	16
Montana	5	2	5	4	16
Alabama	5	3	3	4	15
Connecticut	4	4	5	2	15
Ohio	5	4	4	2	15
Tennessee	5	5	3	1	14
Kentucky	5	4	3	2	14
Michigan	5	4	2	3	14
Minnesota	5	4	2	3	14
Nevada	5	2	5	2	14
Colorado	4	1	5	4	14
Idaho	1	5	5	3	14
Louisiana	4	2	3	4	13
Oklahoma	5	1	3	4	13

The executive budget has also come to the states, but few Governors have the services of budget bureaus resembling the presidential one. In most states there is some form of centralized budgeting under the Governor's control. New York's Governor, for example, possesses fiscal powers approaching those of the President. He can use the budget to present his policies to the legislature and to coordinate the internal operations of the administrative agencies.

Much more commonly, however, the Governor's executive budget is best described as a one-half, sometimes even a one-quarter executive budget. In many states the leading agencies are under independently elected officers who are exempt from the Governor's budgetary controls. Then, too, most states earmark a large percentage of their financial sources for specific programs. A typical illustration is the state gasoline tax. Not only are the receipts from this tax often automatically

	Budget powers	Appointive powers	Tenure potential	Veto powers	Total index
Iowa	5	3	2	2	12
Nebraska	5	3	2	2	12
Wisconsin	5	2	2	3	12
Georgia	5	1	3	3	12
Massachusetts	5	1	2	4	12
Indiana	3	5	3	1	12
Arkansas	5	2	2	2	11
South Dakota	5	2	1	3	11
New Mexico	4	3	1	3	11
Kansas	4	2	2	3	11
Maine	4	1	4	2	11
New Hampshire	5	1	2	2	10
Rhode Island	4	3	2	1	10
North Carolina	4	2	3	1	10
Vermont	2	4	2	2	10
Arizona	2	3	2	3	10
Delaware	1	1	4	4	10
West Virginia	1	3	3	1	8
Florida	1	2	3	2	8
Mississippi	1	1	3	2	7
South Carolina	1	1	3	2	7
Texas	1	1	2	3	7
North Dakota	1	1	2	3	7

Source: From *Politics in the American States: A Comparative Analysis,* Herbert Jacobs and Kenneth N. Vines, Editors. Copyright © 1965, by Little, Brown and Company (Inc.). Reprinted by permission of the publisher. P. 229.

assigned to a special fund for road construction and maintenance, but the fund is frequently administered by a highway board or a commission that is completely beyond the Governor's control. In many states as much as 50 per cent of the tax receipts are not under the Governor's control. In three states—Kansas, Texas, and Colorado—the situation is even more extreme: 80 per cent or more of the public funds are earmarked.

In spite of these serious qualifications, the long-range trend is very clearly in the direction of greater gubernatorial control in the making and execution of the state budget. A number of states have strengthened their central budgetary procedures and established budget offices in the executive branch. The Georgia Assembly, for example, has authorized the creation of a strong Budget Bureau in the Governor's office. Headed by a State Budget Officer directly accountable to the Governor, the

Georgia Bureau is empowered to develop financial policies, coordinate fiscal affairs and procedures, produce plans for improving the organization and operation of state agencies, analyze the financial and administrative aspects of proposed legislation, and provide staff assistance to the legislative appropriation committees. This type of budgetary system is likely to make its appearance in more and more states.

Political Sources of Power

Ultimately, the greatest potential source of power for a Governor or a President is his political skill in maximizing and using his official powers and in activating public support for himself and for his program. The task of a chief executive is to get others to do what he wants them to do. He is not a mere clerk routinely administering a bureaucratic office, but a leader. He wants some laws passed and others defeated, and he wants to apply the discretion inherent in his office toward the fulfillment of certain policy goals. To satisfy these policy wants, he must persuade other political actors to do his bidding. "I sit here all day," President Truman once commented, "trying to persuade people to do the things they ought to have sense enough to do without my persuading them." [10] To be effective the Governor no less than the President must be a successful persuader, and to be a successful persuader he must be a good politician.

Despite their election on party tickets, neither the Governor nor the President derive their major strength from their position as party leaders. In Britain the Prime Minister, who heads the government, leads an essentially unified party and he can usually count on the loyal support of its parliamentary members. But in America, as we know from earlier chapters, this is rarely the case. The Democratic and Republican Parties in most states are internally divided into factional blocs, and in approximately one quarter of the states a single and fragmented party habitually dominates the legislature. In many states, also, the Governor is of one party and at least one of the two legislative houses belongs to the opposition.

A similar situation exists at the national level. The parties are only moderately united on programs, and even divided government is a possibility: during six of Eisenhower's eight years as President he faced a Democratic Congress. President Nixon came into office with majorities of the opposite party in both Houses, nor did the 1970 or 1972 elections substantially alter that situation, despite his campaign efforts. Some Governors and certainly the President do profit from party support, because it is a leading factor in legislative voting. But party alone is rarely enough to guarantee success in a state legislature or in Congress. Party loyalties can help a chief executive, and the strength he brings to a successful election ticket may win him added increments of support from grateful fellow party members.

To the American chief executive it may be more important—and more feasible too—that, instead of the backing of a disciplined party, he have strong public sup-

---

[10] Richard E. Neustadt, *Presidential Power: The Politics of Leadership* (New York: Wiley, 1960), pp. 9–10. The general analysis in this and the next section follows Neustadt's interpretation.

port. He must win elections, but he must also be able to convey to executive subordinates, administrators, and legislators alike the fact (or a very convincing illusion) of continuing popular support for himself and for what he stands for. In part this requires active public backing for specific policy measures that he advocates or undertakes. Only very rarely, however, will even the President enjoy *general* public support for a specific action or series of actions. The type of national climate and of urgency that sustained Franklin Roosevelt during the legendary first "100 Days" of the New Deal and bolstered John Kennedy during the tense two weeks of the Cuban Missile Crisis is, thankfully, unusual. More commonly, a Governor or a President seeks the support of *specific* publics, usually a combination of interest groups and the relatively small minority of persons who are politically attentive, for his specific policies.

Beyond the strength that a chief executive derives from having the backing of specific publics, he needs a more subtle type of general popular support. It can be neither described nor measured precisely, though the regular samplings by the Harris Survey or the Gallup Poll on the extent of popular satisfaction with a President are one useful indication. Nor does public support guarantee the success of a popular Governor's or President's program. John Kennedy, despite his extremely high standing with the public, was generally unsuccessful in carrying out a brave campaign promise to "get the country moving again." Neither is public support merely a matter of having a good personality, though naturally this is a great help. It is, rather, the existence of a widespread popular mood of confidence in the Governor or the President, a feeling that he is knowledgeable, politically skillful, and, to use a colloquialism, in charge.

In the chapter on the legislature it is remarked that public relations is part of the Congressman's job. The same, on a grander scale, is true of the chief executive. The public prestige of Governors and Presidents depends, not only on their actual accomplishments, but on their skill at political public relations. In turn, the former depends partly on the latter. They must handle themselves well at news conferences, give countless addresses, make innumerable personal appearances, and, above all, dramatize themselves and their policies. Herbert Hoover, who once declared, "This is not a showman's job. I will not step out of character," was in many respects a failure as President. Franklin Roosevelt, who was very much in character as a showman, was a success.

A suggestive commentary on presidential public relations in the Nixon era appeared in a *Time* article. It concerned Senator Fulbright of Arkansas, Chairman of the Senate Foreign Relations Committee. Fulbright, according to the article,

assailed the television industry for doing as much to expand the powers of the Presidency "as would a constitutional amendment formally abolishing the [other two] branches of Government." . . . Fulbright's fire at television was prompted by the heavy use of the air waves by President Nixon. He has made 14 appearances in prime time in just 19 months in office. Throughout their Presidencies, Lyndon Johnson enjoyed such exposure only seven times, John Kennedy four times, and Dwight Eisenhower three.[11]

[11] August 17, 1970, pp. 9ff.

The Practice of the Political Profession

By building on his official powers and by exploiting his position as a popular leader, a chief executive can maximize his persuasive power with other political actors. This, however, is merely one aspect of political leadership. In making decisions and re-acting to events the strong chief executive must never lose sight of his own institutional position. Franklin D. Roosevelt, for example, made it clear to the staff in the Budget Bureau, whose job it was to recommend whether he should sign or veto bills, that from time to time he wanted to veto. Once, in vetoing sixteen bills that had Budget Bureau clearance, he told an aide, "The Budget is getting too soft; tell them to stiffen up." Sometimes he would go so far as to ask for "something I can veto"—a way of reminding both department heads and Congressmen that he was a powerful and independent legislative leader.[12]

A President's position is clearly bound up with the success or failure of policies to which he commits the prestige of his office. When Richard Nixon was inaugurated in January, 1969, it was assumed that the biggest test of his prestige would be his ability to end the war in Vietnam. Although this problem turned out to be enormously difficult, the inflationary economy he inherited proved at least as in-tractable. The pressures on the economy, due largely to high levels of expenditure for Vietnam, had caused a steady rise in the prices of consumer goods. This rise in prices in turn generated escalating demands for wage increases, which inevitably pushed manufacturers' costs, and hence prices, up even further.

By August, 1971, it seemingly had become clear to Mr. Nixon that the economy was not responding sufficiently to any of his previous moves. Various spokesmen for the political opposition had been calling for price and wage controls as the only solution and deriding efforts at using indirect or voluntary approaches. In August the President announced on nationwide television one of his most startling moves as President: he informed the nation that, using statutory powers he had previously asserted to be unnecessary, he was freezing all wages and prices for ninety days.

That such a radical initiative should have been taken by a chief executive whom many had thought to be quite conservative is of great interest. Above all, it under-scored again White House concern with the President's prestige and chances for reelection. Barely a year later, of course, the conventions would be over and the campaign would be on in earnest. Mr. Nixon was doubtless impelled to act by these considerations, and specifically by the imperative need either to solve the nation's economic problems or at least to appear to be taking vigorous action against them. By taking as his own the extreme approach his opponents had been urging on him, he of course left them with far less of a political issue than they had had before. The move thus seemed to be extremely adroit politically.

In mid-November, "Phase I," as the freeze had been called, gave way to a "Phase II" of indeterminate duration. On October 7, the President again went on

---

[12] Richard E. Neustadt, "Presidency and Legislation: The Growth of Central Clearance," *American Political Science Review,* XLVIII (September, 1954), 656.

television to announce the policies that would be followed when the ninety-day period expired, or rather, the machinery that would attempt to set such policies. He announced the creation of a Pay Board, made up of five members representing the public, five representing management, and five, labor. (Labor was reluctant to participate, but at length agreed to do so.) He also set up a Price Commission made up of seven public members and a Cabinet-level Cost of Living Council that would superintend the whole economic control program and be under the chairmanship of Secretary of the Treasury John B. Connally. To Connally, in short, the President had delegated overall responsibility in this area, and by so doing made of him somewhat of a lightning rod that might deflect day-to-day "flack" from the White House.[13]

The significance of these startling presidential moves would be hard to underestimate. Because any such program will doubtless prove very hard to dismantle (World War II control programs under OPA came to a logical end with the end of the war, but what logical end could there be for peacetime controls?) without risking a politically devastating upward inflationary surge, President Nixon may have set the nation on a totally new path in regulating the economy. That a Republican Chief Executive should have made these decisions suggests, as do some other policy innovations the administration espoused (some of which will be discussed later), a pretty complete reshuffling, if not elimination, of traditional liberal-conservative patterns in American public policy and politics, and it suggests above all the lengths to which a politically sensitive President will go in dealing with the political imperatives of the office.

[13] Connally later left the government and organized a Democrats for Nixon group in the 1972 campaign.

the president
of the united states

King of the Americans

During the Constitutional Convention rumors spread that the framers were considering the establishment of a monarchy. To counter the rumors, the delegates issued an anonymous statement that declared, "we never once thought of a king." Alexander Hamilton in fact had proposed a monarchy, but the Convention was uninterested; it knew that a constitution that provided for a king would get short shrift from the country. Yet, in creating the Presidency, the framers created an office that eventually became kingly. They rejected a European-style monarchy, but they agreed with Hamilton's contention in *The Federalist* that "Energy in the executive is a leading character in the definition of good government." The "energy" was made possible because the Convention made three crucial decisions when it created the presidential office. It constructed a one-man executive able to act with speed and unity of purpose. It placed the President's election outside of the legislature, which might otherwise have dominated an executive whom it could select. And it endowed the President with his own independent powers.

As early as 1898 an observant newspaperman, Henry Jones Ford, made the essential point:

The truth is that in the presidential office, as it has been constituted since Jackson's time, American democracy has revived the oldest political institution of the race, the elective kingship. It is all three: the prerecognition of the notables and the tumultuous choice of the freemen, only conformed to modern conditions.[14]

Why this should be so is suggested in a comment by the Englishman Walter Bagehot, who wrote earlier in the nineteenth century. Monarchy, he observed, is strong government because "it is intelligible government. The mass of mankind

[14] *The Rise and Growth of American Politics* (New York: Da Capo Press, 1967), p. 293; first published in 1898.

260

understand it. . . . The action of a single will, the fiat of a single mind, are easy ideas: anybody can make them out, and no one can ever forget them." Bagehot, who was writing about the British Constitution, also distinguished between two basic types of governmental institution. There are the *dignified or theatrical parts,* such as the Monarch, "which excite and preserve the reverence of the population." Second, there are the *efficient parts* of government, like the Cabinet and the Parliament, "by which it, in fact, rules." [15] In America, a process of evolution—which included the popularization of the Presidency under Jackson, the decline of the legislature, and the modern need for strong central government—has made the President both the "dignified" and the "efficient" ruler.

Bagehot's English Monarch was a make-believe ruler engaged in trite but "interesting actions" for "the vacant many"; the real government of "uninteresting actions" was carried out by the Cabinet, understood by only "the inquiring few." America's President, however, unites the simple intelligibility and the intrinsic appeal of a king or queen with the practical business of governing. He is both the symbolic chief of the American state and its political ruler. Because, moreover, the people have elected him as *their* chosen representative, his position and power are unmatched in democratic governments. [16]

The President's kinglike position is seen in his many constitutional and political prerogatives, but it is most evident in his great influence over legislation and his control over foreign policy and national defense. He initiates and shapes major legislative decisions, and in relations with other states he leads the nation. He is now such a powerful international leader that President Nixon adopted the practice of giving a State of the World address in addition to the normal State of the Union message each year. One can be sure that every nuance of both is carefully evaluated, not only in Congress, but in Accra, London, and Moscow as well. "I make American foreign policy," President Truman once asserted—and he did.

The wartime President of an armed people is still more powerful. In many instances Lincoln during the Civil War and Franklin Roosevelt during World War II wielded the powers of military dictators. Finally, it is the President who sets the public agenda. True, he often reacts to events beyond his control. But the President alone is able, by his political actions and appeals, to define the issues and to structure controversies. So much is this the case that even Andrew Johnson, a President repudiated by the party that elected him and nearly convicted in an impeachment trial, set the issues of public debate during the mid-1860's.

Dramatically tragic confirmation of the President's hold on the American mind came with the reaction to John Kennedy's assassination. According to the National Opinion Research Center, nine of ten Americans suffered some physical discomfort during the four days between the President's slaying and his burial. Out of a sample of 1,384 persons, two thirds reported feeling tense and nervous, and approximately one half either wept on hearing the news, had difficulty in getting to sleep, or suf-

---

[15] *The English Constitution,* first published in 1857 (New York: Dolphin), Chs. 1 and 2.
[16] France under Charles DeGaulle was an obvious exception. But it is doubtful that the French Presidency will retain its Napoleonic form now that the General has left the scene.

fered a loss of appetite.[17] Perhaps the crude sign on a corner newsstand in New York City the day of Kennedy's funeral best summarized the nation's mood. It read simply: "Closed because of a death in the American family." [18]

Of course a President need not die or be killed in office to evoke a modified version of this kind of response. Professor Fred I. Greenstein, for example, in studying the development of ideas about government and politics among children (their "political socialization"), found that by the time they reached the fourth grade they were universally aware of the existence of the President. Only 30 per cent of these same children, however, could give a reasonably accurate description of his function in the national government. Yet virtually all of them were willing to make some evaluation of the President, and an overwhelming 96 per cent of those doing so judged his performance to be at least "fairly good" if not "very good." In other words, for some reason, perhaps because of a parallel between parental figures and the White House occupant, he is the first governmental personage children come to perceive. Moreover, although vague in its contours, the perception is overwhelmingly favorable.[19]

Adult perceptions are much less unanimously favorable, but still generally more so than electoral majorities would lead one to expect. Understandably, adult awareness of the role of the President is more precise, as is the public view of what that role should be. Professor Roberta S. Sigel, in seeking to measure the citizen's view of the role the President should play in contrast to the role of Congress and the role of the electorate in the political system, posed the following question to a survey sample:

Now, which of the two statements comes closest to your own ideas: "The President is an inspired leader; he has ideas of his own how to help the country. He should be able to make the people and Congress work along with him." or "It is up to the people through their Congressman to find solutions to the problems of the day. The President should stick to carrying out what the people and Congress have decided."

Fifty-two per cent chose the first statement, and only 40 per cent the second. Americans obviously *want* their President to lead. They see him as far more than a mere recorder and implementer of their will or Congress's policy.

This desire for leadership becomes even clearer in the results of a second question Professor Sigel posed to her survey respondents. It asked them to imagine a case in which the President felt troops should be sent to some trouble spot abroad in spite of popular opposition to the move. Should he send them anyway, or should he follow public opinion? (It must be noted that this study was conducted in 1965, well before America had become massively involved in Vietnam.) No less than three quarters of the sample insisted that the President should send the troops in spite of public opposition; only 21 per cent felt he should subordinate his view to opinion in the country.[20]

[17] *New York Times,* March 7, 1964.
[18] *New York Times,* November 26, 1963.
[19] *Children and Politics* (New Haven: Yale University Press, 1965).
[20] "Image of the American Presidency . . ." *Midwest Journal of Political Science,* X, No. 1 (February, 1966), 123–137.

The President's unique hold on the American people suggested by these studies strengthens his ability to lead the nation, yet it also makes him a politically ambivalent figure. On the one hand, he is a politician, elected at the head of a partisan ticket. On the other, he represents the entire nation and embodies many of its highest ideals. This ambivalence is rather graphically illustrated by a comparison between the vote cast for a President and his popularity with the same public shortly after he has taken office. In 1960, for instance, President Kennedy defeated Richard Nixon by a tiny margin, yet a month after his inauguration 72 per cent of a Gallup sample registered approval of his performance. Similarly, within a week of President Nixon's equally narrow victory over Hubert Humphrey in 1968, his popularity was recorded at 59 per cent. Obviously, once elected, a President is perceived as much more than a mere partisan candidate representing a small majority of the population. He becomes instead the nonpartisan leader of a much larger majority of all the people.

The meaning of these patterns for the President as national leader is reasonably obvious. The less partisan or divisive the purpose or object of a President's effort to lead, the more unanimous his following will be. In fact, as the response to Professor Sigel's second question suggests, in an international crisis or in wartime, a President is likely, at least initially, to receive support from *more* of the public than just the segment that agrees with his immediate moves. On the other hand, if the presidential leadership appears to take sides in a narrow way—by supporting his party against the other party, by supporting labor against management, or by favoring the blacks over whites—then quite the reverse may be true. Such a chief executive will lose support, not only among people who oppose his policy, but also among other people within the population. They will be repelled by his partisanship and will resent the fact that he is not fulfilling his obligation to be President of *all* the people. As noted earlier, the failure of a presidential policy (though once popular) can have a similar effect.

The Administration of President Lyndon B. Johnson illustrates in a particularly striking fashion some of these characteristics of the office. As heir to the martyred Kennedy, Johnson inherited overwhelming public support. This, combined with his own instinct for the middle of the political road and for consensus politics, provided near-unanimous approval for his early Administration. Johnson's stature was further reinforced by his massive electoral victory over Barry Goldwater in 1964, but the growing impact of the war in Vietnam soon began to erode his support. As America's involvement became progressively greater in both men and material resources, the public's view of the war polarized. "Hawks" wanted more bombing of North Vietnam and greater efforts to win a speedy military victory; "doves," with a growing intensity and passion, demanded withdrawal. Johnson's policies of steady but controlled escalation pleased neither side, but least of all the doves. Proponents of more vigorous domestic efforts to confront the nation's serious urban and racial problems accused the President of starving the home front to prosecute an immoral and pointless war.

By 1968 the polls had been reporting for some time a decline in Lyndon Johnson's popularity. January figures were typical: they revealed that 41 per cent of the population approved of the way he was doing his job and 47 per cent disapproved. The Johnson consensus had not only broken down, but the division in the nation over foreign policy threatened to become even deeper and more bitter than that between the isolationists and the anti-Nazi interventionists in the 1930's. Johnson, as with most of his predecessors to lesser degree, had become the captive of events and of the logic of the policies he felt it necessary to pursue. He had become, in short, identified with one side of a highly controversial and divisive policy. He thus not only was a target for the concerted opposition of all those who disagreed with the stand he took, but his "partisanship" on the issue of the war in Vietnam distressed more disinterested elements of the public; it violated their deeply held view of the nonpolitical role of the Presidency.

Limitations

Although the President can be an American king, he is far from being an unchecked despot. Current criticism of the office and its occupants focuses largely on the foreign policy sphere. Here, it is charged, there exists a dangerous presidential discretion. However, if the total policy spectrum is taken into account, the picture is rather different. We have already seen that a considerable portion of the influence a President wields rests on such intangible factors as reputation and image, and that this is a fragile base on which to rest presidential power. This fragility is in itself a significant check.

There are, of course, more tangible limits on presidential power. Some are essentially legal. The least important is the possibility that he may be removed by Congress for violating Article II, Section 4 of the Constitution by committing "Treason, bribery, or other high crimes and misdemeanors." First the House must indict him by impeachment, and then he must be tried by the Senate and found guilty by a two-thirds vote of the members present. Only one President, Andrew Johnson in 1867, has faced this ordeal. He was acquitted, though by the narrowest of margins—one vote. Incidentally, at the state level, where the provisions are similar, only four Governors have been ousted since Reconstruction days and none since 1927. The weapon of impeachment, though often called for by irate legislators, is, as one writer puts it, "a rusted blunderbuss that will probably never be taken in hand again." [21]

A President is more effectively checked by the separation of powers and the resulting constitutionally prescribed role of the Congress. As Presidents in recent decades have assumed or have had thrust upon them overall responsibility for the shape of national policy, domestic as well as foreign, this congressional check has grown in importance. In practice, increasing presidential responsibility has entailed setting the legislative agenda for much of the work of Congress. But, as with most state Governors, the national chief executive has few means of compelling congressional acceptance of his proposals or priorities—or even forcing consideration of

[21] Ford, op. cit., p. 288.

them. Presidents can block action with the veto, but they have no constitutionally prescribed way of inducing action.

The party leadership role limits a President as much as it helps him. Even if he enjoys majorities in both houses, he must reckon with the independence of individual members. To illustrate the problem, theoretically the President ought to be in a position to influence the selection of House and Senate candidates of his party. Thus, presumably, he could reduce opposition to his programs from his fellow partisans on the Hill. Actually, Presidents have only on rare occasions had the temerity to endorse publicly congressional candidates in primary elections. Between 1913 and 1960, a careful search of the public record reveals only thirty-nine such occasions. In this same period there were some twelve thousand nominations made in each party for House and Senate seats! In twenty-nine of these thirty-nine cases the President was successful in having his man at least nominated, but he failed in ten.[22]

Clearly, Presidents rarely feel such endorsements are likely to be useful and worth the risk. They are well advised to be cautious. A tremendous furor was kicked up in 1938 when Franklin Roosevelt mounted the most concentrated effort to conduct a purge of hostile Democrats that had yet been attempted. Titular party leader though he may be, the President's hands are usually tied in this area. In the overwhelming number of cases party candidates for Congress are chosen, and will continue to be, on a purely local basis. The President must take pot luck.

In addition to the public relations possibilities inherent in the office, which to some extent can be used for legislative leadership, Presidents have sought out individual members of Congress in quest of support. This may mean efforts to persuade committee chairmen or others in a position to block or advance a bill, or it may mean phone calls to waverers whose votes may turn the tide on a close roll call. There are things in the gift of the President that Congressmen want and that can at times be exchanged for votes. The result is a kind of barter system. Votes, favors, and other "goods" become the currency. Before civil service reform, the main form of currency was patronage jobs. Presidents could use these to "purchase" the support they needed.

In the heyday of patronage, however, Congress did less legislating overall than it does today, and the President was much less involved in the legislative process. Modern Presidents may at times yearn for the return of the bad old days of patronage, but in fact other forms of currency have come into use. Congressmen, for example, need introductions to administrative branch officials for their constituents; they like to be able to arrange special White House tours for key supporters; they want contracts awarded to firms in their district; or they want a military base kept open or a flood control project authorized. The President or the White House staff may be able to influence these matters, thereby building up "credit balances" with members that can be drawn upon later.

When one examines the problems of the President as legislative leader it is

22 William H. Riker and William Bast, "Presidential Action in Presidential Nominations" in Aaron Wildavsky, *The Presidency* (Boston: Little, Brown, 1969).

not surprising that until recently the general view was that he had *too little* power rather than too much. The recent shift in emphasis has grown out of immediate events and the relation of the office to them. Specifically, the war in Vietnam has raised nagging doubts. How can one accept the democratic validity of an office, many are asking, that has the seemingly unfettered power to get the country into such a predicament and keep it involved in spite of a rising clamor of protest? The Presidency as an office must be at fault as well as the individuals who have held it since the mid-1960's.

What our Southeast Asian experience highlights, of course, is the fact that in foreign and military policy, Presidents *do* have very large reservoirs of nearly autonomous power. They can order the armed forces into an area on their own initiative as commander-in-chief and thus leave Congress little alternative but to support the action and pay the bill. As Justice Sutherland wrote in the Curtiss-Wright case: "In this vast external realm, with its important, complicated, delicate and manifold problems, the President alone has the power to speak or listen as a representative of the nation." [23] What of the domestic policy area, however? Here the picture seems sharply different. As Dean Aaron Wildavsky has written, ". . . Presidents have had much greater success in controlling the nation's defense and foreign policies than in dominating its domestic policies." [24] In this sense there are, as Wildavsky indicates, really two Presidencies: there is the powerful and nearly autonomous President-as-architect-of-foreign-policy, whom neither Congress nor the public may seem able to control; and there is the President-as-chief-legislator and initiator of domestic policy, who spends much of his time pleading and bargaining for support in a Congress he has no way of coercing.

Table 7.2 suggests the different levels of success enjoyed by the "two presidents" in terms of congressional action. (Obviously, even in the foreign-defense sphere, the President must often go to Congress for funding or some kind of approval— perhaps after the fact.) It is clear that the President as domestic leader is balked and frustrated far more often than the President as commander-in-chief.

In light of the acute domestic problems confronting the nation in the 1970's— such as those involving the environment, poverty, and race—it may be appropriate to be as concerned about the weakness of the domestic Presidency as about the dangerous power of the foreign policy Presidency. It is not enough to say that if the President as military leader would just end immoral overseas involvements, the resulting release of resources could be plowed into the solving of domestic problems. Agreement would still be necessary on how the problems should be solved, in what order of priority, and with what allocation of resources, *and then* congressional action would have to be secured. These perplexities will tax the domestic Presidency to the limit, quite possibly beyond the limit of its available powers. Without doubt the office calls for thoughtful reevaluation, but the difficulties are not as clear-cut as they might at first appear. "The President," John Kennedy once noted, "is rightly

[23] *U.S.* v. *Curtiss-Wright Export Corp.* 299 U.S. (1937).
[24] "The Two Presidencies," *Trans-Action,* December, 1966.

Table 7.2 *Congressional action on presidential proposals, 1948–1964*

	Pass	Fail	Number of proposals
Domestic policy (resources, labor, agriculture, taxes, etc.)	40%	60%	2499
Immigration, refugees	13%	86%	129
Foreign policy	58%	42%	655
Treaties, general foreign relations, State Department, foreign aid, etc.	71%	29%	445
Defense policy (defense, disarmament, manpower)	73%	27%	90

Source: Congressional Quarterly Service, *Congress and the Nation, 1945–1964* (Washington, D.C., 1965).

described as a man of extraordinary powers. Yet it is also true that he must wield these powers under extraordinary limitations." [25]

President and Presidency

If the President is a man of extraordinary powers and extraordinary limitations, he is equally a man of extraordinary responsibilities. The enormous constitutional and political obligations that come with his office, when measured against the purely human limits on what a single person can do, make it essential that he be given institutional assistance.

This was the purpose of the Reorganization Act of 1939 creating an Executive Office of the President. Basically, the President is given two types of assistance. The first is primarily of a mechanical or routine sort. This includes personal secretaries, telephone operators, and mail clerks to sort and help answer the thousands of letters that reach the President every day. Second, and more significant, the President is given a staff of personal assistants and the help of agencies under his immediate control and intended to be exclusively his executive servants.

Ideally the Executive Office functions as the presidential eyes, ears, and hands; together with the President it comprises the modern Presidency. The original re-

[25] Theodore C. Sorensen, *Decision-Making in the White House: The Olive Branch or the Arrows* (New York: Columbia University Press, 1963), p. xii.

organization assigned certain agencies to the Executive Office and gave the President discretionary authority to reorganize it from time to time in the light of changing conditions and needs. Its components currently number eight specialized subdivisions. Three symbolize the modern President's emergence as the nation's legislative leader and as the protector of its economic and social well-being.

The **White House Office,** as its name implies, ministers to the immediate needs of the presidential office. It also includes a variety of special assistants to the President, such as his press secretary and the special assistant for liaison with Congress.

The **Office of Management and Budget** (until 1970 the Bureau of the Budget), prepares the budget, coordinates the financial and legislative requests of the executive agencies with the President's program, and under its new broader title is to emphasize evaluation of program performance in the executive branch, foster interagency cooperation, plan programs for the development of career executive talent throughout the government, and in general centralize a wide range of management activities.

The **Council of Economic Advisers,** a small office established by the Employment Act of 1946, consists of three economists. They study the latest trends in the nation's economy, advise the President on economic policies, and assist him in preparing the administration's annual economic report to Congress.

The **Domestic Council** was created by the same 1970 reorganization plan that restructured the Bureau of the Budget. As the press release noted at the time, the Council is intended to "bring together under one roof many of the sources for developing domestic policy and designing specific programs." Its members are the President, the Vice President, the Attorney General, and the Secretaries of Agriculture, Commerce, Health, Education and Welfare, Housing and Urban Development, Interior, Labor, Transportation, and the Treasury. It has an executive director and a staff and functions in its area similarly to the National Security Council in the realm of foreign and defense policy.

The **National Security Council** was created by the National Security Act of 1947 to advise the President on how best to coordinate domestic, foreign, and military policies so as to strengthen the nation's security. Only five members are named by law, but there is a permanent secretariat of special assistants, and the President may designate other executive officials to participate in National Security Council meetings. The permanent statutory members of the National Security Council are the President, the Vice President, the Secretary of State, the Secretary of Defense, and the Director of Emergency Preparedness. In addition to its advisory function, the National Security Council is the parent body of the Central Intelligence Agency, a semisecret agency whose espionage and special political undercover operations, it is estimated, absorb at least $2 billion a year.[26]

The **Office of Emergency Preparedness** assists the President in formulating policies and programs for the mobilization of the nation's resources and for civil defense in the event of war.

[26] David Wise and Thomas B. Ross, *The Invisible Government* (New York: Random House, 1964), pp. 259–260.

The **National Aeronautics and Space Council** similarly aids him in undertaking the nation's program of space exploration, and the **Office of Science and Technology** helps him in developing and coordinating programs of scientific and technical research; the activities of both these agencies are closely related to national defense.

A series of other components of the Executive Office of the President need only be listed. In most cases the titles give some clue to their function: The Council for Urban Affairs, The National Council on Marine Resources and Engineering Development, The Office of Intergovernmental Relations, and the Office of the Special Representative for Trade Negotiations.

The **Office of Economic Opportunity** during most of its brief history was the only operating (as opposed to staff) agency in the Executive Office. It managed the so-called poverty program set up under the Administration of Lyndon Johnson. It was located in the Executive Office to afford it the special supervision and protection that a controversial new program needs. Under President Nixon, however, it has been shorn of most of its operating functions but remains as a planning agency.

With a permanent body of around two thousand employees the Presidency has become institutionalized. In fact, some commentators have worried that the President may become a political prisoner in his own Executive Office. Such talk became pronounced during the Presidency of General Eisenhower, who superimposed his famous military staff system on the Executive Office. Except for Secretary of State John Foster Dulles, who had direct access to the President, Sherman Adams functioned as Eisenhower's chief of staff, resolving many policy conflicts himself, passing the more important ones on to the President in the form of brief alternative propositions, and following up on the execution of presidential decisions. In line with this approach Eisenhower consulted systematically with the National Security Council and the Cabinet, though there is no evidence that major Administration decisions were made collegially.

It may be that the Eisenhower Presidency was excessively institutionalized and that his staff system removed him too far from the process of making decisions. (To some critics, Adams was Assistant President, not Assistant to the President.) In the view of a knowledgeable person, former Secretary of Defense Robert A. Lovett, the President ought not to come in only at the final stage, simply ratifying one of two or three alternatives. Instead, policy objectives should be debated in front of him thereby airing all the alternatives and all the obstacles and forcing him "to look down the full length of the hard road and not simply the first few steps of it." [27] Perhaps Eisenhower should not have established a system that apparently cut him off from the political information that is a by-product of vigorous argument and conflict. But what the critics overlooked was that it was *Eisenhower's* staff system. He established it because it suited his needs and his conception of how to run the presidential office. If Eisenhower was captive to the Presidency, it was a Presidency of his own creation.

To be sure, any President must accept the basic structure of the Executive Office as he finds it. The institutionalized Presidency is indispensable. No President would

[27] Testimony before a Senate Subcommittee on National Policy Machinery, *New York Times,* February 28, 1960.

dream of returning the Office of Management and Budget to the Treasury Department or of eliminating his special corps of personal assistants. But if he has any abilities as a political leader, the President can shape the use of his immediate staff, particularly that of the White House Office. John Kennedy's staff system, for example, differed markedly from Eisenhower's. He cut back on the frequency of Cabinet and NSC meetings, and he preferred to use his personal staff in a more informal manner. Each of a small group of broadly talented senior assistants was assigned to particular problems. Lyndon Johnson's staff-working methods appeared to be similarly informal and, like Kennedy, he was more accessible to his senior officials than was Eisenhower. President Nixon apparently has returned somewhat to the more formalized Eisenhower practices. He relies heavily on H. R. Haldeman, who has the role of chief of staff; Henry Kissinger, who is in charge of national security matters; and more recently, George Shultz, Director of the Office of Management and Budget, and then Secretary of the Treasury. In short, each President puts his own imprint on the Presidency.

Table 7.3 illuminates certain aspects of differing presidential styles in the use of staff, as well as indicating the overall trends in recent years. The first two columns of figures are compiled from the *Congressional Directory* for the years indicated; the last column is from figures listed in various issues of the *Statistical Abstract of the United States* under the category of employees in the White House Office. The sharp jump from 61 employees in 1946 to 210 in 1948 reflects a new system of bookkeeping rather than a sudden spurt of 350 per cent. Until the Truman Administration, many White House staffers were borrowed from the traditional executive departments, which continued to pay them and maintain them on their employment rolls. President Truman, however, felt this was not a straightforward way to do business, and he gave instructions to have such staff persons listed under a heading more in accord with their actual function.

The Eisenhower years, as might be expected, reveal a vast expansion in the total number of personnel (column three) assigned to the White House staff. Not all of this reflects the General's style of executive operation; obviously, the burdens and responsibilities of the presidential office grew steadily during these years. A decline nonetheless did set in during the Kennedy and especially the Johnson periods, leaving the Eisenhower period as a high-water mark in the bureaucratization of the office. The same patterns show up in the table's first two columns. These offer a rough measure of functional specialization within the professional portion of the White House staff. Although titles often do not indicate the actual assignment, their multiplication and the marked increase in the total number of titled staffers parallels the growth of special staff assignments.

Another measure of the rising curve of White House activity can be seen in the annual tabulations of press releases issued from the Executive Office. Most decisions, studies, or other specific activities undertaken by the White House staff in the name of the President at some point take the form of a handout prepared for the press. Tabulations show that they averaged about 275 annually under Roosevelt, climbed to just over 500 under both Truman and Eisenhower, and jumped again to 800

Table 7.3 *Growth of the White House Office staff:*
          1938–1968

Year	Number of titles *	Number of persons w/titles †	Total personnel
1938 (FDR)	4	6	
1940	4	9	
1942	6	11	
1944	7	14	50
1946 (HST)	7	12	61
1948	7	12	210
1950	8	15	295
1952	9	12	245
1954 (DDE)	20	26	266
1956	23	40	374
1958	25	46	394
1960	28	47	446
1962 (JFK)	13	21	467
1964 (LBJ)	15	23	349
1966	13	23	289
1968	15	23	273
1970 (RMN)	15	20	340
1972	24	49	508 ‡

* The number of different titles represented in the White House Office listing, e.g.: Administrative Assistant, Special Counsel, Special Consultant, etc.

† Some titles, e.g.: Administrative Assistant, are usually held by several people.

‡ 1971 total.

under Kennedy. The Johnson Administration at least maintained this Kennedy average, the first Nixon year totals were over 1000 (see Table 7.4). In short, the Presidency as an institution has combined in its development an inexorable growth in staffing to match a rising curve and a broadening range of activity and responsibility, with noticeable variations produced by differences in presidential style. This expandability combined with the inherent flexibility of the office represents one of its great strengths.

The Vice Presidency: Anteroom to the Presidency

John Adams, the Republic's first Vice President, described the post he held as "the most insignificant office that ever the invention of man contrived or his imagination conceived." He also pointed to what he could be: "I am possessed of two

Table 7.4

Annual tabulations of press releases

Source: Elmer E. Cornwell, Jr., *Presidential Leadership of Public Opinion* (Bloomington: Indiana University Press, 1965), p. 232, with Johnson and Nixon figures added.

Roosevelt		Truman		Eisenhower	
1933	197	1945	409	1953	463
1934	236	1946	513	1954	486
1935	192	1947	474	1955	402
1936	238	1948	707	1956	501
1937	175	1949	406	1957	419
1938	182	1950	535	1958	513
1939	207	1951	469	1959	557
1940	291	1952	620	1960	566
1941	428	1953	42	1961	141
1942	373				
1943	290				
1944	353				
1945	106				
	3,268		4,175		4,048

Kennedy		Johnson		Nixon	
1961	833	1963	95	1969	1,306
1962	911	1964	974	1970	1,126
1963	649	1965	1,053	1971	
		1966	859		
		1967	796		
		1968	903		
		1969	63		
	2,393		4,680		

separate powers, the one *in esse* and the other *in posse*. I am Vice President. In this I am nothing, but I may be everything."

In recent years, however, the Vice Presidency has risen in popular and political esteem. Vice Presidents today are no longer, as they usually were in the past, aging party war horses enjoying semiretirement in a home for old politicians. Thus, in the months preceding the 1964 Democratic Convention, a baker's dozen of the nation's most prominent Democratic politicians made it clear that nothing would honor them more than to be selected by President Johnson as his vice-presidential running mate. Neither are today's Vice Presidents men who were nominated for the single purpose of reuniting a party split into two political wings. Presidential candidates pick running mates who will broaden their political appeal, but the tickets themselves are not politically schizophrenic. The 1968 presidential tickets of Humphrey-Muskie and Nixon-Agnew, for example, were politically compatible, as was the McGovern-Shriver ticket of 1972. The modern President, therefore, is likely to go into office with a Vice President who has some ability and stature and whose political views are similar to his.

Alben Barkley under Truman, Richard Nixon under Eisenhower, Lyndon Johnson under Kennedy, and Hubert Humphrey under Johnson all illustrate the new practice, though in the eyes of some people Spiro Agnew may be the exception that proves the rule. The Vice President sits in Cabinet meetings, is a statutory member of the National Security Council, makes international goodwill tours, and supervises programs of interest to the President. The extent of such service depends on the President's desires and on the personal relationships that exist between the two men. Yet, useful as they can be, no Vice President can lighten the President's burden. The essence of the Presidency is that it is a one-man job; the ordeal of decision cannot be subdivided.

Despite the change from its earlier obscurity, the comment of John Adams still summarizes the reality of the vice-presidential office: its great significance is that it is a macabre anteroom to the Presidency. Constitutionally, the Vice President has but three duties. The first is to preside over the Senate, and in the case of a tie vote, to cast the deciding ballot. At times he may be in a position to decide an important issue, but such opportunities are infrequent. His second duty is to assume the Presidency when a vacancy occurs. In 1841, when President William H. Harrison died, John Tyler decided that he should become President and not merely be, as the Constitution implies, a Vice President "acting" as President. Ever since then it has been accepted that on the President's death the Vice President succeeds to the full powers of the office, and the Twenty-fifth Amendment writes this understanding into the Constitution. The Vice President's third constitutional duty is to "act as President" temporarily in case the President becomes disabled.

The constitutional provisions on presidential death and disability had long remained vague. The problem was not purely academic: eight of thirty-one Presidents have died in office; three Presidents (Garfield, Wilson, and Eisenhower) were physically disabled for extended periods; and on fifteen occasions there has been no Vice President to succeed the President. Everyone agreed that a President's death meant the accession of the Vice President. Everyone further agreed that it was highly desirable always to have available a Vice President who was informed and able to fill a breach in the Presidency quickly, as Lyndon Johnson did upon Kennedy's assassination. But there long was disagreement on two important subsidiary issues. What was to be done when illness disables a President? Under what circumstances should the Vice President act in his place, and could he do so without irrevocably becoming a full President himself and displacing the incumbent? Second, how should the line of succession run when the vice-presidential office is vacant?

These questions have been finally answered in the Twenty-fifth Amendment to the Constitution. It asserts unmistakably that a succeeding Vice President "shall become President," while Section 2 of the amendment takes the next logical step by providing for the filling of vacancies in the Vice Presidency itself. The President is called upon to make a nomination in such a case, though *both* houses of Congress must confirm by majority vote, not just the Senate as with ordinary presidential nominations. Sections 3 and 4 deal with the thorny problem of disability. The problem is rather simple if the President is in a position, physically and mentally, to transmit a declaration to the President Pro Tempore of the Senate and the Speaker of the House signifying his inability to discharge the duties of his office. It becomes more difficult if he is unable or unwilling to step aside thus voluntarily. Section 4 of the amendment specifies careful procedures for arranging this at the initiative of the Vice President acting either with the Cabinet or with a specially constituted body. Only the President, of course, can terminate such a period of inability and if at any point serious dispute arises, Congress remains the final authority.

Presumably this amendment has solved the problems. The machinery is provided and the principle—never clear before—established that the Vice President may become either President in his own right upon the death of the President, or *acting* President during temporary disability. Actually the practical and political problems that might arise are so delicate and thorny that it is doubtful if the amendment, or any similar statement, can settle them all in advance.

The case of Woodrow Wilson's stroke upon his return from the Versailles Peace Conference is instructive. Mrs. Wilson and Dr. Cary Grayson jealously guarded both the bedchamber and the prerogatives of its occupant. Meanwhile the colorless Vice President, Thomas R. Marshall, lived in terror that he might indeed become President! Under the Twenty-fifth Amendment, either Wilson would have had to certify his own disability, or Marshall would have had to take the lead in having him so certified. Neither was very likely to have happened, and if the latter had, against Wilson's will, a bitter struggle might well have ensued.

Actually, the procedure followed by Presidents Eisenhower, Kennedy, and Johnson prior to the ratification of the amendment, each of whom made an explicit agreement with his Vice President covering such eventualities, still has much to recommend it. Only if the two potential participants in such a temporary transfer of power agree in advance to the steps to be taken is the risk of hard feelings, if not a major political clash, avoidable.

The Legacy of Presidential History

The Presidency, Edward S. Corwin has written, "is still very much a matter of who is President." [28] It is also very much a matter of who was President. For the powers and responsibilities of Presidents today are in large measure a consequence of the precedents established and the expectations aroused by earlier Presidents. The following legacy of presidential history is at once a testimonial to the fact that in the Presidency individual men make a difference and a summary of the main outlines of

---

[28] *The President: Office and Powers 1787–1957,* 4th ed. (New York: New York University Press, 1957), p. 305.

the modern office. Although all such listings are somewhat arbitrary, it seems fair to say that eight of our past Presidents have made significant contributions and have left an indelible mark on the presidential office:

Washington: the President as chief of state

Because he came first George Washington was in a unique position. "Many things which appear of little importance in themselves," he himself perceived, "may have great and durable consequences from their having been established at the commencement of a new general government." Washington established a number of important constitutional precedents, but his contribution was intangible. "There was a seriousness in his manner which seemed to contribute to the impressive dignity of his person," a contemporary reported after meeting the President. "There are persons in whose appearance one looks in vain for the qualities they are known to possess, but the appearance of General Washington harmonized in a singular manner with the dignity and modesty of his public life." [29] Not only did Washington *look* like a President—so too did Warren Harding—but he *acted* like one. Although he articulated no views about his presidential role, preferring to communicate them by his actions, Washington had an intuitive conception of what the President should be.

He was, in the first place, the head of the administration. Washington, as John Adams observed, "seeks information from all quarters, and judges more independently than any man I ever knew." Second, Washington was consciously determined that *the position* of President be recognized as the foremost in the land. He made this clear both by his own inherently dignified behavior and by his insistence that in matters of official protocol the President took precedence. As early as 1789, during a tour of New England, Washington held out until the proud John Hancock, Governor of Massachusetts, called on the President. The President, Washington believed, did not call on a state Governor. Third, Washington, who feared the divisiveness of party factions, devoted himself to promoting national unity. He saw the President as the nation's sober guide and as a unifying force, a role most strikingly illustrated by the magisterial Farewell Address, in which he advised his countrymen to guard carefully "the Union of the whole." By all of these actions, which he infused with the dignity and strength of his character, Washington made the President chief of the American state.

Jefferson: the President as party leader

When Thomas Jefferson assumed office in 1801 the party factions that Washington had feared were dominant. The election of 1800 was the consequence of a sharp party battle between the rising Republicans and the Federalists. Jefferson himself was a leading organizer of the victorious party, and, as Hamilton had predicted, he was no "enemy to the power of the Executive" in cases "which coincided with his views."

[29] Leonard D. White, *The Federalists: A Study in Administrative History* (New York: Macmillan, 1948), p. 98.

Jefferson's preferred method of operation was to work behind the scenes. Presidential commands were given to his party lieutenants who occupied the key legislative posts, discussed in the House and Senate Republican caucuses, and then usually ratified by Congress. "I have proposed in conversation, and it seems generally assented to," Jefferson informed Captain George Rogers Clark, "that Congress appropriate 10–12,000 dollars for exploring the principal waters of the Mississippi and Missouri." With this brief suggestion he set in motion the legislative wheels to support the Lewis and Clark Expedition. Jefferson, a Federalist Senator fumed, "secretly dictates every measure which is seriously proposed and supported." [30] Party government was probably closer to realization between 1801 and 1809 than at any other time in American history. By his leadership and management of a political party, Jefferson created a new presidential role—the President as party leader. Despite the coming decline of two-party competition during the next fifteen years, the expansion of democracy brought a resurgence of party conflict. If Presidents were to be successful in the pursuit of their policies, they would have to be successful party leaders.

Jackson: the President as representative of the people

"He claims to be not only the representative, but the immediate representative of the American people! What effrontery! What boldness of assertion! The immediate representative? Why, he never received a vote from the American people. He was elected by electors—the colleges." The speaker was Senator John C. Calhoun and the year 1832; the object of his wrath was his bitter enemy, President Andrew Jackson, who had dared to veto the bill rechartering the Bank of the United States. Calhoun was technically right—Jackson was elected by the Electoral College—and politically dead wrong: the American people, in choosing electors pledged to vote for him, had directly elected Jackson.

Unlike Calhoun, Jackson understood the source of his political strength. In his Bank veto message Jackson appealed to those he called "the humble members of society—the farmers, mechanics, and laborers." Along with Jackson they blamed the Bank for their economic hardships and disliked it for being a government-sponsored monopoly controlled by an eastern aristocracy. Jackson's opponents, however, were so blind to the political facts of life in a democracy that they stupidly gave his views greater publicity. His foes printed and distributed the veto message, thinking it would harm the President! The peoples' answer came with Jackson's reelection to a second term that confirmed and renewed his popular mandate.

Jackson, like Jefferson, was a party leader, but he was also a self-avowed "direct representative of the American people" charged with the "especial duty to protect the liberties and rights of the people." With "Jackson men" to support him in Congress and with a strong popular base to which to appeal, President Jackson used his executive powers in a truly remarkable fashion. He successfully asserted that the President could veto legislation when he believed it unwise, not merely when

[30] Leonard D. White, *The Jeffersonians: A Study in Administrative History 1801–1829* (New York: Macmillan, 1951), p. 35.

he felt it to be unconstitutional. He ousted Cabinet officials who refused to perform their statutory duties as *he* thought they should. He disregarded the congressional policy expressed in an earlier bank law by removing government deposits from the Bank of the United States. When confronted with South Carolina's nullification and threatened secession over the "Tariff of Abominations," he made unmistakably clear his intention to preserve the Union.

For over twenty years the Presidency had declined in power as Congress, claiming to be the popular organ of government, dominated a parade of weak Presidents. Eight years of Andrew Jackson reversed the legacy of Madison, Monroe, and John Quincy Adams, a legacy of presidential subservience to Congress. Jackson's Presidency showed that, contrary to the earlier distrust of executive tyranny, the President could be the focal point of popular government. (Even Washington had been a reserved and somewhat remote *deus ex machina,* a sort of eighteenth-century DeGaulle; Jefferson had carefully governed under the table—through Congress.) Jackson harnessed popular democracy to the Presidency, and thereby added not only to its powers but to its potential power in the future. Well might another one of his enemies, Henry Clay, speak of "a revolution." Jackson, as Clay so aptly phrased it, "swept over the government like a tropical tornado."

Lincoln: the President as commander-in-chief

In 1860 President James Buchanan sent a message to Congress describing South Carolina's secession from the Union as revolutionary, yet declaring that the executive had "no authority" to act. Even Congress, he said, could not use arms to prevent secession, for this was not among "the specific and enumerated powers" granted to it by the Constitution. Buchanan's solution was a constitutional amendment guaranteeing property rights in slavery. The Union was disintegrating before his eyes, and the President proposed a constitutional amendment!

Buchanan's successor, Abraham Lincoln, took a less restricted view of presidential responsibilities. Not bothering to call a special session of Congress, which might have hindered him, Lincoln increased the size of the army and the navy, spent money for military supplies without congressional authorization, approved the arrest of suspected traitors and suspended the *habeas corpus* privilege, and ordered a blockade of southern ports. Most of these actions violated the Constitution, though Congress later ratified them because it had no choice in the matter. Nor did Lincoln's bold performance end with his eleven-week "dictatorship." He issued the Emancipation Proclamation, undercutting Congress, which claimed the power belonged to it. On December 8, 1863, he also announced a policy of amnesty toward the Confederate rebels. Subsequently, and despite strong congressional resistance, he made clear his intention to dominate reconstruction as he had dominated the prosecution of war.

Lincoln justified his behavior with two arguments. The first was constitutional. According to his interpretation, the constitutional clause making him Commander-in-Chief of the military forces, combined with the one instructing him to "take care that the Laws be faithfully executed," added up to a potent "war power." This power, he insisted, was primarily presidential, not congressional. His oath of office, moreover, was a command to "preserve, protect, and defend the Constitution of the United States." The nation was in a Civil War that threatened the Union; the Constitution and the laws of Congress were being violated—and the President was empowered to act. Lincoln's argument then shaded into his second main point, a practical one. Admitting that his course was not always "strictly legal," he cited his oath to preserve the Constitution as part of "the organic law." "Was it possible," he asked, "to lose the nation and yet preserve the Constitution?" He answered with this powerful contention:

> By general law life and limb must be protected, yet often a limb must be amputated to save a life, but a life is never wisely given to save a limb. I felt that measures, otherwise unconstitutional, might become lawful by becoming indispensable to the preservation of the Constitution through the preservation of the nation.

As Commander-in-Chief Lincoln did even more than mobilize the nation and vigorously prosecute the war. He also concerned himself with the strategy of the war. All of the later "war Presidents"—Wilson, Roosevelt, Truman, and Johnson— have adopted Lincoln's role as Commander-in-Chief. Using the expansive war powers, which ultimately are as expansive as the nation's need for self-preservation, and supported by huge delegations of congressional authority, they have commanded the nation armed for war. The governing precedents came from Lincoln, whose bold actions explain why, as John Kennedy once put it, "there is a Lincoln Room in the White House, and no Buchanan Room."

Theodore Roosevelt: the President as steward of the people

Theodore Roosevelt has been called the first modern President, and in many ways the description fits. He did a little of everything, loudly and with great gusto. Roosevelt succeeded in getting much of his legislative program through Congress, used his executive powers to promote conservation, spurred federal antitrust suits, and stepped into the anthracite coal strike of 1902 determined to force a solution. In international affairs he offered his services as a go-between in international disputes, expanded American influence in the Caribbean, and demonstrated the nation's military power by sending the Navy around the world. And all the while, the ebullient Theodore Roosevelt and his lively young family filled the White House with a "strenuous bedlam" that brought the President unprecedented publicity.

To justify and support his bold actions, Theodore Roosevelt developed a constitutional theory, the "Stewardship Theory," which articulated the Lincoln-Jackson conception of the Presidency and applied it to the twentieth century. As Roosevelt explained it in his *Autobiography:*

> [It was my] theory that the executive power was limited only by specific restrictions and prohibitions appearing in the Constitution or imposed by the Congress under its Constitutional Powers. My view was that every executive office . . . was a steward of the people, and not to content himself with the negative merit of keeping his talents undamaged in a

napkin. . . . My belief was that it was not only his right but his duty to do anything that the needs of the Nation demanded unless such action was forbidden by the Constitution or the laws.

Believing, as did Jackson and Lincoln, that his mandate came from "the plain people" and that "I represent democracy," Theodore Roosevelt was even more outspoken in his private correspondence: "I have," he wrote, "used every ounce of power there was in my office and I have not cared a rap for the criticisms of those who spoke of my 'usurpation of power.' "

One such criticism came from his own hand-picked successor, William Howard Taft. Shortly after leaving the White House, former President Taft argued that the "true view of the Executive functions is that they must be traced or justly implied" from specific constitutional or congressional grants of power. There is, he insisted, no "undefined residuum of Executive power" enabling the President to act in the public interest. He called Roosevelt's view "an unsafe doctrine" that "might lead under emergencies to results of an arbitrary character, doing irremediable injustice to private right." Although Taft admitted that the President should act vigorously when supported by a legal foundation, the essence of his position was that the legislature was the dominant branch of government. Like Clay and Calhoun, who had similarly opposed Jackson, Taft believed that Congress ought to make national policy. The President as its messenger boy—a very dignified one, to be sure—ought to confine himself to executing the congressional will.

Although Theodore Roosevelt's Stewardship Theory has won large acceptance, there are still sharp challenges to the idea of a dominant executive branch. Charges of "executive tyranny" have been routinely hurled at every President since 1932, and in nullifying Truman's seizure of the steel mills in 1952 the Supreme Court gave the President a celebrated constitutional spanking for having exceeded his lawful executive powers.[31] Most students of the Presidency doubt that the *Steel Seizure* decision will be much of a future limitation on bold presidential actions, particularly in cases where the public sense of national emergency is sharper than it was during the Korean War. Nevertheless, the Court's ruling and the rigid separation-of-power views that some of the judges expressed indicate that the ethos of presidential subservience to Congress remains strong.

In fact, the Republican presidential candidate in 1964, Barry M. Goldwater, clearly spoke the language of legislative preeminence. "It is," Goldwater once said, "the job of the legislative branch to legislate and it is the job of the executive branch to administer." During the campaign he described the Presidency as "separated from the legislative branch." He contended that those who "worship" the strong President, because he achieves results that they favor, have adopted "the totalitarian philosophy that the end justifies the means." [32]

[31] *Youngstown Sheet and Tube Co.* v. *Sawyer,* 343 U.S. 579 (1952).
[32] Jack Bell, *Mr. Conservative: Barry Goldwater* (New York: Macfadden, 1964), p. 63; *New York Times,* July 11, 1964; September 12, 1964.

Wilson: the President as legislative leader

Woodrow Wilson would have liked to be remembered as the man who converted the Presidency into a British-style Prime Ministership. This was his academic and political ideal, but it could not work in the American constitutional and political setting. Wilson nonetheless fulfilled and extended Theodore Roosevelt's promise that the President could be the nation's legislative leader. The opposition was divided, a consequence of the Bull Moose bolt from the Republican Party in 1912, but the Democratic caucus was strong. Wilson led it with a sure-footed skill.

Convinced that he had a popular mandate from the country for his New Freedom, Wilson went to Congress in 1913 with a well-prepared program. He did so literally. In an inspired action he revived the Federalist practice of personally addressing Congress, presenting his program in broad and appealing outline instead of the tediously long messages that even Theodore Roosevelt had used. In speaking to Congress, Wilson dramatized his legislative leadership by appealing to the nation for public support. When necessary, he compromised, and the results were impressive. Wilson pushed through such important legislation as the Underwood Tariff Reform Act, the Federal Reserve Act, and the Clayton Anti-Trust Act. During World War I he differed from Lincoln's practice by governing through Congress. The Lever and the Overman Acts gave him virtually dictatorial power to reorganize the executive agencies and to mobilize the nation's resources for war. Even Wilson's later blunders with Congress over the League of Nations Treaty cannot mar the significance of his contribution—the President as legislative leader.

Franklin Roosevelt: the President as public educator

In the course of twelve tumultuous years Franklin D. Roosevelt was the embodiment of all the presidential roles so far discussed. A brilliant politician, Franklin D. Roosevelt refined and extended all the powers of the Presidency, applying them first to combat the Depression and later to prosecute a global war. Yet he too made a significant contribution of his own to the Presidency. Realizing that on major issues the President needed the support of public opinion, Franklin D. Roosevelt systematically played the role of a public educator. The President's task, as he put it in a 1932 speech, was "persuading, leading, sacrificing, teaching always, because the greatest duty of a statesman is to educate."

More than any of his predecessors Franklin Roosevelt seized every opportunity to educate public opinion. He would first try to win public understanding of a problem and next, after a period of maturation, seek support for his proposed solutions. He wanted a social security program—a radical departure from laissez-faire government—but felt in 1933 that "the country is not educated up to all of those things yet." Under his tutelage the nation went to school: he held presidential press conferences to brief the newspapermen and indirectly their readers; he sent a major message to Congress; he engaged in a "fireside" radio chat with the nation; he appointed a commission to study and report on the problem; and he encouraged a barrage of speeches by his Cabinet officials. By 1935 Franklin Roosevelt had apparently convinced the nation that this leading New Deal innovation was "a return" to traditional American values of "home, livelihood, and individual security," which had been "lost in the course of our economic development and expansion." The Social Security Act, which is discussed in Chapter 12, was passed in that year.

Like any President, Franklin Roosevelt could lead only where the nation could be persuaded to go. This is not to say that if Franklin D. Roosevelt had been President in the 1920's instead of the 1930's he would have been only a more colorful and more garrulous Calvin Coolidge.[33] Even in the twenties there were ample public problems to absorb Franklin D. Roosevelt as there had been to occupy his equally energetic cousin, Theodore Roosevelt, in the early 1900's. But a decade of normalcy would have limited Franklin D. Roosevelt's opportunities to lead the public. In 1925 America was content to "Keep Cool with Coolidge," and the President could casually tell a news conference, "I would like it if the country could think as little as possible about the government and give their time and attention more undividedly to the conduct of the private business of our country." Imagine a President—even Calvin Coolidge—handing out such advice in 1933!

During the Depression there existed a political climate in which Franklin Roosevelt could interpret events and lead opinion. But even the master had his difficulties. Roosevelt knew in the thirties that Nazi and Japanese aggression was a threat to all the democracies. Yet, as late as 1937, when he suggested that the entire world had a mutual interest in clamping a quarantine on the nations afflicted with the disease of aggression, the public angrily and unmistakably condemned the President. "It's a terrible thing," Roosevelt commented later, "to look over your shoulder when you are trying to lead—and to find no one there."

He did not make the mistake again, for isolationism and a dread of war were powerfully strong. Patiently and carefully, often with calculated evasiveness, in speeches and press conferences, he gradually educated a wary nation to an understanding of the dangers it faced. The savage sweep of Nazi aggression naturally aided him. After the attack on Poland in 1939, opinion began to move away from the isolationists and toward Roosevelt's position. But he did not merely "ride opinion"; not until the attack on Pearl Harbor was this possible. What Franklin D. Roosevelt did was to guide and instruct opinion in support of his objectives, and he did it with a stroke of genius. Conscription was adopted; Roosevelt described it as "muster," evoking traditional images of embattled farmers at Concord Bridge. Destroyers were turned over to the British without Congress' assent and on dubious authority in return for the use of British bases; his Attorney General described it as a shrewd "Yankee horse trade." A Lend Lease program that was only a step short of a declaration of war was put through Congress. It allowed the President to dispense a vast

---

[33] The image of "Silent Cal" is, however, a public myth, the construction of a shrewd Yankee politician. Actually, Coolidge, with the help of speech writers, gave more speeches in five-and-a-half years than Theodore Roosevelt and Wilson combined; he averaged more "off the record" press conferences per month than Franklin D. Roosevelt! His leadership of opinion, naturally, was directed toward negative policy-making. See Elmer E. Cornwell, Jr., *Presidential Leadership of Public Opinion* (Bloomington: Indiana U.P., 1965), Ch. 4.

and varied quantity of food and war supplies to the Allied nations; Roosevelt told the country that it was no more than the act of one neighbor lending "a length of garden hose" to another whose home had caught fire. It is no exaggeration to say that Roosevelt's leadership of opinion in the bewildering years before World War II ranks as perhaps the most brilliant achievement of his Presidency. Beyond any doubt he provided a model demonstration of the President as public educator.

Truman: the President as international leader

The Presidency of Harry S. Truman is a fascinating one for the contrast it offers between Truman's domestic failures and his international accomplishments. A once common cliché was that some mysterious flaw of character made Truman a Janus-like President, a "statesman" of vision in international affairs, a shabby "politician" in domestic affairs. In reality there was only one Truman, and his problems were not ones of character, but of politics. Postwar America, as it had in the twenties, understandably yearned for a period of tranquility in which to enjoy the hard-earned material pleasures of life. There was also a clear political reaction against the Democratic Party, which appeared to be too much the creature of a selfish labor interest. There was a corresponding gain for the more conservative Republicans and their Southern Democratic allies. The Republican Eightieth Congress elected in 1946 reflected this new balance, and even Truman's surprising and very narrow election victory in 1948 did not change matters. His Southern Democratic–Republican opponents still controlled Congress, and the Fair Deal never became more than a campaign slogan.

Despite these immense political liabilities, Truman's Presidency was exceedingly significant. For the first time a President led the United States into a new and permanent preoccupation with world affairs. The success of his efforts established the President as a powerful international leader. The "Truman Doctrine" supplied economic and military aid to a Greece and Turkey threatened by international Communism, and it committed the United States to containing Soviet expansion. This commitment was vitalized by a series of decisions and programs that Truman carried out during the late forties. Among the most notable were the Marshall Plan for European economic recovery, the "Point Four" program of technical assistance to underdeveloped nations, the Berlin Airlift, the North Atlantic Treaty Organization alliance, and the armed resistance to the Communist attack on South Korea. In addition, throughout this period, Truman, although never disregarding American interests, committed the United States to a leading role in the United Nations.

How, one asks, was all this possible? After all, two of the leading landmarks of Truman's early international leadership, the aid to Greece and Turkey and the Marshall Plan, were possible only because Congress made the huge appropriations to carry them out. Congress was the same "do-nothing Congress" Truman campaigned against in 1948. Once again the answer lies in a complex of political factors. Soviet imperialism was so obviously menacing that, no matter how fervent the wish for a new normalcy, it could not be ignored. The Republican congressional leadership recognized the danger as fully as did Truman, and, convinced that the next President would be Republican, felt the burden of responsibility that comes with power. As Neustadt puts it, "The war was over, Roosevelt dead, Truman a caretaker, theirs the trust." [34] Truman in turn agreed to keep partisan politics out of foreign affairs, appointed prominent Republicans to key international assignments, and allowed the Republican leaders to participate in making the decisions. By contrast, his decision not to seek congressional approval for the Korean intervention undercut his authority once the war went badly and left the Republican Party free to attack "Truman's War."

Truman, however, was no front man for Congress. All of the basic decisions of the Truman Administration reflected his conviction that the President had an obligation to lead the nation into a permanent preoccupation with the state of the world. Because the Constitution gives the chief executive far greater discretion in foreign than in domestic affairs, and because the threat of Soviet aggression seemed real and immediate to most Americans, Truman was able to attain many of his international objectives. Since Truman's years in office, world politics have been changing with revolutionary speed, yet two factors remain unchanged. For over twenty years there has been a permanent—indeed almost routine—sense of international crisis, and the United States has continued its inescapable involvement in world affairs. With equal inescapability, all the Presidents to follow Harry S. Truman have, like him, devoted their major energies to international leadership.

The recent Presidents

All Presidents today perform the roles that the legacy of history has made part of the Presidency. Needless to say, the roles are not interchangeable bright costumes to be worn by the President as he picks and chooses. The listing of roles, rather, reflects the subject matter of his many concerns. At times one concern may tend to crowd out the others, but there is always only one President.

Since Truman's two terms, there have been four Presidents. Although Dwight D. Eisenhower (1953–1961) has been much criticized by many academicians and journalists as a "weak" President, many of the commentaries are both inaccurate and unfair. Eisenhower's conception of the Presidency was less expansive than that of the two Roosevelts, but it was not Taftian either. In international affairs, certainly, there could be no doubt that Eisenhower was the nation's leader. Much of the criticism against Eisenhower as President was actually criticism of his domestic political policies. His critics, for instance, claimed that he did not vigorously support civil rights and that he did not fight hard enough for federal aid to education. But the entire "weak" versus "strong" President classification needs to be handled very cautiously. Was Coolidge, for example, a weak President? In terms of his policy objectives—the promotion of economy in government and of a laissez-faire climate for business—he was eminently successful.

Eisenhower's flaws as President were not so much that he was a weak President, but that he was unsure about his domestic policy objectives. For example, what

---

[34] *Presidential Power,* op. cit., p. 49.

appeared as weakness when he seemingly repudiated his generally liberal budget in 1957 was less weakness as such than a personal uncertainty over the budget's social welfare features and a growing dislike for heavy federal expenditures. In 1958 and 1959, when Eisenhower submitted more conservative budgets that harmonized with what had become his settled conviction on the need to reduce federal spending, he emerged as a strong leader. He proved himself, also, to be an influential public educator on the subject of balanced budgets. The Kennedy Administration, for one, learned that millions of Americans had had their long-standing convictions reinforced by Eisenhower's stern warnings on the dangers of inflation and the wisdom of economy budgets. It had little success when it tried to reeducate the public away from what it called the "myth" that deficit financing was bad.

Eisenhower's uncertainty over some of his objectives sometimes made him seem weak, but his effectiveness was also diminished because of his ingrained distaste for what he contemptuously dismissed as "politics." "I have no great liking for that," he would say. Because of this attitude, he very often was insensitive to the nuances of political power and to the ways in which politicians think and act. Undoubtedly the most popular man to occupy the White House since World War II, Eisenhower was both to himself and to most Americans a great nonpartisan healer. His objective was to unify the nation after the abrasive discords of the New and Fair Deals and to promote peaceful stability abroad.

Ironically, though, his greatest asset, which was the image of a beloved Ike "above politics," was also his greatest liability. He lacked a political power sense, and he often did not seem purposeful in pursuing his objectives in an environment composed of political professionals. Moreover, the objectives themselves, which were intended to foster a spirit of compromise and national unity, necessarily took on a quality of overgenerality and imprecision. Vagueness and imprecision, of course, are no handicap to an experienced politician, but Eisenhower was not an experienced politician. The terse judgment of Eisenhower by former House Speaker Sam Rayburn seems correct: "No, won't do. Good man. Wrong profession." [35]

The Presidency of John F. Kennedy, from 1961 to 1963, was short but revealing. Unlike Eisenhower, Kennedy was at ease in the world of politics and he fully understood the nature of political power. Intellectually, he was the best-prepared man to sit in the White House since Woodrow Wilson. His objectives were as specific as political objectives can be. Abroad he wanted a policy of strength against Communist expansion accompanied by a willingness to negotiate for a détente with the Soviet Union. At home he wanted a liberal and expanded program of social welfare. Yet, continuing a pattern evident since the Truman Presidency, Kennedy's major successes came in international affairs. His Administration launched the widely praised Peace Corps and it undertook the perhaps insuperable task of promoting prosperity in Latin America with the Alliance for Progress. Kennedy blundered in the ill-conceived Bay of Pigs invasion, but recouped with a brilliant exercise in Cold War diplomacy

---

[35] The paragraph follows the interpretation given by Neustadt, op. cit., pp. 161–171; the Rayburn quote is from p. 194.

during the Cuban Missile Crisis. In the summer of 1963 he opened the door to a possible easing of Soviet-American tensions by negotiating a Nuclear Test Ban Treaty and then winning its approval in the Senate.

In domestic affairs, however, the Kennedy record was mediocre. He obtained the Trade Expansion Act of 1962, liberalizing American trade policy, and he achieved a number of modest reforms in social and economic welfare legislation. There were many setbacks also: Congress rejected his "must" program for federal aid to education, Medicare, and major reform of tax laws. The Tax Act of 1964, which was a product of Kennedy's efforts, only cut taxes; its passage was made possible by the elimination of almost all of the reforms that the Administration had proposed.

Kennedy, a polished intellectual, was not always effective in articulating his programs in such a way as to win public support. His rhetoric, although captivating to college professors, lacked the flair for popular dramatization, such as, for instance, in the case of Franklin D. Roosevelt's "garden hose" analogy. In addition, though Kennedy came to the White House from the Senate, he frequently misjudged congressional sentiment. He was almost too deferential to Congress. Kennedy, as John P. Roche has written, "always treated Congress with elaborate solicitude, but it was that of a kindergarten teacher who suspects that one of the children has secreted a hand grenade on the premises." [36]

Kennedy's basic problem, however, was that he sought liberal legislation at a time when the nation was largely indifferent to his reformist objectives. Although Democrats controlled Congress, many of them were conservatively inclined. When, as often happened, southern Democrats allied themselves with the strong Republican opposition, the President was left with something less than a majority. The growing militancy of Negro demands for their full civil rights further complicated Kennedy's problems. His political, not to mention his personal, commitments led him to espouse the Negro cause. His Administration intervened to suppress segregationist resistance to the decrees of federal courts ordering desegregation in Alabama and Mississippi. In the summer of 1963 he sent to Congress the bill that became the Civil Rights Act of 1964. But in taking these actions Kennedy began to acquire the identity of a group partisan. Increasingly the public perceived him as a political ally of the civil rights groups, and in the months preceding his assassination the Gallup Poll recorded a steady decline in Kennedy's popularity. In such an economic and political climate, even a Franklin D. Roosevelt would have had difficulties in getting his programs through Congress.

Lyndon B. Johnson came to the Presidency in 1963 with a background of over twenty years in Congress. His congressional experience included six years as the Senate's Democratic Majority Leader where he established a reputation as one of the ablest Senate politicians in modern history. By succeeding to the Presidency at a time of national shock over Kennedy's assassination, he obtained a strong momentum

[36] "How a President Should Use the Intellectuals," *New York Times Magazine,* July 26, 1964, p. 10.

of popular support. He skillfully retained this initial popularity through his "honey-moon" period in office, and it helped carry him to an overwhelming election victory over Barry Goldwater in the 1964 presidential elections.

Johnson was a "Congressman's Congressman" and a master of political manipulation. Within his first year in office he won major legislative successes by gaining the enactment of the Civil Rights Act of 1964, an antipoverty program, and a Mass Transit Law aimed at some of the difficulties that trouble public transportation.

Until approximately 1967 Lyndon Johnson gave indications of becoming one of the superb politician-Presidents of modern times. His southernness, combined with his northern political support and his presidential commitment to civil rights, put him in a unique position to interpret the North and the South to each other. Like Kennedy, President Johnson promoted civil rights, risking, though also attempting to avoid by his public statements, excessive identification with the civil rights groups. In personal terms he exuded a homely touch that, for many Americans, was initially appealing. His talk of a "Great Society" had elemental appeal, and his political touch seemed deft. In two weeks during the spring of 1964, for example, Johnson subtly united persuasion, pressure, and public appeals in such a way as to get industry and labor to settle a five-year old dispute that threatened a major breakdown in the nation's railroad system.

As time went on, however, his skills and homely touches began to grate on people, especially those who opposed him on such policy issues as the rapidly escalating war in Vietnam. His deftness came to be interpreted as craftiness, the dubious tactics of a "wheeler-dealer," and at times as lack of candor (the "credibility gap") or even outright dishonesty. Increasingly, portions of the original Johnson public consensus moved into an opposition that they voiced as stridently as their counterparts had against Franklin Roosevelt and Harry Truman. By 1968 this opposition had become so intense and pervasive that Johnson decided not to seek reelection; his Presidency had lost its effectiveness. As discussed earlier in the chapter, the nature of the office and public attitudes toward it explain this severe erosion in Johnson's popularity as much as any major shifts in his policy or tactics. When a President presides over, or leads from, a broad base of public agreement, his objectives and his tactics alike win approval. But when the objectives become divisive, the tactics also become sources of bitter criticism. It is also probably true that the Johnson style was bound to become suspect. An Eisenhower-like nonpolitical image is ultimately more congenial than the inevitable Johnson image—that of a complete politician.

With Johnson's withdrawal, seemingly the 1968 election had to bring a change. It did, of course, in the occupant of the White House, but less of a change in policy direction, especially regarding the Vietnam war, than one might have expected earlier in the year. Richard M. Nixon, in attaining his long-standing ambition to become President, did bring to the office, as most new incumbents do, a definite change in style. He has neither the intellectualism of Kennedy, nor the earthy political skills of Johnson. His style, rather, has been that of a chief executive well aware of the acute political problems he faces, and determined to attack them methodically. He is not flamboyant, nor given to the kind of outwardly casual, virtuoso perfor-

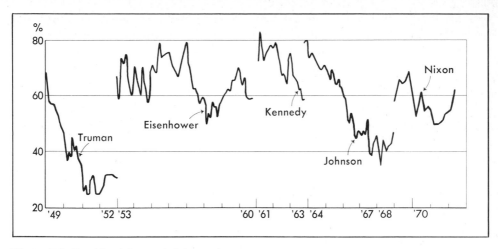

Figure 7.1. Presidential popularity trends

Source: Louis H. Bean in *The New York Times*, January 21, 1968; copyright The New York Times Company. Reprinted by permission. (Subsequently updated.)

mance of a Roosevelt or a Kennedy. More like Eisenhower, he likes to work through regular channels, through carefully structured staff mechanisms, and with deliberateness rather than dash.

For all his caution and careful testing of the political winds, he did, particularly during his third year in office, recommend some rather startlingly innovative domestic policies to Congress. He sought legislation that would completely reform the welfare system, replace the jungle of grant-in-aid programs for state and local governments by block grants of federal money with few strings attached, regroup and fundamentally reorganize the major departments of the national executive branch, and substantially broaden federally sponsored medical care coverage. As this massive legislative agenda was being introduced, there were many who expressed doubts that much would be enacted.

One interpretation of the Nixon legislative leadership style grows out of the fact that he may well serve out his entire period in office with a Congress solidly aligned against him politically. Perhaps acting upon this fact, he decided that he will be judged more by what he proposed than what actually passed. Divided government, as many Governors have demonstrated, can be politically rewarding for the executive if not productive of many policy innovations. If the President (or governor) so situated takes electoral success as his goal, then he can turn his legislative problems into advantages. The trick is to propose measures that will be popular with major elements of the country, advertize them widely, and then await congressional reaction. If party rivals in the legislative branch deny him his policy goals, he can lambaste them at the next election for partisan obstructionism, as Harry Truman did in 1948. If Congress passes his measures, he can reap the credit for having proposed them. He wins either way.

As the Truman example illustrates, this strategy has not been unknown at the national level in previous administrations, but no modern President prior to Nixon has had to base a whole administrative strategy on it. (Eisenhower, whose situation most nearly resembled Nixon's, did have a Republican Congress his first two years, and, of course, never aspired to innovative legislative leadership then or later.) It is an axiom among writers on the American system that divided government does *not* spell automatic deadlock. The Nixon experience may become a clear-cut test of this proposition. If divided government does no more than slow down innovation, this in itself could be a high price to pay for our system of checks and balances in a period of chronic domestic crisis.

We have dwelt on Richard Nixon as domestic policy and legislative leader. Quite possibly his real mark in history will have been made in foreign affairs—his first love. His precedent-shattering 1972 trip to China, and Moscow visit, are likely to have profound long-range affects on American foreign policy, and in the world at large.

The American Presidency: The Center of Power

Whatever the ultimate verdict on a President's tenure in office—and such verdicts must await the passage of considerable time—whoever serves in the office occupies what is certain to remain the nation's central political institution. The twentieth century is one of executive dominance, not only in the United States but all over the world. Any nation, to survive in a complex and dangerous international environment, needs a focus of political responsibility and a leader able to move quickly and decisively. In nations whose governments are dictatorial or autocratic the executive is more than dominant; his power is nearly absolute, and one can meaningfully speak of Mao Tse-tung's China or Franco's Spain.

One cannot speak meaningfully, however, of Nixon's America or Heath's Britain. The very expressions have a strange ring to them, for in the democracies the executive branch may dominate, but it does not dictate. (De Gaulle's France was a partial, though temporary, exception.) Certainly the American President, powerful as he is, is surrounded also by limitations. And this is the way it should be in a democracy. Although the bias of this chapter favors an energetic Hamiltonian executive, instead of a Taftian one, its bias is equally in favor of the proposition that the source of the executive's "energy" should be his skill in the give-and-take of the democratic political process.

The American executive branch, and particularly the Presidency, has come a long way from its eighteenth-century origins. Where once it was an object of anti-monarchical suspicion, today the President reigns as the American "king." Where once the legislature was regarded as the great popular institution, today the President serves as the primary focus of democratic sentiment. Where once the legislature was expected to be the dominant institution of American government, today the President plays the central role. In a political system where power is shared between competing governmental agencies and where a large number of interest groups seek to make government serve their own particular ends, the President introduces the degree of order that makes the system workable. By representing the people in their national interests he is able, at least in part, to harmonize and to integrate the diverse political forces and interests that flourish in a nation of over two hundred million. The tendency, in a consensus democracy, is for most American Presidents to have represented the national consensus most of the time; exceptions have occurred when they have been forced to take sides on deeply divisive issues. When a President is a brilliant politician, he can lead and influence the nation and at the same time implement the popular consensus.

suggested additional readings

Anderson, Patrick. *The President's Men.* Garden City, N.Y.: Doubleday & Company, Inc., 1969.*

Bailey, Thomas A. *Presidential Greatness: The Image and the Man from George Washington to the Present.* New York: Appleton-Century-Crofts, Inc., 1966.*

Binkley, Wilfred E. *The President and Congress.* New York: Vintage Books, 1962.*

Cornwell, Elmer E., Jr. *Presidential Leadership of Public Opinion.* Bloomington: Indiana University Press, 1965.

Cronin, Thomas E., and Sanford D. Greenberg (eds.). *The Presidential Advisory System.* New York: Harper & Row, Publishers, 1969.*

Fenno, Richard F. *The President's Cabinet.* New York: Vintage Books, 1959.*

Hargrove, Erwin C. *Presidential Leadership: Personality and Political Style.* New York: The Macmillan Company, 1966.*

Kallenbach, Joseph E. *The American Chief Executive: The Presidency and the Governorship.* New York: Harper & Row, Publishers, 1966.

Koenig, Louis W. *The Chief Executive,* 2nd rev. ed. New York:

Harcourt Brace Jovanovich, Inc., 1968.

Neustadt, Richard E. *Presidential Power.* New York: New American Library, 1964.*

Ransome, Coleman B., Jr. *The Office of Governor in the United States.* University, Ala.: University of Alabama Press, 1966.

Reedy, George E. *The Twilight of the Presidency.* New York: World Publishing Company, 1970.

Symposium. *Law and Contemporary Problems: The Institutionalized Presidency.* Durham, N.C.: School of Law, Duke University, Summer, 1970.

Warren, Sidney. *The President as World Leader.* Philadelphia: J. B. Lippincott Co., 1964.

Wolk, Allan. *The Presidency and Black Civil Rights.* Cranbury, N.J.: Fairleigh Dickinson University Press, 1970.

* Available in paperback.

8 the legislative

case study

The Draft and the War: Congress Challenges the President

It will be hard to judge for many years which of the effects of the Vietnam war on the American national community was the most profound. A reasonable guess as of 1971 was: the drawing of Congress, especially the Senate, back into the business of trying to control foreign policy. The other side of this coin has been an almost unprecedented questioning of the right of the President to make defense and foreign policy decisions on his own initiative. The resulting shifts of emphasis may well solidify into a new balance between the two branches.

Congress labors under basic handicaps when it tries to ride herd on the executive in any policy area. In foreign and defense policy its lack of expertise, information, and at times public support have usually meant that the President is allowed to have his own way unchallenged. The rising clamor of anti-Vietnam protest, however, has forced the Senate in particular to try to reassert its traditional role of "advising and consenting" as the Constitution puts it. But power once relinquished is very hard to recapture.

All of this, and more, lay behind the nearly eight-month struggle during 1971 over renewal of the military draft authority under the Selective Service System. Officially the fight began on January 28 when

President Nixon sent his second legislative message of the session to Congress. In it he endorsed the widely discussed idea of replacing the draft with an all-volunteer army and suggested a target date of mid-1973 for accomplishing this change. He also asked for a total package of military pay increases amounting to $1.5 billion designed to make the service attractive enough to recruit needed manpower on a volunteer basis. Finally, he asked for a two-year extension of the Selective Service draft authority to cover the period during which the volunteer army ("Volar" in bureaucratese) was being implemented.

This seemingly straightforward and obvious set of proposals masked a series of thorny political and foreign policy issues. Opponents of the Vietnam war had often attacked the draft on the theory that without a conscripted manpower supply for the military, the war could not go on. Young men in the draftable age range had long resented the threatened interruption of their lives that enforced service represented—and above all the compulsion to fight in a highly ambiguous war. It was these same young men (plus their girl friends) who were in the process of being enfranchised and would be voting in 1972. The President could hardly be hurt politically with these people or their parents by substituting Volar for Selective Service. And yet, there was by no means unanimity on the workability or even desirability of the voluntary army idea.

In Congress, at least three distinct points of view had been evident on the Volar-versus-draft issue itself, to say nothing of those who would again seize upon the draft as a way of trying to end the Vietnam conflict. Chairman John Stennis (D–Mississippi) of the Senate Armed Services Committee and his counterpart in the House, Representative F. Edward Herbert (D–Louisiana), were both convinced that a volunteer army could not supply enough military manpower to meet national security needs. At the other extreme, Senator Mark Hatfield (R–Oregon) and Senator Barry Goldwater (R–Arizona) had forced a vote the previous summer on their proposal to end the draft immediately in favor of the Volar principle. They lost but were set to reintroduce the proposal in 1971. (The rather improbable team-up of conservative "hawk" Goldwater with liberal "dove" Hatfield merely proves again that American politics makes strange bedfellows.) They had considerable support among Senate colleagues, and their motion had gleaned thirty-five votes. Third, Senator Edward Kennedy (D–Massachusetts), though liberal and a dove like Hatfield, had taken an adamant position against the volunteer idea. He argued that such a basis of recruitment would burden the poor and the blacks with an even greater share in staffing the military services than the inequitable one they already had. He, and those who agreed with him, could be expected to support the draft principle, while demanding changes to make it more equitable.

Senator Stennis announced that his committee would begin holding hearings on the President's proposals the following Tuesday, February 3. What was destined to become the most intensive review of the military draft since World War II began that day with Secretary of Defense Melvin

Laird as the Nixon Administration's first witness. He and two associates from the executive branch naturally upheld the President's program. During the session it became clear that the chairman had the support of all but three of his fellow committee members in insisting that the Volar concept was illusory and that the draft should be continued—for four years, said Stennis, not just two. The issue had quite completely erased normal partisan and ideological lines on the committee, as some issues tend to do in Congress given the loose party lines. One of the three dissenters was a liberal antiwar Democrat, another a middle-of-the-road Republican, and the third was Senator Goldwater.

On Thursday, February 4, Senator Kennedy appeared before the Stennis committee to testify against the volunteer concept. He also suggested that there be added to the bill a provision limiting draft calls to 150,000 per year. Under this proposal Congress would have to approve any presidential request to exceed that limit. As Kennedy put it, his amendment would "reassert Congressional control over a vital aspect of foreign policy matters." Senator Hatfield testified the same day. Although also a liberal and equally opposed to the Vietnam war, he called for the volunteer idea, an end to the draft when it was slated to expire on June 30, and at least a doubling of the pay package the White House had recommended.

Near the end of the month, simultaneous hearings began on the House side before Chairman Herbert's committee. In fact the scene of action shifted away from the more slow-moving Senate to the other legislative branch for the next few weeks. Much that had been said before the Senate committee was repeated. Representative Herbert did give some hope to volunteer army supporters by expressing the view that higher pay raises than the President proposed were desirable. But it was clear that he too would insist on a continuance of the draft and was skeptical of Volar. As he put this last point, somewhat whimsically one gathers, "I think the only way to get an all-volunteer army is to draft it." With both Stennis and Herbert for the draft extension, and the bulk of their committees in agreement, there was likely to be little difficulty in securing the approval of that presidential recommendation at least.

The House, in any event, moved quickly, as it can in comparison with the Senate. On March 16, about three weeks after Herbert began hearings, the House Armed Services Committee began voting on the bill before them. They defeated 28 to 7 a proposal to let the draft die June 30 in favor of the volunteer concept, and they approved the two-year extension the President had requested. They also agreed to vote on the key pay-raise question two days later. By March 22 the committee had completed its work on the bill, which was then ready to be taken up on the House floor. As a compromise the measure did carry substantially higher total pay raises than the President had asked. Chairman Herbert again expressed doubt that a voluntary army could ever be achieved, but he said of the President's goal: "We're going to give him all the help he wants to implement it. We're going to give him all the rope he wants."

The House began debating the draft-extension legislation on March 30. There was little evidence of widespread opposition among members, and even the White House seemed, from indirect evidence that appeared in debate, unlikely to oppose the part of the bill that raised military pay far above the figures the President had requested. (Interestingly, at about the time the House began debate, Senator Edmund Muskie of Maine, then a leading Democratic presidential contender, took a position similar to Senator Kennedy's: he was for the draft because of the undesirable effect a volunteer army might have.) The outspoken Representative Bella Abzug, a freshman Democrat from New York, spoke for the antiwar point of view, arguing that a continued draft would

guarantee a President sufficient manpower for new or expanded foreign ventures "without the need to go to Congress or to the people." This point won gallery applause.

The appearance of considerable support for the President's request seemed to be borne out by overwhelming votes killing proposals that would have ended the draft on June 30. One such amendment, offered by Representative Michael Harrington (D–Massachusetts), an ardent opponent of the war, was beaten 330 to 62. An even more far-reaching proposal by Representative Abzug garnered only twenty votes in its favor. However, when an amendment was considered, offered by an Ohio Republican, limiting extension of the draft to one year instead of two, a surprising array of both hawks and doves joined the small group of Harrington and Abzug amendment supporters to bring this compromise within two votes of approval. It lost 200 to 198. Clearly, even the normally cooperative House harbored many lukewarm draft supporters. Then, on Thursday, April 1, after the most intensive debate the House of Representatives had yet heard on the Vietnam war, and the most thorough review of the draft in twenty years, the bill passed by the deceptively top-heavy margin of 293 to 99. As *New York Times* reporter David Rosenbaum wrote, this vote "belied the intense opposition in the House to military conscription. There was nothing in the vote that would disclose the scores of Congressmen who took part over the last three days to denounce the war." Some of these spoke out publicly as doves for the first time. As often happens, the earlier vote on the one-year extension was more significant than the final tally on passage.

The scene then shifted back to the Senate wing of the Capitol. Doubtless with the close House vote on the same compromise in mind, Senators Birch Bayh (D–Indiana) and Harrison Williams, Jr. (D–New Jersey) announced a week or so after House passage that they would introduce a one-year extension amendment in their own branch. Three weeks after the completion of House action, the Senate Armed Services Committee, working now with the bill as passed by the other body, voted to approve the two-year extension but also voted to cut by more than half the military pay raises the House had adopted. The membership of the committee is generally more conservative and promilitary than the full Senate, so these actions in no way guaranteed what would happen on the floor. Before the bill had been put in final form by the committee this conservative stance weakened enough—to the surprise of observers who had given the 150,000-per-year draft limit little chance with Stennis's group—to adopt the Kennedy proposal in somewhat modified form. Instead of congressional approval being required to go above the ceiling, under wording written into the bill the President must issue an executive order citing urgent national security reasons for drafting more than 150,000 men. Perhaps the Senate committee, sensing the opposition tide among their colleagues, felt this concession would buy some floor support.

The press account of the opening of debate on the draft bill noted that it immediately broadened out to cover the Vietnam war and even American military contingents in Europe. Draft extension gave every sign, even on the first day, of becoming *the* major piece of controversial legislation for the session. The floor leaders resigned themselves to a debate lasting weeks rather than a few days, as in the House. Senate rules allowing unlimited debate could ensure that long a debate. Senators were waiting with amendments to cut the extension to one year, end it immediately, prohibit sending draftees to any "war" not authorized by Congress, and set a date for the withdrawal of all troops from Vietnam. Senator Mike Mansfield (D–Montana), the Majority Leader, was even preparing to call for a reduction of American troops under NATO command in Europe. Chairman Stennis recognized the situation

when he opened the debate by telling the Senate that the underlying issue was not the draft but whether Congress was to use the issue as a means of trying to end the war in Vietnam.

The first of these many lines of attack on the bill to preoccupy the Senate was the Mansfield amendment, which, as proposed, required a 50-per-cent cut in American NATO strength. Republican leaders feared they could not block its approval despite public White House opposition. Viewing this as a most serious matter, the President's aides swung into feverish action. Conferences on strategy were held, more statements were issued, but differences of view developed between GOP Senate leaders, who counseled compromise, and the President's staff, led by Henry Kissinger (National Security Advisor), who did not want the amendment in any form. The second day of this "legislative crisis" saw the White House taking the no-compromise position firmly, and Senator Hugh Scott (R–Pennsylvania), the Minority Leader, predicting a presidential veto of the bill if it contained any such limitation. The President was adamant, because he saw this as a potential diminution of his foreign policy powers. Or, as Scott put it, the Administration would "not accept any alternative that would have the effect of Congress determining the foreign policy of the United States toward NATO." A whole bevy of former secretaries and under secretaries of state, NATO commanders, and similarly prestigious figures from past administrations were called to the White House and asked to lobby against the amendment.

The following Monday (debate had begun a week earlier on May 10) saw a confusing welter of compromise amendments introduced, all designed to modify the Mansfield proposal and make it more acceptable to those, including the White House, who would not go as far as the Majority Leader. The President still stood firm, however, rejecting all compromise.

Wednesday brought the first showdown on the bill. Each of the more moderate alternatives was defeated in turn. It seemed clear that there was a majority in the Senate that did favor European troop reductions, but there was reluctance to impose this on the President by congressional fiat. This reluctance, coupled with a desire not to tie the hands of the administration in negotiating bilateral troop reductions with the Russians, brought the White House ultimate victory in the shelving of the Mansfield amendment itself by a vote of 61 to 36. Whether this success was as important as the new level of involvement in foreign and defense policy that the Senate claimed by pressing the issue is a moot point. Though Mansfield lost, he had succeeded in using the draft bill to force debate on a seemingly unrelated aspect of national policy, and he had forced the President to mount a massive effort to protect his prerogatives. Another time the Senate critics might win.

On Thursday, May 20, six weeks before the government draft authority was due to expire, debate was resumed. Even more than previously, signs pointed to a long debate, so much so that Senators Scott and Stennis both warned that they might attempt to invoke cloture if debate dragged. (This decision must have come hard for Stennis, whose southern colleagues have always cherished their right to talk to death measures they felt inimical to their region.) On May 25 an amendment by Senator Gaylord Nelson (D–Wisconsin) that would have prohibited sending drafted personnel to Vietnam without their consent was defeated 52 to 21. The next day a blow was seemingly dealt the volunteer-army concept by the rejection of an amendment that would have again increased sharply the levels of military pay. With an eye to developments on Capitol Hill, President Nixon, in a news conference June 1, replied to a question that the sending of draftees to Vietnam would soon be minimal.

As the June 30 expiration date crept nearer, the Senate debate heated up still more. June 4 saw a major test on the whole question of draft renewal. The members first voted 67 to 23 to defeat Senator Hatfield's amendment, which would have cut off the draft completely upon its expiration, and then, by a much closer vote, they beat back an effort to limit extension to only one year instead of the requested two. This tally was 49 to 43. On June 8, the volunteer-army advocates won a round by securing approval of a very large increase in military pay, thus erasing their previous defeat and more than wiping out the cut made by the Senate committee in the House version of the pay provisions. Following that development, in an effort to limit debate by taking up the most important of the remaining amendments, the Senate agreed to turn its attention to the Hatfield-McGovern proposal (co-sponsored by Senator Hatfield and Senator George McGovern of South Dakota, the first announced Democratic presidential candidate for 1972), which required that the President withdraw all troops from Vietnam by the end of 1971. On June 11 debate on this amendment opened.

On June 16, after the rejection of a compromise on the Hatfield-McGovern principle that would have set the deadline for troop withdrawal at June 30, 1972, instead of the end of 1971, the amendment itself was voted down, 55 to 42. That so dramatic a proposal won 42 votes, eight short of half the membership of the United States Senate, is some measure of the intensity of feeling about the Vietnam war that had become focused on this bill. But the defeat of the Hatfield-McGovern amendment by no means ended debate. Senate consideration ground on through a bewildering array of additional proposals for modification too numerous to catalog. On June 22, however, what proved to be a key development took place with the approval of an amendment proposed by Senator Mansfield calling for withdrawal of all American troops from Vietnam within nine months of the release of American prisoners of war by the North Vietnamese.

The next day, just one week before the expiration deadline, in the face of filibuster threats aimed at delaying passage of the bill past that deadline, the Senate voted 65 to 27 to impose cloture—only the fifth time since 1927 when this had been done. Senators are always reluctant to silence colleagues by this means, if for no other reason than that someday the shoe may be on the other foot, and they themselves may want to use the filibuster to achieve some cherished objective.

The Mansfield amendment now became the key issue. White House aides let it be known that in the President's view he could sign the bill and ignore the limitation because Congress had no constitutional right to direct the Commander-in-Chief on the disposition of the armed forces. On June 25, after a flurry of last-minute amendments, the Senate, now acting under limited debate, passed the bill with its two-year extension provision. The debate had lasted more than seven weeks but because the differences between House and Senate versions must be ironed out by a conference committee, the end was not yet really in sight. Many predicted, rightly, a stormy conference stage because of the Mansfield amendment. In fact, before the end of June, the conferees reached agreement on all differences between the two bills *except* that amendment. There the deadlock was firm and the prospects of breaking it dim in the view of Chairmen Stennis and Herbert, who presided over the conference committee. With the impasse still dragging on, the committee decided to recess for a week on July 12.

Finally, at the end of July, compromise language for the Mansfield provision was worked out. The new language read in part that it was

the sense of Congress that the United States terminate at the earliest practicable date all military operations of the United States in Indo-China, and provide for the prompt and orderly withdrawal of all United States military forces at

a date certain subject to the release of all American prisoners of war.

In a word, what had first been phrased as a binding directive to the President was changed to a "sense of Congress" suggestion. Even so, if adopted, this language would be the first time Congress had gone specifically on record in favor of troop withdrawal. The House promptly approved the bill as reported by the conference committee on August 4. Opposition, not surprisingly, was expected from the Senate to the watered-down language. Again, expectations were not disappointed.

It was mid-September before the seven-month struggle finally wound up (a month's congressional recess had intervened in August). By September 16 a coalition had emerged in the Senate bent on blocking the conference report, and they seemed to have enough votes to do it. The group included about twenty who opposed extension of the draft in any form, twenty to thirty who felt so strongly about the original wording of the Mansfield amendment that they would not approve the bill without it, and a small number led by Senator Gordon Allott (R–Colorado) who were demanding changes in the pay schedule in the bill to concentrate the larger increases in the lowest ranks. Senator Mansfield himself, in his capacity as Majority Leader, as an act of courtesy to Senator Stennis, agreed to a day's delay in the vote on a motion to send the bill back to the conference committee. This generosity gave the Nixon Administration time to put on the heat. It did, especially on Senator Allott, who was persuaded to withdraw his opposition. (Allott was up for reelection in 1972.) Also, at a press conference on the same day—September 16—President Nixon chastised those who wanted the draft to lapse permanently, describing this as "one of the most irresponsible acts on the part of the United States Senate that I could possibly think of." It still took a second imposition of cloture before final passage was secured by the Senate, 55 to 30, paving the way at last for presidential approval. This final vote came on September 21.

Little by way of summary need be said about this long and drawn-out sequence of events. The fundamental issue was a clash between a President bent on exercising traditional executive prerogative to carry out his foreign and military policy free from interference, with a Congress —especially a Senate—that had come more and more to reflect rising public hostility to the Vietnam war and that was seeking to reassert a role in this policy area that had largely atrophied over the years. In waging its side of the struggle the "Greatest Deliberative Body In the World," as the Senate likes to call itself, wheeled out and used—or various of its members did—all of the ancient and venerable weapons in its unique parliamentary armory. Many of these weapons are clumsy or ill suited to the task at hand, but at the very least they enabled their users to force the chief executive to be on the defensive in an area in which Presidents in the past have seldom been challenged and to stage a lengthy public airing of the policies they sought to change.

SOURCES

New York Times and *Providence (Rhode Island) Journal* (various issues covering the period of the case).

american legislatures

The Legislative Function

What function, precisely, has been entrusted to the American legislature? It is much too simple merely to say that it makes laws. Superficially, all legislative bodies do that. They all, each in its own way, exercise a degree of supervision over executive organs and bureaucracies, keep on the lookout for misconduct by office holders, conduct investigations, have the final say in financial matters, and even, in rare instances, crank up the obsolescent impeachment machinery. But to say all this is not to differentiate a distinctly American legislative function or style from that of any other democratic system.

It is helpful to begin again with the assertion that American legislative bodies are, first and foremost, lawmaking organs. They are this to a unique degree among their sister institutions in other countries. Behind this lies the distinction between our presidential-congressional system and the British-invented cabinet-parliamentary system, which most other successful democracies have copied. (Only the rather less successful Latin American democratic regimes are based on the American model.) Still further back, however, lies the theory of popular or democratic government itself.

Thinkers like John Locke found the roots of popular government in natural communities whose members delegated a portion of the sovereignty, which rightfully resided with them, to bodies of representatives who would act in their name. These bodies then governed as agents for their principals, and thus exercised the lawmaking power. Such a scheme left no room for divine right kings, and of course, was designed that way deliberately. Nor, however, did it leave any clear-cut role for executive officials generally. Locke himself, in his *Second Treatise,* did recognize an executive role responsible for executing the laws, conducting foreign relations, and acting in emergencies. One suspects that he could not help looking over his shoulder at the monarchical institutions of seventeenth-century England, in which he was writing. There did remain, after all, functions that were ill-suited to legislatures to perform.

The divergence of the British and American legislative traditions stemmed from the paradoxical fact that, for a variety of reasons, the Constitution's framers here accepted Locke in toto. Kings were decidedly out of favor and colonial assemblies had been used to check and thwart royal governors. Such tradition as we had prior to 1787 was thus a legislative one. Quite naturally, then, Congress (and the state legislative bodies even more so) were assumed to be *the* source of governing initiative. Britain, meanwhile, in spite of the fact that Locke was writing for his own countrymen, adapted their monarchy into a cabinet executive that bore the same relationship to Parliament that the King had had earlier: it held the governing initiative while Parliament ratified or rejected. This is what Leopold S. Amery meant when he wrote, "Parliament is not, and never has been, a legislature, . . . [its] main task . . . is still what it was when first summoned, not to legislate or govern. . . ." [1]

We begin, therefore, with the proposition that American legislatures really legislate and do not merely ratify executive governance. This fact has profound consequences both for the whole shape and operation of our institutions and for the role the individual legislator is seen as playing, and sees himself playing. Above all that role—or more precisely, that cluster of interrelated roles—is defined in terms of the theoretically paramount and autonomous function assigned to the institution of which he is a part. The role of the British Member of Parliament, on the other hand, is defined largely in terms of his relation to entities outside Parliament, primarily his party and the Cabinet as executive. As a consequence, there are some general points about the role of the American legislator and the characteristics of legislative institutions on this side of the Atlantic that deserve emphasis.

Getting Along

Sam Rayburn, Speaker of the U.S. House of Representatives for two decades, always had a standard counsel for the freshman representative: "Don't try to go too fast. Learn your job. Don't ever talk until you know what you're talking about. . . . If you want to get along, go along." The rewards of going along are often both tangible and intangible: better committee assignments, greater effectiveness in legislative matters, and satisfying acceptance by the House oligarchs. No list of "do's" and "don't's" is handed the newcomer, but by observing and listening to informal advice he soon becomes politically socialized; he learns the norms, the rules of the game, whose acceptance precedes internal effectiveness within the legislative institution.

The most striking thing about the norms is their pervasiveness and their similarity in both state and federal legislatures. Virtually every representative in a study of the California, New Jersey, Ohio, and Tennessee legislatures identified at least one specific norm; more than half named at least four. Table 8.1 gives the results. Despite their informal nature, five copybook rules seem to be universally important:

[1] *Thoughts on the Constitution* (New York: Oxford U.P., 1948), p. 12.

Table 8.1 *"Rules of the game" perceived by legislators in four states* *

Rules of the game	Percentage of respondents naming rule			
	Calif. N = 104	N.J. N = 78	Ohio N = 160	Tenn. N = 119
1. *Performance of obligations:* Keep your word; abide by commitments.	64%	47%	28%	24%
2. *Respect for other members' legislative rights:* Support another member's local bill if it doesn't affect you or your district; don't railroad bills through; don't appear before another committee (than your own) to oppose another member's bill, don't steal another member's bill; respect the rights of a bill's author; accept author's amendments to a bill.	32	26	24	47
3. *Impersonality:* Don't deal in personalities; don't make personal attacks on other members; oppose the bill, not the man; don't criticize the moral behavior of others; address other members through the Chair; don't refer to another member by name; observe the "Golden Rule."	30	27	32	31
4. *Self-restraint in debate:* Don't talk too much; don't speak about subjects on which you're uninformed.	17	9	18	59
5. *Courtesy:* Observe common courtesies; be friendly and courteous even if you disagree, even if you are of opposite party to opponent.	19	19	24	16
6. *Openness of aims:* Be frank and honest in explaining bills; don't conceal real purpose of bills or amendments.	24	8	22	12
7. *Modesty:* Don't be a prima donna, an individualist, an extremist, or a publicity hound; don't talk for the press or the galleries.	9	19	23	21
8. *Integrity:* Be honest, a man of integrity, sincerity.	13	19	18	11
9. *Independence of judgment* (being independent of outside control): Be objective; don't be subservient to a political organization, a boss, a machine, an interest group, lobbyists, or clients.	16	19	11	14
10. *Personal virtue:* Exhibit high moral conduct, no drunkenness or immorality.	13	0	24	8
11. *Decisiveness:* Take a stand; don't be wish-washy; don't vacillate.	10	8	11	15
12. *Unselfish service:* Don't be a careerist, an opportunist, or overambitious; don't use your legislative position for your personal advantage.	5	19	14	4

* Percentages total more than 100 because most respondents named more than one rule.

Source: John C. Wahlke, et al., *The Legislative System: Explorations in Legislative Behavior* (New York: John Wiley & Sons, Inc., 1962), pp. 146–147.

	Percentage of respondents naming rule			
Rules of the game	Calif. N = 104	N.J. N = 78	Ohio N = 160	Tenn. N = 119
13. *Advance notice of changed stand:* Notify in advance if you are going to change your stand or can't keep a commitment.	26	9	6	1
14. *Openness in opposition:* Don't conceal your opposition; notify in advance if you're going to oppose or introduce amendments.	17	4	13	2
15. *Sociability:* Be sociable; develop and maintain friendships with other members.	6	6	9	11
16. *Conciliation:* Be willing to compromise; don't be a perfectionist; accept half a loaf.	7	12	10	5
17. *Agency for party or administration:* Support the Governor, administration, party leaders (of own party); don't vote to override a veto by Governor of your own party.	1	6	20	0
18. *Restraint in opposition:* Don't fight unnecessarily; don't be opposed to everything.	4	1	11	13
19. *Application:* Be punctual and regular in attendance at sessions, caucuses, committee meetings; don't leave after your own bill has been considered.	5	3	13	5
20. *Respect for other members' political rights:* Respect the incumbent status of other members; don't campaign against a member in his district; don't do anything that would embarrass him in his district; build him up before his constituents.	23	5	3	1
21. *Objectivity:* Be fair, show good judgment, maturity, responsibility.	4	5	13	4
22. *Agency for legislative party:* Follow caucus or conference decisions; go along with majority of your party.	1	23	7	0
23. *Gracefulness in defeat:* Keep your temper; accept defeat gracefully, learn to take a licking; don't take opposition personally.	10	4	4	9
24. *Ability and intelligence:* Show ability, intelligence; not ignorance, stupidity.	2	8	9	5
25. *Nonvenality:* Don't sell vote; don't take money; don't introduce cinch bills, shakedown bills.	6	4	3	13
26. *Restraint in bill-introduction:* Don't introduce too many bills or amendments.	2	1	5	2
27. *Maintenance of confidences:* Don't divulge confidential information; don't violate confidence of caucus, committee, executive session.	1	19	5	3
28. *Avoidance of trickery:* Don't engage in parliamentary chicanery, tricky maneuvering.	8	4	6	4
29. *Apprenticeship:* Respect older members; (new members) don't try to accomplish too much too soon.	5	10	8	1

Table 8.1 (continued)

	Percentage of respondents naming rule			
Rules of the game	Calif. N = 104	N.J. N = 78	Ohio N = 160	Tenn. N = 119
30. *Caution in commitments:* Don't commit yourself too soon; be cautious about making promises; study bills before you decide how to vote.	4	0	3	8
31. *Commitment to job:* Take the job seriously.	4	6	1	7
32. *Institutional patriotism:* Defend legislature and members against outsiders; don't do anything to reflect on the legislature as a body.	12	1	3	0
33. *Respect for opposition groups:* Don't be too partisan; be considerate of minority members.	6	8	3	0
34. *Negotiation:* Recognize the necessity and/or acceptability of log-rolling, horse-trading, swapping-out.	0	0	3	7
35. *Limits to negotiation:* Vote according to the merits of the bill; don't horse-trade, log-roll, or swap-out.	0	3	1	6
36. *Seniority:* Respect the seniority system.	3	1	3	1
37. *Acceptance of committee system:* Respect committee jurisdiction; don't vote to discharge a committee, withdraw a bill; don't vote to amend budget on floor.	7	3	1	0
38. *Self-restraint in goals:* Don't be overeager; don't try to accomplish too much at one time.	2	4	2	1
39. *Senatorial courtesy:* Observe senatorial courtesy (in a narrow sense—control of appointments, etc.)	0	9	0	1
40. *Compliance with group:* Go along with majority when ⅔ vote is necessary; don't refuse unanimous consent.	2	5	0	0
41. *Limits to partisanship:* Don't delay by being too partisan, too political.	3	0	2	0
42. *Abstinence from dilatory actions:* Don't call attention to absence of a quorum; don't demand call of house at inconvenient times.	2	0	1	0
Miscellaneous others	3	28	11	30

1. Do your legislative work.

The everyday work of a legislature is routine and unexciting—and vital to the operation of the institution. Legislatures depend on members who do committee work and master a subject area. In turn, most members will want to devote much time to servicing the requests of their constituents.

2. Specialize.

To establish his credentials the legislator must become an expert in one legislative subject. Preferably his specialty should develop from one of his committee assignments, although exceptions are made for matters that pertain to his constituency, and for the floor leaders who necessarily are generalists.

3. Don't talk too much.

Hard working specialists must ration their time sparingly. There is in the federal House of Representatives and most American legislatures a marked bias against members who talk too much. "Basically," comments one congressman, "I think the House type is an infighter, an operator. . . . He may speak, but he does not speak frequently." [2]

4. Reciprocate—make your word your bond.

Legislation is politics, and the stuff of politics is bargains and deals. A legislator who hopes to be effective must, whenever possible, accumulate credit by voting for his colleagues' favored projects or by doing other favors. Like a banking system, a system of political reciprocity depends on a high degree of trust. "Don't violate your word," a state legislator says. "You may be a thief and a crook, but on the floor your word must be unquestionable." [3] Moreover, the intricacies of parliamentary procedures are workable only because most legislators most of the time do not abuse their privileges.

5. Be courteous.

Discourtesy in legislative affairs is useless; it breeds needless hostility among those whose support or neutrality someday may be welcome. But courtesy is cheap, never harms a legislator's effectiveness, and softens the inevitable conflicts. Legislators therefore customarily envelop their operations in a cocoon of procedural courtesies that, despite a heavy dosage of pomposity, blunt tensions and promote internal harmony.

Without sanctions these informal rules would be meaningless, and the legislator who refuses to go along suffers some subtle yet real punishments. He will be excluded from the circles of the senior and influential men who dominate legislative

[2] Charles L. Clapp, *The Congressman: His Work as He Sees It* (Washington, D.C.: The Brookings Institution, 1963), p. 23.

[3] John C. Wahlke, et al., *The Legislative System: Explorations in Legislative Behavior* (New York: Wiley, 1962), p. 144.

Table 8.2 *Legislative effectiveness in the 83rd and 84th Congresses: The less a Senator talks on the Senate floor, and the narrower a Senator's area of legislative interest and activity, the greater is his effectiveness*

	Index of legislative effectiveness				
	High	Medium	Low		
Level of floor speaking					
High	0%	33%	67%	100%	(9)
Medium	3	68	29	100	(31)
Low	15	59	26	100	(39)
Index of specialization					
High	23%	69%	8%	100%	(13)
Medium	10	62	28	100	(29)
Low	8	51	41	100	(39)

Source: Donald R. Matthews, *U.S. Senators and Their World* (New York: Vintage Books, 1962), p. 115.

proceedings, and he may be denied choice committee assignments or the opportunity to head a subcommittee. Most important, the maverick will find it more difficult to get his bills enacted. The study of the four state legislatures found that the most common sanction employed against deviant representatives was the obstruction of their bills. "These are all sorts of tricks," one legislator commented. "You give 'em false leads, run 'em around in circles, not vote for their bills, give them no place on subcommittees, don't get their bills out of . . . committee." [4]

The customary rules have a still deeper significance, supplementing and complementing the more formal written rules of procedure. Without a network of both formal and informal rules—a prescribed routine for passing bills *and* a custom of courteous respect for the rights of all members—the legislative system would become inoperable. In short, the rules of the legislative game are functionally necessary. They help to limit disruptive conflicts, make the legislative process reasonably stable, and expedite the processing of proposed laws. As one major study concludes, the informal rules "maintain the working consensus essential to legislative performance." [5] Put another way, going along serves far more than the legislators' self-serving interests: if legislators did not go along, the legislature could not get along.

Above all, these customary rules underscore the uniqueness of the American legislative tradition. Clearly (and naturally) they dovetail with a legislative style that emphasizes a positive policy-making role with corresponding responsibilities for

[4] Ibid., p. 153.
[5] Ibid., p. 168.

members. They also suggest a tradition in which there is a considerable degree of freedom from tight party discipline, and not a little rugged individualism that must be softened and curbed. The fact that the prime sanction used to encourage conformity to the rules is obstruction of the legislative projects of the individual member carries special significance. Not only is the American tradition one in which the legislative institution as an institution retains much policy initiative, but it encourages a kind of free enterprise activism among its members. No higher premium is placed on any achievement by the American legislator than success in piloting his own cherished bills onto the statute books. He is, in short, encouraged and expected to legislate.

Lawmaking in America: The Fundamental Variables

In the United States there are fifty state legislatures and Congress (not to mention thousands of city councils), each sharing the common tradition, but each with its own distinctive combination of political factors. One must speak, therefore, of legislative processes, for the many variables that influence legislative policy-making will have different consequences in different political systems. A sophisticated study of the legislature in Illinois, for instance, requires an examination of the state's entire political structure. Although it is obviously impossible to examine the politics of individual states in a general textbook, the more fundamental variables common to Congress and the state legislatures can be identified.

1. The legislative institution

The legislature itself, its organization, procedures, and mode of operation, shapes the legislative process. Legislatures can be organized so as to concentrate power and centralize control. Probably the best illustration of this is the British House of Commons, where the leadership of the majority party, institutionalized as the Cabinet, dominates the legislative proceedings. It is a legislature organized for majority rule: party leaders control the timetable of business, committees expedite the legislation sought by the Cabinet, and individual members are subject to strict party discipline and limited in their freedom to introduce bills and take part in floor debate.

American legislatures nowhere approach the centralization of the British House. Party loyalties are also weaker, a pattern consistent with the values of American political culture, discussed in Chapter 1, which favor independence from intense partisanship. In some state legislatures, however, the parties are relatively cohesive, more so even than in Congress. In such states as Connecticut and New Jersey the legislature's formal organization has been adapted to strong party government. The majority party caucus makes major policy decisions and these are then ratified by the official machinery of the legislature. Moreover, the internal organization and the actual practice of most state legislatures favor centralized leadership. Strict limitation on debate makes it virtually impossible for even the most determined minority to talk a bill to death as can be done in the United States Senate. Nor are the standing committees the independent centers of power they are in Congress; their chairmen can usually be counted on to cooperate with the legislature's dominant political group. In the typical lower house at the state level, power is concentrated in the Speaker; in the upper house it customarily accrues to the majority floor leader. Very briefly, the real powers of these leaders parallel their formal powers: they assign both the members and the chairmen to committees, determine which bills are to be referred to what committees, and generally manipulate the proceedings on the house floor.

This concentration of power within both houses of the typical state legislature is reinforced by the high turnover of legislators. Because salaries are low and legislative service burdensome, many retire voluntarily after a single term. (In contrast, almost all Congressmen seek reelection, and normally less than one member in five is a freshman.) As a consequence, only a handful of veteran state legislators, the floor leaders and their coterie, acquire the specialized knowledge and the political savoir faire that are the prerequisites of legislative influence.

Despite the power of the legislative leaders, many state legislatures remain poorly organized for party government. The leaders, though powerful, are often not party leaders. They are the leaders of a coalition responsive sometimes to the Governor and the urban interests that in most states he tends to reflect, or they are the managers of a coalition responsive to rural and allied interests. In either case, access to the state legislative process on matters of major policy must be through the formal leaders. But in Congress, for reasons to be examined, power tends to be more dispersed. The point to be noted here, however, is that the organization and working habits of Congress, like those of the state legislatures, necessarily influence the legislative process.

2. Constituencies

Legislators make their voting decisions by reacting to the reality that they perceive and the pressures they feel; their own attitudes and beliefs are also a basic ingredient influencing the way they vote. Unquestionably, one of the primary—if most illusive—relationships in a legislator's voting decision is the one that exists between him and his constituency. Congressmen, for example, are, or at least aspire to be, genuinely sensitive to the needs and demands of their constituents, particularly the majority that elected them and the majority that may reelect them in the future. Usually the Congressman does not and cannot respond directly to his constituency's desires, either because it is socially and economically heterogeneous and therefore may speak with two or three voices, or, as is most likely, because it communicates no position on the legislative issue. Nevertheless, Congressmen are ever conscious that their present behavior may become controversial by election time and open to exploitation by their political foes. To quote one Congressman keenly aware of the electorate's power: "You must be as smart in prospect as they are in retrospect." [6]

In most cases Congressmen, as well as state legislators, are potentially free to

---

[6] Clapp, op. cit., p. 158.

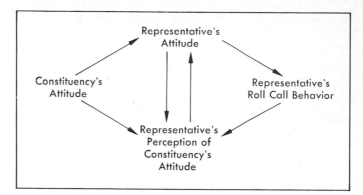

Figure 8.1. Connections between a constituency's attitude and its representative's roll call behavior

Source: Warren E. Miller and Donald E. Stokes, "Constituency Influence in Congress," *American Political Science Review,* LVII (March 1963), p. 50.

vote along party lines or according to their own inclinations, because most constituents are ignorant on legislative issues and even more ignorant of the voting records of their representatives.[7] A member of the Committee on Agriculture of the U.S. House of Representatives has touched perceptively on the heart of the problem:

> If I know the views of the constituents I will vote these views—as a representative I must—but when I don't know I substitute my best judgment. There is not one case in a hundred where I do know their views fully. I figure if they knew what I know . . . they would understand my vote. Most of us vote what we believe is sound, based on the information and our judgment. This can be changed if the people express themselves clearly enough. This, however, is improbable and doesn't happen very often.[8]

A significant study of Congressmen and their constituencies by Professors Warren E. Miller and Donald E. Stokes, which almost certainly is pertinent to the behavior of state legislatures as well, concludes that on certain major policy issues a Congressman's constituency does indeed shape his decision on roll-call votes.[9] The relationship, however, is complex, and it depends on a number of subtle interconnections that are portrayed in Figure 8.1. The constituency attitude makes its impact on the representative's ultimate vote through one of two paths, either through his own attitude, which may parallel that of the constituency, or through his response to the perceptions he has of the constituency's attitude. These two paths are not necessarily mutually exclusive, for the legislator's own attitudes undoubtedly shape his

---

[7] Donald E. Stokes and Warren E. Miller, "Party Government and the Saliency of Congress," *Public Opinion Quarterly,* XVI (Winter, 1962), pp. 531–546.

[8] Charles O. Jones, "Representation in Congress: The Case of the House Agriculture Committee," *American Political Science Review,* LV (June, 1961), p. 365.

[9] "Constituency Influence in Congress," *American Political Science Review,* LVII (March, 1963), pp. 45–56. For a partial revision of the Miller-Stokes study see Charles F. Cnudde and Donald J. McCrone, "The Linkage between Constituency Attitudes and Congressional Voting Behavior: A Causal Model," *American Political Science Review,* LX (March, 1966), pp. 62–72.

perceptions of the constituency; conversely, his perceptions over a period of time may lead to changes in his personal attitudes.

Miller and Stokes, using the facilities of the University of Michigan's Survey Research Center, conducted interviews into the attitudes and perceptions of incumbent Congressmen, their election opponents, and a sample of constituents drawn from a probability sample of 116 districts in the 1958 congressional elections. These attitudes and perceptions were then measured against the Congressmen's voting behavior in three major areas of contemporary legislative policy: social welfare, civil rights, and foreign policy. The study found that in two of the three policy areas, civil rights and social welfare, a discernible connection exists between the constituency and its representative. In the case of civil rights issues, the legislator's personal attitude and his perception of the constituency's desire are significantly aligned with the constituency's basic attitude toward Negro claims. On social welfare issues the relationships are weaker, but there appears to be a statistically significant link between the legislator's attitudes and perceptions and the attitudes of the electoral majority that placed him in Congress.

In this latter case, the Congressman's own attitude on the role of government in social welfare matters predominates, and his party affiliation guides both him and his constituents. Because the parties tend to differ on these matters, the legislator can guide his voting behavior by noting the proportion of Democratic and Republican votes in his district; in turn, the constituency receives important cues as to a congressional candidate's position on social welfare issues from the mere fact of his party affiliation. In the area of foreign policy, however, Miller and Stokes could find no relationship between the Congressmen and their constituencies. There is little effective communication of foreign policy views from the constituency to the representative, and he must look elsewhere for guidance—either to his own personal convictions or evaluations or, most commonly, to the President and his Administration, which in the twentieth century are clearly dominant on matters of foreign policy.

One final point from the study should be noted. Contrary to a common conception that Congressmen from highly competitive (marginal) districts are most prone to follow their constituency's sentiments, whereas those from one-party (or safe) districts presumably are electorally secure and hence freer to vote as they please, the opposite appears to be true. The sentiments of a competitive district are far more obscure than those of a safe, one-party district, which is more homogeneous in its socioeconomic composition. It is precisely those Congressmen from these safe districts who can perceive most clearly their constituency's attitudes and represent them most accurately. Thus, a northern Democrat from a noncompetitive urban district is not free to vote against social welfare legislation. Neither are the vast majority of southern Democrats from rural districts free to vote for civil rights legislation, an issue area in which, as we have seen, Congressmen feel especially sensitive to their constituencies' sentiments. J. William Fulbright, for example, the international-minded Arkansas Senator who led the political dissent to American policy in Southeast Asia, has nevertheless compiled a consistently illiberal record on civil rights. "I am proscribed," he has explained, "from leadership or initiative by the strong preferences of my constituency." [10] He has felt no such proscription with regard to foreign policy issues and, as a consequence, has followed his own judgment in his capacity as Chairman of the Senate Foreign Relations Committee.

State legislators apparently act in a manner similar to that of Congressmen, although the scholarly literature is as yet inconclusive on the precise manner and extent of constituency influence as it operates in fifty state legislative systems.[11] Except in occasional and rare instances in which an issue cut deeply or broadly in his district (the residents of state legislative districts are even less informed than those of congressional ones as to the issues before their legislature and their representative's doings), the state legislator is free to take other factors into account—his party's position, the Governor's appeal for support, an interest group's persuasive demand, and, indeed, his own policy preferences. Many legislators, however, are elected from districts whose socioeconomic composition is homogeneous, and in this general sense they represent their constituency's characteristics. In the words of one sophisticated state legislator,

Basically you represent the thinking of the people who have gone through what you have gone through and who are what you are. You vote according to that. In other words, if you come from a suburb you reflect the thinking of people in the suburbs; if you are depressed people, you reflect that. You represent the sum total of your background.[12]

3. Parties

The relationship of parties to the legislative process does not lend itself to easy generalization, a difficulty that is compounded by the ambivalence toward political parties in the American political culture.[13] In the twenty-five states that are under one-party or modified one-party control, party is a negligible factor. In the remaining states that are politically competitive, however, the legislature is subject, in varying degrees, to party control.[14] Party caucuses elect their floor leaders, and the majority party organizes each chamber by electing its officers and controlling committee assignments. Beyond this, Democrats and Republicans are almost certain to divide on such issues of social and economic policy as the question of unemployment benefits for striking workers. The parties divide also in the normal and largely unprincipled struggle between "in's" and "out's" and on matters such as legislative apportionment, which affect their organizational interests.

Countless other state issues are controversial, too, but not on party lines. No one should expect party members to make a partisan issue of bills to make the maple the official state tree, or to require tests for phenylketonuria in newborn

[10] *The Arrogance of Power* (New York: Vintage, 1966), p. 64.

[11] For a judicious survey see Malcolm E. Jewell and Samuel C. Patterson, *The Legislative Process in the United States* (New York: Random House, 1966), pp. 435–439.

[12] Wahlke, et al., op. cit., p. 253.

[13] See Ch. 1, pp. 5–6, 25–26.

[14] The subject of party voting in legislatures, like the closely related question of the relationship between legislators and their constituencies, is complicated and the subject of a large and growing literature. See below, pp. 345–346.

babies, or to bar the possession of firearms by the mentally ill. Where, however, the clash of interests is strong and of statewide importance, it will, in the competitive states, normally be channeled through the medium of the parties. However, no self-respecting U.S. Congressman would ever boast, as did the First Lord of the Admiralty in Gilbert and Sullivan's *H.M.S. Pinafore*, "I always voted at my party's call, and I never thought of thinking for myself at all." Even the most party-minded member likes to think, and to have others think, that he is independent of party.

The test of admission to a party caucus is as simple and casual as the test by which the average citizen "joins" a party. Once the Representative or Senator calls himself a Democrat or a Republican his credentials are rarely challenged. Nor is there any effective way in which he can be bound by a caucus decision to vote with his party. The Republicans have specifically ruled out any binding vote in their party conference, as they prefer to call their caucus, and the Democrats will excuse any member who claims that he is either committed to a contrary stand or is doubtful about its constitutionality. Understandably, the party leaders are reluctant to use the caucus too often for fear of advertising their party's disunity. Sam Rayburn, for many years the Democratic Speaker of the House, whose job it was to preside over one of the world's most quarrelsome parties, believed that caucuses were "a waste of time" in which "you lose more votes than you gain." [15]

Despite the lack of discipline, party remains the primary influence in congressional voting. Although, as the closely related question of their relationship to constituencies demonstrates, Congressmen try to vote in accord with the attitude of their district or state, they generally perceive no conflict between their constituency and party interests. Except where a proposed bill runs counter to their district's attitudes (or their perception of district attitudes), legislators tend to support the party position. A Congressman is most likely to deviate from the majority of his party colleagues when the district he represents deviates from the demographic characteristics that typify his party's congressional districts, for example, socioeconomic status as measured by the percentage of owner-occupied dwellings, race as measured by the percentage of nonwhites, population density as measured by the average population per square mile, and locale as measured by whether the district is urban or rural. A Republican Congressman from a district whose characteristics tend to make it a liberal-type district, which might be expected to vote Democratic (because of its low percentage of owner occupancy, substantial nonwhite population, and so on), will tend to vote with a majority of Democratic Congressmen more often than Republican Congressmen from districts with conservative-type characteristics. The same, of course, applies in reverse for Democrats who represent conservative-type districts atypical of their party's basic strength and orientation.[16] In spite of the deviation of such Congressmen and the American ambivalence toward political

[15] Neil MacNeil, *Forge of Democracy: The House of Representatives* (New York: McKay, 1963), p. 109.

[16] Lewis A. Froman, Jr., "Inter-Party Constituency Differences and Congressional Voting Behavior," *American Political Science Review, LVII* (March, 1963), pp. 57–61.

parties, a group or a cause that wins the determined support of a party's leaders in Congress has moved a giant step in the direction of legislative success.

4. Interest groups

Without interest groups the democratic legislative process would be lifeless, for in a sense all legislation is interest legislation. Every law embodies the hopes and preferences of certain groups and the fears and dislikes of others. At times, in fact, legislatures do little more than passively record the legislative policies desired by the most powerful groups. In Illinois the legislature routinely adopts injured workmen's compensation bills, unemployment compensation bills, and occupational disease bills after labor and management groups have worked out their differences and agreed on a draft bill. Such instances, however, represent a special adjustment to unusually technical bills; the normal legislative process is infinitely more complicated.

Interest groups vary greatly from one legislature to another and from one issue to the next in their organization, techniques, and effectiveness. Where parties are strong, as in Britiain, interest-group activity is in greater evidence before and after: *before* the formal introduction of bills in Parliament and *after* the legislation is being implemented. These forms of interest-group activity are also very evident in America. But because the parties are weaker, interests are equally prominent *during* the consideration of legislation, though their overall strength will also depend on the total political situation. When there is no effective opposition party, the situation in one-party states, interest groups tend to be more active and influential than they are in the politically more competitive states. Especially when matters dear to their pocketbooks are at stake, interest groups become front-rank combatants in the legislative struggle. But they are only *a part* of a total process. Either singly or in combination, they have seldom been able to reduce a legislature merely to registering their views.

If legislators often seem to do the bidding of interest groups, it is not usually because they have been bought or pressured with threats of defeat at the polls. Their past or present group affiliations, their personal convictions, their friendships, and their customary reliance on an electoral coalition composed of particular groups lead them to identify, consciously or not, with certain interests. Lobbyists, as a matter of fact, communicate almost exclusively with already sympathetic legislators to map out a common strategy. An exhaustive study of the congressional battles over foreign trade policy in the 1950's, for example, concluded that the protectionist initiative and leadership came from *within* Congress and not from the outside.[17]

In turn, legislators view interest groups as invaluable sources of information and political support. At one level interest groups can supply them with technical information explaining the impact of proposed legislation on the affected interest. At another level interest groups provide political information that lets the legislator know something about the electoral strength of competing groups and how strongly they feel on particular issues. "From many lobbyists," a leading New York State Senator has observed, "I got information I can't get just from reading a bill. I listen

---

[17] Raymond A. Bauer, et al., *American Business and Public Policy: The Politics of Foreign Trade* (New York: Atherton, 1963), Parts IV and V.

to both sides and discount the self-interest of each." [18] Indeed, in their more reflective moments legislators might well regard their main function as the accommodation of group demands.

Still, it will not do to ignore the seamier side of the legislative process. Although on major issues conflicting group demands are often compromised in a manner tolerable to the public interest, it is also true that many minor laws reflect a one-sided interest. This is especially the case with state laws that intimately regulate many facets of business life. When an issue means a great deal to a particular industry and comparatively little to other interests, a well-organized industry may be well-nigh irresistible *on that issue*. For example, legislation guaranteeing minimum prices to package stores is vitally important to the liquor interests, but, though it costs them money, it is not a life-and-death matter to a state's unorganized drinkers.

Neither can it be overlooked that some legislators benefit personally by using their inside position to serve their outside interests. Conflict of interest problems plague Congress. The revelations of the tangled cases of Bobby Baker, former secretary to Lyndon B. Johnson when he was the Senate Majority Leader, and of the late Senator Thomas J. Dodd of Connecticut, are spectacular instances of a distressingly common state of affairs. These problems may be even more troublesome in the part-time state legislatures. Consider, for example, this observation by an Illinois Democratic legislator with long experience in the state's House and Senate:

> My colleague, Republican Representative Noble W. Lee, who is Dean of the John Marshall Law School in Chicago and has served eleven terms in the House, estimates that one third of the members accept payoffs. In the light of my observations, I agree. Most of these are recorded as legal fees, public-relations services, or "campaign contributions," though a campaign may be months away. If questioned, the recipient simply denies that the payment had anything to do with legislative activity. This makes it technically legal. A somewhat smaller number of payoffs are not veiled at all; cold cash passes directly from one hand to the other.[19]

Such "inside" lobbying and log-rolling may in certain cases facilitate cooperation between interest groups and the government. More likely than not, however, it is noxious and subtly corrupting, a serious and unresolved problem in the American democracy.

5. Executives, administrators, and judges

Executives, administrators, and judges, each in their own distinctive ways, inevitably engage in lawmaking as they go about the performance of their duties. But they not only "make law" on their own, they participate, directly or indirectly, in the more central lawmaking of the legislature. This is particularly true of chief executives. As any Governor or President will ruefully concede, they by no means always dominate their legislatures, but they unquestionably are the central figures in the modern legislative process. Both this chapter and the last demonstrate that

[18] *New York Times,* February 19, 1964.
[19] Paul Simon as told to Alfred Balk, "The Illinois Legislature: A Study in Corruption," *Harper's Magazine,* September, 1964, p. 74.

Governors and Presidents, by drawing on their constitutional powers and their pre-eminent political position, initiate much legislation and are able to influence the rest significantly. In some respects the state chief executives surpass even the President in their capacity to dominate the legislative process, for the state legislature is typically disadvantaged by infrequent sessions, inadequate staff support, and the inexperience (lack of seniority) and low prestige of many legislators. The Governor may—and often does—enjoy remarkable success in gaining the adoption of his legislative programs, especially when he is adept at forging a winning election coalition and at building coalitions within his legislative party—two preconditions of legislative success that, of course, frequently go together.[20]

Although their roles are normally more passive and usually less visible than those of the chief executives, administrators and judges are also participants in the legislative process. The administrative bureaucracy—those regulatory and service agencies, like the Interstate Commerce Commission or the United States Army Corps of Engineers, that are not under the immediate or effective control of the chief executive—is typically a partner of the legislature. Because they must necessarily pass general laws, modern legislatures openly delegate lawmaking authority to administrators. Viewed realistically, major laws today are passed in two stages, one formal and the other informal. In the first the legislature enacts the broad outlines of a law. In the second stage the administrators, by interpreting and applying it, issue the specific rules that actually apply to the citizen. Administrators, it should also be noted, are concerned with defending their own institutional interests, and the behavior of the administrator as lobbyist is a flourishing subbranch of the legislative process.

Judges act much the same way as administrators. Although the courts perform most spectacularly when they void legislation or announce a new constitutional rule, it is in their interpretation of statutes that they make their greatest impact on legislation. Conversely, in passing laws legislatures often take into account the potential judicial response. Many laws are framed in such a way as to turn back challenges to their constitutionality and to anticipate, if possible, questions of statutory interpretation. Nor, as Chapter 9 shows, is legislative buck-passing uncommon. Legislatures often enact laws so general or even ambiguous that the courts have no choice but to determine their meaning and effect.

A listing of the primary institutions and the fundamental variables that affect the legislative process usefully identifies the basic ingredients of lawmaking in America. Yet there is always the danger that any such listing is too neat and too symmetrical and that it will make a complicated and sometimes invisible process appear delusively simple. Legislators, it must be cautioned, do not react to any set of three, five, or ten factors, and no diagram or flow chart can capture the reality of lawmaking within its four corners.

The American legislative process is not a one-way street with the legislators

---

[20] Sarah P. McCally, "The Governor and His Legislative Party," *American Political Science Review*, LX (December, 1966), pp. 923–942.

simply responding to external stimuli. It is much more like a two-way street with the legislators acting with and reacting to external forces. Each legislator responds to chief executives, administrators, judges, parties, constituents, and interest groups, and they react to him. This may lead to further reactions among other political actors, and these reactions in turn may lead to a further feedback to the legislature. Perhaps the legislative process is not a street at all, but a complicated traffic intersection! Moreover, because on many issues the legislators are not subject to cues *requiring* them to act in a particular fashion, they, and most significantly their leaders, are free to exercise discretion in directing the legislative traffic. In consequence, sometimes it moves smoothly, and sometimes there is a traffic jam. The U.S. Congress exemplifies both situations—both the flow and the deadlock.

The questions many are asking these days are: Can the United States afford so tortured and complicated a legislative process? Does it somehow, through its labyrinthine twists and turns—or perhaps in spite of them—represent the desires of the community? If not, what needs to be changed to make it more truly representative? These questions in themselves pose others: How does one measure the representativeness of a legislative body? And if one can measure it, and finds deficiencies, can one identify specific reforms that will bring improvement, and can one forecast and measure that improvement precisely? And, of course, the final question is whether legislatures as we know them, reformed or otherwise, are the only choice available for true self-government. We shall be able to answer only a few of these questions, and those only partially, in the pages that follow. They must be posed, however, even if answers prove elusive.

the congress
of the united states

Bills into Laws:
The Obstacle Course

The U.S. Congress reflects the basic character of the American political system. Aside from the few cases in which a two-thirds vote is required, nothing in the Constitution *theoretically* inhibits rule by a simple congressional majority. However, in its rules of internal organization and its customary procedures for passing important laws Congress is not an instrument normally adaptable to the speedy adoption of legislation. Its mode of operation makes simple majority rule difficult; yet it is relevant to note that most of the restraints on simple majoritarianism are ones self-imposed by the Representatives and the Senators.

In the House, which organizes itself anew every two years, formal rules can be changed by a simple majority. In the Senate, a continuing body whose rules carry over from year to year, motions to change the rules at the beginning of each new Congress are themselves subject to filibusters that can be broken only by two thirds of those voting. The main significance of this procedural barrier is that it protects the filibuster (Rule 22), which permits a minority of Senators to talk controversial legislation to death. This provision in favor of unlimited debate can be altered only when two thirds of all Senators present and voting agree to close further debate for the purpose of voting on a specific legislative proposal. So far, as Table 8.3 shows, closure or cloture motions have succeeded only ten times in fifty-eight attempts. More often than not the filibuster has been used to block civil rights legislation, and for this reason the rule has been a favorite target of liberal legislators and interest groups. On occasion, however, liberals have themselves used the filibuster to good profit.

Some Senators have argued that the filibuster rule is unconstitutional, and in 1957 Richard Nixon, then Vice President, gave an advisory opinion as the Senate's presiding officer, stating that its rules could be changed by a simple majority vote

Table 8.3 *Cloture votes, 1919–1971*

There were 58 cloture votes following the adoption of Rule 22 in 1917, up to September 1971, only 10 of which have been successful. There have been 3 successful cloture votes on civil rights bills: the omnibus bill of 1964, the Voting Rights Act of 1965, and the omnibus bill of 1968, which included a fair housing provision. The successful votes appear below in dark type.

Issue	Date	Vote	Yea votes needed
Versailles Treaty	Nov. 15, 1919	76–16	**62**
Emergency tariff	Feb. 2, 1921	36–35	48
Tariff bill	July 7, 1922	45–35	54
World Court	Jan. 25, 1926	68–26	**63**
Migratory birds	June 1, 1926	46–33	53
Branch banking	Feb. 15, 1927	65–18	**56**
Disabled officers	Feb. 26, 1927	51–36	58
Colorado River	Feb. 26, 1927	32–59	61
D.C. buildings	Feb. 28, 1927	52–31	56
Prohibition Bureau	Feb. 28, 1927	55–27	**55**
Banking Act	Jan. 19, 1933	58–30	59
Antilynching	Jan. 27, 1938	37–51	59
Antilynching	Feb. 16, 1938	42–46	59
Anti-poll-tax	Nov. 23, 1942	37–41	52
Anti-poll-tax	May 15, 1944	36–44	54
FEPC	Feb. 9, 1946	48–36	56
British loan	May 7, 1946	41–41	55
Labor disputes	May 25, 1946	3–77	54
Anti-poll-tax	July 31, 1946	39–33	48
FEPC	May 19, 1950	52–32	64 *
FEPC	July 12, 1950	55–33	64 *
Atomic Energy Act	July 26, 1954	44–42	64 *
Civil Rights Act	March 10, 1960	42–53	64
Amend Rule 22	Sept. 19, 1961	37–43	54

Source: Adapted from *Congressional Quarterly Weekly Report,* March 1, 1968, p. 379; Sept. 18, 1970, p. 2239; and Sept. 25, 1971, p. 1975.

at the opening of a new Congress. But despite repeated efforts by antifilibuster Senators, the Senate majority has been unwilling to eliminate or significantly modify the rules favoring unlimited debate. The most recent expression of this sentiment, which defends the filibuster as an instrument for the protection of minority interests, came with the opening of the Ninety-second Congress in January, 1971.

From January 26 until well into March the Senate was tied up in its regularly

Issue	Date	Vote	Yea votes needed
Literacy tests	May 9, 1962	43–53	64
Literacy tests	May 14, 1962	42–52	63
Communications Satellite Act	Aug. 14, 1962	63–27	**60**
Amend Rule 22	Feb. 7, 1963	54–42	64
Civil Rights Act	June 10, 1964	71–29	**67**
Legislative reapportionment	Sept. 10, 1964	30–63	62
Voting Rights Act	May 25, 1965	70–30	**67**
Right-to-work repeal	Oct. 11, 1965	45–47	62
Right-to-work repeal	Feb. 8, 1966	51–48	66
Right-to-work repeal	Feb. 10, 1966	50–49	66
Civil Rights Act	Sept. 14, 1966	54–42	64
Civil Rights Act	Sept. 19, 1966	52–41	62
D.C. Home Rule	Oct. 10, 1966	41–37	52
Amend Rule 22	Jan. 24, 1967	53–46	66
Civil Rights Act	Feb. 20, 1968	55–37	62
Civil Rights Act	Feb. 26, 1968	56–36	62
Civil Rights Act	March 1, 1968	59–35	63
Civil Rights Act	March 4, 1968	65–32	**65**
Fortas nomination	Oct. 1, 1968	45–43	59
Amend Rule 22	Jan. 16, 1969	51–47	66
Amend Rule 22	Jan. 28, 1969	50–42	62
Electoral College	Sept. 17, 1970	54–36	60
Electoral College	Sept. 29, 1970	53–34	58
Supersonic transport	Dec. 19, 1970	43–48	61
Supersonic transport	Dec. 22, 1970	42–44	58
Amend Rule 22	Feb. 18, 1971	48–37	57
Amend Rule 22	Feb. 23, 1971	50–36	58
Amend Rule 22	March 2, 1971	48–36	56
Amend Rule 22	March 9, 1971	55–39	63
Military Draft	June 23, 1971	65–27	**62**
Lockheed Loan	July 26, 1971	42–47	60
Lockheed Loan	July 28, 1971	59–39	66
Lockheed Loan	July 30, 1971	53–37	60
Military Draft	Sept. 21, 1971	61–30	**61**

* Between 1949 and 1959 the cloture rule required the affirmative vote of two thirds of the Senate membership rather than two thirds of those Senators who voted.

recurring hassle over Rule 22. Predictable moves had been made with predictable lack of success. Senator Jacob Javits, liberal Republican of New York, offered a motion that if adopted would have allowed the Senate to change its rules by a simple majority at the start of a new Congress. This lost 55 to 37, prompting Javits to declare that the Senate had again refused to "undo its own shackles." He went on, "One day, perhaps when I'm long dead and gone, we'll face some supervening national issue that will shake this country to its foundations and one-third of the Senate will stand in the way of action." [21] As February and the first week in March dragged on, the Senate voted no less than four times, in efforts to invoke cloture under the old two-thirds rule, in order to be free to vote on a new rule that would have allowed three fifths to shut off debate. Finally, after losing again on March 9, 55 to 39, the reformers gave up for another year and set their sights on 1973.

The practical effect of the rules and customs under which Congress operates is to make the passage of legislation difficult. Whatever the other flaws in our political system, no one can complain that it encourages hasty lawmaking. Bills supported by a clear and persistent national majority usually become laws, but they must survive a process that is partly a labyrinth and partly an obstacle race. In each house they must thread their way through a long and elaborate maze, and at the same time they must clear a number of formidable hurdles. [22]

Not surprisingly, there are differences in the way the two chambers process legislation. The Senate is small enough to permit its members great freedom—a fact that the right to filibuster dramatically symbolizes. Senators may speak as often as they gain recognition, and they are free to propose amendments on the floor. It is also relatively easy to get bills voted on, particularly when they are supported by the policy committee of the majority party; it controls the legislative calendar. In practice the majority and minority party leaders normally cooperate in calling up bills that a majority of the Senators wish to consider.

By contrast, the House, which has more than four times as many members, is run like a taut ship, and its inner life is highly organized. When considering a measure, the House voluntarily binds itself with rules that severely restrict the time allowed for debate. A member is fortunate to speak for five minutes, and his right to propose amendments on the floor is sharply limited by the rules recommended (and invariably accepted) by the Rules Committee.

This powerful House committee deserves a few words of explanation. It has the power either to release bills to the House floor or to deny them access, and it sets the length of time for their debate and determines whether or not they may be subject to amendment from the floor. In this respect the Rules Committee serves as an indispensable traffic cop, but it also uses its procedural authority to influence the content of legislation—for it has often extracted changes in proposed legislation as the price for giving it a ticket of admission to the House floor. Few Congressmen actually object to its intervention on substantive legislative matters, but there has been strong conflict over the particular policy orientation of the committee's members and over the question of whether the committee should be responsive to the majority party's leadership or to its own view of the sense of the House.

In 1965 an enormously enlarged Democratic majority (a consequence of the

---

[21] *Providence* (Rhode Island) *Journal,* March 10, 1971.

[22] Two of the most significant informal influences on the congressional lawmaking process, the committee system and the seniority rule, are discussed at length later in this chapter.

Goldwater-Johnson election) anxious to facilitate the passage of liberal legislation, forced the adoption of a "twenty-one day" rule that weakens the Rules Committee's powers. This new rule allowed the Speaker to recognize a committee chairman or ranking committee member in order to bring bills before the House that have been stalled in the Rules Committee for twenty-one days. (The rule was abandoned again in 1967.) It has always been possible to bypass the committee through various procedures, of which the most prominent is the "discharge petition." By signing a special petition a majority of the House membership can get a bill to the floor. But discharge petitions are infrequent, though their threat has sometimes loosened the Rules Committee's hold on controversial legislation. The House membership prefers orderly procedures, and it is often extremely content to let the committee bury or postpone controversial proposals. Although the Rules Committee has now been weakened and the leadership strengthened, it continues to process all bills; it remains one of the significant obstacles that proposed legislation must overcome.

Naturally, the two houses of Congress do not operate in isolation from each other. By law all money or revenue bills and by custom all appropriation bills must originate in the House. As a consequence, the Senate tends to function as an appeals court on appropriation bills, frequently revising upward the reduced appropriations favored by the more cost-conscious House Appropriations Committee. All other legislative proposals may originate in either chamber, and the House and Senate have adopted a method for reconciling legislation that each has passed in different form. The solution is a conference committee whose members are appointed by the presiding officers of each house from the senior membership of the committees that processed the bill. Each set of managers, as the conferees are called, must agree before the bill, sometimes substantially revised, returns to the two chambers. Conference committees are usually, though not always, able to work out a compromise. If the managers are bound so strictly by instructions from their respective houses that they cannot compromise on a disputed point, the bill may die in conference.

One final hurdle still remains to be cleared, and for some bills it is the most formidable. This is the constitutional requirement that the President approve all laws. After a bill has cleared the two houses in identical form, it is sent to the President. If he signs it, it becomes law; if he takes no action on it for ten days and Congress is still in session, the bill becomes law without his signature. If he disapproves of the bill, he may veto it, returning it to Congress with a message listing his objections. For the bill then to become law, both houses must repass it by a two-thirds vote. Late in the session the President has another type of veto that cannot be overriden. If within ten days of the time the bill was sent to him Congress has adjourned, he may "pocket veto" the bill by taking no action at all. In this way the President is not only spared the need to explain his veto, he can be sure it will stick.

The veto, coupled with the extraordinary majority needed to override it, gives the President a powerful weapon in bargaining with Congress. He may also use his veto message as the occasion for a memorable political appeal to the nation—

Jackson's successful veto of the Bank Bill in 1832 and Truman's unsuccessful veto of the Taft-Hartley Act in 1947 were two such events. Presidential vetoes do get overridden (Andrew Johnson was rebuffed fifteen times by the Radical Republican Congress), but the advantage is overwhelmingly with the President. According to one count, between 1789 and 1936 only 1 per cent of the private bills and 16 per cent of the public bills vetoed have been overturned.[23] Indeed, when for the first of only two times during the Eisenhower Presidency Congress rejected one of his 181 vetoes—a "pork" appropriation bill, the daily bread of most Congressmen—the uniqueness of the event warranted a front-page story in the *New York Times*.[24] None of President Kennedy's 21 vetoes were overridden, and all of President Johnson's vetoes prevailed. President Nixon, however, was overridden twice in his first two years in office.

We like to think that national majorities *can* enact their legislative proposals, but to do so they certainly must have the determination and strength to take bills through the obstacle course within the labyrinth that is the legislative process in Congress. When a bill stumbles along the way, a case can be made that it lacks majority support. However, critics of Congress have for a long time been arguing that this assumption that majorities can work their will is not well founded. They note all of the points in the process at which a minority can block action. If, therefore, one is to believe that majorities win, one must at least recognize that these need to be overwhelming majorities, not just 51 per cent. Even here, on some issues like gun control, which has very broad support according to opinion polls, these numerous supporters do not get their way. Moreover, when national majorities do at length win, they do so not so much because there is a one-to-one relationship between their strengths in the electorate and the votes their bill musters in the Congress, but rather because wielders of minority veto power in Congress give in. And they give in, presumably, because they fear that total intransigence will cause them to lose their power for future battles. In short, the reflection of national majorities in congressional action is as indirect and convoluted as the legislative processes themselves. Perhaps, as some have argued in defense of Congress, this is the price we must pay for the ability to govern a vast polyglot nation at all.

The Leadership:
Congressional and Presidential

In neither chamber is Congress as tightly controlled by its party leaders as the British House of Commons is controlled by the Prime Minister and his lieutenants. In both House and Senate the leaders must lead by manipulating and cajoling. They must combine persuasion, rewards, and sanctions with a delicate sense of timing. As the late Representative Clem Miller wrote, the leadership leads only where and when it can:

[23] Edward S. Corwin, *The President: Office and Powers 1787–1957,* 4th ed. (New York: New York U.P., 1957), p. 282.
[24] September 11, 1959.

> If they cannot be certain of winning, they don't want to go. Latent power, negative power, is so much better than power committed that lacks victory as a capstone. Hence, the legislative timidity of the Congress. . . . Hence, the great time lags for the consideration of legislation, stretching into years in many cases, while the Leadership waits for the pressures to build—pressures that will produce success. . . . Righteousness with victory is a fine thing. Righteousness with defeat is nothing much at all.[25]

Why is this so? Would it not improve Congress's effectiveness and perhaps its representativeness of popular will if it had more effective leadership? Perhaps so, but any reform in this direction would confront formidable obstacles. In the first place, the American political culture elevates independence and individualism as virtues for legislators (as well as for everybody else), rather than loyalty to leader or to team play. The emphasis in the British culture is almost the reverse. Furthermore, there is the not unrelated weakness of party ties. In other words, if there were a tradition of follow-the-leader in Congress, or if party loyalty and cohesiveness were more compelling, or both, leaders who could command support and deliver the goods might exist. But one can hardly expect acceptance of reforms that are so out of phase with the cultural milieu.

There are also solid and immediate reasons why Congress does not tighten its leadership. Members assert independence not merely because that is the accepted norm, but also because they have little choice politically. Strong, disciplined parties, such as those of the British system, might guarantee a legislator's reelection, thus enabling him to follow the party line and ignore local pressures. In the absence of such parties, each member must contrive his own election and reelection. His chief reliance must be upon the ties and the support he can develop in his district or state. Accordingly, he goes to Washington, not as a member of a tight party battalion, but as an ambassador from the folks back home.

This being the case, and because his first concern must be to protect local interests, he is bound to be at least ambivalent about strong and centralized congressional leadership. To be sure, it would be wonderful if strong leadership could push through the bills his constituents wanted. Suppose, however, that a strong leadership was unsympathetic to the problems of the urban, lower-income district that the member represented? He would then find himself continually checkmated in battling for his constituents' interests. He and other members who chafed under the strong leader's power would have the choice either of trying to pull down the unsympathetic leader and putting a more congenial one in his place, or of abolishing the leadership position that is causing the trouble. More often than not they will choose the second tactic, in part because it is easier, and in part because, in the long run, it is safer.

If there is *no* strong leader—no position from which highly centralized leadership can be exercised—then everyone is on the same footing. Every group or point of view or philosophical persuasion has a more or less equal opportunity to put together a victory. With a strong leadership role in being, the chance of controlling

[25] *Member of the House: Letters of a Congressman* (New York: Scribner's, 1962), pp. 91–92.

it to your advantage is probably more than overbalanced by the risk that it will be controlled by your opponents to your disadvantage. Furthermore, if you are of a liberal persuasion, you face a better than even chance that power positions will gravitate into the hands of unsympathetic conservatives. It becomes more logical, therefore, to keep the power divided up, the stakes of the leadership game lower, and the chances to win more equitably distributed.

The history of the filibuster issue already alluded to illustrates this line of reasoning. Traditionally, the filibuster has been a weapon in the hands of minorities that could be used to prevent their being overrun by a Senate majority. It enabled them—the southerners, for instance, bent on blocking civil rights legislation—to protect the vital concerns of their constituents and their region against a hostile majority. It is hardly surprising that Rule 22 is so difficult to change.

Two episodes on the House side point up the same moral.[26] A truly classic battle over the shape and power of the House leadership took place in 1910. At issue were the very substantial powers that had gravitated into the hands of the Speaker, and that had been used with skill and devastating effect by Joseph Gurney Cannon. "Uncle Joe" had been Speaker since 1903, and by his day the Speaker's powers were substantial indeed. He was Chairman of the Rules Committee, then a very small group of only five members, all of whom the Speaker appointed. As Champ Clark noted at the time, ". . . the committee is made up of three very distinguished Republicans and two ornamental Democrats . . . there never would be a rule reported out of that committee that the Speaker and his two Republican colleagues do not want reported." [27]

There was also a close and cooperative relationship between Cannon and the Chairman of the Ways and Means Committee, who also served as Majority Leader. Moreover, in those days, the Speaker appointed the members and chairmen of all committees. This did not mean a 100 per cent change each Congress; in fact, seniority was the general rule followed. What it did mean, though, was that the Speaker could use his power to make key appointments in such a way as to influence the committees in their dealing with legislation. In more than one case Cannon chose men as chairmen who had never even served on the committee they were to lead—over the seniority claims of long-time members. Furthermore, as Charles Jones has written, "He was not above delaying the appointment of committees until his wishes on legislation had been met." [28] One year he appointed only the Ways and Means Committee and the Rules Committee at the start of the session. Five months later, after a tariff bill with which he was concerned was safely nearing enactment, he finally appointed the other committees.

These powers, and the rest of the awesome array that Cannon could command, were used to exercise close control over the total output of the House, and in-

[26] The next few pages draw heavily on Charles O. Jones, "Joseph G. Cannon and Howard W. Smith: An Essay on the Limits of Leadership in the House of Representatives," *Journal of Politics,* August, 1968, pp. 617–646.

[27] Ibid., p. 620.

[28] Ibid., p. 621.

directly of Congress. This control, however, was heavily conservative, reflecting the wing of the Republican Party that Cannon led. The liberal Republican insurgents and the Democrats were obviously at a permanent and serious disadvantage. In 1910 these two unhappy groups mounted a successful revolt. The Speaker was shorn of much of this arbitrary power, particularly his membership on the Rules Committee and his authority to appoint the members of all committees.

The rhetoric used in the debate over the powers of the Speaker is as interesting as the results of the battle. Cannon himself, after the fateful vote had been taken, summed up his position:

This is a government by the people acting through the representatives of a majority of the people. Results cannot be had except by a majority, and in the House of Representatives a majority, being responsible, should have full power and should exercise that power; otherwise the majority is inefficient and does not perform its function.[29]

His case was for straight party government, that is, majority government exercised through parties. The model in effect was that of Britain, which has so fascinated a couple of generations of American political scientists, starting with Woodrow Wilson.

Representative John Nelson, a Republican insurgent from Wisconsin, stated the other side just as forcefully during the debate. He challenged the notion of a dominant party majority, insisting that in any event it was really the Speaker and his chief lieutenants who had arrogated to themselves the right to call themselves the majority party. He continued by saying, "We are no less Republicans because we would be free Members of Congress. We do not need to be kept on leading strings. We are free representatives of the people, and we want freedom here for every Member of every party."[30] And, in fact, this approach to the role of the member accords much more closely with basic elements in the national political culture. It also takes little reading between the lines to see its correspondence to the long-term interests of congressional minorities and of individual Congressmen.

A second episode that closely paralleled the dethronement of the strong Speaker took place in early 1961, when, by a vote of 217 to 212, the House added three new members to the Rules Committee, bringing its total membership up to fifteen. Since the 1930's the committee had been dominated by Republicans and southern Democrats. This fact had been mitigated somewhat under the liberal though weak chairmanship of Adolph Sabath of Illinois (1939–1952). The conservative influence of the committee was consolidated, however, under the famous Representative (Judge) Howard Smith of Virginia, who chaired it from 1955 until his defeat for reelection in 1966.

When the Kennedy Administration came into office in 1961, the new President insisted that only if the Rules Committee's obstructionism could be curbed would he be able to carry out his campaign promises. The liberal contingent in his own party in the House, plus some liberal Republicans, had been feeling the same way for a long time. Representative John Blatnik of Minnesota, head and spokesman for the

---

[29] Ibid., p. 631.
[30] Ibid., p. 633.

(liberal) Democratic Study Group argued for the Rules Committee change in terms strongly reminiscent of Nelson, fifty years earlier: [31] "My constituents did not cast a free ballot for the office of U.S. Representative to Congress to have the functions of that Office limited by one or two or even six other Members." [32] If the concentrated power of the Rules Committee and its chairman was a thorn in the President's flesh, it was even more a source of frustration to liberal members. Both would benefit if the Rules Committee could no longer use its power to block measures its conservative majority did not like. Leaderlessness was again preferable to hostile leadership.

If, then, Congress will not tolerate strong leadership, there is no alternative pattern save the tentative and timid sort described earlier by Representative Clem Miller. A major source of such power—or better, influence—as the leaders do have to exercise comes from their control over committee assignments. Nothing is more important to the Congressman than his committee assignment, for there is a well-recognized ranking that separates the prestigious from the less prestigious committees. In the Senate, for example, there are four highly desired elite committees—Appropriations, Armed Services, Finance, and Foreign Relations—that concern themselves with broad national and international policy. There are also five interest committees oriented to bread-and-butter domestic questions, though their desirability varies; many Senators prize a seat on the Agriculture Committee as fully as one on Foreign Relations. But Judiciary, Commerce, Banking and Currency, and Labor are less desirable, with Labor being the least prestigious of the interest committees. Nonelite Senate committees include District of Columbia, Government Operations, and Post Office. In the House, the desirability of committee assignments is explicitly recognized in the Legislative Reorganization Act of 1946. It provides that members who serve on any one of three *exclusive* committees (Appropriations, Rules, and Ways and Means) can serve on no other committee. It further recognizes ten *semiexclusive* committees, such as Agriculture, Armed Services, and Banking and Currency; a member can serve on one of these and on one of seven *nonexclusive* committees—a category that includes District of Columbia, House Administration, and Merchant Marine and Fisheries. (A House member who does not sit on a semiexclusive committee may sit on any two of the nonexclusive ones.)

The influence of the House and Senate leaders over legislative policy is in large part derived from their ability to manipulate committee assignments. House committee assignments are made, for the Democrats, by their members on the Ways and Means Committee, who are themselves elected by a party caucus. Republican assignments are made by a specially constituted Committee on Committees consisting of one Representative from each state contingent who is usually selected on the basis of his seniority. Senate Democratic assignments are made by the floor leader (the Majority Leader or the Minority Leader, depending on his party's status)

[31] For the history and functioning of the Democratic Study Group, see Mark F. Ferber, "The Formation of the Democratic Study Group," in Nelson W. Polsby, *Congressional Behavior* (New York: Random House, 1971), pp. 249–269.

[32] Jones, op. cit., p. 640.

through a Steering Committee dominated by members he has selected. Similarly, Republican assignments are made by the floor leader in his capacity as chairman of the party conference or caucus. Despite some variations in their manner of operation, each of these committee-assigning bodies is dominated by a small number of House and Senate leaders; their nominations are automatically endorsed by the party caucuses, and the formal appointments to the committees are then voted by the House and the Senate.

The leaders' powers are further strengthened by the fact that they control the proceedings on the floor and can often dispense favors—perhaps favored consideration for a desired bill or an appointment as a congressional delegate to an international conference. How their power is brought to bear was illustrated by one of the crucial votes of the House Ways and Means Committee on the 1964 Tax Act. Speaker John W. McCormack picked up a decisive vote by asking Representative Martha W. Griffiths not to destroy the faith he had in her when, for the first time, he placed a woman on the most prestigious House committee. The lady vindicated the Speaker's faith.[33] Above all, in an institutional setting that exalts experience, the leaders *have* experience.

The leadership directs with a light touch and with a sensitive appreciation of the honorableness of compromise and of the members' needs. It is leadership played pianissimo; fortissimo would be too jarring in the halls of Congress. Because the leaders do not make insistent demands too often, their infrequent appeals are doubly effective. How effectively they work is revealed in this account of House Speaker Sam Rayburn by a House Democrat:

> As a substitute for the caucus, the leadership attempts to exert a personal persuasive influence. I have only experienced this on two issues, one of which was the farm bill just prior to the 1956 election. My district opposes the party position on farm policy. The Speaker called me and said, "This is very vital to the party, particularly with the national election approaching. Can you possibly go along with us?" It was a personal appeal from the Speaker on the day of the vote. I told him that I had a strongly Democratic district, and if my vote would make the difference I would vote with him, but, if possible, I wanted to wait until the second round on the roll call, and if my vote was not needed, vote my district. He said, "That is fine. That is all I want." Friends told me he talked to them also. In effect he buttoned the thing up by that type of personal appeal. He could have gotten us all in a caucus and made a speech that wouldn't have been half as effective as ten or twelve phone calls.[34]

One obvious characteristic of this kind of highly personalized leadership is that its effectiveness depends on the individual leader. This is nowhere more evident than in a comparison between Lyndon Johnson's tenure as Senate Majority Leader (1955–1960) and that of his successor, Mike Mansfield of Montana (1961–   ).[35] Johnson seized and exploited every opportunity that the office provided. He devised

[33] Eileen Shanahan, "Tax Reform. Anyone?" *New York Times*, February 27, 1964
[34] Clapp, op. cit., pp. 288–289.
[35] See John G. Stewart, "Two Strategies of Leadership: Johnson and Mansfield," in Polsby, op. cit., pp. 61–92.

the "Johnson rule," whereby he sought to give one choice committee assignment to each freshman, thereby incurring long-term gratitude. He took into his own hands all of the threads of authority and decision-making, leaving little even for his Whip (Mansfield) to do. He bargained for, argued for, and at times virtually demanded the votes of members whose support he needed. Johnson even went so far as to control the Democratic Senatorial Campaign Committee in order to make sure that its aid was channeled to candidates in such a way as to maximize his influence.

Senator Mansfield's approach is as different as night from day. One observer has summarized it by commenting that Mansfield believes his primary function is to maintain a system that permits individual and coequal Senators the opportunity to conduct their affairs in whatever ways they deem appropriate.[36] Where Johnson was the harsh realist, Mansfield appeals to senatorial institutional pride and interest in personal participation. He has deliberately refrained from using even the fragments of power that pertain to the offce, and he is prepared to allow the legislative process to proceed with relatively little interference from the party leadership. Johnson, of course, sought to orchestrate and minutely control each step.

Given these two diametrically opposite leadership styles, one would assume that either one or the other must be clearly and demonstrably superior in results. Actually, this is not the case. As Table 8.4 shows, the Mansfield period has been even more productive than the Johnson period, although any such comparison is very difficult to make. There are too many factors that could affect apparent performance and that are quite beyond the control of the Majority Leader, as for example, the fact that Johnson served only under a Republican President and Mansfield served under a Democratic President until 1969. Even when these factors are taken into account, however, it seems clear that the leadership role is sufficiently unstructured and amorphous that it can be approached in more than one manner and still yield roughly comparable results. On party unity votes (when a majority of one party opposed a majority of the other), Mansfield's record is better than Johnson's, and there is a slight edge for Mansfield on party cohesion.

When a party controls both Congress and the White House, though *controls* is not precisely the word, it has additional advantages. For then the President assumes the leadership. Working closely with the Speaker and the House and Senate Majority Leaders, the President pushes his legislative program by making public appeals and by pressuring reluctant Congressmen. The pressure may be applied verbally in the course of a personal phone call or during a chat in the White House Rose Garden. There are also blunter weapons. The administration has available to it twentieth-century patronage: the power to influence such matters as the awarding of lucrative government contracts and the location and continued operation of military installations. When, for example, the first federal grants under the Model Cities Program, which was intended to assist cities in rebuilding their urban slums, were announced by the Department of Housing and Urban Development, critics were quick to note some striking correlations between the grants and key Democratic Congressmen who

[36] Ibid., p. 69.

Table 8.4 *Comparison of Johnson's and Mansfield's Senate majority leaderships*

	Congresses:			
	85th LBJ	86th LBJ	87th MJM	88th MJM
Democratic victories on "party line" roll-call votes	50%	70%	96%	84%
Index of cohesion	26	41	40	45

Source: John G. Stewart, "Two Strategies of Leadership: Johnson and Mansfield" In Nelson W. Polsby, ed., *Congressional Behavior* (New York: Random House, 1971), pp. 85 and 86.

assisted in the enactment of the legislation and the appropriations for this Johnson Administration Great Society measure. Among the sixty-three cities selected to receive money was Smithville, Tennessee, the home of Democratic Representative Joe L. Evins, who chaired the subcommittee that handled the appropriation and who played a significant role in winning House approval for the controversial Model Cities legislation. Another city receiving funds was Texarkana, Texas, the home of the influential Democratic Representative, Wright Patman, whose House Banking and Currency Committee authorized the legislation. (In contrast, neither Cleveland nor Los Angeles received funds in the initial grants.)

One index of the effectiveness of presidential leadership, summarized in Table 8.5, shows Congress' response to a President's position on legislative issues. Thus, the heavily Democratic Eighty-ninth Congress (1965–1966) enacted 530 of President Johnson's 840 legislative requests, a presidential batting average of 62.3 per cent.[37] (Tabulations of this kind, of course, are only a crude quantitative measure of presidential legislative leadership: they do not allow for the fact that some of the President's requests are much more important to him than others, and they do not measure the extent to which a presidential request that is scored as successful has had to be altered or compromised in order to gain its passage.) Following the 1966 elections, which reduced the Democratic majority, President Johnson's legislative leadership proved less effective. After 1965 the rapid escalation of the human and financial costs of the unpopular war in Vietnam made it increasingly difficult for Johnson to persuade Congress that it should also adopt his expensive domestic programs. Thus, in the Ninetieth Congress (1967–1968) only 51 per cent of the President's legislative requests became law. President Nixon's first Congress gave him only 40 per cent of his requests. There will always be, naturally, an element of

[37] Data in this paragraph from *Congressional Quarterly,* December 2, 1966, p. 2911; January 12, p. 43; and November 15, 1968.

Table 8.5   *Legislative scores—1954–1971*

Legislative scores for President Eisenhower in the 83rd Congress (1953–54, Republican *), 84th Congress (1955–56, Democratic), 85th Congress (1957–58, Democratic) and 86th Congress (1959–60, Democratic); for President Kennedy in the 87th Congress (1961–62, Democratic); for Presidents Kennedy and Johnson in the 88th Congress (1963–64, Democratic); for President Johnson in the 89th Congress (1965–66, Democratic) and the 90th Congress (1967–68, Democratic); and for President Nixon 91st Congress (1969–70, Democratic) and 92nd Congress (1971–72, Democratic).

	Year	Proposals submitted	Approved by Congress	Approval scores
Eisenhower	1954	232	150	64.7%
	1955	207	96	46.3
	1956	225	103	45.7
	1957	206	76	36.9
	1958	234	110	47.0
	1959	228	93	40.8
	1960	183	56	30.6
Kennedy	1961	355	172	48.4
	1962	298	133	44.6
	1963	401	109	27.2
Johnson	1964	217	125	57.6
	1965	469	323	68.9
	1966	371	207	55.8
	1967	431	205	47.6
	1968	414	227	55.0
Nixon	1969	171	55	32.7
	1970	210	97	46.2
	1971	202	40	20.0

Source: Adapted from *Congressional Quarterly,* January 12, 1968, p. 43; November 15, 1968, p. 3131; February 5, 1971, p. 307; and February 19, 1972, p. 375.

* The score for 1953 is not comparable to those for subsequent years. Before 1954, CQ used a different system, grouping Presidential requests in relatively broad categories.

unevenness in the presidential leadership and of uncertainty in the congressional response. The Constitution, in the apt expression of one scholar, "joins the President and Congress for better or worse. But there is no pledge to love, honor, *and* obey." [38]

[38] Pendleton Herring, *Presidential Leadership: The Political Relations of Congress and the Chief Executive* (New York: Rinehart, 1940), p. 127 (emphasis in original).

"Why, it's Senator Matson! I *heard* he was back home to mend his fences."

Figure 8.2. Mending the fences back home: the Congressman as constant candidate
Source: Drawing by Mirachi; copyright 1956, *The New Yorker Magazine, Inc.*

The Committee System:
Seigniors and Seniority

"Congress in session," Woodrow Wilson wrote in 1885, "is Congress on public exhibition, whilst Congress in its committee rooms is Congress at work." These words come from his classic book, *Congressional Government,* notable for its criticism that in Congress "power is nowhere concentrated" but is scattered "into forty-seven seigniories, in each of which a Standing Committee is the court-baron and its chairman lord-proprietor." Some of Wilson's descriptions have become outdated. The congressional parties are now more cohesive and better organized than in his day, and—because of Presidents like Wilson—power is more centralized. But his basic observations remain correct: the standing committees are still the focal points of legislative activity and their chairmen constitute the power elite of Congress. The essence of the congressional system is captured in this observation by Wilbur D. Mills, one of the contemporary "lord proprietors":

> I was always taught by Mr. Rayburn that our whole system was to settle disputes within the committees. It's a waste of time to bring out a bill if you can't pass it. I just don't like to have a record vote for the sake of having a vote. Last year [1967] we lost the debt ceiling bill the first time around because the committee hadn't reduced the Administration's figure the way we did every time before.
>
> They told me downtown that they couldn't take a lower figure; so I brought the bill to the floor because I wanted to show those people downtown what the feeling about Government spending was up here. I knew what would happen to that bill. I visit with the members. Remember that you can always do more in the cloakrooms around here than on the floor.[39]

Unlike the House of Commons, whose committees are largely unspecialized by policy area, and unlike many state legislatures, in which the committees are administrative conveniences useful to the dominant party or clique, the congressional committees are permanent, semiautonomous, and specialized. Nineteen House and fifteen Senate standing committees provide an essential division of legislative labor, each committee sifting an average of one thousand bills a year. The committees themselves are subdivided into more than 250 subcommittees, and these almost defy description. Because normally every bill must be reported out of committee before it can be voted on by the full house, the committee is in a position to exact a heavy toll, even to the point of killing the bill then and there. Three out of every four bills, in fact, get no further than the committee to which they are referred.

Most discussions and studies of congressional committees, including the foregoing paragraphs, treat them as a system and imply that all play basically similar roles. Up to a point that is true, but there are significant variations of style, operation, and tradition. Policy specialization accounts for a portion of this variation. Not only do committee areas of concern differ, but the kinds of issues and strategic problems, to say nothing of the intrinsic importance of the subject matter involved in each, differ widely. From the point of view of the member, too, they are by no means all alike. Some are far more prestigious and sought after than others, some offer one type of opportunity, and some another. For example, one committee may be valuable in enabling a Congressman to serve his constituents and thereby help assure his re-election, another may give him stature and influence in the house in which he serves, and a third may allow him to indulge his personal policy interests.

A study done by Professor Richard Fenno, which in turn is based on earlier work on individual committees, provides an excellent insight into a sample of House committees from several of these perspectives.[40] Fenno also studied the patterns of internal organization, operation, and leadership of the committees involved. He chose for examination two committees from the top of the pecking order, that is, two

---

[39] Quoted in Julius Duscha, "The Most Important Man on Capitol Hill Today," *New York Times Magazine,* February 25, 1968, p. 73. The reference is to Sam Rayburn, who served as Speaker of the House from 1940 to 1947 and from 1949 to 1962.

[40] The next several pages draw on a paper by Professor Fenno entitled "Congressional Committees: A Comparative View," delivered at the American Political Science Association meetings, Los Angeles, September, 1970.

of the most prestigious: the Ways and Means Committee and the Appropriations Committee. The four others in his sample, in descending order of their desirability in the eyes of House members, are the committees for Foreign Affairs, Education and Labor, Post Office and Civil Service, and Interior and Insular Affairs.[41]

There are few things in relation to his career that are of greater importance to a member of Congress than his committee assignments. In general, all prefer to be on important committees at the upper end of the pecking order rather than on committees with less prestige. This concern, however, may be discounted by other career decisions made by the Congressman. These decisions involve weighing constituency interests and demands against committee prestige, as well as personal preferences. For example, Congressmen who choose the Appropriations Committee or the Ways and Means Committee tend, on the whole, to rank "power in the House" higher in their scheme of values than the chance to serve constituents or the opportunity to become engaged in policy problems per se. Membership on such prestigous committees in itself makes one a person of importance, sought out and courted by colleagues. This is so in part because these two committees do many things that can benefit or harm fellow Congressmen or their constituents, and also in part because the Representatives on those committees form a kind of elite within the House.

On the other hand, what about the member who is less concerned about power in the abstract and who is more anxious to play a role in the making of policy in some area in which he has long been interested? Under these circumstances, either the Foreign Affairs Committee or the Education and Labor Committee will be especially attractive. When questioned, none of the Congressmen on these two committees told the interviewer that they sought out this assignment because it would confer influence in the House. Foreign Affairs Committee members felt that their committee role would have no effect on their chances for reelection, and Education and Labor Committee members actually felt, in some instances, that the committee would adversely affect their chances.

If career security—that is, reelection—is really uppermost in a member's mind, then he is far more likely to seek out the Interior Committee or the Post Office Committee. As Fenno writes, summarizing interviews with members of these two committees, "In place of talk about power, prestige, and importance, one hears almost exclusively about district interests to be served, projects to be authorized and political help to be gained." [42] Western Congressmen are particularly attracted to the Interior Committee because of the special interests of their districts. There is no such readily identifiable constituency for the Post Office Committee, but it is obviously sought by Congressmen who have sizable numbers of civil servants among their constituents, who, if given special attention, can be expected to add a welcome dividend of votes at election time.

Committees differ in their relationship to their environment and the strategies they must pursue to come to terms with it, as well as in the kinds of attractions they have for prospective members. Theoretically each committee must deal in some de-

---

[41] The pecking order used here is found in Jewell and Patterson, op. cit., p. 206.

[42] Fenno, APSA paper, op. cit., p. 6.

gree with its fellow House members, with elements of the executive branch, with clientele (interest) groups outside, and with the political parties and specifically their leaders. Generally speaking, however, each committee is likely to find its concern focused on only one or two of these and be relatively unconcerned with the others. Appropriations and Ways and Means must be concerned, above all, with their fellow Congressmen because influence in the House, which the committee members seek, can be secured only if the committees' performance accords with what the House expects.

The House Foreign Affairs Committee has a quite different environmental focus. Its subject matter is peculiarly executive in derivation because the executive has a long-recognized predominance in the making of foreign policy. Given the greater scope accorded the Senate Committee on Foreign Relations in dealing with this subject matter, the range of activity of Foreign Affairs is quite narrow. In fact, it is pretty much limited to dealing with the annual foreign aid legislation, the approval and passage of which is therefore the committee's prime strategic concern. Education and Labor, the other committee in the sample with a predominantly policy orientation, has, as does Foreign Affairs, an area in which the rest of the House is quite disinterested. In its case, also, the executive forms an important element in its external environment: the President's top domestic concerns are likely to involve either education policy or labor questions. But perhaps the most crucial factor in this committee's environment is the political parties because its subject matter is almost invariably partisan. In short, the Education and Labor Committee may have the broadest and most diffuse range of environmental concerns and, in consequence, the most difficult strategic problems.

The external concerns of both the Interior Committee and the Post Office Committee are obviously as clear-cut and focused as those of the Education and Labor Committee are diverse: these concerns are constituents and local interests. The Interior Committee must deal with the largest glut of bills faced by any committee, approximately 50 per cent of all bills introduced in the House. Its strategy could hardly be anything other than trying to secure passage of all the bills that are constituency supported and member sponsored. A closely related strategic concern is to try to protect the interests of (western) resource users against pressure from (eastern) conservation interests. The equation that the Post Office Committee must try to solve is simple but difficult: it must balance the pay demands of its clients (the Post Office and civil service unions), which the Committee is always prone to grant, against the rate increases the executive wants, which the committee is reluctant to approve. (The new government corporation that is taking over the postal service, the United States Postal Service, will doubtless change the pattern of forces playing on the committee.)

As might be expected, the internal structure and operations of the committees vary. Committee operation can most usefully be envisioned in terms of whether partisanship and party alignments play a major role, or whether these cleavages are muted in favor of a nonpartisanship or bipartisan emphasis. The Ways and Means Committee and the Education and Labor Committee are similar in these respects.

Both are highly partisan, but the former engages in a high degree of partisanship only at the decisional stage, when final determinations are being made on bills; most of the rest of its deliberative work is conducted on an intentionally nonpartisan basis. By contrast, the Education and Labor Committee is partisan throughout its process of deliberation. Comparing the two committees, a Ways and Means member noted that "we always try for a consensus. . . . They never try for a consensus; they battle it out." [43] Or, as an Education and Labor Committee member put it, "You can't get a resolution praising God through this Committee without having a three day battle over it." [44]

The other four committees in Professor Fenno's study engage in considerably less partisanship than the first two. Appropriations tries to minimize party battling at both the deliberational and the decision stages, and it enforces a strong tradition against the filing of minority reports. Foreign Affairs has operated in recent years in a bipartisan manner. Because its only major recurring concern is foreign aid, and because all but two or three of the Democrats and a majority of the Republicans support the program, this consensual stance has been easy to maintain. A different makeup of the committee membership would, of course, alter the situation. Both the Post Office Committee and the Interior Committee are low in partisanship, in large part because both deal with relatively monolithic clientele groups whose interests would be harder to serve if the committees got bogged down in partisan fighting.

The internal subcommittee structures of the six committees reveal similar variations. Appropriations, for example, divides its work among a dozen or more subcommittees, each with jurisdiction over a cluster of administrative agencies. Interior also has a durable subcommittee structure resembling that of Appropriations; its members are involved in the committee's work primarily through these subcommittees. Education and Labor did not have a permanent set of subcommittees until 1959, and even today its subcommittees—unlike those of Appropriations or Interior —are less autonomous, can claim less freedom from interference by other committee members, and must submit to having their decisions more thoroughly reviewed by the full committee.

Ways and Means is one of the few congressional committees that does not work through subcommittees at all. It does its work solely in the context of the full membership. Foreign Affairs is second only to Ways and Means in doing the bulk of its work in the full committee. This is in part because of the fact that all members want to be involved in the one major bill the body deals with each year. There is a rather elaborate set of standing subcommittees, but they do very little. Post Office also makes relatively little use of its subcommittees, of which there were four before 1965 and eight subsequently. One of the problems faced by this committee is that its members evince relatively a much lower level of interest in its work than is true of most other committees.

Table 8.6 summarizes some interesting comparative information on the six committees that are being examined. The comparison of the number of meetings held by

43 Ibid., p. 55.
44 Ibid., p. 56.

Table 8.6

	Number of subcommittee meetings	Number of full committee meetings	Total important bills reported
Appropriations	590	24	154
Education and Labor	363	40	96
Interior	374	82	82
Post Office	119	44	42
Foreign Affairs	186	135	66
Ways and Means	0	180	144

Source: Richard Fenno, "Congressional Committees. A Comparative View," paper delivered at the American Political Science Association meetings, Los Angeles, September, 1970, pp. 54 and 62.

the subcommittees and the full committees provides a graphic picture of their internal operation, at least as far as the subcommittee role is concerned. The last column, which tabulates important bills reported out, gives an approximate notion of the committees' work load. (In interpreting these figures we should note that only those bills deemed important enough to be tabulated by the *Congressional Quarterly* were included, not all bills reported out.)

The final dimension of the committee system to be discussed is the role of the chairman. The position of the committee chairman is much like that of the leader in the parent house: it is highly personalized and therefore reflects the personality and style of the individual who holds the position. Wilbur Mills, for instance, doubtless the best known of all recent committee chairmen, clearly dominates the decision-making process in Ways and Means. Yet he does not impose his will; instead he works to promote a consensus. His enormous influence with his colleagues rests in large measure on his expertise in the field and his very sensitive feeling for what the House desires. Wayne Aspinall, the Chairman of the Interior Committee, dominated his committee in much the same way. He operated through rigorous and impeccably fair application of the rules of the committee, which are comprehensive and designed to guarantee fairness all around. Aspinall, too, was a consensus chairman before his primary defeat in 1972.

The Appropriations Committee also has had consensus chairmen. Representative George Mahon, however, is a less dominant figure than either Aspinall or Mills. Appropriations, with its set of highly autonomous and seniority-structured subcommittees, functions, as Table 8.6 indicates, largely through these subgroups. The chairman plays his most important role in relation to his own subcommittee by manipulating subcommittee appointments to gain influence with his colleagues and by being the only member who fully understands the overall scene involving the committee's work. Education and Labor has had a series of highly diverse chairmen in recent years. Graham Barden, a reactionary southerner opposed to most of the bills that came before the committee, was succeeded by Adam Clayton Powell, a black from Harlem, who was at the opposite end of the political spectrum. Of Barden and Powell, Fenno has written that "both lived by the Committee's harsh rules of policy combat and were eventually deposed by majorities invoking those rules against them."[45] The Education and Labor Committee, in fact, must operate within a harsh jungle of partisan policy cleavages that precludes the kind of tight leadership that Wilbur Mills can exercise in his committee. Both Foreign Affairs and Post Office have had relatively weak chairmen in recent years. Neither has had aggressive leadership, and in the eyes of members, both have been less effective than they could be.

In sum, committee operation and effectiveness, and the role a committee plays in the total congressional decisional process, are a product of many variables. All committees share certain common characteristics imposed on them by the system of which they are a part. But they also differ sharply among themselves, in part for reasons that are inherent in the role each is called upon to play in policy-making, in part by virtue of the varied traditions that have evolved within each, and in part because of accidental reasons of personality. This last comment serves as an appropriate introduction to the perennial question of the seniority system.

The Seniority Rule

We have already encountered the problem of assigning members to committees in the discussion of the downfall of Speaker Cannon. In place of his prerogative, each party in the House provided itself with a Committee on Committees to do the job of making initial appointments. Once on a committee, each member gradually works his way up the seniority ladder. If he survives long enough and does not switch to a more desirable committee, he can aspire to the chairmanship.

The political effect of this informal but deeply ingrained chairman selection tradition is clear. It means that the member who is able to maintain good health wins the ultimate prize largely because he comes from a constituency that is noncompetitive. In the past such districts have been largely rural northern in the case of Republicans and rural southern in the case of Democrats. Beyond doubt, the net effect of the seniority rule plus persistent regional one-partyism has been to overrepresent those interests fortunate enough to be concentrated in one-party regions. On the whole the system has favored a coalition of Democratic and Republican conservatives, rural rather than urban in their orientation, and, at the very least, indifferent to the civil rights and social welfare legislation sought by the more populous urban areas.

The seniority rule is as entrenched with Congress as the committee chairmen whose power it confirms; yet its political significance may be gradually changing. Increasingly, as Table 8.7 demonstrates, many congressional seats in northern states have become noncompetitive. Nearly 50 per cent of northern House seats, many of

---

[45] Ibid., p. 84.

Table 8.7 Congressional seats won by Democrats by at least 65 per cent of the two-party vote, by year and region—1946 through 1964

Year	North Urban No.	Per cent	North Rural No.	Per cent	South Urban No.	Per cent	South Rural No.	Per cent	Total seats won by 65% No.	Per cent	Total Democratic seats won
1946	16	15%	7	6%	11	10%	76	69%	110	100%	118
1948	31	23	14	10	12	9	78	58	135	100	263
1950	25	19	13	10	12	9	79	61	129	99 *	235
1952	24	20	4	3	12	10	78	66	118	99 *	213
1954	40	28	14	10	9	6	79	56	142	100	232
1956	32	26	8	7	13	11	68	56	121	100	234
1958	61	35	20	11	20	11	75	43	176	100	283
1960	57	36	12	8	19	12	70	44	158	100	260
1962	53	39	10	7	10	7	64	47	137	100	259
1964	81	49	25	15	12	7	48	29	166	100	294

Source: Raymond E. Wolfinger and Joan Heifetz, "Safe Seats, Seniority, and Power in Congress," *American Political Science Review*, LIX (June, 1965), 347.

* Does not sum to 100 because of rounding

which are located in urban areas, are noncompetitive; northern Democrats with seniority will soon be as numerous as southern Democrats.[46] Already a considerable number of House chairmen come from urban districts, whereas in the Senate the seniority escalator is steadily lifting a group of liberals to the threshold of committee power. Recent elections have also expanded the liberal contingent to the point where former Senator Joseph S. Clark, a sharp critic of the conservative Senate "Establishment," could predict that Democratic and Republican liberals are "within striking distance of obtaining control of the committee system." [47] Aiding this development is a harsh fact of life: southern Democratic committee chairmen are older than their northern challengers, and their ranks will be thinned that much sooner.

In a society so given to the cult of youth, it is paradoxical that Congress should defer to the aged. Many political scientists and other commentators condemn the seniority rule as foolish (as a senility rule) and as irrational—irrational from the point of view of party government that requires committees and chairmen subservient to the majority party leadership. But the seniority rule is in part an effect, not a cause, of the absence of strong and centralized parties. Moreover, it is but one of a number of developments (such as the growth of a staff system, the creation of specialized agencies of party leadership, and the settling of contested elections on a merit instead of partisan basis) that reflect the adoption by Congress of certain automatic patterns of behavior that make its internal processes stable and maximize its ability to bring specialist influences to bear on the political system.[48]

It is, therefore, possible to argue that, for the American Congress, seniority is rational. Because it is automatic it provides a simple and harmonious means of selection, and it avoids the disruptive conflicts that the free election of chairmen would bring. And it works. Occasionally an incompetent (who can be circumvented) heads a committee, but the typical chairman brings with him not only years of legislative specialization and political experience, but considerable ability as well. Nor, contrary to a widespread belief, are the chairmen unrepresentative of their parties. One study shows that in their voting records between 1946 and 1956 the committee chairmen were only slightly below the average member in their degree of party and presidential support.[49]

Despite the case that can be made for the seniority system, its critics remain unconvinced—and have gradually gathered strength inside as well as outside Congress. In fact, the Ninety-second Congress (1971–1973) made some concrete if modest progress in modifying the seniority dogma. During 1970 a committee of House Democrats worked on revisions to be presented to the Democratic caucus with the opening of the Ninety-second Congress. Republicans, for their part, also promised during the 1970 congressional election campaign that they would adopt modifica-

[46] Raymond E. Wolfinger and Joan Heifetz, "Safe Seats, Seniority, and Power in Congress," *American Political Science Review*, LIX (June, 1965), pp. 337–349.

[47] Joseph S. Clark, *The Senate Establishment* (New York: Hill and Wang, 1963), p. 99.

[48] Nelson W. Polsby, "The Institutionalization of the U.S. House of Representatives," *American Political Science Review*, LXII (March, 1968), pp. 144–168.

[49] George Goodwin, Jr., "The Seniority System in Congress," *American Political Science Review*, LIII (June, 1959), pp. 428–429.

tions. The Democratic committee proposals were modest, featuring a provision that would mandate a caucus vote on any chairmanship designation if demanded by a member with the backing of ten others. The committee also urged a limitation of one subcommittee chairmanship for committee chairman. Other more radical reform proposals had also been prepared for presentation to the Democratic caucus, including one that would bar all committee chairmen after they reached the age of seventy, or after having served as chairman for eight years. This would have had the effect, if adopted, of ousting eleven of the twenty-one chairmen, including the heads of Appropriations, Ways and Means, and Rules.

The Republican House caucus, meeting on January 20, 1971, adopted a rule that would automatically provide a secret ballot on all nominations brought in by the Committee on Committees for the ranking minority members on committees. (The ranking minority member on a committee becomes its chairman if his party wins control of the chamber.) That same day the Democrats adopted their study committee's proposals. By limiting chairmen to one subcommittee chairmanship they opened up to thirty or more such positions for more junior House members. Later, however, when the Democratic liberals tried to use the new weapon to oust Representative John L. McMillan of South Carolina from the chairmanship of the District of Columbia committee and thereby elevate a northern black Representative, Charles C. Diggs, Jr., of Michigan, they lost 126 to 96. But the very fact that it is now possible to call for such a vote, and come that close to success, represents progress. (The voters eliminated McMillan in the 1972 primaries.)

A straw in the wind at the other end of the capital should also be noted. When, at the opening of the Ninety-second Congress, Mike Mansfield, the Senate Majority Leader, was faced with the choice of a new member for the Democratic Steering Committee, he took the unprecedented step of naming a freshman. Normally that committee has been the private preserve of the Senate's patriarchs, which usually has meant senior southern Democrats. In naming Lawton Chiles, newly elected from Florida, Mansfield passed over the claims by seniority of such notables as James O. Eastland and John Stennis of Mississippi, Herman E. Talmadge of Georgia, Russell B. Long of Louisiana, and B. Everett Jordan of North Carolina. This, however, was not the first innovative appointment made by Mansfield to the Steering Committee. He has added several younger and less conservative members such as Edward M. Kennedy of Massachusetts, Quentin N. Burdick of North Dakota, and William B. Spong, Jr., of Virginia. This liberalization will have its effect in time on the rest of the Senate establishment.

Parties and Legislatures

The relationship between political parties and Congress, which so far has been mentioned indirectly, is also a significant factor in the working of Congress. To be sure, American parties play a less important legislative role than do their British counterparts at Westminster. Nevertheless, their significance in the legislative process is by no means marginal.

In actuality, political parties form one of the most important and enduring links between the legislative apparatus and its constituents—the public at large. Parties preside over the choice of congressional and other legislative candidates, though, of course, the extent to which they can actually control choices depends on a variety of factors, such as the primary laws in force in a given jurisdiction. Election campaigns for Congress are also party contests in almost every instance. The choices posed to the electorate are essentially party choices, however much individual candidates may play down their party labels for immediate electoral advantage, whether real or presumed. As we have already seen, American legislatures are organized by the party groups, their officers chosen by party votes, and their committees structured in proportion to party strength and chaired by members of the majority party.

Finally, because it is well established that party affiliation is more significant in determining roll-call voting behavior than any other single influence, parties do play a key role in legislative policy-making. In general, there is a basis for assuming that perhaps two thirds to three quarters of all voters consider themselves members of one or the other party and vote their party preference more consistently in legislative elections than in elections for Governor or President. These consistent patterns in the electorate parallel party voting within Congress. Just as the member of Congress is at times responding to specific constituent interests when he votes contrary to his party position on a particular measure, by the same token he is responding to general patterns of voter sentiment when, under normal circumstances, he *follows* his party leadership.

The process through which one gets elected to Congress is, however, essentially an entrepreneurial venture. This is especially true in the case of being nominated; parties are involved, but much depends on the aspirant himself. With the exception of a few districts, House candidates promote themselves and do their own legwork. Not surprisingly, the incumbents enjoy great advantages. Two factors seem indispensable: prior political experience and an existing core of supporters. Backing can come from a large collection of friends, a civic organization, an interest group, or a party faction; but whatever the source, it is essential. Indeed, one reason that so many House members are lawyers is that legal practice provides time to gain contacts and to build a following. A typical tale of entrepreneurial nomination was related in this interview by a Congressman:

I grew up in politics. My Dad was a district captain and my brother was a county leader. When I got out of law school, I sought the assembly post against the organization, but withdrew when a friend got the organization designation. Later I moved to another district and got an opportunity to serve in the state senate. After eight years there, I challenged the Democratic Congressman in the primaries and beat him.[50]

If there is a good chance of victory in the general election, a would-be Representative will probably have to win his party's nomination (at least the first time) in a primary. A few local machines, however, are still strong enough to control

---

[50] Clapp, op. cit., p. 36.

nominations absolutely. Mayor Daley's Chicago organization is the prime example, although vestigial power survives in the Democratic parties of New York City and Albany and in the Republican party of rural Pennsylvania. These machines pass out nominations to ambitious young men whom the old-line leaders want shipped out of town (to a ward-based politician, Washington is a remote and unimportant center) or to loyal old men who need a comfortable sinecure. What machines give, they can also take away. Both the Chicago and the Pennsylvania parties have announced the retirement of several incumbents before notifying these worthies.

One Congressman explained how he got an organization-controlled nomination:

I went to see our national committeeman and asked him if I would get party support if I wanted to run for Congress two years later. He said that was two years away, that he thought they had a candidate for the race coming up, but suggested I take a flier in the primary. Following his advice, I went down to a small town and talked to the district chairman. I said, "I want to run for Congress and I think I can win." "Well, let's go around and meet some folks," and we did. That night he drove me back to the city where he had a date with his old law school classmate, the national committeeman. The next day I went in to see the latter again and he looked up and smiled and said, "I hear you have been traveling around the countryside. Well, there are some people I want you to see. At this point I knew he had changed his mind about me. . . . Thus I was able to get the party endorsement. . . . It was just a case where the guy who happened to be very powerful decided, "You are our boy." [51]

Senate nominations are ardently sought wherever there is the remotest chance of winning the general election. Senate service brings greater prestige and influence than any office in American politics except the Presidency or a Supreme Court justiceship. More than half of the Senators are lawyers who grew up in middle- or upper-middle-class families. High-status ethnic origins and religious affiliations are disproportionately represented, but the Senate is not entirely a closed club. There are Catholic and Jewish Senators, and Edward W. Brooke (R–Massachusetts) is the first Negro to have been elected since Reconstruction. More than 85 per cent of the Senators are college graduates, and many of them possess advanced degrees. At one time, 24 per cent of the Democrats and 14 per cent of the Republicans were Phi Beta Kappas. Where brainpower and motivation are concerned, the Senate is a home for awesome achievers.[52]

Senators are recruited from other positions in political life. A classic study of the Senate (based on data for the years 1947 to 1957) revealed that 28 per cent came from the House, 22 per cent from governorships, 17 per cent from government administration, 15 per cent from attorney-general jobs, and the rest from lesser governmental posts. As the Senate becomes more and more the staging ground for Presidents, its members are likely to be drawn even more from those who are prominent before they run. Would-be nominees are often entrepreneurs who expand already solid cores of support. Few party organizations are strong enough to con-

---

[51] Ibid., p. 37.
[52] Donald R. Matthews, *U.S. Senators and Their World* (New York: Vintage, 1960), Ch. 2.

trol nominations, and contests for the Senate can be as expensive and extensive as any gubernatorial primary.

Thousands of people are elected to the state assemblies, town councils, and county boards that are the legislative bodies of the states and local communities. How are they nominated? As the public visibility of an office recedes, party control over the nomination increases. Public interest in these posts is less, and nominations are generally the outcome of bargaining between hopeful candidates and local party leaders. Primaries are rare outside the South. Sometimes endorsements go to entrepreneurs who seek out the appropriate ward, district, or county committee members and ask to be nominated. Sometimes, where the party is in the minority (many districts at these levels are solidly in the hands of one party because they contain homogenous populations), the party managers will have to search to find someone to *accept* the nomination. Although some people find satisfying careers in state and local legislatures, these positions are far less desirable than service in Congress or in state or local executive positions. As a consequence, there is less competition for such nominations and greater turnover of personnel.

Campaigns for Senate and House seats differ from each other. Senate campaigns resemble gubernatorial contests in their statewide scope and expense. Seriously contested Senate elections engage ambitious and attractive personalities in controversy over a strange but typically American mix of trivial and important local and national issues. In one-party southern states, all of the campaigning, until very recently, took place before the Democratic primary elections. General elections merely ratified the decisions made then, and the campaigns preceding the November voting were dull. As southern Republican parties mount more potent candidates, this pattern is likely to change.

House campaigns take place in a particularly circumscribed electoral environment. First, most House seats are safe seats, even in those states that are competitive in presidential, gubernatorial, and senatorial elections. A candidate of the minority party in the district has almost no chance to win. Second, in *all* districts, the incumbent has an unusual advantage. Few voters make any effort to follow House politics. About 46 per cent of those who vote in congressional elections have not heard or read anything about either candidate; these people vote automatically for their own party's man. Of those who do know the names of both candidates, 83 per cent still cast ballots on straight party grounds. Only when a voter can recognize the name of the opposition candidate, but *not* of the incumbent, is there a chance of defection from the party label—a 40-per-cent chance, to be exact.[53] As a consequence, party identification is the most important variable in voting for a member of the House of Representatives, followed by simple name recognition. In his roundtable discussions, Professor Clapp found that

Although members of Congress are inclined to talk about re-election campaigns in terms of the problems involved, they agree that as incumbents they possess extraordinary ad-

---

[53] See Donald E. Stokes and Warren E. Miller, "Party Government and the Saliency of Congress," op. cit., pp. 531–546.

vantages over their opponents. There is a tendency to believe that, aside from isolated instances where an over-riding issue is present, there is little excuse for defeat.[54]

Many House members campaign constantly, making the process normal rather than exceptional in their lives. As one Congresswoman explained:

I have the feeling that most effective campaigning is done when no election is near. During the interval between elections you have to establish every personal contact you can and you accomplish this through your mail as much as you do it by means of anything else. At the end of each session, I take all the letters which have been received on legislative matters and write each person telling him how the legislative proposal in which he is interested stands.

Personally, I will speak on any subject. . . . Generally I speak at nonpolitical meetings. I read 48 weekly newspapers and clip every one of them myself. When there is a particularly interesting item about anyone, that person gets a note from me. We also keep a complete list of the change of officers in every organization in our district. Then when I am going to town, I know exactly who I would like to have at the meeting. . . . I budget 17 trips home each session and somehow I've never managed to go less than 21 times.[55]

When House seats are seriously contested, the costs may reach $50,000 for a single campaign. Each party has a House Campaign Committee (and a Senate Campaign Committee), and these money-raising and field units can provide each candidate with from $2,000 to $4,000. The incumbents have the additional advantage of the postal frank, which allows them to send mail free to constituents; they also have an established staff on the federal payroll.

Much more than in Great Britain, where seats in Parliament reflect a national campaign and national trends, House seats are won and lost in dozens of isolated campaigns. Nonetheless, the outcomes in the ninety seats seriously contested in any election are affected by the swing of presidential politics. Especially when he is at the top of the crest of a wave of public opinion, a popular President can "carry in candidates on his coat tails." Johnson, for example, swept seventy-one new Democrats along with him in 1964. In off-year elections, the trend traditionally flows the other way and the party in power normally loses seats. Despite concentrated efforts to aid and save his seventy-one new followers (who backed him on 82 per cent of all roll calls while they were in the capital), President Johnson saw twenty-six of them fall by the wayside in 1966. In 1970, though his party was already in a minority, and though he campaigned valiantly, President Nixon saw the GOP House contingent shrink further with a net loss of nine seats. There is little that a House candidate can do about the effect of shifts in public opinion except to try so to imprint his identity on the voters' minds that victory will come from personal recognition.

The tactics of House campaigns vary. In the geographically broad districts of the less populated states, candidates rely heavily on their personal contacts, the news media, and the party organization. In the more congested and spatially smaller urban districts, the media cannot focus on a particular Congressman's constituency.

[54] Clapp, op. cit., p. 374.
[55] Ibid., pp. 375–376.

No TV station, to illustrate, serves only a *part* of Los Angeles. Under these conditions, candidates rely heavily on direct mailings to voters, on party organization and interest-group support, and on handshaking tours.

Individual campaigns for seats in state legislatures and city councils have even less effect on election outcomes than congressional campaigns. Districts for these offices are usually homogeneous and devoid of party competition. Intensive struggles occasionally occur in primaries, but the general election campaigns are usually dull contests between candidates whose names are unknown to most voters. (How many readers can name their state representative?) Victory is a consequence of party label and only broad shifts in party loyalties can bring substantial changes. State legislatures, in fact, have been especially susceptible to national election trends, such as the 1952 Eisenhower and 1964 Johnson sweeps. In the last instance, formerly Republican legislatures in Illinois, Maine, and Iowa were solidly captured by the Democrats.

The proof of the pudding comes, of course, in legislative roll calls in which parties are actually in a position to influence public policy. Studies of congressional roll-call votes prove that significant differences over policy divide the parties.[56] On many roll calls, it is true, a majority of Democrats and Republicans vote the same way. In the 1967 congressional session more than half (65 per cent) of the combined House-Senate roll calls were nonpartisan.[57] In some instances the nonpartisan character of the roll call stemmed from the fact that the issue was one of foreign policy or of defense, in which there usually has been a strong national consensus. In other instances a nonpartisan vote was possible only because the real core of partisan controversy had been settled in an unrecorded vote. Nevertheless, the Democratic and Republican congressional parties cannot equal the inner cohesiveness of their counterparts in most other nations. Compared to the British House of Commons, for example, in which 90 per cent of the members take opposite stands on 95 per cent of all votes, the American House of Representatives has parties that differ that sharply in approximately only 15 per cent of all roll-call votes.

Even with these qualifications, the congressional parties frequently show their partisan colors. A study of roll-call votes in six selected sessions of the House between 1921 and 1944 found that the average cohesion of both parties was 65 per cent.[58] This is less cohesion than the major British and French parties demon-

---

[56] One useful measure of party unity is the statistical analysis of legislative roll calls so as to determine a party's index of cohesion. For instance, if all Republicans in Congress voted together on a roll call the index of cohesion would be 0. An index of 50 would mean that three quarters of the party voted together. What counts, of course, is the average cohesion on a large number of roll-call votes. There are, however, limitations to the utility of roll-call analysis. The most important limitation is that the analysis can be applied only to those issues whose eventual legislative resolution takes the form of a roll-call vote. Many political conflicts are not settled by roll calls, and even when roll calls do occur it is possible that the formal pattern of voting masks the struggles and compromises that preceded the open voting.

[57] *Congressional Quarterly*, December 29, 1967, p. 2643.

[58] Julius Turner, "Responsible Parties: A Dissent from the Floor," *American Political Science Review*, XLV (March, 1951), 143–152; and see generally his *Party and Constituency: Pressures on Congress* (Baltimore: Johns Hopkins U.P., 1951).

Table 8.8 *Two parties' divergence on federal role questions, 1967*

| | 90th Congress, 1967 only | | 89th Congress | |
	Dem.	GOP	Dem.	GOP
Larger federal role				
Both chambers	72%	41%	75%	38%
Senate	69	52	78	47
House	73	39	75	36
Smaller federal role				
Both chambers	25%	56%	21%	58%
Senate	26	46	18	51
House	24	58	22	60

Source: *Congressional Quarterly,* February 10, 1961, p. 212.

strated during a comparable period, but it does indicate the existence of significant party differences. The division, moreover, occurred over such important issues as tariff protection, business regulation, tax policy, civil rights, and farm supports, while the routine matters usually failed to divide the parties. More recently, studies published by the *Congressional Quarterly* document the fact that serious differences divide the parties. Thus, in the 1966 legislative session a majority of Democratic and Republican Congressmen opposed each other on 46 per cent of some 428 roll calls; most of these partisan conflicts were over the establishment and funding of President Johnson's Great Society programs. In 1967, however, partisan voting dropped to 35 per cent (198 of 560 roll calls), the lowest figure in over a decade. This low percentage has persisted in recent years. In 1968 it was 33 per cent, in 1969 it was 34 per cent, in 1970 it was 32 per cent.[59]

Another revealing measure is provided by votes where one of the issues is the extent of the federal government's role. An analysis of twenty-two Senate and twenty-three House roll calls in the Eighty-ninth Congress, each one offering a choice between a larger or a smaller federal role in a wide range of politically controversial subjects, showed that as a group Democrats voted for a larger federal role twice as often as Republicans. In turn, Republicans were almost three times more likely to favor a smaller role. As Table 8.8 shows, these differences narrowed somewhat in 1967 (the first session of the Ninetieth Congress), but the two parties' divergence on federal role questions remains clearly evident.

On many issues the congressional parties divide along conservative-liberal lines. For example, a study by the University of Michigan Survey Research Center of all House roll-call votes on social welfare questions in the Eighty-fifth Congress (1957–1959) classified Congressmen on a nine-point scale ranging from most conservative

[59] *Congressional Quarterly,* December 9, 1966, p. 2989; December 29, 1967, p. 2662; January 29, 1971, p. 238; January 15, 1972, p. 87.

to most liberal. (This was done on the basis of the Congressmen's votes on each of the social welfare issues.) Almost half, 47 per cent, of the Republicans fell in the most conservative third of the scale; but only 1 per cent of the northern Democrats were in this category. On the other hand, 97 per cent of the northern Democrats, in contrast to 21 per cent of the Republicans, were in the most liberal third of the scale.[60] Southern Democrats, however, were distributed evenly throughout the scale, statistical evidence that much of the confusion about party differences is due to the schism within Democratic ranks. As the South moves closer to a two-party system, it seems likely that southern conservatives will tend to gravitate toward the Republican party, making it likely that party lines, at least on social welfare issues, will become sharper.

Can Congress Do the Job?

Before we answer the question as to whether Congress can do the job it will be called on to do in the 1970's, we must define again the dimensions of that job. First and foremost, of course, it is the job of passing legislation—making the policy decisions and adopting the problem solutions that the society requires. Much of the material in this chapter addresses itself, either directly or indirectly, to this question. Definitive answers, however, are elusive because American legislative machinery, and particularly the Congress itself, is so complex in structure and operation.

In addition to lawmaking, other major responsibilities are assigned to Congress. One of these is underscored by an injunction in the Legislative Reorganization Act of 1946, which directs each committee to exercise "continuous watchfulness" over the administrative agencies within its jurisdiction. Difficult as this objective may be, the intent of Congress is certainly clear. It wants assurance that legislative policies are being carried out faithfully and efficiently. Is this ideal realistic? More than five hundred Congressmen cannot—in addition to representing their constituents, tending to the business of legislation, and getting themselves reelected—oversee a dozen major executive departments and perhaps four times that many other agencies, which together employ more than two and a half million people.

Congress can hire experts to help it do its jobs, and it has done so. The Legislative Reference Service located in the Library of Congress provides members with special reports and information, and the reforms of the Legislative Reorganization Act have led to a great increase in the staff assistance available to individual Congressmen and the committees. Allowances vary; Representatives average seven office employees and Senators, twelve. (The more affluent hire additional aid out of their own pockets.) In addition, the House and Senate committees retain over one thousand staff members, some of them highly trained specialists. But good staffing is an aid, not a panacea. Congress cannot match the executive, expert for expert. Even if it could, the creation of a huge legislative apparatus would only double

---

[60] Austin Ranney, "Republicans and Democrats: Principles and Perversities," in Alfred J. Junz, *Present Trends in American National Government* (New York: Praeger, 1961), p. 52.

Congress's problem: it then would have to contend with two bureaucracies—an executive *and* a legislative bureaucracy.

Robert Sherrill, in an article in the *New York Times Magazine,* noted a promising trend in congressional staffing.[61] Congress has sought to solve its problems by multiplying its staff—some staffs have tripled in size in the last two decades—and yet numbers alone are not the answer. One negative result has been the increasing insulation and isolation of the Congressman from those who want to do business with him personally. Even important constitutents find it harder and harder to have a personal word with the Senator or the Representative, blocked as they are by layers of staff aides. The promising trend, according to Sherrill, is the recruitment for at least some staff positions of truly bright, hard-driving, and imaginative young people. These energetic staffers often turn out to be the idea men, as well as the researchers and ghost writers, behind some of the most important investigations and initiatives taken by their congressional bosses.

A dramatic illustration of the impact that can be made by aggressive and intelligent staff aides occurred in the fight to block or limit the deployment of the Anti-Ballistic Missile (ABM) system. Sherrill reports that this effort first began with a note passed to Senator John Sherman Cooper of Kentucky during a debate late in 1968 by William Miller, his aide for foreign affairs. Miller later told Sherrill, "I had got very interested in the ABM after I had talked to one of its inventors and he said it wouldn't work like the Administration said." The note passed to Senator Cooper contained a suggestion that he introduce an amendment to the bill under consideration that would delay deployment until the Pentagon proved its cost and performance assertions. An amendment was then scribbled on the spot, introduced, and narrowly beaten by a vote of 31 to 28. The impact of this near miss was electrifying.

Anti-Pentagon Senators started thinking that something might be done after all. In order to assemble more data, they began meeting with experts who also disapproved of defense proposals. Congressional aides began attending seminars on military gadgetry. As an aide to Senator George McGovern said of this crash education, "By developing a competence on the ABM, members and their staffs saw that the issue of arms wasn't that complicated. It could be understood. One of the things that had held members back was that they had not wanted to be made a fool of by [Senator] Stennis [of Mississippi, Chairman of the Armed Services Committee]. We felt that we had discovered ABM by accident, and that if it was that bad, other weapons systems must be worse."

Sherrill recounts numerous similar examples of staffers' probing in the executive branch and then prodding their bosses to use the material they uncovered. As in the case of ABM, however, staff activity of this kind can never be more than a spot check, a sort of hit-or-miss prescription for administrative surveillance. The executive branch is too vast, its programs too numerous and often obscure, and its bureaucratic defenses too elaborately constructed to permit easy penetration. Nevertheless, the fact that Congress and some of its relentless staffers do exist and may dig up and

[61] "Who Runs Congress?" November 22, 1970.

broadcast embarrassing information is bound to serve as a partial check on the government's executive agencies.

Although Congress cannot *control* the executive systematically, it can *influence* its actions. As the legislative institution Congress acts as a foil to the executive. Its great power is its negative one over legislation and monetary appropriations—the power to ratify or reject policy proposals—which enables it to check and balance the executive. Moreover, in a specific, if disjointed and haphazard, fashion, Congress can affect executive decisions. At times some Congressmen and certain committees manage to exercise control over administrative agencies, but this falls far short of the utopian ideal of unified and systematic control. Chairmen of the legislative committees must be consulted before new administration bills are introduced, and the views of the powerful chairmen of the appropriations committees and subcommittees are respectfully solicited by executive officials. Leading Congressmen, moreover, may sometimes dictate low- and middle-level administrative decisions—where to locate a military base, for instance—but this is influence, not control.[62]

In the final analysis, if there is to be real control, it must come through Congress's power to appropriate money. Without money—approximately $229 billion by 1971—the executive could not function and no federal programs could be carried out. Theoretically, then, the power of the purse is the golden key to executive control. Congress annually passes on the executive budget; it votes appropriations, very often paring down an administration's requests, occasionally giving more than was asked. Does it not, therefore, control the executive by manipulating the purse strings?

The answer is No, not in a systematic sense. When Congress cuts budgetary requests, it frequently employs what is graphically called a *meat-axe* approach—an across-the-board percentage slash of an agency's funds as recommended by one of its appropriations subcommittees. Arbitrary, unpredictable, and perhaps punitive, a ragged series of meat-axe slashes do not add up to comprehensive legislative control of the budgetary process. Nor is this grand objective achieved by the tendency of appropriations subcommittees to concern themselves with trivia when reviewing the executive budget. Thus, one year a House Defense Appropriations subcommittee devoted more time to an appropriation for the National Board for the Promotion of Rifle Practice than it did to the impact of the defense budget on the North Atlantic Treaty.[63] Similarly, the House Appropriations subcommittee responsible for the State Department budget has often given much time to examining the requests for diplomatic entertaining—what, not so diplomatically, has been described

---

[62] In recent years Congress sporadically has sought to institutionalize its power to influence executive decisions by passing laws that delegate authority to the executive on a conditional basis—conditional in the sense that the decision delegated to the executive is subject to the possibility of a subsequent veto by either the entire Congress, a single house, and, in some cases, a single committee. Known as the *legislative veto* and the *committee veto*, these procedures are extremely controversial and increasingly are being resisted by modern Presidents. For a full discussion see Joseph P. Harris, *Congressional Control of Administration* (Washington, D.C.: The Brookings Institution, 1964), Ch. 8.

[63] Jewell and Patterson, op. cit., p. 504.

as the "cookie-and-booze allowance." This is not to say that Congress has no impact on the budget, for Richard Fenno's meticulous study of the House Appropriations Committee, which traced the appropriations histories of thirty-six bureaus from 1947 to 1962, found that Congress's final appropriation conformed to the Bureau of the Budget estimate of required funds in only 15 per cent of the cases; in 67 per cent of the 444 cases tabulated the final appropriation was less, whereas in 18 per cent of the cases it exceeded the Budget Bureau estimate.[64]

Congress, however, is simply not organized for comprehensive budgetary control, and it shows little interest in accepting the long-standing invitation of some scholars that it produce a unified "legislative budget" to counter the executive budget. Instead, in the future as in the past, it is almost certain that responsibility for the authorization of expenditures, the making of appropriations, and the raising of revenues will continue to be parceled out among innumerable legislative and appropriation committees and subcommittees of the *two* chambers. Whatever budgetary unity exists will be the unity of the executive budget—which is itself the product of variegated political pressures and compromises of all kinds and which represents many conflicting policy tendencies (as in the allotment of money to the Public Health Service for research against cancer and the giving of agricultural subsidies to tobacco growers).

This partial and haphazard legislative intervention on budgetary matters is not necessarily undesirable, for Congress does not have the qualifications to engage in broad program management of the executive branch. As an assembly of 535 men, it lacks the prerequisites of effective budgetary management—expertise, self-direction, cohesiveness, and the ability to work with dispatch. For that matter, it is not at all clear that the executive branch lives up to the ideal of coherent budgetary management, and there is great force to an observation by Richard Fenno, Jr.: [65]

To relegate Congress to the making of broad policy decisions and to oversight in terms of broad program management is to prescribe precisely those tasks which Congress is least capable of performing. To criticize Congress for intervening in a specific and detailed fashion is to attack it for doing the only thing it can to effectively assert its influence. Specifics and details are the indispensable handles which Congressmen use to work inductively toward broader kinds of oversight judgments. Specifics and details are what concern the constituents on whose behalf Congressmen must intervene with the bureaucracy. . . . The profusion of committees and subcommittees makes possible a degree of specialization which gives to Congressmen the detailed and specific information they find most useful in influencing executive behavior.

Specific and detailed controls by individuals and small committees give Congressmen

---

[64] This statistic is presented in Jewell and Patterson, op. cit., pp. 504–505. Although Congress frequently appropriates less than the Bureau of the Budget requests, the actual amount appropriated generally represents an increase over the previous year's final appropriation.

[65] Review of Harris, *Congressional Control of Administration, American Political Science Review,* LVIII (September, 1964), 674. And see Aaron Wildavsky, "Toward a Radical Incrementalism: A Proposal to Aid Congress in Reform of the Budgetary Process," in Alfred deGrazia, *Congress: The First Branch of Government* (New York: Anchor, 1967); Wildavsky quotes Fenno sympathetically, while elaborating his own useful discussion of Congress and the budgetary process.

their maximum influence because these controls are best adapted to the realities of executive decision-making. If executive decision-making is basically piecemeal, incremental, and marginal, then congressional control, if it is to be effective, must be basically piecemeal, incremental, and marginal.

Perhaps the most relevant fact of all is that so much of the federal budget today consists of fixed expenses and that Congress must therefore make, in effect, automatic appropriations. The federal government has numerous binding commitments, such as its obligation to make interest payments on government bonds or to pay military veterans their pensions. There are, in addition, countless governmental programs and services that are virtually permanent. Sophisticated studies of the federal budgetary process further reveal that the primary factor in determining the amount of money Congress will appropriate to an agency is the going level of expenditures for the previous fiscal year. There are annual incremental changes to the previous year's dollar base, and the general pattern for a large number of non-defense agencies studied in the period 1947 to 1963 was a steady rise in the absolute level of their appropriations.[66] There is, in short, little doubt that there is only a relatively narrow arena in which Congress can make budgetary alterations.

Congress, in short, must ratify *new* programs, but it cannot dictate new executive policies, and it really has only a partial leverage over the *old* programs that it has already approved. Although the power of the purse, the great legacy of English parliamentary history, enables the committees of Congress to influence some policies and to exert an erratic (though useful) check on the executive department, it does not serve as an instrument of systematic legislative control.

Grand Inquest:
The Power of Publicity

Yet another mechanism through which Congress has been able to exercise influence over executive decisions and policies is the investigating committee. Every year Congress undertakes over two hundred investigations. They are, to be sure, subject to all the factors that keep congressional control over the purse from being a systematic check on the executive, particularly when measured against the idealized and unrealistic goal of "continuous watchfulness." Nevertheless, the power to investigate gives Congress one of its most formidable weapons. Investigations can bring publicity, and executives and administrators are sensitive to bad publicity.

Not all investigations are directed at the executive branch, although they are usually the most spectacular. The investigators may be motivated by partisanship or a self-seeking desire for publicity, though a good guess would be that congressional motives are usually mixed, a blend of public and personal concerns. Whatever the motives, congressional surveillance through investigation has repeatedly publicized, and thereby corrected, corruption, waste, and mismanagement. During World War II, for example, the Senate's War Investigating Committee led by Harry S.

66 Otto A. Davis, et al., "A Theory of the Budget Process," *American Political Science Review,* LX (September, 1966), pp. 529–547.

Truman helped to speed the production and delivery of defense matériel while stopping wasteful practices—and helped to make him Vice President. In the late 1940's a Commerce Committee probe uncovered influence peddling in the Federal Communications and Federal Trade commissions. In 1963 a House Public Works subcommittee studying the $41 billion federal highway program issued a well-documented report that concluded that right-of-way acquisition in Massachusetts was honey-combed with gross incompetence, downright collusion, and fraud. More recently, the hearings on the war in Vietnam by the prestigious Senate Foreign Relations Committee under the chairmanship of J. William Fulbright provided a national forum for a searching critique—literally a grand inquest—into the Johnson Administration's policies in Southeast Asia.

Investigations not only expose official wrongdoing; they also help to build popular sentiment in support of new legislation and of major national objectives. At their best, then, congressional investigations are the Grand Inquest of the Nation and an invaluable aid in keeping big government responsive. At their worst, as were many of the investigations during the era of Senator Joseph R. McCarthy, they bring Congress and representative government into disrepute.

Many specific criticisms can be made about Congress's inadequacy as a legislative organ, as a supervisor of the executive branch, or as the nation's chief financial watchdog. Nevertheless, in a broad sense, Congress and all national legislatures (and American state legislatures, too, for that matter) have long suffered from the effects of a basic and probably insoluble problem. The pace and intricacy of modern life, and the governance it requires, have conspired to shift more and more responsibility to the executive and have left legislative organs at an ever-more serious disadvantage. Only executive organs can have and utilize the staff necessary to cope with contemporary problems; only the executive has the singleness of purpose, the focused leadership, and the capability for swift action; and only the executive enjoys at least partial insulation from localized and parochial pressures, enabling it to pursue integrated programs.

If this assessment is correct, it follows that only part of the problem of congressional reform lies with uprooting the filibuster, modifying seniority, and generally making Congress a more responsive legislative body. The larger challenge is how to make Congress capable of discharging the full range of its responsibilities while preventing it from becoming a mere appendage to the emerging administrative state. A significant component of this challenge is the disadvantage faced by the amateur when pitted against the expert or professional. Traditionally, the Congressman has been the generalist, the amateur, while increasingly he confronts an army of expert professional talent in the executive branch. The ABM episode suggests that the Congressman need not be as intimidated nor feel as inferior as he often does. Nonetheless, his position is likely to remain a difficult one in relationship to the expertise and talent that can be mobilized by the executive branch and by the labor unions.

The chief response Congress as an institution seems to be making as it struggles to maintain itself in this increasingly difficult environment is typified by the trends in staffing. Congress must equip and is equipping itself to fight fire with fire. The tax experts available to the Committee on Ways and Means are, for instance, said to be the equal of any the Treasury can field. If the Armed Services Committees would similarly equip themselves, instead of continuing their past posture of elaborate subservience to the top military brass, they could hire numerous civilian experts on military hardware.

A broader and parallel form of response that the legislative branch is making is its increasing institutionalization in overall terms. This can be seen particularly clearly in an analysis of congressional careers by H. Douglas Price.[67] The primary point made by Professor Price is that in the present century the role of a member of Congress has become a full-time, and for many, a life-time career. In the nineteenth century, the turnover in House membership ranged from 30 per cent to 60 per cent at every election; the Congress elected in 1900 was the first in American history in which the turnover was less than 30 per cent and in which the average number of terms of prior service among the members was more than two.

The current situation is in sharp contrast. In the 1970 midterm elections, no less than 88 per cent of the incumbent House members were reelected and only 12 per cent of the body that convened in January, 1971, were freshmen. This tiny margin of turnover has been the case for a long time. In the Ninetieth Congress, the average number of prior terms served by the members was nearly five. Coupled with this trend toward vastly longer tenure, sessions have grown progressively longer. Around the turn of the century, it was normal for Congress to be in session for perhaps 350 of the 730 days that comprised its two-year term. In recent years the total has often approached or even passed 500 days.

In short, not only is Congress as an institution becoming professionalized with the addition of sophisticated staff, but the Congressman himself is becoming a professional legislator who intends to make a career on Capitol Hill. As Professor Price points out, whereas men often left the House during the nineteenth century for other elective offices, such shifts are extremely rare these days. The significance of this state of affairs, of course, is that long tenure and full-time, year-round application to congressional duties builds expertise, experience, and knowledge of the intricacies of the federal government. A legislature composed of part-time and amateur "in and outers" could not hope to match this experience. Clearly, such a professionalized Congress (the Senate went the same route much earlier than the House) has a far better chance of being able to cope with the executive bureaucracy and the range of legislative problems that face Congress than it might otherwise have.

On the other hand, what does this new state of affairs do for the representativeness of Congress? Can it be possible that as of November 1970, the electorate really felt that 88 per cent of House members were doing a sufficiently satisfactory job to be returned for a new term? It seems unlikely. What seems to be happening, paradoxically and, indeed, ironically, is that Congress, in order to cope with the modern

---

[67] "The Congressional Career Then and Now," in Polsby, op. cit., pp. 14–27.

administrative state that is the federal government, is itself becoming institutionalized, bureaucratized, and professionalized. In the process, it is probably growing progressively farther removed from its clients, the citizenry. Is this price worth paying? One wonders. Again, as is often the case in politics, we are faced with a trade-off. Which value should we seek to maximize in Congress, professionalization or representativeness? It seems difficult to have both.

suggested additional readings

Barber, James D. *The Lawmakers: Recruitment and Adaptation to Legislative Life.* New Haven: Yale University Press, 1965.*

Bauer, Raymond A., et al. *American Business and Public Policy: The Politics of Foreign Trade.* New York: Atherton Press, 1963.

Congressional Quarterly Service. *Congress and the Nation,* Vol. I, 1945–1964; Vol. II, 1965–1968. Washington, D.C.: Congressional Quarterly Service.

Crane, Wilder, and Meredith Watts. *State Legislative Systems.* Englewood Cliffs, N.J.: Prentice-Hall, Inc., 1968.*

Froman, Lewis A., Jr. *The Congressional Process: Strategies, Rules, and Procedures.* Boston: Little, Brown and Company, 1967.*

Goodwin, George. *Little Legislatures: Committees of Congress.* Amherst: University of Massachusetts Press, 1970.*

Hanson, Royce. *The Political Thicket: Reapportionment and Constitutional Democracy.* Englewood Cliffs, N.J.: Prentice-Hall, Inc., 1966.*

Jewell, Malcolm E., and Samuel C. Patterson. *The Legislative Process in the United States.* New York: Random House, Inc., 1966.

Manley, John F. *The Politics of Finance: The House Ways and Means Committee.* Boston: Little, Brown and Company, 1970.*

Matthews, Donald R. *U.S. Senators and Their World.* New York: Random House, Inc., 1962.*

Mayhew, David R. *Party Loyalty Among Congressmen: The Difference Between Democrats and Republicans, 1947–1962.* Cambridge: Harvard University Press, 1966.

Ripley, Randall B. *Majority Party Leadership in Congress.* Boston: Little, Brown and Company, 1969.*

———. *Power in the Senate.* New York: St. Martin's Press, Inc., 1969.*

Shannon, W. Wayne. *Party, Constituency, and Congressional Voting.* Baton Rouge: Louisiana State University Press, 1968.

Wahlke, John C., et al. *The Legislative System: Explorations in Legislative Behavior.* New York: John Wiley & Sons, Inc., 1962.

* Available in paperback.

9 the judiciary

case study

The Appointment Process: The "Mediocre" Deserve Representation

In 1969, Richard Nixon charged that the Supreme Court, by a majority of one, had erected a "barbed wire of legalisms . . . to protect a suspect from invasion of his rights [and] has effectively shielded hundreds of criminals from punishment."

In 1970, G. Harrold Carswell charged that his Senate rejection to a seat on the United States Supreme Court was due to a combination of an "ultra liberal coalition" of the northern press and "its knee-jerk followers" in the Senate. "I agree with Vice-President Agnew. It was the greatest hatchet job in the history of the Senate."

One of the most significant struggles over the confirmation of an aspirant to the Supreme Court occurred between the time span of the above quotations. Why such heated words over a seat on the Court? The story begins in the 1968 election campaign.

Richard Nixon, the Republican candidate for President in 1968, charged that the Warren Court had unwisely broadened the rights of suspects in criminal cases. He promised, if elected, to put "strict constructionists" on the Court. This term was used to define men who interpret the Constitution conservatively. In

speeches across the country, Mr. Nixon promised to name men to the Court who would "interpret the law, not make it." Statements such as these are rhetorical legerdemain, for when the justices "interpret" the law they are in fact "making it." The key issue, of course, is *how* the justices interpret the law. Mr. Nixon was—and is—adamant in his belief that the Warren Court had gone too far in interpreting constitutional provisions in favor of the accused and against police and public prosecutors.

According to some political commentators, Mr. Nixon was following a "southern strategy." Southern electoral support was essential to his 1968 victory; it was also seen as pivotal in 1972. Critical to the success of this strategy was cementing the allegiance of southern states to the Republican party. The appointment of a southerner to the Supreme Court would signal an increased importance for Dixie. Political foes charged that the Nixon Administration wanted to "pay off" the southern states for their 1968 electoral support, while undercutting Governor George C. Wallace's strength in the 1972 election.

It was against this background that President Nixon in 1969 nominated the

359

first southerner to the Court in twenty years, Clement F. Haynsworth from South Carolina, who would have filled the seat left vacant by the resignation of Mr. Justice Abe Fortas. After a vigorous three-month debate the Senate voted 55 to 45 against confirming Haynsworth. The major reason given by Senators was that Judge Haynsworth had decided certain cases (to his advantage) while holding a financial interest in the companies involved. There were, it was charged, clear indications of conflict of interest, or, at the very least, an insufficient care in separating his judicial opinions from his personal business interests. Moreover, Haynsworth's senatorial opponents contended that he had consistently voted against civil rights and labor causes while on the bench.

Attorney General John N. Mitchell commented that labor's concentrated effort to defeat the nomination had caught the Administration off guard, and the president himself was furious. He defended Judge Haynsworth's integrity as "unimpeachable." He "deplored" the attacks on the judge's character, scolded the Senate's liberal critics, and pledged to offer another candidate whose legal philosophy would "restore the proper balance" to the Court. "The criteria I shall apply for this selection," Mr. Nixon affirmed, "as was the case with my nomination of Judge Haynsworth, will be consistent with my commitment to the American people before my election as President a year ago." Implicit in this statement was Nixon's belief that he held a mandate from the people to appoint conservatives who would curb the liberal decisions of the Warren Court.

Judge G. Harrold Carswell from Florida was the man selected to restore the "proper balance" and legal philosophy to the Court. Attorney General Mitchell, whose advice Mr. Nixon followed in recommending Judge Haynsworth, was

much more careful in doing his homework. Mitchell, in briefing Senate Republican leaders, stressed three points: Carswell's record suggested no economic conflict of interests like those that had crippled Haynsworth; he had no stigma of antilabor bias that might turn powerful union groups against him; and he was a "moderate" on civil rights. Republican leaders and southerners seemed satisfied with Mr. Carswell's qualifications. Senate Minority Leader Hugh Scott saw no problems, predicting that Senate confirmation would be quick. The late Senator Richard B. Russell could not conceive of a "more appropriate choice." Judge Carswell "would get the Court back in its proper function as a judicial body." Senators from both parties seemed to want to avoid another prolonged and politically bruising battle like the one that had recently ended with the defeat of Judge Haynsworth. The mood of the Senate was overwhelming to accept whomever Mr. Nixon wanted to put on the Court. Seventeen out of forty-three Republican Senators (40 per cent) had voted against Haynsworth. They had no desire to cross party lines and thwart the President again.

Judge Carswell enjoyed a reputation of being intelligent, quick-witted, and charming. He had served almost twelve years on the federal bench, eleven years as a trial judge and six months on the Circuit Court of Appeals. Judge Carswell was regarded as a conservative with judicial views closely parallel to those of the President. Carswell—like the President—believed in judicial self-restraint. In his years as a judge Carswell had hesitated to use judicial power unless the need was clear and demanding. His conservatism was also expressed in his inclination to settle disputes by invoking long-established precedents. Shortly after becoming a judge Mr. Carswell summarized his judicial philosophy: "Established law, with its imperfections, must nevertheless be applied as it is and not on the predilections of the court." His legal philosophy, prior judicial experience, and southern support made it appear that Senate confirmation would be routine. Pundits and practitioners alike were surprised when it turned into a political cause célèbre.

The Federal Bureau of Investigation, in charge of screening the backgrounds of all judicial nominees, had failed, however, to uncover several embarrassing incidents in Judge Carswell's career. The FBI apparently did an even sloppier job on the Carswell investigation than it had on Haynsworth's. The publication of these episodes in Carswell's background was used as ammunition to attack his qualifications.

The first incident became public during the Senate Judiciary Committee hearings on the nomination. A reporter searching old clippings in a defunct newspaper discovered that Harrold Carswell had made a white supremacist speech in 1948 while running for a seat in the Georgia legislature: "I believe that segregation of the races is proper and the only practical and correct way of life in our states. I have always so believed, and I shall always so act." Carswell stated further that he would always be governed by the "principals of white supremacy." Carswell explained to members of the Judiciary Committee that he had only been twenty-eight years old at the time of the speech and that the words were spoken in the heat of a political campaign. He lost the election, in part, because he was the most liberal of the three candidates in the race. Carswell was emphatic in his denunciation of "the words themselves and the thought they represent; they are abhorrent." Senator Philip A. Hart, Democrat of Michigan, baited a trap when he asked Mr. Carswell whether he believed what he said at the time concerning white supremacy. The question did not have to wait for an answer before the trap sprung closed. Judge Carswell either had to admit that he had once been a liar or had once been a racist. The judge was put in an unenviable position and answered, "I suppose I believed it."

Two relatively minor matters that touched on racism appeared in the press. In 1953 Carswell chartered a Florida State University Booster Club to raise funds for athletic teams. The club opened membership to "any white person." In 1966 he sold land with a restrictive covenant (white only) provision. Both the chartering of the club and the land sale attracted very little public attention.

The next incident, however, attracted national headlines and much attention in the Senate. While serving as United States Attorney in 1956, Mr. Carswell allegedly played a major role in changing the lease of a Tallahassee municipal golf course to a private segregated club. The course had been built with $35,000 in federal funds and was leased to a private organization for $1 a year. Charges were made that this move was clearly made to circumvent a Supreme Court decision that prohibited segregation in municipal recreation facilities. Carswell insisted in the hearings before the Judiciary Committee that he had been unaware that the private club was organized to exclude Negroes. The conservative columnist for the *Washington Evening Star*, James Kilpatrick, saw Carswell's testimony as an "evasive account." Kilpatrick stated that if Carswell did not know that private clubs were commonly used as a ruse to evade desegregation compliance, "he was the only one in north Florida who didn't understand it."

The golf club episode became even more embarrassing when hints of duplicity appeared. The night before his appearance before the Judiciary Committee Carswell had been visited by two members of the American Bar Association and shown photostatic copies of incorporation papers for the golf course bearing his signature. On the next day he had told Senators, under oath, that he was utterly unfamiliar with the contents of these papers. When these facts became public in a *New York Times* article, several Senators raised doubts as to whether they had been deceived.

When President Nixon was asked about Judge Carswell's role in the transfer of the Tallahassee golf course, he skillfully deflected the main thrust of the question: "If everybody in government service who had belonged to, or does belong to, restricted golf clubs were to leave the service, this city would have the highest rate of unemployment in any city in the country."

By mid-March anti-Carswell sentiment in the Senate began to grow noticeably. Senator Birch Bayh, Democrat of Indiana, had assumed active leadership of a loose coalition of Senators who saw the President's choice for the Supreme Court as pedestrian at best and racist at worst. Senator Edward Brooke, an early convert to the "defeat Carswell" cause, was particularly important. He had been largely responsible for organizing the seventeen Republican Senators who voted against Haynsworth. The pro-Carswell Senate leaders were Hugh Scott, Minority Leader, and Robert Griffin, Minority Whip. White House support of Judge Carswell was low-keyed. Administration officials acted as if Senate confirmation was a fait accompli. Most of the political cut and thrust took place on the Senate floor and in the press.

A major break for the anti-Carswell forces came when Senator Roman Hruska, Republican from Nebraska, dropped a verbal bombshell. Hruska, in a fit of anger over a Senate debate,

made the following statement to a radio interviewer: *"Even if [Carswell] were mediocre there are a lot of mediocre judges and people and lawyers.* They are entitled to a little representation, aren't they . . . ?"* (emphasis added). This astonishing statement was seized upon as a defense of mediocrity. Hruska's political blunder was used again and again to try to persuade wavering Senators that Carswell would reduce the stature of the Court. Senator Robert C. Byrd of West Virginia, a Carswell supporter, did not help his candidate's chances when he said that some judges sitting on the "present court" are "mediocre."

Up to this point Judge Carswell and his supporters had weathered several public reverses. The white supremacy speech could be excused as a youthful error. The golf club incident could also be written off as an effort to save a public course that was going bankrupt. Senator Hruska's ill-chosen remark—although damaging—could be explained as an unfortunate slip of the tongue. Cumulatively, however, the critics that charged that Judge Carswell was a lackluster nominee appeared to have gained ground. Yet in mid-March Senator Griffin confidently predicted that Judge Carswell would win confirmation with at least sixty Senators supporting him.

Griffin's comment may have overlooked, or underestimated, serious criticism from within the legal profession. Law professors, deans of law schools, and practicing lawyers publicly criticized Judge Carswell's partiality in civil rights cases. A group of civil rights lawyers charged that Judge Carswell had been discourteous and even hostile to civil rights lawyers who appeared before him in court. The major brunt of the charge was that Carswell had delayed school integration cases by failing to rule on them. When forced to rule, he issued decisions that were "palpably wrong and quickly reversed."

There are numerous illustrations of the intensity of the anti-Carswell interest-group activity. A group of 457 prominent members of the legal profession urged the Senate to reopen the hearings, charging that there was strong evidence of segregationist leanings by the nominee. Another group—as unusual as it was select—of 196 former clerks to Supreme Court justices opposed the nomination, saying that Judge Carswell's record "shows him to be of mediocre ability." A law school dean said that Carswell shows "little grasp of the fundamental issues of American society." The dean of the Yale Law School after reading a number of Carswell's opinions went even further by stating that he presented "more slender credentials than any nominee to the Supreme Court put forth in this century." Specialists in various legal fields and heads of local bar associations wrote letters challenging Judge Carswell's competence. Carswell was invited by the Senate Judiciary Committee to reply to these charges and vigorously denied them all. Over the years there had never been a "suggestion of any act or word of discourtesy or hostility on my part."

Judge Carswell had handed down decisions that frustrated civil rights lawyers and provoked criticisms that he delayed desegregation. One example occurred in the Pensacola area when parents of black children sued to break up the segregation of faculty and staff in the formerly all-black schools. Judge Carswell wrote an opinion in the case that stated, in part, "the Brown cases," referring to the Supreme Court landmark school decisions in 1954 and 1955, "hold that the segregation of white and Negro *children* on the basis of race denies to Negro children equal protection of the laws guaranteed by the 14th Amendment to the

Constitution" (emphasis is in the original). He went on to say that these decisions, and subsequent ones, did not reach the question of faculty desegregation. In sharp contrast, civil rights lawyers argued children *and* faculty must be desegregated as a natural extension of the Brown rulings. These lawyers charged that judicial self-restraint was used to cloak segregationist sympathies.

Every few days a Senator would announce his intention to support or oppose Judge Carswell's nomination. Interestingly, these "spontaneous" announcements, usually at a press conference, were carefully timed to maximize their impact. The plan—or rather the hope—was that an announcement by a key Senator would start a bandwagon effect. No stampedes occurred. On March 26 one Republican Senator, favoring Carswell, commented that he thought the nomination was lost unless President Nixon turned on the pressure. Other Senators saw the confirmation vote as extremely close. The virtual absence of White House liaison with the Senate was puzzling. There had been a conspicuous absence of presidential lobbying. The President was quoted by his press secretary as being "firm in his support for Judge Carswell. . . ." Yet this support seemed lukewarm. Little enthusiasm had been shown for Carswell's qualifications. *Competent, well qualified,* and *experienced* were the strongest adjectives that the Administration could muster.

On April 1—just eight days before the confirmation vote—President Nixon brought up his heavy guns. He charged that the Senate was threatening his appointment powers. "Those who wished to substitute their own philosophy or own subjective judgment" for his own choice were jeopardizing his constitutional powers. He further alleged that the Senate was denying him the "right of choice in naming Supreme Court justices." President Nixon's statement indicated a shift of focus from his nominee's qualifications to a recognition of presidential prerogative. Several Senators strongly objected to the President's rejection of their constitutional role in the appointment process. Senator Bayh, for example, said the President was "wrong" in his interpretation of constitutional law, history, and public policy. More than 1 presidential Supreme Court nomination in 5—28 out of 129—failed to get Senate confirmation.

Senator Griffin countercharged that Senate liberals were trying to prevent President Nixon from carrying out his campaign pledge to place a conservative on the Court. Senator George D. Aiken added that he saw the anti-Carswell effort as a political vehicle to damage the standing of the President: "I will not be a party to downgrading or embarrassing him. . . ." Speaking directly of Judge Carswell, Aiken raised a silent issue: "We need some law and order and to stop apologizing to every criminal."

This verbal charge and countercharge gave way to parliamentary maneuvering in the Senate. Timing had been a crucial factor in the seventy-odd days since President Nixon had sent down the name of his nominee. It had been particularly crucial in late February, when Senator Mike Mansfield announced that the nomination would not be brought to the floor until the Voting Rights Act * was voted on. Putting the Voting Rights Act in front of the nomination vote was a clever procedural

* This Act, passed in 1965, had enfranchised nearly a million blacks in the South and had led to the election of about five hundred black officials in four years. The Act was up for renewal.

ploy to prevent a southern filibuster —and to expedite passage of the Act. Delay, as previously indicated, worked in favor of anti-Carswell forces. Stalling tactics, therefore, were counterproductive for Senators who favored the confirmation of Judge Carswell. Two southern Senators, however, Strom Thurmond and James B. Allen, filibustered, thereby giving Carswell opponents a month to find needed support. Ironically, two Senators who strongly favored Judge Carswell were, at least in part, responsible for his defeat.

On April 1 the outcome of the Senate's vote on confirmation was very much in doubt. Senators in the anti-Carswell coalition were ostensibly trying to recommit the nomination to the Judiciary Committee. Recommital of a nomination, which takes a majority vote of the Senate, usually means its defeat. White House liaison with the Senate increased, and pressure on eight wavering Senators was strong. Allegations of Administration arm-twisting were made by a few Senators. Threats of strong opponents in their next primary campaign, a slowdown of patronage, and a loss of access to the President were allegedly used. Attempts to invoke party loyalty were also employed by White House officials. What the White House did not know was that several Senators had given their pledge to vote against Judge Carswell on the confirmation vote. Senator Bayh had given up hope of recommitting the nomination (and thereby probably killing it), and in a secret tactical switch concentrated all his energy on the final vote. The White House assumed—erroneously—that the recommittal and confirmation votes would be roughly the same. All Administration efforts were directed toward defeating the recommittal motion. Therefore, when recommittal failed on April 7 by a vote of 44 to 52, there was a strong belief by Administration supporters that Judge

Carswell's nomination would be confirmed. Four key senators—Hiram Fong, Thomas Dodd, Robert Packwood, and Charles Percy—had all voted against killing the nomination via recommittal; yet, all four had promised Bayh to vote against confirmation.

In a dramatic moment on April 9, 1970, the Senate gallery erupted into wild applause. Judge G. Harrold Carswell was defeated 51 to 45 (thirteen Republicans voted against the nomination and were joined by thirty-eight Democrats; seventeen Democrats and twenty-eight Republicans voted for Judge Carswell). Seven Senators who had voted against recommittal switched sides and opposed his nomination. Most of the Senators mentioned that the public faith in the Supreme Court might have been shaken by the confirmation of a nominee who was accused of racial bias and mediocrity.

The vote against the confirmation of Judge Carswell was a major Administration setback. Mr. Nixon had made the final test a matter of personal loyalty and presidential prerogative. He lost. He had suffered his second defeat within six months. In each instance he was angered and lashed out at his Senate foes in terms reminiscent of the bitterness displayed toward the press after his 1962 gubernatorial defeat in California. In words that conveyed this anger and bitterness President Nixon accused his Senate opponents of "vicious" tactics and regional discrimination against southerners. He said that the South deserved "proper representation" on the Court, which the Senate had willfully denied.

I will not nominate another Southerner and let him be subjected to the kind of malicious character assassination accorded both Judge Haynsworth and Carswell. . . .

But when you strip away all the hypocrisy, the real reason for their rejection was their legal philosophy, a philosophy that I share, of strict construction of the Constitution, and also the accident of their birth, the fact that they were born in the South.

Senator John Sherman Cooper seemed to put the furious battle into perspective, "I'm sure the debate showed the people, including the people in the Congress, what the Supreme Court should be and what the Senate could be." Perhaps it also showed the people an interesting, if harsh, view of the President. It has been shrewdly noted that one can often learn more about "the President from his Supreme Court appointments than by any other single index."

SOURCES

Black, Charles L., Jr., "A Note on Senatorial Consideration of Supreme Court Nominees," *Yale Law Journal*, LXXIX (March, 1970), 657–664.

"Carswell Nomination to Court Rejected by Senate," *Congressional Quarterly Almanac*, 1970, pp. 154–162.

Harris, Richard, *Decision* (New York: E. P. Dutton and Co., Inc., 1971).

The New York Times, various issues, January, 1968, through July, 1970.

courts and judges

Law in America: Trial by Jury

During the 1964 election campaign the Republican candidate, Barry M. Goldwater, assailed the Warren Court's decisions requiring federal and state law-enforcement officials to meet strict standards of due process when arresting and prosecuting suspected criminals. Goldwater criticized the Court for decisions that seem to say that "a criminal defendant must be given a sporting chance to go free, even though nobody doubts in the slightest that he is guilty." [1]

As a matter of fact, the American and British legal systems operate under the fundamental assumption that, until convicted through a fair and impartial trial, a suspected criminal *is* innocent, even though his accusers do not "in the slightest" doubt his guilt. All legal systems derived from England are deliberately constructed so that each side in either a civil or a criminal action is given "a sporting chance" to win the case. Originally the sporting nature of the common law was rather grim. Trials were a physical battle in which armed contestants fought it out, the assumption being that God would strengthen the innocent fighter. Defeat was rough on the losing party: he lost his case—and sometimes his life. Such crude means of settling legal disputes, whose accuracy was somewhat doubtful, gradually fell into disuse. More and more the truth in a controversy was sought through the mechanism of formal pleadings before a court. Judges and juries would hear attorneys representing the contestants and then settle their dispute by deciding the factual issues and applying the law.

Despite its refinement over the centuries, law in America retains the adversary character derived from its English heritage. Trial by combat—legal combat to settled rules—is its core notion. The mode of operation is best described as accusatorial. Charges made against one party are weighed before a neutral third party, the judge and jury, who depend on the opposing sides to reveal the truth in the course of their

[1] *Congressional Quarterly,* October 23, 1964, p. 2539.

natural conflict. A different method, the inquisitorial, which is based on the more detailed and codified Roman civil law, prevails in continental Europe. There the judge plays an active role as part of the state's prosecuting machinery, interrogating witnesses himself in an effort to elicit the truth. Under the inquisitorial system the accused criminal is assumed to be guilty until proved innocent.

It is useful to keep in mind that differing variants of law are applied to legal disputes in the United States. The most abstract is *natural law,* a set of general principles supposedly rooted in the will of God or in the fundamental laws of nature. Those who believe in natural law view it as a higher law that ought to govern human relations even when it conflicts with the lower law—the earthly commands of mortal lawmakers. Thus, the American Declaration of Independence justified the revolutionists' defiance of British parliamentary law by addressing an appeal to "the laws of nature and of nature's God." In the same tradition, Martin Luther King, the martyred civil rights leader, asserted that integrationists have "a moral responsibility" to disobey statutes supporting segregation. They are, he claimed, "unjust" laws that are "out of harmony" with "the moral law or the law of God." [2] Natural law has no legal standing and its content is imprecise; yet there can be no doubt of its influence. The entire body of American law and constitutional practice is suffused with the assumption that the natural or God-given rights of all men must be respected. On occasion the courts have even voided legislative acts because of their conflict with "general principles . . . common to our free institutions." [3] Moreover, the concept of due process of law, which figures so prominently in modern American constitutionalism, reflects a natural law commitment to what is popularly called fair play.

Despite the great ethical influence of natural law principles, most lawyers and judges are thinking of something much more tangible and specific when they refer to "the law." They are thinking, first, of the *common law,* an enormous body of judge-made law from which the legal system as a whole derives its name.

In time, the common law became too enmeshed in technicalities and its remedies narrowly limited. In civil cases the only remedy available to a person injured by another's lawful action was a lawsuit for damages; this, however, required him to sustain the injury before he could do anything about it. Gradually, over a period of several centuries, the common law was supplemented by a body of law called *equity.* In its broadest sense equity means "fair-dealing," but in the English-American legal tradition it refers to the body of rules by which justice may in some circumstances be preventive as well as remedial. A homeowner, for instance, whose meticulously built Japanese rock garden will be washed away as a consequence of a neighbor's plan to divert a small stream, could probably sue for damages after the flooding occurred. But the gardener will probably be interested in preserving his garden, not in collecting a fine. Equity provides him with a meaningful preventive remedy. He can go to court and obtain an order (an injunction) that enjoins his

---

[2] "Letter from Birmingham City Jail," *New Leader,* June 24, 1963, p. 6.
[3] The quotation is from *Fletcher* v. *Peck,* 6 Cranch 87, 139 (1810), an early United States Supreme Court decision overturning an act of the Georgia legislature.

neighbor from diverting the stream in such a way as to damage his property. (A party who disobeys an injunction invites very severe penalties.)

Common law and equity have been worked and reworked by generations of judges, but the bulk of American law is *statutory*. Because modern society is complex, its laws require constant additions and readjustments, a process best handled by the direct means of legislative enactments. Because court decisions usually decide only the particular conflict that gave rise to the case, the judge-made common law necessarily evolves slowly and on a case-by-case basis. This usually limits its applicability to specific circumstances. By contrast, legislatures can (when inclined and effectively led by the chief executive) move with speed in enacting comprehensive new laws whose scope will include a wide variety of personal and institutional relationships.

Statutory law, it should be noted, includes many of the legal rules derived from the common law and from equity, usually amended in the light of changed social and economic conditions. Very often, of course, legislative statutes repeal or sharply modify outmoded common law rules such as, for instance, the old law of primogeniture decreeing that all of a deceased father's property should go only to the eldest son. The superior status of statutory law is consistent with democratic ideals, which require that, in the final analysis, legislative rules take precedence over judicial rules.

A few additional terms common to legal discussion deserve brief explanation. *Civil cases* are legal disputes primarily concerned with private controversies. Although the government may be a party to civil cases, most of them are concerned with disputes between private litigants over such matters as automobile accidents, business contracts, and unsuccessful marriages that end in divorce proceedings. *Criminal cases,* on the other hand, are exclusively a governmental responsibility. When a person violates a federal, state, or local law intended to secure the public order and safety, he risks official prosecution by the government and, if convicted, punishment, including imprisonment and sometimes death. In addition to these two basic types of legal actions, one can also usefully speak of *administrative law cases* and *public law cases*. The first, a product of the highly regulated industrial state that the United States has become, is derived from the elaborate set of rules made by the state and federal regulatory agencies by virtue of the executive, legislative, and judicial authority delegated to them. The second, a main concern of this chapter, refers to those administrative, civil, and criminal cases that stimulate American courts to define the powers and responsibilities of government agencies by interpreting the public laws and, ultimately, the constitutions under which they operate.

It is important, finally, to keep in mind that all of the different kinds of law and cases that come before the American courts serve a common purpose: they provide a peaceful and orderly mechanism for settling the individual and group conflicts of a large and diverse population.

One part of the American legal system, the jury, is unique in that it is staffed, not by judges and lawyers, but by citizens untrained in the law. Every year it is estimated that more than one million citizens serve on juries. The jury's origins are venerable, for the jury developed out of the practices of feudal England. Today, amid a growing debate over its usefulness and accuracy, the jury performs two functions. First, in the federal jurisdiction and in some state jurisdictions a grand jury, usually composed of between twelve to twenty-three citizens, must indict a criminal suspect before he can be brought to trial. Second, in federal and state trials a twelve-man petit jury decides questions of fact in civil and criminal actions. Jury trial is a right guaranteed in the federal and state constitutions, but an accused criminal or the parties to a civil case may waive the privilege and be tried by the judge alone.

Juries supposedly bring a touch of democracy to the courtroom by returning verdicts on the basis of popular common sense. Defenders of the jury, fondly recalling the days when fearless jurymen returned popular verdicts that stayed the tyrannical prosecutions of Tudor and Stuart kings, still quote Blackstone's tribute to "the grand bulwark of everyman's liberty." But critics of the jury claim that, because American and British judges are no longer cowed servants of tyrannical kings, the institution has outlived its usefulness. They argue that it is unwise to entrust the determination of complex facts to untrained laymen who may easily be swayed by irrelevant emotional appeals.

The State and Federal Judiciaries

The laws that prevail in America, including the provision for indictment and trial by jury, facilitate the orderly solution of personal and group conflicts. But the primary institutional mechanism for applying legal rules to human controversies is the system of courts and judges. At the state level the legal machinery appears complicated, for the court systems of the fifty states reflect a bewildering variety of organizational patterns and of jurisdictional and appellate arrangements. This diversity is reminiscent of the kaleidoscopic structure of the state party systems, which are also products of the decentralization that is bred into the American federal system.

It is nevertheless possible to identify some general similarities in the organization and jurisdictional structure of the state judiciaries. In virtually all states there is a distinction between the courts of general jurisdiction and those of limited (special) jurisdiction. The courts of general jurisdiction are responsible for major civil and criminal cases. These include trial courts, which are frequently called *superior courts* or *circuit courts,* and appellate courts of various kinds. All states have an appellate structure that culminates in a supreme court (called a *supreme court* in forty-two states and by different names in the others); nineteen states also sandwich in an intermediate appellate court between their trial courts and their highest tribunal.

Even greater diversity exists among the courts of limited jurisdiction, which are essentially of two types. The first are local courts whose jurisdiction is limited to minor civil and criminal matters. They are called *municipal courts* in twenty-six states and *county courts* in twenty other states. In addition, many cities have magistrate or police courts to deal with traffic violations and misdemeanors normally punished by small fines and imprisonment for periods of under six months. It is at this jurisdictional level, also, that one finds the rural justice courts staffed by justices

"What makes it so confusing is they've
all sworn to tell the truth."

Figure 9.1. Juries: the people decide

Source: Von Riegen in *The Saturday Review,* July 1964.

of the peace, who are usually untrained in law and largely uncontrolled. These courts, which had their origin in feudal England when justices of the peace enforced the king's peace, seem anachronistic in a complex industrial society. They are gradually disappearing from the judicial scene. The second basic type of limited jurisdiction courts are special courts that deal exclusively with one kind of a legal problem. Thus, in many states there are juvenile courts, domestic relations courts, and probate courts which examine the wills of deceased persons.

State judges, as Figure 9.3 shows, are selected in a number of ways. Each method has its own variations, and many of the states use different selection methods for different levels of courts. In general, though, most state judges are chosen by popular election, an inheritance from the Jacksonian period. Elections are both partisan and nonpartisan. There are three other principal methods: executive appointment, which is subject to the approval of one branch of the legislature; legislative election, which was widely favored during the Revolutionary period but now survives in only four states; and nonpartisan selection, which is conducted by special

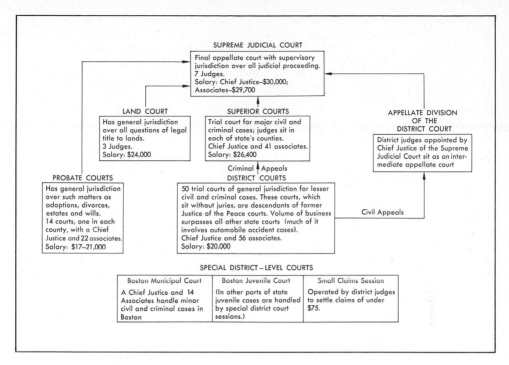

Figure 9.2. A relatively simple and centralized state court system: the judicial structure of Massachusetts

nominating commissions composed of lawyers, ranking judges, and distinguished lay citizens. Under this last method, known as the Missouri Plan, the appointed judge subsequently runs nonpartisanly on the question of whether he should be retained in office.

At the federal level the judicial machinery, in contrast to that of the states, is less complicated. There are a handful of specialized courts that deal in a semi-administrative fashion with certain legal problems, such as customs and patent matters. Apart from these tribunals, whose decisions may be reviewed by the United States Supreme Court, the federal courts are organized in a three-layered pyramid. As Figure 9.4 indicates, almost all of the cases arising under United States law are settled in the ninety-one federal district courts. Their basic authority for deciding cases, like that of all federal courts, is found in the jurisdictional provisions of Article III of the Constitution. The most important are those extending "the judicial power" to "all cases, in law and equity, arising under this Constitution, the laws of the United States, and treaties made . . . under their authority" and to controversies "between citizens of different states." Congress, however, regulates the conditions under which this jurisdiction comes into effect. In 1958, for instance, it passed a law requiring that the financial amount in dispute had to be at least $10,000 before citizens of two or more states could have their conflict adjudicated in the district courts.

Figure 9.3. Methods of judicial selection

Source: Victor G. Rosenblum, "Courts and Judges: Power and Politics." From *The Fifty States and Their Government,* by James W. Fesler. © Copyright 1967 by Alfred A. Knopf, Inc. Reprinted by permission of the publisher. Pp. 418–419.

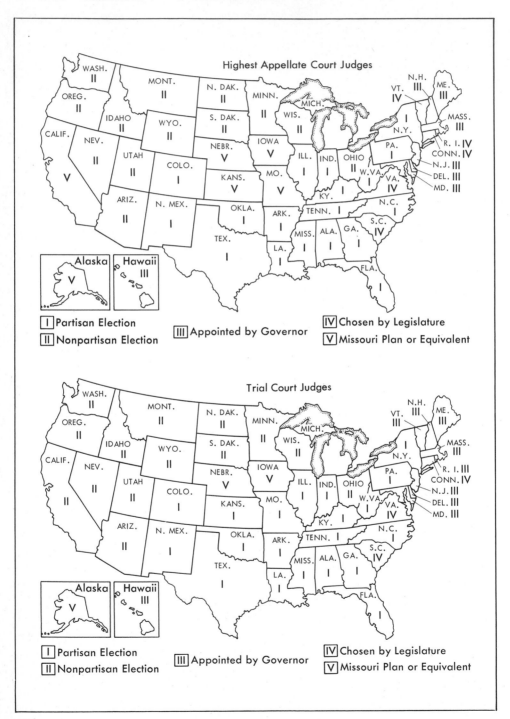

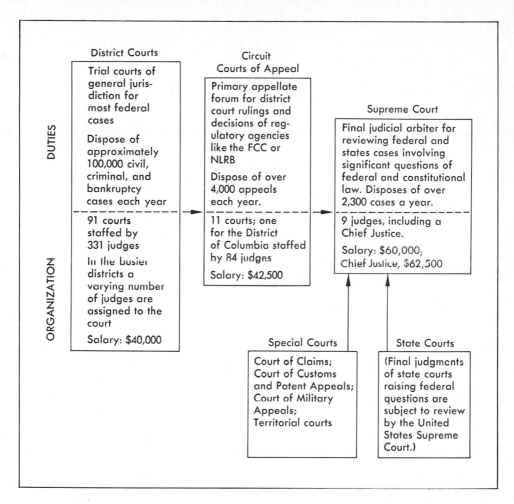

Figure 9.4. The federal judiciary

Eleven circuit courts of appeal review the conclusions of the independent regulatory commissions and of the district courts whenever one of the contestants wishes to appeal an adverse decision. (Federal prosecutors, however, may not contest the acquittal of criminal defendants.) The highest federal court, the Supreme Court of the United States, receives its cases from two separate avenues. The Supreme Court hears cases on appeal from the circuit courts, and, in a few special situations, from the district courts. In addition, because the Court operates under a broad constitutional and statutory grant of jurisdiction that embraces *all* cases raising questions of federal law, it also decides appeals taken from the state judicial systems.

Despite its unique constitutional and political significance, the Supreme Court's presence does not make the American judiciary hierarchical. In matters of purely state law, and these include the vast majority of legal disputes, the Supreme Court has no authority. Even within its area of jurisdiction there are severe physical limitations on what the Court can do. It is but a single tribunal of nine men who hand down full opinions in no more than 100 to 150 cases a year—well under one one-hundredth of one per cent of the approximately two million cases decided annually in the nation's courts. (The Supreme Court, however, disposes of nearly 3,000 cases a year; in most instances this means that, after a fairly cursory examination, it concludes that the appeal lacks merit.) It can decide cases and issue decrees to the subordinate federal and state courts, but the Court cannot force other judges to do its will. Although its decisions are customarily obeyed, the Supreme Court's judicial policies, as the discussion later in the chapter will bring out, are not automatically enforced.

Federal judges are appointed by the President subject to the consent of the Senate. The practice of "senatorial courtesy," however, means that especially in the case of district judgeships the Senators in the state where the judge is to serve have a veto power over appointments. As a consequence, the appointment of federal judges typically leads to complicated political bargaining between the Justice Department (which represents the President's interests), the Senators from the state where the judge will serve, and the local party leaders. Once appointed, federal judges enjoy a security of income and of tenure that insulates them from overt political pressures. Article III, Section 1, of the Constitution prevents their salary from being reduced, and their term of office is constitutionally prescribed as being indefinite "during good behavior." In effect, they serve for life but can be removed for cause if impeached by the House and convicted by the Senate, following a special trial.

Politics on the Bench

American judges, in contrast to the career civil servants who serve as judges in European countries, are politicians on the bench. Particularly on local courts, the judges are political in a narrow sense of that word. They dispense favors and rewards—sometimes in response to corrupt pressures. A few years ago the *Philadelphia Inquirer*, after a series of articles examining the city's magistrate courts, concluded that some of the magistrates were guilty of "bribery, fixes, and disregard for ordinary simple justice." [4] At the time sixteen of the twenty-six magistrates were former party ward leaders who had remained politically active. Even higher courts are not always immune to such pressures. In 1965 three Oklahoma Supreme Court justices were implicated in a spectacular bribery scandal.

In spite of such incidents, direct judicial corruption is an infrequent occurrence. But political patronage in the form of judge-made appointments—the "honest graft" so beloved by politicians—as distinguished from favoritism in decisions, is no stranger to state and local courts. Lower court judges are frequently in a position to select a whole range of auxiliary judicial personnel, such as bailiffs, clerks for the courts and the judges, and secretaries. Although there is a growing tendency to

[4] *Christian Science Monitor*, October 9, 1964.

place court positions under civil service, the amount of open patronage is still sub-stantial. State and city judges in the New York metropolitan area, for example, fill close to five hundred positions with party workers. Some of these posts, such as county clerkships and public administrator jobs paying $15,000 a year, are tasty political plums. It is estimated that more than one third of the city's District Leaders and County Chairmen occupy positions in the court system.[5] Similarly, a survey made of Rhode Island's five-judge Family Court revealed that at least half of the court's fifty-two staff and clerical employees owed their position to political con-nections. The inquiry was prompted by the action of a state administration, defeated at the polls, in creating twelve new court jobs to accommodate some of its outgoing personnel.[6]

Courts also have it in their power to dispense less visible types of patronage. In civil cases, local, state, and federal judges often designate referees specially qualified to decide intricate technical questions. They also appoint receivers to operate bank-rupt businesses and executors and guardians to oversee the estates of persons who die without making wills. These jobs, which are financed from fees paid by the litigants, are well paid. New York City's Surrogate Courts, whose jurisdiction em-braces wills, estates, and guardianships, annually appoint thousands of guardians, executors, and administrators; the total fees are worth several millions of dollars. In Manhattan alone two surrogate courts process wills with an annual gross value of nearly one billion dollars. The judges on such courts, though normally restricted in that they have to appoint competent personnel, are free to appoint, as the case may be, competent Democratic or Republican lawyers.[7] The federal courts, where tenure is for life and where the tradition is strong that the judge sever his former political ties, are the least likely to dispense patronage in a partisan manner. On occasions, however, even federal district judges have been suspected of making appointments for political reasons.

Judges are political also in a broader sense. Most state and federal judges, for instance, have been politically active prior to going on the bench; the backgrounds of federal Supreme Court Justices reveal that virtually all have been at least modestly active in politics before their appointment. Especially when they decide public law cases, which turn on the powers and obligations of government, judges are likely to be influenced by their political affiliations and values. It is always difficult, however, to pinpoint the precise political origins of a judge's judicial behavior. For one thing, only rarely is a simple cause-and-effect relationship apparent between political factors and court decisions. For another, there are two different sorts of political influences that work on the courts. Both are subtle. There are, first, the pressures within the judges. Second, there are the legal and political forces of the outer world that influence the judges' perceptions and structure their reactions.

[5] Wallace S. Sayre and Herbert Kaufman, *Governing New York City* (New York: Russell Sage Foundation, 1960), p. 541.

[6] *Providence Evening Bulletin,* February 21, 1963.

[7] Robert E. Tomasson, "The Surrogate's Role: Protector of Widows and Orphans or Dispenser of Patronage?" *The New York Times,* May 29, 1966.

Judges: The Inner and the Outer Pressures

The most intimate pressures that can be brought to bear on a judge are those he generates himself. Because most American judges are selected directly or indirectly on a party basis, one might expect Democratic and Republican judges to differ somewhat in the way they perceive—and decide—certain types of cases. This expectation is confirmed in a study by a political scientist, Stuart S. Nagel. After analyzing the decisions of 298 federal and state appellate judges in 15 typical areas of adjudication, he concluded that there were significant differences between Democratic and Republican judges.[8] Democratic judges were distinctly more prone than their Republican colleagues to cast their votes in a liberal direction. They were more likely, for example, to side with defendants in criminal cases, with administrative agencies in business regulation cases, with claimants in unemployment compensation cases, and with the libertarian position in free speech cases. A study of decisions by the eleven federal courts of appeals provides further evidence; Democratic judges are more likely to vote in a liberal direction, especially in cases involving economic and property issues.[9] It would be wrong, however, to conclude that Democratic or Republican judges vote differently because of a conscious intent to follow party lines. They vote differently because they hold different personal standards of value, the same standards that help to account for their original party affiliation.

Most judges, while deciding cases in partial response to their personal and political values formed during their precourt careers, are also sensitive to the *changing* environment in the outer world of law and politics. Put another way, the decisions of most judges are a product of the interplay between their internal values and their external environment.

To cite but a few of many possible examples, Justice Oliver Wendell Homes (1902–1932), a believer in economic laissez faire, voted repeatedly to uphold government regulations, the wisdom of which he privately doubted. In his classic dissent in *Lochner* v. *New York,* where he voted to sustain the constitutionality of a state law limiting working hours in bakeries, Holmes insisted that "my agreement or disagreement" with an economic theory "has nothing to do with the right of a majority to embody their opinions in law." [10] Similarly, Justice Louis D. Brandeis (1916–1939) voted to sustain state laws limiting business competition despite his strong opposition to them, because he also believed that in a time of change courts should not prevent the states from engaging in social and economic experiments.[11] Justice Felix Frankfurter (1939–1962), who was revolted by "a State's insistence on its pound of flesh," nevertheless cast the deciding vote in a case that sent a man to the electric chair for a second time after an electrical malfunction spared the prisoner's life in the first attempt to electrocute him. To decide otherwise, he wrote,

[8] "Political Party Affiliation and Judges' Decisions," *American Political Science Review,* LV (December, 1961), 843–850.

[9] Sheldon Goldman, "Voting Behavior on the United States Courts of Appeals, 1961–64," *American Political Science Review,* LX (June, 1966), 374–383.

[10] 195 U.S. 45, 75 (1905).

[11] Dissenting in *New State Ice Co.* v. *Liebmann,* 285 U.S. 262 (1932).

would be to enforce "my private view" rather than the "concensus of society's opinion." [12]

During the 1950's and early 1960's the response of southern federal judges to civil rights cases provided a particularly fascinating illustration of the impact of internal and external pressures on judicial decisions. Few, if any, of the approximately seventy-five southern district and circuit judges in those years could have been classified as personal advocates of racial integration. Most of them undoubtedly preferred the traditional segregationist system under which they were reared. Some made little effort to conceal their attitudes. Judge Harold Cox of Mississippi's Northern District Court publicly referred to the efforts of civil rights groups to increase Negro voting as "a bunch of niggers on a voter drive." [13] Such expressions of distaste for the civil rights cause were not limited to speeches or off-the-cuff courtroom remarks. In one case Judge E. Gordon West of the District Court for Eastern Louisiana reluctantly ordered school desegregation in East Baton Rouge but could not forbear adding a private comment. After describing the Supreme Court's original school segregation ruling as "one of the truly regrettable decisions of all times," Judge West denounced it as an unbelievable "substitution of so-called 'sociological principles' for sound legal reasoning." [14]

Federal district judges, in fact, are closely tied to a local environment. In part this is because federal law requires them to live within their judicial district. Even more important is the fact that they typically owe their judgeship to the recommendations of state and local party leaders and that much of their professional career has usually been built on a network of state connections. A study of southern district judges shows, for example, that 56 per cent had attended law school in their home state and that 89 per cent had previously held a government position in the state.[15] Once on the bench, of course, they have the security of a lifetime tenure. Yet, as a federal circuit judge has explained, this

does not protect them from the unconscious urge for the approbation of their fellow-man, and fellow-man most often means those of like interest and backgrounds, business and professional experiences and predilections and even prejudices.[16]

Under certain circumstances district judges, like Congressmen, may "vote their constituencies." In the South politicians from areas with a small black population have generally been the most progressive in civil rights. Politicians from areas with a heavy concentration of blacks—where the whites fear black domination and where black voting has traditionally been low—have shown the greatest resistance to the expansion of civil rights. The decisions of the district judges in the late fifties and early sixties roughly paralleled those of the elected politicians: judges in districts

---

[12] *Louisiana ex rel. Francis* v. *Resweber,* 329 U.S. 459, 471 (1947).

[13] *The New York Times,* March 8, 1964.

[14] *New Republic,* July 20, 1963, p. 5.

[15] Kenneth N. Vines, "Federal District Judges and Race Relations Cases in the South," *Journal of Politics,* XXXVI (May, 1964), 346–347.

[16] Jack W. Peltason, *Fifty-Eight Lonely Men: Southern Federal Judges and School Desegregation* (New York: Harcourt, 1961), pp. 9–10.

with low black populations had a distinct tendency to hand down a greater percentage of pro-civil-rights rulings than judges in districts with high black populations.[17]

Politics, in short, influences judicial decisions. It does so through both the inner
political values of the judge and the external pressures that impinge on the courts.
This may seem clearest when one examines a single, locally oriented, district judge
in the Mississippi Delta during the early sixties. But it is just as true for the exalted
Supreme Court. Its jurisdiction is national, and because the pressures and attitudes
that influence the Court are contradictory and frequently cancel each other out, the
relationship between the politics of its environment and the decisions it reaches is
more subtle. It is nonetheless evident that the judges of the Supreme Court, too,
usually respond to the general movement of their society's underlying social,
economic, and political forces. When they do not, as happened in the mid-1930's,
a constitutional political crisis becomes inevitable. More commonly the Court's
major decisions reflect—and at times even anticipate—the political realities at work
in the nation.

[17] Vines, op. cit., pp. 346–347. It is very possible that the impact of the Voting Rights Act
of 1965 on black voting in the southern states will gradually change the behavior of the region's
white politicians.

the american
supreme court

The Third Branch of Government

On May 17, 1954, the Supreme Court of the United States decided a case, *Brown v. Board of Education* (also known as one of the *School Segregation Cases*), by ruling that the states could no longer require racial segregation in their public schools. This landmark decision ignited political fires throughout the nation. It challenged the traditional white southern way of life and provoked resistance that sometimes became violent; it gave new strength and direction to the campaign of civil rights groups against segregation; and it forced the nation to confront the problem of the black man's status in American society. It may even be that the decision aroused unrealistic expectations among American blacks as to forthcoming improvements in their lives and social conditions, unrealistic in the sense that the American political system has so far been unprepared to facilitate immediate and true racial equality.[18] Although it would be foolish to attribute the recent growth of black nationalist extremism and of violent rioting in the urban ghettos to the *Brown* decision, it seems reasonable to believe that the Court's historic ruling has contributed significantly to the black men's awareness of the enormous disparity between their formal constitutional rights and the harsher reality of their day-to-day life.

Since 1954 the Supreme Court has extended the ban against racial discrimination to all public facilities, and it has denied local school boards the right to sponsor religious exercises in the public schools. In addition, it has repeatedly invalidated state legislative and administrative policies censoring allegedly obscene books and movies. The Court of Chief Justice Earl Warren (1953–1969) also decreed that the national House of Representatives and both houses of every state legislature must be apportioned so as to reflect population equality. In other recent decisions the Court has strengthened the rights of the criminally accused, declaring, for example, that the states must provide legal counsel to poor persons accused of crimes and that

[18] See Ch. 13.

the states may not use evidence in criminal prosecutions obtained through unlawful searches and seizures.

The American Supreme Court does not give advisory opinions on theoretical questions. It established a lasting precedent in 1793, when the Justices politely but firmly informed President Washington, who had asked the Court's advice on certain questions of international law, that "our being Judges of a Court of last resort" is "a strong argument against the propriety of our extra-judicially deciding the questions." [19] The Court's decisions occur in the context of flesh-and-blood disputes between specific adversaries. They often come at a stage in the political process after other governmental agencies have already acted and when, therefore, the decision may have a profound impact on the contending parties.

Unlike the high courts of other nations, the American Supreme Court is primarily a public law tribunal.[20] Almost all of its cases are of two general types. First, the Court tests state actions against federal law, including the Constitution, laws, and treaties of the United States. And second, it interprets the meaning and passes on the constitutionality of actions by the Congress, the President, and the administrative agencies. As Chapter 3 indicated, the ideal of limited government under the restraint of a written constitution has deep roots in America's history and political culture. Very early in the life of the new Republic the Supreme Court began to emerge as the principal institution for enforcing (according, naturally, to its own reading) the Constitution's limitations. In the case of *Marbury* v. *Madison* (1803), the Court of Chief Justice John Marshall asserted the power of judicial review by voiding a section of an act of Congress; the power, though often challenged, has been confirmed and expanded in significance through seventeen decades of practice and public acquiescence.

Most cases that reach the Supreme Court are initiated by private parties, but they have a public significance. *Baker* v. *Carr* and other *Reapportionment Cases* serve as another illustration. These decisions have had an influence on many political interests, and they are causing a major reorganization of the nation's legislatures. Yet they were initiated by the suits of private American citizens.

Because its decisions are so significant the U.S. Supreme Court has a place alongside the Congress and the President as an active political partner. It is a third branch of government. Perhaps the greatest tribute to the Court's central role is the fact that it is a focal point of activity by private interests who calculate that it may bless them with judicial decisions favorable to their political cause. A good example

[19] Charles Warren, *The Supreme Court in United States History,* Vol. I, (Boston: Little, Brown, 1926), pp. 110–111. The supreme courts of five states, most of them in New England, are required to give advisory opinions, usually on the request of either the Governor or the legislature.

[20] The supreme courts of the states, of course, perform functions analogous to those of the federal Supreme Court, but there are important distinctions between them. First, they are inferior to the federal Court on all questions of federal law—which covers an increasingly broad category of cases. Second, like the foreign high courts, much of their work concerns private legal disputes. The federal Supreme Court is almost exclusively a public law tribunal that passes on cases raising questions of statutory interpretation and of basic constitutionality.

is the American Liberty League, organized during the 1930's by large business corporations and citizens anxious to limit governmental regulation of property. This well-heeled lobby, manned by a phalanx of able attorneys, initiated and encouraged hundreds of court suits against the social and economic legislation of the Roosevelt Administration. Until 1937 the League found a sympathetic ally in a conservative Supreme Court that struck down major parts of the New Deal and challenged Franklin D. Roosevelt's stewardship of the nation. Since then, the NAACP (the National Association for the Advancement of Colored People) has had even more impressive success in obtaining judicial decisions invalidating all federal and state laws and policies that either established or permit racial segregation. The high point of the NAACP drive came with its victory in the *School Segregation Cases.* In similar fashion *Baker* v. *Carr* and the *Reapportionment Cases* were products of systematic campaigns by urban and suburban interests who went to the Supreme Court when it became obvious that the malapportioned legislatures would not reapportion themselves.

If law applied by courts is a peaceful means for settling essentially private disputes, in America it is as much a means for settling political conflicts. "Scarcely any political question arises in the United States," Alexis de Tocqueville observed as early as 1835, "that is not resolved, sooner or later, into a judicial question." Although many conflicts of interests and of values are settled in the more openly political executive and legislative branches and through the quiet adjustments of the administrative bureaucracy, it is nevertheless true that a remarkable number of major political disputes wind up in the nation's courts and ultimately in the Supreme Court of the United States.

The Court at Work

Every once in a while an irate citizen is heard to vow that he will fight a case "all the way to the United States Supreme Court." There is much bravado and little realism in such talk. Even if he is willing to spend the $15,000 or more that this would cost, there is no guarantee that the appeal will be heard. The Court disposes of nearly three thousand cases a year; yet less than 20 per cent of these are actually decided on their merits. In four cases out of five the Court's sole decision is a decision not to decide the case.

There are three avenues for getting cases before the Supreme Court. Under the first, which is known as *original jurisdiction* and is provided for in Article III of the Constitution, the Court may act as a trial court, hearing and deciding cases for the first and last time. Cases involving foreign diplomats stationed in the United States technically fall within this original jurisdiction, though in practice few such cases are tried before the Court. Not only do diplomats enjoy immunity from criminal prosecution, but Congress, with the Supreme Court's approval, has provided that cases involving diplomats can be heard in the federal district courts. The only controversies occasionally tried by the Supreme Court are those between one or more states or between a state and the national government. Although infrequent, these cases often concern substantial interests. In 1963, for example, the Court decided a major case involving the lengthy dispute between Arizona and California over water rights to the Colorado River.[21] In 1966 it sustained the key provisions of the Voting Rights Act of 1965 that had been challenged by South Carolina and five other southern states in a case tried directly before the Supreme Court.[22]

The other two jurisdictional avenues to the Supreme Court have been established by Congress, and they account for almost all of the Court's work. Whenever the state courts declare an act of Congress unconstitutional or deny an alleged federal right that appears to have a strong foundation, the aggrieved party has a statutory right of appeal. A similar right exists when a lower federal court invalidates either a federal or a state law. The third route is that known as *certiorari,* literally meaning "made more certain." Each term the Court is petitioned to grant writs of certiorari in over two thousand cases. The losing side in the lower federal or state courts may ask the Court to hear a case in order to correct an asserted error of legal or constitutional interpretation. If four Justices agree that there is a serious question worthy of examination, the writ is granted and the appeal will then be considered.

Despite the difference between the seemingly mandatory appeals and the discretionary writ of certiorari, the Court has complete control over its docket. In this, as in so many other respects, it is unique among appellate tribunals. Neither the federal circuit courts nor the state supreme courts nor the foreign high courts have the right to decide what cases they wish to hear. Even when confronted with mandatory appeals, the Supreme Court can avoid a decision by ruling that there is a want of "a substantial federal question" in the case. The Court wriggles through this loophole in more than half of the approximately 150 appeal cases that come to it each term.

The certiorari power, by contrast, is wholly discretionary. "A review on writ of certiorari," one of the Court's administrative rules informs the bar, "is not a matter of right, but of sound judicial discretion." [23] It is not surprising, then, that only a fraction of the approximately three thousand cases that reach the Court each term are decided with written opinions after a full consideration of legal briefs and oral arguments. The citizen who eventually walks away from a controversy with a Supreme Court opinion in his hip pocket has achieved a statistical miracle: in the 1970–1971 Term of Court only 126 cases were decided with a full judicial opinion on the merits of the case.

Once the Court has agreed to hear a case, there are normally three phases in its processing—argument, decision, and public announcement. All cases are assigned

---

[21] *Arizona* v. *Califorina,* 373 U.S. 546 (1963).

[22] *South Carolina* v. *Katzenbach,* 383 U.S. 301 (1966). In this case South Carolina, anxious for a speedy decision, invoked the Court's original jurisdiction by suing Attorney General Katzenbach as a citizen of another state. The Supreme Court need not grant such requests, but in this instance the Justices undoubtedly agreed that the urgency of the question justified an early decision.

[23] Robert L. Stern and Eugene Gressman, *Supreme Court Practice,* 3d rev. ed. (Washington, D.C.: Bureau of National Affairs, 1962), p. 545.

to a docket, and those accepted for decision are usually argued at least one year from the time they first reached the Court. Occasionally the Court agrees to a speedy hearing of cases raising questions of extraordinary public importance. When, late in the spring of 1971, *The New York Times* and other major newspapers began publishing excerpts from the top secret Pentagon Papers, a great legal and political debate over the First Amendment and the nation's security interests broke across America. The papers documented the behind-the-scenes record of the nation's involvement in the Vietnam war, and the Department of Justice immediately sought a federal court injunction forbidding any further publication of the Pentagon Papers with the claim that "irreparable injury" would be done to the United States. Within the space of eleven days this issue was reviewed by a federal district court, a court of appeals, and, finally, by the Supreme Court, which lifted the injunction on the ground that the government had failed to prove that publishing the Pentagon Papers would damage the national security.

Although elaborate legal briefs accompany the cases, the customary one hour for oral argument that is allotted to each side can be crucial. Good arguments clarify the issues and direct the judges' attention to the crux of the dispute. The oral argument is an attorney's golden opportunity. If, as Justice John M. Harlan has written, he "is able to enlist the favorable interest of even one member of the Bench, his cause will have advocacy in the Conference debate." [24]

Sometimes the oral argument provides a clue as to how the Justices are thinking because they frequently pepper the attorneys with revealing questions and comments. An excellent example occurred in one of the *Reapportionment Cases,* the Colorado case that involved a challenge to the constitutionality of a scheme apportioning the lower house according to population but giving special weight to sparsely settled areas in the state senate. The strongest point in favor of the Colorado plan was that it had been approved in a statewide referendum. The Justices seemed unimpressed as they fired question after question at the state's attorney:

Justice White: Why does one area need more representation than others?
Justice Goldberg: Why is it assumed that if both houses were on a population basis, and the urban majority had a majority in both houses, it would be less solicitous of the people as a whole than the rural minority?
Justice Black: The people of a state can no more violate the constitution by referendum than by law. I don't see what the [popular] reference has to do with it.[25]

Three months later, when the Court released its decision in this and five other reapportionment cases, the majority opinion took the position that "one man, one vote" was the unequivocal command of the Constitution.

On Fridays of the weeks when they hear oral arguments the Justices meet in private conference with the Chief Justice presiding. The Court first votes on the numerous petitions for certiorari, most of them so trivial and obviously erroneous

---

[24] "A Glimpse of the Supreme Court at Work," *University of Chicago Law School Record* (Spring, 1963), p. 6.

[25] Anthony Lewis, "Justices Question Inequities in Colorado Apportionment Plan," *The New York Times,* April 2, 1964.

that they are quickly disposed of. Then it considers the cases argued during the week. After a discussion led by the Chief Justice, the Justices vote on the merits of the case. If one of them is ill or if he feels that a personal involvement with some aspect of the case may cause doubts about his impartiality, he is excused from the decision. At least six Justices must be present and qualified for a decision to be made. When the Court divides evenly on a case—a 4 to 4 or 3 to 3 vote—it issues only a statement that the decision of the next lower court has been affirmed.

If the Chief Justice is in the majority, he assigns the preparation of an opinion to one of his colleagues; otherwise the assignment is made by the senior Justice voting with the majority. The conference vote is not necessarily conclusive because the judges are free to change their minds at any point prior to the public announcement of the decision. A lively debate frequently continues after the conference as the opinion writers research questions for themselves and reexamine their original conclusions. Justices sometimes shift positions, and it has happened that the judge preparing a majority opinion in a 5 to 4 decision ends up filing a dissenting opinion for a four-man minority!

The judge who prepares the majority opinion studies the briefs, which cover in greater detail the points developed in the oral argument, and he consults with his colleagues. When a draft is ready, it circulates among all the Justices and must be

Figure 9.5. Judging: the influence of nonrational factors

Source: Drawing by Ed Fisher; © 1965 *The New Yorker Magazine,* Inc.

"It's constitutional,
it's unconstitutional,
it's constitutional,
it's unconstitutional . . ."

approved by everyone in the majority. An opinion for the Court, though it bears the imprint of the man who wrote it, is the product of collective thought and deliberation. It often represents the lowest common denominator acceptable to a majority coalition of judges; in short, it is not unlike a negotiated treaty in which the various parties make concessions.

A judge who agrees with the majority decision but not with its reasoning may file a concurring opinion explaining his position. Alternatively, he may want to explain more fully his reasons for voting with the majority. "The importance of the issue and deep conviction with which views on both sides are held," Justice Brennan wrote in a concurring opinion to one of the *Prayer Cases,* "seem to me to justify detailing at some length my reasons for joining the Court's judgment and opinion." Brennan was not exaggerating: his opinion ran to 77 pages bolstered by 410 footnotes—the equivalent of an M.A. thesis on the constitutional problems surrounding church-state relations.[26] Dissenting opinions are likely to be especially pungent. The dissenter is unrestrained by the need to compromise, and he may be profoundly disturbed by the majority's decision. Justice Harlan, dissenting in one of the *Reapportionment Cases,* described the majority decision as historically and logically "unsound" and "a disservice" both to the Court and "to the broader values of our system of government." [27]

Why does a Justice dissent? In good conscience, he cannot accede to what the majority has done and said, and he hopes that his dissent may strike a favorable response among the bar and those who are concerned with the Court's work. Above all, he hopes that eventually—perhaps in a few years, perhaps in a few decades—the Court will reconsider its position and adopt his view. Few dissenters become honored prophets, but the possibility always exists. The eloquent dissenting opinion of the first Justice John M. Harlan (1877–1911) in *Plessy* v. *Ferguson,* where he described the Constitution as "color blind" in arguing that states could not segregate their citizens,[28] became the law of the land half a century later when the Supreme Court decided *Brown* v. *Board of Education.*

More recently, the late Justice Hugo L. Black enjoyed the satisfaction of rewriting some of his dissenting opinions of the 1940's as majority opinions of the 1960's. In *Gideon* v. *Wainwright* (1963) Black elevated his 1942 dissent in *Betts* v. *Brady* to majority status, writing an opinion that declared the Sixth Amendment to require each state to provide indigent criminal defendants with an attorney.[29] In *Wesberry* v. *Sanders* (1964) Black again accomplished the same feat by writing a majority opinion that invalidated malapportionment in the national House of Representatives. He thereby reversed the 1946 decision in *Colegrove* v. *Green,* in which he had filed a strong dissent.[30]

[26] *Abington Township* v. *Schempp,* 374 U.S. 203, 232 (1963).
[27] *Wesberry* v. *Sanders,* 376 U.S. 1, 22, 48 (1964).
[28] 163 U.S. 537, 559 (1896).
[29] 372 U.S. 335, reversing *Betts* v. *Brady,* 316 U.S. 455 (1942).
[30] 376 U.S. 1 (1964), reversing *Colegrove* v. *Green,* 328 U.S. 549 (1946).

Figure 9.6. The dissenting opinion: an appeal to the future

Source: Drawing by Whitney Darrow, Jr.; © 1965 *The New Yorker Magazine*, Inc.

"Well, we lost the appeal, but you'll be delighted to learn
there was a brilliant dissenting opinion in your favor."

The Chief Justice

The justices' freedom to concur or to dissent typifies their independence. The Court is not one but nine deliberative bodies. Each judge is his own decision-maker, united with his brethren only by a sense of institutional and professional responsibility and the common task of deciding cases according to the forms and practices of the law. The Chief Justice is more of a coordinator than a leader. His position brings him $2,500 more a year (the Associate Justices are paid $60,000 annually), and it gives him a special place of honor. But he has no sanctions to hold over his associates.

In spite of these limitations, a Chief Justice who is a good administrator and a shrewd manager of men can provide leadership. By presiding over the conference room deliberations he can structure the discussion of cases. Chief Justice Charles Evans Hughes (1930–1941), a man of strong intellect and forceful personality, made the most of this opportunity. He came to the conference room thoroughly informed on the cases up for consideration. He knew just when and how to call for a vote and cut off discussion when it began to meander or to fray judicial tempers.

Hughes's successor, Harlan F. Stone (1941–1946), was a less fortunate choice as Chief Justice. He was a talented judge, but he lost control of the conference room. Tensions and feuding among the Justices—Stone wryly referred to them as "my team of wild horses"—rose sharply, aggravated by the troublesome questions they were being asked to decide. Stone contributed to this problem because of a temperamental inability to curb the judges' freewheeling arguments and his own inclination to debate for the sake of debating. "Jackson, that's damned nonsense," or "Douglas, *you* ought to know better," he would blurt out in conference. Unlike Hughes, Stone was not, his biographer writes, "born to command equals." [31]

A second source of potential influence available to the Chief Justice is his right to assign opinions whenever he is in the majority. Hughes, whenever possible, assigned liberal justices to write conservative opinions and conservative justices to write liberal opinions. In a similar vein, his predecessor, William Howard Taft (1921–1930), strove mightily to "mass the Court" behind its decisions. Taft disliked dissenting opinions, and he abhorred 5 to 4 rulings because he felt they weakened the Court's image as the interpreter of a Constitution whose meaning was clear and certain. Wavering judges, who seemed inclined to dissent, were subjected to unremitting campaigns of persuasion in order to bring them around, as Taft put it, to "the proper view." [32]

Although a Chief Justice can add to his influence and promote harmony among headstrong brethren by assigning opinions wisely, the task can also bring no end of troubles to a poor Court manager. Chief Justice Stone kept significant cases out of the hands of judges whose abilities he doubted or whose judicial approach he distrusted, creating resentment among the neglected judges. In the assignments he did make, Stone, in contrast to Hughes, sometimes betrayed an insensitivity to sound judicial politics.

Stone's handling of *Smith* v. *Allwright* (1944), a decision invalidating the white primary that had long been prevalent in Democratic party primaries in southern states, provides a striking example. Blacks were excluded from voting in Democratic primaries, and, because in those days Democratic nomination was tantamount to election, they were effectively denied the right to cast a meaningful ballot. Until over-

[31] Alpheus T. Mason, *Harlan Fiske Stone: Pillar of the Law* (New York: Viking, 1956), pp. 795–796.

[32] Ibid., pp. 255–259. Taft worked to curb dissents from another angle too: President Harding consulted with him on judicial appointments. The Chief Justice was able to veto potential candidates whom he feared would not contribute to the Court's "teamwork." See the fascinating account by Alpheus T. Mason, *William Howard Taft: Chief Justice* (New York: Simon and Schuster, 1965), Chs. 7 and 8.

shadowed by *Brown* v. *Board of Education,* the *Smith* v. *Allwright* decision that this exclusion violated the Fourteenth Amendment stood as one of the modern Court's most significant civil rights rulings. It strengthened Negro efforts to build up a base of political power, and it antagonized the race-conscious white South.

Had Chief Justice Stone been politically tactful, he would have chosen a spokesman least likely to offend the South. Instead, Stone assigned the opinion to Justice Felix Frankfurter, prompting a frank letter from Justice Robert H. Jackson to the Chief. Asking forgiveness for "intruding into the matter of assignments," Jackson got to the point:

> I wonder if you have not overlooked some of the ugly factors in our national life which go to the wisdom of having Mr. Justice Frankfurter act as the voice of the Court in the matter of *Smith* v. *Allwright.* It is a delicate matter. We must reverse a recent, well-considered and unanimous decision.[33] We deny the entire South the right to a white primary, which is one of its most cherished rights. It seems to me very important that the strength which an all but unanimous decision would have may be greatly weakened if the voice that utters it is one that may grate on Southern sensibilities. Mr. Justice Frankfurther unites in a rare degree factors which unhappily excite prejudice. In the first place, he is a Jew. In the second place, he is from New England, the seat of the abolition movement. In the third place, he has not been thought of as a person particularly sympathetic with the Democratic party in the past. I know that every one of these things is a consideration that to you is distasteful and they are things which I mention only with the greatest reluctance. . . . With all humility I suggest that the Court's decision, bound to cause bitter resentment, will be much less apt to stir ugly reactions if the news that the white primary is dead, is broken to it, if possible, by a Southerner who has been a Democrat and is not a member of one of the minorities which stir prejudices kindred to those against the Negro.[34]

Stone immediately agreed. He withdrew the opinion from Frankfurter and reassigned it to Stanley F. Reed—a Democrat, a Kentuckian, and a political moderate.

The Jackson letter is instructive. It is a commentary on Stone's weaknesses as a Court manager, and it is also a pointed demonstration of one of the main themes of this chapter—that political thinking necessarily permeates the Court's work. It also shows that the Justices are concerned lest they needlessly weaken the force of their decisions. They can decide cases without fear or restraint, but their edicts are not self-executing judicial thunderbolts: there are, after all, limits to the Supreme Court's power.

The Limits on Judicial Power

Ironically, the most effective limitation on the Supreme Court's power comes, not from without, but from within the judicial branch of government. Much as the President often finds his policy decisions modified or even resisted by the administrative bureaucracy, which is nominally subordinate to him, so too does the Supreme Court

---

[33] Only nine years earlier in *Grovey* v. *Townsend,* 295 U.S. 45 (1935), the Court had upheld the constitutionality of white primaries.

[34] Mason, *Stone,* op. cit., p. 615.

depend on the lower courts to implement its decisions. Even the expression "lower courts" is something of a misnomer. On paper the American judicial system is hierarchical, a neat triangle that culminates in a Supreme Court. But in practice the Supreme Court is something less than a military commander-in-chief. It must fight in order to make good its commands, in part because of the independence enjoyed by all judges and in part because of the political fragmentation inherent in the federal system (see Figure 9.7).

Although the Court can speak the final *words* on all federal questions, it is the federal district courts and the state courts that must actually execute the decisions. In most cases the Supreme Court ruling is put into effect, but there is nothing automatic about this process. The Court's rulings, moreover, technically apply only to the specific cases that prompted them. No matter how similar subsequent cases involving the same issue may be, they are legally different if only because the parties and the precise factual situations differ. Stare decisis is only a general rule to be applied by each judge at *his* discretion. A trial judge who ignores the relevant precedents can always be reversed by the appellate courts, but only in the rarest instances can he be ordered to dispose of a case without any leeway on his part. In the federal judicial system a circuit court can give a mandamus (order) to a district judge to issue a specific decree in a case. This strips the judge of his jurisdiction or discretion over the case. The remedy is extremely rare: 1) a judge can be issued a mandamus only if a plaintiff is willing to proceed against him, and most litigants are reluctant to antagonize a judge whom they may well appear before in future cases; and 2) higher court judges dislike imposing such a drastic sanction on a fellow judge.

The Supreme Court has even less control over state courts, because in reviewing their decisions it passes only on the federal issue and then remands the case to the state court for the final disposition. On remand the state courts have sometimes been ingenious in raising new questions based solely on state law and then issuing decrees that evade the effect of the Supreme Court's decision. According to one study, in the decade from 1941 to 1951 the Court remanded 175 cases to state courts. In 46 of these cases there was further litigation and in 22 the party that had won in the Supreme Court finally lost—in the so-called lower courts! [35]

In one major case that the Supreme Court first decided in 1958 it took six years to overcome the resistance of the executive and judicial branches of the Alabama state government. The case, *NAACP* v. *Alabama*, involved a determined effort by Alabama to prevent the National Association for the Advancement of Colored People from operating within the state. When the Supreme Court issued its first decision in the *NAACP* case, it reversed a $100,000 contempt judgment and remanded it to the Alabama Supreme Court "for proceedings not inconsistent with this opinion." [36] The Alabama court, however, chose to proceed in a manner inconsistent with this judgment, declaring that the Supreme Court had been "mistaken" in its understand-

[35] Note, "Evasion of Supreme Court Mandates in Cases Remanded to State Courts Since 1941," *Harvard Law Review*, LXVII (May, 1954), 1251–1259.

[36] *NAACP* v. *Alabama*, 357 U.S. 449, 467 (1958).

Figure 9.7. The judicial structure

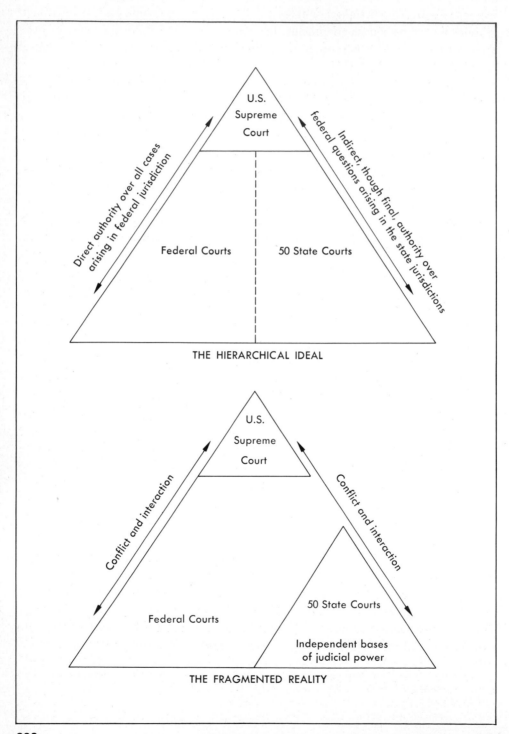

ing of the case. This ruling, in turn, was appealed to the Supreme Court. Once again the NAACP won, but the state courts pursued delaying tactics that required two more trips to Washington before the NAACP finally won a decision ordering Alabama to let it operate in the state. In 1964 the Supreme Court told the Alabama Supreme Court to remove the disqualifications against the NAACP. If prompt compliance were not forthcoming, the Court sternly added, it would allow the NAACP to apply for a final and specific decree not requiring implementation in the Alabama courts.[37]

The Supreme Court finally prevailed in the *NAACP* case, but it took six years and four decisions. It is important to note that the ultimate victory depended as much on the NAACP's combativeness as it did on the Justices' stamina. If the NAACP had not continued the litigation, the decrees of the Alabama courts would have stayed in force. Without litigants to activate its decisions, the Court is helpless, and this is one of the greatest limitations on its power. It cannot reach out and issue pronouncements in cases that are not on its docket, not even in cases that were once on its docket. Before it can make decisions it must be appealed to, for the Supreme Court functions like the proverbial well-behaved child: it speaks only when spoken to.

Federal district judges are more directly under the control of the Supreme Court. Almost all of their decisions are based exclusively on federal law. Administratively, they are supervised by the circuit courts, whose judicial values tend to parallel those of the Supreme Court. Yet even the federal district courts can resist their superiors because every judge has great discretion. He can hear a case promptly—or delay the hearing. He can grant a motion for an injunction preventing public officials from pursuing some course of action—or he can deny it. He can give a favored position to the motions of one side—or he can favor those of the other side.

Curbing the Court

These undramatic internal checks of the federal and state "judicial bureaucracy" are probably the most effective limits on the Court's power. In addition, there are five ways in which interests disappointed with its decisions can seek to have them reversed.

1. Amending the Constitution

Judicial decisions on basic constitutional questions can be changed by the amending process. This is such a formidable undertaking that it is rarely feasible. In fact, the difficulty of amending the Constitution is one reason that the Court plays such a significant role in constitutional interpretation. Only three decisions of the Court have ever been reversed by constitutional amendment and none since 1914. Nevertheless, when all other measures have failed, critics of the Court have not hesitated to seek constitutional changes. In recent years the Court's rulings in the *Reapportionment*

---

[37] *NAACP* v. *Alabama,* 377 U.S. 288 (1964).

Cases and on the subject of public school prayers have stimulated unsuccessful campaigns for new amendments.

2. Changing the Court's composition

In the normal course of events the composition of the Court changes as judges retire or die. Like the amending process it can be frustratingly slow. During the 1968 presidential campaign George Wallace, the third-party candidate, made criticism of the Supreme Court one of his main themes. He proposed a remedy: As attrition takes its toll, he promised to "appoint people differently oriented from those on the present Supreme Court." [38] Yet not all Presidents are fortunate enough to have vacancies to fill. Warren G. Harding made four appointments in two and one-half years; Franklin D. Roosevelt had to wait four years to make his first one.

Understandably, it was Franklin Roosevelt who sought legislation increasing the Court's membership by the addition of one new Justice for each incumbent over the age of seventy who refused to retire. Roosevelt's New Deal, after all, was being systematically voided by a hostile judiciary. As one New Dealer quipped, not only were the "nine old men"—six of them were over seventy—scuttling the reform program, they had also declared the mortality table unconstitutional! Despite Roosevelt's great political popularity, his proposal to remake the Court into an institution more friendly to the New Deal enjoyed little public support, and it was decisively rejected in a Congress heavily controlled by his own party. The Court-packing plan had the appearance of a fundamental attack on American constitutionalism and its separation of powers. Its overwhelming defeat places any similar plan for arbitrarily changing the Court's composition beyond the range of realistic alternatives open to its critics.

One other potential check on the Court's membership is, if anything, even more unworkable. This is the removal of Justices through the impeachment process. Tried early in the history of the Republic, it was found to be an ineffective method for purging Justices whose decisions were politically objectionable. In 1804 the Jeffersonian Republicans sought to oust Justice Samuel Chase, who really appeared vulnerable: he had used his charges to juries as occasions for delivering Federalist speeches. Chase was impeached but acquitted, and President Jefferson rightly concluded that impeachment for political reasons was a "scarecrow" and "a farce which will not be tried again." [39]

Presidents nevertheless gradually shape the Court's composition by their appointments as vacancies occur. Between 1968 and 1972, Richard Nixon made different appointments than Hubert Humphrey would have made. After eight years the effect of a President's choices will almost surely be reflected in the general direction and emphasis of court rulings. In the long run, though not in the short, the Court's composition can be significantly changed.

[38] *Christian Science Monitor,* October 12–14, 1968.
[39] Warren, op. cit., I, 295. Since 1789 only nine federal judges have been impeached. Four were convicted and one resigned.

3. Reenacting legislation

When one of its laws has been declared unconstitutional, Congress (or a state legislature) may respond by repassing the law in slightly altered form. In some cases minor retailoring will eliminate the constitutional defect. Reenacting a law can also serve as an effective demonstration of how resolutely Congress and President desire a particular legislative program. It is in effect an urgent request that the Justices reconsider their position. The final power of constitutional interpretation, however, remains in judicial hands. After the Court struck down the National Industrial Recovery Act in 1935, Congress reenacted essentially the same scheme for industrial regulation in the coal industry: within a year the Guffey Coal Act also lay dead at the Court's feet. One year later, however, the Court reversed its position and began to sustain the New Deal legislation.

A much more common type of interplay between the judicial and the executive and the legislative branches takes place when the Court makes unwelcome statutory interpretations. Congress may then amend the law in order to erase the judicial gloss. In the intricate field of federal taxation the Court must often answer questions about the meaning of the internal revenue code that did not occur to Congress when it passed the disputed section. Once the Court has made an interpretation, the administration and the revenue-raising committees of Congress may decide that corrective legislation is needed. Such judicial-legislative interaction is fairly routine and usually does not imply congressional annoyance with the Court.

In other legislative fields congressional action may be a reaction to unpopular judicial decisions. Thus, in 1953 Congress passed legislation reversing Supreme Court decisions of the previous decade that had assigned title to the rich oil fields within three miles of the California, Florida, Louisiana, and Texas coasts of the United States. The Submerged Lands Act fulfilled one of the states' rights pledges of the Republican party made in the 1952 presidential campaign, and it demonstrated that if interests disaffected with legislative decisions can appeal to the courts, so also can interests disaffected with judicial decisions appeal to the legislature. More recently, in 1966, Congress passed a Bank Merger Act sharply qualifying *United States* v. *Philadelphia Bank* (1963), a ruling by the Supreme Court that interpreted the federal antitrust laws as being applicable to national banks. The Bank Merger Act of 1966 immunized from further antitrust prosecution three major bank mergers consummated prior to the 1963 decision, and it required that mergers arranged subsequent to the decision be judged according to standards that permit anticompetitive mergers when these are "in the public interest" in meeting the "convenience and needs of the community." (The federal courts, however, still have discretion to evaluate whether or not a particular merger is in the public interest.) Not surprisingly, the banking industry was a major influence behind the Bank Merger Act. The American Bankers Association, which represents virtually all United States banks, campaigned vigorously for it, and two of the three banks directly exempted by the law, the Manufacturers Hanover Trust of New York and the Continental-Illinois National Bank and Trust Company of Chicago, engaged lobbyists to work for its passage. Among the hired lobbyists was former Representative Albert Rains of Alabama, who until 1965 had been the second-ranking Democrat on the House Banking and Currency Committee.[40]

Such reversals of Court decisions are not uncommon. Between 1945 and 1957 Congress passed legislation correcting the Court's statutory interpretations forty-seven times; twenty-six of these were in the field of taxation, where the intricate and frequently ambiguous or contradictory nature of the federal tax laws makes judicial interpretation especially difficult. One study of these 1945–1957 reversals in the nontax area concluded that they restored a "common understanding" existing prior to the Court's decision. Nearly all of these understandings, moreover, enjoyed almost unanimous support from strong and articulate interest groups.[41]

A later study for the period 1957 to 1961 found that Congress reversed the Court in forty of forty-four legislative decisions involving twenty-seven judicial rulings. (Some of the legislative decisions took the form of bills passing the two houses in differing versions that were not reconciled in conference committee and did not finally become law.) This second study empirically tested and confirmed the earlier conclusion that Court decisions are most likely to be reversed by Congress when this objective is supported with near unanimity by the politically articulate interest groups concerned with the issue area.[42] Naturally, when judicial statutory interpretations produce mixed interest-group reactions—by far the most common situation—disaffected interests find it difficult to obtain a congressional reversal. Congress does not easily place its imprimatur on controversial legislation. Important as it is, congressional correction of judicial interpretations is scarcely a day-to-day remedy for curbing a politically errant Court.

4. Defying or evading the ruling

The Supreme Court can also be curbed informally by resistance to the enforcement of its policies, a practice that usually involves collusion between disaffected public officials and a large number of aggrieved persons more or less directly affected by the decision and thus able to resist it. These circumstances develop only in spectacular cases with broad political consequences, and they are infrequent: if they were common it would imply a severe pathology in the legal-political system. Such resistance did of course succeed in nullifying the *School Segregation* decision for nearly a decade in the southern states, and political scientists have examined other instances in which public defiance has curtailed the implementation of a controversial judicial policy.[43]

[40] *Congressional Quarterly,* January 28, 1966, pp. 286–288; February 11, 1966, pp. 357–359.

[41] Note, "Congressional Reversal of Supreme Court Decisions: 1945–1957," *Harvard Law Review,* LXXI (May, 1958), 1324–1327. The study designated as reversals those bills that passed Congress, regardless of whether or not the President approved them.

[42] Harry P. Stumpf, "Congressional Response to Supreme Court Rulings: The Interaction of Law and Politics," *Journal of Public Law,* XIV (1965), 377–395.

[43] For a model study of this type see Frank J. Sorauf, "*Zorach* v. *Clauson:* The Impact of a Supreme Court Decision," *American Political Science Review,* LIII (September, 1959), 777–791.

One recent instance of substantial, though by no means total, resistance to a Supreme Court decision involves the refusal of many local communities to obey the ruling in *Abington Township* v. *Schempp* (1963) against the constitutionality of Bible-reading exercises in the public schools. The study summarized in Table 9.1 shows the impact of *Schempp* within approximately a year of the decision in states where Bible reading had been required or, alternatively, was permitted; in these latter states the study categorized the extent of pre-*Schempp* Bible reading either as being widespread, occurring in about half of a state's schools, or being only a scattered practice. Clearly, *Schempp's* impact was mixed. In only five states had Bible exercises ended completely, though they had been substantially reduced in fourteen others. With the failure of various attempts to reverse formally the Court's ruling through a constitutional amendment, this pattern of mixed resistance may gradually decline, though it still persists in most southern states.

5. Curtailing the Court's jurisdiction

Article III of the Constitution assigns appellate power over all federal questions to the Supreme Court—subject to "such exceptions, and under such regulations as the Congress shall make." Here is the judicial Achilles heel. It enables Congress to confer, and hence to withdraw, virtually all of the Supreme Court's power to hear significant cases. The jurisdictional sanction has been used only once, but on that occasion it worked with deadly effectiveness. In 1868 the Supreme Court was considering, under a jurisdictional grant to review certain types of circuit court judgements, a Mississippi case challenging the validity of the congressional program for

Table 9.1 *The impact of* Schempp *in states where Bible reading took place in the public schools* *

Before *Schempp*		After *Schempp*			
Extent of practice		Practice completely stopped	Practice all but stopped	Practice continues as before	Practice unknown
Required	(9)	4 (44%)	2 (22%)	3 (33%)	—
Widespread	(9)	1 (11%)	4 (44%)	1 (11%)	3 (33%)
About half	(3)	—	3 (100%)	—	—
Scattered	(8)	—	5 (62.5%)	2 (25%)	1 (12.5%)
Totals	(29)	5 (17%)	14 (48%)	6 (21%)	4 (14%)

Source: Ellis Katz, "Patterns of Compliance with the Schempp Decision," *Journal of Public Law*, XIV (1965), p. 402.
* The study is based on responses to questionnaires sent out to the chief educational officers of each state, forty-one usable questionnaires were returned. Numbers in the table refer to states.

reconstructing the South. These were days of bitter sectional feeling, and the Radical Republican Congress suspected the Court of being pro-southern. Afraid that the case would be the vehicle for invalidating the Reconstruction laws, Congress quickly passed a law that repealed the Court's authority to hear cases of its type. The next year, despite the fact that the Mississippi case had already been argued and was awaiting decision, the Supreme Court bowed: it ruled that Congress's action ended its power to decide the case.[44]

Nearly one hundred years later a group of Congressmen, supported by an essentially conservative coalition of interest groups, again sought to attack the Court along the jurisdictional avenue. During the 1956 and 1957 terms the Warren Court issued a number of highly controversial decisions. The Court interpreted federal laws as superseding state antisubversion laws, and it seemingly cast the pall of unconstitutionality on congressional investigations of subversive activity.[45] It also interpreted a federal antisubversion law, the Smith Act, in such a way as to make it almost impossible to prosecute Communists.[46] In another case the Court handed down an interpretation of a federal law for the District of Columbia that gave added protection to criminal suspects.[47] These decisions antagonized those who insisted on a strict internal security program and who favored a "tough" line in criminal law enforcement. They also gave southern Congressmen, who were aroused over the *Brown* v. *Board of Education* decision, a convenient outlet for their anger.

The Court's critics responded with a powerful two-pronged attack. They proposed legislation revising the judicial statutory interpretations and reasserting a broad congressional power to investigate. They also sought to change the Court's jurisdiction so as to eliminate its authority to decide certain types of civil liberty cases. These proposals, which constituted the most severe attack on the Court since Franklin Roosevelt's war with the nine old men, won partial approval in the House. In the Senate, however, the proposals were beaten back, thanks largely to the deft maneuvering of the then Majority Leader, Lyndon B. Johnson.

The threat of congressional retaliation probably made an impact on the Court. Two of the Justices (Frankfurter and Harlan) who in 1957 had voted to limit congressional investigations and to restrict state antisubversion programs shifted their position in similar cases decided in 1959. As a consequence, the Court, by 5 to 4 margins, asserted that Congress had a broad investigatory power and that the states could also protect themselves against subversive activity.[48] In 1961, and again by a 5 to 4 vote, the Court refused to declare the McCarran (Internal Security) Act unconstitutional.[49]

As in the case of other controversial legislation that divides powerful political interests, it is difficult for Congress to limit the Court's established jurisdiction. Ever

---

[44] *Ex parte McCardle,* 7 Wallace 506 (1869).

[45] *Pennsylvania* v. *Nelson,* 350 U.S. 497 (1956); *Watkins* v. *United States,* 345 U.S. 178 (1957).

[46] *Yates* v. *United States,* 354 U.S. 298 (1957).

[47] *Mallory* v. *United States,* 352 U.S. 449 (1957).

[48] *Barenblatt* v. *United States,* 360 U.S. 109 (1959); *Uphaus* v. *Wyman,* 360 U.S. 72 (1959).

[49] *Communist Party* v. *Subversive Activities Control Board,* 367 U.S. 1 (1961).

since the attacks on the Warren Court began in 1957, liberally inclined Congressmen, scholars, and newspaper editors have been arguing that punitive changes in its jurisdictional authority violate the Constitution. Those who make this argument go on to claim that the Court's retreat during the 1868 jurisdictional attack was "an unfortunate episode in our history." [50]

Were Congress to pass legislation denying *any* form of relief in *any* federal court in cases in which federal rights were allegedly denied, the Supreme Court might declare it unconstitutional. Even here there is an area of doubt because Congress has historically exercised full dominion over the jurisdiction of the federal courts; the Constitution, moreover, is quite explicit in conferring this power on Congress. At the very least, it would seem that Congress can reenact controversial legislation and simultaneously strip the Supreme Court of *its* jurisdiction. The sanction is clumsy, because it could lead to conflicting interpretations by the coordinate circuit courts. It is nevertheless an effective means for curbing—or at least for threatening to curb—a politically maverick Court.

From Warren to Burger: From Bold Reform to Judicial Restraint?

Chief Justice Earl Warren resigned after the 1968 term of the Court. An era ended. The Warren Court for sixteen years had probably been the most activist and controversial one in the nation's history. It was the Court—not Congress—that had been a major catalyst of reform. The Court had taken on the role of national conscience, handing down decisions that attempted to correct social and political inequities. It was the Court that ordered an end to segregation in public schools, trains, buses, parks, and other public facilities. It was also the Court—not Congress or the state legislatures—that revised many provisions in the code of criminal justice to strengthen the rights of the criminally accused. Finally, it was the Court —not Congress—that virtually rewrote the representative laws of the political system by its famous reapportionment decisions.

After his retirement, Chief Justice Warren called his ruling that "one man's vote should mean as much as another man's," the most important decision in his Court career. If people have equal representation in government, Warren said, they can solve most problems "through the political process rather than through the courts." Critics frequently disagreed. Judges, they argued, are beyond the reach of the elected political leaders and, therefore, should leave such matters as reapportionment to the political process. Few observers, however, could dispute that the Supreme Court had been a creative force in American law and politics. Chief Justice Earl Warren had played a major role in making a revolution—a legal revolution to be sure, but one that made fundamental changes in shaping the national destiny.

[50] A group of prominent legal scholars in a statement issued to combat attempts to limit the Court's jurisdiction in the wake of the *Reapportionment* decisions. *The New York Times,* August 10, 1964.

Professor Philip B. Kurland offers two possible interpretations of Chief Justice Earl Warren and the Court he symbolized.

. . . if a great Chief Justice is one who presided over a Court that has written, and repealed large segments of the law of the land—constitutional as well as statutory and judicial—then Warren clearly qualifies for the accolade. If, on the other hand, reliance is to be placed on Warren's individual contributions to American jurisprudence as revealed in his opinions, it will be difficult indeed to justify such laurels.[51]

Kurland cautions students not to attribute great power, or responsibility, to Earl Warren for the Court's work. There is no evidence, he argues, that indicates that Chief Justice Warren's power went beyond his one vote. Unlike two of his predecessors, Harlan Fiske Stone and Charles Evans Hughes, Warren was not regarded as an intellectual or forensic superior of any of his brethren. He does not appear to have had the force or sagacity to draw his brethren together. The members of the Court probably shaped the Chief Justice rather than vice versa. Kurland's critical appraisal concludes with two admonitions: do not confuse Earl Warren the Chief Justice with the institution that he presided over; and do not lionize him.

Another scholar presents a more laudatory critique of the Court. Archibald Cox, a former Solicitor General, offers a personal evaluation of the Warren era.

. . . I am confident that historians will write that the trend of decisions during the 1950's and 1960's was in keeping with the mainstream of American history—a bit progressive but also moderate, a bit humane but not sentimental, a bit idealistic but seldom doctrinaire, and in the long run essentially pragmatic—in short, in keeping with the true genius of our institutions.

But my view is deeply prejudiced. One who has sat in the Supreme Court almost daily awaiting oral argument or the delivery of opinions acquires both admiration and affection for the Court and for all the justices. The problems with which they deal are so difficult, the number and variety of cases are so overwhelming, the implications are so far-reaching, that one sits humbled by the demands upon them. That the institution of constitutional adjudication works so well on the whole is testimony not only to the genius of the institution but to the wisdom and courage of the individual justices.[52]

The bold reforms and judicial activism of the Warren Court are briefly outlined in Table 9.2 in three major categories—reapportionment, criminal due process, and race relations. There were other constitutional conflicts, such as freedom of religion, in which important decisions were made, but the three areas mentioned comprise the foundations of the Warren Court's legacy.

The decisions summarized in Table 9.2 provoked criticism from many quarters. Richard Nixon was one of the most prominent and outspoken critics of the Warren Court, especially in the explosive area of criminal due process. As the Carswell case study demonstrates, he had campaigned for the Presidency on a pledge to

---

[51] "Earl Warren, The Warren Court and the Warren Myths," *Michigan Law Review,* LXVIII, pp. 353–358.

[52] *The Warren Court* (Cambridge: Harvard University Press, 1968), p. 133. See also Anthony Lewis, "Earl Warren," in Leon Friedman and Fred L. Israel, *The Justices of the Supreme Court 1789–1969,* Vol. IV (New York: Chelsea, 1969), pp. 2721–2736.

change the Court by appointing conservative justices. He had told many audiences that the Court had gone too far in weakening law-enforcement agencies. "Coddling criminals" and "hamstringing" the forces of law and order must cease. Nixon said he would correct this permissiveness by using two criteria for judicial selection: "strict interpretation" of the Court's role and a thorough versing in criminal law and procedure. Even as President, he has frankly stated that he wanted men who reflected his political and judicial philosophy. With Earl Warren's retirement, he had his first opportunity to put his philosophy into practice. The appointment of a new Chief Justice was, according to the President, the

most important that a president makes. Our history tells us that the Chief Justices have probably had more profound and lasting influence on their times and on the direction of the nation than most Presidents have had.[53]

President Nixon chose Warren Earl Burger, who had been a judge for thirteen years on the United States Court of Appeals for the District of Columbia. The fifteenth Chief Justice of the United States was sixty-one years old, a "strict constructionist," and a "conservative" on questions of criminal law. Burger had a reputation as a man opposed to judicial activism. He had publicly criticized the Warren Court's criminal due process decisions saying that some of the "bitterness" in society can be laid at the Supreme Court's doorstep.

Burger was confirmed by the Senate on June 9, 1969, by a vote of 74 to 3. An interesting example of his judicial philosophy—and one which provides a contrast with his predecessor—is found in the *Powell* v. *McCormack* [54] decision. The late Representative Adam Clayton Powell, a flamboyant New York Democrat—and one of the few black men in Congress—was excluded by a Select Committee of the House from taking his seat in the Ninetieth Congress for embezzling money. The case was heard on appeal from a three-judge court of appeals for the District of Columbia. Warren Burger was Chief Judge of this court and had been the author of an opinion that denied federal jurisdiction. For Burger the central question was one of justiciability—whether the Court should choose to decide the matter. His answer was No. The Court should stay out of the "political thicket." Chief Justice Warren disagreed. Warren, writing for a seven-man majority with Justice Potter Stewart dissenting, reversed the lower court. He wrote that the "House was powerless to exclude any Member-elect who met" the constitutional obligations. Both Warren and Burger agreed that the federal courts had the jurisdiction to act. The disagreement was over whether this jurisdiction should be exercised. The *Powell* case illustrated the different judicial philosophies of the two jurists. A change of Chief Justices, or one decision, does not necessarily forecast a curbing of the expansive attitude of the Warren Court. Yet, unexpected changes followed Warren's resignation.

On May 14, 1969, Justice Abe Fortas resigned from the Supreme Court, becom-

[53] "A New Chief Justice: A New Court Era," *Congressional Quarterly Weekly Report,* May 23, 1969, pp. 797–800.
[54] *Powell* v. *McCormack,* 395 U.S. 486 (1968).

Table 9.2 *Significant Warren Court decisions in three areas: Reapportionment, criminal law, and race relations, 1953–1969*

REAPPORTIONMENT

Baker v. *Carr,* 369 U.S. 186 (1963)

The Supreme Court held that federal courts might properly hear and decide cases on whether state legislatures are fairly apportioned. State failure to apportion seats in state legislatures to correspond to population shifts constitutes denial of equal protection of the law.

Gray v. *Sanders,* 372 U.S. 368 (1963)

Political equality means "one man, one vote."

Wesberry v. *Sanders,* 376 U.S. 1 (1964)

The "one man, one vote" rule applies to congressional districts. States must realign congressional districts to have "as nearly as practicable" equal population.

Reynolds v. *Sims,* 377 U.S. 533 (1964)

The "one man, one vote" rule applies to both houses of state legislatures.

Kirkpatrick v. *Preisler,* 394 U.S. 526 (1969)

States must strive to create congressional districts with precisely equal populations. Any variance from the mathematical average must be justified by the state.

CRIMINAL DUE PROCESS

Elkins v. *U. S.,* 364 U.S. 206 (1960)

Evidence obtained during any illegal search is not admissible in federal courts.

Mapp v. *Ohio,* 367 U.S. 643 (1961)

Evidence obtained by illegal search and seizure cannot be used in state prosecutions.

Escobedo v. *Illinois,* 378 U.S. 478 (1964)

An accusatorial investigation by police—without allowing the defendant counsel and advising the defendant of his right to remain silent—is unconstitutional.

Miranda v. *Arizona,* 384 U.S. 436 (1966)

Before questioning a suspect in custody, police must advise him of his right to remain silent and to have a lawyer—and provide one if he is indigent—and delay questioning until a lawyer is present. No confession can be used in court unless police comply with these rules.

In Re Gault, 387 U.S. 1 (1967)

Juvenile defendants must be given the same due process protections as those given adults.

Katz v. *U.S.,* 389 U.S. 347 (1967).
Electronic eavesdropping is unconstitutional as authorized in a New York state law. Police must obtain a warrant before using electronic surveillance, even if no physical trespass is involved.

Duncan v. *Louisiana,* 391 U.S. 145 (1968)
The Fourteenth Amendment extended the right to trial by jury to states in all cases in which federal courts would grant the right to jury trial.

Terry v. *Ohio,* 392 U.S. 1 (1968)
On reasonable suspicion but without probable cause for arrest, police officers may detain a citizen briefly on the street and search him for weapons.

Alderman and Aldesasio v. *U.S.,* 394 U.S. 165 (1969)
Defendants may examine the entire record of illegal electronic surveillance without preliminary screening of that record by the judge.

RACE RELATIONS

Brown v. *Board of Education of Topeka,* 347 U.S. 483 (1954)
"Separate education facilities" for white and Negro pupils are "inherently unequal" in denial of the equal protection of the laws guaranteed by the Fourteenth Amendment.

Brown v. *Board of Education,* 349 U.S. 294 (1955)
Local school officials must move "with all deliberate speed" to end segregation in public schools.

Gomillion v. *Lightfoot,* 364 U.S. 339 (1960)
Political redistricting along racial lines violates the Fifteenth Amendment.

Peterson v. *Greenville,* 377 U.S. 244 (1963)
Private segregation practices under a city ordinance or a city executive requiring segregation constitutes unconstitutional state action.

Anderson v. *Martin,* 375 U.S. 399 (1964)
A state requirement that a candidate's race be noted on the ballot violates the equal protection clause of the Fourteenth Amendment.

Griffin v. *Prince Edward County School Board,* 377 U.S. 218 (1964)
There had been "entirely too much deliberation and not enough speed" in school desegregation. The closing of schools to avoid desegregation is unconstitutional, in violation of the equal protection clause of the Fourteenth Amendment.

Harper v. *Virginia State Board of Elections,* 383 U.S. 663 (1966)
Poll taxes in state elections are unconstitutional in violation of the Fourteenth Amendment.

Jones v. *Mayer,* 392 U.S. 409 (1968)
The Civil Rights Act of 1866 prohibited all racial discrimination, private or public, in the sale or rental of property.

ing the first man in history to leave the Court under public pressure and threat of impeachment. Careless personal dealings, such as a suspicious connection with a stock embezzler, led to strong congressional pressure to institute impeachment proceedings. Fortas resigned to save the Court—and perhaps himself—from a damaging political battle.

Within six months of becoming President, Richard Nixon had his second Supreme Court vacancy to fill. His efforts to fill Abe Fortas's vacant seat were frustrated not once but twice by strong Senate opposition. On November 21, Clement R. Haynsworth was defeated, and less than six months later, on April 8, Nixon's second choice, G. Harrold Carswell, was also denied Senate confirmation. A point that merits repetition is that President Nixon believed that the defeat of his two nominees—both southerners—was due largely to the prejudice of northern Senators. This was not only "regional discrimination," according to the President, but it denied him an electoral mandate to reconstitute the Supreme Court as a more conservative body.

President Nixon's third nominee to fill Fortas's seat was Judge Harry A. Blackmun from the Eighth Circuit Court of Appeals. Like the two previous nominees, Blackmun was a "strict constructionist" who came from the federal appeals bench. His credentials, however, were impeccable and public debate over his confirmation was minimal. On May 12, 1970, the Senate unanimously voted to confirm Blackmun's appointment. For the first time since the Hughes Court a majority of the justices had been appointed by Republican Presidents. Mr. Blackmun was an old and close friend of the new Chief Justice. Burger was alleged to have urged his nomination on the Attorney General. Their common background, judicial philosophy, and geographical roots led some to dub the pair the "Minnesota twins."

Within two years, the Burger Court began to reveal a distinctive character and judicial philosophy. Under Burger's predecessor, Earl Warren, there had been a fairly consistent majority of six justices who had sought to broaden the rights of criminal defendants, consisting of the Chief Justice and Justices Fortas, Douglas, Marshall, Brennan, and Black. With Warren and Fortas replaced by Burger and Blackmun, this liberal majority disappeared. The pattern that is slowly emerging is the "Burger majority," composed of the Chief Justice, Justice Blackmun, and three Justices who were frequent dissenters during the Warren era—John Harlan, Potter Stewart, and Byron White.

An indication of a new pattern of decisions—though certainly not a sharp change of direction—is seen in the area of criminal law. During the last term of Chief Justice Warren, 1968–1969, the Court heard and decided twenty-six appeals that came under the heading of "criminal law and procedure" as listed in the legal periodical *United States Law Week*. The prosecution won only eight (31 per cent). By the end of Chief Justice Burger's first term, however, twenty-nine cases in the criminal area had been heard on appeal and the prosecution had won eighteen (62 per cent). More significantly, the cases decided after Burger became Chief Justice dealt with the conduct of trials rather than efforts to control police behavior through procedural rules. A study by the American Jewish Congress of civil rights and civil liberties decisions of the Supreme Court after Warren Burger's first year as Chief Justice revealed that individual claims were recognized in slightly more than 50 per cent of the cases compared to 81 per cent during the last year under former Chief Justice Warren. The new Chief Justice differed with his brethren on civil rights and civil liberties appeals. Of the fifty-two appeals studied, Burger favored persons asserting constitutional rights sixteen times—or in 31 per cent of the cases. This was the lowest percentage of any Justice and contrasted the most sharply with Justice Douglas, who voted for the person asserting constitutional rights in forty-one of the cases (79 per cent).

By contrast, the first case under Chief Justice Burger clearly announced that there would be no retreat from the Warren Court's famous school desegregation decisions. In a one-paragraph per curiam opinion, the Court announced that the "all deliberate speed" decision of 1955 was replaced with an order to integrate "at once."

Tho quootion prooontod io ono of paramount importance, involving as it does the denial of fundamental rights to many thousands of school children, who are presently attending Mississippi schools under segregated conditions contrary to the applicable decisions of this Court. Against this background the Court of Appeals should have denied all motions for additional time because continued operation of segregated schools under a standard allowing "all deliberate speed" for desegregation is no longer constitutionally permissible. Under explicit holdings of this Court the obligation of every school district is to terminate dual school systems at once and to operate now and hereafter only unitary schools.[55]

The message in *Alexander* v. *Board of Education* (1970) was unmistakable: integrate now, litigate later. The new standard of immediate compliance affected fourteen districts in five southern states and about 300,000 children.

A case more indicative of the new direction toward judicial restraint is found in the area of criminal law. Over one third of the cases disposed of by full opinion in the 1971 term of the Court dealt with criminal matters. It is in this sensitive area that Chief Justice Burger is particularly forceful in stressing that "policy is not the business of judges." It is here that the Chief Justice wants to "lower the profile of the Supreme Court." In *Harris* v. *New York* [56] the Court, in a 5 to 4 decision, limited the famous *Miranda* v. *Arizona* decision. Chief Justice Burger, who wrote the majority opinion, held that statements made by defendants could be used in trial— so long as they were voluntary—to impeach a defendant's creditability if he should contradict that statement when testifying in his own behalf. Justices Blackmun, Harlan, Stewart, and White (the latter three dissenters in *Miranda*) joined the Chief Justice in his opinion. The *Miranda* doctrine, wrote Chief Justice Burger, "cannot be perverted into a license to use perjury." The benefits of exposing false testimony outweigh "the speculative possibility that impermissible police conduct will be encouraged" by this holding. The decision upheld the narcotics conviction of a New York man, Vivien Harris. After his arrest, Harris gave a statement to the police, who had not warned him of his rights. At his trial, Harris contradicted this statement from the witnooo otand. Tho prooeoutor admittod that tho pretrial otatement was inadmissible as evidence but argued that it could be used to point out that the

[55] 369 U.S. 19 (1969).
[56] 401 U.S. 222 (1971).

defendant had perjured himself. Five justices—the "Burger Majority" agreed, with Brennan, Marshall, Black, and Douglas dissenting. Justice Brennan's vigorous dissent stated that the *Harris* decision "goes far toward undoing much of the progress made in conforming police methods to the Constitution."

Even the shift to a less activist role in criminal law decisions has some notable exceptions, suggesting that the change in judicial direction may be partial rather than total. For example, in *Whiteley* v. *Warden* the Court ruled that it was unconstitutional for police to arrest someone on the basis of information broadcast over a police radio when the information had been considered insufficient by a judge for grounds to issue an arrest warrant. In another search and seizure case, *Bivens* v. *Six Unknown Agents of the Federal Bureau of Narcotics,* the Court held that if a person's constitutional rights had been violated by federal agents acting in their official capacity, then grounds exist for a damage suit against the government. The *Bivens* decision, decided by a 6 to 3 vote, however, drew a dissent from Chief Justice Burger, who contended that Congress alone could create a damage remedy against the federal government:

We would surely preserve the important values of the doctrine of separation of powers—and perhaps get a better result—by recommending a solution to the Congress. . . . Legislation is the business of the Congress, and it has the facilities and competence for that task—and we do not.[57]

The philosophy of judicial self-restraint, which holds that cases should be decided on the narrowest possible grounds and that the Court should shy away from politically entangling cases, is central to the thinking of Chief Justice Burger. He has championed a twin theme of judicial self-restraint and judicial reform in his off-the-bench activities, which stand in sharp contrast to Earl Warren's judicial activism. Improvements in criminal and civil procedure, Burger maintains, should be done by Congress or state legislatures because "judicial decision is the worst possible way to do it." Similarly, he has cautioned against the needless overburdening of the federal courts, proposing that Congress eliminate direct appeals from three-judge Federal District Courts to the Supreme Court. In his second "State of the Judiciary" address to the American Bar Association in July, 1971, Chief Justice Burger said that the Court was confronted with 1,100 cases in 1940, and 1,300 in 1950, but in the 1971 term, more than 4,000 cases were filed. Figures on the increase in the number of cases disposed of by the Supreme Court over a three-year period are found in Table 9.3. In almost every category there has been a sharp increase from 1968 to 1970 in the number of cases decided. According to the Chief Justice, "either the quantity or quality of the work of the Court must soon yield to the realities."

Whether the "quality or quantity" of the Court's work will change is open to question. But the addition of two Nixon appointees indicates that there will be some changes in the direction in the pattern of Supreme Court decision-making even though there has, so far, been no pronounced movement toward judicial self-restraint. "Our Constitution," Justices Black and Douglas wrote in a recent dissent,

[57] *Criminal Law Reporter,* IX (June 23, 1971), 3195.

Table 9.3 *The number of cases filed, disposed of, and remaining on dockets at conclusion of October terms, 1968, 1969, and 1970*

	Original			Appellate			Miscellaneous			Totals		
	1968	1969	1970	1968	1969	1970	1968	1969	1970	1968	1969	1970
Number of cases on docket	9	15	20	1,559	1,758	1,903	2,350	2,429	2,289	3,918	4,204	4,212
Number disposed of during term	0	5	7	1,288	1,433	1,613	1,863	1,971	1,802	3,151	3,409	3,422
Number remaining on docket	9	10	13	271	325	290	487	458	487	767	793	790

	Terms		
	1968	1969	1970
Cases argued during term	140	144	151
Number disposed of by full opinions	116	105	126
Number disposed of by per curiam opinions	14	21	22
Number set for reargument the following term	10	18	3
Cases granted review this term	135	150	161
Cases reviewed and decided without oral argument	130	113	192
Total cases to be available for argument at outset of following term	73	94	107

Source: United States Law Week, XL (July 13, 1971), p. 3035.

"was not written in the sands to be washed away by each wave of new judges blown in by each successive political wind which brings new political administrations into temporary power." Yet, as those two veterans of different political winds fully realize, political changes have come in the past—and they will certainly come in the future.

Strong—and unexpected—indications of future changes occurred in September, 1971. Two judicial giants—Justice Hugo L. Black and Justice John Marshall Harlan—suddenly resigned from the Court. Both were compelled to leave the bench because of serious illness. Both Justices were men of stature, craftsmen of the law, who had served long and distinguished careers. White House sources indicated that the two vacancies would be filled by a southern conservative and a woman—a first in the Court's history.

The President's nominees to fill the Court's vacant seats have been widely criticized for lacking legal, scholarly, or personal stature. Two judicial candidates, one of whom was a woman, were even given "unqualified" ratings by the American Bar Association. In order to avert another Senate battle and possible humiliating defeat, President Nixon changed his mind about a woman appointee and nominated two conservative, legally distinguished male lawyers: Lewis F. Powell, Jr., sixty-four years old, from Virginia, and Assistant Attorney General William H. Rehnquist, forty-seven years old, from Arizona.

Appointments to the Supreme Court can become President Nixon's most enduring memorial—one that shapes policy outcomes long after he leaves the White House. Only the future will tell if President Nixon's appointments will endure as a living memorial or provide a legacy of criticism. In any event, what Winston Churchill once called "the most esteemed judicial tribunal in the world" shows no signs of sliding into obscurity.

The Supreme Court and National Majorities

The pages of American history record many attacks on the Supreme Court; most of them failed. When an entire section of the country is strongly hostile to the policy embodied in Court decisions—southern reaction to the desegregation rulings is a recent example—widespread defiance may, at least for a while, nullify the judicial policy. If such defiance persisted for long on a major issue, the entire political system and not just the Supreme Court would be endangered. Despite the initial evasions of *Brown* v. *Board of Education,* federal court decrees ordering desegregation are now being enforced. Equally significant, the Court has gradually picked up overwhelming national support for its antisegregation stand. A 1963 national opinion survey of twelve hundred white people found that nearly two thirds of them approved of the Court's decision.[58] The most impressive evidence of the

[58] William Brink and Louis Harris, *The Negro Revolution in America* (New York: Simon and Schuster, 1964), p. 143. White Americans, however, still resist intensely many Negro civil rights demands. See Ch. 13.

ultimate national acceptance of the *Brown* decision, however, came when Congress enacted the Civil Rights Act of 1964 and the Voting Rights Act of 1965.

On two historic occasions the Supreme Court has been checked. In 1857 its *Dred Scott* decision declared that Congress lacked constitutional power to prevent the spread of slavery into the territories, thereby denying the possibility of using national power to settle the most urgent political problem of the period. It also struck at the raison d'être of the new Republican party, which had been expressly formed to bar slavery from the territories. A specific conflict over *Dred Scott* was never joined, but President Lincoln and the Republican party came to power in 1861 making it absolutely clear that they did not feel themselves limited by the ruling. Significantly, the ensuing Civil War was a time of judicial ebb as the Lincoln Administration played fast and loose with the Constitution's provisions. And it was in the bitter Reconstruction period that the Radical Republican Congress passed the only law ever stripping the Court of its jurisdiction over a line of cases. Not until the 1870's and 1880's did the moderate Waite Court, under the leadership of a prudent Chief Justice, restore judicial prestige.

In 1937 the Supreme Court, which had challenged the constitutionality of the New Deal, was again curbed. Franklin Roosevelt had the strength of his forty-six-state victory over Alfred Landon in 1936, and his Administration's legislation was backed by heavy congressional majorities. As in the *Dred Scott* case, the pre-1937 Court denied Congress and the President the right to use national power to solve national economic and social problems of the first magnitude. Roosevelt lost his battle to increase the Court's membership, but even as Congress was rejecting this plan the Court was backing down. In March, 1937, it began upholding the New Deal legislation. Two months later one of the conservative Justices resigned, providing the President with his long-desired opportunity to infuse the Court with what he described as "new blood."

The *Dred Scott* and New Deal episodes share a common characteristic: on both of these occasions the Justices denied power to national majorities and, more specifically, threatened the institutional prerogatives of Congress and the President. The Court, apparently, has learned the lessons of the *Dred Scott* case and of the New Deal period. During World War II it sanctioned the forcible evacuation of more than 100,000 West Coast Japanese and their internment in concentration camps euphemistically labeled as "relocation centers." It is now uniformly agreed that these events were the ignoble consequence of a massive national racial prejudice against the Japanese-Americans. In the middle of a global conflict, however, the Supreme Court placed discretion over valor and weakly acquiesced in a presidential policy (strongly supported in Congress) rooted in the hatreds and fears of wartime.[59] That the Court risks retaliation when it challenges the other branches of the federal government on major policy issues is clear enough. The intensity of the 1958 attack on the Warren Court, which very nearly prevailed, was primarily motivated by the

---

[59] The two principal Japanese evacuation cases were *Hirabayashi* v. *United States,* 320 U.S. 81 (1943) and *Korematsu* v. *United States,* 323 U.S. 214 (1944).

Court's apparent limitation on one of Congress's most vital powers—the power to investigate.

The Supreme Court is inevitably criticized, for many of the decisions it is asked to make admit of only controversial answers. Because it now consistently imposes *national* constitutional standards on all levels of American government, the modern Court often provokes the ancient cry of states' rights. It has, for example, applied the most important guarantees of the Bill of Rights to both federal and state governments. Its rulings in the *Reapportionment Cases* imposed a national standard on all fifty state legislatures. Although these decisions antagonized many state interests, such interests, by definition, are the interests of one or a few states, and even those are rarely monolithic within a state. Unless the Court profoundly antagonizes a broad coalition of major national interests—in short, a national majority—it suffers little danger of being seriously curbed. An occasional decision or judicial policy may be reversed, or, more likely, qualified, but the Court's fundamental institutional prerogatives are almost certainly secure.

Survey research evidence is also relevant, for it indicates that public knowledge about the Supreme Court's decisions is very low, even in this period of high and often controversial judicial activism. A survey of Wisconsin residents brings out that few people have an accurate idea of even the topics that the Court is confronting. Approximately one quarter of the sample incorrectly attributed to it decisions on urban renewal and the John Birch Society, and approximately 50 per cent made the same mistake on federal aid to education and Medicare. Only the Court's involvement in school segregation and prayers in the public schools seems to have acquired saliency for most persons—in contrast to the low level of knowledge concerning the Court's intervention in two other major policy areas, reapportionment and the rights of the criminally accused. Even though it used an extremely generous definition of "high knowledge," the Wisconsin study found that only 15 per cent of its sample fell into this category of knowledgeability about the Supreme Court. Equally significant, this survey, as well as national opinion polls, reveals that, until recently, the population's overall evaluation of the Supreme Court has generally been favorable. These factors, when coupled with the highly impersonal relationship between judicial decisions and the public's consciousness, may well help to explain the Warren Court's success in gaining compliance with its innovating policy decisions in such areas as legislative apportionment.[60]

Impact of Supreme Court Decisions

"Does anybody know . . . ," the late Justice Felix Frankfurter asked, "where we can go to find light on what the practical consequences of these decisions have been?" An indispensable segment of the judicial process is what happens—if anything— to a Supreme Court ruling after it is handed down. Total or immediate compliance rarely, if ever, occurs. The Court's decisions have been met by a variety of responses,

[60] Kenneth M. Dolbeare, "The Public Views the Supreme Court," in Herbert Jacob, *Law, Politics, and the Federal Courts* (Boston: Little, Brown, 1967), pp. 194–212.

from massive resistance in the case of school desegregation, to evasion in the case of school prayer, to acceptance in the case of reapportionment. The degree to which parties accept a Supreme Court decision is an empirical question—one that can be studied to ascertain if the Court was obeyed, and if so, by whom, and to what extent.[61]

Research on the impact of the *Miranda* v. *Arizona* decision provides several interesting examples of how different police organizations responded to an important change in the law. One study of the impact of the *Miranda* decision stationed observers in police headquarters in New Haven, Connecticut, for an eleven-week period. These observers—Yale Law School students—witnessed 127 police interrogations and conducted 40 interviews with persons who had been interrogated. The purpose of this study was to discover if the *Miranda* decision had had any appreciable effect on the police and/or the suspects. Was law enforcement hampered, as critics charged, because suspects had to be warned of their rights? The bedrock of the decision rests on the Supreme Court's five-man majority's conviction that police intimidation often compels a suspect to incriminate himself. The protections, outlined in the majority opinion, known as the "Miranda warnings" attempt to prevent police intimidation or coercion. These warnings state that a suspect: 1) must be informed of his right to consult a lawyer; 2) is entitled to have a lawyer present during questioning; 3) has a right to remain silent; and if he does say anything, it can and will be used against him; 4) will have a lawyer appointed by the Court, if he cannot afford one; 5) may, if he wishes, remain silent at any time, at which point the interrogation must cease.[62] The authors of the New Haven study found that only 25 out of 118 (21 per cent) suspects received all the warnings listed. Twenty-six (22 per cent) suspects received no warnings at all. This failure to give the "Miranda warnings," according to the authors, was partly attributed to the ignorance of the officers. When detectives did adhere to the letter of *Miranda,* however, they often violated the spirit by changing words, or making the statement appear so routine or bureaucratic that there was a tendency among the suspects to disregard it. An extensive analysis of the data found that warnings were helpful in protecting suspects' rights, but they could not eliminate the "inherently coercive atmosphere" that exists in the police station. An accused person, frightened and confused and in an unfriendly atmosphere, may unwittingly give up his "privilege of silence."

The suspect arrested and brought downtown for questioning is in a crisis-laden situation. The stakes for him are high—often his freedom for a few or many years—and his prospects hinge on decisions that must be quickly made: To cooperate and hope for leniency, to try and talk his way out, to stand adamantly on his rights. . . .

The likely consequences of the alternatives open to him are unclear—how much leniency cooperation may earn, how likely fast talk is to succeed, how much a steadfast

[61] Theodore L. Becker (ed.), *The Impact of Supreme Court Decisions: Empirical Studies* (New York: Oxford U.P., 1969), passim; Richard M. Johnson, *The Dynamics of Compliance* (Evanston, Ill.: Northwestern U.P., 1967), pp. 3–9; Stephen L. Wasby, *The Impact of the United States Supreme Court: Some Perspectives* (Homewood, Ill.: Dorsey, 1970), pp. 28–34.

[62] Michael Wald, Richard Ayres, David Hess, Mark Schantz, and Charles H. Whitebread, II, "Interrogations in New Haven: The Impact of *Miranda," Yale Law Journal,* LXXIV (July, 1967), 1523, 1535, 1568, 1613–1616.

refusal to talk may contribute to a decision by the police, prosecutor or judge to "throw the book" at him.[63]

The authors concluded that "not much has changed after *Miranda*. Despite the dark predictions by the critics of the decision, the impact on law enforcement has been small."

In contrast with the above study, the Institute of Criminal Law and Procedure of the Georgetown University Law Center concentrated on how the *Miranda* decision affected suspects' perceptions of their right to a lawyer. The study was conducted in the District of Columbia. Data were gathered from questionnaires administered to lawyers who had volunteered to assist suspects who had been arrested. Forty per cent of those arrested during 1967 reported that they gave statements to the police. Another central finding was an "astonishing" small number of persons—1,262 out of 15,430, or 7 per cent—who requested the assistance of lawyers. The figure is inflated, because only about half of those arrested were interrogated, but even with this adjustment less than 15 per cent of those interrogated requested counsel. Attorneys were readily available, twenty-four hours a day, seven days a week. Interviews were also conducted with 260 suspects who had been arrested during 1965 and 1966, 175 (67 per cent) of the suspects had been arrested prior to the *Miranda* decision and 85 (33 per cent) had been arrested after *Miranda*. Almost two thirds of the post-*Miranda* suspects who received warnings asked for counsel. Yet, over one third of those interviewed chose not to ask for a lawyer. (Only 2 of the 175 pre-*Miranda* defendants requested a lawyer.) [64] Sixty per cent of the post-*Miranda* defendants who were given warnings gave no statements to the police; 40 per cent, despite the warnings, did give statements. Interviews with 85 post-*Miranda* defendants disclosed that "15 per cent . . . failed to understand the right to silence warning, 18 per cent failed to understand the warning of the right to the presence of counsel, and 24 per cent failed to understand the warning of the right to appoint counsel." A number of defendants expressed cynicism or misunderstanding about the warnings. Some of the defendants thought they were "merely a formality." Typical misinterpretations of the warnings were

> The police "had some lawyer of their own who was working with them."
> It means that "I would have to pay for a lawyer."
> They planned to "appoint someone at court."
> "I just have to write for one and wait for him to answer." [65]

An important lesson that emerges from these defendants' comments speaks directly to the question of Supreme Court impact: the *Miranda* decision and its self-incrimination protections may never reach the suspect in the station house. A suspect, therefore, may not avail himself of his constitutional rights. Why? Two commentators writing about *Miranda* observed,

---

[63] Ibid., pp. 1613–1614.
[64] Richard J. Medalie, Leonard Zeitz, and Paul Alexandes, "Custodial Police Interrogation in Our Nation's Capital: The Attempt to Implement *Miranda*," *Michigan Law Review*, LXIV (May, 1968), 1352–1362.
[65] Ibid., p. 1375.

To predict how a suspect's insistence on his right will affect his chances of avoiding prosecution requires an intimate knowledge of the system which cannot be conveyed by a warning, however improved. . . . The suspect . . . does not know if his request for counsel will annoy the police, the prosecutor or a jury. The fact that he has been warned as required by *Miranda* may have little bearing on his decision whether counsel should be waived. . . . A suspect may well choose not to be a "wise guy" who will land in jail as a reward for his insistence on his rights.[66]

Two additional studies of *Miranda* v. *Arizona* illustrate the variety of responses to the decision. A statistical study conducted in Pittsburgh in 1967 shows a significant decline in the number of suspects that confessed to crimes after the *Miranda* decision. The figures in Table 9.4 reflect a decline of 16.2 per cent in the number of suspects who confessed to crimes before and after *Miranda*. Yet, even with this sharp decline in confessions, the authors found no evidence of a corresponding decline in the conviction rate. Thus "*Miranda* has not impaired significantly the ability of (Pittsburgh) law enforcement agencies to apprehend and convict criminals." [67] Another study of the administration of criminal justice in

[66] Quoted in idem.
[67] Richard H. Seeburger and R. Stanton Wettick, "The Miranda Decision: Effects on Confessions and Convictions," in Norman Johnston, Leonard Savitz, Marvin E. Wolfgang, *The Sociology of Punishment Correction,* 2nd ed. (New York: Wiley, 1970), pp. 112–114, 127.

Table 9.4   *Confession rate among suspects before and after* Miranda

		Number of suspects who confessed	Number of suspects who did not confess	Per cent of suspects who confessed
Homicide	Pre-*Miranda*	54	37	59.3
	Post-*Miranda*	6	13	31.6
Robbery	Pre-*Miranda*	167	106	61.2
	Post-*Miranda*	26	64	28.9
Burglary	Pre-*Miranda*	185	217	46.0
	Post-*Miranda*	37	62	37.4
Auto larceny	Pre-*Miranda*	62	81	43.4
	Post-*Miranda*	3	7	30.0
Sex	Pre-*Miranda*	20	78	20.4
(forcible)	Post-*Miranda*	3	11	21.4
Total	Pre-*Miranda*	488	519	48.5
	Post-*Miranda*	75	157	32.3

Source: See footnote 67.

Illinois found that prosecutors were trying harder, and using more pressure, to get guilty pleas because of the reduced rates of guilty verdicts by judges. The *Miranda* decision had the unexpected result in Illinois of more people pleading guilty, thereby negating the very principle that the case hoped to establish. The problem raised by authors of this study is that the prosecution may be "able to neutralize *Escobedo* and *Miranda* by offering yet more radical charge and sentence reductions." [68]

Although these studies have not provided data that are applicable to the entire nation, three conclusions seem noteworthy: 1) those who have minimized the impact of the *Miranda* decision seem to be correct; 2) suspects still seem to waive their right to remain silent and their right to counsel; 3) and police interrogations are still an important part in the investigation of a crime. These conclusions return us to a fundamental, yet important, point in the study of the judicial process: patterns of compliance (and defiance) with Supreme Court rulings may vary from decision to decision, from community to community, and from station house to station house. Far from being automatic, then, compliance to Supreme Court decisions is a part of the political struggle that hammers out law on the anvil of experience.

Along with the emphasis on studying the impact of Supreme Court decisions, a relatively new generation of scholars has made major contributions to the study of courts and the legal system. Fred Kort, Stuart Nagel, Harold Spaeth, S. Sidney Ulmer, and especially Glendon A. Schubert have stressed statistical techniques to study judicial behavior. These judicial behaviorists employ quantitative methods that lead to the systematic and objective classification of judicial behavior by quantifying such information as attitudes, values, and votes. Mail questionnaires, interviews, attitude surveys, game, factor, and content analysis are used in an effort to lend statistical precision to the study of judges and the judicial process. The judicial behaviorists, for example, study the voting pattern of judges, the conservative/liberal nature of this voting pattern, and the tendency of certain judges to vote together as a bloc on certain issues. In addition, their studies have expanded the frontiers of judicial research. Where once the Supreme Court and its Justices served as the primary laboratory for analysis and study, the contemporary behavioral effort is now directed toward the lower federal courts and the state trial and appellate courts.[69]

Democracy and Judicial Review

Measured against the theory of majoritarian democracy the power of the American Supreme Court is an anachronism. It is, as John P. Roche writes:

a Platonic graft on the democratic process—a group of wise men insulated from the people have the task of injecting truth serum into the body politic, of acting as an institutional

---

[68] Dallin H. Oaks and Warren Lehman, *A Criminal Justice System and the Indigent* (Chicago: University of Chicago, 1968), pp. 80–81.

[69] Students may wish to sample the rich and provocative research of the judicial behaviorists by examining two books: Samuel Krislov, *Judicial Process and Constitutional Law: A Laboratory Manual* (Boston: Little, Brown, 1972), and Walter F. Murphy and Joseph Tanenhaus, *The Study of Public Law* (New York: Random House, 1972).

chaperone to insure that the sovereign populace and its elected representatives do not act unwisely.[70]

This is true enough, but it is beside the point. The government of America, like that of all modern industrial democracies, is characterized by regulatory and social welfare programs and vast bureaucracies to administer them. Tens of thousands of nonelective officials, although nominally subordinate to Congress and President, make significant political decisions. The power of the judges is great, but it is not qualitatively different from that exercised by a Federal Trade Commission examiner or a bureau chief in the Interior Department.

The criticism that the Court's power interferes with the purity of the democratic process skirts the fact that the American political system is one of consensus democracy within a framework of constitutional limitations. Before major innovations in public policy can be adopted they must have the support, or at least acquiescence, of popular and legislative majorities. There are, in addition, certain policies that no majority—no matter how large—can adopt. In the words of Justice Robert Jackson, "One's right to life, liberty, and property, to free speech, a free press, freedom of worship and assembly, and other fundamental rights may not be submitted to vote; they depend on the outcome of no elections." [71]

The American Constitution and the Bill of Rights deliberately place limits on what popular majorities and their governing representatives can do. Yet, to be effective, limitations on government, such as the guarantee that freedom of speech will not be abridged, must have institutional support. The Supreme Court, by reviewing the constitutionality of legislative and executive decisions, serves as the institutional guarantor of those rights and liberties that are beyond public regulation. Its function, therefore, is a logical extension of the belief in constitutional limitations that is a basic feature of the American political culture.

At times judicial review has been used to block the desires of legislative majorities in areas that have little to do with fundamental rights to life, liberty, and property. Particularly in the years between 1895 and 1937 the Supreme Court frequently invalidated federal and state legislation. These decisions were unpopular with certain interests, but it is doubtful whether, with the exception of the Court's conflict with the New Deal, its constitutional policies violated the national consensus. Whenever the Court strikes down a piece of legislation it acts counter to the desires of *some* majority, if only those legislators who voted for the bill. Such judicial invalidation is not, however, necessarily identical to judicial action violating the desires of "the" popular majority; as earlier chapters have noted, in the United States there are often many majorities built around diverse policy issues. Much legislation, moreover, is enacted in response to minority demands in areas where the majority is essentially indifferent.

During much of the period from 1895 to 1937 the majority political preferences

[70] *Courts and Rights: The American Judiciary in Action,* 2nd ed. (New York: Random House, 1966), pp. 121–122.

[71] *West Virginia State Board of Education* v. *Barnette,* 319 U.S. 624, 638 (1943).

of the American nation were oriented to conservative Republicanism, and the Court's conservative posture roughly harmonized with the majority consensus. The year 1895 is often cited as the bench mark indicating the emergence of a Supreme Court committed to a full-blown judicial conservatism. That year the Justices voided the federal income tax law, seriously weakened the Sherman Anti-Trust Act, and allowed business employers to break labor union strikes through the use of judicial injunctions. The Court angered the nation's strong progressive forces, but in the mid-1890's the nation's conservative forces were even stronger: it was, after all, the Republican William McKinley, not the progressive Democrat and "Great Commoner," William Jennings Bryan, who won the historic election of 1896. A famous quip about the Supreme Court is that it follows "the election returns"; it is just as accurate to say that it often anticipates them—and without the aid of Gallup Polls.

The outcome to the constitutional crisis of the 1930's further suggests that the Supreme Court cannot long stand in opposition to the sentiments of dominant majorities on matters that are of urgent interest to the entire nation. As severe as the New Deal crisis was, it lasted for but two years (1935–1936), and it was followed by a complete capitulation on the part of the Court. It is true of course that the decisions of the Court are not easily reversed; yet means do exist for either reversing its decisions or limiting its powers. Congress's authority to regulate the Court's jurisdiction is a healthy potential check. And there is always in the background the possibility of using the amending process if the Justices ever persist in holding to decisions that are in irreconcilable conflict with the ultimate popular consensus.

The school segregation ruling of 1954 was initially controversial, but within ten years the entire nation ratified the principles of *Brown* v. *Board of Education* when it accepted the Civil Rights Act of 1964. Soon after this act was passed the Court found itself in the happy position of giving it the blessing of constitutionality.[72] In a sense the Court's decision upholding the Civil Rights Act confirmed a national policy decision that the Court's own earlier rulings—by giving stimulus to the civil rights movement—had helped to bring about. The decisions in the *Reapportionment Cases,* although also controversial, do not cut against the grain of majoritarian sentiment. Quite the contrary, the "one man, one vote" ruling has elemental popular appeal, especially when it is contrasted with the opposite position, which in effect says "two votes for me, one vote for you." It allows national and state legislatures to make policy in response to majority desires and, not surprisingly, has won the approval of a 3 to 2 majority in the Gallup Poll.

The Supreme Court is controversial. It is a primary arbiter of political conflicts in legal dress, and its decisions interpreting laws and ultimately the Constitution are inescapably political. Because the Court performs political functions, the attacks questioning its decisions and the motives of the Justices are to be expected. Such attacks are really a testimonial to its significant position in the American system of government.

---

[72] *Heart of Atlanta Motel* v. *United States,* 379 U.S. 241 (1964).

During the 1968 presidential campaign George Wallace denounced the Supreme Court as a "sorry outfit" that "ought to be put in its place." [73] If elected, the American Independent candidate promised to work for a constitutional amendment that would require all federal judges to be reconfirmed by the Senate every six to eight years. Yet even Wallace was not above soliciting the aid of a tribunal he supposedly despised. When Ohio's rigid election laws barred Wallace's name from the state ballot, his attorneys successfully carried an appeal to the federal Supreme Court— relying on the legal principles laid down in the "one man, one vote" *Reapportionment* decisions! [74]

Those who sympathize with the Supreme Court's decisions and who value its role in the American democracy may be distressed by the harsh political attacks it engenders. Such attacks, though often abusive and extremely farfetched, are however an inescapable consequence of the Court's intimate involvement in the living political process. A Supreme Court that makes decisions on such vital public subjects as law enforcement, legislative reapportionment, and race relations cannot be—and, in a democracy, should not be—immunized from the oversimplifications of the political marketplace. It is naïve to expect that a Court, which is continually issuing controversial decisions affecting the fortunes of major interest groups, will have its work evaluated according to Marquis of Queensberry rules. Not so long ago, when the pre-1937 Court had an image that was starkly conservative, New Deal Democrats were vehemently denouncing the "heartless" and "reactionary" nine old men. Their language, too, was suited, not to legal journals, but to the tabloid press.

In its history of over one hundred and eighty years the Supreme Court has aroused passionate loves and violent hates. It has rarely stimulated dispassionate and disinterested evaluations of its judicial-political decisions, and the reason is plain. The Supreme Court is a unique judicial tribunal: it responds to the conflicting forces that contend in the American democracy with decisions that mix law and politics, thereby contributing to the formation of national policy and influencing the direction of political change.

[73] *The New York Times,* September 21, 1968.
[74] *Williams* v. *Rhodes,* 37 **LW** 3113 (1968).

suggested additional readings

CASES IN AMERICAN
CONSTITUTIONAL LAW
One of the primary sources for the study
of the American judiciary is the opinions
of the courts in the cases they are asked
to decide. Each state has its own official
case reports, and there are regional
reports, such as the *Southern Reporter,*
which bring the decisions of four to six
states into one volume. The decisions of
the Federal District Courts are reported
in the *Federal Supplement,* and those of
the courts of appeal may be found in
the *Federal Reporter.* United States
Supreme Court decisions are available
in a number of formats; the official
version, published by the Government
Printing Office, is known as the *United
States Reports.*

Students who wish to examine what
American courts have done or said on any
subject or issue should consult *American
Jurisprudence* and *Corpus Juris
Secundum.* These are multivolumed
legal encyclopedias that contain
measured statements on hundreds of
topics. There are, for example, sections
on the law of civil rights or of
corporations. The best shorthand guide
to current American legal developments
is *United States Law Week,* published by
The Bureau of National Affairs
(Washington, D.C.). Among a number
of constitutional law casebooks intended
for students in political science are the
following:

Becker, Theodore L. *Political
Behaviorism and Modern
Jurisprudence.* Chicago: Rand
McNally and Co., 1964.*

Grossman, Joel B. *Lawyers and Judges:
The ABA and the Politics of Judicial
Selection.* New York: John Wiley &
Sons, Inc., 1965.

Jacob, Herbert. *Justice in America:
Courts, Lawyers and the Judicial
Process.* Boston: Little, Brown
and Company, 1965.*

———. *Law, Politics and the Federal
Courts.* Boston: Little, Brown and
Company, 1967.*

Kalven, Harry, Jr., and Hans Zeisel.
The American Jury. Boston:
Little, Brown and Company, 1966.

Lewis, Anthony. *Gideon's Trumpet.*
New York: Random House, Inc.,
1964.*

McCloskey, Robert G. *The American
Supreme Court.* Chicago: University
of Chicago Press, 1960.*

Magrath, C. Peter. *Morrison R. Waite:
The Triumph of Character.* New
York: The Macmillan Company,
1963.

* Available in paperback.

————. *Yazoo: Law and Politics in the New Republic, The Case of* Fletcher v. Peck. New York: W. W. Norton and Company, Inc., 1967.*

Mason, Alpheus T. *Harlan Fiske Stone: Pillar of the Law*. New York: The Viking Press, Inc., 1956.

————, and William M. Beaney. *American Constitutional Law,* 4th ed. Englewood Cliffs, N.J.: Prentice-Hall, Inc., 1968.

Murphy, Walter F., Jr. *Elements of Judicial Strategy*. Chicago: University of Chicago Press, 1964.

————. *Wiretapping on Trial: A Case Study in the Judicial Process*. New York: Random House, Inc., 1965.*

Peltason, Jack W. *Fifty-Eight Lonely Men: Southern Federal Judges and School Desegregation*. New York: Harcourt Brace Jovanovich, Inc., 1961.

Schmidhauser, John R. *The Supreme Court: Its Politics, Personality and Procedures*. New York: Holt, Rinchart and Winston, Inc., 1960.*

Schubert, Glendon A. *Judicial Policy-Making*. Chicago: Scott, Foresman and Company, 1965.

Shapiro, Martin. *Law and Politics in the Supreme Court*. New York: The Free Press, 1964.

10 bureaucratic politics in a federal system

case study

Tragedy off Gay Head

Ever since the heyday of sailing ships, international practice has accepted the three-mile limit as a nation's territorial waters. Three miles was the maximum range of the smooth-bore, muzzle-loading cannon of the day. Nothing, however, in the mid- and late twentieth-century calls more insistent attention to the absurdity of this long-outmoded rule than the overseas fishing activities of the Russians, the Japanese, and, indeed, the Californians off South America. This case has to do with the Russians off the coast of New England.

It is true, of course, that even before permanent settlements had been planted in North America, fishermen from Europe began coming across the ocean to take advantage of the rich fishing grounds off the Grand Banks. There is nothing new about transoceanic fishing. What was new—and became a kind of cause célèbre in New England fishing ports during the 1960's and into the 1970's—was the devastating efficiency and grand scale of the fish-harvesting efforts of the Russians. They sent over virtual fleets of very modern, electronically equipped trawlers and huge factory ships capable of processing the enormous catches just out of the water. Americans and others who habitually used the fishing grounds

off the New England and Canadian Maritime coasts became alarmed at the growing danger that overfishing would permanently reduce or destroy this age-old resource.

In the fall of 1970 negotiations had been going on with the Russians aimed at securing their compliance, pursuant to earlier agreements designed to limit catches of fish in the interest of conservation, to new quotas on the take of yellow tail flounder. At the suggestion of the Russians that the conversations be completed at the scene, one of their factory ships was invited to come for a conference within the three-mile limit off Gay Head, at the western end of the Island of Martha's Vineyard. It is, of course, this three-mile limit that poses the basic problem. A whole series of delicate questions of international intercourse have arisen because the interests of nations have long since extended far out to sea beyond this narrow and arbitrary limit. The fishing rights of nationals versus foreigners and the protection of fishing grounds from destructive exploitation are only two of these. Others range from offshore drilling for oil and gas to pirate radio stations based on shipboard that harass the state-owned networks of European countries. If international practice allowed the United States to control as a matter of right the seas one hundred or even fifty miles off her coasts, many problems would be solved, and the tragedy off Gay Head might never have occurred.

Actually there were much more immediate human and organizational causes for that tragedy, but we are getting ahead of the story. Let us return to the conferences at sea on November 23, 1970. On board the Coast Guard Cutter *Vigilant* were representatives of the U.S. Bureau of Fisheries and the regional fishing interests, including, significantly, Robert M. Brieze, president of the Seafood Producers Association of New Bedford and himself a post-World War II refugee from Soviet-controlled Latvia. The cutter and the Soviet factory ship rendezvoused. Lines were passed over to secure the ships side by side, with fenders in place to prevent them from damaging each other as they rode the swells.

The conference was scheduled to be held on the Soviet ship, and the Americans, including some Coast Guard personnel, crossed the ten feet or so of water that separated the vessels in a breeches buoy (a kind of sling in which a man can be pulled from ship to ship on a pulley line). All was enormously cordial and the discussions were carried on in the midst of traditional Russian gastronomic hospitality. Vodka was plentiful. There was a buffet spread of sardines, cold cuts, and dark bread. The Russian fleet commander gave the Americans gold tie pins, and when the talks were successfully concluded, veal cutlets were served. The hosts accepted the restrictions on flounder catch and even agreed to allow local inspectors aboard their ships to check compliance.

Accounts of the grave incident that was developing as a kind of counterpoint to this international encounter, so apparently successful politically and socially, are

hard to fit together precisely. It began, however, when the Lithuanian radio operator of the Soviet vessel got close enough to one of the Coast Guard officers from the *Vigilant* to tell him that he, the radio man, planned to flee and ask the Americans for asylum. This information was apparently relayed with little delay to Commander Ralph Eustis, the captain of the cutter. From then on, though it takes but a few minutes to tell the story, the actual events happened in what must have appeared to be slow motion to many of those involved, with much waiting about and conferring in the intervals. It was not, in other words, the kind of crisis that requires instant response and snap judgment.

At 12:43 P.M. Commander Eustis prudently radioed Coast Guard District Headquarters in Boston that there was an 80 per cent probability that there would be a defection in the course of his close contact with the Russian ship. It was actually four hours later, however, before Simonas Kudirka jumped. He had intimated to the officer earlier that he would jump into the sea and allow himself to be pulled in by the crew of the *Vigilant*—saying (he had a limited command of English) that the water was not so cold that a man could not survive a short time. As it turned out, he elected to jump directly from the higher deck of the Soviet ship to the deck of the cutter. This he did at 4:30 P.M.

Commander Eustis' message calls for brief explanation of the bureaucratic chain of command that linked him on his small vessel riding the swells off Martha's Vineyard with the rest of the government. His immediate superior was the Commandant of the First Coast Guard District in Boston, Admiral William Ellis. He actually dealt directly with Captain Fletcher Brown, Chief of Staff of the First District, because Admiral Ellis was at home recuperating from surgery. Admiral Ellis' superior was Admiral Chester R. Bender, Commandant of the

Coast Guard in Washington. His immediate supervisor was Secretary of Transportation John Volpe. The President, of course sat at the apex of this chain of command.

As we shall see, however, the direct chain of command was not the sum total of the bureaucratic apparatus that became involved in the incident. Presumably Eustis' message went to Captain Brown, who, at some early point, telephoned his commanding officer, Admiral Ellis, for instructions. Ellis or Brown then got in contact with the office of the Commandant in Washington, Admiral Bender. The latter subsequently testified before the House Merchant Marine Committee that he had received two messages about the incident, one early in the afternoon, and the other at 7:45 P.M., after the final decision had been made and was apparently being carried out on the spot. Sometime around 3:00 P.M. the Soviet desk in the State Department received the first of the three calls it was to get during the events from the Coast Guard intelligence staff, who were seeking guidance. Edward Killham, a Soviet specialist on duty, advised, "Don't encourage him to defect, but if he does, let us know and we will send further guidance." The State Department asked to be kept informed. This message was relayed to Coast Guard Intelligence at 3:15 P.M.

A little over an hour later Kudirka jumped. This information seems to have been transmitted to Boston. At about 5 P.M., with surprising speed in light of the pace of events up to then and for the rest of the evening until midnight, Admiral Ellis is said to have given his "first order" to the Captain of the Vigilant, which ultimately resulted in the forceable return of Kudirka to the Soviet ship. It is not clear if Ellis was aware of the communication that had been received from the State Department and even if he had been, it would not have been much help. No one had had

any opportunity either to encourage or to discourage the defection. The Admiral might, however, have taken the State Department up on its offer of further guidance, but for whatever reason, he did not. The State Department heard again about developments at about 4:00 P.M. to the effect that at that point no further information was available. Then at 7:45 P.M. both the Coast Guard Commandant and the State Department reported afterward they were informed that the defection had taken place and that the seaman was being returned.

If the overall pace of events was leisurely, there were periods of intense and agonizing drama on board the Vigliant. Kudirka had jumped believing implicitly that the Americans would give him protection and allow him to claim asylum. When the American negotiators returned from the Soviet vessel they were confined to Captain Eustis' cabin while he sought Headquarters guidance. The Soviets responded to the defection by requesting Kudirka's return, and permission to come aboard and speak with him. At one point they alleged that he was wanted for theft of the equivalent of $2,000 from his ship's funds.

At length a party from the Russian ship was allowed to come aboard to talk with the defector. Instead of verbal communication, they apparently substituted a beating with a rope and efforts to seize him. Kudirka broke away from the Russian party and tried to escape. He even tried to leap into the water, but was restrained by two American sailors. He is also said to have pleaded for a knife so that he could kill himself rather than go back. By this time he had obviously concluded that the Americans were not going to grant him automatic asylum and indeed were going to acquiesce in his return. Brieze, the naturalized Latvian from New Bedford, reported hearing him pleading with his reluctant hosts: "He was crying 'help' and was on his knees praying and begging them to save his life. But the Captain said he was just following orders."

After he broke away initially he dashed about the cutter trying to elude his pursurers, who were being cheered on by his shipmates gathered along the rail of the factory ship. From their vantage point they shouted instructions to the Russian boarding party when Kudirka seemed about to find a hiding place. During all of this, save for the intervention to keep the defector from jumping overboard, the American crew members of the cutter apparently stood aside and watched. The spectacle must have been an incredible one indeed: Russians being allowed the run of an American quasi-military vessel to capture a frantic defector. At some stage Kudirka did manage to find concealment below, but the determined posse flushed him out in time, and he was securely bound amidst a severe beating and an alleged effort to strangle him into unconsciousness.

Again the time sequence, as one attempts to reconstruct it, becomes one of the more bizarre aspects. The subsequent testimony had the State Department and the Coast Guard Washington headquarters being informed at about 7:45 P.M. that the decision had been made and was being carried out to return the seaman to his ship. It was not until after midnight that the return was finally effected. The American ship had been cast off from the Russian ship for fear, it is said, that if Kudirka did jump overboard he might be crushed between them. Unaccountably, the *Vigilant* obligingly provided a small, manned boat, in which the Russians were taken back, their captive trussed up in a blanket, having been literally thrown in the bottom.

Following the first press report of the incident (it did not appear in the *New York Times* until November 29), the reaction from many quarters was predictable and violent. As President

Nixon himself noted in answering a press conference question on December 10, the circumstances and cause of the episode could hardly have been more embarrassing to Americans: "The United States of America for 190 years has had a proud tradition of providing opportunities for refugees and guaranteeing their safety. And we are going to meet that tradition." Picketings and demonstrations took place in several American cities. Even the United Nations complained to the American government that the return of Kudirka was a clear violation of Article 33 of the Geneva Convention.

What had taken place was a bureaucratic snafu of the first magnitude. Bureaucracy may be the most technically efficient form of human organization, but for all its normal efficiency it can produce unimaginative and even horrendous results on occasion. The results here were both. Admiral Ellis, according to later testimony and reports compiled on the incident, justified his action by attributing it to "consideration of delicate international discussions being carried on regarding fishing problems. The progress could have been endangered by any other course of action." Clearly he had weighed, in a rather simplistic manner, the broader interests of the United States in concluding the sought-after agreement, against the welfare of a single foreign seaman. What the Admiral seems to have failed to take into account was either the broad "philosophical" interest that the nation had in the principle of free asylum for the oppressed, or the public relations implications of the decision he was making, or, indeed, the possibility of stalling for time until the alternatives could be sorted out more carefully.

The Coast Guard investigating board recommended to the Secretary of Transportation that Ellis and Brown be court-martialed. Secretary Volpe refused to follow that course, arguing that no useful purpose would be served. He did accept the finding that Ellis was **primarily** to blame for what had quite clearly been a wrong decision, and that the Admiral was to be criticized for offering "advice" to Brown and Eustis (as he apparently claims to have done) that, though not in the form of an order, he should have known would be taken as tantamount to an order. Finally, Ellis was criticized for assuming an authority that was beyond his competence, though the investigating board noted that the State Department had not furnished "adequate, helpful or timely advice." In the final upshot, the officers directly involved were punished with reprimands. Brown and Ellis were allowed to retire from the service, and Eustis was relieved of his command of the *Vigilant* and reassigned.

Bureaucracies usually punish those lower down on the totem pole and gloss over the responsibility of those higher up, despite the fact that authority is supposed to be hierarchical. Certainly both the Commandant in Washington and the State Department were derelict, or at best, unimaginative. Either or both should have taken the initial word from Boston District Headquarters as a warning of possible trouble and should have followed up with a good deal more vigor than they did. (Actually, the fact that the Coast Guard as a branch of one Cabinet Department found cooperation with a part of the notoriously ponderous State Department bureaucratic machinery difficult will come as no surprise to those acquainted with interdepartmental relations.)

Bureaucratic rigidity as well as lack of imagination were well documented at the Washington end of the drama. By way of lame excuse, the Coast Guard (possibly with some legal principle in mind) made the incredible suggestion that the chance of granting the seaman asylum would have been better if he had jumped into the water and been fished out by the cutter's crew rather than jumping directly to the *Vigilant*'s deck!

As Admiral Bender said, the United States should "not permit our ship to be used as a means of defection." It is difficult to see a difference between using the ship and allowing the use of the line and life preserver by which Kudirka would have been pulled aboard if he had sought escape in the approved manner. The State Department, for its part, primly insisted that they could only have given definitive guidance once the defector was actually aboard, a fact of which they were not apprised until it was too late.

The President's reaction has already been suggested by the quote from his press conference. The rest of his reply, when he was asked to give the assemblage his personal view on the defector problems of this Lithuanian who was beaten on the Coast Guard cutter, ran:

Well, as I have already indicated, I was, as an American, outraged and shocked that this could happen. I regret that the procedures, the Coast Guard informing the White House, were not adequate to bring the matter to my attention. I can assure you it will never happen again.

The sequence of White House involvement in the aftermath of the incident began with a presidential call for a "very full and immediate investigation" on November 30. Press Secretary Ron Ziegler reported that the President was incensed about the way the incident was handled and the fact that the White House was not informed.

On December 1, probably on White House orders, the Voice of America used its full facilities to tell the world that the bungle off Martha's Vineyard did not represent a change in American refugee policy. On December 2, Mr. Nixon was reported to have received the reports he had requested from the State and Transportation Departments, and after studying them he would issue new and clear policy guidelines on refugees. On December 3, the White House announced that henceforth it was to be informed about defectors immediately. On December 7, it released the departmental reports it had received, and then on December 10 the news conference comment already quoted put the capstone on presidential involvement.

Obviously this was the kind of international flap that, though seemingly tiny and isolated, could have ballooned into a major international complication. The White House had to take this possibility into grave account. But also, it was the kind of occurrence that had many complex domestic political overtones. Mr. Nixon might have been acutely embarrassed by it in a quite direct political way had he not responded decisively and adroitly. This he seems to have done. Indeed, as one correspondent suggested, he was so vigorous in his expressions of anger and dismay that he may have wrung political advantage out of the blunderings of some of his lesser subordinates.

Bureaucracy not only characteristically ties officials together in a tight hierarchical chain of command and obedience, responsibility and subordination, but it also can be used to insulate decision-makers and keep blame for ineptitude or misjudgment carefully confined to a small part of the organization and prevent it from tainting the rest. This paradoxical fact is well illustrated here, along with many of the other characteristics of the bureaucratic form of organization. Finally, and almost too obvious to require mention, is the fact, abundantly illustrated in this case, that bureaucrats *make* policy; they are far from being mere automatons who do no more than carry out the orders of political superiors. If the Coast Guard officers had been somewhat less willing to make policy decisions here, things might have gone better.

SOURCES
The New York Times, issues for
November 29 and 30, and for December 1, 2, 3, 4, 5, 6, 7, 8, 9, 10, 11, 12, 14, 22, 23, 27, 30 and 31, 1970.
Newsweek, "Defectors: 'Nightmare' off Gay Head," December 14, 1970, pp. 46 and 51.

the federal bureaucracy

The Administrative State(s)

"Government" as we most often visualize it has been covered in the three preceding chapters on the executive, the legislative, and the judicial organs. Traditional students of public administration made a firm distinction between politics and administration, assigning the former—policy-*making*—to these three "political" organs (or at least the first two of them), and policy implementation, the carrying out of the political decisions, to the administrative apparatus. The latter, under this highly formalistic theory, did not make policy, but rather was the servant of the political organs. Actually, in recent years students of administration have jettisoned this set of artificial and unrealistic categories. They now insist, properly, that the administrator makes policy every bit as much as does the elected executive or the legislator. Even the policeman on the beat "makes policy" in the very act of deciding, when he sees a minor infraction of the law, whether to make an arrest or to look the other way. Officials all up and down the line exercise discretion in almost every action they take, and such discretion *is* policy-making.

Even this perspective on the administrative role understates the full importance of that role. In a very real sense the administrative bureaucracy *is* the government in any political system. Legislatures, executives, courts, and, of course, political parties do govern, but the pervasiveness of their roles and the depth of their penetration into the body politic can hardly compare with the omnipresence, to say nothing of the sheer numbers, of the bureaucracy. A moment's reflection suggests the point with little need for further elaboration. The permanent officials of government— the nonelected clerks and functionaries, that is—are encountered by the citizen at every turn. Yet he may have no contact with or even know the names of the representatives and governors he himself chooses at the ballot box.

An important way of underscoring the point emerged in the first chapter, which stressed the similarities between government in a democracy and in a totalitarian system. We noted that modern states, regardless of their philosophical persuasion, require vast amounts of governing. All such national communities, in other words, *must* and do take the form of administrative states. The point is not how broad policy is set—whether by elections, legislatures, and referenda, or by dictators and monolithic parties. The point is that policy, however set, must be implemented, and implementation requires bureaucracy, no less (more, in fact) in the Soviet Union than in the United States. It might even be argued persuasively that to an extent bureaucracy can govern when no one is setting policy at all! There were times during the hectic lives of the French Third and Fourth Republics when the political organs were deadlocked in immobility and the only element of effctiveness and continuity in the political system was the administrative corps.

In much of the world the history of the development of government has been the history of the development of bureaucratic administrative machinery to replace rule by local tribal chiefs, feudal lords, or royal favorites. Winston Churchill has written of Henry I (1100–1135):

Henry realized that royal servants who were members of the minor baronage, if formed into a permanent nucleus, would act as a brake upon the turbulence of the greater feudatories. Here were the first beginnings, tentative, modest, but insinuating, of a civil administrative machinery, which within its limits was more efficient and persistent than anything yet known. These officials soon developed a vested interest of their own . . . entrenched themselves in the household offices, and created what was in fact an official class.[1]

Gradually and painfully Henry and succeeding British monarchs, building on the foundations laid by William the Conqueror, forged the kind of simple put effective central administration that enabled them to overcome feudal pluralism and rule a united nation.

The full-blown model of the administrative state, at least in the West (Egypt and China produced highly developed bureaucratic mechanisms before Europe had emerged from barbarism), was Prussia. Under Frederick William I (1713–1740) there was systematized a pattern for a professional administrative corps, which embraced many of the characteristics now generally accepted as normal adjuncts to the public service. Selection, for example, was by competitive examination upon the completion of specialized training, and career tenure was the normal expectation. It was really this extremely efficient government mechanism, as much as any other single factor, that enabled Prussia to emerge as the dominant force in the congeries of competing German princedoms that existed until the late nineteenth century. This model was emulated by other continental nations, most notably France—the latter under the centralizing leadership of Napoleon. Its essence is centralized authority exercised through a hierarchical structure of offices and officials and uniform throughout the nation; it follows elaborate patterns of law and rules administered by a professionalized career corps.

Britain's governmental evolution followed this model only to a limited extent, and that of the United States hardly at all until very recently. Yet even in Britain, through long centuries the development of government *was* the development of administrative structure and personnel. The often-cited emergence of the role of Parlia-

[1] *The Birth of Britain* (New York: Dodd, Mead, 1956), p. 184.

ment as a prototype of democratic legislatures hardly belies this assertion. The long, painful struggle for Parliamentary supremacy, which culminated, constitutionally speaking, in the Glorious Revolution of 1689, was at bottom a struggle to control the centralized governing apparatus that successive kings had developed, as much as it was to control the monarch himself. Obviously the monarch could rule only through his servants in the administrative structure: control of the one could not be asserted without control of the other.

America's political development owes much to Britain, and in this area our experience was more like that of our English cousins than like the continental model. The new nation, with its simple economy, relatively sparse population, wealth of resources, and remoteness from the broils of the old world, in fact needed but a minimum of government of any kind. At the local level government followed traditions of direct citizen involvement symbolized by the New England town meeting, which minimized the need for full-time professional public servants to supplement the work of part-time citizen functionaries. And even as government grew more complex, the characteristic pattern of staffing was to add more elective offices at the state level. This approach began in the Jacksonian era and made auditors, treasurers, highway superintendents, directors of public instruction, and many other offices elective rather than appointive; it served for a long time as an alternative to the development of a career service at the upper levels of administration, just as patronage did at all levels.

As a consequence, the democratization of the American system of government posed different problems than those faced abroad, and was accomplished in different ways. In the first place, America had no significant heritage of indigenous autocracy to overcome. Long before the Revolution, traditions of popular participation had become firmly established. And obviously, no administrative machine, no bureaucratic state-within-a-state had developed over which control had to be established. In fact, quite the reverse was true. The nation began with representative and political institutions, and extemporized additions to these later to fill such modest administrative needs as became manifest. This was really the meaning both of the patronage pattern and of the Jacksonian insistence upon the election of as many public officials as possible.

The problem of administrative development that America faced was, therefore, one of overcoming a tradition hostile to bureaucracy and deeply rooted in a political culture that stressed equalitarianism, equal opportunity, and a militantly antielitist approach to staffing the political system. When the time finally came to require a more professional and reliable public service than patronage and popular election could produce, the resistance was long and at times bitter. George Washington Plunkitt of New York's Tammany Hall summed it all up in one of his strictures: "This civil service law is the biggest fraud of the age. It is the curse of the nation. There can't be no real patriotism while it lasts." [2] Eventually civil service reform did bring the bureaucratization of the American public service and the adoption, by the

---

[2] William L. Riordon, *Plunkitt of Tammany Hall* (New York: Dutton, 1963), p. 11.

same token, of much of the European model administrative state. Some such development was inevitable, yet America adopted the bureaucratic model subject to many of its own modifications, which the following pages will describe.

The Personnel of Administration

As with all political institutions, but even more than most, the administrative apparatus can be viewed either as structure or as people, and of course it must be viewed from both perspectives. The only question is where to begin. If the structural form represents the framework within and around which activity is oriented, the life-blood of the system is the people who staff the departments and agencies. It is therefore most appropriate to begin with these people and to turn later to the structural questions.

During the first hundred years of American history, administrators were selected and obtained tenure either as a consequence of popular elections or partisan preference through an elaborate patronage system; the characteristics of a professionalized bureaucratic service on the European model were conspicuously absent. But beginning in the 1880's, with the growing if reluctant acceptance of civil service principles, trends were reversed, and the current high level of professionalization of the public service was slowly and at times painfully attained.

As already noted, the evolution of the personnel system in the federal service was greatly affected by the major themes in the national culture. Nevertheless the personnel system under the Constitution of 1787 got off to a mildly elitist start. The document itself, in several important respects, provided for a kind of indirect and filtered popular rule, which was to mean initially concentration of much power in the hands of the well-born and the well-to-do. (It is interesting to note that Robert A. Dahl in his study of the political history of New Haven, Connecticut, found the same trend there: rule until recent decades by a small circle of leading families who had quite a tight monopoly of political power.) [3] The Federalists, at least those who were prominent in public life in the 1790's and the early 1800's, certainly held to the view that the "gentry" should rule. President Washington, in his filling of the offices created by the new government, used criteria that led to this result. He looked for men of reputation and public esteem who would be a credit to his administration, and, quite naturally, men who had supported the adoption of the Constitution in the first place were, therefore, presumed to be loyal to it. Washington was far less concerned than we might be today with seeking men with technical competence. But then, government in his day was infinitely less complex than it later became.

Washington's political acuteness, as well as his need for information about likely candidates, to say nothing of the right of the Senate to confirm appointments, led him to consult extensively with members of Congress. For this and other reasons, many of the tendencies toward partisan personnel practices began during Washington's Administration. As Professor Herbert Kaufman has written:

[3] *Who Governs?* (New Haven: Yale University Press, 1961).

The partisan considerations, the preferments for veterans, the maintenance of territorial representativeness (over-riding questions of merit), the battles between the legislative and executive branches of the government—all these made their appearance at the very beginning.[4]

On the other hand, Washington's preference for Federalists and men of stature produced a state of affairs that was modified by patronage practices initiated by Jefferson, Jackson, and their successors. With the first party change in the Presidency in 1801, there naturally developed pressure from the now-triumphant Republicans for a share of the offices. Jefferson himself noted that: "Out of about six hundred offices named by the President there were six Republicans only when I came into office, and these were chiefly half-breeds." [5] In practice, though, Jefferson was moderate and cautious in working to redress the balance and there were no wholesale dismissals. Jefferson's appointments included men outside the gentry class and thus provided representation for other elements in the community, but even this tendency was very limited.

Jefferson's successors down through the 1820's found even less reason to make large-scale changes among the administrative personnel. In this respect, Professor Leonard D. White points out that:

stability and continuity thus became as conspicuous features of the public service under the Republicans as under the Federalists. Employment legally at pleasure became in practice employment during good behavior.[6]

In other words, the first four decades of development under the Constitution saw the emergence of a kind of career service, based primarily on elite recruitment and proprietary class control of public office.

The change came under President Andrew Jackson. But even this was not a complete change in practice as much as it was a change in rhetoric. Instead of filling offices with his partisans quietly and apologetically, Jackson did it openly. He set forth his rationalization in his first annual message to Congress:

The duties of all public officers are, or at least admit of being made, so plain and simple that men of intelligence may readily qualify themselves for their performance; and I cannot but believe that more is lost by the long continuance of men in office than is generally to be gained by their experience. . . . In a country where offices are created solely for the benefit of the people no one man has any more intrinsic right to official station than another. . . . The proposed limitation [to four years incumbency] would destroy the idea of property now so generally connected with official station, . . . by promoting that rotation which constitutes a leading principle in the Republican creed.[7]

Implementing this philosophy, Jackson made many changes—far more than his predecessors, but considerably fewer than his successors, who enthusiastically practiced the principle of rotation. The Whigs condemned Jackson for his excesses, but

---

[4] "The Growth of the Federal Personnel System," in Wallace Sayre, *The Federal Government Service* (Englewood Cliffs, N.J.: Prentice-Hall, 1965), p. 14.

[5] Leonard D. White, *The Jeffersonians* (New York: Macmillan, 1951), p. 348.

[6] Ibid., p. 375.

[7] Leonard D. White, *The Jacksonians* (New York: Macmillan, 1954), p. 318.

under Harrison embarked on precisely the same tactics. When Harrison took office no less than thirty to forty thousand office seekers are reported to have descended on Washington in quest of spoils. Polk did the same when he led the Democrats in a return to power. The pendulum again swung in the other direction with the new Whig success under Taylor. The spoils system took a new turn when Fillmore, upon succeeding the deceased Taylor, removed the latter's appointees, even though they were of the same party as himself, replacing them with partisans of his particular party faction! Lincoln made the cleanest sweep of all when he came to office in 1861.

The significance of the Jacksonian revolution in the public service is considerably more than the civil service reformers have been prepared to grant. In their rather oversimplified view, Jackson replaced the desirable Washingtonian precedents with a system that exalted political greed into a credo. In fact, however, the public service under the early Presidents left much to be desired in its degree of efficiency and honesty. Above all, the principles on which it had evolved came into increasing conflict with the growing democratic spirit of the nation. Jackson was clearly right when he insisted that rotation in office was a leading principle of the American Republican creed—and that the previous class-bound elitism was not.

But the Jacksonian system also had severe limitations. Jackson's easy optimism about the essential simplicity of the tasks in the public service and the adequacy of a rapidly rotating system of nonprofessional staffing could hardly survive the growing complexity of governmental activity. Yet the vested interests of the parties in that status quo, well illustrated by Plunkitt's expostulation quoted earlier, long hampered the efforts of the reformers. Not until the assassination of President Garfield in 1881, by a man whose twisted mind blamed the President for his failure to secure a patronage position, did the public become sufficiently aroused to demand change.

Reform efforts had actually begun as early as the 1830's, though with little success. After the Civil War, President Grant, perhaps to the surprise of modern readers, did more than any of his predecessors for the civil service cause, though again with an absence of notable or long-lasting results. President Rutherford B. Hayes (1877–1881) had pledged himself to civil service reform as a candidate and once in the White House did succeed in advancing the cause in significant ways. But it was left to Garfield's successor, Chester A. Arthur, himself a former chief spoilsman as head of the notorious New York custom house, to sign the Pendleton Civil Service Act in 1883.

This legislation embodied the basic elements sought by the civil service advocates in quest of their goal of a neutral, professional public service staffed on the basis of merit. Positions were to be filled by competitive examination designed to test the fitness of the candidate in a practical manner for the position he was seeking. Appointments could then only be made from among the top three qualifiers. Political harassment or activity involving officeholders was proscribed. The battle had by no means been won, however. Initially only 10 per cent of the total federal employees were covered, and it was left to subsequent Presidents to broaden coverage. A kind of pendulum rhythm became normal: when a new party took office it naturally took advantage of all the leeway the existing system allowed for spoils, and it often yielded to the temptation to declassify jobs in order to increase the supply. Then, upon learning that it too would soon be replaced in office following ill fortune at the polls, the lame duck President often created new categories for officeholders who had attained their posts by patronage, so that they would enjoy protection in the days of political adversity that lay ahead. Followers of the new President would, of course, cry "foul" and undo as much of this deathbed conversion to the virtues of civil service as they dared, and the cycle would begin over again. With all of this backing and filling, there was still an upward trend in coverage within the classified service (see Table 10.1).

The rapid development at forced draft of the alphabet soup of New Deal agencies (AAA, CCC, HOLC, FDC, FSA, WPA, and a host of others) made it both necessary and politically expedient to staff them with non-civil-service recruits. It probably would have been impossible to recruit enough people fast enough through the somewhat cumbersome methods used by the Civil Service Commission. Furthermore, the President and his associates reasoned that to make new and novel programs work, and to infuse them with the necessary imagination and philosophical commitment, recruitment had to be more flexible than the civil service system allowed. This same

Table 10.1 *Extension of the competitive civil service*

	Total employees	Number in classified service	Per cent in classified service
1884	131,208	13,780	10.5
1891	166,000	33,873	20.4
1895	189,000	54,222	28.7
1901	256,000	106,205	41.5
1905	300,615	171,807	57.2
1910	384,088	222,278	57.9
1915	476,363	292,291	61.3
1920	691,116	497,603	73.0
1925	532,798	423,538	79.5
1930	580,494	462,083	79.6
1935	719,440	455,229	63.3
1940	1,014,117	726,827	72.5
1947	2,128,648	1,733,019	81.4
1950	1,966,448	1,687,594	85.8
1955	2,397,268	2,004,814	83.6
1960	2,398,705	2,050,939	85.5
1963	2,527,960	2,164,163	85.6

Source: Herbert Kaufman, "The Growth of the Federal Personnel System," in Wallace S. Sayre, *The Federal Government Service* (Englewood Cliffs, N.J.: Prentice-Hall, Inc., 1965), pp. 41–43. Kaufman compiled the data from Commission on Organization of the Executive Branch of the Government, *Report on Personnel and Civil Service* (February, 1955), pp. 97–98; and U.S. Civil Service Commission, *Annual Report* 1955–1963.

reasoning dictated the setting up of entirely new agencies in many cases rather than the entrusting of these functions to line departments.

There was nevertheless a steady trend toward incorporating these new recruits into the classified system, and by 1947 the percentage covered again reached 80. The total in numbers, however, was by then 1,733,000, or nearly four times the civil service total fifteen years earlier. In 1951 the percentage grew to an all-time high of 87, but declined to just over 83 in 1955, during the Eisenhower years; it climbed again to over 85 per cent in the 1960's. Once again a change of party, together with other factors, had caused a dip, but this did not appreciably affect the long-run trend. At the present time there is little basis for criticizing the system for lack of sufficiently broad coverage. The bulk of those jobs not covered are outside the system for good reasons. Many fall into the top policy-making categories and should, of course, be available to be filled by an incoming President to enable him to secure administrative compliance with his policy preferences.

The present-day federal personnel system is characterized by a number of significant technical features. One of the most basic objectives of the civil service reformers, for example, was equal pay for equal work. Patronage and the kinds of favoritism it engendered produced vast inequities among individuals doing essentially the same kind of work in different agencies. Techniques of objective job classification are designed to meet this problem. All of the hundreds and thousands of jobs in the public service were studied and put into categories on the basis of similarity of content, difficulty, and responsibility. These various categories were then ranked in hierarchical fashion so that the more difficult and responsible the position the higher up the scale it would fall. Thus, all individuals doing the work of a clerk-typist, or of an accountant, or of an agronomist are classified in identical categories, with the clerk-typists placed relatively low on the scale, the agronomists quite high, and the accountants somewhere in between.

A series of grades, each with its own pay scale, has been contrived and each position fitted into it. The basic federal system of grades is called the "General Schedule," with designations of GS-1 for its lowest step and GS-18 for its highest. Within each of these grades there are currently ten "steps" or pay grades, ranging for GS-1 from $4,125 to $5,358. GS-2 begins at $4,621 and runs up in ten steps to $6,007. (The grades thus overlap in pay range in order to reward seniority.) Those in GS-17 could rise through five steps from $30,714 to $34,810; and if promoted to the "super grade" of GS-18 would earn $695 more, with no step increases provided. The General Schedule is not the only graded pay and promotional system in the federal service. The United States Postal Service has its own system, with twenty levels and as many as a dozen steps within the lower ones. The Foreign Service has its own, as do medical personnel in the employ of the national government. These autonomous career systems guard their autonomy jealously, just as bureau and agency autonomy is cherished and carefully protected.

Admittedly, in many ways, the total system is incredibly complicated. Its underlying rationale is to guarantee not only freedom from political pressure and to afford the protection of tenure, but to establish fairness within the system as to compensation, promotions, and levels of responsibility. It has also had the partially unintended effect of producing a public service that has placed a high premium on matching the skills of an individual with the job for which he is being examined, rather than on testing for general intelligence, ability, and capacity for growth and later supervisory responsibility. In other words, it has tested and recruited specialists for particular jobs, rather than seeking generalists capable of adapting to a variety of roles during their careers.

The British Alternative

The British, in contrast, contrived a different system based on different premises, which are, of course, derived from another political culture. Instead of emphasizing specialized recruitment and equality of opportunity for all those who could meet the requirements of the particular job in question, they stressed the recruitment of generalists. People have been fed into the British public service at several levels, depending on their level of educational attainment. University graduates have usually been recruited into an administrative class whose members were marked from the beginning for high supervisory positions. Recruitment into this class especially is carried on through general tests of intelligence and overall ability. The British theory holds that there is no telling in what particular departments or governmental activities candidates will eventually work. And it is based on the further assumption that if these recruits are indeed the cream of the university graduates, they will learn easily the technicalities of any agency sufficiently to perform the necessary supervisory functions.

Supervisory personnel in the American system have tended to be recruited from outside the government, as in the case of presidentially appointed assistant secretaries and bureau chiefs, or alternatively, promoted from the ranks. For the most part such promotion has meant elevating individuals, who were originally recruited on technical criteria, to supervisory roles. Thus, a chief of the Bureau of Animal Husbandry in the Department of Agriculture may be an individual who originally came into government service by passing an examination in veterinary medicine. This has often been portrayed as a serious problem. Many have argued that it is better to recruit, as the British do, people specially chosen for their supervisory potential. Because, however, this would mean the kind of multilevel recruitment used in Britain, it has class overtones to the sensitive ears of Americans.

Efforts were made, however, during the 1930's and the 1940's to meet this problem. One of them was the Junior Professional Assistant examination first offered in 1939. Even this examination was still specialized in twenty-two categories, one of which, however, was the Junior Administrative Technician. After World War II this program gave way to the JMA (Junior Management Assistant) examination. This was an improved version of the JPA, but the extravagant Communist-hunting activities of Senator Joseph R. McCarthy and particularly his charges of rampant disloyalty in the federal government during the early 1950's damaged the concept of federal service as a highly professional career. In 1954, the Federal Service En-

Table 10.2 *Paid civilian employment in the federal government by agency, 1955 and 1970*

Agency	1955	1970
ALL AGENCIES	2,397,309	2,929,276
Legislative branch	21,711	29,193
Judicial branch	4,136	6,796
Executive branch	2,371,462	2,893,287
EXECUTIVE OFFICE OF THE PRESIDENT		
White House Office	290	340
Bureau of the Budget	444	572
Executive Mansion and Grounds	70	72
National Security Council	28	69
Office of Economic Opportunity	(X)	2,320
Office of Emergency Planning	1,015	418
Office of Science and Technology	(X)	61
All other	63	217
EXECUTIVE DEPARTMENTS		
Agriculture	85,503	104,332
Commerce	46,077	34,349
Defense		
Office of the Secretary	1,954	2,354
Department of the Army	461,986	464,918
Department of the Navy	410,564	398,838
Department of the Air Force	312,076	319,321
Other defense activities	—	66,551
Health, Education and Welfare	40,405	106,481
Housing and Urban Development	11,082	14,782
Interior	54,322	67,800
Justice	30,686	37,091
Labor	5,051	10,499
Post Office	511,613	727,645
State	27,495	41,464
Agency for International Development	(X)	15,186
Peace Corps	(X)	1,323
Transportation	(X)	62,670
Treasury	79,180	95,383

Source: Statistical Abstract of the United States (Washington, D.C.: U.S. Government Printing Office, 1970).

— Represents zero.
(**X**) Not applicable.

Agency	1955	1970
INDEPENDENT AGENCIES		
American Battle Monuments Commission	775	407
Arms Control and Disarmament Agency	(X)	175
Atomic Energy Commission	6,076	7,256
Board of Governors, Federal Reserve System	588	921
Canal Zone Government	2,487	3,420
Civil Aeronautics Board	528	637
Civil Service Commission	3,864	5,342
Commission on Civil Rights	(X)	167
Equal Employment Opportunity Commission	(X)	666
Export-Import Bank	148	338
Farm Credit Administration	1,078	228
Federal Aviation Agency	(X)	(X)
Federal Communications Commission	1,094	1,509
Federal Deposit Insurance Corporation	1,127	2,243
Federal Home Loan Bank Board	(X)	1,212
Federal Maritime Commission	(X)	218
Federal Mediation and Conciliation Service	357	425
Federal Power Commission	657	1,070
Federal Trade Commission	584	1,256
Foreign Claims Settlement Commission	161	37
General Services Administration	25,729	38,051
Information Agency	10,145	10,499
Interstate Commerce Commission	1,822	1,785
National Aero-Space Administration	7,508	32,501
National Capital Housing Authority	276	(X)
National Labor Relations Board	1,150	2,216
National Mediation Board	110	119
National Science Foundation	170	1,062
Panama Canal Company	12,833	12,839
Railroad Retirement Board	2,344	1,709
Renegotiation Board	540	219
St. Lawrence Seaway Development Corporation	33	(X)
Securities and Exchange Commission	666	1,389
Selective Service System	7,123	9,104
Small Business Administration	736	4,211
Smithsonian Institution	986	2,552
Soldiers' Home	1,020	1,095
Tariff Commission	198	242
Tax Court of the U.S.	141	
Tennessee Valley Authority	19,854	20,657
Veterans Administration	177,656	166,314
Virgin Islands Corporation	785	
All other	209	593

trance Examination was initiated, designed to measure general intelligence and ability. The very best qualifiers were then invited to compete for Management Intern positions. Professor Frederick C. Mosher has pointed out that the select few who make the grade are appointed at higher levels and can anticipate rapid advancement to positions of high administrative responsibility.[8] At length, it seemed that the problem of staffing for administrative leadership and supervision was on the way to solution. Something more nearly similar to the British recruitment pattern for the filling of top administrative positions had been introduced.

Yet the British have now begun to doubt the wisdom of *their* administrative class of "generalists" and to move in the direction of a more American-like system. In 1968 the Fulton Committee Report rejected the "cult of the generalists," long taken to be the gospel in British public service, and the notion of the "ideal administrator," who ". . . is still too often seen as the gifted layman who, moving frequently from job to job within the Service, can take a practical view of any problem, irrespective of its subject matter. . . ." Such civil servants, in the view of the Committee, "lack the fully developed professionalism that their work now demands," and they "do not develop adequate knowledge in depth." [9] Combining recent American and British thinking one concludes that some balance point between the generalist and the specialist concepts is being sought in both countries, and that the result will be more nearly similar patterns of staffing than existed in the past.

Current Personnel Trends and Problems

On February 2, 1971, President Nixon sent Congress a message recommending the establishment of a new "Federal Executive Service" designed to solve another facet of this same problem of providing top-level leadership for the public service. The difficulty the President had in mind stemmed in large part from the unique extent to which the upper management levels have traditionally been staffed by political appointees brought in from outside, in-and-outers who are not part of the career service and have no intention of making government a career. Reliance on this kind of recruitment is of course a holdover from the Jacksonian era. The fact that top management has been divided into two groups, those in the highest three GS supergrades (GS-16, GS-17 and GS-18) on the one hand, and the group of in-and-outers on the other, has come to pose increasing difficulties.

The new Federal Executive Service, if established, will comprise some seven thousand in total, including those currently in the three supergrades, plus non-career people not in the General Schedule. These individuals, incidentally, are increasingly professional people. Forty-five per cent are in science, engineering, and allied fields; another 15 per cent are professional social scientists or lawyers. The generalist manager, in the old sense, seems to be in a decreasing minority, though

---

[8] "Features and Problems of the Federal Civil Service," in Sayre, op. cit., p. 183.

[9] *The Civil Service,* Vol. I: *Report of the Committee 1966–68,* Chairman Lord Fulton (London: Her Majesty's Stationery Office, June, 1968), quoted in Felix A. Nigro, *Modern Public Administration,* 2nd ed. (New York: Harper, 1970), pp. 280ff.

some 75 per cent of the total group are program managers in one way or another. In many respects the distinction between career and noncareer people is to be maintained in the new FES, but the three civil service supergrades will be abolished and both categories will be paid on a case-by-case basis within a general salary range.[10] The overall objective is to create a flexible and interchangeable pool of top executive talent that can be used by agency heads in the most efficient manner, unhampered by present limitations.

Two issues that have boiled to the surface during recent years relating to staffing the public service deserve note. One is the employment of blacks and other minority groups, and the other is the matter of unionization, strike action, and collective bargaining. As of November, 1970, the latest figures available showed 137,919 blacks employed by the federal government out of the total of 1,289,114 covered by Civil Service regulations. This works out to 10.7 per cent, which is less than the 12.9 per cent estimated in the 1970 census as the black proportion of the total population.[11] Clearly, progress has been made in the direction of equal governmental employment opportunity, but there is still a long way to go.

Figures show that more blacks than ever are moving onto the federal roster in the middle and upper middle positions, and filling professional slots. But this is where the record is the weakest. In 1970, as they had been for decades, two thirds of all black civil servants were still to be found in the five lowest-paying and lowest responsibility classifications, such as messenger, clerk, or secretary. There were roughly 135 blacks in policy-making positions, but they represented only 1.2 per cent of the individuals in the three supergrades and others of equivalent rank. In November, 1967, there were 4,655 blacks in the top seven civil service grades (less than 2 per cent); by 1970 another 1,856 had been added to that figure.

The basic difficulty seems to be that progress is uneven from agency to agency. If all agencies were equally zealous, far more would be accomplished. Secretary of Transportation Volpe, for instance, has an outstanding record. His department has 14 blacks out of 270 individuals in the supergrades, more than any other department. The Department of Justice, on the other hand, has 16 fewer black lawyers than it had before the change of administration in January, 1969—a total of only 45 out of between 1,900 and 2,000. Only 7 out of 102 in the Civil Rights Division are black! [12]

If increasing employment of blacks in the federal public service has been considerably slower than it should have been, the rate of acceleration in the area of public employee unionization and collective bargaining has been anything but slow. As Irwin Ross has written, "as recently as 1959, public employees were damned for picketing a state Governor during nonworking time. . . . [In 1967] over 300 full-scale strikes of public employees—including policemen and fire fighters—racked

[10] Seymour S. Berlin, "The Federal Executive Service," *Civil Service Journal,* April–June, 1971, pp. 7–13.

[11] "Blacks Seek Tougher Equality Standards for Federal Hiring and Promotion," *New York Times,* November 15, 1970.

[12] Ibid.

public services across the nation." [13] The rate of unionization shows the same trend. Felix Nigro writes that "From 1956 to 1966, union membership increased 88 per cent in federal, state, and local governments (from 915,000 to 1,717,000), compared to only 12 per cent in the private sector." [14] We all recall the federal postal strike of 1970 and the garbage and transit strikes that have plagued New York City, among other communities.

This trend has been accompanied, as it had to be, with a growing official recognition that public employees have most if not all of the rights that labor has in the private sector. Prior to 1959 there were relatively few collective bargaining agreements in force at the state or local level, and such agreements were doubtless considered illegal in many jurisdictions. In 1959 Wisconsin passed a law that required local units to bargain with their employees, and by 1967 nine other states had followed suit. Some additional ones permit such bargaining, and in many states it is carried on nowadays in the absence of explicit legal sanction. At the national level there were very few such agreements prior to 1962. The Tennessee Valley Authority was one of the few federal agencies that dealt with its employees in that fashion. As early as 1912 legislation allowed federal employees to organize, but not until President Kennedy, pursuant to a campaign pledge he had made in 1960, issued Executive Order 10988 in January, 1962, were collective bargaining rights confirmed. Under the impact of this order, in five years the number of federal employees who were members of employee organizations doubled to about 1,500,000.[15]

It is not possible here to do more than note some of the implications of this almost revolutionary trend. It was spawned by a new militancy among public employees parallel to that of many other segments in society during the same period. Such groups as teachers, firemen, and especially policemen came to feel themselves to be among the people most affected by the new ferment in society; they saw themselves deserving of compensation commensurate with the burdens and risks they were called upon to bear. Conversely, there has been a decrease in the control exercised by the taxpayer and his representatives over major segments of government cost, especially at the local level. Town councils, school committees, and similar local entities have increasingly found themselves faced with the results of collective bargaining in the form of salary scales and total compensation costs that, as a practical if not a legal matter, they have little choice but to accept.

Another basic problem is summarized in a comment by Professor Nigro. "The difficult question," he notes, "is which phases of merit systems should be determined by collective bargaining and which should not be so determined." [16] It is one thing to acquiesce in the setting of wage rates and fringe benefits through collective bargaining, but should the same process apply, for instance, to promotions? Until now the traditional civil service doctrine has required that promotions be handled

[13] "Those Newly Militant Government Workers," *The Public Employee,* XXXIII, No. 9 (September, 1968), p. 6, quoted in Nigro, op. cit., p. 315.

[14] Op. cit., p. 315.

[15] Ibid., pp. 315 and 319.

[16] Ibid., p. 337.

by examination or generally on merit. Many public employee organizations, as with their counterparts in the private sector, are, however, insisting that seniority determine promotions. Yet another emerging issue deals with the role of employees in making policy for their agencies. Certainly social workers can legitimately expect to be able to negotiate over case loads, but should they, as in New York City a couple of years ago, attempt to negotiate over substantive policy issues such as the clothing and other allowances their clients were to receive? The City Welfare Commissioner pointed out that he did not have the authority to negotiate on these issues because they were governed by federal and state regulations.[17]

Whatever the outcome in some of these areas of present controversy, it is clear just from the trends cited in the foregoing paragraphs, that the current decade will see substantial alterations in the role and position of the public servant. Revolutionary as these changes may become, they will probably do no more than parallel and reflect upheaval and reform in many other aspects of society. The American political system cannot function without countless thousands of public employees at every level. It can, however, function with a corps of employees organized and utilized on a far different basis than that dictated by the legal and civil service orthodoxies of the past. And it probably will find itself using the services of people who are increasingly program oriented and assertive about implementing their own values in the work of public service.

Administration as Structure

The structures in and through which the administrators we have been discussing carry on their duties are important, directly and indirectly, for a variety of reasons. One can say this without falling into the trap that many students of government in days gone by fell into: thinking that structure is the *only* important factor to study in governmental arrangement. Institutional forms are not all important, but neither are they wholly without significance. They are especially crucial in shaping the overall texture of public policy and in determining what programs and functions will overlap and/or conflict with what other functions, or on the other hand, which will mesh with and complement which others. Structure has much to do in determining the extent to which the total effort of government in coping with the problems of the economy, the quality of life for less advantaged citizens, or the physical environment functions either as a coordinated whole or, instead, generates cross-pressures and dysfunctional conflicts that inhibit goal achievement.

The structural units of the federal government range all the way from the individual subagency, such as the bureau, to the total federal system as a policy-implementing structural framework. In between are the various departments and departmentlike units that make up the administrative branch, clusters of entities with parallel program concerns in the states, and indeed the whole American political system down to the local level. Each of these requires at least brief examination.

[17] Ibid., pp. 339ff.

The Federal Administration

Beginning with the federal administrative establishment, its primary units are the eleven departments, whose heads carry the title Secretary and who enjoy Cabinet rank. There are also, however, a host of commissions, boards, agencies, administrations, corporations, and whatnot numbering upwards of fifty. The proliferation of different names and designations in itself is an interesting commentary on some of the cultural forces that shaped the system's evolution.

As a nation America was repeatedly caught between the imperative of national development, which demanded new functions performed by new administrative agencies, and its aversion to "government" in general and bureaucratic government in particular. Time and again Americans have tried to contrive structural formulae that would enable them to squirm out of this dilemma. The independent regulatory commissions provide a pertinent example. The first of these was the Interstate Commerce Commission set up in 1887 to regulate railroad rates. The notion of setting up a commission of several members, independent of any other agency—and to a degree of both President and Congress—was born of these conflicting motives.

On the one hand it was quite obvious that the practice of allowing Congress to set detailed policy was out of the question in a delicate area of this kind, however much it had become normal practice in other areas (e.g., the location of post roads and military bases). Yet there was apparently little desire to follow the European practice of confiding this authority in the professional staff of a normal bureau. Instead, a semijudicial, semilegislative hybrid was contrived, which was to be independent, yet representative of the community, nonprofessional and also nonpolitical. Such a commission would be, presumably, in a position to make policy free from pressure from political or special interests, and yet would somehow be responsive to the community at large.

Not surprisingly, this effort to avoid at one and the same time the Scylla of politics and the Charybdis of bureaucratic control succeeded in avoiding neither in the long run. As more such commissions were set up they successively came under the influence of the interests, or at least a portion of the interests, they were to regulate. Each, of course, also developed in time a skilled professional staff, steeped in the technical concerns of its industry. In fact, the commissioners themselves often lost their neutral and nontechnical status in practice, if not in form, and became professional experts in the field, as did Joseph Eastman of the Interstate Commerce Commission.

The government corporation was devised as another approach to the same dilemma. An early prototype was the Panama Railroad Company, which came under United States government control in 1904. The most famous subsequent use of this device was the Tennessee Valley Authority, which though not called a corporation, had all the attributes of one. The idea here was to copy a widely used administrative form from the admired business world with the hopes that some of its virtues could be transplanted to government. In a political system that made popular control (usually legislative or patronage) a major feature of all aspects of its public life, the independent management found in the business world was normally out of the question. The government corporation seemed to be the answer.

In other words, by the conferring of budgetary and managerial autonomy on an agency that imitated the autonomy of the firm, politics could be curbed and the admired entrepreneurial freedom and initiative of business acquired. The report of the first Hoover Commission on Reorganization of the Executive Branch (1949) recommended tighter controls over such enterprises. Interestingly enough, the Post Office, though more like a private business in the services it renders than most government agencies (yet chronically inefficient and unbusinesslike), was not a serious candidate for government corporation status until quite recently. Its political involvements with the White House, Congress, and local politicians had always been too important. Legislation was finally passed, however, under which, in 1971, the Post Office finally shifted from departmental to autonomous quasi-corporate status. No longer would Congress have to pass on rate and pay increases, and other administrative details. The change finally was enacted doubtless because the rapidly mounting costs of the service counterbalanced as a political liability the traditional patronage advantages the service had represented.

Most puzzling of all among America's bureaucratic labels and structural forms are the so-called agencies and administrations. Thus, according to the *U.S. Government Organizational Manual,* the Federal Security Agency (FSA) was created in 1939 to bring together "those agencies whose major purposes were to promote social and economic security, educational opportunity, and health." [18] Here, clearly, was a department in everything but name. Why not, then, call a bureaucratic spade a spade? The answer lies in the history of the creation of some of the other departments and the motives behind them. Departmental stature somehow had become the preeminent status attainable in the executive branch. Several of the departments created after the advent of the first few with their obvious and essential functions came into being at the behest of powerful sectors of the community, which sought representation in the councils of the nation. This was clearly true of the Department of Agriculture, and later of the Department of Commerce and Labor, soon divided into two separate Departments. (In 1967 President Johnson proposed a remerger of the two, which, predictably, encountered little enthusiasm.)

In recent decades, new services and functions have developed outside of the old-line departments as often as or oftener than within their limiting and conservative confines. As with the FSA, groups of these have been brought together for coordination and more effective supervision. But why not a *Department* of Federal Security in 1939 rather than the Federal Security *Agency?* Surely the services represented reflected the needs of major segments of the community as much as did the services rendered by Agriculture. The reasons are to be found both in the jealousy with which the title "Department" is guarded and in the resistance by opponents of welfare programs, such as the American Medical Association, to the conferring of such lofty representation on welfare beneficiaries; the AMA, for example, feared an ex-

[18] Washington, D.C.: G.P.O., 1967, p. 687.

pansion of medical programs. Not until the safe and conservative (as it appeared) Eisenhower Administration came into office and promised special safeguards, particularly to organized medicine, was Congress willing to transmute the FSA into the Department of Health, Education and Welfare (HEW).

During the 1960's there was a new spurt of department-creating activity, and the Department of Housing and Urban Development (HUD) and the Department of Transportation were born. Both were the product of a long struggle that is reminiscent of the establishment of HEW. In the case of HUD, urban and civil rights interests had for many years been demanding Cabinet-level representation of the cities. President Kennedy, sympathetic to their claims, included in his legislative program a request that Congress elevate the Housing and Home Finance Agency (HHFA) to departmental status as a Department of Urban Affairs. Opposition stemmed generally from elements in Congress, often with rural constituencies, that were generally unresponsive to urban problems. It also became known that if the department were created, the President would probably appoint Robert Weaver, a Negro (then administrator of the HHFA), as its head. This would make Weaver the first Negro to sit in the Cabinet, and it alienated southerners. The upshot was that two Kennedy attempts to secure the new department failed. In the course of the second effort, a press conference assertion that he would in fact appoint Weaver backfired on the President. He had hoped it would put Congress on the spot and force passage, but instead the tactic angered the prospective department's opponents, who rallied and defeated the administration bill. Not until three years later, under Lyndon Johnson, did a Department of Housing and Urban Affairs finally emerge from Congress.

In ways such as these administrative structures have evolved in America, responding far less to textbook definitions and patterns than to the traditions and folkways of an essentially antibureaucratic political culture. Yet these forms of resistance could not halt but only deflect the development of the labyrinth of forms and euphemisms that today make up the gigantic "fourth branch" of the American federal government.

Bureau Autonomy:
The Quest for Security

Clearly, in many ways the individual bureau or agency is the focus of administration. Each at one time came into being at the behest of some set of forces in the community that sought the services it could provide. Its birth probably at the same time alerted future enemies to mobilize. Its early months and years of life had to be devoted not only to developing the technical and procedural aspects of its appointed role, but to building its defenses. Once firmly established, the bureau or agency cultivates its clients and gives them both reasons for gratitude and means of expressing it. It needs to develop friends in Congress, especially on the Appropriations Committee, and it must maintain cordial relations with the President, while seeking to avoid the necessity of choosing between the President and Congress as rival masters. It must be ever alert to checkmate efforts by competing agencies to absorb it and its functions. It must watch reorganizational efforts constantly lest it lose its identity in some superdepartment.

Autonomy is in many ways the key objective. In the best of all possible bureaucratic worlds, the agency will have been set up as an independent establishment in the executive branch responsible to the President. It will thus have, if not the status, the freedom and direct White House access of a Cabinet department. In another sense, too, it will have a great deal of real autonomy. Direct responsibility to the President in practice means virtual freedom from effective supervision save in periods of crisis involving the agency's work. With all the agencies that report to him and all of the other demands on his time, it is obvious that the chief executive can spend little time dealing with the problems of any single agency. And any such agency is bound to resist reorganizational moves that seek to place it within a larger department whose head would then be the immediate focus of responsibility. Such a Cabinet-level superior would of course represent a source of more direct and continuing supervision than the White House, and further, he would represent a barrier between the agency (now bureau) head and the President, should the former need support from this ultimate source.

Many agencies, naturally, begin their administrative life as bureaus in a larger organization. Under such circumstances what, specifically, is the bureau chief's relationship to his superior—and to the President? Is he appointed by the department head (with, of course, presidential approval), or is appointment vested directly in the chief executive? Are the powers and functions of the bureau formally vested in the bureau chief, or are they vested either in the department secretary, who delegates them in such form as he may see fit to his subordinate? Or, alternatively, are its powers vested in the President, making a two-step delegation necessary to bring them to the operating bureau level? From the bureau's point of view, the ideal situation is for its powers to be vested directly in the bureau chief. This enables him to argue that he is really responsible not so much to his nominal superior as to the Congress and the President. He will be responsible, in other words, to the secretary of his department only in regard to certain housekeeping matters, and not really so far as substantive programs are concerned. By the same token, genuine program coordination by the departmental secretary will then be limited. When any threat to a bureau looms on the horizon—that it is to be moved from one location into another department, or that its relationship to its department head is to be changed in the name of more effective coordination—the issue will often center on this very question as to where its powers should be vested.

Needless to say, others besides the bureau and its chief are equally concerned with its autonomy and freedom of action. Outside interests may perceive that vital stakes are at issue both in terms of the agency's program and its organizational integrity. Such interests obviously do not want the agency and its functions abolished, but neither do they want a new supervisory situation to be instituted that will rival the influence they have developed over its activities. "Consumers" of the services of the Army Corps of Engineers, for instance, resist any merging of Corps functions with those of other project-building agencies. They know full well that the head of any such merged enterprise would have wider responsibilities for the setting of priorities and the balancing of relative claims than the Chief of Engineers, and "good" projects could well fall victim to his coordination efforts. (See further discussion of the Corps later in this chapter.)

Professor Kaufman has made a highly suggestive point as to the roots of the "politics of administration" that relates closely to the foregoing discussion:

Originally, civil servants (in the days of patronage) engaged in political activity to further the cause of a particular candidate or group of candidates. After the installation of the merit system and the growth of agency consciousness and professionalization, the end of political collaboration was defense of the agency and its program, and was practiced by both parties. This was politics of a different kind.[19]

Obviously the growth of civil service unionization and collective bargaining has further intensified the trend that Kaufman notes. In short, if the bureau or the agency is the key unit, the permanent, professional personnel of the bureau hold ultimate importance. Now that their loyalty need no longer be to a party or to another outside group (except, in a growing number of cases, their union), their particular subdivision of the federal establishment becomes the focus of their loyalty. The agency in a sense takes on the character of an interest group and in structural terms, its form and status become in themselves important characteristics to its members.

This orientation poses problems for top administrators such as the President or the secretaries of departments in their efforts to enforce coordination and singleness of purpose. It also poses problems for the agency or bureau chief himself. Janus-like he must face two ways. He must transmit and enforce orders from his superiors, the logical consequence of his position in the governmentwide hierarchy. But he must also act as ambassador and guardian for his own people, representing them at higher echelons and defending their interests. If he leans too far either way he is likely to be in trouble. Too keen an espousal of the role of "President's man" or "Secretary's man" will lose him support and leverage with his own people to the point, perhaps, of making his position untenable. Of the two, becoming the committed spokesman of his own staff is the safer. This may cause him serious problems with his bureaucratic superiors, but if his agency accepts his leadership and has a strong outside supporting clientele, he might well survive and even thrive in the face of presidential or Cabinet secretary displeasure.

Nor do the problems stop here. The agency head who is a prisoner of his own staff and its corporate desires loses most of his ability to innovate in, or even control, his own establishment. It is difficult enough for such an official, inevitably viewed by his people as a bird of passage, to grasp the threads of real power in his agency. If he either alienates the agency's personnel or allows them to take him into camp and thereby neutralize him, his chances of doing anything creative during his tenure are proportionately reduced. Somehow he must statisfy both his superiors and his own troops sufficiently to stay on good terms with both, all the while grasping and mobil-

[19] Op. cit., p. 57.

izing enough power to exert genuine control. This is indeed a difficult task. Bureau chiefs and other middle-management people need little reminding that, however remote they may or may not be from partisan politics, they are deeply and continually immersed in the politics of administration.

The Chief Executive: Budgeting and Coordination

Up to this point the worm's-eye view, as it were, of administration has been portrayed. Essentially the same phenomena can also be viewed from the top down—from the vantage point of the President as the chief administrator and as the chief architect of national policy. The development of administrationwide coordination and of modern budget practices, themselves controlling and coordinating mechanisms, suggest the political-administrative problems faced by recent White House incumbents.

Until approximately the New Deal (with the partial exception of periods of wartime crisis) most of the federal administrative functions were modest and essentially autonomous. Thus, a problem such as the need for railroad rate regulation, steamboat inspection, or rural mail delivery would be identified. A decision would then be made that the government should try to provide a solution and an agency would be created with a mandate to implement the new policy. The implementation of such policies could be carried on relatively autonomously as far as the rest of the government or even the rest of the executive establishment were concerned. The President himself, in his capacity as chief administrator, also played a very modest role. Most of these piecemeal governmental functions could run with a minimum of supervision or direction, because they *were* autonomous programs contrived to deal with special problems.

The most graphic illustration of this pluralist stage in national administration is provided by the budgetary arrangements that existed up until 1921. Prior to the passage of the Budget and Accounting Act in that year, each agency prepared its own estimates and transmitted them to the Treasury, where they were assembled and sent in turn to the appropriate congressional committees. Each agency then dealt directly with Congress in its quest for funds. This system provided for no process of central review and evaluation and no point at which programs could be compared for relative importance, for overlap and duplication, or for their correspondence with any overall budgetary or policy plans. This system involved, furthermore, no explicit role for the President as ostensible head of the executive establishment.

World War I, with its administrative and financial stresses, focused attention on the deficiencies inherent in a decentralized and headless budget system and led to the passage of the Budget and Accounting Act of 1921. This enactment provided for the first time that there be a unified executive budget prepared under the direction of the President by a Bureau of the Budget (now the Office of Management and Budget) set up especially for that purpose. The doubts and reservations that still persisted in Congress regarding this major innovation were reflected in the fact that the Bureau was put in the Treasury Department, even though it was made directly responsible to the President. This represented a kind of compromise, at least symbolically, between the former decentralized system and the new centralized budget procedure. (It should be noted, however, that there was in 1921 no Executive Office of the President to which the Bureau could have been attached. The White House establishment was to remain small and lacking in formal structure until Franklin Roosevelt set up the Executive Office of the President in 1939, and, signficantly, included the Bureau of the Budget as one of its major parts.)

In 1965 President Johnson initiated a major revision in the executive budget system designed to make it into an even more refined and effective tool for executive oversight of agencies and programs. The new scheme was called the Planning-Programming-Budgeting System and was derived from the pioneering innovations developed in the Department of Defense under Secretary Robert S. McNamara. Its keynote was a shift from summarizing money requests agency by agency and bureau by bureau in favor of the use of program headings. In the Defense Department this meant shifting from listings under the separate departments of the Army, Navy, and Air Force to such headings as "Strategic Retaliatory Forces," "Continental Air and Missile Defense Forces," and "General Purpose Forces." Breakdowns by administrative subdivisions are of course available, but they are not emphasized.

From the bureau point of view, this new approach meant that it must think in terms of programs, and defend its means of achieving assigned program goals by use of supporting "cost effectiveness" data that demonstrated the inappropriateness of possible alternative ways of doing the same job. From the supervisor's point of view, forcing subdivision chiefs to justify their requests in depth, and to lay out their planned work in program terms—instead of so much for salaries, so much for heat and light, so much for paper clips, and so much for typewriters—has obvious advantages. Now they had to demonstrate that, in terms of actual cost, their proposal for doing a particular job was more effective than any possible alternative.

It was this approach that President Johnson ordered applied to the entire executive establishment. Budget Bureau Bulletin No. 68-2 set forth the elements of the system under three headings:

a. Program Memoranda which succinctly present the agency head's major program recommendations to the President within a framework of agency objectives, identify the alternatives considered, and support the decisions taken on the basis of their contribution to the achievement of these objectives;
b. A comprehensive multi-year Program and Financial Plan which is periodically updated and presents in tabular form a complete and authoritative summary of agency programs (initially those recommended by the agency head and subsequently those adopted by the President) in terms of their outputs and costs; and
c. Special studies which provide the analytical groundwork for decisions reported in the Program Memoranda.[20]

Obviously, a system of this kind puts into the hands of the President, as it did earlier

[20] Bulletin No. 68-2, Executive Office of the President, Bureau of the Budget, "Planning-Programming-Budgeting," July 18, 1967.

in those of the Secretary of Defense, a versatile set of tools for centralizing, coordinating, and monitoring the activity of the federal administrative establishment.

The adoption and continuing refinement of a modern executive budget system has paralleled other major efforts to coordinate the activities of the executive establishment. These were given their initial impetus by the Great Depression. The most important long-range impact of this enormous financial crisis was the conviction that it implanted in the minds of citizens and officials alike that government need not stand idly by and let the economy right itself as best it could. By the early thirties this laissez faire attitude had become politically untenable and completely undesirable on humanitarian grounds. Even so, public intervention of the scale and with the variety of approaches attempted by the Roosevelt Administration made unprecedented demands on the administrative branch of the government.

For the first time in peace, the government attempted to develop and implement a broad policy that affected most of the national economy and involved many, if not most, of the existing agencies and programs. Despite the fact that new agencies were often set up to carry out various anti-Depression measures, the old-line departments were also directly or indirectly engaged. This created a vast problem of coordination, one without precedent in the previous era of limited and piecemeal administrative activity. For the first time the work of the whole federal bureaucracy had to be meshed into a coordinated pattern. As a consequence, all Presidents since 1933 have been increasingly active in their role as chief administrator. They have had to develop overall economic, welfare, and regulatory policies, and they have had to exercise the kind of political and administrative control over the agencies of the executive establishment necessary to blend their efforts into a consistent implementation of these broad policies. The modern President's preoccupation with such matters underscores the extent to which public administration is part of the political process.

The development of an imperative need to extract unified policy emphases and directions from a formerly highly pluralistic bureaucratic establishment found little machinery available for its accomplishment. The Cabinet, long the only pretense at coordinating machinery, held but modest promise. Franklin Roosevelt, the first President to confront this new situation, made a series of moves, some short-lived and others of lasting importance, in his efforts to direct the energies of the executive establishment toward the goals of his Administration. The first of these was the inauguration of the Executive Council, soon to become the National Emergency Council. The NEC (the more important of the two) was in effect a super-Cabinet that contained the heads of both the old-line departments and also of the new emergency agencies.

With the creation of the Executive Office of the President, a further step was taken in the direction of centralized policy supervision and control. It provided the chief executive with an institutional base from which to play his role as chief administrator. The new administrative assistants gave him extra sets of presidential eyes and ears for liaison purposes, while the shift of the Bureau of the Budget into the Executive Office of the President confirmed once and for all the availability of the budget as a management tool for executive control and leadership.

These and many other suggestions for streamlining the executive establishment and bringing it firmly under presidential control emanated from the landmark report of the President's Committee on Administrative Management. The Committee, consisting of three administrative experts commissioned by Roosevelt, took as their primary objective the meshing of the administrative branch into an instrument for executive leadership; they sought means by which the President could use his new staff tools to secure implementation of his Administration's goals. Not all of their ideas found acceptance, but this is the invariable fate of reorganization efforts. The philosophy of a unified executive establishment headed by a President equipped to direct its coordinated energies was the Committee's major contribution.

Administrative Reorganization

The topic of administrative reorganization is usually handled in standard treatises on administration as a separate area of concern. From all that has been said up until now, however, it is readily apparent that it cannot be separated meaningfully from the politics of administration, whether viewed from the perspective of the bureau or agency, or from the exalted perspective of the President. Beneath what may appear to be abstract exercises in rationalizing structure and improving management lurk intense and significant political involvements. A classic illustration is the so-called Hoover Commission, a massive reorganization effort mounted in 1949 by a presidential-congressional commission under the chairmanship of former President Herbert Hoover. It issued a formidable series of task force reports and final reports on all of the major sectors of the federal establishment and it made numerous recommendations for the realignment of functions; the creation, abolition, and the merger of agencies; and the improvement of methods of central control. Yet only part of its carefully worked out scheme of reform was put into effect. The reasons for this only partial success reflect the network of political motives and relationships that underlie any administrative structure. For instance, would-be reformers frequently insist that coordination of related functions is essential to good government. But in the minds of the agency officials whose programs are to be coordinated, often through merger into a department or subordination to a common superior, this seemingly desirable goal is likely to be suspect for the same reasons that autonomy is bureaucratically desirable. Coordination, after all, means compromise and loss of autonomy. Compromise means that one party must give up something, and another party must also give up something in the name of some larger objective. But unless both are persuaded of the merit of that larger objective, they are almost certain to conclude that the price is too heavy to pay; they will prefer their own uncoordinated ways.

Yet demands for coordination are frequent and predictable responses to the chaotic results of normal democratic policy-making processes. In the nature of things, most policy-making is piecemeal. Some group decides that this or that private activity needs to be regulated "in the public interest." The attendant legislative and administrative decisions will be made amid the thrust and counterthrust set in motion by the proposal among interested parties. A new set of vested interests, institutional and interest group, will be born. If this example is multiplied a dozen or more times, the activity of government in any major policy area then becomes a series of these little policy-making subsystems. Sooner or later pairs and clusters will interact—either negatively through competition, duplication, or working at cross purposes, or, less often, positively through ad hoc cooperation. Overall policy thus becomes an unplanned collage partaking as much of wasteful competition as of conscious integration. Coordination is often demanded when someone or some group concludes that too many such clusters exist in a given policy area. Or perhaps a major reorganizational effort like those recommended by the two Hoover Commissions (the second in 1955) will map a blueprint for the rationalizing of administration and supervision in all major policy areas.

A typical example that illustrates much of this process of mushroom growth and often unsuccessful effort at rationalization centers on the Corps of Engineers of the U.S. Army. Years ago the Army Engineers were the only civil engineers readily available to the government. When the now-familiar federal policy of underwriting local improvements—waterways, harbor improvements, and so on—began, it was the Army Engineers who did the technical work. In time this became more or less their prerogative. There gradually evolved a tight network of relationships linking the Engineer Corps with the Rivers and Harbors Committees of the Congress, other Congressmen who wanted or might someday want a federally financed improvement in their home district (which includes most Congressmen), and various private interests who benefited from such projects. These latter might include local government units, chambers of commerce, shippers, barge owners, sportsmen, yacht clubs. The process of approving proposed projects clears the way for Corps implementation. It involves congressional committee authorization of an investigation, hearings in the local area that afford an opportunity to those who would be affected to voice support, and ultimately inclusion of the by now popular and heartily approved project in an omnibus rivers and harbors bill (*pork-barrel bill* in popular terminology) along with many other similar projects. In actuality, the Corps plays a far from completely neutral role and serves instead as a catalytic agent in these deliberations. The very friendliness of its relations with interested parties inside and outside of Congress turns it into an ally rather than a mere bystander. Unquestionably, too, the Corps often fosters both the initiation of projects and the stimulation of support for them.

In recent decades other federal programs have developed that also construct dams and undertake resource development projects. The Bureau of Reclamation in the Department of the Interior has the most important of these. It was established in 1902 (at the height of the interest in conservation sparked by Theodore Roosevelt) to "construct, operate, and maintain works for the storage, diversion, and development of waters for the reclamation of arid and semi-arid lands in the Western States." [21] Dams are also constructed by the Corps of Engineers for flood control or navigational purposes. Why not, one might ask, put the functions of these two agencies together in the hands of a single department or bureau? The primary reason lies

[21] *U.S. Government Manual,* op. cit., p. 258.

in the enormous political power that can be mobilized in Congress in defense of the present status of the Corps. Though nominally responsible to the Secretary of the Army and through him ultimately to the President, the Corps considers itself really responsible to Congress regarding these civil functions—they are, in their own phrase, "Engineer Consultants to the Congress." Any effort to insert a supervisory layer between the Corps and its close congressional associates, or to reorganize its operations so as to give the President genuine control, is met by a solid wall of legislative and interest-group opposition.

As a matter of fact, there have been occasions when the Corps has had the temerity to defy the direct instructions of the President himself. In a famous case involving the construction of a dam in the central valley of California to supply irrigation water, the Corps went ahead on the basis of its solid congressional and local support, even though President Franklin D. Roosevelt had made it abundantly clear that he wanted the Bureau of Reclamation to do the job. It is not therefore surprising that reorganization is so difficult. With the exception of the Federal Bureau of Investigation and the U.S. Marine Corps, few agencies can mobilize the massive political backing that is ever ready to rush to the support of the Engineer Corps. Most agencies, however, have built such defenses-in-depth as they could to fend off would-be reformers, hostile private interests, or predatory bureaucratic rivals.

An illustration of the image consciousness of government agencies, even those with the impregnable base of the Corps of Engineers, came in an August, 1971, news story headlined: "Army Corps Strives to Join Ecology Camp." The Engineers had often been in the bad graces of the conservation and ecology groups because of their militant refusal to be swerved from projects that were criticized as ecologically harmful. In an astute shift of program emphasis designed both to blunt such criticism and to hoist the Corps aboard the environmental bandwagon, its facilities are being turned toward problems of water-waste management in five major metropolitan areas of the country (Boston, Cleveland-Akron, Detroit, Chicago, and San Francisco). As a spokesman put it: "In the 1970s we have to go where the people are, that's where the environmental problems are, not in the bayous." [22] In this new role, the Corps will be working closely and doing detailed planning for the Environmental Protection Agency in a consultant relationship on the construction, supervision and operation of water treatment facilities.

Recent Reorganization and Coordination Proposals

President Richard M. Nixon may go down in history as one of the most innovating Presidents ever to sit in the White House, at least so far as the number and scope of his proposals for reform and restructuring are concerned. How many will actually find their way onto the statute books before the end of his tenure in office is and will remain an open question for some time. (See also the discussion of the Nixon

[22] *Providence* (Rhode Island) *Journal,* August 9, 1971.

proposals for welfare reform in Chapter 12.) In his State of the Union message to Congress in January, 1971, the President indicated his intention of proposing the most far-reaching reorganization of the departments and programs of the federal government, at least since the first Hoover Commission. In sweep and scope his proposals might actually have to be compared with the impact of the New Deal. In a nutshell the plan, as finally submitted in detail to Congress, called for the elimination of seven of the present Cabinet-level departments, and the reallocation of their functions among four new departments to be named Natural Resources, Human Resources, Economic Affairs, and Community Development. These four, plus State, Treasury, Defense, and Justice (minus Post Office, which is now an autonomous corporate entity) would constitute the new Cabinet.

The plan makes considerable sense as a step toward promoting the consolidation of functions into more meaningful clusters and hence their more effective coordination within the new departments and ultimately by the President. Much of the piecemeal, ad hoc, formless growth of generations, and the anomalies and conflicts it has created would be eliminated or rationalized. The new Department of Natural Resources, for example, would have five functional divisions: land and recreation resources; water resources; energy and minerals resources; oceanic, atmospheric, and earth sciences; and Indian and territorial affairs. It would comprise 110,700 employees and have a budget of something over $5 billion. Its component parts would come from the present Department of the Interior primarily, but some also from the Department of Agriculture (e.g., the Forest Service and the Soil Conservation Service) and other sources.[23]

The Department of Human Resources would be composed largely of elements of the present Department of Health, Education and Welfare plus some Office of Economic Opportunity functions. Its employment roster would doubtless top 100,000 and its budget would be in the vicinity of $70 billion. Economic Affairs revives a proposal by President Johnson to combine the present Departments of Labor and Commerce, but it adds elements from Agriculture, Transportation, and such independent agencies as the Small Business Administration and the Tariff Commission. The Department of Community Development would have as its core the Department of Housing and Urban Development, and it would also include programs and staff from Agriculture, HEW, and the Office of Economic Opportunity. Its mission would in effect be broadened from HUD's present focus on the problems of the cities to community development problems across the land, in rural and small communities as well as in urban settings.[24] A useful synoptic view of the whole plan, together with a listing of the major programs and the agencies assigned to the proposed new departments, is to be found in Figure 10.1.

The political pitfalls that lie between the proposal of this sweeping reorganization and its implementation are suggested by the comment of President John Kennedy to a gentleman who proposed to him a splendid new way to handle a Federal program. "That's a good idea. Now let's see if we can get the Government to

[23] Ibid., March 26, 1971.
[24] Ibid.

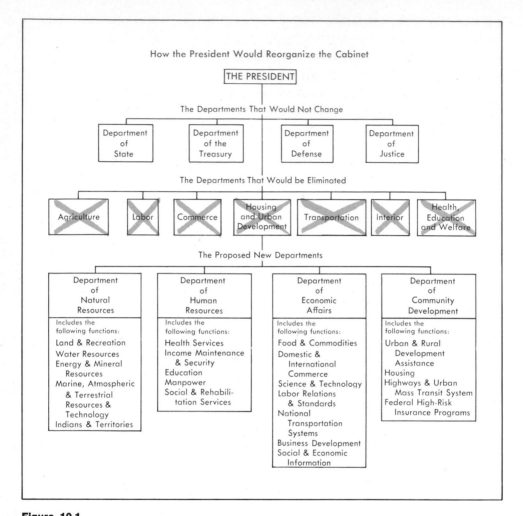

Figure 10.1.

Source: The New York Times, March 28, 1971. Copyright by The New York Times Company.
Reprinted by permission.

accept it." [25] The White House was not unaware of the various hornet's nests into which it was thrusting its proposals. For example, as late as four days before the plan went to Congress the President compromised one of the hottest issues likely to come up: the location of the so-called civil (dam and water resource projects) functions of the Army Engineers. The political power of this agency has already been discussed at length. As Robert Sherrill wrote in the *New York Times,* "Devotees of Congressional warfare are also looking forward to the attempt to take the civil functions . . . and put them—along with the residue of the Interior Department and some other agencies—into the new Department of Natural Resources. That

[25] Robert Sherrill, "Every U.S. President Wishes He Could Act Like One," *New York Times,* March 28, 1971.

should supply plenty of excitement." [26] At the last minute the President decided to cut the excitement level a bit by transferring only the planning and related functions, leaving the construction personnel attached to the Department of Defense.

One of the major sources of opposition to the whole reorganizational idea is bound to come in time from the congressional establishment's concern for its own prerogatives. The committee structure is, of course, geared to the present allocation of functions and departmental jurisdictions in the executive branch in order that the committees may perform their overseeing role in a systematic fashion. The Nixon plan would force a basic reshuffle of much of the committee structure. As another *Times* correspondent noted, Senator Herman Talmadge of Georgia "would probably not look too kindly on the prospect of seeing the Agriculture Department, and thus presumably his committee," in effect reorganized out from under him.[27] Although the Nixon effort to secure better program integration and coordination, better executive management, and greater rationality in the federal administrative structure makes good theoretical sense, not much of it is likely to come to pass, at least in the short run. Representative Chet Holifield of California, whose committee will have jurisdiction over the proposals, estimated it would take his group at least four years to process the legislation!

[26] Ibid.
[27] John W. Finney, "Political Purpose for '72 Is Suggested by Holifield," *New York Times,* January 24, 1971.

bureaucratic relations in a federal system

The Problems of Intergovernmental Coordination

If problems of coordination in the federal administrative structure have proved to be complex and intractable, the still broader problems introduced by the framers of the Constitution when they adopted the federal structural principle to govern the relations between the national authorities and those in the various states have been even more complicated for a longer time. As noted earlier, it was really not until the impact of the Great Depression and the New Deal innovations that the need to mesh the total policy output of the national government was fully recognized and at least partially dealt with. State versus national problems of coordination even predate the Constitution, and on at least one occasion, provoked a bloody Civil War. Curiously and significantly, however, the most crucial problems of coordination among the levels of government (including local as well as state and national) have developed during the second half of the twentieth century.

Conflict and Cooperation

The placid phrase "intergovernmental relations" conceals some of the stormiest conflicts as well as some of the most constructive cooperative efforts in the American political system. Intergovernmental relations are the interactions between the overlapping units of government characteristic of American federalism: the national government in Washington, the fifty states, and the thousands of counties and cities. The Civil War was conflict, in part, among parties, leaders, and citizens who held irreconcilable views about the federal system of government. In our own times, there have been smaller but dramatic confrontations between national authority and resisting state leaders in Little Rock, Arkansas, and Oxford, Mississippi. Thus, in 1957 President Eisenhower federalized the state militia to enforce school integration in a Little Rock public high school; in 1962 President Kennedy sent in the Army to quell riots at the University of Mississippi that were obstructing the enforcement of a federal court order demanding the admission of a black student, James H. Meredith; in 1971, Governor George Wallace of Alabama tried to overturn federal court orders on school busing by executive order.

Happily, there is another parallel thread to intergovernmental relations besides the ones of violent conflict. Since our earliest days the various levels of government have cooperated in solving common problems in education, financing, and administration.

Not only have "intergovernmental relations" embraced some of the major issues, events, and problems of American politics, but they have also included some of the nation's most important and colorful political leaders. Federal-state relations have involved such Presidents as Lincoln and Kennedy and such Governors as Wallace and Barnett. Moreover, Governor after Governor has gone to Washington to testify as to his state's needs and to propose appropriate federal programs. Sometimes in agreement with the Governors, but often not, big city mayors also arrive regularly in Washington to explain their problems and to seek the superior financial and planning resources of the national government. In the process, many mayors, from former Mayor West of Nashville to Mayor Lindsay of New York, have openly expressed the sentiment that they are more inclined to look to the federal government for help than to their own state capitals. As a consequence, far-reaching domestic programs, which have been hammered out through negotiations involving the officials of numerous layers of government, depend for their day-to-day administration upon leaders both in and far away from Washington. The Elementary and Secondary Education Act of 1965 requires cooperation between federal bureaucrats in the Office of Education, state education agencies, and thousands of local school boards and school systems. It is only one example among many.

As even an introductory survey of the realm of intergovernmental relations reveals, it would be difficult to devise a governmental system at once more confusing, complex—and flexible—than that under which Americans live. Yet, more often than not we seem to have made the necessary day-to-day adjustments. Americans live under, bargain with, and alternately influence and are influenced by an incredible profusion of government units: there are ninety-two thousand tax-levying units in the United States. Perhaps this variety is inevitable in a nation composed of heterogeneous citizens and diverse local political cultures. Surely there are enough cracks and open joints in the system for people with views as different as those favoring "centralized government," "states' rights," or "grassroots democracy" to coexist and prosper most of the time. The branches of government in the United States are so diverse and their points of contact with one another so overlapping that it is incorrect to visualize intergovernmental relations as something conducted between separate, clearly defined "layers" of government. Rather, the system as it operates is best described by Morton Grodzins' apt term: "a marblecake."

Within this marblecake individual citizens are served by overlapping units of government. A resident of Park Forest, Illinois, for example, pays taxes to all of the following governments: the United States of America, the State of Illinois, Cook County, Cook County Forest Preserve District, Suburban Tuberculosis Sanitary District, Rich Township, Bloom Township Sanitary District, Non-High School District 216, Rich Township High School District, Elementary School District 163, and the South Cook County Mosquito Abatement District.

Those who live and work in the metropolitan Philadelphia area, which stretches from Trenton, New Jersey, to Wilmington, Delaware, may find themselves in contact with 11 counties, 21 cities, 218 townships, 138 boroughs, and 3 state governments, not to mention numerous independent school districts and special authorities.

In addition, the different units of this governmental marblecake are connected to each other in many complicated ways. Most of the civilian employees of the national government are based, not in Washington, but in America's regions in such a way as to facilitate their work with their counterparts in countless state and local agencies, bureaus, and departments. Since the end of World War II Washington has had an increasing number of direct relationships with city governments. Further, in the Delaware Basin Compact, the federal government functions as a partner within a contractual arrangement involving a number of state and local governments.

Washington, finally, is a party to only a fraction of the intergovernmental relations of the country. States have relations with other states, separately and in groups; there are now some twenty-three interstate compacts that provide for cooperation among the state governments in policy areas ranging from education to water pollution. The state governments are also typically involved with local governments within their own boundaries in much the same way that Washington is related to the states; state transfer and aid payments provide large portions—from 10 to 40 per cent—of the budgets of city governments and local school boards. One way to understand how the marblecake developed is to begin with a look at the subject of federalism.

Federalism

Numerous countries of the world, among them Brazil, Canada, Mexico, the Soviet Union, and West Germany, along with the United States, possess "federal" as opposed to "unitary" systems of government. Simply put, federalism means that more than one unit of government will have partial responsibility for a citizen living in any part of the nation. A more formal definition has been offered by Professor Daniel J. Elazar. Federalism, he writes, is

The mode of political organization that unites smaller polities within an overarching political system by distributing power among general and constituent governments in a manner designed to protect the existence and authority of both national and subnational political systems, enabling all to share in the over-all system's decision-making and executing process.[28]

Why did the early leaders of our nation switch from the confederational system of the Articles to the more centralized federalism of the Constitution? The answer to this significant question begins with an examination of the general conditions

---

[28] *American Federalism: A View from the States* (New York: Crowell, 1966), p. 2.

under which federal systems emerge. It requires, too, some consideration of the particular political conditions that led to the construction of the Constitution of 1787.

Professor William H. Riker has delineated the two conditions under which a federal bargain is likely to be struck among political leaders holding local and national orientations:

1. The politicians who offer the bargain desire to expand their territorial control, usually either to meet an external military or diplomatic threat or to prepare for military or diplomatic aggression and aggrandizement. But though they desire to expand, they are not able to do so by conquest, because of their military incapacity or ideological distaste. Hence, if they are to satisfy the desire to expand, they must offer concessions to the rulers of the constitutent units. . . .
2. The politicians who accept the bargain, giving up some independence for the sake of union, are willing to do so because of some external military-diplomatic threat or opportunity.[29]

In Riker's view, these two conditions existed when the Constitution of the United States was adopted. The concrete motivations behind the urgings of those national leaders who wanted to move beyond the ineffective government of the Articles, and those strong state leaders who were willing to give up some of their own power, come together in what Riker calls the "Military Interpretation of the Constitution." Although this analysis need not be accepted as an exclusive explanation of the origins of the Constitution, it presents a useful interpretation more in harmony with the facts of American political life in the 1780's than explanations that describe the framers as tools of a mystical "manifest destiny" or as agents of some base "economic" interests.

Under the "Military Interpretation," the era of the 1780's is primarily viewed as one of great international tension. American politicians perceived their fragmented country as gravely threatened by both the hostility and the superior resources of the British, French, and Spanish, all of whom had military garrisons in North America. To Washington and to Madison, a stronger system of centralized government was necessary in order to deal with these foreign threats. As a consequence, Madison, with Washington's tacit support, wrote a proposed document for the Constitutional Convention—the famous Virginia Plan. This plan came close to proposing a unitary form of government: it relegated the states to an essentially administrative role by providing that their laws could be "negatived" by the federal Congress and by authorizing the enforcement of congressional commands with national troops.

Leaders from other states at the Convention were not, however, willing to go quite as far as Madison proposed. They were nonetheless prepared to bargain away some state authority in return for the presumed advantages of a more centralized system; this led to a compromise, creating a relatively centralized national government, but leaving the states with an important role in the composition of that government and also with important reserved powers. What did the compromise document actually provide? Although contemporary federalism can only be understood through

[29] *Federalism: Origin, Operation, Significance* (Boston: Little, Brown, 1964), p. 2.

Table 10.3 *1787: The terms of the federal bargain*

I. Limitations on the states	II. Guarantees to the states
INDIRECT	
Establishment of strong federal, executive, and legislative branches.	Guaranteed equal representation in the United States Senate and proportional representation in the United States House of Representatives. Ultimate control of the amending process rests with the states.
DIRECT	
States prohibited from making treaties, alliances, or confederations or making war—no state foreign policies.	Guarantee against division or consolidation against their wishes.
No interstate or foreign trade compacts without consent of Congress—no external independent economic policies.	Protection against invasion and internal violence. Guarantee of a "republican" form of internal government.
States cannot tax other state's products—no state protectionism.	Retain right to maintain militias. Equal treatment for their ports and their citizens from federal government and other states.
States bound to accept federal Constitution and statutes as superior to their own constitutions and laws—in case of controversy, federal policy rules.	Citizens accused of violating federal laws will be tried within their home states. Federal judiciary will decide disputes between citizens of different states, or between the different states themselves.

an examination of the many subsequent Supreme Court decisions, the alterations wrought by historical developments, and the actual patterns of present-day politics, a look at the Constitution as framed and amended provides some initial insights into the shape of the federal system. Table 10.3 summarizes the terms of the 1787 compact.

To begin with, the new Constitution imposed a set of limitations upon the states. One set, the establishment of a generally strong federal executive and legislative branch, was indirect. There were also some distinctly defined limitations. The states were prohibited from entering into treaties, alliances, or confederations, or engaging in war on their own; they could not participate in interstate or foreign compacts without the consent of the national Congress; they were forbidden to levy import taxes on one another's products; and they were bound to accept the Constitution and all acts of Congress as the law of the land superior to their own acts. Subsequent amendments have prohibited the states from denying the right to vote on the basis of race or sex, from denying the equal protection of the laws, and from interfering with life, liberty, or property without due process of law.

At the same time, the states extracted a substantial set of guarantees from the Constitutional Convention. They could not be divided or consolidated against their wishes, they were guaranteed protection against invasion and domestic violence by the federal government, and they were guaranteed a republican form of government. Furthermore, the states retained their right to maintain militias; they were pledged equal treatment for their ports and reciprocal privileges and immunities for their citizens in the courts of all other states; they received a pledge that federal criminal trials would be held within their own boundaries and that the federal judiciary would mediate disputes between them or between citizens of more than one state. Most important, they were each given two Senators and a number of Congressmen proportionate to their population. And finally, the states retained ultimate control over the process of amending the Constitution itself.

States' rights advocates then and now took comfort in the language of the Tenth Amendment, which provided that powers not delegated to the national government were "reserved" to the states. Yet, even when the wording was adoptd by the Congress in 1789, an attempt to insert the phrase "expressly delegated" was rejected, indicating from the outset that Congress did not intend to limit itself or the President rigidly in terms of the future use of power in unforeseen or new circumstances.

This partial listing of the powers of the national government in relation to the states is intended only to illustrate the bare bones, the starting point, of the federal system. Yet it indicates that all levels of government have certain responsibilities and that the vagueness of the constitutional language makes overlap and conflict unavoidable.

Contemporary Intergovernmental Relations

Starting roughly at the time of World War I the traditional pattern of "division of labor" in the federal system began to change decisively. Until then, most of the relatively few functions and services that government performed for the citizen were the responsibility of the state and local governments. The national government dealt with the public directly only in a very few areas. Before 1913, the states spent more than the national government: $2 billion to $700 million. All governments put together spent $26 per capita on various services. By 1946, the balance had shifted. Washington spent $60 billion and the states only $10 billion. Overall per capita spending had reached $518. In 1915, Washington made grants and transfer payments to the states of $5 million; by 1946, the comparable figure exceeded $1 billion. Clearly, between 1913 and 1948 the level of overall government spending vastly increased, and the level of Washington's expenditures increased far more rapidly than that of the states. In a very real sense this shift reflected the federal government's superior fiscal resources and its ability to respond more rapidly to problems that were beyond either the capacity or the inclination of the states to solve. At the same time the citizenry accepted, indeed demanded, that the national government play the preeminent role among the myriad government units of the country. One revealing sign of the growing change in general attitudes during this period is the behavior of the Supreme Court. From 1913 until 1937 the Court frequently struck down efforts of the Congress to deal with various problems of regulation and to extend the activities of the federal government. The Court declared unconstitutional acts ranging from the regulation of child labor to the establishment of national industrial pricing boards. But beginning in 1937, the Court reversed itself, approving broad regulation of economic activities, Social Security, and farm price supports. In its decisions, the Court recognized the extent of the changes in the body politic and the ensuing new relationships of governments. In short, it added its approval to that of the public.

If any single word can describe contemporary intergovernmental relations, it is *complexity*. All governments have expanded their activities. In the process, they have more to do with one another and with their citizens. More and more, there has come to be a noticeable overlap in the activities of the national, state, and local governments.[30] Table 10.4 indicates the direction of present control. Certain functions historically performed exclusively by Washington remain in its control. Many other services now are provided predominantly by the national government although the states still share a quite significant secondary role. A contemporary assessment of the federal-state balance also reveals the two levels of government sharing about equally in some other areas. The states still are predominant actors in some fields but with a substantial secondary federal role. The states, finally, still maintain their traditional exclusive jurisdiction over a few policy areas.

Increasingly, those areas that used to be equally shared between Washington and the states now see Washington predominate; those that used to see a predominant state role now see an equal responsibility; those that used to be the states' alone now see a rising federal involvement. The last two decades have seen the expansion of federal standards through Supreme Court decisions, acts of Congress, and various instances of presidential leadership and administrative decision in the executive branch. Many of these federal advances have, of course, been bitterly resisted by the southern states, and states and localities in all parts of the country have refined their own methods of imprinting local needs on the federal programs.

As happened within the national administrative establishment itself, the pattern of programs that make up the intergovernmental "layer cake" reached the point during the 1960's at which coordination became an urgent necessity. For years individual grant-in-aid and similar schemes have been enacted aimed at solving specific individual problems. Cumulatively they came to cluster in various policy areas, but without any systematic coordination. The 1960's saw new developments within this amorphous intergovernmental framework in the shape of broad attacks on fundamental, wide ranging social, economic, and urban problems. There was urban renewal in its various forms, the Poverty Program in 1964, and Model Cities in 1966, to note the outstanding examples.

---

[30] This evaluation draws upon W. H. Riker's interpretation in *Federalism: Origin, Operation, Significance, op. cit.*, pp. 82–84.

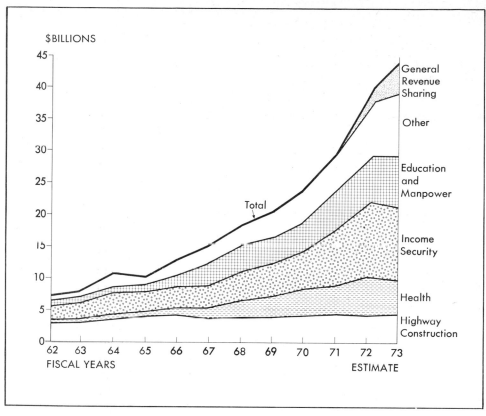

Figure 10.2. Distribution of federal aid to state and local governments by programs

Source: Bureau of the Budget. Special Analysis P: Federal Aid to State and Local Governments. Budget of the United States, 1972, p. 239.

James Sundquist and David Davis of the Brookings Institution make the point when they begin their study *Making Federalism Work:*

In the nineteen-sixties the American federal system entered a new phase. Through a series of dramatic enactments, the Congress asserted the national interest and authority in a wide range of governmental functions that until then had been the province, exclusively or predominantly, of state and local governments. The new legislation not only established federal-state-local relations in entirely new fields of activity and on a vast scale but it established new patterns of relationships.[31]

In part this development took the form of a dramatic rise in the number of grant-in-aid programs sponsored by the federal government. Such assistance to state and/or local government was available in only ten areas of activity before 1930; another seventeen were added during the New Deal years; twenty-nine were added during the first decade and a half after World War II; and *thirty-nine* came into being in

[31] Washington, D.C.: The Brookings Institution, 1969, p. 1.

Table 10.4 *Contemporary intergovernmental relations: Level of government controlling different policy functions*

I. *Exclusive control with national government:*	Foreign affairs; defense; regulation of money and credit
II. *Primary control with national government/strong secondary role to states:*	Support and regulation of transportation, communication, production, distribution; natural resource management; welfare; support of basic research
III. *Equal control between national and state governments:*	Maintenance of civil rights and liberties; support of recreation and health facilities
IV. *Primary control with state government/strong secondary role to national government:*	Public safety and police activities; protection of property rights; regulation of utilities; support of public education
V. *Exclusive control with state governments:*	Public morals; divorce, marriage, abortion

just the six years starting with 1961.[32] Table 10.5 shows the dramatic growth also in the amount of money spent annually for this kind of aid program in the period between 1958 and 1970.

It has not been just a matter of multiplication of grant programs or the total increase in dollars. Again, to quote Sundquist and Davis:

Before 1960 the typical federal assistance program did not involve an expressly stated national purpose. It was instituted, rather, as a means of helping state or local governments accomplish *their* objectives. . . . Characteristic of the legislation of the 1960's are forthright declarations of national purpose, experimental and flexible approaches to the achievement of those purposes, and close federal supervision and control to assure that the national purposes are served.[33]

The key changes are, specifically, the breadth of the new objectives sought (e.g., the elimination of poverty), the fact that these are now explicitly national objectives being superimposed on local programs, and finally, the decision (need?) to seek these goals by working with and through local and state levels of government rather than through direct unmediated contact between federal bureaucrats and the client groups.

Actually, there is a theoretical range of three possible approaches to areas of policy concern like poverty, the salvaging of the core cities, or the cleaning up of

[32] Ibid., p. 2.
[33] Ibid., p. 3.

Table 10.5 *Growth in the volume of federal aid expenditures, 1958–1970*

Fiscal year	Amount of federal aid (in millions of dollars)	Federal aid as percentage of		
		Total federal expenditures	Domestic federal expenditures *	State-local revenue †
1958	4,935	6.1	14.6	12.0
1959	6,669	7.4	16.6	14.6
1960	7,040	7.8	17.2	13.8
1961	7,112	7.4	15.7	13.2
1962	7,893	7.5	16.4	13.5
1963	8,634	7.7	16.4	13.7
1904	10,141	8.6	18.2	14.8
1965	10,904	9.3	18.8	14.8
1966	12,960	9.9	20.3	15.7
1967	15,240	9.9	20.7	16.7
1968	18,599	10.4	20.9	17.8
1969 ‡	20,813	11.3	22.0	17.9
1970 ‡	25,029	12.8	23.6	n.a.

Source: Special Analysis Budget of the United States, Fiscal Year 1970, Table O.3, p. 209, in James L. Sundquist and David W. Davis, *Making Federalism Work* (Washington, D.C.: The Brookings Institution, 1969), p. 2.

n.a. Not available.

* Excluding expendiures for national defense, space and international affairs and finance.

† Based on compilations published by Governments Division, Bureau of Census. Excludes state-local revenue from publicly operated utilities, liquor stores, and insurance trust systems.

‡ Estimate. The 1970 estimate is that of President Johnson's final budget and does not take account of President Nixon's revisions.

the environment. The federal government may take existing grant-in-aid programs, supplement them with necessary new initiatives, and weave the whole into a coordinated pattern of federal-state-local cooperation to achieve objectives that are set in Washington. Second, the national bureaucracy, as noted, could bypass the other levels of government and deal with the groups involved directly; or, third, through the kind of bloc-grant revenue-sharing initiated by the Nixon Administration, Washington could indicate problem areas to the states and localities, but leave them to frame their own specific programs and guidelines for solution.

The second of these possibilities can be readily ruled out. If it did not in fact violate the federal provisions in the Constitution, it would face all of the monumental political opposition that appeals to the "spirit of the federal system" can generate. The third seems certain to become increasingly important in the next few years, with the enactment of revenue sharing in 1972. The first received its most elaborate test under the Johnson administration's Model Cities program.

The Model Cities approach involved calling on each city to take the initiative in preparing and submitting to Washington its own comprehensive program, including consideration of the physical improvements needed: housing, transportation, education, manpower and economic development, recreation and culture, crime reduction, health, and social services. Fifty or more existing federal programs administered by seven Cabinet departments plus the Office of Economic Opportunity were listed for possible inclusion in the cities' plans.[34] The essence of the planning phase, then, was federally prompted local initiative to do broad-based planning that would make integrated use of existing federal aid programs.

A final word on the long-term impact of the Nixon Administration's revenue-sharing program is necessary. The presumed outcome of adopting a set of bloc grants in place of the dozens of very specific program grants currently made to states and localities will be to shift both goal-setting initiative and implementation largely to the state and local levels of government. This will have a fragmenting effect on policy, and almost certainly a conservative impact. It seems obvious that national standards will give way to varying local emphases based on local cultural patterns—and prejudices. It is almost equally obvious, in light of the court battles in recent years to force states and communities to accept prescribed levels of integration or welfare aid or procedural fairness, that many jurisdictions would turn back the clock if freed from present detailed federal directives. Local elites, the elements of local power structures, can usually get their way much more easily in dealing with city or state officials than with the federal bureaucracy or courts. The other side of the coin represented by the remoteness and inaccessibility of Washington, is a relative insulation from the special pleading of local vested interests.

The State and Local Level

As the foregoing pages demonstrate, it is not possible to talk about problems of administration in the American political system without saying a good deal about the levels of government below the national. Administrators at all levels are forced into what is often an uncomfortable and unenthusiastic cooperation. Hence, there is little that need be said specifically about state and local administrative problems, though a few illustrative points will serve to round out the discussion in the chapter.

For one thing, we must not leave the impression that broad policy is made in Washington and then handed to the states and localities as Moses brought down the commandments from Mount Sinai. The local political units may well have a considerable voice, though perhaps an indirect one, in shaping the policy before it reaches the implementation stage or when it is being reviewed and revised by the federal government.

It is sometimes difficult for those affected to perceive accurately what the consequences of any new program will be. (See the discussion of the Poverty Program

[34] Ibid., p. 83.

in Chapter 12.) After a while, however, the picture becomes clearer. If there is widespread dissatisfaction, then the disaffected parties will try to alter the program basically during the yearly congressional review. If there is general acceptance of the program, minor changes may still be sought at the level of executive administration. Continuing adjustments in ongoing programs are common. Another type of activity has nothing to do with the substance of either legislation or administration, but is part of a continuing struggle to have federal money for research or installations spent within particular boundaries. This is the conflict, pure and simple, over the allocation of earmarked resources.

When *basic alteration* is the goal, the requests before Congress are for fundamental changes in who will administer a certain program or how much money it will get. In recent sessions of Congress the state governments have demonstrated considerable resourcefulness in having control turned over to them in a number of areas. Some examples may illustrate the point. State departments of education are more conservative than the United States Office of Education in the Department of Health, Education and Welfare, primarily because the state education agencies, unlike the national one, are largely dominated by the viewpoints of professional education associations. Consequently, to take a program away from the federal office and place it under the direction of the states is to move from an innovative to a more conservative administration and outlook. In 1967, when several titles under the Elementary and Secondary Education Act of 1965 came up for review, state-oriented interests persuaded Congress to place these titles under the control of the states. At the same time, the recruitment and selection responsibility in the administration of the Teacher Corps, a program that sends talented volunteer teachers into slum schools, was transferred from Washington to the states, and the program's budget was halved. Thus, this innovative program was simultaneously curtailed and made more amenable at the level of teacher selection to the standards favored by tradition-bound state education leaders—the very officials whose previous failures in dealing with slum schools had motivated the original establishment of the Teacher Corps. By careful application of pressures in Congress and by waiting for the proper moment, the states won major victories and basically altered major federal programs. Legislation in the fields of urban development, poverty alleviation, and education has been similarly subject to this sort of yearly change.

Other areas of legislation affecting intergovernmental relations are so established, however, that the political action bypasses the Congress. Pressure is applied to the great Washington bureaucracies—HEW, HUD, and the Departments of Labor, Commerce, the Interior, and Agriculture. The process, one of *continuing adjustment,* is characterized by pressures from the states and cities to amend, alter, or relax the administrative rules that the agencies have the power to set under permissive authority delegated to them by the Congress. Sometimes state intervention is at high levels, as when southern governors in 1967 asked HEW Secretary John Gardner to change the guidelines under which aid to state departments of education was being distributed. More often, however, the process is what most people have in mind when they refer to cooperative federalism. There is a continuing effort on the part of administrators in Washington and their counterparts in the states and cities to accommodate the others' needs and demands.

This process of bureaucratic accommodation goes on at many levels. Federal officials in most fields, including those of health, highways, housing, and welfare, have the power to review state utilization of federal funds through the devices of prior approval, on-the-spot inspection, and postaudits. These federal officials also have the legal authority to withhold funds when federal requirements are not met by state or city administrative recipients. When there is a discrepancy between federal rules and state or local performance, negotiations begin and both sides look for ways to make the programs work. The federal officials are anxious that their programs have users—satisfied and effective ones at that. They thus make every effort to persuade the erring state or local officials to mend their ways, and they generally specify explicitly how this can be accomplished. On the other side the method, tried and often true, of the state and city bureaucrats is to try to convince their federal counterparts that they have in fact followed the rules and devised a workable program—if only the rules would be interpreted to allow certain procedures. In some cases a state or local promise to mend erroneous ways will suffice to keep the funds flowing; in others, formal negotiations and conferences must be held to work out new agreements. In practice, though, the threat of withholding funds is used far more often than it is carried out.

A great amount of energy is consumed in Washington over *resource allocation*. If the objective is a federal grant to support a state or local program—whether the construction of a mental health center or a sewer—the locality making the application will follow standard procedures up to a definite point. Thus, applications are constructed by professional bureaucrats at the state and local level; these men will also collect the necessary endorsements from other units of government, industrial groups, and civic-action agencies. Then elected officials sign the applications, which are sent to Washington or to a regional office of the appropriate federal agency. At this time the subtle political shadings characteristic of American intergovernmental relations come into play. The mayor of a city may fly to Washington to find out what the chances of approval are for his community's proposal. He is likely to plead his case in person at the appropriate department. Not coincidentally, the mayor will talk with his Congressmen and Senators, letting them know about his proposal; finally, the Congressmen may call the department to inquire about the status of the application and to outline the city's arguments once again.

The rules of these encounters are understood by all. The bureaucrats cannot change the rules under which they must decide, but important areas of discretionary decision-making are available to them. They can act with greater or lesser haste, give explanations that befuddle or clearly indicate the path to success, or interpret an ambiguous point in one way or the other. The personal intervention of elected officials from the states, cities, and Congress is thus carefully noted. When the interest is expressed by a Congressman who sits on the department's appropriation subcommittee, the executive response is likely to be especially sympathetic.

Even such a seemingly nonsensitive agency as the Weather Bureau must be on guard at all times. Once it tried to stop providing reports to northeastern cities about the weather in Savannah, Georgia. Savannah drew a portion of its income from northern tourists, and its Congressman chaired the subcommittee that oversaw the Bureau's annual appropriations. The following exchange reveals the impact of personal intervention by an important Congressman:

Congressman Preston: I wrote you gentlemen . . . a polite letter thinking that maybe you would [restore it] . . . and no action was taken on it. Now Savannah may be unimportant to the Weather Bureau, but it is important to me.
Bureau Official: I can almost commit ourselves to seeing to it that the Savannah weather report gets distribution in the northeastern United States.[35]

Decisions over the allocation of federal resources appear to depend upon a variety of criteria. Some federal establishments simply are put in districts whose Congressmen handle the appropriations of the agency doing the building. Most American domestic military bases are in the southern states and southerners have been chairmen of both the House and the Senate Armed Forces Committees since the 1930's. Other types of federal contracts, particularly for aerospace or defense materials, appear to go to the most industrialized and technologically advanced sections of the country because the major private firms are there and also because of effective lobbying on the part of state industrial and political leaders. California's preeminence in aerospace and Massachusetts's in electronics provide two striking illustrations.

Some federal installations are, of course, located on sites chosen on the basis of relatively objective technical criteria. Thus, the Atomic Energy Commission, which visited hundreds of places before deciding to build its Bevatron Reactor in Weston, Illinois, considered everything from land costs to the proximity of existing scientific facilities and personnel. Before building a research center in the Florida Keys, the Environmental Sciences Administration measured average water temperatures and the days of annual port accessibility in a number of potential locations. Under these circumstances the mobilization of state and local support and congressional interest is usually sufficient only to guarantee a hearing for the applying community.

In general, the administrative problems that exist at the federal level are duplicated in varying degrees and in varying forms in the state capitals and in all communities large enough to have full-time officials. Problems of department and agency organization and problems of recruitment and patronage are found everywhere. It is probably safe to generalize that in most respects most state governments are less advanced than the government in Washington. Civil service systems based on merit have reached high levels of development in some states like New York, but they are rudimentary or totally absent in many states except where they are required by the federal government. Some federal grant-in-aid programs carry as conditions the re-

[35] Quoted in Aaron Wildavsky, *The Politics of the Budgetary Process* (Boston: Little, Brown, 1964), p. 81.

quirement that the recipient state or local community establish certain minimum personnel standards. Undoubtedly, this policy has had a significant overall impact in broadening merit-system coverage in places where it had not existed before.

The range of variation in the structuring of the units in state and local administrative branches is, however, very great, and generalizations are difficult. Unlike the national government, states have often frozen into their constitutions specifications about the number, titles, functions, and other characteristics of their administrative agencies. This was usually a response to some of the same cultural influences that have helped to shape the national executive establishment—the fear of government and a desire to provide iron-clad limits and safeguards, as well as more specific motives applying to specific functions or agencies. In Michigan, for example, when the state rewrote its constitution in 1964, an effort was made to alter or abolish the constitutional office of the highway superintendent, who had long been popularly elected. The efforts failed, however, because the vested interests that were accustomed to the existing arrangement blocked the proposed innovation; the office remains a constitutionally protected one today. Similarly, in Kentucky, certain county officials are popularly elected by constitutional mandate. A Constitutional Revision Commission proposed that this provision be deleted to allow the legislature to provide for appointment if it saw fit. The ensuing political furor was so great that the whole revision effort went down to crushing defeat in a referendum.

Thirty-two of the fifty states are listed as having some sort of general-coverage civil-service system, including all of the six with the largest numbers of public servants save for Pennsylvania. Eighty-three per cent of cities with more than 25,000 population have some degree of a formal civil service system, including most of the largest cities (having a population of over 250,000). Yet clearly progress on this front has been spotty; many so-called merit systems are quite feeble by any objective standards and easily circumvented for political purposes. The elimination of spoils has gone much further at the national than at the state and local level, with important implications for the functioning of national politics versus politics at lower levels. Old-style forms of reward for political services are much more often available to mayors and Governors than to Presidents.

One final illustration will complete this brief discussion of state and local administration. It involves the serious problem of the bureau or agency head trying both to command the loyalty of his personnel and to control their activities. Professors Sayre and Kaufman, in their classic study of New York City government, analyze the administrative problems of selected city department heads, among them the Fire Commissioner. This official heads a municipal service that is perhaps as typical of the activities of the local government as any that could be chosen. The New York Commissioner heads a department of some thirteen thousand persons, most of them in the uniformed ranks. The department's missions are fire fighting and fire prevention through its inspection and licensing powers.

The formal powers of the Commissioner certainly look adequate. The city charter reads:

> The Commissioner shall have sole and exclusive power and perform all duties for the government, discipline, management, maintenance and direction of the fire department and the premises and property in the custody thereof.[36]

Specific functions are then listed. He is appointed by the Mayor and serves at his pleasure, which ordinarily means that he is closely allied with his superior. A non-career Commissioner bent on innovation or on seizing the initiative in his department faces three major obstacles. The first is that operational control over the department's forces is vested in a career chief. This official stands at the top of a tight chain of command that the Commissioner cannot pierce or bypass. Secondly, the tradition-bound personnel system of the department deprives the Commissioner of any real opportunity to recruit or promote personnel who might share and support his ideas. Third, as the authors write, "the Uniformed Fireman's Association, and the allied officer groups, have the power, if not to make the Commissioner do what they want, to prevent his doing what they strongly disapprove." [37]

The rigidities that these three factors introduce into the situation make it difficult if not impossible in practice, in spite of the city charter's words, for the Commissioner to do the kinds of things that in theory almost any agency head has the power to do. Presumably the Commissioner should be able to alter the program emphasis of his department (increase the effort devoted to fire prevention, for example), bring about the acceptance of new technological developments faster than the glacial pace at which the closed departmental bureaucracy is willing to accept them, or reform the agency's organizational structure. Sayre and Kaufman, however, point out the reality:

> He cannot abolish a special Brooklyn office, although successive studies have shown its irrelevancy to the fire fighting and fire prevention functions. He cannot organize, redistrict, or reduce in any significant degree the number of fire districts, fire station houses, and fire companies, although studies have convinced him that present arrangements are obsolete and inefficient. He cannot secure the data for a critical analysis of the Department's present performance, nor can he establish systems of statistical and other analyses for the forward planning of fire fighting and fire prevention programs. He cannot do these things because he cannot persuade his organization to agree to, and support his proposals. He encounters instead a variety of opposition, ranging from the doubts and delays of high officers, through the increasing resistance of line officers, to the often strident and public hostilities of the organized fire bureaucracies.[38]

These kinds of problems are not unique to the New York Fire Commissioner. Whenever found, departmental and agency bureaucracies almost invariably develop this sort of esprit, in-group loyalty, suspicion of their temporary political chiefs, and ability to resist changes not deemed to be in their interests.

Max Weber, the great German sociologist and student of bureaucracy, contended

---

[36] Wallace S. Sayre and Herbert Kaufman, *Governing New York City: Politics in the Metropolis* (New York: Norton, 1965), pp. 265ff

[37] Ibid., p. 267.

[38] Ibid., p. 268.

that bureaucracy was the most efficient form of human organization. In light of the problems of the Fire Commissioner, one is tempted to paraphrase Churchill's aphorism that democratic government is the worst form of government—except for all of the others. Bureaucracy is the most *in*efficient form of human organization imaginable—except for all the others. As bad as the organization of the New York City Fire Department may be, it is still infinitely better than any attempt to protect the city with a volunteer, amateur band of firefighters, such as many small towns use, or to encourage the citizenry to buy garden hoses and to shift for themselves. The running of a large-scale organization, or the provision of services that require a large organization, really admits of no other mode of functioning but through a trained, professional bureaucratic corps. Governing the modern state would be impossible without the bureaucracies that carry so much of the day-to-day burden.

suggested additional readings

Dror, Yehezkel. *Public Policymaking Reexamined*. San Francisco: Chandler Publishing Co., 1968.

Elazar, Daniel J. *American Federalism: A View from the States*. New York: Thomas Y. Crowell Company, 1966.

Gawthorp, Louis G. *Bureaucratic Behavior in the Executive Branch*. New York: The Free Press, 1969.*

Grodzins, Morton. *The American System: A New View of Government in the United States*. Chicago: Rand McNally and Co., 1966.

Hovey, Harold A. *The Planning—Programming–Budgeting Approach to Government Decision Making*. New York: Praeger Publishers, Inc., 1968.

Mosher, Frederick C. *Democracy and the Public Service*. New York: Oxford University Press, 1968.*

Nigro, Felix A. *Modern Public Administration*, 2nd ed. New York: Harper & Row, Publishers, 1970.

Redford, Emmette S. *Democracy in the Administrative State*. New York: Oxford University Press, 1969.

Riker, William H. *Federalism: Origin, Operation, and Significance*. Boston: Little, Brown and Company, 1964.*

Sayre, Wallace (ed.). *The Federal Government Service*. Englewood Cliffs, N.J.: Prentice-Hall, Inc., 1965.*

————, and Herbert Kaufman. *Governing New York City: Politics in the Metropolis*. New York: W. W. Norton & Company, Inc., 1965.*

Seidman, Harold. *Politics, Population, and Power: The Dynamics of Federal Organization*. New York: Oxford University Press, 1970.*

Sundquist, James, and David Davis. *Making Federalism Work*. Washington, D.C.: The Brookings Institution, 1969.*

Wildavsky, Aaron. *The Politics of the Budgetary Process*. Boston: Little, Brown and Company, 1964.*

Wheare, Kenneth C. *Federal Government,* 4th ed. New York: Oxford University Press, 1964.*

* Available in paperback.

11 urban politics: where the crisis is

case study

Conflict in Chicago: Civil Rights in the Schools

The Chicago public school system is a gigantic organization with 580,000 students, over 20,000 teachers, and hundreds of separate schools in the city's seventy-five different neighborhoods. The system is run by an eleven-member nonpartisan Board of Education, the members of which are chosen by the Mayor for four-year terms. The Board selects the Superintendent, who has operating responsibility for the entire system. In 1953 the Board hired the highly esteemed Buffalo, New York, Superintendent, Benjamin A. Willis, to manage Chicago's schools. By paying Willis $48,500 a year, the Board made him the fourth highest paid public official in America. Active in various professional education associations, Willis was a cold, efficient specialist. He believed that educational decisions rightly belonged in the hands of experts like himself. Yet to the Board's clients—teachers, students, parents, Chicago citizens—school policy in some respects involved highly personal values. Whenever elements of the American citizenry feel that way about a subject, it is likely to become an issue in the political process. Elected public officials inevitably are drawn into the controversy. This case is a study of a four-year battle over school policy in Chicago.

In January, 1962, black Alderman Leon M. Depres, an Independent, accused the Chicago Board of Education of pursuing a policy of racial segregation. By organizing schools on neighborhood lines, the Board, he charged, kept blacks in segregated and overcrowded schools. Seven months later, twenty-two black parents brought suit in a federal court to have the neighborhood-boundary policy declared unconstitutional. The parents employed as one of their lawyers the well-known Rochester, New York, civil rights specialist Paul Zuber. Meanwhile, the Board of Education was upsetting the black community by constructing mobile classrooms in black neighborhoods to solve overcrowding; this method was seen as an objectionable alternative to switching the black students to less crowded schools in white areas. Civil rights leaders called the mobile units "ghetto carts" and "Willis wagons." A minister said, "To segregate Negro children in ghetto carts today is to nurture hate, fear, and mistrust."

As the 1963 spring semester ended, the Congress of Racial Equality (CORE) decided to protest against the Board's policies. Its method was typically direct: it set up demonstrations and pickets at the Board's offices. For seven days the marches went on until the police stepped in, acting at the request of Board president Claire Roddewig, who said the situation was "bordering on anarchy." The police

477

arrested seven men and three girls and charged them with unlawful assembly and trespass. What CORE wanted was "open enrollment," but its main target was Superintendent Willis. Willis missed the demonstrations because he was in Boston in his capacity as a $32,500-a-year consultant to the Massachusetts Board of Education.

Mayor Richard J. Daley, however, was in town. Daley, undisputed leader of the country's most powerful city political organization, supported the police action, observing that "we can't let anybody physically take over city offices." Typically, Daley touched bases with the other side of the argument too. He voiced his view that orderly demonstrations were proper means of expression, and announced that in response to his personal plea the Chicago Building Trades Council had agreed to provide more apprenticeships and union jobs for blacks. Unsatisfied, the Chicago director of CORE said, "Chicago is on the verge of mass demonstrations and there is bound to be violence."

Daley also tried to defuse the conflict. He met with a group of civil rights leaders, and helped to arrange a meeting with the Board of Education. The meeting, however, was eminently unsuccessful. Superintendent Willis, back in Chicago, listened to the rights leaders' case for two hours, but then refused to make any statement about his philosophy on the relationship between education and segregation. Neither side was satisfied.

By August, 1963, the demonstrations had taken a nasty turn. Protesting on the sites of mobile classroom construction, some rights advocates set fires, sat in front of bulldozers, and scuffled with police. The direct action attracted national publicity when the famed comedian Dick Gregory, known for his ascerbic humor and his appearance on the "Tonight" show, first joined, then led, the protests. Arrests continued as police and demonstrators

were hurt. Willis recommended that the construction continue anyway, and, after a stormy meeting, the Board supported him by an 8 to 2 vote. Raymond W. Pasnick, a white labor leader, and Warren H. Bacon, a black member, voted to halt the building. Another black Board member, Mrs. Wendell E. Green, abstained. Police Chief Orlando Wilson, a man noted for his fairness and incorruptibility, felt constrained to warn demonstrators that disorderly conduct would be met with police force.

Nonetheless the struggle continued to grow in ugliness. Demonstrators appeared at the homes of Mayor Daley and four Board members. More fires were set in the mobile units. Thirty ministers joined the pickets at the sites. Once more Daley tried to bring peace by agreeing to meet again with demonstration leaders. As if in response, Willis proudly released a statement explaining that his efforts had made room for thirty thousand more students in the classrooms for the fall term than there had been the year before. Many of these, of course, would be in the nineteen mobile units.

Suddenly, the Zuber lawsuit, begun the previous year, reappeared. A federal appeals court ordered the suit heard by a lower court. Rather than go to trial, the Board of Education agreed to a carefully drafted peace pact. It would issue a statement "recognizing" that racial imbalance caused educational problems and that such imbalance existed in Chicago schools; a blue-ribbon committee would be appointed to study the entire system. Further, the Board agreed to a "moratorium" on mobile classroom construction. The black parents, in return, would drop their suit. Zuber, in a conciliatory statement, said that "if the Board would keep open its communications levers," good relations with civil rights groups and a stable situation could be maintained.

This compromise was announced on August 28, but on September 2 the Board moved its mobile units to a different South Side black area and renewed construction. The truce was over. Black Alderman Charles Chew, Jr., a faithful Democrat, observed angrily, "We've been double-crossed." The Board of Education blandly replied that its action was nonpolitical, a move undertaken solely on the advice of its real estate committee. As civil rights leaders met to plan a citywide school boycott, the demonstrations started anew. Young children were sent through police lines to protest the construction. Superintendent Willis said the mobile units were going to stay. He issued a statement: "This has been going on for a long time. I didn't come here to become a political liability. I came to be superintendent of schools and that is what I am."

Mayor Daley intervened again to try and bring harmony. He met with black leaders and appealed for negotiations in "a spirit of cooperation." He wanted to bring the Board and the rights leaders together for talks. As Daley tried to dampen the conflict, another incident fueled the flames. Willis had promulgated a plan whereby a student in the top 5 per cent of his class could attend any one of twenty-four "receiving" high schools scattered around the city. In protest, *white* parents picketed the Board. Willis responded by reducing the number of "receiving" schools to nine. Now black groups bitterly counterprotested, and the Board, against Willis's advice, put two schools back on the "receiving" list. Charging that the Board had taken a "discriminatory" action against him, Willis resigned. At that time three-quarters of Chicago's population was white, and there was little doubt that most whites wanted Willis to stay on as Superintendent. Pressures were placed on the Board from two sides to bring Willis back. White parents protested his leaving. The North Central Association of Colleges and Secondary Schools threatened to remove Chicago's accreditation because the Board, in "forcing" Willis to resign, had acted counter to the Association's

professional criteria. The Board, retreating again, voted 8 to 2 *not* to accept Willis's resignation. Willis returned, but he set conditions: new guidelines specified the lines of authority between himself and the Board, and these were not to be transgressed. Thirteen days after leaving, Willis was back as superintendent.

The entire sequence of events left civil rights groups appalled. They called for a boycott, and on October 23, 1963, nearly 225,000 pupils—half the city's enrollment —stayed away from school. This by far exceeded the 125,000 figure predicted by the most optimistic rights leaders. In addition, on boycott day 8,000 people picketed City Hall and the nearby Board of Education offices. The boycott leaders had a list of thirteen demands. At the top was Willis's dismissal. They also wanted integration of students and staff and elimination of the neighborhood school policy.

The boycott was so much a success that civil rights leaders from other cities flew to Chicago to observe it. The national publicity left Mayor Daley visibly discomfited, but he declined to issue a statement. The year ended with the Board of Education's refusing, on a close 4 to 3 vote, to endorse a resolution supporting school integration in principle. Board members opposing the resolution said they had already voted years before for a statement condemning segregation; they would not be pressured into further action. The meeting ended in a chaotic shouting match between the Board president and a group of rights advocates who were in the audience.

The battle lines were clearly drawn. Willis was in command of the Board. Daley, mindful that whites then outnumbered blacks three to one in Chicago and four to one in terms of registered voters, gave Willis at least tacit support. Observers of Chicago politics felt that without Daley's backing Willis could not survive. Yet, the rights groups had demonstrated their ability to capture headlines and to mobilize the black community en masse for direct action. Blacks, moreover, had been loyal supporters of Daley's political organization too. What would happen?

The civil rights groups announced another boycott for February 25, 1964. For the first time, Daley openly fought back by mobilizing his famous Democratic ward machines to prevent another successful boycott. U.S. Representative William L. Dawson, "boss" of four black wards, and his local agent Alderman Kenneth E. Campbell were known to be passing the word to "stop it." Arguing that "your children need all the education they can get," Dawson and Campbell organized "The Assembly to End Prejudice, Injustice, and Poverty" to work against another stay-home. The Daley tactics divided the civil rights movement. The National Association for the Advancement of Colored People and the Urban League declared themselves against another school strike. The widely read black newspaper, *The Chicago Defender,* came out for the boycott, and criticized those "second rate" black politicians who were trying to block it. A federation of twenty-one groups called the Coordinating Council of Community Organizations began planning the boycott.

As the threatened boycott drew nearer, the Board of Education took two steps. It sought a court injunction prohibiting another school strike. And, by a vote of 5 to 2, it endorsed a statement favoring racial integration in the schools. The statement's wording had been worked out in meetings between Alderman Campbell and Board member C. H. Adams. The prospects for compromise were set back, however, when Board president Roddewig announced his intent to resign. Roddewig, a close associate of Mayor Daley, had also remained on friendly personal terms with black leaders. Now, reportedly tired from Willis's continued refusal to yield an inch and faced with the prospect of getting caught in the middle again, Roddewig

declined to serve another term. Willis said:

The major issues in today's urban school, whatever they might be, are clouded by civil rights or whatever people may mean by civil rights. The administrator who must stand harassment will sometimes wonder if the light is worth the candle.

During the second Chicago boycott some 172,350 pupils absented themselves from school. Many attended one of the 112 "freedom schools" staffed by area college students, and the schools in Alderman Campbell's ward were 90 per cent empty. Mayor Daley denied that the boycott had any political implications for him personally; he added that "nothing that keeps children out of school is a success." Little changed in the school system as a result of the boycott, but in May the report authored by the blue-ribbon committee appointed at the time of the Zuber compromise was turned in to the Board. Drafted by Philip A. Hauser, Chairman of the Sociology Department at the University of Chicago, it predicted twenty to thirty years of racial turmoil if changes were not made. It proposed "clustered" schools and abandonment of the neighborhood system, but its recommendations were ignored. A fall newspaper report noted that blacks, for the first time, comprised a majority of the public school pupils.

City controversies often continue for years. One side or the other may win or lose individual encounters without there ever being a definite settlement. Such certainly seemed to be the case in the fight over integration in the Chicago public schools. By the end of 1964, two boycotts and hundreds of demonstrations had not changed the system nor forced Willis's firing, nor deterred the civil rights groups from continued efforts. In May, 1965, the Board of Education faced a new decision: whether or not to renew Superintendent Willis's contract.

Rumor had it that Willis did not have majority support within the Board but that the Board was afraid to release him outright. Word of a Daley-negotiated compromise was also in the wind, and on May 27 it was announced. Willis would receive a new contract, but instead of serving the full four years, he would retire when he reached sixty-five, on December 23, 1966. Negro leaders promptly scheduled a boycott for June 7. One leader said, "We think we can force him to quit. We're pulling out the plugs."

This boycott was stopped cold, however, by an injunction issued by an Illinois Circuit Court, which the rights leaders agreed to obey. Then the demonstrations started again—at City Hall and in rush hour traffic. Albert Raby, leader of the Coordinating Council, explained, "There is not a person in town who doesn't know that Willis is there because Daley wants him there." Arrests followed, at the rate of 150 a day for almost a week. On television, Mayor Daley said, "As long as I am Mayor, there will be law and order in Chicago." Still, the Mayor sought a way to restore civil peace. He met with clergymen representing the pickets, and with other rights leaders. Nothing changed. Daley, frustrated and tired of conflict, hinted darkly that the demonstrations were part of a plot against him financed by the Republican Party. Willis said that the marches did not disturb him. New York Congressman Adam Clayton Powell revealed his plans to investigate discrimination in the Chicago schools in his capacity as Chairman of the House Committee on Labor and Education.

By July the struggle had achieved a new point in mutual bitterness. The demonstrators continued their protests, and the police were hauling them away regularly. Dick Gregory was arrested almost every day. Raby was arrested also. After an unusually acrimonious session with the Board of Education, the civil rights leaders announced a new tactic. They would seek to persuade the federal Office of Education to cut off its $30-million-a-year aid to the Chicago

school system on the grounds that the Board was violating Title VI of the 1964 Civil Rights Act banning assistance to segregated facilities. The section had been invoked before against southern cities but never in the North. Congressman Powell announced his support of this maneuver. Mayor Daley called in reporters to say that police files showed that many Communists were aiding in the demonstrations.

As the hot month of July dragged on, the scales began to tip against Willis. First, Reverend Martin Luther King decided to make Chicago the site of his first full-scale northern integration drive; he was going to work closely with Raby's Coordinating Council. Then, a group of forty-seven leading white businessmen issued an unprecedented public statement demanding a "quick and bold stance" by the city in the direction of "vigorous public school integration." The signers came from Chicago's largest corporations: Inland Steel; Chicago and North Western Railways; Foote, Cone and Belding. The statement was made even more striking by the industrialists' tactic of releasing it from the offices of the Urban League. In direct contradiction of Willis's position, the businessmen accepted the League's contention that 90 per cent of Chicago's black students were in segregated schools. The businessmen's statement was widely interpreted as a rebuff to Mayor Daley as well as a challenge to Willis.

The Board of Education again reacted ambivalently. Its new president, Frank Whiston, criticized the business spokesmen. The Board also voted 8 to 3 to appoint immediately an assistant superintendent in charge of integration. While the pressure remained on the Board, the temperature at the Mayor's headquarters was rising even faster. Martin Luther King led thirty thousand marchers to City Hall. Not only was Mayor Daley's support among leading businessmen and Negroes alike eroding, but he was subjected to personal harassment. Pickets marched in front of his modest home in Bridgeport, a white lower-middle-class neighborhood where the Mayor was born and where he still lived. As Daley's white neighbors shouted racial epithets at the marchers, the beleaguered Mayor dourly observed that "some people are trying to create tensions."

On September 29 a new actor—the federal government—entered the proceedings. Acting under Title VI of the Civil Rights Act of 1964, Commissioner of Education Francis Keppel ordered a freeze on the $30 million allocated to Chicago's schools. No money was to be released until complaints about segregation were "satisfactorily resolved." A wounded howl went out from City Hall. Daley asked the White House why Chicago, which voted overwhelmingly for a Democratic President, was getting such "shoddy treatment." Representative Dawson, Chairman of the House Government Operations Committee, threatened a full-scale investigation of Keppel's agency. The Chicago congressional delegation was joined by Senate Minority Leader Everett Dirksen of Illinois in outraged protest.

The support of the Chicago Democractic organization is important to any Democratic President, whereas the Commissioner of Education controls few votes. Not surprisingly, within four days the word came down to "negotiate a settlement and do it fast." Department of Health, Education and Welfare Undersecretary Wilbur Cohen was sent to Chicago for a secret meeting with Daley's chosen bargainer, Board of Education president Whiston. The meeting was held at night in Whiston's real estate office. The terms were a total victory for Daley. All federal investigators were to return to Washington. All the money was to be unfrozen immediately. The Board, in a meager counterconcession, agreed to appoint a new study commission. Chicago

Congressman Roman Pucinski gleefully described these results as "an abject surrender" by Keppel and a great victory for "city's rights."

Still, the victory was less than permanent. Once involved, the federal bureaucracy is difficult to dislodge. Its responsibilities are great and so too are its resources. On the last day of 1965, Health, Education and Welfare Secretary John Gardner quietly announced yet another investigation into Chicago's school system. He declared that he was acting in response to continued complaints of discrimination.

Early in January, 1966, new federal researchers arrived in Chicago. Superintendent Willis declined to assist them, demanding to know, "What are the issues?" The Board, however, was weary of obstruction. After receiving assurances that the inquiry would proceed slowly and that no sudden decisions would result, it agreed to cooperate fully. On still another front, Martin Luther King hinted that school boycotts might be one tactic in his continuing Chicago integration campaign. Then, on May 11, a Board of Education Recruitment Committee made public its choice for a new superintendent to succeed Willis—Dr. James F. Redmond of Syosset, Long Island, New York. Until Willis retired in December, the two men would serve concurrently.

The Board unanimously approved the recommendation to hire Redmond. Two weeks later Benjamin Willis announced that he would retire on August 31, four months ahead of schedule, but gave no reasons for his decision. Civil rights leaders could hardly contain their joy. Mayor Daley praised Willis as "a fine administrator." Board president Whiston called him "one of the greatest school superintendents in the United States." Nonetheless, Daley and Whiston were both obviously relieved. They had a record $195 million school bond issue up for voter approval at an election in three weeks. The last such issue had been defeated, and the Mayor and the Board needed all the backing they could possibly attract. Civil rights leaders were quick to voice their support for the bond issue.

The new superintendent had different qualifications from the man he was replacing. Willis had come to Chicago with a reputation as a builder. He had fulfilled that expectation well, adding 277 schools and 5,601 classrooms to Chicago's school plant while reducing construction costs from $21 a foot to $16 a foot and taking the schools off double sessions for the first time in the twentieth century. But while he was improving the physical aspects, the needs of the system had shifted. Redmond seemed to have the background to meet the new demands. Before going to Long Island, he had been superintendent of the New Orleans schools. There he had defied the Louisiana legislature in a staunch and courageous defense of integrated public schools. On Long Island he was best known for his skillful community relations and for working closely with parents' groups. Like Willis before him, Redmond came in with the full approval and full support of the Mayor.

SOURCE
The New York Times, 1962–1966.

the setting of
urban politics

The Development of a
Metropolitan Society

The United States is a vast and diverse country, and there are many differences among its great cities. New York, San Francisco, and Houston have their own distinct flavors. Still, there are uniformities. One of the most striking trends of the twentieth century has been the steady, relentless urbanization of our country, the accelerating tendency for people to live in cities. In 1790, the United States had only four urban communities with 2,500 or more persons, and urban residents numbered only one-twentieth of the total national population. It took a full 130 years, until 1920, for the number of urban dwellers to exceed 50 per cent of the population. Between 1930 and 1940, the trend was temporarily slowed by the Depression, but it began again with World War II and since then has continued at an ever more rapid pace. The 1970 census showed almost 75 per cent of our population as urban. Four fifths of the population growth of the last decade has taken place in urban areas, which are now continuous belts of settlement conveniently labeled "Standard Metropolitan Statistical Areas" (SMSA's) by the Census Bureau.

As defined by the Census Bureau, Standard Metropolitan Statistical Areas contain a core city of 50,000 or more in population plus a surrounding belt of suburbs, villages, and towns. To look at the 230 Standard Metropolitan Statistical Areas is to confront head on America's urban growth. They range in size from the New York Standard Metropolitan Statistical Area, with over 10½ million people and 600 local governments, to the Meriden, Connecticut, Standard Metropolitan Statistical Area, with 52,000 people and few governmental units. Those Standard Metropolitan Statistical Areas with over one million inhabitants each now contain nearly half of America's urbanites, and only three states are without at least one Standard Metropolitan Statistical Area.

These metropolitan areas have certain characteristics that sharply differentiate them from the hinterlands. Size alone is not their distinguishing mark, nor are they necessarily discrete and unified political entities. What distinguishes metropolitan areas is that they contain a spreading conglomeration of people who are uniquely *interdependent* in their daily lives. The *independence* among the citizens of a metropolitan area is a two-way street. The central city depends upon the outlying residential areas for much of its labor force, especially for white-collar workers and management personnel. Downtown city merchants, despite the proliferation of suburban shopping centers, still draw a large percentage of their customers from the ring districts. New York is the extreme example: over 3 million people daily commute into Manhattan to work, to shop, and to be entertained. Conversely, the suburbs rely heavily upon the core cities for a vast store of items: newspapers, television stations, symphony orchestras, specialty shops, department stores, hospitals, universities, and pro-football teams.

Decentralization is the second characteristic of modern metropolitan areas. This decentralization is the result of a long process of development. Suburbs located twenty or more miles from the downtown section of the central city are possible only when technology makes commuting by car or train physically possible and only when a high standard of living makes it economical in money and time. The flight to the suburbs began in earnest in the 1920's when mass production made possible the distribution of inexpensive private automobiles. Suburban growth slowed in the 1930's, but boomed after World War II. By building highways and underwriting cheap long-term home loans, the federal government played a major role in the decentralization process. Originally, people moved away from the city in the pursuit of better housing, more space, and greater social status. To these values the contemporary white suburbanite has added the desire for better schools and the urge to escape the blacks who migrated to the core cities from rural areas. The dispersion seems permanent. The French demographer Jean Gottman, who coined the word *megalopolis* to describe continuous belts of settlement, has written:

we must abandon the idea of the city as a tightly settled and organized unit in which people, activities, and riches are crowded into a very small area clearly separated from its non-urban surroundings. Every city in this region (the Northeast) spreads out far and wide around its original nucleus; it grows amidst an irregularly colloidal mixture of rural and suburban landscapes; it melts on broad fronts with other mixtures, of somewhat similar though different texture, belonging to the suburban neighborhoods of other cities.[1]

The third metropolitan characteristic is *specialization*. This means that parts of the core cities and often entire suburbs are devoted exclusively to one use. City neighborhoods become residential, commercial, or industrial. Some suburbs exist largely for private homes, for sprawling shopping areas, and for light manufacturing. Some specialization in land use is deliberate, the result of planning and zoning by governmental agencies or even private developers. But much is the outcome of informal social processes. Through self-selection, members of the same ethnic groups or people with similar incomes settle in the same neighborhoods or suburbs. Dis

---

[1] *Megalopolis* (Cambridge: M.I.T. Press, 1964), p. 5.

crimination in the sale and rental of housing forces black people into certain districts. As a consequence of this specialization every metropolitan area possesses a distinctive spatial pattern, and the land use becomes a way of distributing social values. Property values, densities, prestige—these determine where the different elements in a metropolitan population will live.

The modern metropolis is noteworthy, fourth, for the *fragmentation of legal authority* over its area. Many factors bind the parts of the region together in a common destiny and perhaps even a sense of community, but unified government is not one of them. Of course, the federal government affects all the residents within a metropolitan area, but a given Standard Metropolitan Statistical Area may fall within the boundaries of as many as three states and thirteen counties. Furthermore, the number of local governments for any given Standard Metropolitan Statistical Area may be astronomical. At the time of the defeat of a plan to consolidate government in the St. Louis area, the affected portion of the Standard Metropolitan Statistical Area contained ninety-eight municipal governments, the city administration, a country government, twenty independent fire protection authorities, twenty-seven separate school districts, and one metropolitan sewer district.

The fifth and final characteristic of the metropolitan areas is that they are *open-ended political systems*. By open-ended political systems, we simply mean that ideas, people, groups, issues, and resources may enter a city from outside to shape its political life. Much of the earlier political science literature has tended to treat urban politics as if it takes place in a vacuum. Yet cities are directly connected to the national political culture and the national political system, which is, of course, one reason they are of interest to us. The concept of "nonviolent resistance," as applied by civil rights organizations, affected southern cities throughout the early 1960's. More recently, the idea of "community control" has altered northern communities. Similarly, to consider resources, a community may be rebuilt by private capital raised in the national financial market, as parts of Los Angeles have been. Even a federal installation, such as the monstrous National Aeronautics and Space Administration facility in Houston, can have a great impact on a local area.

What all this means, in the language of communications theory, is that "inputs" for urban political processes come from our national political, economic, educational, and social processes. Some inputs are useful to cities—a federal research institute or a new plant in a technological or defense-supported industry brings multi-million-dollar payrolls and thousands of educated, law-abiding, tax-paying residents to a community. Some inputs, however, bring disruption. Cutbacks in federal aerospace spending may devastate employment in such cities as Los Angeles or Seattle. Mechanization of southern agriculture sends black migrants to Detroit and New York; if those migrants cannot find permanent work, they may wind up on the public welfare rolls. Still other inputs have mixed consequences. The federal highway program has raised land values in suburbs and made feasible fast commuting and locating new factories along suburban roads. Central cities, however, have seen land removed from their tax rolls and the exodus of jobs and middle-class persons accelerated. As the chapter on public policy indicated, few decisions benefit or penalize all categories of people equally. The same rule applies to communities.

Central Cities and Suburbs: Crucial Variations Within the Metropolis

The impact of growing American urbanization has not been uniform. In fact, certain crucial differences in rates of growth and racial distributions set the social background for the "urban crisis." Most population growth since World War II has taken place in the suburban rings, and increasingly most new commercial and industrial development has been in these newer communities. For example, between 1960 and 1969, central city populations grew by about 1 per cent (Oklahoma City and Houston were notable exceptions), whereas suburbs grew by 27 per cent. At the same time, central cities have become increasingly black. Table 11.1 documents the process. Twelve of sixteen of our largest central cities have seen a net decline of white population. All have seen high black growth rates, and today 56 per cent of

Table 11.1 *Racial changes in central city populations, 1960–1970*

City	Black percentage of total population, 1960	Black pecentage of total population 1970	Rate of growth of black population, 1960–1970	Rate of growth of white population, 1960–1970
Boston	9	16	+66	−17
Chicago	23	33	+36	−19
Cincinnati	22	28	+15	−17
Cleveland	29	38	+15	−26
Dallas	19	25	+63	+14
Detroit	29	44	+37	−30
Houston	23	26	+47	+26
Kansas City	10	22	+35	Not available
Los Angeles	14	18	+50	+ 5
Milwaukee	8	15	+68	−10
New York City	14	21	+53	− 9
Philadelphia	26	34	+24	−13
Pittsburgh	17	20	+ 4	−18
San Francisco	10	13	+29	−15
St. Louis	29	41	+19	−32
Washington, D.C.	54	71	+31	−39

Source: U.S. Department of Commerce.

all black people live in central cities, compared to 26 per cent of all whites. Conversely, 38 per cent of all whites live in suburbs compared to only 15 per cent of all blacks.

It should be noted that growth rates and race are not the only differences between central cities and suburbs. There is something to the image of the suburbs as the happy watering grounds of the educated, school-oriented, and child-bearing middle class. Median incomes are higher, $9,367 for the suburban family compared to $7,813 for the central city family in 1967. School expenditures are greater, $573 per student in the suburbs compared to $449 per pupil in central cities. And there are fewer aged persons and more children in suburbs.

On the other hand, the stereotype cannot be carried too far. Within each metropolitan area, there is great variation in the characteristics of individual suburbs. The variation, as urban theorists have suggested, gives individual residential and industrial consumers a choice in levels of services and costs among locations.[2] For example, in his classic study of the one thousand four hundred local governments of the New York Metropolitan Region, Robert C. Wood found that one municipality spent $4.30 per capita for services, whereas another spent $351.20. One community taxed $24.60 per capital whereas, at the other extreme, another taxed $376.89.[3] Suburbs vary widely in the costs of homes, in age, in the amount of industry, and in social status or social rank. Sociologists distinguish, on the basis of land use, among dormitory, industrial, service, recreational, and educational suburbs.

Furthermore, the Advisory Commission on Intergovernmental Relations has reported that

for a number of population characteristics the differences *among* metropolitan areas are far larger than the differences between central cities and their suurrounding area. For most characteristics it is possible to generalize about disparities only for particular kinds of metropolitan areas. . . . While racial disparities are large everywhere, the other elements of the dichotomy—education, income, employment, and housing—fit the stereotype only in the largest metropolitan areas and those located in the Northeast.[4]

The Commission noted that in southern and western SMSA's, the pattern ran exactly opposite to the northeastern trend. People with high socioeconomic status live in core cities, whereas "nonwhite poverty and underprivileged" people are found in the suburbs. Interestingly, in a study of political attitudes and activities differences among individual metropolitan areas were found to be more significant than nationwide city and suburban cleavages.[5] Despite the homogenizing impact of a national political culture and national communications networks, regions and metropolitan communities retain many distinctive features.

[2] See Vincent Ostrom, Charles M. Tiebout, and Robert Warren, "The Organization of Government in Metropolitan Areas: A Theoretical Inquiry," *The American Political Science Review,* LV, No. 4 (December, 1961), pp. 831–842.

[3] *1400 Governments* (Garden City, N.Y.: Doubleday-Anchor, 1964), p. 29.

[4] *Metropolitan Social and Economic Disparities: Implications for Intergovernmental Relations in Central Cities and Suburbs* (Washington, D.C.: G.P.O., 1965), p. 11.

[5] See Joseph Zikmond, "A Comparison of Political Attitude and Activity Patterns in Central Cities and Suburbs," *Public Opinion Quarterly,* XXXI, No. 1 (Spring, 1967), pp. 69–75.

The Historical Development of American Urban Governments

The metropolitan setting is one part of the environment of urban politics; another part consists of the actual units of local government. An understanding of why we have the kinds of local governmental arrangements we do today can come only from a brief historical sketch of several colorful and indigenous trends in American municipal self-government.

At the time of the American Revolution local governments were modeled on those of Britain. Local rule was by an elected legislative council. Britain has retained the same approach to this day, but our country has traveled down some different paths. During the 1820's, local communities began to separate the city executive from the council by introducing the popular election of mayors; this trend toward elected executives accelerated in the 1840's when other offices—such as town clerks and treasurers—also became elective. This separation of powers at the local level was in frank imitation of the widely admired federal system.

Only the smallest towns rejected the concept of separating local executives and legislatures into a mayor and council. They tended to keep power in the city council —an approach still favored today in small-town America. When smaller communities in the nineteenth century did elect mayors, they preferred what we now call the "weak mayor-strong council" system. Under it councils retained the authority to appoint such department heads as there are, to prepare budgets, and to watch expenditures. And weak mayors are given the secondary responsibilities of presiding over council meetings, proposing ordinances (local laws), and, on rare occasion, exercising a veto.

After 1850, there were major changes in local governmental forms and in the relationship between the various parts of the government. In terms of structure, the councils began to subdivide themselves into upper and lower houses; by 1900, about one third of our cities had two houses or bicameral councils. Along with multiplication came increased size: Philadelphia's Common Council, for example, had 149 members. In addition, in a number of cities the powers of the elected mayor were substantially strengthened. These steps, in the direction of what is now known as "strong mayor-council systems," gave the mayor appointment authority over department heads and strong legislative vetoes. Many citizens came to believe that stronger mayors offered one solution to a dilemma that faced many post-Civil War American cities—the dilemma of the political machine.

Nineteenth-Century City Machines

City machines can develop only when certain conditions are present in the urban environment. They arose in the nineteenth century for four reasons. First, the period from 1850 to 1900 was characterized by meteoric urban growth: city populations increased sixfold. The new populations necessitated a rapid expansion of city plant and services. Second, the formal governmental structures of the era, with weak executives and fragmented and decentralized authority, were unable to cope with the tasks of absorbing the many newcomers into the community. Third, the new populations had more than material needs; they wanted friendship, recognition, and a sympathetic education in the ways of the New World. Fourth, in this era of rapid commercial and industrial expansion, business firms had a variety of demands, both licit and illicit, which city governments were in a position to grant. These included, for example, contracts for public work, charters for railways and utilities, and freedom from plant inspection laws, or police enforcement of vice regulations.

The post-Civil War city was ideal for the machine. The machine was a political party organization; it operated as an order-creating broker, exchanging services and sympathy in return for votes with the new immigrants, and favors and concessions in return for cash with the businessmen. Devoid of interest in issues or ideology, the machine was a political business, working on a profit motive, trading on a quid-pro-quo basis, and centralizing authority in itself in the vacuum that otherwise existed. Machines gave the immigrants welfare services and kindness. With the immigrant votes, the machine placed its party operatives in the offices of city government and managed, however inefficiently and corruptly, to run the town and expand the services. While in government, the machine's leaders would typically sell everything salable to the avaricious businessmen of the day. In this era the pursuit of wealth was almost a religious dogma, sanctioned by a crude but popular philosophy of Social Darwinism that emphasized the economic "survival of the fittest." Thus, it was not surprising to find politicians following the same paths of personal enterprise. The machines were in keeping with the times.

Each machine had a boss. The classic machine was the Tammany Hall political club of New York City, and it possessed the archetypal boss in the "Honorable" William M. Tweed, "grand sachem" of the club from 1868 to 1871. Like most bosses, Tweed did not run for public office; instead, he held a series of important party offices plus selected appointive city jobs. These kept him out of the public eye, but in a position to control those resources and individuals necessary to his power. Tweed's machine was a pyramid-shaped organization, with himself at the top and an army of precinct and block captains at the bottom. From his positions as head of the Hall, Deputy Street Commissioner of New York, and later as City Public Works Commissioner, Tweed dispensed patronage to keep his thousands of underlings loyal—an easy task because he maintained them on the city payroll. They, in turn, were charged with making sure that their neighbors voted for Tweed's front men, the slate of Tammany candidates. Tweed's methods were effective: at one time his men simultaneously occupied the Mayor's office, three important city judgeships, and all the city's major elective offices, not to mention governorship of the state and many of the seats in the legislature.

Tweed was finally brought to heel by *The New York Times*. The paper ran an exposé series on the boss's notorious "ring," a group of Hall insiders who charged all those doing business with the city a straight 65 per cent commission in return for a promise that all bills submitted to the City Board of Auditors would be approved, whatever the amount. Tweed ended his career in jail. In the sources and manipulation of his power, he typified bosses of his era and subsequent periods, whether they operated in Cincinnati, Jersey City, New Orleans, Philadelphia, Pittsburgh, San Francisco, St. Louis, or in any one of countless other cities.

Today we realize that, along with their evils, the machines did develop the cities and assimilate vast new populations. But the excesses of the machines provoked a reaction. A group of reformers, who thought of government in issue terms and who valued honest impartial service and efficiency, entered the fray. Most of these people were upper- and middle-class citizens of native Anglo-Saxon stock. They disliked not only the spoils politics of the machines, but also the politicians and immigrants of foreign origin associated with them.

The National Municipal League, founded in 1894, was the most important organization in the reform movement. It instigated and then provided national coordination for the dozens of local citizens associations that sprang up from coast to coast. Another reform organization was the Short Ballot League; once headed by Woodrow Wilson, its moving spirit was a young New York advertising man, Richard S. Childs. In 1917 Childs brought the National Municipal League and the Short Ballot League together, while persuading both to support his own creation, the "council-manager" system of government. He helped to popularize this governmental system through a widely distributed Municipal League publication, the *Model City Charter,* and through extensive personal appearances. Childs became the merchandising expert for the reform drive. Selling the idea of a new direct democracy, an arrangement where no parties intervened between voters and city officials and where no "politics" disturbed the conduct of local government, Childs maintained an active career in municipal reform from the 1890's to the 1960's.

The Reform Ideology and Program

Childs and the Municipal League offered a straightforward rationale. They saw the objective of city government as the provision of such services as police, fire fighters, and water. Their ideal was simple, businesslike administration, in which political considerations of friendship or party support or recognition would play no part. On those issues where there was conflict or disagreement as to how something should be done, the reformers felt that a policy in the public interest rather than the interest of any one group could certainly be found. The reformers had a detailed program. The short ballot was to reduce voter confusion and thus voter reliance upon party advice. At-large election of council members was to eliminate the control minorities had over council members elected from small, geographically defined wards or districts. The nonpartisan election system eliminated party labels from the ballot. The council-manager system was grandiosely intended to remove "politics" from the community entirely.

Nonpartisan elections had—and have today—a particular appeal to reformers. The nonpartisan ballot was first used in municipal elections in Louisville, Kentucky, in 1888; Dallas adopted it in 1907; and Boston became the first large eastern city to take the step in 1909. In 1914, *all* local communities in California were brought under the nonpartisan scheme, a status they have retained ever since. When the first comprehensive nationwide report on local electoral systems became available in 1929, reform achievement was evident: 57 per cent of all cities with more than thirty thousand population were utilizing the nonpartisan ballot.

In a council-manager system, an elected city council—often elected on an at-large, nonpartisan basis—hires a professional administrator or manager. In theory, the council makes policy and then the manager carries it out. The council-manager plan was devised by Richard Childs when he drew up a proposed new charter (which was never adopted) for Lockport, New York, in 1911. Childs's scheme actually combined two lesser-known municipal devices. As early as 1908, Staunton, Virginia, had hired a professional manager to oversee some of its city services. And numerous cities had councils that made policy through a system of government known as the *commission plan.* In commission plan cities, elected commissioners acting together as a council first made policy, then, acting individually as department heads, actually administered the government. Childs called his program a marriage of the manager and the commission systems.

In 1912, Sumter, South Carolina, became the first city to adopt a council-manager government. Between 1912 and 1914 the plan spread slowly as only seven cities adopted it. But then, late in 1914, Dayton, Ohio, became the first large city —it had a population of over 100,000—to adopt the council-manager government. The dramatic Dayton victory, in which Childs played a major part, led to one hundred more adoptions over the next five years. From then on expansion was steady, if not spectacular. After World War II the rapid formation of new suburbs led to a renewed growth of council-manager communities.

Contemporary Patterns of Municipal Government

The landscape of municipal governments today is a blend of machine remains and reform encrustations. Two generalizations outline the overall scene. First, larger cities use the mayor-council system that is built around a strong mayor. Second, the medium-sized and smaller communities favor manager-council systems, with the council usually elected on a nonpartisan ballot.

The data in Table 11.2 substantiate these assertions. Sixteen of the twenty cities with a population of more than half a million and fifteen of the thirty-one cities with between 250,000 and 500,000 people have mayor-council forms of government. Further, in all but two of these thirty-one largest cities, the mayor is a strong executive in the sense that he possesses considerable legal authority in relation to the council. Only in Minneapolis and Los Angeles is the mayor a legally weak figure. In other words, our major cities—including Atlanta, Chicago, Detroit, New Orleans, New York, Philadelphia, and St. Louis—have mayors who act as chief city executives in much the same way that state Governors are leaders of the political and administrative aspects of state governments.

At the same time, as the size of the city declines, the popularity of the council-

Table 11.2 *Forms of urban governments*

City size	Number of cities	Mayor-council		Commission		Council-manager	
		Number	Per cent	Number	Per cent	Number	Per cent
Over 500,000	20	16	80	—	—	4	20
250–500,000	31	15	48	4	13	12	39
100–250,000	79	30	38	10	13	39	49
50–100,000	192	73	38	21	11	98	51
25–50,000	391	139	36	47	12	205	52
10–25,000	1,013	474	47	98	10	441	43
5–10,000	1,281	821	64	57	4	403	32
Totals	3,007	1,568	52	237	8	1,202	40

Source: *Municipal Yearbook, 1965*, Orin F. Nolting and David S. Arnolds (eds.) (Washington, D.C.: International City Managers Association, 1965), p. 114.

493

manager form increases (until one reaches the very smallest communities). The yearly rate of adoption of the manager form underwent a great increase between 1945 and 1960; nearly seventy-five communities a year were added to the rolls. Since then, the spread of the manager form has slowed, at least in the major cities. Those four largest cities having it, Cincinnati, Dallas, San Antonio, and San Diego, adopted it during the 1930's and 1940's, before they reached their present size. Yet, even where the traditional mayor-council form has been retained, *some* of the reform goals have been achieved. Almost half of the mayor-council cities elect mayors and councilmen on a nonpartisan basis, and 46 per cent of these select councilmen on an at-large rather than a district basis.

Urban Environments, Governmental Forms, and Local Policies: Some Relationships

Despite many changes in underlying institutional relationships and functions, the federal government has essentially the same structure as prescribed by the Founding Fathers in 1787. One reason is that the system has proved adaptable to changing political demands; another is that the Constitution has insulated structural forms from day-to-day political conflicts. In contrast, governmental forms in metropolitan areas have proved less successful and have been far less insulated. It is not just policies but also institutional arrangements that are the meat of group conflict. Thus, the political machine served as a mechanism for providing services demanded by immigrants and profits for entrepreneurs in the fast-growing cities. Later, the reform movement became a middle-class counterattack, bringing about changes in the form of government aimed both at ending corruption and at diluting the political power of the immigrants and their leaders.

Political scientists have wondered whether more than historical political controversies underlie the distribution of urban governmental forms. Does the form of urban government matter? Strong mayors seem to be found in larger cities, where one also finds the greatest diversity of people and the most severe social conflict. Is there a uniform national correlation between these characteristics, mayor-council government, and social diversity? Further, one argument in favor of mayor-council government is that it is more responsive to the demands of community groups. The mayor is elected. The councilmen, often from ward districts and elected on a partisan basis, are easily accessible to neighborhood interests, be they ethnic or racial or class-based. Is the mayor-council system in fact as responsive to demands as it is supposed to be? Is it more responsive, for example, than manager-council systems?

Council-manager systems seem to be utilized in middle-sized and smaller cities. Is this because such communities are more socially homogeneous, less divided by various class, ethnic, or racial conflicts? Is there a uniform national correlation between manager-council government and social homogeneity in cities? Further, one of the reformers' arguments in favor of council-manager government was that it reduced governmental responsiveness to separate groups and substituted administration for politics. Are council-manager systems in fact less responsive to the group demands within their communities?

Various research findings on these questions are by no means unanimous, but they are nonetheless well worth examining. Thus, three studies have found correlations between high social status, homogeneity, and the utilization of council-manager government in American cities. When Sherbenou ranked seventy-four Chicago suburbs on the basis of median home values, eighteen of the top twenty with the most expensive homes had city manager governments. None of the thirty-one suburbs with the least expensive homes had the manager system.[6] Another study by Schnore and Alford analyzed the characteristics of 300 suburban cities in 25 Standard Metropolitan Statistical Areas. The conclusion was that communities with council-manager governments were more likely to have fewer Negroes, fewer aged people, more people in white-collar occupations and with at least a high school education, and more rapid population growth.[7] Alford and Scoble found connections between manager systems and city homogeneity and between mayoral systems and population diversity in still another analysis, observing that "white, Anglo-Saxon, Protestant, growing, and mobile cities are highly likely to be manager cities; ethnically and religiously diverse but nonmobile industrial cities are highly likely to be mayor-council cities."[8]

Two other projects have not supported these findings. Using 309 cities of over 50,000 population, Wolfinger and Field found that geographical region was a better predictor of what type of government a city would have than was the socioeconomic composition of its population. Only in the Midwest did they find some connection between homogeneity and manager government.[9] The Lineberry and Fowler analysis of 200 cities with over 50,000 people also concluded that the differences in the populations of council-manager and mayor-council cities were not very great, as a rule much less than one might have expected.[10]

Different studies have also come to different conclusions about the correlations between the social characteristics of a city, its type of government, and the public policies it pursues. Wolfinger and Field felt that geographical region was a better predictor of expenditure for programs such as urban renewal than either population homogeneity/diversity or form of city government. Lineberry and Fowler, however, found a series of significant connections among some socioeconomic variables, governmental structure, and policy as measured by comparative levels of spending and taxes. They found that as the percentage of owner-occupied dwellings

[6] Edgar L. Sherbenou, "Class, Participation, and the Council-Manager Plan," *Public Administration Review,* XXI (Summer, 1961), 131–135.

[7] Leo F. Schnore and Robert R. Alford, "Forms of Government and Socio-economic Characteristics of Suburbs," *Administrative Science Quarterly,* VIII (June, 1963), 1–17.

[8] Robert R. Alford and Harry M. Scoble, "Political and Socio-economic Characteristics of Cities," *Municipal Yearbook,* Chicago, 1965, p. 95.

[9] Raymond E. Wolfinger and John Osgood Field, "Political Ethos and the Structure of City Government," *American Political Science Review,* LX (June, 1966), 306–326.

[10] Robert L. Lineberry and Edmund P. Fowler, "Reformism and Public Policy in American Cities," *American Political Science Review,* LXI (September, 1967), 701–716.

(private homes and duplexes as opposed to rental apartments) increased, community expenditures for services went down; most important, this relationship had a greater effect when found in council-manager cities than in mayor-council cities. As the proportion of religious and ethnic minorities in a community's population increased, so did both spending and taxes; this relationship had its greatest significance in mayor-council cities. These authors concluded:

The more important difference between . . . cities is in their behavior, rather than their demography. . . . The translation of social conflicts into public policy and the responsiveness of political systems to class, racial, and religious cleavages differs markedly with the kind of political structure.[11]

Local Governments and Policies: Some Other Patterns

The discussion so far has considered patterns in 3,000 or so largest cities. But these are not the only local governments in the United States. In fact, the country has some 81,248 local governments, almost all with taxing power and at least some service functions. Eighteen thousand and forty-eight are municipalities; 3,049 are counties; 17,105 are townships; 21,782 are school districts; and 21,264 are "special districts." The special districts may exist within single communities or span a multistate metropolitan region. Sometimes they do no more than manage a sewage or water supply system; in other cases, as in the mammoth New York Port Authority, they may own and operate bridges, bus systems, bus terminals, airports, commuter trains, and office buildings. Metropolitan areas have more than their share of these overlapping local governments; the 230 SMSA's have over 20,000 governments. Table 11.3 indicates the pattern for particular communities. The Chicago SMSA has the most governments, 1,113, including 6 counties, 113 townships, 250 municipalities, 327 school districts, and 417 special districts.

Students of urban politics distinguish problems of the entire area from those of individual communities by the terms *areal* and *local*. Although these are distinctions of degree, areal functions are usually said to include air and water pollution control, water supply, sewage disposal, mass transportation, and highway construction. In the popular literature, local functions are listed as police and fire protection, welfare, public health, education, and recreation. The areal functions are designated as metropolitan problems because few individual communities in a sprawling Standard Metropolitan Statistical Area can cope with them singlehandedly. Most separate cities and towns lack the requisite planning staffs, financial resources, and, certainly, legal authority to meet areal challenges. Even where one city can act, because it cannot operate on its neighbors' turf it can only cure a part of the pollution, sewage backup, or traffic jam.

Nonetheless, the general American pattern has been to allow each local government to struggle with each areal problem as best it could, without cooperation with

---

[11] Ibid., p. 715.

Table 11.3 *Local governments in metropolitan areas*

SMSA	Population *	Number of local governments †
Boston	3,239,000	226
Chicago	6,815,000	1,113
Cincinnati	1,376,000	266
Cleveland	2,068,000	207
Dallas	1,459,000	192
Detroit	4,127,000	242
Houston	1,876,000	214
Kansas City	1,231,000	272
Los Angeles	6,860,000	233
Milwaukee	1,344,000	174
New York	11,551,000	551
Philadelphia	4,829,000	876
Pittsburgh	2,387,000	704
San Francisco	2,999,000	312
St. Louis	2,327,000	474
Washington, D.C.	2,751,000	84

Source: U.S. Statistical Abstract (Washington, D.C.: U.S. Government Printing Office, 1970).

* 1968 data, rounded to nearest 1,000.

† 1967 data.

or attention to the needs of neighbors. There have been five kinds of efforts at metropolitan action, which are, at best, only half successful.

First, a number of communities have set up *metropolitan regional councils*. These are voluntary associations of elected officials from the local governments of an entire metropolitan area. Until 1965, these outfits were largely engaged in research and the design of joint plans. Since then, a federal requirement that regional planning boards must approve some forty categories of federal programs intended to benefit individual communities has breathed new life into these boards. Over one hundred such boards or councils now operate as clearing agencies in the federal grant-seeking process.

Second, in Dade County, Florida, there is a unique government that is actually a *federation* of the region's local governments. Known as the Miami Metro, the federation shares power with twenty-seven municipalities within its area; its history since its birth in 1957 has been shaky. Nonetheless, in many ways, the Metro has been a developing success.

Third, although proposals for actual *consolidation of city and county governments* into one unit were defeated in twelve out of thirteen referenda in different states, in 1962 such a plan was finally adopted for Nashville, Tennessee. The Nashville government has two districts. The urban services district provides complete governmental services to the core city only. The general services district offers areal benefits for the entire county. This arrangement is very similar to the "Unigov" of Indianapolis.

Fourth, another metropolitan structure utilized with some success is the *urban county*. Here a traditional county government sells services on a contract basis to other local governments. It may sell everything from water to electrical inspection to police and fire protection, as Los Angeles County in fact does. Los Angeles County has one thousand five hundred contracts with seventy-five municipalities, which buy from four to forty-five services each.

Fifth, about one fourth of the Standard Metropolitan Statistical Areas contain *metropolitan special districts*. These units perform one or more areal functions for the central city and also for the most heavily populated nearby suburbs. Such districts have an impressive record in handling complicated administrative problems; for example, the St. Louis Metropolitan Sewer District provides pipes and central disposal plants for a large area.

The Significance of Local Governments

Local governments are not only numerous, but they also affect every citizen. Despite the more publicized activities of the federal government in defense and world politics, it may very well be that, except in time of war, local governments touch the citizen more directly. Schools are locally run and largely still locally financed. Police are completely locally managed and largely locally financed, as is fire protection. Water and waste disposal are local tasks that have little to do with either the federal or the state governments. Many local governments build and maintain local roads and run municipal or county hospitals. Table 11.4 shows how municipal revenues are distributed among various functions. All told, local governments spend 40 per cent as much as the federal government, over $80 billion a year, and employ more people than Washington and the state governments combined. Further, local governments, despite increased state and federal aid in the past decade, still raise close to two thirds of their own revenues from local sources. The main source, for over 80 per cent of the money, is the property tax on homes and business.

Local governments are thrust into the center stage of national concerns for a reason that goes beyond the scope and expense of their activities: they make crucial qualitative decisions. Will the police be an integrated force treating all racial and economic classes equally? Or will it, instead, be an all-white operation viewed by ghetto residents as an army of occupation? Will the zoning board set standards opening the community to a variety of races and income groups, or will it require home construction of such quality on lots so large that only those with incomes over $50,000 a year can live there? Will local businesses be underassessed on their taxes and unregulated on pollution, or will tax burdens be distributed fairly and the environment strictly and honestly protected? None of these problems is strictly monetary. All are largely within the purview of local decision-makers. Indeed, to raise

Table 11.4
*The expenditure
patterns of local
governments*

Service	All municipalities (per cent)	Twenty-five largest cities (per cent)
Education	15	18
Highways	10	6
Welfare	8	15
Health and hospitals	7	10
Police	11	10
Fire protection	7	5
Housing and urban renewal	4	5
Sanitation collection	10	n.a. *
Parks	5	n.a.
All other expenses	25	30

Source: U.S. Statistical Abstract (Washington, D.C.: U.S. Government Printing Office, 1970).

* Subsumed in "Other Expense Category." Not available separately.

these issues takes us beyond a description of metropolitan development and the distribution of governments. We turn now to the politics of urban areas, beginning with a fundamental question: Who rules the cities?

who rules the cities?

The Special Role of the Federal Government

We can begin to understand the position of local governments by looking first at the role of the federal government. Many federal decisions, made in all branches of its government, have exceptional impact on local communities. The Supreme Court's school desegregation decisions, starting with *Brown* v. *Board of Education* in 1954 and continuing to the present day, have relentlessly struck down segregated classrooms organized by state and local governments. On the other hand, the Court's refusal to strike down segregation occurring as a consequence of neighborhood residential patterns or economic differentiation has protected many northern forms of urban discrimination. The Court's approach has also increased the attractiveness of suburbs to whites, who find racial protection in distance and homogeneity within small legal enclaves. Similarly, various congressional programs have had a direct impact on local communities. The antipoverty program to organize the poor, the Civil Rights Acts of 1964 and 1965, which desegregated hotels, restaurants, and theaters and opened up voting registration, have all had an immediate impact at the local community level. In addition, various programs passed under executive leadership and now administered by executive agencies have significantly affected local communities. The Federal Highway Administration has built thousands of miles of urban highways and suburban connectors; the effect of these roads has been to make commuting cheaper in time and money, thereby encouraging and subsidizing the exodus of families and industries from central cities. The new roads have also frequently destroyed low-cost city housing occupied by minorities, and have had the further effect of reducing city tax rolls.

The urban areas, it should be observed, are hardly pawns in these processes. Their Congressmen represent them, as "ambassadors" to Washington, intervening for categorical grants from agencies to build facilities and underwrite special programs and working for general-purpose bills. Urban officials are themselves also organized into Washington lobbies, particularly through the U.S. Conference of Mayors, which represents the larger cities, and through the National League of Cities. Some cities even maintain their own Washington lobby offices to work for federal grants. Still, for a variety of reasons, efforts to induce a strong federal-city format into the traditional federal-state form of American federalism has been something short of a success.

There have been some direct federal-city programs. The federal aid programs for hospital and airport construction were two early efforts, and the original 1965 Poverty Program was a later one. But state governments, jealous of their own powers and more conservative and more oriented to rural and suburban interests, have fought the extension of direct federal-city relationships. Their success is marked in provisos in law requiring approval by the governor or by gubernatorial-appointed planning boards for federal grants intended for city projects. A further complicating factor is that the politics of urban federalism is often blurred by the conflicts between suburban and central city interests. As suburbs grow more rapidly than central cities and become larger in absolute terms, a trend marked for the first time by the 1970 Census, the political split will widen not only at the local level, but in the representation of local views in Washington. The political problem of organizing a coherent urban position may be made insurmountable by demography.

Meanwhile, decisions made in Washington will continue to affect every metropolitan area. Some will have an impact in the absence of explicit planning and calculations of loss or gain, though they will nonetheless be "policies." This, apparently, was the way the FHA housing program and the federal highway program were converted from simple goals—more housing and better roads—into aids to suburbanization and decentralization. Other programs, such as revenue sharing, are better understood in terms of their urban effects from the beginning. Revenue sharing, for example, returns a portion of federal tax revenues directly to the state governments which pass the monies on a formula basis directly to city governments to use as they please within broad guidelines. The city governments understood from the beginning how this effort would benefit them.

The Special Role of State Governments

State governments have influence in municipal politics because they have complete legal authority over all local governments.

The legal hold of the state derives from the cities' subordinate position as municipal corporations. Whatever powers local governments do possess are derived from grants of power or charters issued by the state. (Of course, the states can only grant authority not inconsistent with the federal Constitution.) Some commentators on municipal government have argued for an inherent right of local self-government, but this has been a distinctly minority position. Most state governments have rejected the inherent-right doctrine in favor of the famous dictum of Judge John F. Dillon of Iowa, who wrote:

It is a general and undisputed proposition of law that a municipal corporation possesses and can exercise the following powers, and no others: First, those granted in express words; second, those necessarily or fairly implied in or incident to the powers expressly granted; third, those essential to the accomplishment of the declared objects and purposes of the corporation—not simply convenient, but indispensable. Any fair, reasonable, substantial doubt concerning the existence of power is *resolved by the courts against the corporation and the power is denied.*[12]

"Dillon's Rule" is one of narrow construction of municipal powers. It has had enormous political consequences: 1. state legislatures, traditionally malapportioned in favor of rural areas until the reapportionment cases of the 1960's, have watched over cities closely and regulated them minutely; 2. wherever legislatures have been liberal in granting cities power, the state courts have been almost uniformly restrictive in interpreting it; they have typically returned much of the authority to the legislatures. Many legislatures have given cities the right to home rule, namely the right to make changes in their own charters and to act independently on local matters, yet the courts have rendered home rule almost meaningless. Although almost two thirds of all cities with a population of over 200,000 possess home rule, they still find themselves restrained and must continually run to the legislature for authorization to act.

State governments also control metropolitan governmental organization. The state legislatures can make it easy or impossible for central cities to annex surrounding territories. They can make it easy or impossible for developers to incorporate independent governments in newly settled areas. Only in a few southwestern states, where the social distance between central cities and suburbs is small, have legislatures allowed much annexation. In most states, annexation is effectively blocked by two devices. First, all affected places are required to approve annexation in a referendum. Second, new incorporations are made easy and already incorporated areas, even if they were formerly the smallest villages, are given great protection. It is an interesting question whether state legislatures will take a more benevolent view toward annexation in the decades ahead when many central cities will have black majorities. In that context, forced consolidation of central cities and surrounding suburbs would dilute black power with white votes. The possibility has already been raised in Georgia, where the legislature has considered merging Atlanta, which has a black majority, with the primarily white county that surrounds it.

There are numerous examples of state governmental participation in local politics. The states provide about one third of all local governmental revenues; most of this aid goes for schools, welfare payments, and highways.[13] To cite some specific illustrations, the Governor of Missouri appoints the Police Commissioner for the city of St. Louis, and the City Council must, by law, appropriate whatever city funds the Commissioner requests. All of the city employees in Massachusetts are in a civil

---

[12] *Commentaries on the Law of Municipal Corporations* (Boston, 1911), p. 448. Italics added.

[13] See James A. Maxwell, *Financing State and Local Governments* (Washington, D.C.: Brookings Institution, 1969).

service system run by the state. When the Mayor of New York wishes to add new taxes, on city residents or on commuters, he needs not only the approval of his own city council, but also the approval of the state legislature and the Governor in Albany.

State courts, in fact, have declared the regulation of juke boxes, apartment houses, sewers, transit systems, and plumbers to be state rather than local matters. As a consequence, city officials depend upon state legislators elected from their community to represent them at the capitol and to help put through a "city program" every session. Such dependence gives the legislators a continuing voice in city affairs, and Governors are always involved as well, often in the most minute details of urban budgeting, schools, and police services. A good rule of thumb in city governmental decision-making is that anything important will eventually require recourse to the state capital, where the outcome will be a result of bargaining and compromise—in short, of politics.

Decision-Making Within the Cities

For the past fifteen years a heated academic debate has raged over the question of what groups, classes, interests, officials, or individuals possess the power to influence different kinds of decisions in our cities. As conflict in urban areas has increased, the question of who rules has increasingly become a practical one. In many ways, the argument over who has power, and the effort to find out and prove a case, has its analogies in the debate over national politics. Are national policies made by elected officeholders who are responsible to the people? Or are these officeholders merely a front for private economic interests? If officeholders are a front, do they act as the conscious or unconscious agents of the real "power structure"? If there is a national power structure, a "military-industrial-labor-academic complex," for example, does it operate directly in day-to-day politics? Or does it, indeed, engage in manipulative actions that actually prevent the important questions from ever appearing on the agenda of politics, and thus, secure in the knowledge that no serious challenges are possible, allow a politics of triviality open to all to go on at a surface level? If that happens, then, is not politics simply a symbolic ritual, aimed at reassuring deceived mass publics, while, behind the scenes, the pie is divided up by powerful and barely visible elites? [14]

Sociologists have developed a model of local decision-making known as the *power-structure theory.* Their data come from "reputational" surveys, in which prominent citizens name others whom they think are influential. A ranking is constructed of those named most frequently, and a tabulation is then made of who they are and what they do. Floyd Hunter's Atlanta study, *Community Power Structure,* was the pioneer in this genre.[15] Hunter and his followers have found the cities they study controlled by interlocking sets of business and industrial leaders—hence

[14] For a detailed exposition of this line of analysis, see Murray Edelman, *The Symbolic Use of Politics* (Urbana: University of Illinois, 1964).

[15] Chapel Hill: University of North Carolina, 1953.

the "power structure," terminology. This power structure is allegedly hidden from public view, and its members dictate policy from behind the scenes to civic activists and city officials who act as their willing agents. The hidden power structure supposedly controls the community's significant economic, civic, and political resources, and can use its power on ongoing issues or to keep issues out of politics entirely.

Although disapproving of the reputational methodology, one team of political scientists, Bachrach and Baratz, has come to essentially the same conclusion about local politics.[16] They argue that the "mobilization of bias" in any local community is to keep some groups deprived and to protect others who benefit from the status quo. The prime device is the "nondecision," the process by which the main questions of politics—what the rules, processes, and divisions of benefits are going to be in the first place—are kept out of visible political conflict. In an extensive study of Baltimore, these authors demonstrated how nondecisions kept black interests out of the arena of public decision-making for many years. Their research also suggested that federal aid, black protest, and changing white attitudes did gradually bring forth black issues into the main institutions over a harsh decade.

Many other political scientists reject both the power structure and the non-decision-making explanations of urban politics. They question the reliability of informants in detecting influence in others, and also the absence of studies of real decisions in many power structure studies. And, with regard to the approach that focuses on nondecisions, they ask a pertinent question: How is it possible to observe and verify an exercise of power that, by definition, is covert and perhaps not even conscious? On the other hand, these critics accept the dominance of business elites in some cities, particularly in the South and the Southwest, such as Dallas, and in general accept the argument that private groups outside government play a major role in urban politics. Taking as their methodology the observation of specific controversies in different cities, this group has derived a "pluralist model" of the distribution of power. Studies in New Haven, Syracuse, and Chicago all led to similar conclusions.[17] Instead of a hidden yet all-powerful elite, they found a shifting cast of political and civic actors, depending upon the issue and the stakes. City officials, political parties, neighborhood leaders, civic associations, and businessmen all had very real influence on the outcome of some conflicts, yet none could—or tried to—enforce their preferences on every issue.

The pluralists feel that outcomes are always the product of a complex set of variables. These include the expertise a group can claim on a subject in question, the allies available, the votes and economic resources behind each set of protagonists, and the position taken by elected governmental officials. In the pluralist view, the problem is not who rules, but if anyone does rule. Power appears hard to come by, fragmented, and shifting as controversies change.

Various scholarly efforts have been made to consolidate alternative theoretical

---

[16] See their *Power and Poverty: Theory and Practice* (New York: Oxford U.P., 1970).

[17] See Robert A. Dahl, *Who Governs?* (New Haven: Yale University Press, 1961); Roscoe C. Martin, Frank J. Munger, et al., *Decisions in Syracuse* (Bloomington: Indiana U.P., 1961); and Edward Banfield, *Political Influence* (New York: Free Press, 1961).

explanations as to how urban communities are governed. Terry Clark combined aspects of the power structure and the pluralist decision-making methodologies along with various environmental data in a study of fifty-one communities of all sizes and locations.[18] He found considerable variation among cities in the level of decentralization of decision-making authority, i.e., in whether a small power structure or a variety of actors held power. He also found that decentralization—the pluralist model—fits best in cities that were more economically diversified, were larger in size, had more civic associations, and were least reformed. In these communities, too, overall budget expenditures and urban renewal expenditures were greater. In a secondary analysis of 166 communities, Claire W. Gilbert found:

> The evidence supports the notion that increasing scale of society is reflected in the political structure of local communities. It appears that power—i.e., the ability to make binding decisions for the community—is less and less in the hands of a privileged few and is increasingly dependent upon the broker, be he elected official or not, who can bring together (to the extent he can bring together) the various elements in the *community*.[19]

An appealing theory, which synthesizes key elements in the other explanations we have outlined, is Robert Salisbury's hypothesis of the controlling force of *the executive coalition*.[20] He argues that important decisions in urban politics are made by a coalition of influential individuals and interests, with the most important single participant being the mayor of the city. The two most significant supporting units in the coalition are the professional technocrats in city hall and the business leaders downtown. Voters are an indispensable third element, but insofar as policy-making is concerned, they stand at least several steps removed from the center of the coalition.

The politically skilled mayor becomes the leader of the coalition, once he is in office, through two devices. First, highly aware of the complexity of modern city government, he relies heavily upon the professional technocrats for counsel and for programs. Second, he utilizes his various resources to obtain and maintain the support of the businessmen, who in turn work with him because he is vital to the development programs necessary to their own economic well-being. The mayor thus has the political appeal to get elected, the intelligence to utilize top-grade aides, and the power to bring the private resources of the business community behind him. Having a series of common interests, the coalition makes policy.

In the executive coalition, business emerges with a major role, but not a controlling one. Its influence is narrow and circumscribed: it supports the mayor who works toward its development goals. The mayor is the catalyst who holds the government together, but even his influence is *relative* to that of other groups. He is the

---

[18] "Community Structure, Decision-Making, Budget Expenditures, and Urban Renewal in 51 American Communities," reprinted in Charles M. Bonjean et al., *Community Politics: A Behavioral Approach* (New York: Macmillan, 1971), pp. 293–313.

[19] "Some Trends in Community Politics: A Secondary Analysis of Power Structure Data from 166 Communities," reprinted in Bonjean et al., op. cit., p. 215.

[20] "Urban Politics: The New Convergence of Power," *Journal of Politics*, XXIV (November, 1964), pp. 775–797.

central figure in all negotiations—be they over a racial riot or a new building scheme. Yet the power that makes him loom large compared to other participants does not seem great compared to the magnitude of the problems confronting him. Salisbury has wryly observed that:

the Mayor cannot determine by fiat or, apparently any other way, that the economic resources of the city shall increase, that crime and poverty shall decline, that traffic shall move efficiently. He only has rather more to say about how the problems shall be approached than anyone else.[21]

Participants in Urban Politics: Big-City Activists

Whatever the correct theoretical model of urban politics, certain community-based elements are predictably the participants. The list is different for big cities and for suburbs. In the larger cities, the major activists, in different roles of course, are the mayor, the agencies of the city government itself, the voters, the political parties, the economic interest groups, the racial and ethnic blocs, the civic associations, and the newspapers. In beginning with the mayor, a useful approach is to assess cities in terms of how much power is centralized in the city government. In broad terms, mayors seem to face three kinds of environment.[22]

The **extremely decentralized city government** is the first type, with Los Angeles and Seattle as the foremost examples. To illustrate, the mayor of Los Angeles shares his executive branch with a City Attorney and a Controller who are elected independently. Nineteen of the twenty-eight city departments are not under his direction, but are run by independent boards; these include schools, welfare, transportation, employment, health, and housing. Although the Mayor can appoint the heads of some of the boards, he can remove them only in the most unusual conditions. Once they are in, his influence is severely circumscribed. Nor does the Mayor find assistance among the councilmen. They are elected on a nonpartisan basis for staggered terms and respond largely to interests in their own districts. To fragment the government further, many important questions are settled by the voters directly through referenda.

In this situation, how does the Mayor of Los Angeles manage to sail his own ship? The only reply is that to a large degree he presides rather than governs. Because the Mayor is elected on a nonpartisan basis and has no strong party behind him, he must mobilize informal support in the community at large in order to influence city decisions. The usual approach for a Los Angeles Mayor is to sell his program personally through the mass media. Using the hard and concentrated sell, he must put together shifting majorities in the public on an ad hoc basis and then, with this backing, try to deal with the Council issue by issue. Leadership in an environment such as this is difficult, involving strenuous activity and long-shot gambles on the Mayor's part—and often it is impossible.

[21] Ibid., p. 790.
[22] The following categories are adapted from those used by Edward C. Banfield and James Q. Wilson in *City Politics* (Cambridge: Harvard University Press, 1963).

The **partially centralized city government** is the second type, and it is manifest in such cities as Boston, Detroit, and New York. In Boston the Mayor does possess at least two kinds of political resources. First, his formal authority is considerable. He can appoint and remove his own department heads, prepare and control the levels of the city budget, and appoint various city employees. Second, although he is elected on a nonpartisan basis and is not especially close, generally, to the city Democratic Party, from which he invariably comes, the Mayor still finds it relatively easy to mobilize informal support. As a popular figure, he can count on public backing. In Boston's predictable and manageable group structure, he can pick up allies from outside City Hall. At the minimum, the combination of his formal resources and informal popularity allows the Mayor to dominate the members of the City Council.

On the other hand, the Mayor of Boston is still something less than the complete executive. The tool of party is unavailable to him as a control device in dealing with the Council. Like many nonpartisan mayors, he is isolated from the mainstream of state and national party politics. Leading Massachusetts Democrats often have their own personal bases of support in Boston and, as a result, view the Mayor as a competitor rather than an ally. When these party-based leaders control the state legislature, they can make life exceedingly difficult for the Mayor, especially because the Massachusetts legislature possesses great legal power over Boston city affairs. Through a number of special agencies, the state oversees the city's liquor stores, amusement centers, and restaurants. A state finance commission is the watchdog for city fiscal affairs.

The Mayor of Boston, moreover, does not control the functions of water supply, sewage disposal, parks, and public transit; these are all managed by independent and legally autonomous special districts. The ruling boards of the districts contain city representatives, but they also include representatives of the state and the outlying suburbs. Finally, although he can usually overwhelm his own Council, the Mayor cannot stop it from harassing him on any one of a number of sensitive budget items.

The third type is the **effectively centralized government.** The classic present-day example is Chicago, ironically enough a nominally nonpartisan city. As the Willis case indicated, however, the Mayor of Chicago keeps strong hands on all the political levers. The Mayor's power lies in his informal rather than his legal authority. The strange truth is that there is *no* American city with a government effectively centralized in terms of legal structure alone. In Chicago, the City Charter forces the Mayor to coexist with a City Treasurer and a City Clerk who are independently elected; and he must divide responsibility with 341 other city and county officials whose jurisdiction overlaps his own. In addition, there are numerous independent boards and special districts in Chicago, including the Board of Education. Finally, important issues are often decided by the voters in referenda, and the council members, who are elected within districts on the basis of neighborhood sentiment, can, in theory, oppose the Mayor.

But the theoretical possibilities in Chicago have little relation to the reality of government. The Mayor runs the tightest ship and the most centralized government in America. How does he do it? He is either "the last of the bosses," or, in Mayor

Daley's own words, "The first of the new leaders." [23] His source of power is the Chairmanship of the Cook County Democratic Party. The party is a tightly controlled pyramid, held together by patronage in the form of city jobs, stretching from block to precinct to ward organizations and on up to the Mayor himself. The responsibility of the lower units is to deliver voting support for the Mayor, the candidates he endorses, and the referenda he proposes. Those in the lower echelons who deliver the most votes get preferred treatment when the Mayor dispenses jobs, legal business, and contracts. As many as five hundred jobs may be filtered through an individual ward leader.

As the leader, the Mayor controls some twenty-five thousand city positions. This allows him to rule the party organization. At the same time, because he can grant contenders for state offices the party endorsement, he also is able to dominate the forty-two-man Cook County delegation to the state legislature in Springfield. Illinois Governors, Democrats or Republicans, remain intensely sensitive to the Mayor's wishes, in recognition of his potent "clout." Further, the nine members of Congress from Chicago are, if not the creations of the Mayor, among his most loyal political friends.

The Roles of Other Big-City Activists

Next to the mayor, **agencies of the city government** itself may be the most visible actors in city politics. Especially when organized in municipal unions, police, teachers, and sanitation personnel are increasingly prone to strikes and direct-action tactics. Their interest in city policy is partially material, focusing on wages and job conditions and security.

The concerns of most city workers are also symbolic, for they define themselves as professionals and seek autonomy over their spheres of operation. Conflict with other segments of the community is not uncommon. Policemen and black groups often disagree on what constitute reasonable tactics. Teachers and parents' groups fight over methods in the classrooms. The activism of city agencies today vividly illustrates the axiom that no bureaucracy merely "administers" in a neutral fashion policies that are established by other instrumentalities of government. All government employees have their own values, goals, and claims, and they fight for them in the cities as they do in Washington or in the state capitals.

Voters communicate with decision-makers in government in a variety of ways; it may be the primary form of participation for most of our citizens. Municipal elections attract less interest than presidential or state contests. In a city election, a turnout of 50 per cent of those eligible is high, 30 per cent the probable average. Nonpartisan election systems are correlated with the lower turnouts. The choices facing the voters in these nonpartisan cities are between individuals backed surreptitiously by the parties and openly by various civic and interest groups whose influence

[23] For one view, see Mike Royko, *Boss: Richard J. Daley of Chicago* (New York: Dutton, 1971).

tends to supersede that of the parties. Finally, in many cities voters have a particular type of direct influence on policy because many referenda—"yes" or "no" choices on various improvements and bond issues—are placed before them on the ballot.

Political parties, in nonpartisan cities, are forced either to operate behind the scenes or to concentrate on state and national goals. The most extensive empirical examination we have of big city parties, Samuel Eldersveld's study of Detroit, uncovered the expected situation for a nonpartisan city: the parties were loosely organized and very fluid networks of socially heterogeneous activists.[24] Their primary orientation was toward county and state elections, not toward the city. Detroit parties are almost the exact opposite of those in Chicago. Where partisan systems do exist in big cities, the parties generate votes, socialize those seeking access to the political system (the training-ground function), and distribute governmental rewards such as jobs, contracts, and social status to their supporters.

Economic interests are participants in city politics in the form of organized and usually professionally staffed groups. The range of these groups is narrower than in national politics. Thus, it is *local* businessmen who are active. Large corporations do only as much as their absentee owners and mobile plant managers feel is necessary for minimally harmonious relations and an acceptable image. But for the local bankers, department store owners, and real estate operators, the stakes of city politics are high. Their firms have major financial investments there, usually in the downtown section. Their families occupy high social positions and in many instances they feel a sense of responsibility. Since the end of World War II, such local businessmen have banded together in many cities in new civic progress organizations. The main goal is usually restoration or redevelopment of the central city.

National labor unions like their corporate counterparts, are indifferent to local politics. The crafts unions—plumbers, carpenters, and bricklayers—who are concerned about licensing and construction regulations tend to be the most involved. There are, however, important exceptions. The Teamsters in St. Louis, the United Auto Workers in Detroit, and the Central Labor Council in New York City all play intense roles in local affairs.

Racial and ethnic blocs represent the major cleavages in the broad publics of big cities today. The range of black participation, for example, is extensive. It includes the riots of the 1960's in cities as disparate as Atlanta, Dayton, Omaha, New York, and San Francisco. It also involves traditional party politics played by black ward chiefs in Chicago, New York, and St. Louis, and full-fledged mayoral campaigns in Cleveland, Detroit, Los Angeles, Newark, Gary, and elsewhere.

Black organizations are also diverse. They range from "community-control"-oriented neighborhood organizations interested in school procedures and city services to the Black Panthers and the Muslims, the latter each having their own complete ideologies. There are also traditional groups such as the National Association for the Advancement of Colored People (NAACP) and the Urban League. The last two have middle-class values and depend upon a mixed black-white base of support.

---

[24] *Political Parties: A Behavioral Analysis* (Chicago: Rand McNally, 1964).

The goals of black urban activity also vary. For many, the capture of offices and positions is the primary first objective; for others, integrating schools and other public and private institutions, housing, and white-collar jobs. Still others seek policies that will enhance "black power"—housing, schools, hospitals, and more jobs, preferably under their own control.

Increasingly, those whites remaining in some of the larger cities are blue-collar working-class people who are highly conscious of their own ethnic identity, as, for example, the Italo-Americans and the Polish-Americans. Because they feel challenged by blacks and deserted by middle-class whites, they have formed their own organizations, through neighborhood, church, and union associations. These ethnic groups have sought to extend their influence through alliances with "law-and-order" police and political forces in many cities.

Civic associations, such as affiliates of the National Municipal League and the League of Women Voters, are always to be found in city politics. Some, especially taxpayers' "research groups," are actually fronts for those who wish to keep property taxes down. A few of the civic associations serve as the local spokesmen for the reform ideology, but most frequently they take the form of ad hoc operations created to espouse or oppose a particular cause with fervor—a new school, a neighborhood center, or a redevelopment plan. Once the issue is settled, the association vanishes. A new kind of civic association is the National Urban Coalition, which, through local chapters, tries to bring together local businessmen, blacks, and ethnic leaders.

Newspapers occupy a special place in the political life of most cities. They are supposed to be impartial reporters of events, and although the amount of space devoted to local problems varies enormously, many do an exceptionally fine job. But at the same time, the papers are themselves a local business with large fixed investments in plant and a definite dependence upon department-store advertising revenues. Not surprisingly, most major city dailies are supporters of civic progress development proposals and of the reform ideology in city affairs. Their actual influence varies. It is greatest in nonpartisan cities and on bond referenda, when alternative sources of advice to the voters are less available.

Participants in Urban Politics: Suburban Activists

The main participants in surburban politics are the city managers, the city council and the other agencies of the government, the voters, the parties, local businessmen, and civic clubs. The manager plays a unique role. Two types seem to be recruited: the local comes from the community and has no special training; the professional is attuned to the standards of the International City Managers Association, is geographically mobile, and has advanced degrees.[25] Although in theory **city managers** act as hired administrators acting on behalf of the city council, in fact they appear to

[25] See Gladys Kammerer et al., *City Managers in Politics* (Gainesville: University of Florida, 1962).

define their role as policy initiation and advocacy.[26] The problems that arise can be understood by an analysis of three types of managers in different community settings.

The *administrative manager* is found primarily in homogeneous communities. He may be a local or a professional, but whatever he is, his position is one of considerable strength. He does not have to worry about politics or conflict, because there are none in the community. His decisions deal with routine, and routine matters are always administrative.

The manager who is a *factional agent* is found in communities that have diverse interests, one of which is dominant. The dominant faction may consist of businessmen or a civic caucus, but whatever it is, if the manager is its agent, he will find himself in a position of considerable personal strength. Although local managers may survive, the delicacy of the context and the need for extreme sensitivity frequently require the direction of a professional manager. As factional agents, professionally oriented managers can create fine careers for themselves. If the faction loses its majority, of course, the chosen manager goes.

In some council-manager cities there exists a multiplicity of interests, and none is strong enough to dominate. Here a third type of manager, the *tightrope artist,* is required. Whether he is a local or a professional, this type of manager must be able to maintain a delicate balance between warring factions. To retain his job he must carefully avoid their crossfire, and he must be extremely cautious in recommending any particular course of action. Not surprisingly, in communities that require a tightrope artist manager there is frequently a stalemate on policy issues and the manager has little personal authority.

City councils in suburbs apparently attract amateur activists with little ambition for professional political careers.[27] Councilmen do take their jobs seriously, and, as Table 11.5 shows, have some built-in role conflicts with their managers. The attitudes of the councilmen—what they think the problems are and what they want for their communities—have an independent impact upon public policy.[28] As for the rest of suburban government, it is likely that the main agency is the school department. The archetypal employee may be the school superintendent.

The Roles of Other Suburban Activists

As to **voters,** popular myth to the contrary, all suburbanites are not Republicans. In national elections, of every six suburbs, three are Republican, two Democratic, and one evenly split. The socioeconomic composition of the suburb is the key variable. In local contests, turnouts, which generally correlate with home ownership

[26] See Ronald O. Loveridge, "The City Manager in Legislative Politics," *Polity,* I (Winter, 1968), pp. 214–236.

[27] See Kenneth Prewitt, "Political Ambitions, Volunteerism, and Electoral Accountability," *The American Political Science Review,* LXIV (March, 1970), pp. 5–17.

[28] See Heinz Eulau and Robert Eyestone, "Policy Maps of City Councils and Policy Outcomes: A Developmental Analysis," *The American Political Science Review,* LXII, No. 2 (March, 1968), pp. 124–143.

Table 11.5   *Role expectation disagreements between city managers and councils*

	City managers (%)		Per cent disagreement	City councilmen (%)	
	Agree	Disagree	%	Agree	Disagree
1. City manager as policy administrator					
	22	78	66	88	12
2. City manager as policy innovator					
	88	12	46	42	58
3. City manager as political leader					
	53	47	41	12	88
4. City manager as policy neutral					
	24	76	40	64	36
5. City manager as political recruiter					
	44	56	21	23	77
6. City manager as budget consultant					
	31	69	18	49	51

Source: Ronald O. Loveridge, "The City Manager in Legislative Politics," *Polity,* I, No. 2 (Winter, 1968), p. 230.

and higher educational levels, should be higher in many suburbs than in the central cities. Still, even this is not uniformly the case. If cities suffer from problems so great that they may be insoluble, many suburban communities suffer from a trivialization of politics. In homogeneous towns with no conflicts, no issues, and nonpartisan and businesslike manager government, few voters bother to turn out.

Political parties in the suburbs have a restricted role. Suburbs are more likely than cities to have nonpartisan governments. Electoral conflicts are over personalities in the typical suburb. In suburbia, furthermore, the professional politicians and the political managers of the big cities are absent. More often than not, suburban politics is a game played by spirited amateurs. To the degree that the party politician exists there at all, he is what Robert C. Wood has labeled the "suburban boss."[29]

The suburban party leader often holds the post of county party chairman. This allows him to do his job, but also permits him to maintain a hands-off position on

[29] *Suburbia: Its People and Their Politics* (Boston: Houghton, 1959).

town government issues. He knows he must let the manager administration go its own way, and he does, often spouting a form of good government jargon that pleases his constituents.

Suburban group life does not have the numerous and tightly organized interests of the city. Instead, one finds a few permanent organizations of **local businessmen** and an astounding number of civic clubs that come and go with the issues. The local businessmen do not own great enterprises, but shopping centers, retail stores, gas stations, and restaurants. They are concerned with tax rates, zoning, and parking facilities to make their establishments more convenient for shoppers. Business politics in suburbia is mostly "boosterism." Those large industries lured to suburban industrial parks are captured through lush concessions and, once in, they rarely pay any attention to the community. Suburban newspapers are, more than in the city, an extension of community commercial life.

Civic clubs are omnipresent features of suburban political life. Sometimes they are dominated by housewives, sometimes not. These clubs form in response to issues when they arise, such as, for example, whether a neighborhood should be beautified, a new park developed, or a new school constructed. Leaders tend to be self-selected enthusiasts or members of small and self-perpetuating civic-minded cliques. Since the school tends to be the focal point of suburban interest, many such groups form around educational controversies.

Politics and the Future of the Cities

What will happen to the cities? What will happen to the suburbs surrounding them? Will some sort of civil peace with justice be achieved? Or will the suburban communities become armed white encampments containing the society's wealth and jobs, while the core cities serve as dumping grounds for the alienated—the black, the old, and the hippie? What impact can political decisions at all levels of government have upon the urban future? How much of what will happen is already set beyond changing, either by present social arrangements or by an unyielding technology? These questions are of interest to every student, every politician, and every urban dweller. Research into the urban future has made a beginning, but the possibilities and the main factors are by no means perfectly clear.

It is certain that reversing the decentralization of urban life will be difficult if not impossible. The old central cities drew their immigrants and their industry because of the advantages of their location; they were close to river and rail transportation routes and had a cluster of people and firms who could carry on necessary communications with each other easily. Today, however, highways and airports are the main transportation routes, and they have made suburban areas more attractive than core cities for most middle-income residents and an increasing percentage of firms. Moreover, the availability of computer, telephone, and television communications makes face-to-face contact less and less necessary. From a technological perspective alone, the central cities would seem to have little hope of regaining their former preeminence. In fact, the human capital that used to supplement the cities' natural advantages—the trained middle-class work force—has already moved out.

The political interests of the suburban citizens also seem to portend continuation of the present suburbanization trends, with limited possibilities for much consolidation of existing units into strong metropolitan governments. Existing cooperative efforts have been mainly in the areas of airports, electricity, roads, sewers, and water, which Oliver P. Williams has aptly described as system maintenance functions.[30] On issues in which the life style of suburbanites is at stake, there has so far been little cooperation. This is because suburbanization, i.e., the creation of legally protected, homogeneous, specialized units, protects the two most important bulwarks of the residents' life style—the value of their land and the quality of their schools. Land values are protected by zoning practices that keep out low-income dwellings, whether privately or governmentally sponsored. The schools can be run at a high level because the social homogeneity of the small community makes it possible to concentrate on academic work, and equalization formulas in state school aid programs underwrite much of the cost. As Alan A. Altshuler has pointed out, whereas blacks in the central cities are fighting for "community control," whites in the suburbs have already achieved it.[31]

Despite their protection of middle-class life-style values, the suburbs have problems. As they grow older, some will decline. Because these suburbs lack diversity, the decline cannot be counterbalanced by resources elsewhere in the same community, and people will simply move away. In addition, the suburbs have enormous capital expenses in building new *plant,* that is, their schools, administrative facilities, and secondary roads. Even if few amenities are provided, tax burdens are sure to become heavier.

The federal government, by contrast, is impaled upon the horns of a severe political dilemma. The Republicans nationally depend upon and the Democrats seek the votes of suburban whites. Nonetheless, under both parties since the mid-1950's there has been an uneven, but undeniable, progression toward using federal power to further racial equality. The dilemma comes from the fact that suburban life styles rest on racial exclusion. Between 1960 and 1970, although the number of blacks living in suburbs increased, black residents as a percentage of all suburbanities actually *declined.* Even if governments do not act to ameliorate racial exclusion from the suburbs, the conflict is sure to be severe.

What will happen? Few observers are optimistic. Edward C. Banfield, famous conservative scholar and adviser to the Nixon Administration, believes that in time the raw growth in the economy will do much to alleviate urban poverty.[32] He also feels that descriptions of urban deprivation are exaggerated. Banfield attributes much urban violence to the presence of a lower class, largely male and young, predisposed to a street life-style. Their destructive activities will diminish with a

[30] "Life-Style Values and Political Decentralization in Metropolitan Areas," in Bonjean et al., op. cit., pp. 56–64.

[31] *Community Control: The Black Demand for Participation in Large American Cities* (New York: Pegasus, 1970).

[32] *The Unheavenly City* (Boston: Little, Brown, 1970).

demographic decline, and the proportion of this group in the total city population will not decline until the 1980's. Time, rather than social strategies, is advised as the solution.

At another level, some see hope in the emergence of black leadership in many cities to positions of real power. But, without resources, what good can office be? Most mayors, including black mayors, feel that, with their limited resources, the best hope is a change in federal policy priorities leading to a change in the amounts of federal aid. This viewpoint is substantiated in research showing that, insofar as spending is concerned, the key variable is the resources a community has to start with. If those resources are slight, or declining, then only outside help can save the cities. On the other hand, other research suggests that on nonmonetary issues, political variables do count.[33] This finding suggests that the form of government, local parties, civic leaders, and individual politicians may be able to make a difference on urban questions not requiring cash. What difference they will make in practice, and whether the difference will matter, hinges on what they choose to do and what support the beleaguered big-city leaders find among other elements within American society.

[33] See James W. Clarke, "Environment, Process, and Policy: A Reconsideration," *The American Political Science Review,* LXIII, No. 4 (December, 1969), pp. 1172–1182.

suggested additional readings

Bachrach, Peter, and Morton S. Baratz. *Power and Poverty*. New York: Oxford University Press, 1970.*

Banfield, Edward C. *The Unheavenly City*. Boston: Little, Brown and Company, 1970.*

———, and James Q. Wilson. *City Politics*. New York: Vintage Books, 1963.*

Bonjean, Charles M., et al. (eds.). *Community Politics*. New York: The Free Press, 1971.*

Dahl, Robert A. *Who Governs?* New Haven: Yale University Press, 1961.*

Danielson, Michael N. (ed.). *Metropolitan Politics*. Boston Little, Brown and Company, 1971.*

Downs, Anthony. *Urban Problems and Prospects*. Chicago: Markham Publishing Co., 1970.*

Dye, Thomas R. *Politics in States and Communities*. Englewood Cliffs, N.J. Prentice-Hall, Inc., 1969.

Goodman, Jay S. (ed.). *Perspectives on Urban Politics*. Boston: Allyn & Bacon, Inc., 1970.*

Hunter, Floyd. *Community Power Structure*. Garden City, N.Y.: Doubleday-Anchor, 1963.*

Lineberry, Robert L., and Ira Sharkansky. *Urban Politics and Public Policy*. New York: Harper and Row, Publishers, 1970.*

Maxwell, James A. *Financing State and Local Governments*. Washington, D.C.: The Brookings Institution, 1969.*

Sayre, Wallace S., and Herbert Kaufman. *Governing New York City*. New York: W. W. Norton and Company, Inc., 1965.*

Wood, Robert C. *1400 Governments*. Garden City, N.Y.: Doubleday-Anchor, 1964.*

Yin, Robert K. (ed.). *The City in the Seventies*. Itasca, Ill.: F. E. Peacock Publishers, Inc., 1972.*

* Available in paperback.

12 the welfare state

case study

*The Poverty Culture: America's Poor**

There in the shade of the hamburger stand was the guitar player—dark glasses, tin cup, strumming loosely, singing loudly—the popular image of the remaining poor in America: the exceptional unfortunate one, the irreducible special case. He was scarcely noticeable in the surrounding crowds who wandered into Five-and-Tens and department stores on their consuming rounds.

The scene framed by the window of my rented car was in downtown Columbia, South Carolina, but it could have been in a thousand American cities. To the motorized middle-class American eye, the poor hardly exist.

The thought had occurred to me an hour earlier as the plane lowered over the lovely spring countryside. Where on the landscape below were the signs of poverty? Not on the big concrete highway where the cars and their slanting afternoon shadows raced past new shopping centers and geometric clusters of painted cottages. But if the eye left the main valley to go up a side road to a smaller valley, to still another dirt road that splayed out on a

* From Ben H. Bagdikian, *In the Midst of Plenty* (New York: New American Library, 1964), pp. 1–6, 103–104, 106–111. Copyright © 1964 by Ben H. Bagdikian. Reprinted by permission of Beacon Press.

sudden uptilt of eroded land, there they were: the collapsing shacks, the tilting privies, the rotting farm buildings with smoke curling out of a roof-pipe, hidden from the eye of the automobilized citizen, out of sight and out of mind, the ill-fed and ill-housed forgotten fifth of America.

The impoverished are forgotten because, among other reasons, the automobile and the airplane are new wombs for personal withdrawal, private capsules that impel their passengers along predetermined paths of affluence.

As I drove the car through downtown Columbia I knew very well that somewhere behind the big buildings were the row houses of the urban Negro poor. But I was curious to test on the ground what I had seen from the air. I drove by graceful homes aglow with azalea, through the outskirts with their Dairy Queens and root beer stands, until there was only field and forest. Then I took the first side road I could find, then another, each time choosing the smaller of every fork until I turned into one lane just wide enough for the car and had to stop short.

When the dust settled, the chromium-plated car dominated a tiny scene. On the side was a weary garden hemmed in by rusted hoops of wire, some tired white iris still

519

nodding from the rush of the car. On the other side was a tin-roofed cottage, tipped slightly as it rested on loose brick piles. From under a worn front stoop came two ambivalent mongrels, unsure whether they were frightened or frightening. Out of the door came a tall, scrawny Negro woman. The porch boards gave a little under her step. She had grey kinky hair, her upper teeth were mostly eroded away, and she looked me straight in the eye. Driving at random, guided only by the impulse to get off the beaten path, I met Rebecca Franklin. It was, it so happened, her birthday.

Inside the living room of the five-room shack the younger children giggled in from the kitchen. To make excuses to see the visitor they brought in empty paper bags and folded towels as gifts to tease their mother. "Happy birthday, Mama." After a time this irritated her. She looked steadily at the children and then sighed in resignation. "I'm 48," she said. "I know I look older."

Her husband died from injuries in an automobile accident six years ago and left her with twelve children, ages six to twenty-seven. The youngest eight are still at home. Because she is a widow with dependent children whose husband was under Social Security she gets $70 a month in federal survivors insurance. She earns about $100 a month cleaning and cooking for white families in town. The older married children outside the state send her about $100 in cash a year. For a family of nine $2200 a year is poverty.

Because she cooks for others, Mrs. Franklin assumes that her own food costs nothing. She spends $30 a week for the children's food, or 70 per cent of her income. At times she has enough for the 25 cents a day the children need for a hot lunch at their school but usually they are limited to 3 cents a day for milk. If there have been "extra" expenses during the month, on the last few days before the check they eat only bread, salt pork

and cane syrup. The children have never been to a doctor or a dentist. They have no television set. In the evening they cut wood for the kitchen stove and if, after that and homework there is still time, they go to a neighbor's house to watch some TV. There is no running water in the house, but there is a World Book Encyclopedia, its payments made by a daughter in Connecticut, and there is an electric refrigerator, its payments made by a son in Philadelphia.

Mrs. Franklin may be eligible for welfare aid but she doesn't get it. "After my husband's insurance gave out I went down and applied. I answered all their questions and then got a letter saying I hadn't proved to them I needed welfare. I told them everything they asked. I'm not going to lie for welfare. I'm not going to take a white person to speak for me. So I decided to work and take a chance the children would be all right while I'm out."

She held her head stiffly. "Well, all my grown children but one finished high school, and that one quit after the eleventh grade because he had to go to a sanitarium with the TB. And the younger ones will finish too. My tenth grade girl needs a pair of shoes right now if she's going to finish school this year. I got a dollar for my birthday from my pastor, and $2 from the lady I work for, and $5 my older children sent me by mail. So my girl will get to finish tenth grade; I'll get her a pair of tennis shoes."

She pursed her lips and straightened a magazine on the living room table.

"Here it's almost the end of the school year but already it seems like the awful months."

The awful months?

"Yes. The awful months. August. December. March. August you got to find clothes if the kids are going to school that year. December you just have to find some money somehow for Christmas presents. March is usually Easter and everyone else will have new clothes and you've got to try to find some little thing bright and new so the kids won't be ashamed to go to church or to school."

There is more to Rebecca Franklin's story, but though she is better off than most in spirit and in strength she is a reflection of the majority of the American poor, engaged in the desperate struggle to maintain the framework of civilized life against the crush of brute survival. For the country at large there are wry jokes about Christmas bills and standard complaints about school clothes, but after this ritual is completed there is no question that school is taken for granted as the required gate to opportunity, and that the Christmas and Easter seasons are times for renewal and joy. These are real for most of the poor but for them they are also terrible reminders that the symbols of civilized life are fading away and their families are losing their foothold on normal American culture. They become "the awful months."

In Rebecca Franklin's tilting home were the standard elements of life among the poor; the awful months, the pinch of real hunger at month's end, the regular economic catastrophe of disintegrated shoes, the absence of medical care, and in the countryside the universal leaky roof.

But the worst ghost of all is loneliness and isolation. There are curtains that separate the poor from their countrymen, symbolized by the hills that shield the valleys of misery, and the dirt roads that discourage fast-moving cars, and the ugly decrepitude that keeps respectable people out of the slums. But these are physical manifestations. The real isolation of the poor is from the warmth and hope of ordinary life. This is a paradox in a rich and compassionate country. It should not

be economically difficult to give meaning to the lives of the 6 out of every 100 workers who are unemployed, nor for the 94 to reach out in human help to the 6. But this does not happen in any effective way, not because Americans are cruel but because they are looking the other way. The poor have drifted out of the national consciousness. Had I stayed on the big highways and the busiest streets I would have missed most of the poor.

.   .   .

Edmund MacIntosh was depending on the theory that hard-boiled eggs and opened cans of Spam need no refrigeration. And he was sick.

He had also depended on the theory that if you work hard, live frugally, and mind your own business, you'll get by without help. And now he was seventy-four years old and needed help.

Mr. MacIntosh depended on hard-boiled eggs because his hotel room has no refrigerator and he can't afford to eat out. He is trying to live on his $50-a-month Social Security check. Room rent is $38.50 a month, which provides a room with clean linen every two weeks and clean towels every day. The remainder goes for food and chewing tobacco. Every week friends on the same floor buy him two dozen eggs, seven small cans of V-8 juice, two cans of Spam, a carton of dry cereal (because the box says, "minimum daily requirements of vitamins") and his tobacco. He boils his eggs all at once and eats them morning and evening. He stretches a can of Spam for three days or so. It has cost him violent nausea to discover that hard-boiled eggs and opened Spam need refrigeration in warm weather.

He was trying to eat on $11.50 a month, or 38 cents a day. The Department of Agriculture thinks that the cleverest shopper for the minimum needs of an old man has to have a dollar a day.

It came as almost as shattering a blow that his other theory about self-reliance also has flaws. He has worked hard in his time, lived frugally, minded his own business, but somehow at age seventy-four this has not been enough. He is slowly starving to death, hastening the invasion of age.

A lot of old Americans will recognize the world of Edmund MacIntosh. He has a solid, dignified manner, even as he lies on his bed, propped on an elbow, his square-jawed face turning ashen. His third-floor room in a Los Angeles hotel is painted a vague green. Torn curtains at the window are tied in a knot to let in some light and provide a view of an eroding dirt hillside and the side of a concrete bridge.

He was born in North Carolina, was graduated from high school, finished two years of a military institute. During World War I, in the Merchant Marine, he married a girl from Georgia. They had a daughter. The MacIntosh life was never luxurious but he seemed to earn money adequately. After the first war, he bought a newsstand in Times Square for $200 and cleared $2500 a year from it. When the Depression shrank that income below tolerable limits he went to work in a Baltimore hospital and finally went to Washington, D.C., where he worked in a newspaper distributing office and made $3000 a year. This was not enough to keep the whole family together happily and his wife and daughter went to live with one of his relatives while he worked things out in Washington. The day after Pearl Harbor, Mr. MacIntosh, then fifty-two, volunteered and because of his World War I experience was shipped out as a merchant seaman. He saw his wife before he left.

"I kissed her goodby when I left and gave her a hug and went. I was in Midway when I noticed the letters were coming farther and farther apart. First they was once a week, then every two weeks, then once a month. I was on a ship when

it finally came. I wasn't surprised. It was a notice she was filing for divorce. I read it once and tore it up into little pieces and dropped the pieces over the side. That was that."

After the war Edmund MacIntosh went it alone, working steadily and minding his own business. After his discharge he became a civilian guard at an Oakland Air Base at $38 a week, room free. He left that to become a railroad guard on the Southern Pacific at $80 a week, the high point of his working career.

"Ah, those were the best days. The pay was good. The work was good. I was doing what I liked. I had friends and saw shows. I was living in a San Francisco rooming house where railroad men stayed, for a dollar a day. Then in '54 the railroad started laying off men. I came down here to Los Angeles after that. It's warmer and it's supposed to be cheaper living."

He went from his pleasant railroadman's rooming house to a Los Angeles flophouse at 60 cents a night. He did odd jobs. By now he was sixty-four and nobody wanted to put him on a regular payroll. Mostly he cut lawns in Los Angeles, and cleaned cellars and garages. He lived on $1.50 a day. "I could get a good breakfast, eggs and bacon for half a dollar, I'd have no lunch, and a snack for supper, you know, eggs or a hot dog. I was getting by. I had enough to see a picture show once a week."

Then, about a year ago, after almost ten years as the old man who always came around cutting lawns, automation hit Edmund MacIntosh. He was made obsolete by power lawn mowers.

"They was using more and more of them. I couldn't afford one and when I used the people's mower it took only half the time as with a hand mower and by and by my people realized that, hell, they might as well do it themselves. I don't blame them. With a power mower it's no work at all.

But I just wasn't getting enough work to stay alive. That's when I went to the Social Security people. I knew I had Social Security coming to me when I reached sixty-five but I was getting along cutting grass so I went to the Social Security people and asked them if I'd lose anything by not taking it right then. They told me no, it would just pile up, so I let it. But when those power mowers came in and I wasn't making enough to eat, I went to the Social Security people. I didn't mind doing that. Now, welfare, that's charity and that's something else. But Social Security that's yours, you work for that yourself.

"So last year I went to the Social Security. They was awfully nice and I picked up my back pay and started by $50 a month. I try living on the $50 but it just doesn't work. Some months it's all right, some months it's not. I have to use all my money in the bank from my Social Security saving because it's all I've got. But now I need help."

Mr. MacIntosh was lucky. Only because he was over 72 did his uncollected Social Security pension accumulate. He was also lucky he could steadily withdraw money from this nest egg to augment his monthly payments.

He spit some tobacco from his reclining position. He didn't quite make it to the green plastic wastebasket on the floor. "Well, they've told me about welfare and I didn't much like the idea of that. But I've done about everything I can to cut out my outgo. I moved to a cheaper hotel here and now they're going to tear this one down. I sold my TV for $15.50 and I miss it now. Maybe I'll have to go to welfare. But I don't know where to go and I'm not able to go out any more. If I try walking my head swims and I'm afraid if I go outside I'll fall down and the cops will think I'm a wino.

"This is a tough neighborhood. I had a friend, older man like myself, good fellow, didn't drink. He had dizzy spells now and then and one day he had a spell and stopped to lean against a lamppost. Well, the cops picked him up for a drunk. You get one telephone call when they pick you up and I was the only man he knew so he called me. He said he needed $21 to make bail but $21 was more than I had or could put my hands on. He spent thirty days in jail. So I've been afraid to try walking much outdoors.

"The last time I left this city was seven years ago. Last time I left this block was two weeks ago. I took a cab to Third and Main for a haircut that cost me 50 cents. Cab cost 85 cents. I get my hair cut at the barber school. But they don't seem to have no taxi school for a cheap ride."

Sometimes in the evening, Edmund MacIntosh will walk to the elevator on his floor and ride down to the "lobby" of his hotel, a corridor of depression where ashen old men sit in torn plush sofas beside a row of orange steel barrels marked "scrap."

Most of the time he lies on his bed, listening to a cracked plastic radio, mostly to news and discussion programs.

"I like the radio, though I miss my TV. I don't have the money to buy a newspaper. The janitor here's a nice fellow and he brings me an old one now and then. On the radio I like to hear political talks. Best thing I like is the President's press conference. I'm a Democrat in politics. My daddy was and my granddaddy was. We believed all Republicans go to hell when they die and I didn't want to go to hell. I voted last year for Governor Brown and Mayor Yorty. I voted for Kennedy. I've voted all my life ever since I was old enough. Fact is, I was accused once of voting because I was not old enough. I was nineteen years old, pretty near old enough."

He fears the day when even his walking to the elevator will stop and the time when he will not have kind friends. As it is, a couple on the floor look in on him every day. The janitor brings him old papers. Another man does his shopping every week. But the hotel will be torn down and Edmund MacIntosh will be moved among strangers.

"What I need most is a doctor. But I don't know no doctor I can call. I need something for my eyes. Four years ago I went to the hospital and they scraped them and I could read a newspaper without glasses. Now if I shut my right eye I can't see that doorknob over there. My hearing's going, too."

I asked him what things he missed most, now that he is alone in his hotel room. He pulled with his arm against the steel rod of his headboard and let himself look out the window at the bare earth hill and the grey concrete that made his view of the world.

"Things I miss? You haven't got enough paper."

He was silent for awhile. He was good-natured and matter-of-fact.

"My eyes are getting dimmer. I keep having these dizzy spells. I get sick to my stomach. There's not a thing on my stomach right now. I guess what I want more than anything else is a doctor. Some good medicine."

He paused some more.

"I'd like to go to church. I went a year ago but I don't know if I'll be able to go again. I can't right now and it's a little hard for me to tell when I will again. If I will again. Straight up, that is. I need a suit of clothes. I'd love to go to a picture show. That may sound like asking for everything in sight, but I miss things like that."

He chewed some more and spit again. He missed again.

"All right. A man ain't going to have everything all his life. Sure, I'd like to be able to walk around without getting dizzy. And go to church. And go to a picture show. But maybe if I just had some good company I guess that would be all right, too. I ain't had a letter in twelve months. And that was from the bank about my account."

The man referred to in this chapter as "Edmund MacIntosh" died three months after this interview. The coroner's report said death was from "apparent natural causes."

public welfare in america

The Traditional American Approach

This chapter and the next complement one another. In this chapter the focus is on a range of issues that fall under the general heading of the "quality of life" and the relationship of government and governmental programs to its maintenance and enhancement. The next chapter will also concentrate on issues and policies that determine the quality of life, using the term broadly, but the emphasis will be on the legal and symbolic dimensions that affect the American citizen. There will be an examination of the rights of the citizen, his fundamental liberties, and the ways in which government through its action (and inaction) impinges on these rights and liberties. The role of government in regard to the courts, but also as manifested in the role of the police, will receive special attention.

A textbook on American government written a hundred or perhaps even fifty years ago would certainly not have included this chapter, and it probably would not have included the subject matter of the next chapter either. Although the safeguards of the Bill of Rights have been in the Constitution virtually from the beginning, and despite the fact that the Civil War was fought in part over the rights of the black man, only in the last two or three decades have these issues become sufficiently significant in a political and governmental sense to warrant extended attention in the textbooks.

Moreover, the vast array of programs and policy issues discussed in this chapter under the quality-of-life heading was but dimly foreshadowed as recently as the 1920's. And a hundred years ago it was totally foreign to the American system of government. Even at the state level, where most new experiments in domestic policy developed, governmental involvement in fostering directly the welfare of the citizen was almost totally lacking or left up to local communities. All levels of government, of course, promoted the pubic welfare *in*directly by maintaining order, providing a stable currency, regulating commercial relationships, providing for the common defense, and generally maintaining a social and economic environment in which the citizen could work out his own destiny free from governmental interference.

A close examination of the General Laws of Rhode Island for 1872 dramatically illustrates the point. Only four of the thirty-five titles deal with matters that would today be labeled *welfare*, even under a very broad use of the term. Thus, Title IX referred to "Public Instruction," XI to the "Settlement and Support of Paupers, and the Prevention of Pauperism," and XIII to "The Insane"; another title dealt in part with the care of the blind and deaf.

Only Title XI addressed itself to the type of problem that is the subject of our complex contemporary structure of Social Security and public welfare legislation. Its provisions and phrasing are of more than antiquarian interest for students of the development of welfare policy as a major concern of the American political system. The whole thrust of the individualistic, equalitarian, and antigovernmental beliefs of the American political culture has traditionally been against the public assumption of welfare responsibilities. Where these responsibilities were assumed, they were a function of local government, as they had also traditionally been in England since the days of the Elizabethan poor laws. A century ago this was the unvarying pattern not only in Rhode Island but in all of its sister states.

Even this local responsibility was assumed grudgingly by a society that believed deeply in private individual and family self-help. Most of the three brief chapters comprising Title XI strive to limit the responsibility of the towns as narrowly as possible. Only bona fide residents were entitled to long-term assistance, and the longest chapter is labeled "Of Keeping Out and Removing Paupers." The principle of private responsibility was firmly stated in Chapter 65, Section 5: "The kindred of any such poor person if any he shall have, . . . shall be holden to support such pauper in proportion to such ability." [1] This is followed by a series of provisions whereby relatives can be compelled to render aid if they do not do so voluntarily.

Conspicuously absent from these provisions is any discussion of the nature and level of the aid to be given. Only minimal subsistence was contemplated and, so far were the policies of that day from any concept of a *right* to a basic standard of living for all, that paupers were often confined to workhouses as virtual prisoners. This underscored the contemporary view that moral or other deficiencies within the individual explained his penurious state. Such an explanation was naturally appealing in a society in which all men were asserted to have been created equal, to enjoy equal opportunity for self-development, and—because of the frontier—to have endless chances for a new start if they were dissatisfied with their lot. The contrary idea that certain classes of people suffered under special handicaps not of their own making could not be reconciled with the dominant beliefs of the nineteenth-century culture.

As a consequence, until the Great Depression, welfare programs were rudimentary, almost invariably local in their implementation, based on need rather than on

---

[1] The General Statutes of the State of Rhode Island and Providence Plantations, 1872, p. 150.

right, minimal in their benefits, and invariably grudging often to the point of being punitive. (The fact that Rhode Island found it necessary to provide in Section 15 of Chapter 65 that "Corporal punishment, and confinement in dark rooms, or in dungeons, are prohibited at all asylums and houses for the poor" [2] is appalling evidence of this punitive attitude.) Clearly, the modern welfare state could not emerge before a whole series of adjustments, not merely in public policy but in fundamental cultural attitudes, had first come about.

During its first century of existence, when the Republic was essentially an agricultural society with an abundance of free land, the precept of self-help was more natural and meaningful. Men such as Thomas Jefferson, for whom those who labored in the earth were "the chosen people of God," provided the intellectual basis and persuasive phrasing for a matrix of cultural values that centered on the virtues of rural life and an agrarian economy. "Cultivators of the earth," wrote the Sage of Monticello, "are the most vigorous, the most independent, the most virtuous [citizens]. . . ." [3]

And yet, as much as Jefferson ardently wished his country would let her "workshops remain in Europe," industrialization came in the years following the Civil War —and even earlier in the states of New England. The factory worker, unlike his rural counterpart, had nothing upon which to rely for income save the labor of his hands. He owned no land from which he could draw income and upon whose produce he could subsist in periods of economic adversity. He was completely tied to the fluctuations of an economy that might leave him for months without employment and hence with no resources beyond his own savings (if any) or the meagre provisions of the local community. Unemployment in this stark form is virtually unknown in a rural society.

In a factory-centered civilization, moreover, old age also became a haunting specter. On the farm the elderly could live out their years with relative security in the family homestead, now turned over to the younger generation. The land produced enough to feed them, and thus they were not a severe burden to their families. These elderly preserved their self-respect both through the fact that they had enriched the land patrimony their children were now inheriting and that there were always light chores they could perform as a contribution to the common enterprise. In the city, when age or infirmity forced older persons to leave the factory, their ability to contribute to their own or their family's income ceased abruptly and completely. They became an unrelieved burden on their children, with all the loss of dignity that such dependence entails, and there was only one degrading alternative—the poorhouse.

The plight of the factory worker and of the elderly, to say nothing of those with disabling physical handicaps, in a society that was both industrialized and yet still wedded to the policies of an agricultural past, can indeed be painted in lurid colors. But when change finally came, it was not motivated by humanitarian sentiment alone.

---

[2] Ibid., p. 151.
[3] A. Whitney Griswold, *Farming and Democracy* (New York: Harcourt, 1948), p. 31.

Quite the contrary, the social and political credo of "survival of the fittest" enunciated by such writers as William Graham Sumner (1840–1910), who reworked the ideas of Charles Darwin, provided powerful counterarguments to any sentimental pleas on behalf of the industrial poor.[4] Social Darwinism reinvigorated and carried to their logical conclusion many of the beliefs already characteristic of the American cultural ethos. Any effort to succor the unfortunate, so the argument went, would disrupt the process of natural selection that, as in nature, must be allowed free rein in the social and economic spheres. The utility of such a theory (or rationale) to those anxious to avoid government regulation or the institution of expensive welfare schemes is obvious.

The welfare aid tradition America inherited from Britain emphasized local responsibility, and until the 1930's that is where the responsibility remained. Constitutional problems centering on the federal allocation of powers seemed to preclude a national role, even if such a role had recommended itself to policy-makers. As a consequence, general tradition and constitutional provisions reinforced each other in underscoring local responsibility.

Even the states made few moves into this policy area. Although constitutionally free to do so, they were in practice inhibited because, by taxing their citizens and local business enterprise to support social welfare schemes, they would place themselves at a competitive disadvantage in relation to their neighbor states. Despite this problem, experiments with social insurance were launched in what Justice Louis D. Brandeis once called the insulated laboratories of the states. In 1914 Arizona enacted the first noncontributory old-age-pension scheme, but this law was soon invalidated by the state's Supreme Court. The movement to provide care for the aged under state auspices nevertheless made headway. By 1931, seventeen states had some kind of assistance program for the needy elderly, but only a few were really pension schemes in any strict sense. In most of these states the full cost of the "pensions" was still borne by the local governments, in only one (Delaware) by the state alone, and in the rest by the two levels of government jointly. Actually, these laws hardly represented much more than some liberalization in the traditional approaches to the support of the poor.

The First Great Turning Point

The stresses and strains on the social and economic fabric of life imposed by an industrial society were bound to bring change in the locus and magnitude of the welfare or quality-of-life responsibilities of government. Other industrial nations had moved toward comprehensive national social welfare systems much earlier: Bismarck's Germany in the 1880's enacted programs for health, accident, and old-age insurance; Denmark, New Zealand, and Great Britain instituted old-age pensions in

[4] Sumner, a sociologist, took Darwin's ideas about the evolution of species in the animal kingdom and applied them to the development of human society. These patterns must be allowed to work themselves out by natural selection of the fittest individuals, he argued. See Richard Hofstadter, *Social Darwinism in American Thought,* rev. ed. (Boston: Beacon, 1955).

1891, 1898, and 1908, respectively.[5] France and the United States did not launch such systems until the 1930's.

The Great Depression, which struck the United States in full force in the aftermath of the 1929 stock market crash, brought the need and the demand for welfare reform to a head. In 1933, the year Franklin D. Roosevelt entered the White House at the height of the economic crisis, a California doctor, Francis E. Townsend, proposed a flat $200 per month pension for all persons over sixty to be financed by a national sales tax. So receptive had the elderly, at least, become to the notion of government underwriting of security of old age, that within two years 4,550 Townsend Clubs had sprung up across the nation.

General pressure for the federal government's involvement in aiding the destitute and the millions of unemployed produced by the unprecedented economic collapse was rendered irresistible by the total inability of the local authorities to cope with the situation. Not surprisingly, voluntary agencies also quickly came to the end of their resources in the face of the overwhelming demand. Several states, led by New York under Governor Franklin D. Roosevelt, established state emergency relief programs in an effort to backstop the desperate local communities. A few hesitant national steps were even taken by the cautious Administration of President Herbert Hoover before it left office in March, 1933; for example, it made some federal resources available to support local relief efforts. The new Democratic Administration of Franklin D. Roosevelt, however, came in with a clear mandate to take far more vigorous national action.

The Roosevelt Administration quickly put into effect a variety of emergency programs providing direct assistance to the foundering state governments, supporting local relief efforts, and making possible work relief on construction projects. More important and more lasting was the impetus that this period of economic disaster gave to the movement for permanent social insurance. In 1934 the President appointed a Committee on Economic Security to bring in recommendations aimed at protecting Americans from destitution and dependency. The Committee's report, which was sent to Congress in January, 1935, led to a Social Security Act that was signed into law on August 14, 1935. Although not embodying all of the Committee's far-reaching proposals, it established a compulsory old-age insurance program to be administered by the federal government, a system of grants-in-aid to the states so they could assist those aged not covered by the insurance provisions, a scheme of unemployment insurance essentially under state auspices, and a program of financial grants to the states enabling them to aid needy dependent children and to provide for maternal and child welfare and aid to the blind.

This New Deal legislation was a great turning point in America's approach to welfare problems. When later tested in the courts it was upheld as a valid exercise of the power of the Congress to tax and spend for the general welfare. Prior to 1937 the Supreme Court's decisions frequently imposed constitutional limitations on the

[5] See President's Commission on Income Maintenance Programs, *Background Papers* (Washington, D.C.: G.P.O., 1970), pp. 31–37, for some discussion of the recent development and present status of welfare programs in selected European countries.

federal government's authority to undertake social and economic welfare programs. Less obvious and in some ways more important, however, was the process by which the *idea* of such deep and comprehensive involvement by federal governmental agencies in areas once held to be the responsibility of the individual, private charitable organizations or, where absolutely unavoidable, the task of local authorities, came to be accepted. Businessmen and other opponents of the Social Security proposals, when testifying before congressional committees, had strongly argued that individual initiative and thrift would be destroyed, and that no one would any longer have the incentive to work if such schemes were put into effect. As late as the mid-1930's this was still the accepted view.

But the nation and especially its millions of unemployed and destitute were ready for change. The remarkable growth of the Townsend Movement was a signal that the traditional nineteenth-century beliefs were crumbling. However, it was by no means clear to President Roosevelt and his advisers how much change would prove acceptable. It was nevertheless likely that unless he proposed major innovations Congress might be stampeded by the advocates of such appealing, if impractical, schemes as those advocated by the California doctor. With these considerations in mind, Roosevelt proposed a Social Security system that would have the greatest chance of broad acceptance, while at the same time going far enough to forestall vocal demands that still more be done.

In public utterances between the appointment of the Committee on Economic Security and the introduction of the legislation, the New Deal President often discussed the nation's welfare problems. Typically, Roosevelt's discussions were couched in terms that clearly indicated his awareness of the shift in values that the new program represented, and his desire to effect this transition as smoothly as possible. He repeatedly insisted that no new values *were* being created, and that in actuality a Social Security program was quite in line with some of the most basic traditions of the American people. In a message to Congress on June 8, 1934, which foreshadowed the introduction of the Administration's proposals the following January, the President declared: "This seeking for a greater measure of welfare and happiness does not indicate a change in values. It is rather a return to values lost in the course of our economic development and expansion." [6]

Once they were written into law, there was never any serious question about the acceptance of the social welfare and social insurance principles that the new legislation embodied. In fact, Congress has periodically broadened coverage and increased benefits—doing so at the behest of both Democratic and Republican administrations. The one major barrier yet to fall before the advance of this concept of state responsibility for citizen welfare was that which protected the sphere of medical care. Although urged to include medical care in the legislation he proposed to Congress, Roosevelt prudently declined, fearing that the opposition of the American Medical

[6] *The Public Papers and Addresses of Franklin D. Roosevelt,* Vol. III: *The Advance of Reform and Recovery,* 1934 (New York: Random House, 1938), p. 292. For an analysis of Roosevelt's efforts to "sell" Social Security, see Elmer E. Cornwell, Jr., *Presidential Leadership of Public Opinion* (Bloomington: Indiana University Press, 1965), pp. 128–131.

Association would endanger his primary objective of a basic Social Security system. Later, in the 1940's, when President Truman tried to secure approval for a comprehensive scheme of national health insurance, the legislation never even got out of committee in Congress. A serious first step in the direction of medical care (restricted to elderly persons) had to await the Kennedy-Johnson presidential period.

The completeness of the shift in public attitude toward the role of the government in the area of welfare is most clearly demonstrated in some studies of popular attitudes. Robert E. Lane of Yale, for example, after conducting lengthy interviews with a small sample of urban, lower-middle-class respondents on their attitudes toward government and public policy, concluded that an attitudinal reorientation had taken place. Lane attributes this change to the innovations of the New Deal period: "By the change in policy so dramatically effected in the thirties," he comments, "the government became, with certain residual doubts, an ally, a friend." [7] Another study, by Herbert McClosky and his associates from the University of Minnesota, traces in greater detail public attitudes toward the role of government in economic and welfare matters, and in other policy areas. A national sample, broken down into those who viewed themselves as Democrats and those who viewed themselves as Republicans, were asked a series of questions. In each case the query was as to whether the government should increase, decrease, or retain at the same level its involvement in a particular policy area. A selection of the results is presented in Table 12.1.

One striking revelation is the massive support for Social Security, with only 3

Table 12.1   *Public attitudes toward the role of government*

Area		Dems.	Reps.
Social Security benefits	Increase	69%	57%
	Decrease	3	4
	Same	28	39
Federal aid to education	Increase	75%	72%
	Decrease	6	8
	Same	19	20
Government regulation of business	Increase	19%	8%
	Decrease	33	46
	Same	48	46
Regulation of public utilities	Increase	39%	26%
	Decrease	11	12
	Same	50	62

Source: Herbert McClosky et al., "Issue Conflict and Consensus Among Party Leaders and Followers," *American Political Science Review,* LIV (June, 1960), 412.

[7] *Political Ideology* (New York: Free Press, 1962), p. 474.

per cent of the Democrats and 4 per cent of the Republicans favoring a decrease, and upwards of three fifths to two thirds favoring increased government benefits. The picture is nearly the same with respect to aid to education, though in this area, for various reasons, the involvement of the national government has come much more slowly. The public, apparently, was ready for a federal role in education long before Congress passed the Elementary and Secondary Education Act during the Johnson Presidency. One major factor delaying federal involvement was the opposition of Roman Catholic groups and politicians to assistance that excluded parochial schools, and the corresponding resistance of non-Catholic groups to federal aid to Catholic-related schools. On the other hand, McClosky's study found that few persons desired greater governmental involvement in the regulation of business, and substantial numbers felt that involvement had already gone too far. In the utilities field, an area often viewed as a natural monopoly and hence a suitable subject of regulation, the role of government is viewed more favorably.

It is apparent that the cultural values that the public accepts have changed substantially in the field of welfare. The nation has come to expect the government to maintain a minimum level of security for most citizens, and, moreover, it has wanted this level raised periodically. The Cassandras who saw the introduction of America's modest welfare state as the opening wedge for complete socialism in the Marxist mold would have difficulty explaining why McClosky's sample of citizens still insist on viewing less favorably the regulatory role of the government in America's traditional free-enterprise economy. Obviously, the American people are capable of far more selectivity in holding on to some values and at the same time adjusting others to meet changing conditions, than they are sometimes credited with. Interestingly, too, party affiliation has little significance when it comes to attitudes on these questions, for there is a broad national consensus instead of a series of highly partisan responses.

Welfare Programs:
From the Thirties to the Seventies

The opening chapter discussed the essential "classlessness" of American society as Americans insist on viewing it. Actually, as numerous studies have shown, Americans really see themselves as a *middle-class society*. It is this term, or some variation of it, that most poll respondents choose when asked to identify the class to which they feel they belong. This pattern of middle-class identification may help to explain why the welfare-state concept took so long to win acceptance in the United States. It also explains the almost exclusively middle-class nature of the welfare programs adopted in the 1930's and elaborated upon during the next third of a century.

An essentially bourgeois society steeped in the myths exemplified by such stories as those of Horatio Alger so popular in the late nineteenth century—that hard work and pluck could lead any American boy from rags to riches—was bound to look askance at government efforts, however well intentioned, to help the individual to do what he should really do for himself. This was the prevailing popular ethos, at least until the middle class found *itself* engulfed in a tidal wave of economic insecurity and distress brought on by the Great Depression.

Solid citizens who owned their own homes or farms, no less than tenement-dwelling workers, lost their jobs. Many of the former saw their life savings either quickly spent or lost in a bank failure, and they lived under the shadow of mortgage foreclosure. The Townsend Movement was undoubtedly made up far more of middle-class retirees than of the elderly poor. It was the middle class that demanded government action most insistently, and it was toward the solution of their security problems that the New Deal directed much of both its short-term emergency legislation and its long-term programs. Thus, the Home Owners Loan Corporation for mortgage refinancing, the Federal Deposit Insurance Corporation (which guaranteed bank deposits), the Works Progress Administration projects that were designed to provide work for skilled craftsmen and professional people as well as laborers, and the price-support programs for farmers typified the essentially middle-class orientation of the New Deal's programs.

The farm programs, for example, benefited the family-owned-and-operated farm and the large farming enterprise far more than they assisted the tenant farmer or the sharecropper. A similar emphasis is discernible in much of the Social Security and related legislation. Protection against unemployment was an area that called insistently for a uniform national program to overcome the reluctance of the states to tax their own industries in order to provide benefits. Accordingly, under the Social Security laws both levels of government shared responsibility for a system of compensation payable to the unemployed for a number of weeks to tide them over until they could secure another job. The tax-rebate device was used to induce state cooperation. A percentage tax was levied on payrolls, nine tenths of which was forgiven if the state in turn imposed a tax of its own to support such a compensation system. Part of the remaining money collected by Washington was then returned to finance the administration of the program at the state level. The states were thus allowed, within federally established limits, to set up the standards and mode of implementing the program that they felt to be most appropriate in the light of local conditions. They also provided state employment services that attempted to place the unemployed in new jobs.

Many of the features of this system suggest the middle-class bias of the welfare laws. In the first place, unemployment insurance under Social Security was really a program designed to solve the short-term problems of people who, basically employable, are ready and eager to work. It was not designed to deal with chronic unemployment of the sort that plagues the urban poverty ghettos. Many of the regularly employed are not covered, simply because they work in establishments that are too small to qualify for coverage or are exempt from coverage. The benefits, furthermore, are low, once again on the assumption that this is strictly an emergency measure for people who may well have some resources of their own to help tide them over a short-lived crisis.[8]

---

[8] See President's Commission, op. cit., p. 71 for a discussion of the differences between middle-class views of work and those of other groups.

Probably the best-known part of the Social Security system is the provision for Old Age and Survivors (and Disability) Insurance.[9] This is a nationally administered program intended to provide old-age security in an era when support by one's family has frequently become totally impractical. It involves a basic insurance principle under which the employee contributes, during his working life, a percentage of his earnings that is matched by the employer. Benefits payable at sixty-five (or at sixty-two on a reduced basis) are then calculated on the basis of previous earnings and number of dependents. The OASI coverage is now very broad. It encompasses the self-employed, those employed by nonprofit organizations, employees of governmental units, and even those in domestic service if they earn up to a certain amount. An effort has been made through a series of amendments to make the OASI system into as universal a basis for underwriting the security of the elderly as possible, but it still is predicated on a more or less stable employment record. In short, it still presupposes employability. OASI symbolizes perhaps most clearly the fundamental change in policy direction represented by the Social Security and welfare-state pattern of legislation that emerged in the New Deal. It places the government squarely in the business of helping the individual to underwrite his retirement security. But it also reflects a pervasive middle-class bias. OASI was not a program of direct government handouts, but rather, using quasi-insurance principles, a more systematic supplement to traditional middle-class thrift—the practice of saving for a rainy day.

Professor Lane, whose study was cited earlier, provides indirect support both for the notion that cultural values had changed enough to permit the acceptance of such a new departure in policy, and for the notion that, at the same time, the middle class retained much of its former orientation toward self-help. The shift was subtle rather than radical. In a chapter suggestively entitled "The Mind of the New Collectivism," Lane argues that although his respondents strongly supported government welfare programs of the New Deal sort, they by no means had acquired the "socialistic" outlook that conservative critics insisted would become prevalent. The "Eastporters" with whom Lane talked made a sharp differentiation between the government's merely serving as a backstop to persons in moments of adversity and the government's actually providing a permanent income or a ready-made way of life.

Eastporters, for instance, ready as they were to see many kinds of government regulation and aid, did not want the government to tell business how to conduct its affairs, nor did they want the government to provide jobs for those who needed them. Instead, they looked to government for indirect assistance. They wanted public authority to maintain the stability of the economy, to make available government contracts to keep business humming, and otherwise to enable employers to prosper. Lane's Eastporters wanted employers able to supply jobs that would permit workers to earn a living for themselves as a consequence of their own labor, strongly pre-

---

[9] Excellent and current discussions of the various Social Security and welfare programs are in President's Commission, op. cit., and Gilbert Y. Steiner, *The State of Welfare* (Washington, D.C.: Brookings Institution, 1971).

ferring this approach to any system of direct income payments by government agencies.

These conclusions, together with McClosky's finding that three fifths of the electorate agree that "there will always be poverty so people might as well get used to the idea," seem to confirm a basic thesis of this chapter. Not until President Kennedy proposed a war on poverty and President Johnson secured adoption of pioneering legislation did public policy *begin* to reflect a different value orientation: concern with the very poor, who do not share middle-class status or, indeed, do not wholly share middle-class values. President Nixon's proposals for a major restructuring of the welfare assistance system (to be discussed later along with the poverty program) represent further recognition of the problems faced by the very poor. An interesting question relates to the extent to which the public will ultimately accept these recent policy innovations and accommodate them to themes in the traditional American culture.

It should, however, be noted that some parts of the original Social Security system were designed to deal with the problems of needy people who fit less neatly into the solid middle and upper working-class categories. These include aid to the aged who do not come under OASI, to dependent children, and to the blind. Much of the money disbursed under these programs is federal, with only a small fraction supplied by the local governments and another portion by the states. This minimal local role, incidentally, indicates how far the United States had come from the pre-1930 era of almost total dependence upon local units of government for the provision of welfare benefits. The figures in Table 12.2 show the dramatic realignment in the contributions of the three levels of government.

The share of local governments, long the only source of aid to the needy, dropped in a short half dozen years from 90 per cent to around 10 per cent; the

Table 12.2   *Public expenditures for assistance and work programs*

Year	Total amount (thousands)	Share of federal	Share of state	Share of local
1930	$ 98,024	1%	9%	91%
1932	421,370	17	22	61
1934	1,779,313	76	10	14
1936	2,505,580	77	14	9
1938	2,827,300	73	17	10
1940	2,309,068	68	21	11

Source: Adapted from Herbert Jacob and Kenneth N. Vines (eds.), *Politics in the American States* (Boston: © Little, Brown and Co., 1965), p. 377. Reprinted by permission of the publisher.

states' share remained more or less the same; and the federal government assumed the lion's share of the rapidly growing expenditures. This reversal of roles is hardly more dramatic than the shift in public attitudes that it reflects. Figure 12.1 shows the same shift of responsibility to the national government in more detail. Washington's involvement in social insurance programs and services for veterans, for example, preceded by many years its entry into the area of education.

The number of aged in need of assistance outside the OASI scheme has steadily declined as more persons covered by the insurance system have reached retirement age. With the progressive broadening of coverage, the decline is likely to continue. On the other hand, though individual OASI payments have steadily increased in size as Congress periodically reviews the program, they still are often too small for subsistence. As a result, some of the aged who are covered must receive supplemental assistance. In the case study, Edmund MacIntosh's plight graphically exemplifies this problem.

The program most clearly illustrative of the areas as yet inadequately covered by America's welfare state is Aid (and Services to Needy) Families with Dependent Children (AFDC). This is assistance to families in which a parent is mentally or physically incapacitated, has died, or has been continuously absent from the home (see Table 12.3). It was also the skyrocketing numbers of AFDC recipients and program costs during the late 1960's and the early 1970's that brought on the "crisis in welfare," prompting the Nixon Administration to propose its radical new plan for

Figure 12.1. Social welfare expenditures under selected public programs, 1940–1969

Source: Chart prepared by Department of Commerce, Bureau of Census. Data from Department of Health, Education and Welfare, Social Security Administration.

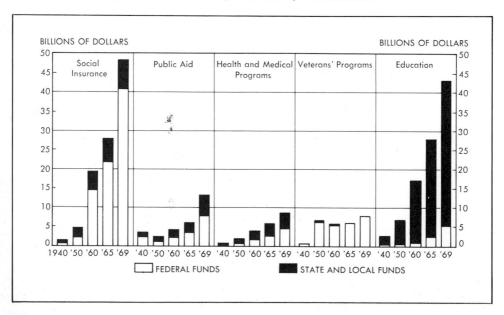

Table 12.3
Status of fathers of AFDC families, 1961 and 1967

Status	Percentage of total 1961	1967
Dead	7.7	5.5
Incapacitated	18.1	12.0
Unemployed	5.2	5.1
Absent from the home, total	66.7	74.4
Divorced	13.7	12.6
Legally separated		2.6
Separated without court decree	8.2	9.6
Deserted	18.6	18.2
Not married to mother	21.3	26.8
In prison	4.2	3.0
Other reason for absence	0.6	1.4
Other status	2.2	3.0

Source: U.S. Department of Health, Education, and Welfare, National Center for Social Statistics, Report AFDC-1 (67), p. 9. From Gilbert Y. Steiner, *The State of Welfare* (Washington, D.C.: The Brookings Institution, 1971), p. 42. © by The Brookings Institution.

Table 12.4 AFDC recipients and payments, 1964 through June, 1970

Year	Average monthly number of recipients	Child participation rate per 1,000 *	Average monthly payment	Total expenditure
1964	4,118,000	45	$30.30	$1,496,525,000
1965	4,329,000	47	31.65	1,644,096,000
1966	4,513,000	49	34.15	1,849,886,000
1967	5,014,000	55	37.40	2,249,673,000
1968	5,705,000	63	41.25	2,823,841,000
1969	6,706,000	75	44.10	3,546,668,000
1970, Jan.–June	7,912,000	—	46.35	—

Source: U.S. Department of Health, Education, and Welfare, National Center for Social Statistics, Report A-2 (3/70), and monthly statistical reports. From Gilbert Y. Steiner, *The State of Welfare* (Washington, D.C.: The Brookings Institution, 1971), p. 32. © by The Brookings Institution

* Number of children participating per 1,000 children in total population under 18.

Table 12.5 *Social welfare expenditures by source of funds and public program, 1969*

Program	Federal	State and local
TOTAL	$68,595	$58,206
SOCIAL INSURANCE	40,824	7,896
Old-age, survivors, disability, health insurance	33,389	(X)
Health insurance for the aged	6,598	(X)
Railroad retirement	1,547	(X)
Public employee retirement	4,739	2,740
Unemployment insurance and employment service	932	2,021
Railroad unemployment insurance	45	(X)
Railroad temporary disability insurance	58	(X)
State temporary disability insurance	(X)	635
Hospital and medical benefits	(X)	58
Workmen's compensation	114	2,500
Hospital and medical benefits	17	833
PUBLIC AID	7,851	5,592
Public assistance	6,389	5,592
Vendor medical payments	2,186	2,235
Other	1,462	—
HEALTH AND MEDICAL PROGRAMS	4,497	4,321
Hospital and medical care	1,967	2,827
Civilian programs	200	2,827
Defense department	1,766	(X)
Maternal and child health programs	192	190
Medical research	1,401	73
School health (educational agencies)	(X)	204

Source: *Statistical Abstract of the United States* (Washington, D.C.: U.S. Government Printing Office, 1970).

— Represents zero.

(X) Not applicable.

welfare based on the income-maintenance principle. Recent developments in connection with this program deserve special attention.

After World War II, AFDC rose to a peak (for those days) of 2,246,000 recipients by 1950. The total then declined somewhat—dipping below 2,000,000 in 1953 —but thereafter it rose gradually. A more rapid increase between 1960 and 1962, which coincided with a recession and rising unemployment, caused the Kennedy Administration to push through a reform in the law. This reform allowed the states, at their option, to adopt a special AFDC program for families in which both parents were at home but the father was unemployed (AFDC-U). Besides the obvious motivation behind this innovation, there lay the added and often-cited problem of

Program	Federal	State and local
Other public health activities	551	527
Medical facilities' construction	386	500
Defense department	59	(X)
Other	327	500
VETERANS' PROGRAMS	7,996	40
Pensions and compensation	5,041	(X)
Health and medical programs	1,585	(X)
Hospital and medical care	1,478	(X)
Hospital construction	54	(X)
Medical and prosthetic research	53	(X)
Education	671	(X)
Life insurance	503	(X)
Welfare and other	197	40
EDUCATION	5,079	37,954
Elementary and secondary	2,472	31,963
Construction	34	4,620
Higher	1,943	5,100
Construction	431	1,100
Vocational and adult	514	891
HOUSING	446	110
OTHER SOCIAL WELFARE	1,903	2,293
Vocational rehabilitation, total	431	127
Medical services and research	116	31
Institutional care	26	1,495
School meals	624	171
Child welfare	50	500
Special OEO programs	647	(X)
Social welfare, not elsewhere classified	124	(X)

desertion by the male parent. Seemingly, in many cases, fathers left home when they could not find work or could not earn enough in poor-paying jobs to support their families, thereby rendering the remaining spouse eligible for AFDC. AFDC-U, hopefully, would cut the incidents of this solution to the financial problem.

One of the problems with the new AFDC-U legislation was that only twenty-two states saw fit to exercise the option offered them. In the remaining twenty-eight the program could obviously have no effect. Whatever might have happened had the program been instituted on a nationwide basis, the AFDC case load climbed steadily during the 1960's, and at a sharply accelerating rate during the period beginning in 1968. (See the figures presented in Table 12.4.) The reasons for this sharp climb are not easy to identify. Unemployment did increase after 1968, and obviously it accounts for a major portion of the steep AFDC rise. However, an examination of the trends during the earlier years of the decade clouds the explanatory picture considerably. In 1961, about the time the Kennedy reforms were being passed in Congress, there were 3.5 million AFDC recipients and unemployment was also high at a figure of 6.7 per cent. By 1968 unemployment had declined (although it soon moved upward again) to a record low figure of 3.4 per cent. *But* the AFDC recipient total had gone up from 3.5 million to 5.7 million during this same eight-year period.

If further proof were needed that there was a substantial poverty substratum in the national society that had not been reached, or at least had not been lifted from its chronic poverty status by any existing programs, AFDC provided it all too clearly. Furthermore, as the *New York Times* editorialized on January 3, 1969, noting a low unemployment rate in New York City, yet a welfare load that had reached a million out of the total city population: "It becomes increasingly clear that the welfare rolls have a life of their own detached from the metropolitan job market."

To round out the catalog of social welfare legislation on the books as a result of the 1935 revolution in attitude and governmental role, we list aid to the disabled and aid to the blind. There is also a complex and largely separate set of programs that predate 1935 by many years designed to deal with the problems of veterans of the nation's wars. These include pensions, a network of medical care facilities, insurance systems, and education and rehabilitation programs. It has always been easier, given the cultural values of the society, to make generous provision for needy veterans as a special class to whom gratitude was felt to be due, than to the general needy population. The latter, of course, not only had no special claim on public aid, but characteristically had been viewed as deserving censure as much as minimal aid.[10] Most catalogs of government welfare activity also include various efforts that have been mounted since the New Deal to upgrade housing. Although important legislation and difficult problems exist in this realm, we shall not devote detailed attention to them in this chapter.[11] Table 12.5 presents in summary form a listing of all federal, state, and local programs that fall under the general welfare heading, together with expenditure figures.

[10] See Steiner, op. cit., Ch. 7.
[11] See ibid., Ch. 4, and also Harold Wolman, *Politics of Federal Housing* (New York: Dodd, Mead, 1971).

the problems of poverty

The War on Poverty

Precise identification of the intellectual and political roots of the Poverty Program is less important for our purposes than the fact that it represented a major new turning point in the evolution of the national government's concern with quality-of-life issues. In essence the program was designed to deal with the problems of the hard-core poor, the people who have not been reached adequately by the traditional welfare services. It represented a recognition that there were major groups among the poor that could not be dealt with as basically middle-class people who had fallen temporarily on hard times. These poor obviously had never been part of the great American middle class, did not necessarily share the values and aspirations associated with such status, and would require a far more intensive effort to bring them into the mainstream of the middle-class culture than mere temporary financial assistance. Hence the thrust of the poverty program was essentially remedial rather than custodial as former programs had been for the chronic poor.

This approach to the poor as a severely disadvantaged segment of the American society came with the growing realization that a combination of factors had intensified their plight in spite of rising levels of social services. Shifts in occupational patterns in the society have been steadily in the direction of increasing the proportion of skilled jobs requiring more general and specialized education. Fewer and fewer manual labor positions have remained in the wake of the widespread introduction of automated and computer-directed processes in business and industry. The undereducated, in consequence, have found few purchasers in the labor market for the unskilled labor they can provide.

The civil rights ferment set in motion by the Supreme Court's school desegregation decision of 1954 has called increasing attention to the further fact that blacks in America were not only deprived of normal political and social rights, but systematically denied the kind of education that might have put them in a position to make their way successfully in an increasingly technologically advanced society, even as-

541

suming that all barriers of racial prejudice were removed. In every summer ghetto riot the plea was heard that jobs must be provided to assuage anger and alienation. Yet so many of the victims of poverty, black and white, are unemployable in the contemporary American economy.

The consequences of this situation have rapidly approached crisis proportions. Many have come to the belief, which they assert with passion and vehemence, that the government must undertake vast programs of remedial action. Daniel Patrick Moynihan, later to serve as chief architect of the Nixon welfare reforms as a member of the White House staff, was in the vanguard of this group. Its basic thesis was that the alternative to affirmative national action on a massive scale is a society of two nations. There will be—if there is not already—an increasingly affluent middle-class America and an "other America," composed of a progressively more alienated and restive underclass of the poor with its own culture and its own impoverished way of life. The National Advisory Commission on Civil Disorders appointed by President Johnson after the severe ghetto riots of 1967 endorsed this theme, stating in the introduction to its report: "This is our basic conclusion: Our nation is moving toward two societies, one black, one white—separate and unequal." [12] To a very disturbing extent, of course, the alienated underclass and the "black society" are the same people.

One of the early moves that heralded the idea of the Poverty Program was the Kennedy Administration's "mini-poverty program" for Appalachia. This was a logical outcome of the key West Virginia presidential primary, which Senator Kennedy won, thereby consolidating his preconvention claim on the 1960 nomination. When Lyndon Johnson inherited the Presidency in November, 1963, there were pending in Congress—stalled is perhaps more accurate—two or three additional pieces of Administration legislation that were also precursors of the full-blown Poverty Program. [13] One of these pieces of legislation was a proposal for a Youth Employment Act that would establish a youth conservation corps (similar to the Civilian Conservation Corps of the Depression) and that would also have made money available to states and cities to assist them in developing local community service occupations. There was also a pending proposal for a national service corps—a kind of domestic Peace Corps—of the sort that was eventually set up in the VISTA program.

Until January, 1964, it seemed likely that Johnson would, as he had in other areas, lend his weight to pushing these preexisting Kennedy initiatives. However, he decided to launch his own war on poverty on an expanded basis, and he announced this intention in his State of the Union message on January 8, 1964. Soon afterwards he named Peace Corps director Sargent Shriver as his special assistant to develop plans for the "war." Shriver immediately enlisted Adam Yarmolinsky (one of McNamara's "whiz kids" from the Defense Department), Moynihan (then in the Department of Labor), and James Sundquist from the Department of Agriculture as a

[12] New York: Bantam, 1968, p. 1.

[13] This account of the origins of the Poverty Program relies heavily on John C. Donovan, "A President's War on Poverty," in Thomas E. Cronin and Sanford D. Greenberg, *The Presidential Advisory System* (New York: Harper, 1969), pp. 209–219.

task force to prepare the new omnibus bill. The team was definitely eastern establishment in orientation and part of the Kennedy legacy of intellectual liberals drawn into government. Other individuals and many governmental agencies were involved in the process, but this core group, with Shriver very much in charge, was central.

In typical Kennedy fashion, this group turned to such sources of ideas as Paul Ylvisaker of the Ford Foundation, which had an experimental approach called the Gray Areas program that became the basis of the community action program idea; Mitchell Sviridoff, who had worked with Mayor Richard Lee in making New Haven, Connecticut, an urban development showcase; and the staff of the recent President's Committee on Juvenile Delinquency. Shriver's group also heard from church, labor, business, academic, and civil rights spokesmen, but interestingly enough, the poor themselves did not participate in putting together the ideas that went into the Act.

Working against enormous time pressures, the task force was able to put together a draft bill ready for presentation to Congress by March 16. The resulting Economic Opportunity Act of 1964 was, understandably, a mixture of ideas, some old and some very new. As John Donovan wrote:

Title I established three youth programs, two of which differed only slightly from similar provisions in the Kennedy youth employment opportunities bill which had been passed by the Senate and reported by the House committee before languishing in the House Rules Committee. The third youth program, a work-study program for college students, had been considered earlier as a possible amendment to the National Defense Education Act. Title II, on the other hand, bearing the label "Urban and Rural Community Action Program," was without precedent as a legislative matter.[14]

Congress' reception of this massive and innovating legislative proposal was amazingly mild and acquiescent. Hearings were begun before an ad hoc subcommittee of the House Education and Labor Committee chaired by Representative Adam Clayton Powell of New York. Seventy-nine witnesses appeared during twenty days of hearings, with only nine of them hostile (including the U.S. Chamber of Commerce, the National Association of Manufacturers, and the Farm Bureau Federation). The main burden of much of the testimony was quite general, with opponents taking the familiar line that this was just another undesirable welfare "spending" program. Although—as Professor Donovan wrote, "it would be almost impossible to imagine a legislative proposal with a greater potential for arousing congressional anxiety than community action" [15]—Title II, which embodied this startlingly new concept, attracted little attention and came through intact. Even the dangerous "precinct level" potential, so far as the political establishment was concerned, of the "maximum feasible participation" provision in Title II evoked little comment. Attorney General Robert Kennedy's testimony concerning this phraseology—in which he said, "This means the involvement of the poor in planning and implementing programs: giving them a real voice in their institutions"—aroused no reaction.[16]

[14] Ibid., p. 213.
[15] Ibid., p. 215.
[16] Ibid., p. 216.

The part of the bill that did arouse some resistance had to do with the alleviations of rural poverty in Title III. Overall, however, the Administration did have to pay a price for southern support of the bill. This took the form of a gubernatorial veto written into Titles I and II allowing state chief executives to review any proposed projects for their states. Also, because for some reason he had become persona non grata to the Southerners, Adam Yarmolinsky, who had been slated to become the Deputy Director of the new Office of Economic Opportunity that would carry out the provisions of the Economic Opportunity Act, was dropped.

In general, the Poverty Program was preeminently an example of presidential legislative leadership. The congressional role, save for ratifying what the White House presented to it, was minimal. The speed with which the whole process was accomplished was breathtaking: just about six months from drawing board to final passage by the House on August 8, 1964. The radically new nature of many of the proposals in part accounts for this rapidity. Congress is in a better position to deal critically with proposals that are to some degree familiar and whose political impact is known or predictable. Innovations lacking this backlog of experience, such as the Poverty Program, may pass quietly at first and, as their implications become known, generate hostility later. As we shall see, this was the case with the Economic Opportunity legislation.

Although Sargent Shriver and his associates had no dearth of program ideas with which to work, it certainly was by no means clear what ingredients would go to make up a genuinely victorious war on poverty. As the title of the Act itself suggests, the goal of the program was and is to integrate the poor into the mainstream of American life—middle-class American life. The aim, that is, is to equip disadvantaged persons so that they can take advantage of traditional economic opportunities for self-support and self-fulfillment. Whether this can be accomplished without an attempt to reengineer the values and way of life of large numbers of people—brainwashing them, to use a blunt if unpleasant term—is a fundamental and pertinent question. A democratic society by definition places supreme value on the individual, and it denies government the right to manipulate him to fit its own ends, no matter how noble they may be.

The programs that made up the Antipoverty Program during its initial years had as their main objectives education, vocational guidance, and rehabilitation. (Table 12.6 lists the programs in detail with their 1966 budget allocations.) Most of them were entrusted to a newly established agency, the Office of Economic Opportunity, though some were, or later became, the responsibility of established departments and agencies. Setting up the OEO rather than farming all of the new functions out to existing agencies reflected an awareness that the necessary freedom and imagination could better be obtained in that way. Old-line departments might well have smothered the new departures involved under their long-standing traditions and practices. Placing the OEO directly in the Executive Office of the President was an effort to shelter the poverty program's initial political vulnerability in the very shadow of the White House. (See the discussion of the politics of the Poverty Program later in this chapter.)

The programs run directly by OEO itself fell into three categories: Community Action Programs, the Job Corps, and VISTA (Volunteers in Service to America). The first category included programs initiated at the local level by either public or private groups or combinations funded by OEO, and then carried out by their initiators. In 1966, for example, grants were made to some five thousand communities, institutions, and community agencies. The variety among these is, of course, considerable. According to the OEO report, "Education, manpower training, community organization, housing and social services are the broad areas covered by Community Action." [17] Some five hundred multipurpose centers were set up in communities, concentrating in one place assistance to the poor in relation to problems of health, employment, housing, and community services. Other programs provide job opportunities, job and vocational training, and assistance in developing small businesses. Neighborhood health centers were established; remedial educational assistance was made available; legal services were provided; and summer Head Start programs were launched to prepare the culturally deprived child to benefit from his school experience. Assistance was made available for the organizing of credit unions and cooperatives by the poor for their mutual benefit.

The Job Corps was designed to take young men off the streets who could not find work. The idea was to put them in the healthful atmosphere of a camp or a similar setting where they could be paid for useful work on conservation or other projects, while filling gaps in their education and learning useful skills. VISTA was conceived of as a kind of domestic Peace Corps, whose volunteer members work in urban slums or rural poverty areas trying to help the poor help themselves. Closely related to both of these was the Neighborhood Youth Corps program run by the Department of Labor for OEO. Through it part-time jobs were provided for potential and actual high school dropouts designed to help them remain in school or return to complete work for a high school diploma.

The Department of Health, Education and Welfare ran two major parts of the poverty program, Adult Basic Education and Work Experience. The first, as its title suggests, was aimed at raising the educational level of the numerous poor whose lack of adequate formal schooling is the greatest single barrier to their entrance into the employment market. The twelve million Americans with less than a sixth-grade education were the target of this effort. The Work Experience program was designed to meet more directly the problem of the unemployability that haunts so many of the poor. As the annual report put it, "It is designed to take previously unemployable heads of families and funnel them into the labor market through a comprehensive program that includes work experience training and education." [18] Each case was to be handled separately with evaluation of each individual problem and counseling aimed at developing an approach that promised a solution.

The Farmers' Home Administration of the Department of Agriculture was to operate a loan program to help the rural poor. Loans were made both to individuals

---

[17] Office of Economic Opportunity, 2nd Annual Report, *The Quiet Revolution* (Washington, D.C., 1967), p. 11.

[18] Ibid., p. 35.

Table 12.6 *The antipoverty programs of the OEO*
(figures for 1966)

Community Action			
Total Cap:	6,260	Grants	$653,500,000
This Includes:			
Upward Bound	224	Institutions	
	20,418	Students	27,986,000
Legal Services	157	Projects	27,512,000
Foster Grandparents	33	Projects	5,089,000
Migrants (Title III-B)	66	Grants	25,285,000
Neighborhood Multiservice Centers			51,130,000
* Indian Reservation Projects	78	Grants	
	100	Indian Tribes	12,000,000
Health Centers	8	Grants	9,296,000
Head Starts:			
Summer	1,659	Grants	
	573,000	Children	97,000,000 †
Full Year	470	Grants	
	178,000	Children ‡	83,000,000
Job Corps			
28,547 Youths in 106 Centers			
OEO Cost (Obligated)			303,500,000
Centers:			
86 Conservation			
8 Men's Urban			
11 Women's Urban			
1 Special			

Source: 2nd Annual Report of the Office of Economic Opportunity, *The Quiet Revolution* (Washington, D.C., 1967), p. 9.

* Exclusive of $7,747,000 in other OEO grants.

† Plus an additional $14,000,000 obligated in FY 1967.

‡ Includes 18,000 children in follow-through programs.

and to cooperatives for the purchase of equipment needed to put the farm or enterprise on a paying basis, or to enable a farm family to set up a small business to supplement its income. The Small Business Administration operated a loan program that provided the same kind of capital loans for nonrural enterprises. An individual who felt that he had an idea that would earn a profit could thus obtain the needed capital to start. Alternatively, an individual might need money to save an existing enterprise. The owner of a small Chicago rug-cleaning establishment is reported to have secured a loan of $600 with which to advertise his service during the spring rug-cleaning season, thereby bringing in enough new customers to save his business.

Other poverty program projects have included aid of various kinds to some of the 600,000 American Indians, whose income is characteristically exceedingly low; provision of assistance to meet the educational, housing, day-care, and sanitation needs

VISTA		
OEO Cost (Obligated)		15,900,000
Field Service:	*Projects*	*Volunteers*
Migrants	23	271
Indian Reservations	56	301
Rural	86	1,172
Mental Health & Retardation	12	93
Job Corps	31	44
Urban	89	659
Hold Status	—	—
In Training	—	1,053
Total	297	3,592

Neighborhood Youth Corps (Labor)		
1,477 Projects	528,000 Authorized Enrollment Opportunities	$271,000,000

Adult Basic Education (HEW)		
Work Experience (HEW)		
45 State Plans Approved	9 State Plans Pending	35,500,000
147 Projects	38,261 Trainees	53,487,000
127 Renewals	46,559	58,913,000
Total		112,400,000
Rural Loans (Agriculture)		
17,073 Individual Loans		27,264,000
391 Cooperative Loans		5,000,000
Small Business Loans (SBA)		
1,651 Loans		17,000,000

of migratory farm workers; Medicare Alert, which was a public relations effort to inform the elderly of the benefits available to them under the new Medicare program passed as an amendment to the basic Social Security legislation; and a variety of efforts to reach the poor with assistance and counseling that might enable them to improve their lot.

This battery of programs obviously rested on a series of assumptions. Foremost was the assumption that the attack on poverty must be multiform, that no one or two approaches would do the job. Equally obvious, it has been highly experimental since its inception. In the 1930's it was more apparent what programs were necessary to meet the very different welfare and security needs of middle class people such as unemployment insurance and old-age pensions. The problems of the hard-core poor, however, are far more baffling and difficult to solve. Finally, the war on poverty was planned to rely heavily on local initiative, private as well as public, including wherever possible the initiative of the poor themselves. These characteristics of the Poverty Program have guaranteed that its history would be markedly different from that of the Social Security-based portion of the welfare state.

The Politics of Poverty

There could hardly be a better introduction to the politics of welfare than the problems encountered by the Poverty Program. Any welfare program, naturally, involves the redistribution of the society's loaves and fishes; it involves, in short, taking from one group of citizens and giving to another. One can readily imagine the disputes that must have erupted in town meetings of yesteryear when it became apparent that the tax rate would have to be raised to expand the budget of the town poor-farm. The prosperous were being asked to turn some of the fruits of their industry over to their shiftless fellow townsmen—as they doubtless viewed them.

The vastly more elaborate elements of a modern welfare-state program have the same effect, though the complexities involved may conceal the fact. New welfare policies are initiated and survive because the political support they can command or generate is more than enough to offset the opposition of the groups in society who must be taxed for their support. Welfare policies that not only drain off additional tax dollars, but also bid fair to upset existing balances in the community or to disturb existing patterns of power or advantage, live in double jeopardy. The travail of the Poverty Program amply illustrates these generalizations.

The difficulties began while Lyndon Johnson was still in the White House. As might be predicted (but curiously was not when the legislation was passed) the local impact of the Community Action part of the OEO activity accounted for much of the trouble. In the first place, the law was drawn to encourage private groups to develop plans and apply for OEO financing. Activity could thus be set on foot inimical to the interests of local political establishments, and it would be beyond their control. Pursuant to the "maximum feasible participation" mandate in the law, OEO's Community Action Workbook urged that the poor be assisted "in developing autonomous and self-managed organizations which are competent to exert political influence on behalf of their own self-interest." Only the strongest local political organizations, such as Mayor Richard Daley's in Chicago, have been able to maintain control in the face of these provisions. One study showed only 8 per cent representation of the poor on Chicago Community Action Agency policy-making committees against 50 per cent in New York City, whose party organizations are weak and fragmented.[19]

In short, these aspects of the poverty program were early seen as threatening a reallocation of power at the local level. One indirect line of attack chosen by its

---

[19] See J. David Greenstone and Paul E. Peterson, "Reformers, Machines, and the War on Poverty," in James Q. Wilson, *City Politics and Public Policy* (New York: Wiley, 1968); also Paul E. Peterson, "Forms of Representation: Participation of the Poor in the Community Action, Program," *American Political Science Review,* June, 1970.

opponents was to "spin-off" various programs from the OEO, transferring them to politically more conventional and predictable old-line agencies. Adult Basic Education and the program of small business loans were respectively transferred from the OEO to the Department of Health, Education and Welfare and to the Small Business Administration, an independent agency of the executive branch.

To head off a southern Democrat-Republican alliance aimed at redirecting, if not demolishing, the entire Poverty Program in 1967, northern Democratic supporters successfully introduced, to use its colorful unofficial label, the "bosses and boll weevil" amendment.[20] This put the Community Action Program portion of the anti-poverty operations in the hands of local elected officials. Such a shift was designed to short-circuit the private interests, whether made up of alleged do-gooders or the poor themselves, and at the same time satisfy both conservative southerners and big-city mayors by giving them control of these potentially disruptive influences. Skillful maneuvering centering on this amendment saved the day, securing for President Johnson a two-year extension of the Poverty Program.

When the Nixon Administration took office, friends of the program braced themselves for further attacks, now with the blessing if not under the leadership of the White House. Soon after taking office, however, the President surprised observers somewhat by going counter to a campaign promise and indicating that he wanted to keep the Job Corps alive for another year, but removing it from OEO jurisdiction. At the same time Nixon announced that he would switch the Head Start program from the OEO to the Department of Health, Education and Welfare. These moves would cut the agency's budget by about half, and of course represented adoption by the President of the familiar spin-off tactic earlier opponents had used, in place of the more drastic outright abolition of the controversial programs.

These proposals encountered difficulties along the way, including an intramural battle within HEW between the Office of Education and the Children's Bureau over which would inherit Head Start. While the reorganization plans were before Congress, the General Accounting Office issued a report sharply critical of the entire Poverty Program, especially attacking its disorganization and lack of coordination. Representatives Carl Perkins (Dem–Kentucky), Chairman of the House Education and Labor Committee, which oversees welfare and related programs, and a staunch OEO partisan, likened the warm words the President had uttered about the Poverty Program when making his reorganization proposals to the fisherman's "Hold still, little fish. I don't intend to hurt you. I just want to gut you." [21] Ultimately the President's reorganization proposals were allowed to go into effect.

The White House then requested another two-year extension of the OEO's life. If adopted this would enable the agency to continue coordinating what remained of the Poverty Program within its jurisdiction: the 938 Community Action Agencies, 934 Neighborhood Legal Services Offices (themselves highly controversial), 88

---

[20] More generally known as the Green Amendment after its sponsor, Representative Edith Green. For a summary of these developments see *The New York Times,* December 25, 1967, p. 1.

[21] *The New York Times,* March 16, 1969.

migrant programs, 208 projects for the aged, 67 Neighborhood Health Centers, 320 family planning programs, 400 food projects, and 4,600 VISTA volunteers.[22] The Nixon Administration and the congressional liberals agreed on this extension when a bipartisan coalition of opponents introduced an amendment that would have given control over the Poverty Program to the states. (Just as old-line agencies were likely to be more conservative and amenable than the OEO, so state control was seen as more desirable than federal.) Although all signs seemed to point toward success for this effort, and the President did little or nothing to help save the OEO, at the last minute the attack was turned back in the House, and the bill passed as originally proposed. The Poverty Program had squeaked through again—thanks, apparently, to the fact that it has a sufficiently potent constituency to provide last-minute support.

The attacks continue, however, on individual programs if not on the whole bundle. The Nixon Administration in 1970 moved to soften VISTA's image of dedication to confrontation tactics and organizing the poor to achieve specific goals. In 1971 it announced plans to merge VISTA with the overseas Peace Corps in a new volunteer service agency called ACTION. VISTA supporters saw a basic attack on their agency and its policy orientation. In somewhat similar fashion, the legal services part of the OEO's program has also come under attack. Governor Ronald Reagan of California has expressed particular anger at the use of federal funds to pay lawyers to fight cases against the state of California. This kind of situation, and the accusation that the young activist lawyers who staff the legal services offices spend time on New Left cases and causes instead of concentrating on defending the poor, has brought almost continuous hostility.

All major policy innovations suffer a similar vulnerability until they gain really widespread acceptance. Opponents may attack them on grounds of economy, or they may challenge the existence of the new agencies created to carry them into effect by threatening to transfer them to safer hands. Finally, opponents may seek to shift control from Washington to the states or local communities. This latter tactic, which is customarily defended as making possible local administration sensitive to local needs, also means control by the vested community interests that might otherwise be adversely affected by the decisions of a less accessible Washington bureaucracy. Viewed in these terms, the politics of welfare differs little from the politics found in almost any other policy area.

The "Nixon Revolution"

If the Johnson revolution—the war on poverty—had come because of awareness that the programs that had been evolving since the 1930's had proved inadequate, the Nixon income-maintenance "revolution" came because it seemed that even the combination of long-standing welfare legislation *plus* the poverty program was *still* insufficient. There were other and more immediate motives behind the Nixon pro-

---

[22] Figures are from the Office of Economic Opportunity, *Annual Report, Fiscal Years 1969–70* (Washington, D.C., 1971).

posals, which will be examined later. Statistically, by 1967, when Social Security had been functioning for some thirty years and the poverty program had been on the books for three, the picture was at best mixed.

It is true that if one takes the family income levels in dollars that define *poverty* according to the Social Security Administration one finds that the percentage of all persons falling below that line went down from 22 per cent in 1959 to about 13.5 per cent in 1967. The drop was far more rapid for families than for unrelated individuals (from 20.4 to 11.7 per cent as against a decline from 47.4 to 37.2 per cent). Furthermore, by 1967 only 10.3 per cent of the whole white population were classified as having poverty status, whereas 35.4 per cent of all nonwhites, or more than a third, still fell into the poverty group.[23] From these data one can conclude that there has been progress, but that it has been uneven, affecting some groups more than others, and that there is still a very substantial poverty core untouched by all past remedial efforts: 26 million people as of 1967. Finally, nonwhites bulk far larger in the poverty totals than they do in the overall population.

Another way of looking at the picture, this time taking the twenty-year period from 1947 to 1967, is considerably less encouraging than the figures just cited. The analysis in this instance focuses on the distribution of the total pretax income received by individuals and families, and particularly, the portion of that income received by the lowest fifth of the population. That figure has remained almost completely stationary during the two decades examined: standing at 5.1 per cent in 1947 and 5.4 per cent in 1967. Breaking this down one finds that the share of the white income total going to the lowest fifth of whites remained about the same, but that the share of nonwhite income going to the lowest fifth of nonwhites actually declined. In addition, the proportion of nonwhites with incomes that qualified them for inclusion in the bottom fifth of all incomes remained virtually the same—about 40 per cent—during the period.[24]

In short, progress in eradicating poverty from the American national community has been slow, and, measured by genuine income redistribution, minimal. Seemingly, traditional ways of defining and attempting to remedy poverty are inadequate, including the varied and often sophisticated efforts at education and retraining that compose the Poverty Program. Accordingly, during the mid-1960's the call began to be heard for a new approach generally referred to by the overall term of *income maintenance*. A not untypical, if somewhat surprising, enunciation of this new point of view came in a speech by the then President of the Ford Motor Company, Mr. Arjay Miller. He said in part:

I believe strongly that it is now time for us to take a total approach to poverty that would reach all of the poor and not just certain segments. What I have in mind would include both direct income assistance to those in need and measures to increase employment of the disadvantaged.

[23] *Statistical Abstract of the United States, 1969* (Washington, D.C.: G.P.O.), Table No. 484, p. 328.

[24] This analysis is found in Pamela Roby, "Inequality: A Trend Analysis," *Annals of the American Academy of Political and Social Science* (September, 1969), pp. 110–117.

Figure 12.2.

Source: Providence (Rhode Island) *Journal,* July 23, 1971. Copyright © 1966 *The Chicago Sun-Times,* reproduced by courtesy of Wil-Jo Associates, Inc., and Bill Mauldin.

Poverty War

>In my opinion, the proposal that meets these requirements best is one called the negative income tax. Under this plan, a family with a zero income would receive a basic allowance related to the size and composition of the family unit. When a member of the family began to earn income, the basic allowance would automatically be reduced by an offsetting tax, but not by a corresponding amount.[25]

This idea of a negative income tax had been proposed before by both liberal and conservative students of welfare problems, and it has advocates in and out of government. It was first broached by Professor Milton Friedman of the University of Chicago, who served as Barry Goldwater's economic adviser during the 1964 presidential campaign.

The same concept is described in one of the staff studies done for the President's Commission on Income Maintenance Programs, published in 1970. "An income maintenance program . . . [is one that will] provide a money payment adequate to give all persons (or families) the opportunity to have a socially desirable standard of living according to middle-class values. . . ." [26] Acceptance of this notion means dropping many of the traditional attitudes toward the poor and their relief, some of which still infused programs adopted in recent decades. Under the income maintenance theory all persons and families are entitled, as a right, to a standard of living supplied by the government in whole or in part, if necessary, that is above mere subsistence and approaches middle-class standards of adequacy. All considerations of whether the recipient is "deserving" of aid become subordinate to this overall principle. And it is the—admittedly somewhat limited—acceptance of this income maintenance approach that constitutes what we have been calling the Nixon "revolution."

The way in which this revolution seems to have been decided upon and launched is interesting and significant. President-elect Nixon had appointed a preinauguration Task Force on Public Welfare. The report of the group was looked to as important by the new Administration once it was installed in office, because there was little by way of other immediate program proposals available to offer Congress and the country. Also, the welfare area seemed to offer a place to make a mark quickly in an important field that was engendering rising public concern. The Task Force, however, tested the political wind and concluded that a series of adjustments in the existing system of welfare programs represented the most that was politically feasible.[27]

That a much more radical proposal was ultimately sent to Congress seems to be accounted for by the fact, first of all, that the President himself was still open-minded in this area and had not made up his mind on the scope of the welfare program he would propose. Moreover, the fact that there were certain individuals in his entourage who had particular views on welfare and could shape his thinking in their direction was also of obviously key importance. One of these was Robert Finch, the new Secretary of Health, Education and Welfare, who had become acutely aware of welfare problems while serving as Lieutenant Governor of California. It was Finch who categorized the debate that raged around the President as "a classic confronta-

[25] The New York Times, December 1, 1967.
[26] President's Commission, op. cit., p. 12.
[27] See Steiner, op. cit., Ch. 3, for this part of the story.

tion" between "those (including himself) who recognize that the present system is just a disaster and that we had to break out of the old mold, and those who wanted to rewrite the old system." [28] Then there was that perennial figure in welfare discussions, Daniel Patrick Moynihan, who by then was the President's Assistant for Urban Affairs. He had soon become disenchanted with the poverty effort he had helped to put together.

Finally, after repeated delays while the battle presumably went on within the White House, the President went on national television on August 8, 1969, and unveiled his welfare reform package. In place of the hodgepodge of former measures, a basic federal payment of $1,600 per year would now be provided to a family of four. The states could supplement this if they desired. Outside earnings by the family would be encouraged, not discouraged, the President said. He then outlined a formula by which the family could keep the first $60 a month earned without penalty, whereupon for each dollar of outside income, benefits would be cut by 50 cents. At a predetermined point as earnings rose, government aid would cease. In 1967, when forty-eight congressional offices were asked if the guaranteed income idea was a live issue, none felt that it would be legislatively relevant in less than five years, and some said twenty-five. The President's speech obviously provided no guarantee of congressional adoption, but the idea now became instantly feasible.[29]

A Gallup poll published a few weeks later showed that 75 per cent of the sample had heard of the proposal for welfare reform, and of these two thirds approved.[30] It was actually not until October 3, after further hassling in the Administration, that the actual draft bill embodying the President's program finally went up to the Hill for congressional consideration. No one needed to be told that the major key to its success was the attitude of Chairman Wilbur Mills of the House Ways and Means Committee. During the late winter and spring of 1970, Mills did in fact come around. On April 16 the bill was passed by the House, 243 to 155 (140 Democrats and 103 Republicans voting in favor, and 84 Democrats and 71 Republicans recorded against).

It may well be that a behind-the-scenes collaboration between academic research and politics was in part responsible for pushing the measure along.[31] Back in 1968, Dr. John O. Wilson, Director of Research for the OEO, had presided over an experiment designed to test the key argument against the income maintenance idea, namely, that if money were given in this manner to all poor, whether employed or not, it would substantially cut the incentive of the people involved to work at all and discourage their desire to improve their lot. Thirteen thousand and fifty-nine families were chosen at random in three cities to receive income maintenance checks on an experimental basis. Three years later, in August 1971, it was intended that the results be analyzed and recorded.

Early in 1970, while the Nixon plan was stalled in the House Ways and Means

---

28 Ibid., p. 120.
29 Ibid., p. 119.
30 *The New York Times,* August 30, 1969.
31 See Fred J. Cook, "When You Just Give Money to the Poor," *New York Times Magazine,* April 26, 1970.

Committee and the complaints of encouraging shiftlessness were being heard, Moynihan turned to Wilson to see if he had any ammunition that could be used by the White House. Wilson recalled: "I sat down to write a report, and I took it to Pat Moynihan. Pat jumped all over me. He stomped around the room, waving his arms, that Irish temper of his flaring. 'Wilson,' he said, 'you mean to tell me that you've had a $5-million experiment running in New Jersey for almost two years now and you don't know what you've got?" Wilson of course had said that he would really have to wait until the research had run its three years before he would have anything significant to report. Moynihan brushed aside explanations and snorted: "That's the trouble with you economists—you never have any facts until it is too late." [32]

Moynihan's needling made Wilson mad. He went back to his office and mobilized the research team. They got out the data they already had and processed it, and he took the results back to the White House a week or so later. Even the preliminary results showed clearly that the federal payments, far from encouraging slothfulness, actually seemed to stimulate the families receiving them to work harder. Their earnings increased in 53 per cent of the cases, whereas only 43 per cent of the families in the control group not receiving checks increased their earnings.

The Ways and Means Committee and the House may have been convinced, but the Senate Finance Committee was not. In the fall of 1970, it rejected the plan overwhelmingly. The following spring, the House Committee again approved the bill. This time the $1,600 federal income payment went up to $2,400, provisions were included to federalize the cost of welfare generally (in order to steal some of the thunder from another major Nixon proposal, revenue sharing), and the new bill tied the whole package to always-popular Social Security benefits increases. Again the House responded favorably to Chairman Mills's leadership and passed the measure. Again, in midsummer 1971 it became stalled in the Senate Finance Committee by a coalition of conservatives who disliked the whole idea and liberals who felt the benefits inadequate.

In October 1972 the Senate, in a complicated series of votes effectively shelved income maintenance until after the election. But when a Republican President proposes such a seemingly radical departure and can count on more than half of both parties in the House plus the crucial support of the cautious and relatively conservative Ways and Means Committee Chairman, when wide-ranging support from economists, businessmen, and others in the community is repeatedly voiced, the march toward broad national agreement is likely to continue. The gestation period for major social reforms in America is often long.

Welfare and State Politics

The history of welfare policy has been, certainly in the last four decades, one of a steady drift of responsibility and funding to Washington. Local responsibility has eroded rapidly, as we noted at the opening of this chapter. States have found that the

---

[32] Ibid., p. 110.

courts will not even allow them to impose residence requirements for welfare eligibility, nor cut back on federally mandated categories of supplementary payment, though legislative mandates for such policy changes have widespread backing. The national government has virtually preempted the field and will be likely do so even more completely as federal funding of programs becomes more complete in the near future.

As a postscript to this trend—and to this chapter—however, there has been some recent research at the state level that makes possible an approach to the problems of welfare from a somewhat different direction. The authors of one study, Professors Richard E. Dawson and James A. Robinson, sought to identify what factors determine the shape of decisions made in regard to state welfare programs and their financing.[33] By using the fifty states rather than the national government they were able to note patterns of program and expenditure and to seek correlations between these and other variables. Specifically, their concern was with why some states spend more, relatively and absolutely, on welfare programs than other states. Their initial assumption was that welfare spending must be related either to the needs and resources of the state in question, or, alternatively, to the political mechanisms through which appropriation decisions are made. For example, do richer states spend more, relatively speaking, than poorer ones? Do more highly urbanized and industrialized states spend more, either because urban people need more welfare assistance or because a developed economy makes more resources available? Or should one, perhaps, first look at need and then attempt correlations? Do states that have proportionately larger groups of deprived or needy (or foreign-born) citizens devote more resources to welfare in relation to other expenditures?

Dawson and Robinson also speculated that possibly none of these variables was the key one. Instead, might it not be that political considerations and mechanisms override the variables of need and available resources? For example, it could be that states with highly competitive party systems spend more on welfare than states with little party competition. This could be true if one assumed that political parties bid against each other by promising higher welfare benefits to recipient groups in order to win their votes. By this reasoning noncompetitive state party systems would operate in a converse fashion. There politics and elections would center on personalities rather than on bids for group support, and thus would have less effect on welfare expenditure levels. Yet another political variable included for study was that of citizen participation. High voter turnout in a state must mean more poor people voting, because voting-behavior research indicates that turnout declines as income declines. Accordingly, if the needy *are* voting in large numbers in a given state, they are probably using their influence at the polls to secure higher benefits for themselves.

These hunches about the possible relevance of a series of variables to welfare appropriations form the hypothesis of the Dawson-Robinson study. Their next step was to compare each variable with a measure or measures of actual state spending on welfare. Accurate measures are not easily constructed, but, among others, they used

[33] "The Politics of Welfare," in Jacob and Vines, op. cit.

the amount of payment per welfare recipient and the per capita state expenditure. The first permits a comparison of states in terms of how much is paid to an individual beneficiary in one state and how much the same person would get in another. The second measure relates total expenditure to population as a means of putting all states, large and small, on the same footing for comparative purposes.

Dawson and Robinson found a strong positive correlation when they compared welfare expenditures with the relative wealth of the states: the richer the state, the more generous its welfare programs. Level of urbanization also correlated positively with expenditure levels, but state industrial development did not relate very clearly. However, the greater the number of foreign-born people in a state's population, the more was spent on welfare. On the other hand, the comparisons involving the direct measures of need or deprivation showed emphatically negative correlations. States whose people needed the most welfare aid were decidedly *not* the ones that were most generous in providing assistance. Similarly, the two political variables showed only limited levels of correlation. When relative party competitiveness within states or higher voter-turnout patterns were examined, some relation was found with welfare spending, but in neither case was there a really clear-cut correlation.

What does this all mean for students of the politics of welfare? In overall terms, it seems that availability of resources is more important than the political machinery for allocating them. State wealth, either measured directly or through levels of urbanization, is more closely tied to welfare spending than the kind of party system or the level of voter activity. Affluent states have generous welfare programs, one presumes, in part at least because there is a sufficiently large pool of resources from which to draw welfare funds; consequently the resistance to reallocation is lessened. This may well be one of the basic ironies of welfare politics—it is reminiscent of the biblical assertion that unto those who have shall be given. Wealthy states, whose poor are also better off than their counterparts elsewhere, can nevertheless afford to be more generous by virtue of their abundance and the greater political leeway it affords. Poor states, though perhaps they should be under an even stronger compulsion to spread the available resources more evenly, find the political problems entailed in such "leveling" much more inhibiting.

One is tempted to suspect that the high incidence of foreign-born population in states with more generous welfare programs is in part the accidental result of the fact that the richer states, by virtue of their location and greater economic opportunities, have drawn disproportionate numbers of immigrants. By contrast the Deep South states, homogeneously Anglo-Saxon anyway save for their black population, have on balance been exporters of population. The presence of foreign-born population, in other words, seems to be less closely related than state wealth to high welfare appropriations.

suggested additional readings

Bagdikian, Ben H. *In the Midst of Plenty: Poverty in America.* New York: New American Library, 1964.

Bracey, Howard E. *In Retirement: Pensioners in Great Britain and the United States.* Baton Rouge: Louisiana State University Press, 1967.

Dye, Thomas R. *Politics, Economics, and the Public: Policy Outcomes in the American States.* Chicago: Rand McNally and Co., 1966.

Harrington, Michael. *The Other America: Poverty in the United States.* New York: Penguin Books, 1962.*

Kershaw, Joseph A. *Government Against Poverty.* Washington, D.C.: The Brookings Institution, 1970.*

Kramer, Ralph M. *Participation of the Poor: Comparative Community Case Studies in the War on Poverty.* Englewood Cliffs, N.J.: Prentice-Hall, Inc., 1969.*

Moynihan, Daniel P. *Maximum Feasible Misunderstanding.* New York: The Free Press, 1969.*

Piven, Frances F., and Richard S. Cloward. *Regulating the Poor: The Functions of Public Welfare.* New York: Pantheon Books, Inc., 1971.

President's Commission on Income Maintenance Programs. *Report: Poverty Amidst Plenty, The American Paradox; Technical Studies; Background Studies.* Washington, D.C.: U.S. Government Printing Office, 1969–1970.

President's Commission on Urban Housing. *A Decent Home.* Washington, D.C.: U.S. Government Printing Office, 1968.

Stein, Bruno. *On Relief: The Economics of Poverty and Public Welfare.* New York: Basic Books, Inc., 1971.

Steiner, Gilbert Y. *The State of Welfare.* Washington, D.C.: The Brookings Institution, 1971.

Symposium. *Evaluating the War on Poverty, Annals of the American Academy of Political and Social Science.* September, 1969.

Wilson, James Q. (ed.). *Urban Renewal; The Record and the Controversy.* Cambridge: Harvard University Press, 1966.

Wolman, Harold. *The Politics of Federal Housing.* New York: Dodd, Mead, and Co., 1971.*

* Available in paperback.

13 individual liberties and minority rights

case study

*Justice on Trial: The People v. Donald Payne**

The first time I walked into the Criminal Court Building that odor hit me. That combination of sweat and onions and Polish sausage. I wanted to turn around and come out. I saw a guy I knew in law school and I said, "What the f——— is that smell?" And he said, "That's tears."

—Constantine Xinos, an assistant public defender for Cook County, Illinois

It is a melancholy place, flyspecked and grimy, a Hollywood-Egyptian temple squatting heavily and incongruously among the factories, the freight yards and the slum housing projects on Chicago's roiling West Side. Its out-of-the-way location is a monument to the failed business instinct of the late Anton Cermak, the Chicago politician who opened the building on April Fools' Day, 1929, in hopes of sparking a real-estate boom in his home ward. The boom busted, and only the courthouse and its neighbor of convenience, the Cook County Jail complex, are left to Cermak's vision. Through its cavernous courtrooms have passed generations of Chicago's outlaws and outcasts—a faceless

* By Peter Goldman and Don Holt, *Newsweek*, March 8, 1971. Copyright © Newsweek, Inc., March 8, 1971.

succession of bootleggers, bookies, hit men, drifters, thieves, whores, petty Mafiosi and lately the black young so thickly involved in the crime of the city streets. In its corridors, in the smell of food and sweat and tears, the People of Illinois through their agents—the police, the prosecutors, the lawyers, the judges—labor imperfectly toward a rough approximation of justice.

An 18-year-old named Donald Payne came handcuffed and sullen into the building last year—a tall, armed robber and attempted murderer of a white liquor-store owner in a "changing" fringe neighborhood. The police report told it simply: ". . . At 2100 (9 P.M.) . . . Aug. 4, 1970 . . . victim stated that two male Negroes entered his store and the taller of the two came out with a gun and announced that this is a holdup, 'give me all of your money.' With this the victim . . . walked away from the area of the cash register. When he did this, the smaller offender shouted, 'Shoot him.' The taller offender aimed the pistol at him and pulled the trigger about two or three times. The weapon failed to fire. The offenders then fled. . . ." It was a botched job—nobody was hurt and nothing stolen—and so Payne in one sense was only another integer in the numbing statistics of American crime.

561

But the case of the *People* v. *Donald Payne* was in another sense central to the malaise of the nation's decaying big cities. Street crime has contributed powerfully to that malaise—and street crime in urban America has become in large and growing measure Negro crime. The subject has until lately been thought too painful for public discussion; to raise it has been considered treasonable among blacks and racist among sympathetic whites. But the statistics command attention. One little-noted staff study for Lyndon Johnson's commission on violence showed urban arrest rates ten to eighteen times higher for Negroes than for whites in serious crimes of violence—and up to twenty times higher for black teen-agers. Another, a seventeen-city survey, found blacks suspected of 72 per cent of the criminal homicides, 74 per cent of the aggravated assaults, 70 per cent of the rapes, and 85 per cent of the robberies in which the police made arrests. To acknowledge these figures is only to recognize the effect on Negroes of years of poverty and discrimination in what the Negro sociologist E. Franklin Frazier once aptly called "the city of destruction." To suppress the figures is to ignore not only the fears of white people but the pain of the blacks who are the victims of the vast majority of black crime.

.   .   .

A voice said, "I want that." Joe Castelli looked up from the till, and there across the counter stood this tall colored kid with an insolent grin and a small caliber, blue-steel automatic not 4 feet from Castelli's face. Castelli can't remember now what he thought in that split second; maybe it was how he had worked behind that counter for 24 years and how all of it was slipping away. The colored are chasing me out. The thought haunts him still, and so does the image of that pistol. And now, sometimes, Joe Castelli wants to kill somebody.

.   .   .

And finally the tall one with the blue-steel .25 and the scornful half-smile—the one Castelli identified later as Donald Payne. He and another, smaller youth came in the OUT door that cool August evening just as Castelli was stuffing $250 or $300 in receipts from cash register No. 2 into his pocket. "I want that," the tall one said. Castelli edged away. "Shoot him!" the small one yelled. The tall one stared at Castelli and poked the gun across the counter at him. "Mother f____er," he said. He squeezed the trigger, maybe once, maybe two or three times.

The gun went *click*.

The two youths turned and ran. Castelli started after them, bumped against the end of the counter and went down. He got up and dashed outside, but the youths disappeared down a dark alley. An old white man emptying garbage saw them go by. The tall one pointed the pistol toward the sky and squeezed again. This time it went off.

A clerk from across the street came over and told Castelli that a woman had seen the boys earlier getting out of a black Ford. "People around here notice things like that," Castelli says. "They watch." Castelli found the car parked nearby and wrote down the license number. The driver—a third Negro youth—followed him back to the store. "What you taking my license for?" he demanded. "I was just waiting for my wife—I took her to the doctor." He stood there yelling for a while, but some of Castelli's white neighbors crowded into the store, and the black youth left. Castelli went back into the street, flagged down an unmarked police car he recognized and handed over the number, and the hunt was on.

.   .   .

Payne was sleeping when the cops crowded into his little attic bedroom, and he came awake cool and mean. "Get moving," someone said. "You're under arrest." The police started rummaging around while Payne, jawing all the while, pulled on a pair of green pants and red jacket. "You don't have no warrant," he said. As Payne told it later, one of the cops replied, "We got a lawyer on our hands." But Officer Higgins insists he misunderstood— "What I said was we'd *get* him a lawyer."

They marched him out in handcuffs past his mother, took him to the district station and shackled him to a chair while one of the officers started tapping out an arrest report: Payne, Donald m/n (for male Negro) 18 4-19-52 . . . [Officer] Higgins got Castelli on the phone. "It's Joe," he said, "come in— we think we've got the man." Castelli came in with DeAngelo. The cops put Payne into a little back room with a few stray blacks. Castelli picked him out—and that, for the cops, was enough. Payne was taken to the South Side branch police headquarters to be booked, then led before a magistrate who set bond at $10,000. The bounty is a paper figure: the Chicago courts require only 10 per cent cash. But Payne didn't have it, and by midafternoon he was on his way by police van to the Cook County Jail.

Joe Higgins and Tom Cullen by then had worked twelve hours overtime; in four hours more, Tac Unit 660 was due on patrol again. They talked a little about Donald Payne. "He had a head on him," Cullen said in some wonder. "Maybe if he didn't have a chip on his shoulder. Maybe—"

. . .

Connie Xinos disliked Donald Payne from the beginning. They met in October in the prisoners' lockup behind Judge Fitzgerald's courtroom, and all Xinos

had to go on then was the police report and Payne's public-defender questionnaire ("All I know is I was arrested for attempted murder on Aug. 5") and that insinuating half smile. He did it, Xinos thought; all of them except the scared children and the street-wise old pros swear they are innocent, but you get a feeling. And that smile. He 's cocky, Xinos thought. A bad kid. Xinos has been at it less than four years, but four years in the bullpens is a long time. He thinks Chicago is dying. And he thinks thousands of black street kids much like Donald Payne—his clients—are doing the killing.

. . .

[Finding a job after graduation from law school was very difficult.]

The state's attorney had no openings, so he went upstairs to see public defender Gerald Getty, "Don't even pay me," he said. "Give me a dollar a year, I just want to work." Getty asked him to get a letter from a Democratic committeeman for form's sake—practically everyone in the building from janitor to judge has some such connection—and hired him shortly afterward for $7,800 a year to start (and $13,600 now). Xinos arrived bubbling with ideals, like most of the young lawyers coming into the office, but a senior staffer on his way out took him aside and told him: "Six months in those bullpens and you'll want out. You'll go practice probate law." And now Xinos figures he was right.

. . .

Xinos learned fast. "For a while," he recalls, "I used to go out on Clark Street" —in a crime-infested section of storefronts and rooming houses north of the Loop—"and go up to these places and measure off rooms for evidence. People looked at me like I was nuts." So did judges, and after six months or so Xinos quit measuring off rooms like

Perry Mason and started operating—
"swinging"—inside the building.

You learn its folkways. "It's our court,"
Xinos says. "It's like a family. Me, the
prosecutors, the judges, we're old
friends. I drink with the prosecutors.
I give the judge a Christmas present,
he gives me a Christmas present." And you
learn technique. The evidence game. The
little touches: "The defendant should
smile a lot." The big disparities: which
judge gives eighteen months for a wife
killing and which one gives twenty to
forty years. How to make time and the
caseload work for you. "The last thing you
want to do is rush to trial. You let the
case ride. Everybody gets friendly. A
case is continued ten or fifteen times,
and nobody cares any more. The victims
don't care. Everybody just wants to get rid
of the case." Then you can plead your
man guilty and deal for reduced charges
or probation or short time. You swing.

And you get calluses. You discover early
that a lot of crime is black and that the
bulk of it—black crime against black
victims—is taken considerably less
seriously than crime by anybody, black or
white, against white victims. "There's one
kind of law for them," a judge told Xinos
early on, "and another kind for us." It
was a hard lesson—"I was very liberal
when I first started"—but everything, even
the working vocabulary of the building,
confirmed it. You learn that a "nigger
disorderly" means anything up to and
including the murder of one black by
another; you learn that a black man
convicted of raping a black woman may
well get off with the minimum sentence
("Four to five years and everybody's
happy") but a "zebra rape"—black on
white—means certain big time. And, since
the bulk of the rape and murder cases
you handle are black against black, you
learn to swing with the double standard,
too.

. . .

Everybody kept trying to talk him out of

his trial. "Plead quilty, jackass, you could
get away with ten to twenty for this,"
Xinos whispered when they finally got to
trial. "Ain't no need for that," said Payne.
"You really want a jury?" the assistant
state's attorney, Walter Parrish, teased
him. "Or you want to plead?" "I want
my trial," said Payne. Everything in the
building says cop out, make a deal, take
the short time. "They ought to carve it in
stone over the door," an old courthouse
hand, then a prosecutor and now a judge,
told a friend once, "no case ever goes to
trial here." The *People* v. *Donald Payne*
did get to trial, halfway at least. But then
his case went sour, and the deal got
sweeter, and in the end Donald Payne
copped out, too.

Practically everybody does: urban justice
in America would quite simply collapse if
even a major fraction of the suspects
who now plead guilty should suddenly
start demanding jury trials. The Payne
case was only one of 500 indictments on
Judge Richard Fitzgerald's docket last
year; it would have taken him four years to
try them all. So 85 to 90 per cent of them
ended in plea bargaining—that backstairs
haggling process by which pleas of
guilty are bartered for reduced charges
or shorter sentences or probation.
"Plea bargaining used to be a nasty
word," said Fitzgerald; only lately have
the bar and the courts begun to call it out
of the closet and recognize it as not just
a reality but a necessity of the system.
"We're becoming a little more
sophisticated about it. We're saying
'You're doing it, we know you're doing
it and you have to do it; this is the way
it has to be done.' "

The pressures to plead are sometimes
cruel, the risks of going to trial high and
well-advertised. There is, for waverers,
the cautionary tale of one man who
turned down one to three years on a deal
—and got 40 to 80 as an object lesson
when a jury convicted him. Still, Payne
insisted, and Xinos painstakingly put a
defense together. He opened with a pair
of preliminary motions, one arguing that

the pistol was inadmissible because the evidence tying it to Payne was hearsay, the other contending that the police should have offered Payne a lawyer at the line-up but didn't. The witnesses straggled in for a hearing on Dec. 1. Joe Castelli took the stand, and Patrolman Cullen, and, for a few monosyllabic moments, Payne himself. Had anyone advised him of his rights to a lawyer? "No." Or let him make a phone call? "No" But another of the arresting officers, Robert Krueger, said that Payne had been told his rights—and such swearing contests almost always are decided in favor of the police. Everybody admired Xinos's energy and craftsmanship. Nevertheless, Fitzgerald denied both of the defense motions and docketed the case for trial on Dec. 14.

And so they all gathered that wintry Monday in Fitzgerald's sixth-floor courtroom, a great dim cave with marbled and oak-paneled walls, pitted linoleum floors and judge, jury, lawyers, defendant and gallery so widely separated that nobody could hear anything without microphones. Choosing a jury took two hours that day, two the next morning. Parrish, an angular, [Ivy-cut] Negro of 41, worked without a shopping list. "I know some lawyers say fat people are jolly and Germans are strict," he says, "but none of that's true in my experience. If you get twelve people who say they'll listen, you're all right."

But Xinos is a hunch player. He got two blacks on the jury and was particularly pleased with one of them, a light-skinned Urban League member who looked as if she might be sympathetic. And he deliberately let one hard hat sort on the panel. Xinos had a point to make about the pistol—you couldn't click it more than once without pulling back the slide to cock it—and the hard hat looked as if he knew guns.

That afternoon, slowly and methodically, Parrish began to put on his case. He opened with the victims, and Castelli

laid the story on the record: "About ten after 9, the gentleman walked in . . . He had a small-caliber pistol . . . I edged away . . . The other lad came up to me and he said. 'Shoot him, shoot him, shoot him' . . . (The first youth) pointed the gun at me and fired three times or four —at least I heard three clicks." And the gunman—did Castelli see him in court?

"Yes, I do, sir."

"And would you point him out, please?"

Castelli gestured toward the single table shared by the prosecution and defense. "That," he said, "is Donald Payne."

But Xinos, in his opening argument, had promised to alibi Payne. His mother was prepared to testify for him—and now, on cross-examination, he picked skillfully at Parrish's case. Playing to his hard hat on the jury, he asked Castelli whether the stick-up man had one or two hands on the gun. "Only one, sir," said Castelli. "And was that trigger pulled in rapid succession—click-click-click?" Xinos pressed. "Yes, sir," said Castelli, and Xinos had his point: it takes two hands to keep pulling the slide and clicking the trigger. Next came Patrolman Joe Higgins, who remembered, under Xinos's pointed cross-examination, that Castelli had described the gunman as weighing 185 pounds—30 more than Payne carries on his spindly 6-foot frame. Payne had nearly botched that point by wearing a billowy, cape-shaped jacket to court, but Xinos persuaded him to fold it up and sit on it so the jurors could see how bony he really was. The 30-pound misunderstanding undercut Castelli's identification of Payne—and suddenly the People and their Lawyer, Walter Parrish, were in trouble.

Parrish didn't show it: he is a careful, phlegmatic man born to striving parents in the Chicago ghetto and bred to move smiling coolly through the system. He came into it with a Howard law diploma, a few years' haphazard practice and the right sort of connections as counsel to and precinct captain for the 24th Ward regular Democratic organization. He figured on the job only as an apprenticeship for private practice, but he has stayed six years and seems rather comfortable where he is. The black kids over in the County Jail call him "The Devil," and he likes that; he fancied that the edgy hostility he saw in Donald Payne's eyes was a tribute to his hard-guy reputation. He likes his public law firm, too. It pays him $18,000—he guesses he would have to gross $50,000 in private practice to match that—and it puts all the enormous resources of the state at his service. Investigators? The state's attorney has 93 to the public defender's six. Police, the sheriff, the F.B.I.? "All you got to do is call them." Pathology? Microanalysis? "Just pick up the phone. You've got everything at your beck and call."

What he had in *People* v. *Payne* was the Hamilton boys, the two cousins through whom the police had tracked Payne. Parrish had hoped he wouldn't have to put them on the stand. "It was a risk," he said later. "They could have hurt us. They could have got up there and suddenly said Donald wasn't there." But he was behind and knew it. He needed Frank Hamilton to place Payne inside the store, James to connect him with the car and the pistol. So, that afternoon, he ordered up subpoenas for the Hamiltons. "We know how to scramble," said his young assistant, Joe Poduska. "That's the name of the game."

The subpoenas were being typed when Connie Xinos happened into the state's attorney's office to socialize—*it's like a family*—and saw them in the typewriter. Xinos went cold. He had talked to the mother of one of the Hamiltons; he knew their testimony could hurt. So, next morning, he headed first thing for Parrish's austere second-floor cubicle —and found the Hamiltons there. "We're going to testify," they told Xinos, "and

we're going to tell the truth."

Xinos took Parrish aside. "Let's get rid of this case," he said.

"It's Christmas," Parrish said amiably. "I'm a reasonable man."

"What do you want?" Xinos said.

"I was thinking about three to eight."

"One to five," said Xinos.

"You got it."

"It's an absolute gift," Xinos thought, and he took it to Payne in the lockup. "I can get you one to five," he said. Payne said no. Xinos thought fast. It was a deadbang case—the kind Clarence Darrow couldn't pull out—and it was good for a big rattle, maybe ten to twenty years. Xinos went back downstairs, got the Hamiltons, and sat them down with Payne in Fitzgerald's Library. "They rapped," he remembers, "and one of them said, 'Donald—you mean you told them you weren't there?' I told him again I could get him one to five. They said, 'Maybe you ought to take it, Donald.' I said, 'You may get ten to twenty going on with the trial.' And he said, 'Well, even if I take the one to five, I'm not guilty.' That's when I knew he would go."

But Fitzgerald, would he buy it? Xinos was worried. The judge is a handsome 57, with a pink Irish face rimmed with silver hair and creased to smile. "He looks like God would look and acts like God would act if God were a judge," says Xinos. "He doesn't take any s_____." He was a suburban lawyer in Calumet City when Mayor Richard Daley's organization slated him for judge seven years ago, a reward for having backed a Daley man for governor once when it was tough to do so. He started in divorce court and hated it: "I think I'd rather have 150 lashes than go back down there. Jeez—it's a lot easier to give a guy the chair than it is to take five kids away from a mother." He is happier where he is, and he has made a considerable reputation in the building as a solid, early-rising, hard-working judge—no scholar but conscientious and good on the law. He can be stern as well: he isn't the hanging type, but he does think the pendulum has swung pretty far lately in the defendant's favor. "We've clothed 'em in swaddling clothes," he says, "and laid 'em in a manger of bliss." So Xinos fretted. "The judge is the judge," he told Payne while they waited for an audience with Fitzgerald. "He might give you three to eight. You better think about it."

But Fitzgerald agreed to talk, and the ritual began to unfold, Xinos led Payne to the bench and announced for the record that they wanted to discuss pleading—"Is that correct, Donald?" Payne mumbled, "Correct," and, while he went back to the lockup to wait, the lawyers followed the judge into chambers. A bailiff closed the door behind them. Fitzgerald sat at his desk and pulled a 4-by-6 index card out of a box; he likes to keep his own notes. Parrish dropped into a leathery sofa, his knees coming almost to his chin. Xinos sat in a green guest chair in a row along the wall. There were no outsiders, not even a court stenographer. The conference, not the courtroom, has become the real locus of big-city criminal justice, but its business is transacted off the record for maximum flexibility.

Fitzgerald scanned Parrish's prep sheet, outlining the state case. Xinos told him glumly about the Hamiltons. "We look beat," he conceded.

"Walter," asked the judge, "what do you want?"

"I don't want to hurt the kid," Parrish said. "I talked to Connie, and we thought one to five."

They talked about Payne's record—his jobs, his family, his old gas-station burglary rap. "Two years' probation," Xinos put in hopefully. "That's nothing." Fitzgerald pondered it all. He had no probation report—there isn't time or manpower enough to do them except in major cases—and no psychological work-up; sentencing in most American courts comes down to a matter of instinct. Fitzgerald's instincts told him one to five was a long enough time for Payne to serve—and a wide enough spread to encourage him to reform and get out early. "Up to five years" he feels, "that's the area of rehabilitation. Beyond five, I think they get saturated." So he finished and made up his mind.

"Will he take it?" the judge asked Xinos.

"I'll go back and see," Xinos replied. He ducked out to the lockup and put the offer to Payne.

"Let's do it," Payne said. "Right now."

A light snow was falling when they brought him back into court grinning slightly, walking his diddybop walk. A bailiff led him to a table below Fitzgerald's high bench. His mother slipped into place beside him. He spread his fingers out on the tabletop and looked at them. The judge led him through the prescribed catechism establishing that he understood what he was doing and that no one had forced him to do it. Payne's "yeses" were barely audible in the cavernous room.

The choice now was his, Fitzgerald told him. He could go to the pen and cooperate and learn a trade and come out on parole in eleven months; or he could "go down there and do nothing at all and sit on your haunches . . . and you will probably be going (back) down there for twenty or thirty years." Payne brushed one hand across his eyes and studied the tabletop. "I'm giving you the first break you probably ever got in your life," the judge said. ". . . The rest of it, Donald, is up to you. Do you understand that?"

"Yes," said Payne.

And then it was over. Fitzgerald called the jurors in and dismissed them. They knew nothing of the events that had buried Donald; they sat there for a moment looking stunned. Xinos slipped back to the jury room to see them before they scattered. "But you were *ahead,*" one told him.

Payne's mother walked out to a pay phone, eyes wet and flashing. "They just pressed Donnie," she insisted, "until he said he did it." Parrish packed up. "An hour, a day—even that's punishment," he said. "One to five?" he snorted. "S_____. That's no sentence for armed robbery." Xinos went home to his apartment in the suburbs. "One to five," he said. "Fantastic. Payne should go to the penitentiary. He's a bad kid, he's better off there. He's dangerous. He'll be back."

And Payne was sulky sore. He shook hands with Xinos and grinned broadly when the deal went down, but when Xinos told him later what the juror had said—you were ahead—he felt cheated. A break? "The best break they could have given me was letting me go." But there was nothing for him to do just then but go brooding back down the tunnel and to jail. "Everybody do something wrong," he told himself. "Maybe my time just caught up with me."

.   .   .

the problems of
liberty and equality

Liberty

Liberty, Abraham Lincoln once said, "has never had a good definition." To Lord Acton, the nineteenth-century English historian, the trouble was that liberty has had too many definitions—two hundred, he suggested. Like *justice* or *virtue* the words *liberty* or *freedom* stand for an abstract concept. Perhaps a usable, if rough, working definition is to say that a person enjoys liberty when he is both legally free and physically able to do or not to do the things as he wills. The capacity to take advantage of one's rights is a crucial element in the definition of liberty. The steelworker in Gary, Indiana, and the publisher of *The New York Times* live under a Constitution that guarantees them "freedom of the press"; yet surely the publisher is able to take advantage of his freedom of the press far more easily and more effectively than the steelworker.

It is easy enough to demonstrate that the rich have greater liberty in this sense than the poor, but liberties in a constitutional democracy do not belong only to the rich. In a democracy all persons are protected by a set of broadly recognized and legally enforced freedoms. The distinctive quality of this freedom is *legal,* because in one way or another the public authorities place the power of official law and its sanctions behind certain specific freedoms. It is in this sense that we speak of *civil liberties* and *civil rights*. These two expressions are used interchangeably in everyday discourse, and for most persons civil liberties and civil rights are virtually identical. In this chapter references to *freedoms, liberties,* and *rights* are intended to serve as synonyms for the commonly used expressions of *civil liberties* and *civil rights.*

One distinction, however, is worth making: a distinction between individual liberties and minority rights. Individual liberties are the constitutional or legal guarantees that allow each person to do or not to do certain things. These liberties, in turn, tend to have either affirmative or passive qualities and purposes. Thus, the freedom to speak is guaranteed by the First Amendment for affirmative, and sometimes even aggressive, purposes. By contrast, the prohibition against unreasonable searches and seizures guaranteed by the Fourth Amendment is an essentially passive liberty: it is intended to protect the individual against the unlawful intrusion of police officers.

Minority rights, which have their primary constitutional or legal foundation in the guarantee of the Fourteenth Amendment that no person is to be denied the "equal protection of the laws," refer to such rights as the right to vote, the right to open housing, or the right to an equal public school education. These rights, paradoxically, are asserted precisely because they have been systematically denied to certain categories of persons; and they have been denied solely because these persons are members of unpopular minority ethnic, racial, or religious groups. In short, who one *is* in group terms, rather than what one does in individual terms, is the central concern in questions of minority rights. The objective, therefore, in the pursuit of a minority right is to achieve equality in the sense of freedom *from* discrimination, and this, as Chapter 1 argued, is one of the principal quests—and greatest dilemmas—of American political culture.

Probably it is best not to make too much of these distinctions. All freedoms, after all, can be exercised only through individual persons. Nevertheless, in a rough and approximate way, it is useful to note that some of the problems of liberty primarily concern individuals acting (or not acting) in their individual capacities and that others primarily concern individuals acting in their capacity as members of minority groups.

The discussion up to this point may give the false impression that the problems of liberty are primarily an abstract matter. Nothing could be further from the truth. Questions of liberty are at the very center of American politics in the twentieth century, for their recognition and enforcement engages the power of government. The Alabama sheriff who prevents qualified blacks from registering or voting violates federal law, and the United States government can prosecute him as a criminal. The city that undertakes a wide-ranging censorship to suppress controversial, though not pornographic, books violates the First Amendment; if those who are suffering from the censorship fight back, the federal courts have the power to overturn the censorship.

The Free Exercise of Religious Beliefs

Only rarely, if ever, is freedom in any form absolute. Even the right to vote, indispensable as it is to the operation of a democratic political system, is not absolute unless one meets the qualifications set by law. The most that can be said is that certain rights—such as freedom of speech and religion—are to have a privileged status, even to the point of significantly limiting majority rule. A few of these conflicts are selectively examined in the pages that follow, and the balance that has so far been struck by the courts and society is indicated.

Religion, one sometimes hears, is not a proper topic for polite discussion. This dislike for the frank exchange of opinions may be born of exaggerated prudence, but it reflects a mature insight—that religious belief is a peculiarly private concern. The

Constitution elevates this insight into legal doctrine. Article VI states that "no religious test shall ever be required as a qualification to any office or public trust under the Constitution." The First Amendment forbids any laws "respecting an establishment of religion, or prohibiting the free exercise thereof."

Few areas of public policy are more contentious than the relationship between religion and the state. It is nonetheless well to keep a sense of perspective: not so long ago in Europe rival religions warred and the fate of heretics was death at a fiery stake. Even colonial America was troubled with religious strife and persecutions. But men gradually and painfully learned that they could live together without a state-supported religion and with freedom of all sects. Indeed, they learned that only in this way could they live together. As the late Father John Courtney Murray once said, the First Amendment is an article of peace, not of faith. Amidst all the disagreements over its interpretation, it is well to note that it *does* settle a number of important questions. Probably the best summary of the consensus is contained in a statement made by the late Justice Black in *Everson* v. *Board of Education:*

> Neither a state nor the Federal Government can set up a church. Neither can pass laws which aid one religion, aid all religions, or prefer one religion over another. Neither can force nor influence a person to go or to remain away from church against his will or force him to profess a belief or disbelief in any religion. No person can be punished for entertaining or professing religious beliefs or disbeliefs, for church attendance or non-attendance. No tax in any amount, large or small, can be levied to support any religious activities or institutions, whatever they may be called, or whatever form they may adopt to teach or practice religion. Neither a state nor the Federal Government can, openly or secretly, participate in the affairs of any religious organizations or groups and vice versa.[1]

All of the judges on the Supreme Court in 1947 agreed with Black's statement; yet they divided 5 to 4 on the specific question that the *Everson* case asked them to answer. Black and the majority ruled that New Jersey could pass a law allowing its local communities to pay the bus fares of pupils attending Catholic parochial schools without breaching what Jefferson called the "wall" separating church and state. The four dissenters argued that the majority opinion "advocating complete and uncompromising separation of Church from State" was "utterly discordant with its conclusions."

The dispute underlying the *Everson* case raised the issue of federal and state financial aid to church-related schools, one of the most controversial issues in modern American politics. It is clear that government may not directly subsidize the teaching of sectarian religion. But does the establishment clause of the First Amendment prohibit public support for the essentially nonreligious functions of parochial schools and church-affiliated colleges? Is, for instance, financial aid for the teaching of languages or the physical sciences unconstitutional? The Elementary and Secondary Education Act of 1965, which is a continuing federal program, provides various aids of this kind to public and private (church-affiliated) schools, and there have been numerous challenges to its constitutionality in federal and state courts. To date, these

---

[1] 330 U.S. 1, 15–16 (1947).

have been unsuccessful, but the Supreme Court has taken steps that may lead to a constitutional resolution of the major issues. In the case of *Flast* v. *Cohen* it ruled that federal taxpayers may sue to enjoin the administration of federal programs providing aid to sectarian schools; the basic controversy in this case, which challenges many features of the Elementary and Secondary Education Act, will first be adjudicated in the lower federal courts.[2] Although the final constitutional outcome remains uncertain, a decision in another establishment-clause case offers strong encouragement to the defenders of the federal legislation. In the case of *Board of Education* v. *Allen,* which tested the constitutionality of a New York law providing nonreligious textbooks to pupils attending sectarian schools, the Supreme Court ruled 6 to 3 that this assistance was as constitutional as the bus transportation aid approved in the *Everson* case.[3] An important defeat for the aid for parochial school advocates is discussed in the case study that precedes Chapter 3. In *Di Censo* v. *Robinson* (1971), the Court struck down two state statutes that give financial aid to secular teachers in parochial schools. The states, according to an eight-man majority, were involved in "excessive entanglement between government and religion."

Those who argue that assistance to sectarian schools is unconstitutional contend that it amounts to an "establishment of religion." They are unimpressed by the alleged distinction between a parochial school's religious and secular programs. They insist that, even where public assistance is limited to programs without a religious content, it very tangibly, if indirectly, provides a subsidy to the religious denomination. It does so, the argument goes, by freeing financial resources that would otherwise be expended on the more secular programs and allowing them to be channeled into the school's overtly religious functions, thereby aiding the overall sectarian enterprise of the denomination.

Those who benefit from such aid and those who support it as a wise public policy deny that the establishment clause prohibits public aid to what they describe as the "secular" purposes of these educational institutions. They contend that the kind of aid furnished by the Elementary and Secondary Education Act falls far short of establishing any religion in the United States, and they further contend that church-affiliated schools fulfill an educational function that is useful to the public welfare.

Moreover, when non-Catholics and unbelievers claim that they have a constitutional "right" not to support these schools, even for limited purposes, Catholics counter that the free exercise of religion clause of the very same First Amendment gives them a constitutional "right" to such aid. American law, they point out, recognizes the right of all parents to educate their children in church-related schools, so long as these schools conform to certain general state-education standards. In a period of rising educational costs, which has led to a growing federal subsidization of state education programs, the failure to aid parochial schools will slowly but surely destroy them. The ultimate consequence would mean, according to the National Catholic Welfare Conference, "that those who, in conscience, desired education in a church-related school would be forced to participate in a [secular public school] education in unacceptable orthodoxies." This, the National Catholic Welfare Con-

[2] 392 U.S. 83 (1968).
[3] 392 U.S. 236 (1968).

ference concludes, would as a matter of practicality be "a *de facto* denial of free exercise of religion." [4]

Whichever position one agrees with, the dispute over aid to church-related schools shows how easily constitutional "rights" may conflict. Not only are rights—in reality, values—in conflict; the school aid dispute also reveals a tension between the religion clauses of the First Amendment. The establishment clause of the First Amendment protects a passive liberty, freedom *from* religion. It assures Americans that they are free from any public compulsion to support religious creeds. But the free exercise clause guarantees a more positive kind of liberty, freedom *for* religion. It grants to Americans the affirmative liberty to practice freely their religious faith and to proselytize on its behalf.

In theory both the establishment and the free exercise clauses appear to be entirely compatible, but in practice they are often in conflict. Consider, for example, the Sunday-closing laws, the so-called "blue laws," which in a number of states forbid many commercial activities to operate on Sundays. Although these laws were originally enacted to enforce the Christian Sabbath, the Supreme Court has taken the position that they have long since shed their religious motivation. Instead, the Court has ruled that the purpose of these laws is to assure a common day of rest and relaxation, and it has therefore found that the laws do not constitute an establishment of religion.

For many merchants the ruling presents no real hardship, but what about the Orthodox Jews whose religion decrees Saturday as their Sabbath? If they follow the dictates of their conscience, they must close their shops on Saturdays; and if they comply with the law, they must also remain closed on Sunday. As a consequence they lose a day of business and their Orthodox customers, who may have dietary needs, are unable to buy food for two consecutive days. It is not surprising, then, that the Sunday-closing laws have been challenged on the ground that they abridge the freedom of Orthodox Jews to exercise their religion. In *Braunfeld* v. *Brown,* a 6 to 3 decision, the Supreme Court ruled that the closing laws do not violate the religious freedom of Orthodox Jews.[5] Some of the Justices noted that to exempt Orthodox Jews and other Sabbatarians from Sunday closing laws in order to further their free exercise of religion would raise establishment problems from another direction. Would, then, an exemption put Sabbatarians in a favored position in relation to non-Jewish storekeepers who might also desire to remain open on Sundays? [6]

Religious believers in America cannot claim a constitutional right to be exempt from nondiscriminatory criminal codes and public regulations. Mormons cannot

---

[4] Legal Department, National Catholic Welfare Conference, *The Constitutionality of the Inclusion of Church-Related Schools in Federal Aid to Education* (1961), pp. 55–56.

[5] 366 U.S. 599 (1961).

[6] Since these Court decisions were announced, a growing list of states have voluntarily exempted certain categories of stores operated by religious Sabbatarians from Sunday closing. It is possible to view these exemptions as establishing a state preference for Sabbatarian religions. A perhaps wiser, if not doctrinally tidy, view is that such an exemption policy is not really "establishment," because it reflects the considered judgment of the state political system that the Sabbatarians' free exercise claim must take precedence. Nevertheless, the tension between the two religious liberties persists.

practice polygamy, and Christian Scientists may not disregard health quarantines, even though their religious beliefs would have it otherwise. Belief, in short, is absolutely free; its exercise is not. In the reality of everyday life, of course, it is virtually impossible to separate belief and practice. Almost all meaningful religious belief requires an overt behavior of some kind—the conduct of ceremonies, the printing of tracts, or the operation of church schools. The true believer wants to express his belief through his practices, and often he will resent public laws that interfere with his religious scruples. The political majority, although it is not constitutionally compelled to do so, may grant exemptions. Thus, in many states the children of Christian Scientists may be excused from physical examinations in school, and Orthodox Jews may be allowed to open their shops on Sunday. Similarly, the Supreme Court has ruled that the states may not compel Jehovah's Witness schoolchildren to salute the flag, which in their minds constitutes a blasphemous worship of a graven image.[7] In America there is extraordinary religious freedom for a truly amazing variety of sects, creeds, and religious practices. Tensions between conflicting religious and political claims are, we have seen, inevitable. One man's right is often another man's wrong, and in a vast pluralistic society there are many competing rights and wrongs. Yet, paradoxically, the very fact that so many religious claims and counterclaims joust for acceptance is itself a testimonial to the high status that all religions enjoy. For a variety of reasons, practical and political no less than constitutional, the American political system has made religious freedom the rule and restraint the exception.

Civil Rights: The Agonizing Struggle for True Equality

Among the many issues confronting the United States none is more troublesome than that of the black man's place in American society. Whites usually speak of a "Negro problem"; blacks like the writer James Baldwin say with considerable justice that it is a "white problem." Probably it is most accurate to refer to it simply, in former President Johnson's phrase, as "an American problem." In part the problem is subjective, existing in the minds of blacks and whites alike. The black American is handicapped by the discrimination, obvious and subtle, that is a consequence of white racial prejudice.

In large part, too, the problem has an objective reality of its own. By every index of social and economic well-being the black American lags far behind his white fellow countrymen. The differentials are appalling. Black babies are nearly twice as likely as white babies to die; when they grow into childhood they are much more likely than white children to attend inferior schools in squalid black ghettos. Black

---

[7] The right of Jehovah's Witnesses to be exempted from compulsory flag-saluting ceremonies won constitutional recognition in *Barnette* v. *West Virginia Board of Education,* 319 U.S. 624 (1943). Technically, the *Barnette* ruling recognized a political (rather than a religious) right to refuse to salute the flag; in its broad context, however, the exemption of Witnesses from flag-saluting requirements takes its place among the special exemptions that members of small minority sects have won.

Figure 13.1. The black unemployment rate in 1970 was about 8 per cent—much higher than the white rate

Source: Black Americans: A Chartbook, U. S. Department of Labor, Bureau of Labor Statistics, Bulletin 1699 (Washington, D. C.: U. S. Government Printing Office, 1971), pp. 20–21.

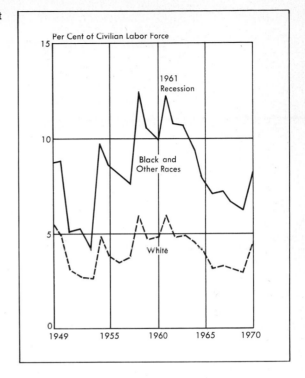

families, which tend to be larger than white families, have only slightly less than half the income of white families. Black men earn salaries that are 40 per cent less than the salaries earned by white workers, and their employment is concentrated in low-skilled jobs that are threatened by automation.

Table 13.1 and Figure 13.1 show the differences in the black and white unemployment rate. In 1970, 8 per cent of the black labor force were out of work and looking for a job. There has been a 2 to 1 ratio of black-to-white unemployment over the last fifteen years. Stated differently, in 1970 blacks made up 11 per cent of the civilian labor force, or about their same share of the total population. Yet their unemployment was nearly double their share in the labor force. It is impossible to assess how much black unemployment is due to racial discrimination by employers.

It is also significant to note that the ratio of black to white family income rose in the late 1960's to the highest on record. Yet the level of black income was still only three fifths of the white. Throughout the nation's history the average (median) income of black families has always been lower than that of white families. Part of this difference is explained by lower educational and occupational attainments. Another part, however, is probably due to the effects of racial discrimination. The Moynihan report documented another problem confronting the blacks: a serious deterioration in the structure of the black family.[8]

The black man's objective plight contributes to his subjective difficulties because

---

[8] Lee Rainwater and William L. Yancey, *The Moynihan Report and the Politics of Controversy* (Cambridge: M.I.T. Press, 1967), pp. 38–124.

Table 13.1 *Unemployment rates by race, 1949–1970* *

Year	Black and other races †	White	Ratio: Black and other races to white
1949	8.9	5.6	1.6
1950	9.0	4.9	1.8
1951	5.3	3.1	1.7
1952	5.4	2.8	1.9
1953	4.5	2.7	1.7
1954	9.9	5.0	2.0
1955	8.7	3.9	2.2
1956	8.3	3.6	2.3
1957	7.9	3.8	2.1
1958	12.6	6.1	2.1
1959	10.7	4.8	2.2
1960	10.2	4.9	2.1
1961	12.4	6.0	2.1
1962	10.9	4.9	2.2
1963	10.8	5.0	2.2
1964	9.6	4.6	2.1
1965	8.1	4.1	2.0
1966	7.3	3.3	2.2
1967	7.4	3.4	2.2
1968	6.7	3.2	2.1
1969	6.4	3.1	2.1
1970	8.2	4.5	1.8

Source: *Black Americans: A Chartbook,* U.S. Department of Labor, Bureau of Labor Statistics, Bulletin 1699 (Washington, D.C.: U.S. Government Printing Office, 1971), pp. 20–21.

* The unemployment rate is the per cent unemployed in the civilian labor force.

† Although these percentages include other racial minorities, blacks comprise an overwhelming majority of the nation's nonwhite population.

his low socioeconomic status makes him appear "undesirable" in terms of the middle-class standards of the more affluent white majority. From another direction, the subjective white prejudice makes it difficult for the black man to escape from a ghetto that is psychological as well as social and economic.

Legally, the black man's status has improved in recent years. He has gained legal support for many of his civil rights claims, winning in effect the right to do those things that white citizens do. Since the Supreme Court's 1954 decision on school segregation, blacks have been able to claim a constitutional right not to be discriminated against in the use of educational facilities. Since 1964 they have been free under the Civil Rights Act to patronize all business and recreational establishments open to the general public, and they have been protected against discriminatory

Table 13.2 *Voting registration figures by race—eleven southern states*

| | Spring, 1968 | | | | Nov. 1964 | |
	White registered	Black registered	% of voting-age whites registered	% of voting-age blacks registered	Black registered	% of voting-age blacks registered
Alabama	1,212,317	248,432	89.6	51.6	111,000	23.0
Arkansas	616,000	121,000	72.4	62.8	105,000	54.4
Florida	2,131,105	299,033	81.4	63.6	300,000	63.7
Georgia	1,443,730	322,496	80.3	52.6	270,000	44.0
Louisiana	1,200,517	303,148	93.1	58.9	164,700	32.0
Mississippi	589,066	181,233	91.5	59.8	28,500	6.7
North Carolina	1,602,980	277,404	83.0	51.3	258,000	46.8
South Carolina	731,096	190,017	81.7	51.2	144,000	38.8
Tennessee	1,434,000	225,000	80.6	71.7	218,000	69.4
Texas	2,600,000	400,000	53.3	61.6	375,000	57.7
Virginia	1,140,000	243,000	63.4	55.6	200,000	45.7
Regional						
Total	14,750,811	2,810,763	76.5	57.2	2,174,200	43.3

Source: Congressional Quarterly, May 17, 1968, p. 1136.

practices in interstate commerce. A series of voting laws, the last and most stringent one passed in 1965, are making it possible for a growing number of southern blacks to enjoy in practice the right to vote that they have enjoyed in theory ever since the adoption of the Fifteenth Amendment in 1870. Table 13.2 provides dramatic evidence of this: more than 55 per cent of the voting-age black population is now registered to vote in the South; in Deep South Mississippi the figure is almost 60 per cent compared to a meager 6.7 per cent in 1964. Many states and cities, in addition, have their own civil rights laws that are intended to guarantee equal employment opportunities and equal access to residential housing.

Despite these advances, the black man remains a frustratingly long distance away from true equality of opportunity, and the desperate cry for "black power" and the wave of destructive summer rioting in the urban slums are two jarring measures of the depth of this frustration. Approximately only 15 per cent of the black school-children actually attend the same schools as white children in the eleven states of the former Confederacy. In Alabama, Louisiana, and Mississippi the rate of integration is closer to 3 per cent. The United States Department of Health, Education and Welfare, which administers the school desegregation provisions of the Civil Rights Act of 1964, has made some progress in its campaign to impose desegregation guidelines on southern school systems. But it has encountered strong, if subtle, resistance in the form of "freedom-of-choice" plans. These recognize the theoretical right of every child, whether black or white, to choose through his parents the school he wishes to attend. In practice the local school authorities generally have discretion to decide how many black youngsters a white-dominated school can accommodate. This, naturally, places the burden of initiating desegregation transfers upon black parents, who often must contend with economic and other pressures that discourage them from trying to enroll their children in "white" schools.

Statistics released by the Department of Health, Education and Welfare show that the number of black pupils attending white public schools in the South doubled from the fall of 1968 to the fall of 1970. More than one out of every three black pupils in the South in 1970 attended a school in which the majority of students were white. This is a sharp increase over the fewer than one in every five who attended white schools two years earlier. The figure in Table 13.3, however, show very little comparable change outside the South. School desegregation is more than a "numbers game." Unless there is a strong commitment to a uniform effort throughout the country, thousands of black children will have to endure unequal, and inferior, educations. The strong language used by the Court in ordering desegregation "at once" in *Alexander* v. *Board of Education* (1970) [9] suggests the frustration of the 1954 *Brown* v. *Board of Education* goal of equal educational opportunity.

The snail-like pace of school desegregation has forced the federal courts to come to grips with the emotionally and politically explosive issue of whether school-children should be bussed outside their neighborhood to advance integration. A few federal judges have ordered bussing when communities have failed to eliminate

[9] 396 U.S. 19.

Table 13.3　*Per cent of black pupils attending* *

Geographical area	0–49.9% minority schools	80–100% minority schools †	100% minority schools
Continental U.S.			
1968	23.4	68.0	39.7
1970 est.	32.8	50.2	16.0
32 North and West (1)			
1968	27.6	57.4	12.3
1970 est.	27.7	57.4	11.9
11 South (2)			
1968	18.4	78.8	68.0
1970 est.	38.1	41.7	18.4
6 Border and D.C. (3)			
1968	28.4	63.8	25.2
1970 est.	29.6	60.3	22.0

Source: Congressional Quarterly Weekly Report, January 22, 1971, p. 199.

(1) Alaska, Ariz., Calif., Colo., Conn., Idaho, Ill., Ind., Iowa, Kan., Maine, Mass., Mich., Minn., Mont., Neb., Nev., N.H., N.J., N.M., N.Y., N.D., Ohio, Oreg., Pa., R.I., S.D., Utah, Vt., Wash., Wis., Wyo.

(2) Ala., Ark., Fla., Ga., La., Miss., N.C., S.C., Tenn., Tex., Va.

(3) Del., D.C., Ky., Md., Mo., Okla., W. Va.

* Districts with fewer than 300 pupils are not included in the survey. The 1970 figures are estimates based on the latest available data and are subject to variation upon final computation.

† Percentage figure includes percentage shown in 100 per cent minority schools.

predominantly black schools. When a northern federal judge ordered school bussing in Pontiac, Michigan, violence and boycotts were touched off. The objective of the bussing order was to disperse Pontiac's black students throughout the city so that no school would be more than 40 per cent black. This was one of the first bussing orders in the North, and it was greeted by a bitter reaction from parents. School buses were dynamited, and racial incidents in schools sharply increased.

The Pontiac School Board claimed that school desegregation was a result of of neighborhood patterns and not of planned discriminatory actions by school officials. The federal judge disagreed, stating that neighborhood schools were intentionally segregated, which violated the Equal Protection Clause of the Fourteenth Amendment. The Supreme Court declined to review the case. The significance of the Court's action is twofold, one legal and the other intensely emotional: there will probably be more federal bussing orders in the North, met by violence and protest by white parents.[10]

[10] "The Agony of Busing Moves North," *Time,* November 15, 1971, pp. 57–64.

"Hang on, kids—we're decelerating."

Figure 13.2.

Source: The New Republic, November 20, 1971, p. 8.

In the northern states integrationists face equally severe obstacles. Residential segregation is so severe that school segregation is actually increasing. It may, in fact, soon exceed that of the South, which, ironically, is more vulnerable to the Civil Rights Act than the North. The Act does not authorize the federal government to promote integration where the school segregation is a result of residential patterns, and most northern Congressmen have stoutly opposed such authorization. Moreover, even the Supreme Court's condemnation of freedom-of-choice plans has so far been restricted to the border and southern states that once officially sanctioned racially segregated school systems. Data collected by the Department of Labor—as seen in Table 13.4—indicate that residential segregation has been increasing in the mid-

1960's. This rather surprising conclusion is based on a special census conducted in fifteen cities. No data are yet available to indicate whether the tendency toward increased segregation has been affected by the new Open Housing Laws.

The real core of the problem is the fact that most black Americans are the victims of a vicious cycle, encircled by their poverty, their lack of education, and the hindering prejudices of many whites. Under these circumstances the struggle for racial equality is a struggle to expand the scope and content of a whole range of civil rights and minority group claims. If the black is to be free from his social, economic, and psychological fetters, his "rights," then, must include much more than the right to vote or the right not to be discriminated against in the use of public facilities. As the late Whitney M. Young of the National Urban League once stated:

The American Negro has been out of the mainstream for more than three centuries and a special effort must be made to bring him into the central action of our society. The effects of more than three centuries of oppression cannot be obliterated by doing business as usual. In today's complex, technological society, a sound mind, a strong back, and a will to succeed are no longer sufficient to break the bonds of deprivation as was the case with minority groups in the past.[11]

To break these bonds, Young called for a domestic Marshall Plan to help close the economic, social, and educational gap separating black citizens from their fellow Americans. A group of civil rights leaders and prominent citizens have proposed a detailed ten-year "Freedom Budget" that would commit the federal government to a massive program for the benefit of poor blacks and whites. The Freedom Budget, whose major aims are the abolition of poverty, a guarantee of full employment and of incomes for those unable to work, and the establishment of full educational opportunities and improved housing for all Americans, would require an increased federal welfare outlay of $355 billion over a ten-year period.[12] Its supporters argue that this could be financed through revenue generated by the nation's economic growth. President Johnson's National Advisory Commission on Civil Disorders spoke in similar terms, calling for a massive public attack against the social and economic roots of the black man's condition.

Black Congressmen have been more unified, and vocal, in their protests about racism and inequality. Thirteen black members of the House of Representatives—called the Black Caucus—told President Nixon in a historic meeting that he must commit himself unequivocally to the goal of equality for all Americans. The President was presented with sixty demands for action to aid 25 million blacks. The caucus members explained that they served as Congressmen-at-large, representing all black Americans in believing that the Nixon Administration, by word and deed, was retreating from Nixon's commitment to equality. Caucus chairman Charles C. Diggs, Democrat from Michigan, commented that black "people are no longer asking for equality as a rhetorical promise. They are demanding . . . the only kind of equality that ultimately has any real meaning—the equality of results." Another member of

11 *To Be Equal* (New York: McGraw-Hill, 1964), p. 27.
12 *A Freedom Budget for All Americans* (New York: Randolph Institute, 1966).

Table 13.4 *Residential segregation in the United States*

(percentage of all blacks in selected cities living in census tracts grouped according to proportion black in 1960 and 1964–1966 *)

City and state	Year	All census tracts	75 or more	50 to 74	25 to 49	Less than 25
		Percentage of all blacks in city				
Cleveland, Ohio	1960	100	72	16	8	4
	1965	100	80	12	4	4
Memphis, Tenn.	1960	100	65	26	5	4
	1967	100	78	14	4	4
Phoenix, Ariz.	1960	100	19	36	24	21
	1965	100	18	23	42	17
Buffalo, N.Y.	1960	100	35	47	6	12
	1966	100	69	10	13	8
Louisville, Ky.	1960	100	57	13	17	13
	1964	100	67	13	10	10
New Haven, Conn.	1960	100	0	33	19	48
	1967	100	16	19	27	38
Rochester, N.Y.	1960	100	8	43	17	32
	1964	100	16	45	24	15
Sacramento, Calif.	1960	100	9	0	14	77
	1964	100	8	14	28	50
Des Moines, Iowa	1960	100	0	28	31	41
	1966	100	0	42	19	39
Providence, R.I.	1960	100	0	23	2	75
	1965	100	0	16	46	38
Shreveport, La.	1960	100	79	10	7	4
	1966	100	90	0	6	4
Evansville, Ind.	1960	100	34	27	9	30
	1966	100	59	14	0	27
Little Rock, Ark.	1960	100	33	33	19	15
	1964	100	41	18	22	19
Raleigh, N.C.	1960	100	86	0	7	7
	1966	100	88	4	2	6
Trenton, N.J.	1960	100	26	9	48	17
	1968	100	24	55	13	8

Source: Black Americans: A Chartbook, prepared by U.S. Department of Labor (Washington, D.C.: U.S. Government Printing Office, 1971).

* Selected cities of 100,000 or more in which a special census was taken in any of the years 1964–1968. Ranked according to total population at latest census.

the caucus was not as moderate in his language when he told the President "the black community has not been blackjacked into silence or lulled into apathy . . . and that he might, therefore, be sitting on a powder keg." [13]

Speaking in a strictly legal sense, the demands for public policies aimed at the social and economic manifestations of racial discrimination do not lend themselves to classification as *civil rights* claims as that term has been traditionally used. These demands, however, are clearly related to the general furor over civil or minority rights and to the long pattern of white discrimination against blacks. Legally, many of the demands are not judicially enforceable rights. But to those blacks making the claims they are simply their due—their right based on centuries of past mistreatment and on their inalienable right to share in the American dream. Indeed, in some situations the courts and the legislatures have agreed that some of the claims, such as those involved in the dispute over open housing discussed later, do involve legally enforceable civil rights. Congress, to take a related illustration, in passing the public accommodations section of the Civil Rights Act of 1964, created a new, legally enforceable right—the right to be free from discriminatory treatment in the use of hotels, restaurants, and other public facilities. In the case of the demands for a basic overhaul of the black man's social and economic status, yet another new public policy, justified as necessary to the implementation of true equality of opportunity and the more formal civil rights, may someday emerge as a consequence of executive and legislative policy decisions.

Some black leaders and their organizations have denied the relevancy of integration and militantly demanded recognition of an independent "black power." Organizations such as the Congress of Racial Equality (CORE) and the paramilitary Black Panther party have concluded that American society is incurably permeated with white racism, and they have identified themselves with an extreme black nationalist position. The small movement clustered around the concepts of black power and black nationalism is often condemned in white circles for preaching a form of black racism and for applauding the riots in the urban slums. Yet the angry cries of the black power advocates serve as vivid testimonials to the frustration and despair of America's largest minority group.

In addition to calling for a massive federal social welfare program to close the gap between the black minority and the white majority, the more conventional civil rights organizations, who still believe in integration, have pressed claims for a whole range of governmentally enforced rights. The black man, they say, must be given the right to join craft labor unions, many of which now exclude black workers, if he is to gain access to the well-paying skilled jobs that these unions control. He must be given the right to purchase or rent any house or apartment he can afford, without being restricted to ghettos because of the prejudice of the white man. He must be given the right to educate his children in integrated schools because segregated schools, whether segregated by deliberate public policy or by the accident of neighbor-

---

[13] "Black Caucus: 60 Recommendations for the President," *Congressional Quarterly*, April 2, 1971, p. 783.

hood, are inferior schools that cripple the potential development of black youngsters.

Whenever such integration claims are made, they invariably conflict with white interests and counterclaims. Many of these claims directly threaten what many whites claim to be *their* rights. The members of specialized craft unions in the building construction industry fear that black members can be admitted only at the cost of their hard-earned job security. Parents whose children now attend predominantly white schools fear that full-scale, as opposed to token, integration will result in a poorer education for their own children. The civil rights organizations, however, attack de facto school segregation—segregation that is the consequence of residential patterns —as segregation nonetheless. Not only, they argue, are black schools inferior in their teachers and facilities, but even if these are equalized, they will still be inferior because segregated education is inherently an inferior education.

The dispute over segregated schooling is a major urban issue, for blacks comprise a large and growing percentage of the population in the largest cities. Although only approximately 11 per cent of the national population is black, Washington, D.C., has a black population of 66 per cent. This is the most extreme case, but it indicates the tread. Chicago has a black population of 28 per cent, Detroit of 34 per cent, and New York of 18 per cent. Aside from the depressed rural areas, as in Appalachia, most of the nation's inferior schools are located in the large urban centers, and these are becoming predominantly black. The American public school problem, in other words, is largely an urban problem that concerns the black American.

A number of solutions are proposed. Some civil rights leaders, convinced that true and complete school integration is years away and concerned with the damaging impact of inferior ghetto schools upon the present generation of black youngsters, demand immediate steps to upgrade the quality of these schools. They also demand community representation in their operation, a claim that is reiterated in an ultra-militant form by those individuals and groups coalesced around the "black power" slogan. Arguing that integration is irrelevant and that it leads to a degrading denial of a prized black identity, the militants insist that the ghetto schools be generously financed and turned over to black representatives selected in their own local communities. These separatist demands, no less than the integrationist ones, involve minority claims upon other forces and interests in the political system.

The more conventional civil rights leaders and their white allies, although not excluding efforts to improve the ghetto schools immediately, still perceive integration as their primary and most meaningful objective. (Surveys among American blacks reveal that a vast majority desire an integrated society.) One of their integrationist proposals requires the bussing of black children into predominantly white neighborhoods and white children into black areas. Another similar proposal calls for the pairing of black and white schools that are relatively near to each other; some students from each school would then be transferred to the previously "black" or "white" school. Other proposals look to the establishment of educational parks to which children from diverse neighborhoods would be brought to receive their education in elementary and secondary school complexes geared to handling a variety of diverse individual needs. Some white parents endorse these plans, but many react the way that residents of a New York City suburb reacted to a low-income housing project planned for their neighborhood.

The caption in *The New York Times* read, "To Be Black *and* Poor Is Not to Be Wanted." The article dealt with the sharp protest of white, liberal, middle-class residents in Forest Hills, Queens, to a low-income housing project about to be built in their neighborhood. The irony of the situation was that a decade ago these same citizens were horrified by TV newsclips of southern racism against black grade-school children. Stones and insults aimed at children had filled the air. Now rocks were being thrown through windows of construction trailers in opposition to a black housing project. The head of the Forest Hills Resident's Association said that "they're [the federal government] transplanting a malignant tumor to a healthy viable community." Residents complained that an infusion of ghetto people would bring drugs, crime, and overcrowded schools. The intensity of the protest was seen when homeowners vowed to be in front of bulldozers to block construction.

Federal guidelines for the 840-unit low-income housing stipulate that it is to be "located so as to provide housing opportunities for minority groups outside areas of minority concentration." In plain language this means poor blacks moving into white middle-class neighborhoods. Protest and lobbying activity against the project may have been successful. George Romney, Secretary of Housing and Urban Development, has decided to review his decision to locate the project in Forest Hills. The fury of the white population may give Washington pause in its resolve to enforce its own rules.[14]

Conflicts over de facto segregation disturb almost every urban center in the North. Neither side has yet won a clear-cut legal victory. The courts generally appear to be taking the compromise position that neither de facto segregation in itself nor attempts to overcome it by shifting students are unconstitutional.[15] This legal standoff, if it continues, leaves both sides free to push their conflicting claims in the political arena—each side claiming that the objectives of the other threaten its rights. Because the issue of de facto segregation usually focuses on only a few specific schools in a large school system, it is typically a dispute between organized minorities with the majority of whites (and many blacks, too), who are outside of a particular community, essentially uninvolved. The disputes over the control and quality of the ghetto schools and over de facto segregation, the conflict over the racial practices of certain labor unions, or the conflicts over the demands of civil rights groups that

---

[14] *The New York Times,* November 28, 1971, Sect. 10, p. 4.

[15] However, the Federal District Court for the District of Columbia has ruled that racial imbalance, regardless of its cause, is unconstitutional under the Fourteenth Amendment and that school authorities must combat this by promoting as much integration as possible and, concurrently, by improving the quality of the predominantly Negro schools. *Hobson* v. *Hansen,* 269 F. Supp. 401 (1967). In 1968, in a case initiated by the Department of Justice, a Federal District Court has ruled that a suburban school district in Chicago, whose facilities and student bodies are de facto segregated, is in violation of the Equal Protection Clause of the Fourteenth Amendment. *United States* v. *School District 151,* 37 LW 2055 (1968).

certain employers give blacks a preference over whites in hiring (to compensate for years of antiblack hiring policies) are like many conflicts between competing claims of liberties and rights: they engage only active minorities of citizens.

The struggle over open housing, as with so many conflicts in the political system, has been by a relatively small number of groups and persons, and the political leadership of the nation—Congressmen, judges, and the President—have, to a degree, been able to lead public opinion. As a consequence, open housing, at least as an official national policy, has come to America. During the late sixties Congress came under strong pressure to enact legislation submitted by President Johnson that would outlaw racial discrimination in the sale and rental of approximately 80 per cent of the nation's housing. It finally did so in voting the Civil Rights Act of 1968, an event spurred by the national revulsion attending the assassination of the Reverend Dr. Martin Luther King, Jr., a Nobel peace prize recipient and America's most admired black civil rights leader. Federal judicial support for the new open housing policy may also prove to be a significant factor in the campaign to make open housing a reality. The Supreme Court has long demonstrated a concern with residential discrimination, and as far back as the case of *Shelley* v. *Kraemer* (1948) ruled that judicial enforcement of racial covenants, which were intended to forbid the sale of certain tracts of land to persons from minority groups, was "state action" in violation of the Fourteenth Amendment.[16] Nearly twenty years later, in *Reitman* v. *Mulkey,* it nullified the California constitutional amendment forbidding the enactment of open housing legislation for the same reason.[17] And shortly after Congress enacted its open housing law, the Court made another dramatic pronouncement in the case of Joseph Lee Jones, a black man excluded from the Paddock Woods development in suburban St. Louis. It declared in *Jones* v. *Mayer* that an almost-forgotten Reconstruction law, which was intended to implement the Thirteenth Amendment by guaranteeing every citizen the right to inherit, purchase, lease, sell, hold, and convey real and personal property, prohibited racial discrimination in all sales and rentals of property.[18] Although this ruling actually has a broader scope than the Civil Rights Act of 1968—because it prohibits *all* housing discrimination—it can only be implemented through expensive and time-consuming legal suits. The congressional law is therefore still likely to be the primary instrument for effecting open housing, but the *Jones* v. *Mayer* decision assures that administrative efforts to end housing discrimination will receive valuable cooperation from the federal courts.[19]

A concerted national effort to enable the black American to have social and economic opportunities fully equal to those of the white man is, of course, an infinitely

[16] 334 U.S. 1.

[17] 387 U.S. 369 (1967).

[18] 392 U.S. 409 (1968).

[19] As has been the case with state and local open housing laws, the new federal policies may have only a limited effect. Relatively few blacks can afford houses in expensive neighborhoods and suburban developments. Moreover, legislative and judicial decrees can often be ignored and subtly resisted, thereby minimizing their impact on those who oppose them. A further factor is that Congress has not yet appropriated sufficient funds to administer effectively the 1968 Civil Rights Act.

formidable hurdle. It is, for example, very much to be doubted if the proposals contained in the report of the National Advisory Commission on Civil Disorders, which might help to bridge the enormous gap between the new constitutional or legal equality of the black American and his day-to-day inequality, can command majority support and, what is most relevant, support in Congress. The recommendations proposing that the federal government create two million new jobs, train the hard-core unemployed, guarantee a minimum income for all Americans through a scheme of family allowances, and construct or improve six million dwellings for persons of low income will also, if implemented, cost billions of tax dollars.[20] As a consequence, and particularly for the duration of the war in Vietnam, the recommendations face severe political resistance in Congress.

Whatever their ultimate fate, President Johnson's establishment of the Commission following the racially "hot" summer of 1967 reflects a preliminary response to the urban riots and the angry minority group demands that they physically symbolize. The President, moreover, assured the Commission's significance by appointing to it such prominent figures as then Governor Otto Kerner of Illinois (the Chairman), Mayor John V. Lindsay of New York (the Vice-Chairman), Senators Edward W. Brooke of Massachusetts and Fred R. Harris of Oklahoma, Representative William M. McCulloch of Ohio, Roy Wilkins (National Director of the National Association for the Advancement of Colored People), I. W. Abel (President of the United Steelworkers of America), and Charles B. Thornton (the president of Litton Industries). The bold proposals made in the report represent an even more explicit response, and in turn they are almost certain to stimulate continuing pressures from the civil rights organizations and from militants in the urban ghettos. It is at least conceivable that if the urban racial unrest continues (and there is every indication it will), the Congress, the President, and the majority of American whites will come to accept the desirability of paying the price and essentially following the Advisory Commission's prescriptions. The alternative—a policy of ignoring the social and economic causes of the urban unrest and of using military forces and harsh repressive measures to attempt to still it—could well lead to persistent rebellions and guerrilla warfare in the nation's cities. The United States, as the Commission feared, very likely does face the danger of becoming frozen into "two societies, one black, one white—separate and unequal." Little has changed since the 1968 Report. President Nixon has not demonstrated any political skill—or legislative program—that would solve America's racial dilemma. He has had a great deal of difficulty redeeming his campaign pledge "to bring the nation together." Indeed, the recommendations and warnings of the 1968 *Report of the National Advisory Commission on Civil Disorders* seem to have been largely ignored.

The black American will not be able to enjoy all the rights he now seeks, including full equality with the white man, until the white majority makes his cause its cause—either out of moral conviction or out of fear of the consequences of worsening

---

[20] *Report of the National Advisory Commission on Civil Disorders* (New York: Bantam, 1968).

civil disorders, or, most likely, because of both. Ultimately, on matters of minority rights and needs, as on matters of individual liberties generally, the national majority in its view of what is moral and of what should be the great public objectives of the society determines their real-life content. The majority may, of course, willingly limit itself by supporting a constitutional policy that guarantees many minority rights and individual liberties; it does this, for example, in the First Amendment area of speech and religion. There often exists, in other words, a public policy that the majority supports (or, at least, tolerates) in favor of certain claims of individual liberties and minority rights. Unfortunately, many of the black demands for economic betterment, for open housing, and in general for those public steps essential to equal opportunity lack majority support, and they often arouse strong resistance from white interests. The day of true equality of opportunity seems distant, and the present situation is one filled with dangers for the American democracy. The most serious is that the frustration of low-income blacks, so dramatically expressed in the urban riots, may have had the ironic "backlash" consequence of hardening white prejudices—thereby adding fresh fuel to the blacks' frustration.

In a broad sense Judge Learned Hand was correct: liberty does lie in the hearts of men and women; it does depend on what rights they value most. And this is true on the issues of minority rights and racial equality, just as it is on so many public issues. There are profound differences in the values and interests that men and women have in their hearts and minds, and the resulting tensions and conflicts promise to remain a central feature of American politics for years to come. Insuring the civil rights of blacks and other minority groups, then, is an agonizing problem for our society. The problems confined to the judicial system are no less severe.

the problems of justice

Injustice and the Law in America

The people who reap the bitter fruit of injustice are often those who are least able to protect their rights. For these minorities the American dream is often a nightmare. A few of the cruel ironies of our democracy are discussed in reference to the judicial system, the invasion of privacy, and equal employment opportunities.

The Poor and the Law: Civil Justice

Justice plays a major role in all countries. In America "equal protection of the laws" is a fundamental tenet of our judicial system. Other ideals of justice are that every man is "allowed his day in court," and that a defendant is presumed "innocent until proven guilty." Yet these ideals are flawed if the poor are treated less fairly than the middle class and the rich. In practice, as we shall see, the "equality before the law" guaranteed by the Fourteenth Amendment resembles the equality proclaimed in George Orwell's *Animal Farm:* "All men are equal, but some are more equal than others." The least equal in American justice are the black, the poor, and the ignorant. Rather than helping the poor surmount their poverty, writes Federal Judge J. Skelly Wright, "the law has all too frequently served to perpetuate and even exacerbate their despair and helplessness." [21]

Hardly a Law Day speech goes by without the inadequacies of the legal system's being criticized. For example, the late Attorney General Robert F. Kennedy in an address delivered in 1964 declared that the poor man "looks upon the law as an enemy, not as a friend. For him, the law is always taking something away." Mr. Kennedy's successor as Attorney General, Nicolas de B. Katzenbach, in a 1965 address stated:

[21] J. Skelly Wright, "The Courts Have Failed the Poor," *The New York Times Magazine,* March 9, 1969, Section VI, p. 26.

Too often the poor man sees the law only as something which garnishes his salary; which repossesses his refrigerator; which evicts him from his house; which cancels his welfare; which binds him to usury; which deprives him of his liberty because he cannot afford bail. . . . Small wonder that the poor man does not respect the law.[22]

Why the apparent unconcern among citizens and college students if justice for the poor is inferior to justice for the middle class? There are, of course, many explanations. One reason—we will touch briefly upon others later—is the myth of courtroom justice. Television shows portray dramatic courtroom battles in which a defense attorney saves his client by a brilliant legal argument, or by producing a surprise witness. Justice is seen in terms of courtroom, fair trial, and the rule of law. For the middle class or the affluent this image of equal justice is true to life; for the poor, it camouflages the fact that the great majority of their legal battles never reach the courtroom.

Low-income consumers are particularly vulnerable to many illegal practices, which rarely even get to a lawyer, no less a courtroom. A few illustrations of the frustrations and fears of low-income consumers suggest the gravity of their problems. The poor frequently get into legal trouble by failing to read the small print in "buy now and pay later" plans. They are overcharged and even cheated by slum merchants. Consider, for instance, the case of Mrs. Ora Lee Williams, a welfare mother of seven children who purchased $1,800 worth of appliances and furniture from the Walker Thomas Furniture Company. After four years of installment payments only $170 remained to be paid. Then the same store sold her a $515 stereo set. When Mrs. Williams failed to meet her payments on the stereo, the store not only tried to repossess it but sought to take back all the other appliances and furniture (merchandise that she had already paid for!). Fine print in the contract she had signed gave the furniture store the right to repossess all other items previously bought by the same purchaser. The trial court and lower appellate court ruled to enforce the contract to repossess all the furniture and appliances. The Circuit Court of Appeals reversed the holding, saying the contract was grossly unfair and commercially unreasonable. Usually, such a case would not even get to trial. The overwhelming majority of merchant-initiated suits for repossession of property end in a judgment in favor of the merchants. For example, 97 per cent of the cases in Harlem end in a default judgment for the store owners.

Low-income consumers are particularly susceptible to abuses that resemble extortion. Jobs are threatened by debt collection agencies acting with the law's support. Sometimes an employer fires an employee rather than be bothered with wage attachments. These attachments (called wage *garnishments*) have been termed "a modern parallel to debtors prison"; the low-income consumer is left without a job and without his household possessions. For the poor man, then, the laws that govern sales contracts are often harsh and discriminatory.

---

[22] Quoted in Walter Gellhorn, "Poverty and Legality: The Law's Slow Awakening," *William and Mary Law Review,* **IX** (Winter, 1967), 298.

Other legal problems of the poor never reach the courtroom. Landlords and welfare agencies are notoriously delinquent in fulfilling their obligations to provide repairs and services. Slums are overcrowded and public housing is appallingly inadequate. Slumlords feel little legal or economic pressure to make repairs, and tenants typically do not know where to complain. Moreover, the tenant himself may be in violation of the law for overcrowding. Slumlords make enormous profits from unfit housing units. Leaky roofs, faulty toilets, and lack of heat are breaches of building code regulations, yet legal enforcement is slow, piecemeal, and occasionally unfair. Landlords rarely pay fines and are seldom sent to jail.

Welfare agencies in many instances also fail the poor. Often these agencies act in an oppressive, rather than helpful, manner. Welfare programs have operated under a degrading theory that welfare is a form of charity, and that the recipients are actually lazy and undeserving. Consider, for example, the impact that a cut of approximately 6 per cent in welfare allowances had a few years ago on one New York family.

> "My children will probably have to starve," said Mrs. Escobar, "because right now, I can't get along on what we're getting."
> Mrs. Escobar and her three children, ages 4–8 (an average welfare family), are presently living on $2,536 a year in relief payments. That includes $100 every three months in a flat grant to pay for essentials not included in the $2,136 basic grant.
> However, because of the Legislature's welfare cut in the budget, $40 of the basic grant will go. And because of a new welfare assistance bill, all of the flat grant will go.
> "It is not enough. The food we've been having is not enough, I would like my children to eat. . . ." [23]

Mrs. Escobar's problems are serious. She does not know who her state assemblyman is; she does not know how to get political assistance; and she does not know a lawyer who might be able to help her. The problem of legal representation for the exploited low-income consumer, the evicted tenant, as well as Mrs. Escobar, is particularly important. Without a lawyer, there is little chance for the poor person to receive assistance. Three interrelated problems tend to isolate the poor from a legal remedy.

1. Awareness of a problem as a legal problem

Low-income people, with limited formal education, do not understand how to exercise their legal rights. David Caplovitz in his book *The Poor Pay More* states:

Many consumers have almost no idea of the complex set of legal conditions embodied in the contracts they sign. The penalties that can be brought to bear on them, such as the loss of possessions already paid for [as in the furniture store's attempt, previously mentioned], the payment of lawyer and court fees, are matters that some families become rudely aware of only when, for whatever reasons, they miss their payments.[24]

[23] *Law and Order Reconsidered*, National Commission on the Causes and Prevention of Violence (Washington, D.C.: G.P.O., 1969), pp. 31–33.
[24] *The Poor Pay More* (New York: Free Press, 1967), pp. 1–31, 155.

2. Willingness to take legal action

Indications are that lower-class people are reluctant to take legal action when they recognize they have a problem. For example, a study of alleged acts of discrimination in Newark disclosed that close to 90 per cent of the black people took no action. There seem to be two factors that explain this reluctance of lower-class people, black and white, to use the law to protect their rights. First, prior contact with the "law" resulted in alienation, distrust, and even hatred; second, there is a general fear of unfairness or reprisal if legal remedies were pursued (e.g., the threat of a "retaliatory eviction," if a tenant complained).

3. Getting to a lawyer and hiring a lawyer

Lower-class people have less access to lawyers, know few private attorneys, and have an apprehension over the high cost of legal service. Moreover, private attorneys may exclude lower-class clients because of their inability to pay fees. When an impoverished litigant does find a lawyer, the legal damage has been done, and it may be too late; a client's goods may already have been repossessed, an eviction notice has already been served, or an arrest has already been made. One indication of the shortage of lawyers is provided by the American Bar Association, which estimates that the poor have a minimum of 5,000,000 legal problems each year (other sources estimate the figure at closer to 10,000,000). The Office of Economic Opportunity lawyers deal with only 600,000 cases annually.

The municipal courts, small claims courts, and police courts in inner cities are seriously overburdened. Cases are handled in assembly-line fashion, sometimes with less than five minutes to a case. Backlogs can run longer than a year. And when cases dealing with the poor come up for trial—say, for example, in small claims courts—they rarely collect from landlords or merchants, but instead are collected from. The systematic hardship undergone by poor litigants prompted a judge in a Washington, D.C., claims court to lament the shoddy treatment of black defendants: "It's a miracle they don't burn down the courthouse. All they see is white people enforcing white laws designed to do them in." [25]

The poor in the area of civil justice have more legal problems than the rest of society and appear to get the least help. A look at the criminal justice system provides further information on the invidious treatment of the poor.

The Poor and the Law: Criminal Justice

Criminal law and its administration is important to all segments of our society because its enforcement seeks to discourage dangerous behavior. It also seeks to protect lives and property. It is important because convicted offenders can be deprived of their property, their liberty, and even their lives. Moreover, the criminal

---

[25] Jerome E. Carlin and Jan Howard, "Legal Representation and Class Justice," *UCLA Law Review* (January, 1965), pp. 424–428. The poor's difficulty in finding a lawyer is covered in the cited pages.

justice system is the major institution to establish justice and to maintain order and stability.

The following discussion is designed to point out some—but certainly not all—of the problems of the poor when they face the criminal justice system. The great majority of those people accused of crime in the United States are poor. They usually come from inner cities that breed despair, racial discrimination, and unemployment. Cities that were once referred to as melting pots for immigrant masses are now powder kegs. Policemen in these large cities are often underpaid, under-trained, and understaffed. It is the poor who suffer the most from these conditions.

For the middle class, the police protect property, give directions, and help old ladies. For the urban poor, the police are those who arrest you. In almost any slum there is a vast con-spiracy against the forces of law and order. . . . [T]he city jail is one of the basic institutions of the other America. Almost everyone whom I encountered in the "tank" was poor: skid-row whites, Negroes, Puerto Ricans. Their poverty was an incitement to arrest in the first place. . . . They did not have money for bail or for lawyers. And, perhaps most important, they waited their arraignment with stolidity, in a mood of passive acceptance. They accepted the worst, and they probably got it. . . . To be impoverished is to be an internal alien, to grow up in a culture that is radically different from the one that dominates the society.[26]

As in the area of civil justice previously discussed, the great majority of criminal cases initiated by police never get into a courtroom. (See Figure 13.3.) The diagram illustrates how few criminals actually ever get brought to trial. It shows how cases are disposed of in the criminal justice system.

Approximately half of the arrests are disposed of outside the traditional trial process, usually by a decision by a public prosecutor to drop or dismiss charges. Nine out of ten of the remaining cases are disposed of without trial because the defendants plead guilty. Thus, a small fraction of those people charged with a crime ever go to trial. Moreover, there is a strong probability that if a defendant does go to trial in a criminal court, especially if he is an indigent, he will lose. The adversary system of justice (the courtroom justice or fair trial model) is based on evenly matched contenders, meeting in the cockpit of the courtroom. Yet how can the indigent, the ignorant, and the victims of racial discrimination hope to be equal adversaries to the state's prosecutor?

If a prosecutor (a very important figure in the criminal process) decides not to dismiss charges and to hold a defendant over for trial, he is entitled to be freed on bail. Because the date of trial may be more than a year away, the defendant is allowed to post bail, usually a cash bond, to assure that he will appear for trial. The Eighth Amendment to the Constitution states that "excessive bail" cannot be re-quired. Yet for poor defendants any cash bail may be "excessive." Ironically, the professional criminal or white-collar thief has little difficulty providing the collateral needed for a bond. According to the findings of a recent government commission that studied the administration of justice, some affluent professional criminals seem to consider the cost of bail a routine "business expense." Numerous studies have

[26] Michael Harrington, *The Other America* (Baltimore: Penguin, 1963), pp. 16–17.

Figure 13.3.

A general view of the criminal justice system

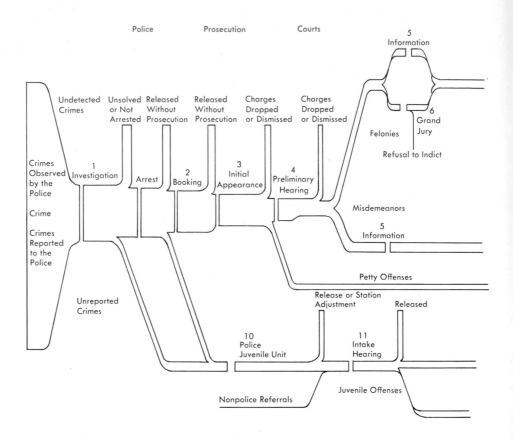

This chart seeks to present a simple yet comprehensive view of the movement of cases through the criminal justice system. Procedures in individual jurisdictions may vary from the pattern shown here. The differing weights of line indicate the relative volumes of cases disposed of at various points in the system, but this is only suggestive because no nationwide data of this sort exists.

Source: President's Commission on Law Enforcement and Administration of Justice, *Challenge of Crime in a Free Society* (Washington, D.C.: U.S. Government Printing Office, 1967), pp. 8–9.

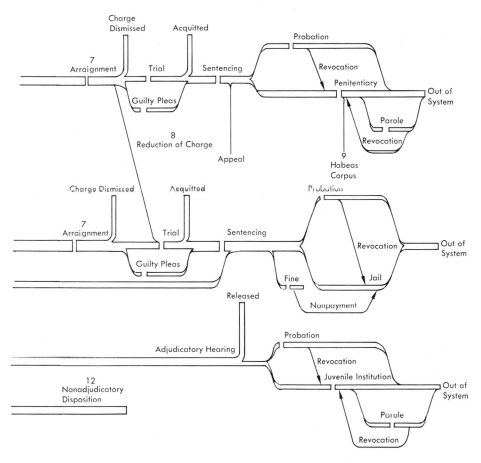

Corrections

1. May continue until trial.
2. Administrative record of arrest. First step at which temporary release on bail may be available.
3. Before magistrate, commissioner, or justice of peace. Formal notice of charge, advice of rights. Bail set. Summary trials for petty offenses usually conducted here without further processing.
4. Preliminary testing of evidence against defendant. Charge may be reduced. No separate preliminary hearing for misdemeanors in some systems.
5. Charge filed by prosecutor on basis of information submitted by police or citizens. Alternative to grand jury indictment; often used in felonies, almost always in misdemeanors.
6. Reviews whether government evidence sufficient to justify trial. Some states have no grand jury system; others

seldom use it.
7. Appearance for plea, defendant elects trial by judge or jury (if available); counsel for indigent usually appointed here in felonies. Often not at all in other cases.
8. Charge may be reduced at any time prior to trial in return for plea of guilty or for other reasons.
9. Challenge on constitutional grounds to legality of detention. May be sought at any point in process.
10. Police often hold informal hearings, dismiss or adjust many cases without further processing.
11. Probation officer decides desirability of further court action.
12. Welfare agency, social services, counseling, medical care, etc., for cases in which adjudicatory handling not needed.

shown that most of the poor are unable to make bail. Early in 1971, for example, there were over eighty thousand people in state prisons who had not been convicted of any crime but could not afford bail.

The problems of a poor defendant who is being detained in prison are exacerbated for several reasons: they cannot investigate their cases or pay anyone to prepare a defense; jails are overcrowded, and detainees are frequently mixed in with hardened criminals, leading Justice William O. Douglas to observe that pretrial detention may be "equivalent to giving a young man an M.A. in crime"; defendants held in prison often lose their jobs and have a great deal of difficulty supporting their families; and finally, studies have shown that imprisoned defendants plead guilty at a significantly higher rate than defendants who have been released on bail.

Former President Lyndon Johnson summarized how the system of money bail discriminates against the poor.

> The defendant with means can afford to pay bail. He can afford to buy his freedom. But the poorer defendant cannot pay the price. He languishes in jail weeks, months and perhaps even years before trial.
> He does not stay in jail because he is guilty. He does not stay in jail because any sentence has been passed. He does not stay in jail because he is any more likely to flee before trial. He stays in jail for one reason only—because he is poor. There are hundreds, perhaps thousands of illustrations of how the bail system has inflicted arbitrary cruelty.[27]

Holding a poor person who cannot afford bail in prison raises a question that is even more hotly contested: preventive detention. This is a term used to describe a procedure whereby "dangerous" defendants are not allowed bail before trial. President Nixon has twice proposed to Congress such a measure that would be used in federal courts; neither bill passed. Supporters of preventive detention, however, continue to argue that the public will be protected from dangerous drug addicts and hard-core criminals who are likely to commit further crime when out of prison on pretrial release. Civil liberties groups argue vigorously that any preventive detention measure may prejudice a jury as to the guilt of the accused. They also fear repression of the free speech of unpopular political groups. Two fundamental questions remain unanswered. Is preventive detention workable; that is, how does one define clearly a standard of dangerousness? Is it constitutional or does the Eighth Amendment forbid imprisonment based on the prediction of a *future* crime?

In sum, the system of money bail and preventive detention discriminates against the poor. Those accused of crime, especially if they are awaiting trial in prison, have a great deal of difficulty locating competent counsel. The problems are similar to those previously outlined in the civil justice section, with a few important differences.

It is estimated that anywhere from 50 to 75 per cent of all criminal defendants are indigents. Unpaid public defender systems are unequipped to handle the job of representing the poor. Lawyer manpower is not available. In the United States about

---

[27] President's Commission on Law Enforcement and the Administration of Justice [*Task Force Report: The Courts*] (Washington, D.C.: G.P.O., 1967), p. 40. Hereinafter cited as *The Courts.*

4 per cent of the total number of lawyers, or about 12,000, are involved in the criminal process. In New York City, for example, there are 50 public defenders to handle 60,000 cases. In most large cities public defenders have huge case loads and small investigative staffs. Court-appointed lawyers have a different set of problems. They often lack the experience and the adequate funds to prepare a defense. As a result of this scarcity of lawyers, judges, and clerks a logjam is created in the criminal courts.

In many criminal courts how is this logjam broken? About 90 per cent of all "convictions" are obtained from guilty pleas (and perhaps as high as 95 per cent in misdemeanor convictions). It has been estimated that between 30 and 40 per cent of these guilty pleas are negotiated. Donald Payne's experience in the case study provides an excellent example. The defendant's lawyer, in effect, "bargains" with the prosecuting attorney. The defendant bargains away his right to a trial by pleading guilty in return for a promise of probation, or a suspended or lenient sentence. The prosecutor benefits by saving the time and expense of a trial, enabling him to concentrate on major felony cases. A few examples of "negotiated pleas" or "bargain-counter justice" follow: a charge of burglary may be reduced to petty theft; assault with a deadly weapon may be reduced to assault without a weapon; a defendant accused of committing homosexual acts may plead guilty to a charge of disorderly conduct. Data are not available on precisely how many "deals" are made for sentence reduction. In New York City, however, four out of every five defendants who originally are charged with a felony plead guilty to a misdemeanor.[28]

The "bargain" or "deal"—as seen in Table 13.5—has marked disadvantages for the impoverished litigant. Fear or bewilderment may cause him to forfeit his rights. Defense counsel pressed for time and with few funds may encourage his client to "cop a plea" and plead guilty rather than demanding a trial in which the prosecutor must prove guilt "beyond a reasonable doubt." Justice in this crucial phase of the criminal process often becomes a question of expedience, and many lower criminal courts merely dispense speedy decisions instead of thoughtful justice. The offense for which guilt is acknowledged, and for which a "deal" is made to avoid a trial, becomes incidental to keeping the business of the courts moving. President Nixon summarized a few of these obstacles to the cause of justice:

The law's delay creates bail problems as well as overcrowded jails; it forces judges to accept pleas of guilty to lesser offenses just to process the case-load: "to give away the courthouse for the sake of the calendar." Without proper safeguards, this can turn a court of justice into a mill of injustice.[29]

Injustice to impoverished litigants does not stop at the courtroom doors. Donald Payne, and others like him, are subjected to dehumanizing treatment after they arrive at the prison. The endless boredom of a daily prison routine is punctuated by

[28] Richard M. Pious, "Pretrial and Nontrial in the Lower Criminal Courts," *Current History*, LX (July, 1971), 22–25.

[29] This is an excerpt of an address by President Nixon given on March 12, 1971, to the National Conference in the Judiciary. See *Current History*, LX (July, 1971), 365.

Table 13.5 *Advantages and disadvantages of bargain justice*

Advantages	Disadvantages
—Defendants avoid lawyer fees for a trial. —Time spent in jail may be credited to sentence. —Prosecuting attorney saves time; he can also boast a high conviction rate. —Cost of operating the criminal system is kept manageable. —Without a steady flow of guilty pleas to reduce crowded courtroom calendars, the criminal justice process in large cities could not function.	—A defendant surrenders his right to a fair trial. —Constitutional safeguards against excess pressure to plead guilty can be threatened; there is an opportunity for undue leniency when a felon pleads guilty to a lesser charge. —Because plea bargaining is "invisible" there is no judicial review. —Defendant has no due process guarantees that the "bargain" will be fulfilled by the judge. —An innocent defendant's attorney "bargaining" in the coercive atmosphere of a station house may agree to plead guilty because of the fear of a harsher sentence if he requests a trial. (Ex.: The threat of a prosecutor to "throw the book" at the defendant unless he confesses.)

inadequate meals, potential violence, and even rape. Rage, frustration, fear, and despair are part of a prisoner's daily bread. Prisoners are beaten, mail is censored, and privileges are taken away. Guards are untrained, uneducated, and often prejudiced. The punishment that a prisoner receives probably condemns him to a life of crime because rarely does any rehabilitation take place. Payne—like thousands of others—will serve his time in an inhuman, anachronistic institution. He will reenter society after a few years with no job skill and consequently with little chance of staying out of prison. A fifth to a third of all prison alumni get in trouble with the law less than a year after they leave prison.

The painfully slow process of prison reform was decried by the warden of Joliet Prison in Illinois: "We're moving ahead about fifty years. We're now up to about 1850." The cause of justice is not served when confinement in prison is so cruel that it becomes a crime against society.

Horrible prison conditions throughout the nation have lead to a series of spontaneous prison revolts and riots from New York to California. The Tombs Prison in New York City and Attica Prison in upstate New York were two penal institutions where rebellions took place. In the Tombs riots ten guards and many prisoners were injured. In Attica nine hostages and twenty-eight prisoners were killed in a massive assault by state troopers to break up a five-day rebellion. Both outbreaks were sparked by prisoners' demanding an end to inhuman conditions. If history is an accurate guide, their demands will have been forgotten shortly after the rubble is cleared away.

For the Donald Paynes, for the poor, the black, and the ignorant, the judicial process, especially the prison system, is blatantly discriminatory. It is an outrage. It runs contrary to every ideal of American justice.

Conclusions and Suggestions for Judicial Reform

Discrimination against the poor in our legal system reflects, in large measure, the same discrimination as in society at large. In withholding fundamental protections from impoverished litigants, America reveals a poverty of its own. The legal system— instead of helping the poor, the victims of racial injustice, and exploited consumers —tends to maintain their underdog position in society. Legal and public defenders and assigned counsel often do an outstanding job in defending indigents' rights. Yet there is pervasive evidence that there are not enough lawyers or resources to provide adequate legal representation for the poor. The nation tolerates a judicial system based largely on wealth rather than on justice or equality. In blunt terms, justice is like many other American commodities; the more one pays, the better the product one gets.

In both consumer protection and criminal justice the courts, in the words of Judge J. Skelly Wright, "have failed miserably" in protecting the rights of the poor. Crowded dockets, overburdened courts, and cumbersome procedures foster a mass-production system of guilty pleas. "The history of liberty," wrote the late Justice Felix Frankfurter, "has largely been the history of procedural safeguards." Those safeguards for an important but defenseless segment of society are threatened.

The furor over momentous Supreme Court decisions such as *Gideon, Escobedo,* and *Miranda,* which broadened defendants' rights to counsel and added protections against self-incrimination, may not be statistically significant. These legal milestones may be irrelevant because of the everyday operations of the criminal process, by which the great majority of all defendants, especially indigents, plead guilty.

The National Commission on the Causes and Prevention of Violence had called for bold revisions of the American judicial machinery, which it called "fragmented, inadequate, and archaic." President Nixon has also spoken of the "urgent need" for judicial reform. The legitimacy of the legal system plays a critical role in American society, and changes seem to be essential if this legitimacy is to be maintained. To date, federal and state judicial reform have been orphans with rich verbal commitments but little financial assistance.

Three key areas of reform warrant brief comment. The most important judicial reform must be one of resolve. The nation must make the goal of judicial reform as compelling as that of putting a man on the moon. One scholar has estimated that the entire criminal process—police, prosecutors, courts, and prisons—claims an annual expenditure of less than $5 billion dollars (or 2 per cent of all government expenditures). This figure is close to the amount spent each year on outer space research and moon explorations. Put differently, on the entire criminal justice system we spend less each year than we do on federal agriculture programs.[30] Immediate steps are:

1. A "judicare" system—similar to Medicare—in which the federal government pays the legal fees for the needy would be a monumental reform in strengthening and revitalizing the judicial system. At present, there are far too few lawyers, both civil and criminal, representing the poor. With "judicare" the poor could find competent attorneys who would have the investigative time, and the financial resources, to protect their rights.

2. An end to the anachronistic system of money bail also seems essential. The Vera Institute in New York City has shown that a careful study of a suspect's roots in the community considered along with the seriousness of the crime charged provides an adequate standard to assure a suspect's return for trial.

3. Finally, federal and state governments should institute a root and branch attack on the dehumanizing and deplorable conditions that exist in most prisons. Much more money must be spent on rehabilitation, case work, and job training. If reforms are neglected, judges should, perhaps, invoke the "cruel and unusual punishment" provision of the Eighth Amendment against the offending prison officials.

Other reforms could be outlined. Yet the judicial system as it stands now is inefficient and discriminatory. The poor get an inferior quality of justice to that given the middle class. Patricia M. Wald, an expert on poverty and criminal justice, summarized the plight of the poor, while suggesting an essential ingredient for reform:

The poor are arrested more often, convicted more frequently, sentenced more harshly, rehabilitated less successfully than the rest of society. So long as the social conditions that produce poverty remain, no reforms in the criminal process will eliminate this imbalance.[31]

The Invasion of Privacy: Wiretapping, Computer Banks, and Army Snoopers

Electronic eavesdropping by police agencies has sharply increased under the Nixon Administration. From 1968 to 1970 the number of court-approved wiretaps tripled; in 1968 there were 147 taps or bugs, whereas in 1970 the number had climbed to 583. Wiretapping and bugging as investigative tools had been largely dormant under the Johnson Administration. Former Attorney General Ramsey Clark called electronic surveillance a waste of "time, effort, and money" because 85 per cent of all police expenditures on such activities are salaries. Clark believed that widespread government wiretapping would erode individual liberties and create a climate of fear.

[30] Jack Ladinsky, "Lawyer Manpower in the Criminal Justice System," *Current History,* LX (July, 1971), 48–49, 56.

[31] "Poverty and Criminal Justice," Appendix C in *The Courts,* op. cit. See also Louis L. Knowles and Kenneth Prewitt (eds.), *Institutional Racism in America* (Englewood Cliffs, N.J.: Prentice-Hall, 1969), pp. 76ff.

The yield in convictions is low, according to Clark, and the risk to the invasion of privacy and repression is high.[32]

John N. Mitchell, who served as President Nixon's first Attorney General, disagrees vigorously with Ramsey Clark. He considers wiretapping the most valuable tool available for fighting crime, arguing that "the only repression that has resulted is the repression of crime." [33] In his view, the grave danger of organized crime activity makes it a necessity for the government to use a crime-fighting tool that is both effective and compatible with constitutional law. About 80 per cent of the telephone calls tapped by the Justice Department in 1970 were incriminating—proof, according to John Mitchell, that the government was not using electronic surveillance for "fishing expeditions." (The majority of these wiretaps were targeted against illegal gambling activities.) As a result of 133 taps in 1970, there were 419 arrests and 325 indictments.

Data on the effectiveness of wiretapping throughout the nation was not as encouraging. In 1970, eavesdrops resulted in 382,061 intercepts, of which 173,888 were incriminating. These intercepts resulted in 1,874 arrests and 151 convictions. The total cost of this effort on the federal, state, and local levels was over $3 million in manpower and other resources. Although not specifically referring to the 1970 data, Alan F. Westin, who has made an exhaustive study of electronic surveillance notes that "it is clear from the data that *most* electronic eavesdropping by local law enforcement agencies involves illegal entry" (emphasis in original). According to Westin, the reason that police use illegal entries into homes and offices so frequently is that better reception and service are attained by the planting of bugs or taps rather than the use of more sophisticated devices that do not require physical trespass.[34]

In 1968, Congress passed the Omnibus Crime Control and Safe Streets Act, which set guidelines for court-approved electronic eavesdropping. Police could plant listening devices for thirty days by showing a judge that they had probable cause that criminal activity was taking place. No court approval for federal taps or bugs was needed in national security cases. The passage of the act raised a controversy over the use of electronic surveillance. This controversy rests largely on a question of values: Is the apprehension of criminals and perhaps the breaking up of underworld activity worth the risk to privacy and personal freedom inherent in government wiretapping?

Allegations of excessive electronic surveillance have caused several prominent people to complain. Representative Hal Boggs, House Majority Leader, charged that the FBI tapped his phone and those of several other members of Congress. The Justice Department denied this charge. There were also allegations by reporters

[32] "Eavesdrops: Number of Cases by Police Up Sharply," *Congressional Quarterly Weekly Report,* August 6, 1971, pp. 1668–1670. Hereinafter cited as "Eavesdrops . . ."; *The New York Times,* October 28, 1970.

[33] "Eavesdrops," *CQWR,* p. 1688.

[34] Alan F. Westin, *Privacy and Freedom* (New York: Atheneum, 1968), p. 132.

that telephones in the White House press gallery are tapped. An atmosphere of suspicion is suggested by a *Washington Post* survey published in February, 1971. The survey revealed a fear of government wiretapping among 25 per cent of the prominent Washington residents who responded to a questionnaire. These people "suspected or believed that they were tapped or bugged or have, in the past, ordered checks on their telephone lines for possible wiretapping." Among the respondents were six Senators and fifty-eight Representatives. Attorney General Mitchell has dismissed many of these fears and accusations as "bogeys." It is difficult to assess how many of these accusations were politically motivated to embarrass the Nixon Administration or the then-Director of the FBI, J. Edgar Hoover. Hoover, in any event, responded by attacking Ramsey Clark for acting like a "jellyfish" in not being an adequate crime fighter.[35]

Beyond the rhetoric and heat generated by charges and countercharges of effective crime fighting, certain fundamental constitutional questions are raised. The Omnibus Crime Control Act, previously mentioned, specially exempts national security cases from the requirements of a court-approved warrant. According to the Nixon Administration, domestic subversives and foreign spies are subject to government wiretaps without court permission. The Attorney General further maintains that he has a constitutional right to keep all details of this type of surveillance secret. In national security cases, the Justice Department's argument is that the President's oath to defend the Constitution supersedes the Fourth Amendment's restrictions against unreasonable searches and seizures. Thus, warrantless searches in national security cases are "reasonable" within the meaning of the Fourth Amendment. The President or the Attorney General, it is argued, have the competence to make judgments about the sensitive nature of national security material, whereas judges—who have the authority to grant warrants—are untrained and unqualified in such matters. The real danger to society, according to Mr. Mitchell, is from "domestic subversion." "Never in our history has this country been confronted with so many revolutionary elements determined to destroy, by force, the government and the society it stands for. These 'domestic' forces are ideologically and, in many instances, directly connected with foreign interests."

Civil liberties groups countered that the government's standards of dangerousness are far too vague. Any dissenter or unpopular political group, they argue, could be classified as "dangerous," and could, therefore, be subjected to electronic eavesdropping. There is no judicial or other review to oversee that government abuses do not occur. The central question is whether the fundamental rights of "dissident elements" are threatened? And this question raises a problem as old as government itself: Who shall guard the guardians?

Another danger to the individual right to privacy is the proliferation of government computers and data banks. The average American—perhaps much to his surprise—is the subject to ten to twenty dossiers in government or private files. These dossiers contain a wealth of information, much of it personal, on marital

---

[35] "Eavesdrops . . . ," *CQWR,* op. cit., pp. 1670–1671.

status, credit rating, present and past debts and their payment history, criminal record, or law suits in which one has been involved. At least fifty federal agencies have substantial investigative and enforcement functions providing a corps of more than twenty thousand investigators working for agencies such as the FBI, the Narcotics Bureau of the Treasury, and Army Intelligence—to name but a few. New data-processing equipment is being added to the federal government at the rate of nearly five hundred computer installations a year. At present, the federal government already has various kinds of sensitive information on about 50 million people. This information ranges from potential presidential assassins to those who might want to "embarrass" the President, from suspected "revolutionaries" to persons who had peace symbols on their automobiles, and from convicted felons to civil rights protestors.[36] At present, there are no published government standards for putting a citizen's name into an internal security computer.

There are, of course, many advantages to the nation of having vital data on individuals readily available. Medical data banks could save lives. For example, if a person falls seriously ill away from home, a local doctor could have immediate access to medical history records and drug reaction from a central medical data bank. In a different area, public officials can be more easily protected by having people who have made threats identified. In law enforcement, where computerized dossiers are having their greatest growth, the electronic processing of information assists law enforcement officials in preventing crime. More important, government data centers could provide enormous benefits to society in the planning and administration of welfare programs.

The risks to an individual's privacy and personal dignity, however, are also great. Government surveillance, storage, and exchange of information on millions of Americans' private lives seriously threaten constitutionally protected liberties. Unknown to most citizens is the growing number of government data banks in existence. There is a national computer file in the Transportation Department on information and offense records of over 2 million people in every state who have had their driver's licenses suspended or revoked. The Justice Department, to cite another illustration, is preparing a computerized list for national distribution to police and prosecutors of all persons ever charged with drug offenses. A drug record, no matter how slight, will become instantly available by a teletyped report to any police agency. Information on the drug offender's acquittal, however, may not be included in this report. Instances of an incomplete or inaccurate record are not infrequent. For example, FBI "rap sheets" containing a suspect's criminal record are often incomplete. In 35 per cent of the cases, data are not furnished on what happened after an arrest. An arrest record—especially if it is incomplete or inaccurate—can be damaging to a person's future and may seriously hurt his chances for employment. Another illustration of infringements on privacy was discovered by Senator Sam J. Ervin, Jr., when he learned that the Department of Health,

---

36 Peter Schrag, "Dossier Dictatorship," *Saturday Review,* April 17, 1971, p. 25; Westin, op. cit., p. 119; *The New York Times,* December 27, 1970, p. 44.

Education and Welfare was using stored information to blacklist scientists for their political views. Certain scientists, in other words, were denied government research grants on the basis of their political ideas.

A striking example of the government's violation of individual freedoms surfaced in 1970, when it became known that the Army was keeping watch over the lawful political activities of prominent politicians. There were charges by former Army intelligence agents that eight hundred Illinois political figures—including Senator Adlai Stevenson III and former Governor Otto Kerner—were under surveillance. The Army's vague criteria for surveillance was "persons of interest." These "persons" and groups covered a wide range of legal protest. A former Army intelligence officer has revealed:

> The Army maintains files on the membership, ideology, program, and practices of virtually every activist political group in the country. These include not only such violence-prone organizations as the Minutemen and the Revolutionary Action Movement (RAM), but such non-violent groups as the Southern Christian Leadership Conference, Clergy and Laymen United Against the War in Vietnam, the American Civil Liberties Union, Women Strike for Peace, and the National Association for the Advancement of Colored People.[37]

The information gathered by the Army is exchanged with other government agencies and is ultimately stored in a central data bank in Fort Holabird, Maryland. Other reports by former intelligence personnel stated that Army agents had infiltrated student groups in major universities on the East Coast. Military agents even attended the 1968 Democratic and Republican nominating conventions.

The Army intelligence apparatus for domestic political groups had originally been called into service to help quell civil disorders in the mid-1960's. However, it expanded and broadened its intelligence-gathering functions until the constitutional rights of many political activists were infringed upon. Sharp criticism from members of Congress has caused the Army to curtail its domestic intelligence-gathering activities and to announce the abandonment of its data bank. But the suspicion lingers that the military branches are continuing—perhaps more discreetly—certain surveillance activities.

A sophisticated national data center—with an eerie resemblance to George Orwell's *1984*—could be capable of a womb-to-the-tomb dossier on every citizen. Individuals in this Orwellian situation would be subjected to the potential of a "dossier dictatorship." Even the knowledge that such dossiers exist could have a chilling effect on the spirit of dissent that characterizes our free society. These files have a potential for intimidating that, at the very least, is unhealthy for a democracy. There is no process for challenging the accuracy of these files. Consequently, sloppy investigating, past mistakes, or omissions may become a part of a person's permanent record. Thus, an unfavorable government report, unknown to its subject, can be distributed to other agencies. Not only may this information be used in a derogatory way, but there is no opportunity for redress.

The Nixon Administration has contended that the danger of misusing com-

---

[37] Arthur R. Miller, *The Assault on Privacy: Computers, Data Banks, and Dossiers* (Ann Arbor: University of Michigan, 1971), p. 40; Westin, op. cit., p. 167.

puterized information is exaggerated, and that self-discipline by the Executive Branch will serve as a sufficient safeguard against government abuses. Senator Ervin and his subcommittee on Constitutional Rights disagree. He believes that rights of privacy and personal freedom need more due process protection. According to Senator Ervin, citizens should have the right to inspect their own files, make factual corrections when appropriate, and be able to challenge or deny derogatory information. He would also place strict congressional limitations on the collection and exchange of personal information by federal agencies. An agency would first have to demonstrate a need to collect personal data, and then gain congressional approval.

"The right to be left alone," in the words of Justice William J. Douglas, "is indeed the beginning of all freedom." The government's unregulated power of surveillance and data collection seems to be eroding this fundamental right. Government computers and data banks, therefore, must come under closer legislative and judicial scrutiny—our continuing struggle to maintain liberty demands it

The "New" Minority: Women

In the years after World War II black people began asserting their rights. These rights were fought for in courtrooms, employment offices, and restaurants. Progress was—and is—painfully slow. Today—as we have seen—poor people, many of whom are black, still face major obstacles in achieving equal justice. Yet there is a larger group in America that faces indefensible discrimination: women and "other minorities." Good jobs in commerce, industry, and government are virtually monopolized by white males. Women, Spanish-speaking citizens, and Indians have only token representation and are largely excluded from the better salary brackets.[38]

Job discrimination against women takes several different forms and seems to operate on all educational levels. A Department of Labor survey documents that the average salary offered to women was less than men in every private company studied, with differences ranging from $20 to $100 per month. Women, who make up approximately 35 per cent of the work force, are highly concentrated in underpaid and menial positions. For example, 70 per cent of all clerical workers are women. Their median income is 65 per cent that of men in the same types of positions. Only 14 per cent of working women have professional or technical positions. These women invariably receive less pay for the same work as males. A study of chemists' salaries, for example, conducted in 1967 found that with seniority held constant, women with Ph.D.'s earned less than men with B.A.'s Data on law school graduates is equally revealing. Upon graduation the average male (again, holding the variables constant) earned 20 per cent more than the average woman: after ten years, male attorneys earned 200 per cent more. The inequities in the job market are so great that the median salary of full-time women workers is only 58 per cent of men's.[39]

In the better salary brackets in business corporations and government, job

[38] John Kenneth Galbraith, Edwin Kuh, and Lester C. Thurow, "The Galbraith Plan to Promote the Minorities," *The New York Times Magazine,* August 22, 1971, pp. 9, 35.

[39] Joreen, "The 51 Percent Minority Group: A Statistical Essay," in Robin Morgan (ed.), *Sisterhood Is Powerful* (New York: Vintage, 1970), p. 37.

discrimination against women is blatant. In 1969 males accounted for 96 per cent of all jobs paying more than $15,000 a year. Only 2 per cent of the employed women made over $15,000. In the public sector 89 per cent of the jobs that paid over $15,000 a year were held by white males. Data at the other end of the economic scale shows that perhaps 32 million women were not working because of home or child-care responsibilities; at least 3 million in this group, according to government estimates, would like to have jobs. More important, although female-headed households represent only 20 per cent of all households in the nation, they constitute 50 per cent of those living in poverty.[40]

In higher education women are frequently victims of various kinds of discrimination. They are encouraged to take "feminine" courses such as teacher education, regardless of their interests or ability. They are often denied scholarships, fellowships, and even loans on the basis of sex, particularly for graduate study. A few quotes from political science professors reveal sex discrimination against women as students and scholars: "Any girl who gets this far has got to be a kook." "I know you're competent and your thesis adviser knows you're competent. The question in our minds is, are you *really serious* about what you're doing" (emphasis in original).

Traditionally women in the United States have been seen as homemakers and childbearers. Like the black man, women were assigned their "place" in society. The general belief to justify lower pay is that a woman's salary is a luxury income that merely supplements that of her husband's. Yet at least 30 per cent of the women of marriageable age are not married and therefore must support themselves. Moreover, many of the women who are married and work do so out of economic necessity.

Sex discrimination has led to the emergence of new "women's liberation" groups. Cries are heard that "women are an oppressed class." Young women radicals who had worked in civil rights and peace movements became tired of typing, running errands, and fixing food. The men were the leaders, while the women did the menial work. Stokeley Carmichael's wisecrack to members of SNCC, that "(t)he position of women in our movement should be prone," represented a sexist attitude that stimulated women to organize groups to combat discrimination.[41]

Like women, chicanos, Puerto Ricans, and American Indians recently gained a public awareness of their oppressed position in society. These groups have complained bitterly about the fruits of discrimination; hunger, malnutrition, and sub-standard housing. These "new" minorities have been denied equal protection of the laws in public and private employment. President Nixon's appointment of Romana C. Banuelos as Secretary of the Treasury acknowledges virtual absence of women and Mexican-Americans in high level government positions. Moreover, the President is seriously considering the appointment of a woman Supreme Court Justice.

What can be done to ensure equal opportunity? John Kenneth Galbraith has

[40] Robert S. Benson and Harold Wolman (eds.), *Counterbudget* (New York: Praeger, 1971), p. 289.

[41] Joreen, op. cit., pp. 39–40; Susan Brown-Miller, "Sisterhood Is Powerful," *The New York Times Magazine,* March 15, 1970, p. 22.

suggested a Minority Advancement Plan (MAP). The essence of MAP is that Congress should pass a law making it a national policy that the employers of women, blacks, Spanish-speaking minorities, and American Indians give better-paying jobs according to their numbers in the population. A commission would be set up to assure that industry and government change their hiring and promotion policies to reflect the reality of a labor market in which minorities are discriminated against. The time allowed for full compliance would vary with the size of the firm. The important point is that after a set number of years all levels of government and all phases of private industry would be penalized for noncompliance.

Every year the cost to society for the underutilization of women and "other minorities" because of discrimination in education and employment can be measured in billions of dollars. The costs in humiliation and suffering are incalculable. Congress and the nation must act more quickly to institute programs like MAP or else this indefensible discrimination will continue. If the 1960's belonged to the blacks to struggle for their rights, the next ten years may see the blacks joined by the "new" minorities raising their voices in protest.

suggested additional readings

Baldwin, James. *The Fire Next Time.* New York: Dell Publishing Co., 1964.*

Blaustein, Albert P., and Clyde C. Ferguson. *Desegregation and the Law,* 2nd ed. New York: Vintage Books, 1962.*

Carmichael, Stokeley, and Charles V. Hamilton. *Black Power.* New York: Random House, Inc., 1967.*

Clark, Kenneth C. *Dark Ghetto.* New York: Harper Torchbooks, 1965.*

Crime and Justice in America. Washington, D.C.: Congressional Quarterly, Inc., 1968.*

Hook, Sidney. *The Paradoxes of Freedom.* Berkeley: University of California Press, 1962.*

Kalven, Harry. *The Negro and the First Amendment.* Chicago: University of Chicago Press, 1966.*

Kurland, Phillip B. *Of Church and State and the Supreme Court.* Chicago: University of Chicago Law School, 1961.*

Lewis, Anthony. *Gideon's Trumpet.* New York: Random House, Inc., 1964.*

Magrath, C. Peter. "Chief Justice Waite and the 'Twin Relic': Reynolds v. United States." *Vanderbilt Law Review,* XVIII. March, 1965, 507–543.

Matthews, Donald R., and James W. Prothro. *Negroes and the New Southern Politics.* New York: Harcourt Brace Jovanovich, Inc., 1966.*

McClosky, Herbert. "Consensus and Ideology in American Politics." *American Political Science Review,* LVIII. June, 1964, 361–382.

Report of the National Advisory Commission on Civil Disorders. New York: Bantam Books, 1968.*

Stouffer, Samuel A. *Communism, Conformity, and Civil Liberties.* New York: Doubleday and Company, Inc., 1955.

Westin, Alan F. *Privacy and Freedom.* New York: Atheneum Publishers, 1967.

* Available in paperback.

14 foreign policy and defense: the united states in world politics

case study

The Nuclear Test Ban Treaty

On May 26, 1972, President Richard M. Nixon signed a far-reaching arms control measure in Moscow with Soviet leaders. The product of two years of SALT (Strategic Arms Control Limitation Talks) negotiations, the United States and the USSR agreed by treaty to limit each country to only two antiballistic missile sites with no more than one hundred antiballistic missile launchers at each one. The nations also agreed to a five-year executive agreement to freeze the number of land-based, intercontinental ballistic missiles (although not the number of warheads) at existing levels and to set ceilings on the number of missile-firing submarines and submarine-launched missiles. The agreement appeared to signal the end of a strategic arms race that had begun at the end of World War II. Both sides accepted a rough parity of destructive power, mutual vulnerability, and the realization that disputes between them could not be settled by nuclear weapons. The Moscow accords followed the Nuclear Nonproliferation Treaty of 1971, in which the nuclear powers (except France and the People's Republic of China) agreed not to disseminate nuclear weapons to nonnuclear powers.

In 1971–1972, progress in arms control marked a turning point in the Cold War. While by no means inevitable, these developments were built upon earlier experience in exploration of technical arms issues and in bilateral and multilateral political negotiation. To understand how the major powers were able to finally turn the corner into new and different relationships, it is useful to look in detail at how they took the first halting step, the treaty of 1963 banning the testing of nuclear weapons in the atmosphere, in outer space, and in the oceans. This first accommodation was the outcome of a long process of hard bargaining, during which, as later on, substantive issues and global politics became intermixed in moving the talks ahead and setting them back.

The idea of a test ban was interjected into American politics during the early 1950's by scientists active in bomb development. As testing on hydrogen bombs proceeded, it became evident that they, unlike the atom bombs that devastated Nagasaki and Hiroshima in World War II, produced radioactive debris—"fallout." The fallout fell to the earth in rain, and it potentially could cause damage to human beings: injury to blood, bones, and germ plasm, and genetic injury were all possible after the accumulated fallout reached certain levels. During the 1956 presidential campaign, Democratic candidate Adlai Stevenson proposed such a ban, but the idea was firmly rejected by the Eisenhower Administration.

Behind the scenes, however, the Eisenhower Administration periodically investigated the technical aspects of a possible ban, including the thorny issues of inspection of the installations of potential violators and the investigation of suspicious underground explosions that could be either tests or earthquakes. More officially, the American government was forced to consider the political aspects of testing beginning in December, 1957, when Chairman of the Council of Ministers of the USSR, Nikolai A. Bulganin, wrote to President Eisenhower. Bulganin, in a long list of other proposals, suggested that the three nuclear powers (at that time Britain, the United States, and the USSR) should stop testing by agreement as of January 1, 1958. Eisenhower, who had met with Soviet leaders in a summit conference in Geneva, Switzerland, in 1955 and subsequently became increasingly wary of Soviet promises and proposals, replied in a series of messages. Rejecting the idea of another summit conference, Eisenhower linked the question of a ban on testing with other items of arms control, including an end to the actual production of nuclear weapons.

The Soviet Union again forced the initiative in the spring of 1958. It did so by first running an extensive series of atmospheric nuclear tests that raised the radioactivity levels around the world. Then, on March 31, 1958, it announced that it was discontinuing testing and would not resume unless other nations tested. Chairman Nikita Khrushchev made this appeal both publicly and in letters to President Eisenhower. As a consequence, the United States was placed in an awkward position, and the Russians harvested a considerable propaganda advantage.

The American predicament developed because the United States was itself planning a series of nuclear tests. President Eisenhower convened a special panel of nuclear scientists and military specialists to analyze two questions. Was it essential to American security that the planned series of tests be held? After that, would it be consistent with American security to negotiate a test ban? The scientists disagreed on the first issue, and the tests were held. On the second question, the recommendation was that the United States could safely risk a test suspension. President Eisenhower then proposed to Chairman Khrushchev that a conference of experts from the Communist and Western powers be convened to work out the technical aspects of a test ban.

Chairman Khrushchev, somewhat to the surprise of the Americans, agreed to Eisenhower's proposal. Thus, on July 1, 1958, the Conference of Experts convened in Geneva. Scientists from the United States, Great Britain, and the Soviet Union met to discuss such questions as the threshold of blast at which an explosion could be detected if it were set off underground, the number of inspections on foreign soil that might be necessary, and the type of international organization required to carry out inspections. The scientists in the American delegation were picked from the "center" of the scientific community: individuals who held either strong antiban or proban views were not sent.

While the discussions at Geneva were proceeding, a so-called Committee of Principals within the Eisenhower Administration was meeting in Washington to discuss what the American position should be following the Conference of Experts, when the actual negotiating with the Russians would begin. This Committee of Principals included the Secretary of State, the Secretary of Defense, the Director of the Central Intelligence Agency, the Chairman of the Atomic Energy Commission, and the

Special Assistant to the President for Science and Technology. In addition, the President's Special Assistant for National Security Affairs and the Director of the United States Information Agency attended various sessions.

The Conference of Experts, which concluded its work on August 22, 1958, agreed in its report that a ban was technically feasible because a satisfactory control system was possible. At this point both the Americans and the Russians began maneuvering for position in the forthcoming negotiations that both sides were committed to. It was agreed that a "Conference on the Discontinuance of Nuclear Weapons Tests" would be convened in Geneva on October 31, 1958. The Americans continued nuclear testing through the summer, and in response the Russians initiated a new series of test blasts that continued right up to October 30. Both sides were clearly rushing to complete as many tests as possible, because both were prepared to call a moratorium on testing—a temporary suspension—when the new talks began. The Soviet Union implied that it would observe such a moratorium as long as the talks proceeded—a position consistent with their overall objective of an end to testing without inspection. The United States implied that there was a time limit as to how long it would refrain from testing in the absence of a signed agreement and an inspection system.

The Geneva talks, however, failed to produce an agreement. For one thing, each side had different objectives. The Soviet Union wanted a permanent and deep commitment from the West, but with only minimum control machinery. The Western powers, although willing to give such a commitment, wanted it to include substantial inspection facilities that would both prevent violations and also "open up" the iron curtain of Soviet secrecy. Both sides suspected the motives of the other, and Western

suspicions were heightened by Russian propaganda efforts.

In addition, even if the positions of the two superpowers were ultimately reconcilable, there was fundamental disagreement within the United States on the desirability of such a ban in terms of American security and development of nuclear weapons. One group of American physicists developed a "decoupling" theory of explosions, which suggested that by setting off bombs in a large underground cavity, any nation could test and evade inspection. The physicists who developed this theory, most notably Dr. Edward Teller, opposed a ban, and they were joined by many in the military services. Furthermore, within the American government there were few strong proponents of a treaty—President Eisenhower was preoccupied with other problems, and the State Department did not push for an agreement.

Such was the situation—stalemate despite continuing talks—when John F. Kennedy was inaugurated President in January, 1961. When Kennedy met with Chairman Khrushchev in Vienna in June of that year, the test ban was one of the major items on the agenda. Kennedy expressed his hopes for an accord—and America's concern with the continuation of an unpoliced moratorium. Khrushchev's response was discouraging. He felt that inspections were basically unnecessary, although the Soviet Union would consider three a year on its soil. Most important, any international control apparatus would have to be managed by a "troika" device, consisting of three individuals, each having a veto. To the Americans, this proposal negated the possibility of meaningful controls. The Russians also wanted, in emulation of an early American position, to tie the test ban to general disarmament measures. But the American position, which had shifted, was that the test ban should come first and be considered separately. Kennedy quoted to Khrushchev the old Chinese maxim: "A thousand-mile journey begins with a single step." He suggested: "Let us take that step."

The Soviet Union, however, rejected Kennedy's initiative for reasons soon to become apparent. After he left Vienna, Khrushchev made statements indicating that he was under internal pressures to resume testing—saying so publicly and also privately to visiting Americans. Kennedy was under similar domestic pressures—from the Pentagon, the Congress, and some segments of the public. He thereupon appointed a special scientific panel, under his Special Advisor, Jerome Weisner, to examine whether there was evidence of resumed and secret Soviet testing and what advantages would accrue to the United States if it should start testing again first.

The Soviet Union resolved the doubt within the American Administration by resuming its own tests on September 1, 1961. The Soviets proceeded to unveil an elaborate series of explosions of exceedingly large bombs in the 50 to 100 megaton range, or two thousand five hundred times larger than the American bomb dropped on Hiroshima. Beyond doubt, the planning for this series had been well along during the Khrushchev-Kennedy Vienna meetings. Kennedy, who just that month had succeeded in having a new Arms Control and Disarmament Agency established in the State Department, was appalled. He felt that he could no longer resist demands to resume testing, and, indeed, the United States began underground but not atmospheric tests.

In the next few months, in close collaboration with British Prime Minister Harold Macmillan, Kennedy tried in the United Nations and behind the scenes to persuade the Russians to stop testing

again. Meanwhile, American preparations were also underway for further atmospheric testing. On March 2, 1962, President Kennedy reported to the American people on national television that the United States would go to the disarmament talks that were scheduled to resume in Geneva prepared to agree to a test ban. If the Soviet Union would sign, Kennedy declared, the United States would not start its tests. Despite this offer, which in effect would have allowed the Soviets a testing period without American response, Chairman Khrushchev rejected the idea. On April 25, 1963, the United States began to test nuclear weapons in the atmosphere.

At this point, it appeared as if the prospects for agreement were gloomier than ever. A basic wall of mistrust—the legacy of a long Cold War—still separated the two sides. Once again the Soviet Union and the United States were blasting away, developing new weapons, and spewing poisonous fallout into the earth's air. Strangely, however, neither side was willing to make the ultimate break and stop the perpetual discussions at Geneva. In fact, the American Ambassador, Arthur Dean, was even more determined that they should continue. Thus, even as the testing continued, the sparring over the terms of a test ban went on. The United States hinted that it would accept a smaller number of annual inspections than it had previously demanded. The Kennedy Administration also began to consider something less than a comprehensive test ban, namely a limited ban. Under a limited ban, all but underground testing would be prohibited. The advantage of a limited ban, which had actually been suggested as early as 1958 by Senator Albert Gore of Tennessee, was that no on-site inspections at all would be necessary. All violations except underground ones were easily detectable by existing national systems—seismographs, space satellites, underwater and air collection vehicles.

A limited ban had the additional virtue of being easier to sell, potentially, to the United States Senate, where a two-thirds affirmative vote would be needed to ratify any treaty; the Senators could be assured that under such a limited ban, the Russians would not be able to cheat.

Suddenly, these discussions and proposals began to bear fruit, and the possibilities of agreement on a treaty drastically improved. All negotiations, however technical they are, in a sense reflect the prevailing international mood in superpower relations. In October, 1962, the Soviet Union and the United States faced each other head-on at the brink of out-and-out nuclear conflict over the Cuban missiles. After this, there was a new mutual recognition of the horror of nuclear war, a realization that the terrible moment had been close, and an apparent desire on both sides to draw back and make such confrontations less likely in the future. In addition, the Soviet spilt with the Chinese Communists now seemed irreparable. Khrushchev wrote to Kennedy that the "time has come now to put an end once and for all to nuclear tests, to draw a line through such tests." In addition, Khrushchev markedly reduced Soviet pressures on the Western sector of Berlin, one of the perennial trouble spots of the Cold War. On the American side, Kennedy tried hard to resolve an apparent misunderstanding that had emerged from private talks between United States and Soviet scientists on the inspection question; he sent a skilled negotiator, Deputy Under-Secretary of State Averell Harriman to Moscow. Kennedy also utilized a magazine editor, Norman Cousins, as a private channel to assure Khrushchev that he really did want a treaty.

During the spring of 1963, Kennedy struggled with problems on two fronts in order to reach an agreement. On the one hand, private talks with the Russians were stalemated over the inspection issue, especially because the Soviet Union felt that the United States had first committed itself to three inspections and then reneged. On the other hand, there was rising domestic opposition within the United States to reaching any kind of agreement. Influential Republican Governor Nelson Rockefellor of New York spoke against a ban, as did Senate Minority Leader Everett Dirksen. Other Congressmen spoke up against it, and the Joint Chiefs of Staff seemed opposed to a ban in general—an opposition they expressed by ruling anything under eight inspections utterly unacceptable from a military point of view. Nonetheless, Kennedy and Prime Minister Macmillan struggled on, drafting new proposals, writing to Khrushchev, and prodding their own governments. Kennedy observed:

If we don't get an agreement this year . . . I would think . . . the genie is out of the bottle and we will not ever get him back in again. . . . Personally I am haunted by the feeling that by 1970, unless we are successful, there may be ten nuclear powers instead of four. . . . I regard that as the greatest possible danger and hazard. . . . I think that we ought to stay at it.

In May, 1963, Khrushchev wrote to Kennedy, suggesting that there be high-level talks in Moscow on the ban. Kennedy seized on this opportunity. He decided to send a high-level delegation to Moscow on July 15, consisting of Under-Secretary of State Harriman and four other carefully chosen representatives, one from the White House national security staff, one from the Disarmament agency, and one each from the departments of Defense and State. Kennedy also received valued political support when thirty-four Senators joined in sponsoring a "sense of the Senate" resolution that backed the idea of a limited ban.

Kennedy was determined that the United

States, having finished a series of tests, would not test again as long as the Soviet Union also abstained. The new negotiations were finally announced publicly by the President in a commencement address he gave at American University on June 10. In that speech, Kennedy addressed himself to the topic of peace, urging not only that the Russians reexamine their views, but also that Americans discard the shibboleths of the Cold War. He pointed to the mutual interest each side had in avoiding a nuclear holocaust, observing that "if we cannot now end our differences, at least we can help make the world safe for diversity." Khrushchev responded by calling this speech the best by an American President since the days of Franklin Roosevelt. In an address of his own in East Berlin on July 2, the Russian leader endorsed the idea of a limited test ban treaty that would outlaw tests in the atmosphere, in outer space, and under water.

Harriman, a former World War II U.S. Ambassador to Moscow and an old hand at hard negotiations with the Soviets, was chosen to head the Western delegation. Kennedy arranged that the delegation keep in close daily contact with him personally, and that the strictest limitations be put on the distribution of information within Washington until the talks were over. Kennedy stressed to his team that this was the last chance to reach an agreement with the Russians that could begin to cut away the many layers of mutual suspicion. Kennedy wanted no stone unturned in the efforts to reach an accord.

The Americans and the British offered two complete treaties as a basis for discussion. The first was a comprehensive treaty with provisions for banning underground tests and for international inspection and control. The second was a limited treaty banning tests only in the atmosphere, in outer space, and under water; it had no inspection provisions.

The Russian interest was confined to the limited treaty, and negotiations were exclusively over its concrete provisions. After ten days of hard marathon talks, agreement was reached on a limited ban. Tests would be prohibited in the atmosphere, in outer space, and under water. On July 25, 1963, the treaty was initialed; Kennedy then made plans to send a formal, bipartisan delegation of executive officials and Senators to Moscow for the formal signing. The President also went on national television to say that since "the advent of nuclear weapons, all mankind has been struggling to escape from the darkening prospect of mass destruction on earth. . . . Yesterday a shaft of light cut into the darkness."

For President Kennedy, however, there still remained the formidable hurdle of Senate ratification. Many important military officials opposed the treaty and so too did many weapons development scientists; these included a former Air Force Chief, a former Chairman of the Joint Chiefs of Staff, the head of the Strategic Air Command, and a former Chairman of the Atomic Energy Commission. The renowned physicist Edward Teller was also opposed.

Kennedy confronted this opposition with a major personal effort to assume the Senate's approval. He worked hard with his own Joint Chiefs of Staff and ultimately won their public support by promising that American underground testing would be continued, that the nuclear labs would be maintained at a high state of ready development, and that overall American vigilance against the Soviet Union would not be relaxed. At press conferences and in numerous public messages, the President worked to develop public support. And there was, indeed, a strong shift in public sentiment between the time the treaty was signed in July and the day it came before the Senate for a vote on September 24, 1963. A Louis Harris poll in July showed that the public was lukewarm in its support of the treaty; but by September, approval for the treaty stood at an overwhelming 80 per cent. No less important, the President personally persuaded certain key Senators, such as the Republican Minority Leader Everett Dirksen, to endorse the ban; Dirksen's floor speech in flavor of the treaty was a high point in the Senate debate. When the Senate vote came, it was 80 to 19 in favor of the treaty, fourteen more votes than the required two thirds. A process that had begun in the Eisenhower Administration five years earlier was finally concluded. President Kennedy called the signing "a welcome culmination of this effort to lead the world once again to the path of peace." Each side had taken some real risks in reaching an accommodation with the other. Nonetheless, an accord had been reached, because those responsible for foreign policy making in both countries believed that the gains outweighed the risks.

SOURCES

Jacobson, Harold Karan, and Eric Stein. *Diplomats, Scientists and Politicians: The United States and the Nuclear Test Ban Negotiations.* Ann Arbor: The University of Michigan Press, 1966.

Schlesinger, Arthur M., Jr. *A Thousand Days: John F. Kennedy in the White House.* Boston: Houghton Mifflin Company, 1965.

Sorensen, Theodore C. *Kennedy.* New York: Harper and Row, Publishers, 1965.

a perspective on american international politics

The Challenge of International Relations

This generation of students is the first to have lived its entire life under the cloud of possible nuclear war, under the day-to-day stress of the Cold War, in an atmosphere of continuous American political and military involvement throughout the world. One result has been a heightened consciousness of the importance of foreign policy values and decisions. Americans know how these decisions affect their own lives in higher taxes, possible military service in far-off Asian places, and the deferment of domestic programs because of military spending. American decisions affect others as well, most of the people of the world in fact, those of the 124 nations with which we have diplomatic ties and also those of the nations with which we have no formal connections.

Few nations have ever been as involved in world affairs as America in the years following World War II. Only Imperial Britain in its heyday is an appropriate comparison. Since 1945 the United States has spent over $1,200 billion for military purposes alone, more than the value of all business and residential structures in the country. Depending upon which accounting system one uses, between 40 and 65 per cent of the annual budget goes for defense. In 1972, the nation maintained over 1.5 million soldiers abroad in sixty-eight foreign countries at 432 major overseas military bases. We are part of a system of formal alliances that girds the globe and, by design, rings the rim of all the major Communist powers. In addition, billions of dollars more are spent in foreign aid; American businesses are the world's largest exporters of capital and largest investors in overseas enterprises; and more Americans are foreign tourists than nationals of any other nation. An amazing 1 per cent of our population currently works or lives abroad.

Policy decisions in foreign affairs present a wide range of opportunities and dangers to our citizens and politicians. By *foreign policy* we mean the goals and the activities America pursues in its relations with the external or international environment. Contact with this environment comes at multiple levels—citizen to citizen, state to state, state to internal organization, and state to citizen. State to state is by far still the most important level. Within that category, our relationship with the Soviet Union, and secondarily with Communist China, is of the greatest concern. In more general terms, foreign policy is often defined as the political pursuit of the "national interest." Most observers agree, however, that it is always difficult to define just what the national interest is as each concrete decision arises. Moreover, within the United States, there is considerable disagreement on the proper "world role" or "national interest" foreign policy-makers should pursue. Even when there is agreement on goals, choosing the proper tactics is difficult.

Some students of international politics, especially Professor Hans J. Morgenthau, have held that the national interest can always best be expressed in terms of "power." In this "realist" view, power, influence over the decisions, resources, and activities of other international actors are the primary foreign policy goal. Even when the specific shape of the national interest is unclear, states will seek to extend their power over other states. Their goal is to obtain or preserve position for future specific needs. Thus, for Morgenthau, the pursuit of power is a constant in the behavior of nation states, Communist and Western alike, throughout modern history.

Others feel that the foreign policy of all countries operates within constraints imposed by the nature of the international system itself. These constraints will differ as the configurations of the international system differ. The balance-of-power world of the nineteenth century was a fundamentally different world than the bipolar world of the 1950's and the multipolar world of the 1970's. In the nineteenth-century pattern, seven or eight nearly equal world powers possessed room for various types of maneuvers. States shifted alliances loosely, tending to arrange themselves into roughly equal competing camps that were kept equal by the availability of a "balancer." The balancer, usually England, consciously shifted from side to side to keep any single coalition from becoming predominant. In this world, ideology did not differentiate states; emotions were kept low because the stakes were frequently remote pieces of territory; and armed conflict did not lay waste the winners and losers alike.

Despite occasional efforts by policy-makers to recreate the nineteenth-century balance of power and the prevalence of talk about the balance in official rhetoric, the post-World War II environment has been substantially different. In a bipolar system, even a loose bipolar system, there are two major antagonists with very little room for maneuver. Whatever happens anywhere in the world is perceived as a gain or loss for one side or the other, so both become global interventionists. There is a deep cleavage of ideology, and each side imputes motives of world conquest to the other. Emotions run high because the stakes are seen as control over whole populations. The very survival of different ways of life, the "free world" or the "socialist camp," is seen as being at stake. Major war between the two major powers will surely destroy winner and loser alike. From 1945 to 1970, this description accurately characterized the environment of competition between the Soviet Union and the United States. The post-1970 environment differs, not only because the competition has diminished but because there are other centers of relatively independent strength, still largely regional, besides the two giants. The emergence of the People's Republic of China and Japan in Asia and of a stronger Western Europe makes the international system multipolar—and more complicated in ways not yet fully clear. This last system change, as others before it, will affect American foreign policy.

In addition, every state's domestic politics influences its choices of what to do and how to act in international affairs, if only because competing domestic groups will act differently when they control the governmental apparatus. The values of a Germany controlled by the Nazis made that country's foreign conduct and goals different from that of its liberal democratic predecessor, Weimar Germany. The foreign policy of the United States under Richard M. Nixon surely differs in its attitudes toward military aid, military involvement, and American overseas commercial activities from a U.S. government controlled by a socialist-minded coalition or by an isolationist antimilitary government concerned only with domestic programs.

Despite the importance of both the international system and the internal variables in shaping state behavior, Morgenthau's "power" theory retains explanatory usefulness. Beyond any doubt, nations acting in international affairs try to maximize something they call the "national interest," and because their pursuit must always be uncertain, they seek to buttress their continuing positions by seeking a generalized extension of their influence. Especially where day-to-day relations among nations are concerned, thinking in terms of power explains a great deal.

Power, of course, is more than a goal of foreign policy. It is also a set of resources that states possess and utilize in seeking to achieve any set of goals. As a consequence, various elements of national power enter into the international pursuit of more influence. Geography, economic resources (especially industrial and technological facilities), population, and military strength (including raw firepower and also overall flexibility), plus such intangibles as viable political institutions, popular support, and national "cohesion" are often listed as such primary elements of national power.

The United States like other nations has to grapple with the problem of deciding what foreign policy goals it should pursue. Defining what our national interest is preoccupied policy-makers and fueled hot dispute in our domestic politics in George Washington's days no less than in Richard Nixon's. President Washington's problem was to persuade the American people and various political leaders that a policy of international noninvolvement should be our aim and that it was essential for Americans to avoid "permanent inveterate antipathies against particular nations and passionate attachments for others." Some in that era wanted us to ally ourselves with Republican France and others thought that it was essential to cultivate a close relationship to England. In his famous "Farewell Address," Washington argued that, "Europe has a set of primary interests, which to us have none, or a very remote, relation." He thought that, "Our detached and distant situation invites and enables us to pursue a different course"; if we could "remain one people, under an efficient government," we would be able to "defy material injury from external annoyance" and "choose peace or war, as our interest, guided by justice, shall counsel."

We can perhaps best illustrate the continuing complexities of foreign policy making, and also the changing roads our nation has traveled, by looking briefly at three historical periods, 1790–1914, 1914–1945, and 1945 to the present.

1790–1914: Combining International Isolation with Hemispheric Dominance

Between 1790 and 1914 the United States changed from being a weak, coastal, agricultural society to being a mighty, continental, industrial society. In 1790, its strength vis-à-vis the world powers was minimal. By 1914, its resources placed it high among the mighty in potential. Yet throughout this long time span America pursued a policy of trying to opt out of the important issues in world politics. Its foreign policy sought to achieve two basic goals: 1) to remain uninvolved in the conflicts of the major powers, namely the European nations; and 2) to carve out a special position of strength in the Western Hemisphere. Over this period the goals remained the same even as the nation's changing domestic development influenced the tactics it utilized in trying to fulfill them.

For the founders of the American Republic, insulating the new nation from European politics posed two problems. First, the United States had to remove its own territory from the category of a prize to be won by competing European nations. Its leaders therefore sought to remove those Spanish, French, and British troops that remained on the continent after the Revolutionary War. Second, the United States had to carve out for itself a recognized diplomatic identity—a particular international role. The specific role that many aimed at was one of a "regional state," concerned with settling its own continent, interested in foreign relationships within its own hemisphere (the New World), and seeking respect for its shipping and trading activities but preferring to stay out of the politics of Europe.

Before continental security could be gained, the United States engaged in a period of active diplomacy, the highlights of which were Jay's Treaty of 1794 (securing the removal of British troops from the Northwest), Pinckney's Treaty of 1795 (giving the United States navigation rights on the Mississippi through agreement with Spain), war with the French from 1798 to 1800, the Louisiana Purchase of 1803, and war with the British from 1812 to 1814. After many Americans settled in Florida with encouragement from our government, we gave Spain the choice of selling us the territory or losing it without compensation. Later, settlers were to be the spearhead of American expansion into Texas, Oregon, and California. Although this settlement was not organized and directed by the American government, it became a sort of "fifth column," a base of support for us within foreign territories. The separation of Texas from Mexico and its later incorporation into the United States bears striking resemblance to some of the contemporary "wars of national liberation." As a "developing nation," the early United States was an expansionist political actor in the areas around its borders. These activities were justified by a doctrine known as "manifest destiny," through which polemicists argued that it was our fate to bring the continent under one government. Even after the War of 1812, many included Canada in that American destiny.

Although the Americans were tenacious and demonstrated considerable hit-and-run military talent, along with an impressive rate of political development, what actually guaranteed its success in detaching itself from the politics of Europe was a change in the system of great power competition. After the 1814 Congress of Vienna, the worldwide conflict among the European powers lost some of its edge, the system stabilized, and military confrontations in Europe and the colonial outposts decreased in frequency. When the pace of European expansion accelerated again after 1870, the United States was already an established and accepted nation.

The United States started early in its history to establish a special role for itself in the Western Hemisphere. This intention was clearly stated in the famous "Monroe Doctrine," which was a part of President Monroe's 1823 State of the Union message to Congress. The doctrine set down a series of objectives, some of which are part of American foreign policy even today. America declared the Western Hemisphere "off limits" to future European colonization and announced that it would oppose any attempt on the part of European powers to interfere with the governments of the independent republics of the New World. Although there were minor or temporary episodes that did not strictly accord with the Monroe Doctrine, it was maintained without major violation, thanks largely to the control of the seas exercised by Britain.

The Monroe Doctrine came to imply that the United States would interpret its own widespread intervention in the commercial, political, and military affairs of the Western Hemisphere as a special right. Before the Civil War, the Doctrine was largely a statement of intent, but in the late nineteenth and early twentieth centuries, our activities expanded widely. Reflecting its growing industrial power and military capability, the United States became more assertive. It openly imitated the imperialism of the Western European powers, who were rapidly dividing up the globe among themselves.

We insisted on the right to arbitrate an 1895 dispute between Britain and Venezuela. We fought Spain over Cuba and in the process extended our Pacific interest by first acquiring the Philippines, and then fighting a bloody counter-insurgency war there to put down nationalist guerrillas. We insisted on equal commercial opportunities in China in the "Open Door" notes of 1899 and 1906, mediated the 1905 Russo-Japanese War, and intervened in the internal politics of a number of feeble Caribbean and Central American countries. Our troops occupied Cuba, the Dominican Republic, Nicaragua, and shortly after 1914, Haiti. American firms and banks received special concessions and control over resources in many Southern Hemisphere countries. Despite all these actions, America still professed disinterest in "power politics." Although American expansionism received much support, especially from President Theodore Roosevelt, there was mixed reaction and dissent in the domestic politics of the era.

1914–1945: Reluctant World Power

President Woodrow Wilson tried to maintain the traditional American foreign policy—to be absent from Europe, to be supreme in the Western Hemisphere. In the first goal, he failed. His campaign in 1916 suggested that he would keep America out of the cataclysm that had engulfed Europe, but by 1917, the United States was in World War I too. Wilson took America into the war after Germany defied his policy of opposing unrestricted submarine warfare, but once the United States was in, the war became a crusade. Wilson felt the war had been caused by the authoritarian governments and that the entire European system needed to be replaced by an arrangement that substituted mutual interdependence—collective security—and cooperation for the power politics of individual states. Wilson saw our effort as part of a war to end war, to make the world safe for democracy, to establish a new world order. America's terms for abandoning its old separation from Europe were stiff: a remade international system.

Wilson was weakened politically when the Treaty of Versailles, including the Covenant of the League of Nations, was defeated in the Senate, and the Republicans scored a decisive victory in the election of 1920. The Europeans paid little regard to Wilson's views in making a punitive peace. As a consequence of these events, during the 1920's and 1930's the avowed goal of American policy was to return to the prior separation from Europe, to be "isolated" once again. At the same time, the European order became precarious and unstable. The balance-of-power arrangement could not be restored. Two of the former great powers, Russia and Austria-Hungary, were out of the new system. Germany was terribly hostile to the terms of the peace of Versailles. The two victorious democracies, Britain and France, were seriously weakened. Neither would respond in proper time to the Nazi threat.

America's goal of noninvolvement actually had the effect of further destabilizing the international system. By any standard, the United States was the strongest single state in the world. By 1938 its Gross National Product was double that of the Soviet Union's, three times that of Germany and Great Britain, and four times that of France and China. It had, moreover, come out of World War I with no domestic damage and the least overall loss. It served as creditor to the world. And yet the United States refused to join the League of Nations and devoted most of its international energies to trying to collect the debts owed it from the war. Ironically, the process of trying to collect war debts put America squarely in the center of the domestic fiscal planning and politics of most of the European countries. America, it is true, did participate in some disarmament conferences, and it sponsored one in Washington in 1921–1922. Perhaps typical of the diplomacy of this era was America's support of the 1928 Kellogg-Briand Treaty, a meaningless document in which virtually every state renounced war as an instrument of national policy, not because they felt they could or should so act, but because the United States insisted that the piece of paper, however hedged with reservations, be signed.

American isolationism was not the exclusive policy of either domestic party. For the first years of his tenure, New Deal President Franklin D. Roosevelt demonstrated the same support for isolationism as had his Republican predecessors. In fact, the Great Depression caused America to look inward even more than before. Its restrictive tariff laws further depressed European economies without saving the American economy. Its so-called Neutrality Acts of 1935 and 1937, forbidding the sale of American arms to any belligerents in combat, had the practical effect of weakening the democratic loyalists in the Spanish Civil War and of depriving Britain and France of the prospect of assistance in resisting Nazi aggression.

America did shift its policies to provide substantial assistance to Britain after Hitler's blitzkrieg in 1940, before the Japanese attack on Pearl Harbor brought us fully into World War II. After American entry into World War II, American policy was more sophisticated than it had been during World War I. There was preparation behind the scenes for full-scale participation in the international politics of the postwar era, for an international monetary system, and for a new international organization, the United Nations. Underlying our participation at the famous 1945 Yalta Conference was the optimistic hope that the great powers, particularly the Soviet Union and the United States, would police the world together.

The Post-World War II World

Interpretations of history are neither self-evident nor entirely objective. Conflicting perceptions of what happened become positions taken by opposing sides in international and domestic politics. Certainly there are differing views about the origins and nature of America's post-World War II involvement, although there is little disagreement on the dimensions of that participation or the changed international system accompanying it. At the end of the war, the United States possessed preponderant power in the world of international politics. It had a nuclear monopoly. Its ongoing economy had a Gross National Product three times that of the war-wracked Soviet Union and at least five times that of any of the battered European nations.[1] Despite the wartime alliance, the United States quickly became locked into a complicated and encompassing conflict with the Soviet Union.

Certain events highlight the emergence of the conflict. Between 1945 and 1948, the Soviet Union achieved Communist hegemony over most of Eastern Europe, climaxed with a pro-Communist coup in Czechoslovakia in early 1948. There were Soviet military probes against Turkey, and in the Greek Civil War one side consisted of indigenous Communists aided by Yugoslavia. In 1948, after months of bickering over policy in occupied zones of Germany among the four powers—the United States, France, England, and the Soviet Union—the latter imposed a blockade on Berlin. The United States countered with an eleven-month airlift to provide all vital supplies to that beleaguered city. The confrontation shifted to Asia when, in June, 1950, Communist North Korea invaded South Korea. Initially the Americans aided South Korea unilaterally but later, after a United Nations Security Council vote for which the Russians were absent, other nations joined in providing some troops and

---

[1] See Bruce M. Russett, *Trends in World Politics* (New York: Macmillan, 1965), pp. 2–5.

materiel. The North Koreans obtained equipment from the Soviets and—from November, 1950, on—were joined on the battlefield by hundreds of thousands of Red Chinese troops.

The Communist Chinese had come to power in 1949 after an intermittent struggle that began in the 1920's and accelerated after 1946. In the last phase of the Communists' civil war with Chiang Kai-shek, the United States had supported the latter's Nationalists with advisers, materiel, and money, all to no avail. Chiang and his army fled to Taiwan (Formosa) in 1949. In 1950, when the Korean war broke out, the United States threw up an armed cordon—the Sixth Fleet—around this island and continued to give Chiang diplomatic recognition as head of the legitimate government of China. Thus, by the mid-1950's, the post-World War II world had its new political outlines clearly drawn: global conflict between the Western world and the Communist countries.

The new international system had two striking features. First, the world was divided into two rival political "blocs" with a "superpower"—the United States or the Soviet Union—at the head of each. The towering relative might of the superpowers led analysts to talk of a "bipolar" world. The superpowers dominated the international scene by virtue of their possession of nuclear weapons, their standing armies, their economic resources, their competing governmental structures, and the very scope and fact of their conflict with each other. The members of each bloc, the Western and the Communist, were heavily dependent upon their superpower for everything from basic military security to economic survival. The fear of the other bloc kept each set of bloc members close to its sponsor, and the units faced each other from behind drawn military lines, the West in NATO and SEATO (Southeast Asia Treaty Organization), the Communists in the Warsaw Pact alliance.

The second distinguishing feature of the post-World War II era has been the Cold War. *Cold war* is a shorthand term for a new style of competition in international politics. The conflict between the superpowers proceeds simultaneously on military, economic, and political levels. Militarily, the superpowers have confronted one another with nuclear weapons targeted against each other—first in the form of aircraft delivery systems and now in ballistic missiles. Further, the superpowers are prepared for military conflict with traditional nonnuclear arms, either directly or through allies and agents in "limited wars."

The political conflicts of the Cold War have taken many forms. Each side has waged an all-out propaganda offensive against the other in an effort to persuade the uncommitted, the developing nations, the neutrals, or "world opinion" that its system of values is superior. The propaganda war is a struggle for men's minds. Both sides have backed their propaganda with various types of overt or covert support of leaders sympathetic to them in other nations—ranging from the lining up of UN votes to the supplying of money and arms for revolutionaries or counterrevolutionaries.

A seamy aspect of the political conflict of the Cold War is the "intelligence" war, the continuing effort by each side to obtain elaborate information about the economic, military and political plans and resources of its opponent. The opponents use the open, written sources about the other nation whenever possible, but spies are used whenever necessary. Sometimes the spies are complicated technical devices, such as high-altitude picture-taking satellites that orbit the globe. Other times the spies are human secret agents recruited by the intelligence services of each nation. The Cold War has witnessed the rise of an American intelligence apparatus of large scope for the first time in history, the massive Central Intelligence Agency, which is aided by an even more shadowy sister, the National Security Agency. Although the intelligence efforts of both superpowers occasionally are directed toward countries other than the opposing superpower, most activities are concerned with the nation perceived as the main threat. For the United States that has meant the Soviet Union. For the Soviet Union that has meant the United States.

As time passed, the superpowers defined some of the lengths to which they were and were not prepared to carry their conflict. The United States built a string of military bases around the world, most of them on the geographical periphery of the Soviet Union and Communist China. On the other hand, it did not intervene in Hungary in 1956, when the Soviets brutally repressed a revolution there; the nonintervention was a signal that America was unwilling to use direct force to influence the internal politics of the Communist bloc. From the other side, a change in Soviet leadership in the late 1950's brought a frank statement that the Russians did not want conflict with the United States to extend to nuclear war. Premier Khrushchev pithily observed that nuclear weapons could not draw class distinctions.

Within the framework of basic competition, the 1960's saw still further change. After the harrowing head-to-head nuclear confrontation of the Cuban Missile Crisis, tensions between the superpowers were distinctly defused. The scope of relations was enlarged because there seemed to be a new mutual recognition that further accommodation had to be established. Thus, agreement was reached on a number of matters ranging from the inauguration of airline routes between the two nations to the test ban treaty described in the case study of this chapter. In addition, both sides tried hard to increase the number of formal and informal channels through which they could communicate with each other, adding, for example, a teletype "hot line" over which the Kremlin and the White House could exchange messages instantaneously.

One result of the lessening of the level of permanent tension between the Soviet Union and the United States was that the cohesion of their respective blocs began to lessen. In the Communist world, the most serious schism was that between the Soviet Union and Red China. Friction between these two Communist giants was evident during the 1950's; by the 1960's it had accelerated to a plateau of public verbal abuse and bitter private antagonism. The Eastern European countries demonstrated varying degrees of independence from Moscow. The Czechs experimented with autonomy to the degree that the Soviets removed the liberal Dubcek government by force in 1968. The Rumanians managed to be assertive on some issues, yet remain uninvaded. (The Yugoslavs had separated themselves from the Soviet bloc as early as 1948.) The Western bloc saw similar changes. The French first withdrew military, then political support from NATO, and they opposed American policy on such issues as a nuclear nonproliferation treaty, Britain's proposed entry into the European Common Market, and the war in Vietnam.

Causes of the Cold War: Differing Interpretations

From the perspective of the present, looking back, two clearly differing interpretations of the causes of the Cold War that dominated the post-World War II world can be outlined. One view might be called the Establishment Position. It views American behavior as a response to Communist aggression and as a disinterested assumption of the mantle of "world responsibility." The other might be called the Dissenting View. It maintains that elements in American society magnified the Communist threat to cover our military and corporate expansion over the globe in the manner of a traditional imperial power. Some of the main points of each of these explanations follow.

The Establishment Position holds that the Russians began the Cold War through their expansionist policies in Europe between 1945 and 1947. They did this through violating the spirit of the Yalta Agreements in bringing Communist regimes to power in Eastern Europe, their military probing in Turkey and Iran, their role in the Greek Civil War, and their export, through indigenous Communist parties in every country, of a revolutionary doctrine of global conflict and Communist hegemony. The American policy of "containment," based upon the ideas of George F. Kennan as propounded in the July 1947 issue of *Foreign Affairs,* was a defensive response to Soviet behavior. The Americans were to meet Russian probing resolutely and, in time, hope that their opponents would mellow and weary of the struggle.[2]

In concrete form, containment became a series of American sponsored economic and military programs. The North Atlantic Treaty Organization (NATO) brought the Western Europeans together in a mutual security military pact; the Marshall Plan brought them together in an economic recovery aid program. The Soviet Bloc then developed its own alliance, the Warsaw Pact. Other American defense agreements followed in Southeast Asia, the Middle East, and Latin America. Military aid in the form of weapons and training in this country for foreign officers, over 256,000 by 1970, was developed as another means of helping non-Communist governments resist either Soviet aggression or the challenge of internal revolutionary opponents. American support of foreign governments, armed intervention in the Middle East (Lebanon in 1958), Latin America (Cuba at the Bay of Pigs in 1962 and the Dominican Republic in 1965), and Southeast Asia (Vietnam from 1960 on), and covert operations against hostile governments or revolutionary movements by our CIA (in Iran, Guatemala, Bolivia, and Laos) were all part of the effort to protect American and free world interests in the global conflict against the Communists.

---

[2] For a good exposition of this interpretation, see John W. Spanier, *American Foreign Policy Since World War II,* 4th ed. (New York: Praeger, 1971).

Richard J. Barnet has characterized the officials in charge of this policy as national security managers—top executives in the White House Department, the Pentagon, the State Department, and the CIA [3]—and maintained they had a cohesive view of the world determining their behavior. The primary enemy is international Communism. The major testing ground is the third world. The dominant value is the maintenance of American military and economic preeminence, which can only be done, these managers reason from their own World War II experiences, on the basis of power and a willingness to use it. There is no way America can avoid its responsibility in the unstable and violence-prone underdeveloped world. American interests are always best protected by the maintenance of order, and the need for order has to be seen in its worldwide context rather than with too much attention to local particulars. In this context, successful violence or disorder against established governments anywhere encourages further such activity, and success in holding the line maintains stability and increases the chances for future orderly progress. Development with order and under conditions of free trade that provide opportunities for American capital are possible and desirable keystones of our national interest.

The Establishment Position, with the views as sketched out, has, in general, dominated the conduct of American foreign policy. It has dominated because national security managers tend to be recruited from a like-minded, similarly trained legal and business elite, because Presidents of both parties have strongly subscribed to these views, and because there has been popular support for this perspective in the Congress and the public. Since the mid-1960's, however, as an offshoot of opposition to the Vietnam war, a core of research, criticism, and political action has produced what might be called the Dissenting View on the Cold War. The Dissenting View has supporters among counterelites in the universities, among students and minorities, and, for some parts of it, in segments of the Congress and the general public.

In the Dissenting View, American policy-makers never gave postwar cooperation with the Soviet Union a fair opportunity. Taken aback by the implications of agreements they had made themselves at Yalta, haunted by the specter of Communist successes in unstable situations around the world, and motivated by the fear that worldwide revolutionary change would destroy the capitalist system, our policy managers exaggerated the threat of Russian behavior. They overacted, in the process deliberately frightening the American public and bringing into being a peacetime war machine. Subsequently, the public became, sometimes enthusiastically, a source of demands and support for further anti-Communist activities. The military gained the first peacetime draft in American history in the landmark flood of national security legislation of 1947–1948, which also established the National Security Council in the White House and the Central Intelligence Agency. Once in business, with control over the lives of millions of young men, an ever-growing share of the national budget (which has seldom dropped beneath 10 per cent of the Gross National Product since the 1950's), and a special set of industries dependent upon it—the military-industrial complex—the Pentagon became an independent source of pressure for a stronger

[3] *Intervention and Revolution* (Cleveland: World, 1968).

anti-Communist policy. Its emphasis, as with all bureaucracies, was upon responses extending its own control, namely military responses.

In the Dissenting View, American officials have been motivated by strong ideological views in their international behavior.[4] But more than that, and more than the mission-seeking behavior of the Defense Department and the CIA, there has been a strong economic aspect to our foreign policy. Some of this dates from the turn of the century when the Marines allowed American investment banks to manage the entire revenue apparatus of Central American countries or the Navy protected American businessmen in China. But in the post-World War II epoch the apparatus is more extensive. The CIA has been used to help American industry in Guatemala and Iran. American firms, following military bases, receive favored trade access. They obtain an above-world-market monopoly on most purchases under our foreign aid program. And, proponents of the Dissenting View maintain, the basic American drive for world order and stability has the effect of reinforcing those who are already powerful. Nowhere is this impact more visible than in the underdeveloped world (Latin America and other areas), where the United States draws out yearly three times more than it invests, as Table 14.1 shows.

Vietnam as a Turning Point in American Foreign Policy

Vietnam was a logical progression of American anti-Communist foreign policy, with its emphasis on military containment, begun in the late 1940's. The Pentagon Papers, a leaked version of the Defense Department's own study of the war, makes clear the

[4] See, for example, Michael Parenti, *The Anti-Communist Impulse* (New York: Random House, 1969).

Table 14.1   *Income from direct investments transferred to the United States, 1950–1965, in billions of dollars*

	Europe	Canada	Latin America	All other areas
Flow of direct investments from U.S.	$8.1	$6.8	$3.8	$5.2
Income on this capital transferred to U.S.	5.5	5.9	11.3	14.3
Net	+$2.6	+$ .9	—$7.5	—$9.1

Source: Harry Magdoff, *The Age of Imperialism* (New York: Monthly Review Press, 1969). Copyright © 1969 by Harry Magdoff; reprinted by permission of Monthly Review Press.

continuity between all of the Vietnam decisions and the twenty years that preceded them.[5] The policy maintained the same world stance, the same reliance on military technology, and the same bipartisan political support. One of the many consequences of America's involvement in the war was the breakdown of the intellectual and political consensus on both the facts and the wisdom of the Establishment Position on foreign policy. The Vietnam war as interpreted through the Establishment Position and through the Dissenting Position reveals bitter and deep-seated conflicts, which may illustrate in specific terms some of the general points we have been presenting.

The facts of America's involvement in Vietnam are clear enough. We financed the French effort to hold onto Indochina as a colony, increasingly from 1948 through 1954, and paid most of the costs of the last years of that bloody struggle against Ho Chi Minh's Viet Minh. When the war was settled by a multination agreement, the Geneva Accords, partitioning the country into two pieces until elections were held, the United States did not sign, but agreed to respect the provisions. We underwrote the efforts of Ngo Dinh Diem to build a non-Communist society in South Vietnam, first with money, then with nonmilitary technicians, then with American military advisers in 1960—and finally with American combat troops: 17,000 in 1962, 250,-000 troops by 1966, and over 500,000 troops by 1968. Then, under President Nixon, America gradually began the slow but steady withdrawal of its forces at a rate of around 100,000 a year. From February, 1965, through October, 1968, we engaged in extensive bombing operations in North Vietnam, unloading on that country about three times the tonnage dropped on Nazi-controlled Europe during World War II. In 1972, extensive bombing of the North was resumed, and the harbors of Hanoi and Haiphong were mined.

While in Vietnam American forces engaged in sweep and destroy missisons, forcible relocations of civilian populations, and chemically induced "scorched earth" tactics to defeat the Viet Cong and their North Vietnamese allies. Americans suffered over fifty thousand dead and a quarter million wounded. After a constant series of coups, an authoritarian military government under General Nguyen Van Thieu came into power in a 1967 election of severely limited competition and was relected under similar restrictions in 1971. At no time did our South Vietnamese allies demonstrate much ability to function on their own, either as a government winning the loyalty of its citizens or as a military force.

In the Establishment Position, our entry into the Vietnam war was a clear case of containing Communism, a test case of the Communist tactic of subversion by using native guerrillas supplied, inspired, led, and supplemented from outside the country being attacked. If we could not protect the South Vietnamese, then Communist insurgents elsewhere would try the same thing and there would be disorder throughout Southeast Asia and a "domino" effect in the falling of legitimate non-Communist governments of the region. Further, to fail to act would call into question American resolve elsewhere. Allies would wonder whether we would honor our commitments to them if they were threatened. If we allowed aggression to succeed

[5] New York: Bantam, 1971.

against our friends in Asia, for whom we had sacrificed so much, what would happen to our standing as a world power? What would happen to those in South Vietnam who had staked their lives on our support? From this perspective, the Vietnam war emerges as a logical activity, designed to shore up the non-Communist barriers of the world, halt violent revolutionary activities, and dissuade local Communists, as well as the Chinese and the Russians, from expansionist behavior.

In the Dissenting View, the war is seen differently. Our intervention is interpreted as support for one side in a Vietnamese civil war, a side which has been consistently corrupt and repressive. The North Vietnamese, because of the role of their leaders in the fight against the French, were the nationalists in the country as well as social revolutionaries. Our success or failure would have no impact upon revolutionaries or world order in other places. We have magnified the Chinese and Russian role in Vietnam out of proportion, have acted more often aggressively than defensively ourselves, and have raised serious moral questions through our use of devastating technology against underdeveloped Asian peoples far less powerful than we. Further, in this view, by no calculation could the war be said to be justified in terms of its costs to the Vietnamese, whom we have destroyed in the process of proposing to save them, not to mention the awesome American casualties, the $200 billion in war expenditures, the dislocation of our domestic politics, and the inflation that has followed. Some dissenting pragmatists have simply argued that we picked the wrong conflict in the wrong place; others, more concerned with ethics, have seriously raised the issues of American violation of international law and commission of war crimes.

foreign policy:
the cold war and beyond

Making Foreign Policy:
The Major Participants

Making foreign policy is a political process, and it is worthwhile examining who participates and how it is done. The major participants in the making of American foreign policy are the President and his personal staff and staff agencies, the regular Cabinet departments of the executive branch, the Congress, and a variety of domestic interest groups. In the emergence of the United States as a primary world power, through World War II and the hot parts of the Cold War, the President has played the preeminently powerful role. In part his authority rested upon the legal justification spelled out by the Supreme Court in the *Curtiss-Wright* case: "in this vast external realm, with its important, complicated, delicate and manifold problems, the President alone has the power to speak or listen as a representative of the nation." [6] The Supreme Court went so far as to argue that the President was "the sole organ of the federal government in the field of international relations." The Court said that this exceptional authority derived not only from the Constitution and various delegations of the legislature, but from the nature of national sovereignty itself. Protection of our sovereignty required information, secrecy, and other attributes that only the presidential office could provide.

The President's role also grew because of the extension of our overseas activities and the tensions and crises of the Cold War. Although the President may be blocked on domestic policies by various opponents, and indeed has no power to remove from office state or local officials who displease him, in the foreign realm he is less limited. There are numerous governments around the world whose economies have been so dependent upon our support, or whose armies could not exist without our donated equipment, that a word from the President could change that country's policies internally or externally, or remove from office officials close to and including the

[6] Quoted in Elmer E. Cornwell, Jr., *The American Presidency: Vital Center* (Chicago: Scott, Foresman, 1966), p. 152.

632

highest. Indeed, foreign governments have been overthrown on the order of American Presidents in a way no mayor could be removed in an American city. Support for the President's preeminence was primarily generated through the Cold War consensus on the establishment position: the Congress acquiesced and the public approved. Those two provided the most powerful supports, but in addition a series of intellectual justifications for the President's role were widely circulated. Professor Richard E. Neustadt's widely read book *Presidential Power,* for example, seems to maintain that whatever is good for the President's personal political position is good for the country as a whole.[7]

Not least of all, Presidents since Franklin D. Roosevelt, with the exception of Dwight D. Eisenhower, have sought more power and carefully extended and guarded their prerogatives in the foreign policy field. They have attempted to manipulate foreign policy news to place their programs in the best possible light, have withheld information about certain activities such as an American war fought in Laos with mercenary troops commanded by the CIA, and have applied very sophisticated public relations techniques to buttress their role. Although the President remains preeminent today, the questioning and conflict generated by Vietnam have brought the exclusiveness of his foreign policy power into question. Especially under attack is his ability to carry the nation gradually into undeclared and limited wars without any explicit statement to the public or approval from the Congress.

The President operates at this pinnacle of foreign policy-making with the help of personal advisers and foreign policy staff agencies housed in the White House itself. Certain individuals and units are intended to serve only him, without having operating responsibilities or bureaucratic clienteles outside the White House. His main personal adviser is the Special Assistant for National Security Affairs. His main staff help comes from the National Security Council, the Bureau of the Budget, and the Office of Science and Technology.

The National Security Council is an institutionalized advisory mechanism established in 1947 to act as a kind of special foreign policy cabinet. Its members include the President, the Vice-President, the Secretaries of State, and Defense, and the Director of the Office of Emergency Planning. The Chairman of the Joint Chiefs of Staff and the Director of the CIA are advisers to the Council, who can be utilized as much or as little as the President chooses.

The President needs personal staff and staff agencies to help him in the foreign policy area in part because his is a unique political perspective, but also in part because he may have differing needs insofar as the *process* of making decisions is concerned. The astute Jackson Senate Subcommittee on National Security Staffing and Operations phrased the problem this way:

What does a President need to do his job?
Essentially he wants to keep control of the situation—to get early warning of items for his agenda before his options are foreclosed, to pick his issues and lift them out of normal channels, to obtain priority attention from key officials on the issues he pulls to his desk, to

[7] New York: Wiley Science Editions, 1962, pp. 183–185.

get prompt support for his initiatives, and to keep other matters on a smooth course, with his lines of information open, so that he can intervene if a need arises.

As top officials meet the President's urgent requirements, their other duties necessarily receive lower priority. Their regular meetings are canceled. They become less accessible to their subordinates. *Ad hoc* procedures are devised. Much is done verbally that would normally be put in writing. This all becomes exceedingly hard on subordinate officials, for it interferes with their handling of the usual run of business.

What do the officials of our vast departments and agencies need to do their job?

Essentially they want orderly, deliberate, familiar procedures—accustomed forums in which to air their interests, a top-level umpire to blow the whistle when the time has come to end debate, and written records of the decisions by which they should be governed.[8]

The major executive branch departments and agencies with policy-making and operational responsibilities in the foreign affairs area are State, Defense, Central Intelligence, Agriculture, Commerce, and the Treasury, along with the Atomic Energy Commission. Among these, the State Department has traditionally held senior rank; it is specifically charged with making and administering foreign policy, and its chief, the Secretary of State, ranks as the senior cabinet officer. Beneath the Secretary, the department's fifteen thousand professional personnel are organized along geographical and functional lines.

Four operating agencies have grown in importance in recent years. The Agency for International Development (AID) administers the foreign aid program—from squeezing the annual appropriations from the Congress to analyzing project proposals to working with foreign governments in administering projects in the field. AID officers are stationed in American embassies abroad. The United States Information Agency (USIA) is the propaganda arm of the American government, handling its worldwide public relations, making films for foreign distribution, and operating the Voice of America radio station. USIA officers are also part of the overseas embassies. The Peace Corps provides technical and educational services to developing nations through its volunteers. Finally, the Arms Control and Disarmament Agency has played important roles in the negotiation of the nuclear test ban treaty, described in the case study to this chapter, the nuclear nonproliferation treaty, and the SALT talks.

The role of the Defense Department in the execution of foreign policy goals is almost self-evident. It administers overseas military operations, from the troops in Asia to the units on assignment to NATO. The department also has military attachés serving in the overseas embassies to observe developments in foreign countries. It maintains Military Assistance Advisory Groups in many embassies to administer foreign grants and sales of American weapons and to advise the military services of friendly governments.

In Washington, the role of the Defense Department in making foreign policy is complicated. Recommendations from the military in the awesome area of strategic

---

[8] Senate Subcommittee on National Security Staffing and Operations, *Administration of National Security: Basic Issues,* in Andrew M. Scott and Raymond H. Dawson, *Readings in the Making of American Foreign Policy* (New York: Macmillan, 1965), p. 215.

policy—the development, procurement, and conditions for usage of nuclear weapons systems—lie at the heart of physical national security. Yet there is no longer any possibility of a shield that would protect more than a small percentage of Americans in case of a nuclear war or "exchange." As a consequence strategic policy revolves around "deterrence," a psychological concept. The idea is that if the United States has sufficient nuclear forces to destroy an enemy, even if he launches a first strike himself, the thought of the destruction of his own society will deter him from taking any such rash action. Whatever the military says in this area, and its advice is usually buttressed by such "think tanks" as the Institute for Defense Analysis and the Rand Corporation, has to be taken very seriously by civilian decision-makers. The technology itself is awesome in terms of its destructive power, sophistication of systems, and costs. The basic drift of military advice, which has seldom been rejected, has led to very extensive armaments. America has over eleven thousand nuclear warheads deliverable to Soviet targets, in arsenals based abroad, in planes constantly in the air, in missile-carrying submarines, and in land-based missiles.

The military has been cautious in its approach to disarmament talks of all kinds, not surprisingly when one considers that its business is defense. Beginning with the Administration of John F. Kennedy, the military's conventional forces were built up to a capability of fighting two and a half wars at any time: a land war in Europe, a land war in Asia, and a small war on some other continent. President Nixon reduced this capability to a one-and-a-half-war readiness posture.

While fighting wars, the military may be the purveyor of purely technical advice to civilian decision-makers. In terms of its overall outlook, however, the Pentagon has been more than a reflector of the Cold War anti-Communism of the Establishment Position. It has actively sold that position, using sophisticated public relations techniques in domestic affairs, in governing, and for those it considers to be "opinion-makers" out of government.[9] It has utilized to the maximum its relationship with defense contractors to build support for military projects, and because at least 70 per cent of this spending is done without competitive bidding and because the dollar stakes are so large, most companies have been eager to cooperate. In addition, the location of large military bases in many parts of the country injects considerable spending into local economies and is translated into support from Congressmen representing such areas.[10]

The Central Intelligence Agency (CIA), established under the National Security Act of 1947, is responsible for the coordination of all the intelligence information-gathering activities of the different departments operating in the national security and foreign policy areas. But it is much more than a coordinating body. For one thing, it does much of its own research. Research involving secondary materials is carried on in the agency's huge headquarters building in Langley, Virginia, in one of the world's best libraries of foreign periodicals and journals. The CIA is also responsible for

[9] See Senator J. William Fulbright, *The Pentagon Propaganda Machine* (New York: Vintage, 1971), and the prize-winning CBS News documentary television program, "The Selling of the Pentagon."

[10] See Bruce M. Russett, *What Price Vigilance?* (New Haven: Yale University Press, 1970).

"And this, just in. A usually reliable Pentagon source, who declined to be identified, has vigorously denied suggesting that published speculation, admittedly based on fragmentary and unconfirmed reports not available to the press, regarding allied troop movements in or near unspecified areas of Indo-China and purportedly involving undisclosed numbers of South Vietnamese, Cambodian, Laotian, and perhaps American armed personnel is false, although he cautioned that such published speculation could be dangerously misleading and potentially divisive."

Figure 14.1.

Source: Drawing by Lorenz; © 1971 The New Yorker Magazine, Inc.

covert intelligence gathering abroad and for covert operations sponsored by the government, including, in the past, the sponsoring of a revolution in Guatemala (1954) and the Bay of Pigs invasion of Cuba (1961). The CIA's top officials are at the core of the foreign policy-making process, as statutory advisers to the National Security Council and as personal advisers to the President. The CIA's budget is generally camouflaged in the larger executive budget, and its operations are watched over by a small, specially selected congressional committee, which itself operates in secret. Thus the agency possesses considerable autonomy and freedom from the kind of visibility and public scrutiny to which other parts of our government are subject.

In addition, the Cabinet departments of Agriculture, Commerce, and the Treasury are involved in foreign policy decisions and operations. The Agriculture Department, through its support and purchase of domestic farm surpluses and distribution of these foodstuffs under Public Law 480—the "food for peace" program—feeds millions of people in developing lands around the world. The Commerce Department works with businessmen in establishing and protecting the billions of dollars of private American investments around the globe. The Treasury is concerned with and involved in the subtleties of America's balance-of-payments problem and other fiscal relationships with foreign countries. Finally, the Atomic Energy Commission, as the Nuclear Test Ban Treaty case indicated, is involved in the design and testing of nuclear weapons systems, and it provides highly technical advice on the subject of arms development and control.

Congressional Participation in Foreign Policy-Making

During the main era of the Cold War, Congress has been eclipsed as a powerful voice in foreign policy by the executive branch. In part this occurred because Congressmen subscribed to the establishment position on the Cold War with little deviation and were content to rubber-stamp executive branch initiatives and Pentagon programs. Many believed the standard arguments about the need for executive preeminence to be empirically true: that crises required secrecy, that only the President had the information to make national security decisions, and that such speed was required that sharing power would not be in the national interest. All of these are simply arguments. No studies have ever been devoted either to proving or to disproving their validity. Nonetheless, they were strong arguments in the Washington atmosphere, especially in the tenseness of a Cold War context.

In a legal-constitutional sense, there is no reason why the Congress could not be as important as the President in foreign affairs, or as powerful as it is in domestic issues. Although it is true that the Supreme Court and the Constitution have given the President a special role, it is also true that the Senate must give its consent before treaties can be ratified, and that Congress alone can declare war. What has happened is that the Senate allowed the treaty power to be eroded by "executive agreements" between the President and foreign governments that do not require its consent. Congress as a whole allowed its war-making powers to be eroded by presidential initiatives in Korea, Vietnam, and elsewhere. Yet Congress could reassert these powers if a majority sought to, and the increasing number of resolutions sponsored in both houses and the challenges by both the Senate Foreign Relations Committee and the House Foreign Affairs Committee are evidence of an increasing restiveness with regard to complete executive control.

In the simplest sense, the Congress could control American foreign policy—short of the most drastic nuclear decisions in response to attack—through its control over the funds of American politics. At the height of the Cold War and the Vietnam war, the Congress ran military budgets through without a murmur while domestic bills were subject to the most agonizing scrutiny. The Congress, in the end, however, is responsible for authorizing and appropriating all of the funds for maintaining our embassies, supplying and paying our troops, developing and buying weapons, underwriting the Peace Corps, and distributing American crop surpluses. Any move toward real congressional control over major decisions of American foreign policy, especially if it involved rearrangements of total governmental priorities between

Figure 14.2. Tall in the saddle

Source: Conrad in the *Los Angeles Times,* reprinted courtesy of The Register and Tribune Syndicate.

domestic and foreign/military costs, would be certain to produce conflict. There would be conflict between the Congress and the executive branch, between domestic groups benefiting from our prior foreign policies and the new beneficiaries, and between the military and the civilian sectors.

Moreover, additional Congressional influence in foreign policy would surely mean a different style of making decisions, whether the substance of policy changed or not. The Congress, for example, operates with much deliberation and little secrecy. Congressional power is decentralized in the dual power system of committees and party. Although the foreign and military affairs committees in both houses are most important, the appropriations committees in each body also have considerable influence. In all, over half of the thirty-six standing committees concern themselves with foreign policy in some way.

The Role of Interest Groups in Foreign Policy

Sometimes it is said that foreign policy requires such special skills that the process of making decisions should be insulated from the judgments of all but the highest officials or the most refined specialists. As is the case with so much that passes for wisdom in the foreign policy field, this seems to be more an argument than a provable description of reality. This argument is also frequently self-serving in that those defined as "fit" often represent a particular point of view rather uniformly. In any case, however much various participants have tried to insulate their authority, domestic groups have become as involved in foreign policy as in domestic policy. The reason is simple. Foreign policy decisions have a direct impact upon the income, power, status, and life chances of different groups. Few are willing to forego having a say in such vital matters. Shippers who depend upon the Agency for International Development for their income, defense contractors with a stake in the Cold War, college students who object to war in Asia and to serving in the military, corporations that gain from America's global power—none simply happily step aside and leave their fate to others in our government, however much they may be urged to do so.

A group's choice of tactics depends not only upon original resources and power, but the range of its concern. Most groups with opinions on foreign policy have very specific objectives. The American Jewish community wants support of Israel. Oil companies with heavy overseas investments want a more pro-Arab policy in the Middle East. Oil companies with primarily domestic facilities want to maintain the oil import quotas, which keep prices for their products artifically high for northeastern and midwestern consumers by strictly limiting the importation of foreign oil. For very specific goals such as these, appropriate tactics are private lobbying of the executive and legislative branches, with a low visibility of the activity of the interest groups. If, in contrast, groups are concerned with broad outlines of foreign policy —Cold War policy and defense spending being the major items—then the tactics tend toward public political articulation.

In any discussion of groups acting in foreign policy politics, it must be remembered that the main "group" is still the government itself. It has the most employees and the largest budget devoted both to the operations of foreign policy and to "public information," or selling whatever the policies are to the public. On the broad issues of foreign policy, private groups and the government are involved in seeking support from individual political leaders, parties, and other groups that might form a coalition. The public is a crucial audience because, in a system based upon consent, an open press, and a minimum of coercion, ultimate public support is essential. Eventually, when there is a well-defined public position, elected politicians will line up on that side. Not surprisingly, then, the group and government struggle over major foreign policy issues is a battle for the hearts and minds of the American people.

The Special Place of Public Opinion in Foreign Policy-Making

As with so much in the foreign policy field, there is disagreement about the American public's relationship to foreign policy. Some scholars have argued that the public is generally poorly informed on policy issues, tends to respond to crises in an emotional way, and is generally reactive to whatever cues political elites put forth, particularly the President. It does seem to be true that the public was broadly "isolationist" until World War II, and that majority opinion, responding to the political leadership of the Truman Administration and its successors, turned strongly anti-Communist during the Cold War. In addition, numerous polls have shown that *any* strong action by a President, whatever its substantive direction, increases his foreign policy support in the short run. One reason is that people, in the short run, take the President at face value and assume he knows what he is doing. Another reason seems to be that by such action the President invokes patriotic feelings that override the specifics of whatever he has done.

On the other hand, collections of polls have shown rather considerable public information on many issues, and some scholars have maintained that, under the circumstances of the cases, the public has kept its cool rather well.[11] On top of that, however much a dose of presidential public relations adrenaline may shoot up Gallup or Harris Poll ratings temporarily, all Presidents have seen their ratings decline as their terms wore on. The most serious eroders of such popularity, next to economic issues, have been foreign policy acts such as the wars in Korea and Vietnam. It seems certain that the public in the 1970's has begun to react experientially to its government's foreign policy. That is, whatever the ideological coating or the urgings of leaders, when foreign policies begin to hurt—in war deaths, in inflation, or in bitter domestic conflict—the public reacts negatively. Conversely, peace or any relaxation of tensions generates widespread approval.

The Process of Foreign Policy-Making

How these participants and the public interact in the process of making foreign policy can be better understood by a look at a typology of the decision-making apparatus. Table 14.2 suggests in schematic form some of the range of variation in the process. The size of the decision-making circle, the openness of the process, the

[11] For a sampling of the literature on diverse aspects of the relationships between public opinion and foreign policy, see Gabriel Almond, *The American People and Foreign Policy* (New York: Harcourt, 1950); Alfred O. Hero, *Americans in World Affairs* (Boston: World Peace Foundation, 1959); James N. Rosenau, *Public Opinion and Foreign Policy* (New York: Random House, 1961); Hazel Erkine, "The Polls: Exposure to International Information," *Public Opinion Quarterly* (Winter, 1963), pp. 658–662; V. O. Key, Jr., *Public Opinion and American Democracy* (New York: Knopf, 1964); Milton J. Rosenberg, "Attitude Change and Foreign Policy in the Cold War Era," in James N. Rosenau, ed., *Domestic Sources of Foreign Policy* (New York: Free Press, 1967), pp. 111–159; Kenneth Waltz, *Foreign Policy and Democratic Politics* (Boston: Little, Brown, 1967); and William R. Caspary, "The 'Mood Theory': A Study of Public Opinion and Foreign Policy," *The American Political Science Review*, LXIV, No. 2 (June, 1970), pp. 536–547.

duration of time allowed for a decision to be made, and the general atmosphere all vary with the issue. In the "war-peace crisis" situation, the crucial nature of the issue and the time pressures that the crisis generates make certain that the number of people involved in any American decisions will be small. They will include the President, a few particular advisers, top officials in the State and Defense Departments, and some ranking executives from the intelligence agencies. America's responses to the Berlin Blockade and the Cuban Missile Crisis conformed to this pattern. In the latter instance, the inner circle included a special ad hoc body, an executive committee of the National Security Council. Internal processes in a war-peace crisis are likely to be secret, because almost by definition it involves a direct and major confrontation with an opponent; the government natually does not want its moves signaled before decisions are made and until after alternatives are weighed. The time span because of the gravity of the challenge, is exceedingly short—weeks at most, days more likely. The gravity of the problem coupled with the short-time parameters means that the overall atmosphere will be one of extreme crisis—characterized by late meetings at the White House and the putting aside of routine affairs. The pressures are heaviest on the President himself. Foreign policy becomes a kind of grisly international chess game, with fateful stakes. His decisions affect the other actor, whose next move shapes America's sequential response.

It is a measure of the nation's adaptation to this environment that the second type of situation can be labeled the "regular-cross-bloc-struggle," implying that, short of direct confrontations, daily challenge from the Communist world is something that has actually become routinized. Regular-cross-bloc-struggle issues include the Soviet military, economic, and political relations with Europe as well as a variety

Table 14.2 *A typology of foreign policy processes*

Issue	Size of decision-making circle	Openness of process	Time span	Atmosphere
1. War-peace crisis	Very small	Secret	Short	Severe crisis
2. Regular cross-bloc struggle	Medium	Partially open	Continuous	Considerable tension
3. Diplomacy with allies and neutrals	Medium	Largely open	Continuous	Relative calm
4. Allocation of American resources	Large	Open	Continuous	Increasing tension

of thorny questions: how to respond to Soviet military and space progress, how to counteract Soviet efforts to extend their influence in neutral nations, how to reach greater accommodation with the Soviets on arms questions, or how to achieve a broader or narrower détente or lessened level of hostility in relations in general. Into this category falls the intense debate over Asia, including the policy choices that America must make in regard to the People's Republic of China. How much more should it soften its approach in hope of more mutual responses?

In regular-cross-bloc-struggle issues the decision-making circle, or at least the decision-debating circle, is likely to be much larger, including not only the President and the White House core, but also numerous sub-cabinet level department officials, important congressional committees, and influential segments of the academic community, the press, and the interested public. Although final decisions may or may not be made in secret, the process of deliberation is relatively open to those who choose to follow it. Sometimes the technical nature of the specific problems limits the range of participants: the Nuclear Test Ban Treaty, for example, required some ability to assess the possibilities of one side or the other's being able to devise a means to cheat and whether or not such possible cheating could be converted to a developmental gain in nuclear weapons design.

During deliberation on regular-cross-bloc-struggle issues, the time parameter is continuous; that is, consideration of policy goes on at various levels all the time without beginning or end. The mood is one that might best be described as semi-crisis. Sometimes the moves of the United States are in response to its opponents' actions, and always the opponents' possible responses are included in America's calculations. Initiative rests with the President and the executive branch, but the Congress follows these issues sufficiently closely and with a sufficient level of expertise to block presidential initiatives and frequently to alter the specifics of presidential plans. Referring primarily to issues of this type, Roger Hilsman has commented:

this process by which decisions on major policies are reached is a political one, even when it takes place entirely within the government and screened from the public view. That is to say, first, that such decisions require the reconciliation of a diversity of goals and preferences as well as alternative means; second, that there are competing groups within the government as well as outside it who are identified with the alternative goals and policies; and, third, that the relative power of the participating groups is as relevant to the decision as the cogency and wisdom of their arguments.[12]

Issues involving "diplomacy with allies and neutrals" are differentiated from other types primarily by the atmosphere of domestic decision-making. Here, although again the process goes on continuously, the mood is one of greater calm. The mood is one of calm for two reasons. However unfortunate a wrong decision, error is not

[12] "Congressional-Executive Relations and the Foreign Policy Consensus," in Andrew M. Scott and Raymond H. Dawson, *Readings in the Making of American Foreign Policy* (New York: Macmillan, 1965).

likely to involve basic national security immediately or to accelerate the nation into a war-peace crisis. Accordingly, the decision-makers have greater leeway. Second, issues in this category involve relations with either friends or at least nonenemies. From a psychological perspective, to work with friends and nonenemies almost always permits the establishment of a more congenial and less tense pattern of interaction than is the case in the confrontation of opponents. It is easier to give consideration to the views of friends or nonenemies and to give in on minor points.

Issues in this category include alliance security policy, as for example, NATO policy. They also include questions of trade, of coordination of policy at the United Nations, and of routine consultations on the entire spectrum of world issues. In relations with nonenemies, the issues are often connected with the amount and nature of American aid programs.

The decision-making circle extends outside the White House by some distance on issues of this sort. Many decisions are made in fact at the middle levels of the government, particularly in the State Department. The process of arriving at a decision is relatively open for those who care to follow it. Lack of interest in many decisions—who but the specialist cares about aid to Nepal?—the routine nature of many other matters, and the technical aspects of many aid questions limit the amount of public consideration given to individual issues. Nonetheless, there is little, if any, deliberate effort to impose secrecy on the process of deciding on these issues.

Finally, there is a recurring set of issues that have serious consequences for our foreign policy, but that are considered almost totally within the framework of domestic politics. These are the "allocation of American resources" cases. Through the 1960's, these tended to be relatively low-key decisions about what was then seen as a never-vanishing pie of goodies: how American overseas aid had to be spent on American products and on which products and sent in which American ships; who among the top fifteen defense or space contractors would get to build the next major weapon in the endless cornucopia of such projects that research could envision into an endless future; where plants, bases, and NASA facilities would be located to bolster the economies of districts of deserving local Congressmen; and which American commodities would get government support in the world trade negotiations against competition from imports.

Since the early 1970's, these issues have generated much more controversy and taken place in an atmosphere of increasing tension. The reasons are simple: competing claims have come to the fore for the resources of the society, and these resources are no longer perceived as unlimited, but as scarce. What happens when a pattern of public policy consisting of the low-visibility dividing of an economic pie among private groups becomes a hotly contested matter is well known. The struggle is escalated into a broad conflict over policies; it becomes, in the schema of Chapter 2, redistributive rather than distributive. Issues of international trade including tariffs, import quotas, and opening new markets have become particularly important.

American Foreign Policy: Some Hard Questions about the Future

The debate over American foreign policy, first centered on Vietnam but later on the entire concept of the American role in the world, involves some basic issues affecting the lives of every citizen for the next twenty years. There are convincing arguments and serious implications on all sides. In the end, the student will have to decide for himself or herself what he or she thinks. In what follows, however, we can raise some of the thorniest issues.

Americans will have to face up to the fact that what some of us call "America's responsible world role" is what other Americans call "imperialism." The labels are simply supportive and hostile connotations for the same behavior: the global extension of American military, economic, and cultural forces over the last thirty years, reaching deep into all nations not in the Communist camp, and encircling those Communist nations with a ring of military bases and nuclear weapons. One issue is: What are the gains and costs of the Establishment Position as it has largely dominated our behavior for most of the time since the end of World War II? Another question is: What constraints will the international system itself impose upon American alternatives in the years ahead? Finally, there is a normative question: How *should* the United States act in the world arena within the realm of the possibilities open to it?

Benefits and Costs

There is no question that post-World War II American world hegemony has had benefits for aspects of the international system and for American politicians, groups, and individuals as well. For the international system, American military and economic power certainly contributed to world stability, at least between 1945 and 1965. Given the damage of World War II and the lessons of instability wrought by the vindictive 1919 Versailles Peace, American policy-makers are deservedly proud of their contribution to the rebuilding of Europe and Japan, whose free, modernized, and prosperous societies today have their roots in our policies in the immediate post-war era. Even in underdeveloped nations, where the American record is more ambiguous, no one can deny that our technical assistance in agriculture has made many countries self-sustaining in food production (the "green revolution" of miracle rice), that the "Alliance for Progress" of John F. Kennedy had the redistribution of income in South America as a real goal, or that the Peace Corps has been as close to a purely altruistic venture as nation-states undertake.

For individual American politicians, especially its Presidents, office-holding has made them automatically "world leaders." It has been a heady atmosphere because few kings in history enjoyed the power and status around the globe of American Presidents. And Presidents and their aides and the executive branch and the Congress have enjoyed the perquisites of their power: the world travel with courteous treatment and the ability to make momentous decisions and carry them out with few impediments in our own free world realm. For American companies, as Table 14.1 made evident, world power has meant profits, and this prosperity has filtered into the general standard of living enjoyed by Americans. Not only have homebound Americans benefited from the economic advantages of our world role, but tourists and others had the benefit of the dollar as the world's strongest currency from 1945 to 1968. As we watch the weakening of that currency, the benefits in cheaper imports and cheap travel are becoming clearer to millions.

At a very basic level, proponents of the Establishment Position on the Cold War can argue that their policies provided physical security for the free world and America during a dangerous era. A nuclear war or a major land war between the superpowers was averted. Although Americans have suffered heavy casualties in Korea and Vietnam, there has been no physical damage to the United States. In addition, the case is often made that American postwar economic affluence depends in part upon the spur of defense spending. The Roosevelt New Deal experts never managed to get the economy going full tilt on a peacetime basis. Thus, in truth, our government has no experience in managing a full-employment nonmilitary economy, nor have our businessmen. Anyone who argues against the short-run economy-priming aspects of defense spending, with its millions of jobs and multiplier effects through hundreds of thousands of firms, has an obligation to have some workable conversion plans available.

As to the costs of the general pattern of American foreign policy in the Cold War era, these can be listed in an order parallel to the benefits. For the international system, the deployment of our military and economic forces, dissenters argue, has served to slow down processes of social justice and economic change, especially in the underdeveloped nations. American arms, in countries such as Greece and Pakistan, have helped maintain in power repressive and undemocratic governments who have only had to claim they were anti-Communist to win our support.

Further, as much as the Soviets, we have been responsible for escalations in the world arms race, which depletes resources that otherwise might go for capital investment or human needs. Indeed, arms spending among the superpowers is interactive—that is, activity by one stimulates a reaction by the other.[13] Several times, especially in the early 1960's, our military strategy, particularly the doctrine of "counterforce" that could have given us a first strike capability, set off counter-deployment by the Soviet Union. Our policy of gearing our military preparedness to the *industrial potential* of the other side—not its actual production or presumed intent—has had the effect of a self-fulfilling prophecy, propelling each side to higher and higher levels of military spending and wilder and wilder weapons. We acted this way in spite of evidence that deescalation of the arms spiral was a real possibility.[14]

For American politicians, concentration on the world role has extracted three kinds of costs. First, Presidents have spent, by a rough estimate, 70 to 80 per cent

[13] See Bruce R. Russett, *What Price Vigilance?*, op. cit.
[14] Charles E. Osgood, *An Alternative to War or Surrender* (Urbana: University of Illinois, 1963).

of their time on foreign policy. Many have known more about the problems of Calcutta than those of Detroit, about the leaders of Saigon than the leaders of Atlanta. On a day-to-day basis, top leadership has neglected domestic problems. Second, in some ways, wielding American power in foreign affairs has been simpler, or at least more attractive, than trying to resolve the tough conflicts of domestic politics. Political leaders have preferred the power and the glory to the nitty-gritty, hard efforts of America's own problems—race, urban decay, and the entire well-known spectrum of other domestic problems. Finally, the secrecy of foreign policy as conducted by executive branch officials and particularly the Vietnam war has surely reduced the credibility of American politicians at a crucial time in our national history. Years of secret war-making coupled with public denials and dissembling erode public confidence and the legitimacy of government. Some of this is reflected in the political culture data cited in Chapter 1.

As for the costs to groups, Professor Seymour Melman has argued that major sectors of our society have been depleted by military spending. He maintains that the low level of technology in basic heavy industries such as steel and machine tools and the chaos in the telephone, transportation, and power systems are directly caused by the channeling of capital and human resources into defense goods.[15] Professor Bruce M. Russett has done a sophisticated analysis of the lost-opportunity costs for other economic sectors brought about by defense spending. Much of defense spending has come out of consumer purchases, but another substantial portion has come out of general capital investment, schools, and medical facilities.[16] Finally, to the degree that the Vietnam war was financed by inflation, those groups hit the hardest were the poor, the aged, and others on low or fixed incomes.

Constraints and Challenges of the Future International System

New arrangements of power in the now-emerging international system are certain to assign a more limited role to the United States. The appearance of additional major powers, with full industrial and nuclear capabilities, by itself reduces our preeminence. The People's Republic of China, Japan (not rearmed yet but able to be at any time), the Europe of the Common Market, and India—all will achieve major power status. The prerequisites of major power status—industrialization, population, and stable government—are much more widely distributed than they were thirty years ago. There is no way for the United States to hold back these developments, and the challenge is to find a new role that fits its capabilities and goals.

In addition to more major powers, the United States will be part of a more complicated set of relationships with the Communist giants, the Soviet Union and the People's Republic of China. The Soviet Union will surely extend its diplomacy beyond its own borders by using its Navy, as we have done ourselves. After twenty

---

[15] *Our Depleted Society* (New York: Holt, 1965); see also his *Pentagon Capitalism* (New York: McGraw-Hill, 1970).

[16] *What Price Vigilance?*, op. cit.

years of American isolation, President Nixon began the reestablishment of contact with the quarter of the globe's people who live in China. The contest between the Soviet Union and China is itself a deadly serious one, almost twenty years in duration and harking back at the leadership level to disputes from the 1920's. How will we thread our way through this three-cornered situation? How will we balance conflict and cooperation between these two?

In the underdeveloped world, as Figure 14-3 suggests, there is likely to be continued instability and violence, which grow from deep social and economic roots. The traditional American preference for order is unlikely to be attained by our or anyone else's efforts, or to be seen as desirable by challenging groups. This, however, does not mean that the Communists, through some strategy of wars of national liberation, will take over the underdeveloped world. In terms of political control, the picture is likely to be very mixed, with indigenous nationalist governments hostile to any intervention in their internal affairs predominating. The Communist great powers—Russia and China—have not been notably successful around the globe. They have provided arms and aid and have supported local Communist parties— and seen very little extension of control as a result. Leaders of underdeveloped nations are willing to take help and arms from all sides; they are adept at playing the major powers off against each other. It is also certain that in the years ahead leaders in such countries will nationalize foreign-owned natural resources within their borders, as Libya and Chile have already done, and raise the prices of such goods to all the resource-importing developed nations wherever they can.

As Americans make the difficult adjustments to a multipower world, and to a world where we deal more often with equals or quasi equals, there will be another change. We have arranged the world during our hegemony in global politics around a Communist-versus-anti-Communist cleavage. But that is not the only possible division, and it may be a division of concern to fewer people than we realize. For example, there are fundamental conflicts between the rich nations of the West, including the Soviet Union, and the poorer nations of Asia, Africa, and South America. For many parts of the world, including the Indian subcontinent, "communal" conflicts of religion, life styles, and values between Hindus and Moslems are the major source of trouble. A revived Islam in Africa could very naturally, on the basis of its community and religious values, be hostile to Communism and Western capitalism alike. All this means is that one consequence of a changing American power role will be a decline in our ability to define for the globe what values are important and what are not.

Some Normative Questions for Americans

The alteration of America's world role does not mean that American policy-makers and the American people are without either power or choice in world affairs. To some degree, what the choices are will depend upon whether our foreign policy is based upon a continuation, albeit a modified one, of the anti-Communism of the Establishment Position, or whether those holding some version of the Dissenting

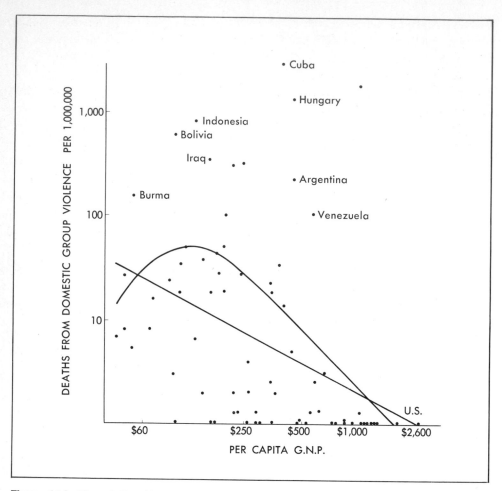

Figure 14.3. The relationship between political violence and national economic development

Source: Bruce M. Russett. *Trends in World Politics.* New York: The Macmillan Company, 1965, p. 137.

View come into political power. In any case, here are some pertinent questions. Are we prepared to reduce our permanent military installations and our pattern of armed intervention if by so doing we would hurt the American standard of living? If American affluence depends in part upon its world role and in part upon defense spending, and if these are reduced, what are the realistic chances for finding political support to help our own minorities raise their status and standard of living?

Are we prepared, in our attitudes and our skills, to protect our interests by bargaining and accommodation in a situation in which our basic economic and military power is insufficient to prevail? Already such problems have arisen in the realm of economic competition with our allies in Europe and Japan. Most important, the Vietnam war and its dislocations have made a reality at home of the economists' lesson of scarcity. If forced to choose between power and influence abroad and spending the same funds for the development of our capital and human resources at home, what will be the decision? Whatever the answers, the conflict will be reflected in America's domestic politics during the seventies. The argument about "national priorities" is in the end a fight over the role of foreign policy, and the intensity of the struggle shows that politics is a seamless web in which external and internal politics are artificial divisions of a single whole.

suggested additional readings

Almond, Gabriel. *The American People and Foreign Policy*. New York: Praeger Publishers, Inc., 1966.*

Barnet, Richard J. *Intervention and Revolution*. Cleveland: World Publishing Company, 1968.*

Brazezinski, Zbigniew, and Samuel P. Huntington. *Political Power: USA/USSR*. New York: Viking Press, 1964.*

Fairbank, John K. *The United States and China*. Cambridge: Harvard University Press, 1971.*

Fulbright, J. Williams. *The Arrogance of Power*. New York: Vintage Books, 1966.*

Hilsman, Roger. *To Move a Nation*. New York: Dell-Delta, 1967.*

Kahin, George McTurnan, and John W. Lewis. *The United States in Vietnam*, rev. ed. New York: Dell-Delta, 1969.*

Kahn, Herman. *On Thermonuclear War*. New York: The Free Press, 1969.*

Kissinger, Henry A. *American Foreign Policy*. New York: W. W. Norton & Company, Inc., 1969.*

Magdoff, Harry. *The Age of Imperialism*. New York: Monthly Review Press, 1969.*

Morgenthau, Hans J. *A New Foreign Policy for the United States*. New York: Praeger Publishers, Inc., 1969.*

Parenti, Michael. *The Anti-Communist Impulse*. New York: Random House, Inc., 1969.

Russett, Bruce M. *What Price Vigilance?* New Haven: Yale University Press, 1971.*

Spanier, John W. *American Foreign Policy Since World War II*, 4th ed. New York: Praeger Publishers, Inc., 1971.*

Waltz, Kenneth N. *Foreign Policy and Democratic Politics*. Boston: Little, Brown and Company, 1967.*

* Available in paperback.

15 new issues and the potential of politics

Where Do Political "Issues" Come From?

Students taking an introductory course in American politics, reading newspapers, and watching nightly TV newscasts must wonder, rightly, "Where do political issues, day-to-day controversies of politics, come from?" A further logical question is, "What issues are likely to be important in the years ahead?" These are crucial questions. On the answers hinge who will get what benefits out of our society and who will pay the costs, what kind of society we can expect to live out our lives in, and, ultimately, what sort of future the political system has.

Some of the answers, we hope, have become clear in the preceding chapters. Some political issues emerge from the nonpolitical structures and subsystems of the society. Thus, a certain number of political issues are generated in the economy, independent of government efforts to manage it. Questions of inflation, employment, distribution, and levels of governmental control, in a modified free-enterprise system, are still largely affected by the functions of that system. Similarly, with racial differences in our society, set by the eighteenth century, and with attitudes solidified by the nineteenth century, it would seem inevitable that our social system would produce racial issues. Likewise, wide-scale nineteenth- and early twentieth-century immigration of various European Catholic and Jewish immigrants into a Protestant society set the basis for our clanlike and lingering ethnic solidarities.

Economic and social arrangements do not become issues automatically. They are translated into political demands and programs by organized groups, political parties, and individuals. What gets translated may change over time on the basis of what people *perceive* as important. That is, in the early twentieth century, poverty for a family may have been perceived as "fate" or at least as something unalterable to be accepted passively. Today, with a welfare system inscribed in law, a widely televised version of an "affluent" society, a circulated political ideology of full employment, and organizations of the poor, such as the National Welfare Rights Organization, passive acceptance is less likely. In other words, changing perceptions about what is acceptable and what is possible cause change in what people consider to be legitimate political questions. In a highly educated, mass-communication society such as our own, in the end every subject may become "political." Health care, drugs, abortion, the role of women in society, the work ethic—it is hard to think of some topic that is not somehow now a political issue at some level.

There are also other sources of issues, many of great importance. An electoral competition that relies heavily upon advertising and a hard sell, puts politicians constantly in the position of "marketing" issues. What else are they supposed to talk about? And the need of the media for news provides a means of dissemination. Probably more important, officeholders generate issues in two ways. Particularly in the executive branch, the government both causes and responds to foreign events. Foreign policy perspectives and issues are heavily dominated by the President and although there are circumstances in which initiation begins with the public, they are less frequent than first moves by government itself. On top of that, on a continuing basis, issues are brought forth by internal bureaucratic needs and competition. Agencies in being need missions. Agencies with some functions sense the possibility of new roles. They seek publicity and support. Perhaps the clearest example is when a branch of the military seeks a new weapon, which becomes a source of public controversy. But poverty agencies, environmental agencies, health care agencies, and educational agencies, in terms of fundamental patterns of behavior, are not much different. They constantly spin off new ideas, "issues." Those analysts who favor a systems approach call this initiation-from-the-inside process "withinputs," because the impetus is from within government itself.

In this chapter we will discuss some subjects that seem to us to be hotly controversial public problems of the 1970's: crime, pollution, housing, school busing, and some additional aspects of foreign policy. Some of the analysis will be factual, but a lot will be purely speculative. The aim will be to suggest questions that any student might want to pursue further for herself or himself. The list is in many ways arbitrary. We have omitted topics already covered, including incomes policy and civil rights and liberties. There is simply not enough space to pursue other issues, including such items as zero-population growth, or national health insurance, national systems of no-fault auto insurance, problems of the aged or various aspects of educational reform. After looking at our admittedly abbreviated list, we will turn to some even larger speculative questions, including the potentials and limitations of politics for resolving human needs, and the likely future of the American political system.

Crime as a Political Issue

When most people think about crime, what they appear to have in mind are personal attacks on individuals or their property: homicide, muggings, armed robbery, breaking and entering, and burglary. Crime of this sort, and the fear people have of it, has generated a special kind of political issue: "law and order." What *law and order,* which first appeared in the 1964 Republican presidential campaign of Barry Goldwater, seems to mean is that the resources of society, particularly the police, should be used more strongly against criminals who commit personal or property crimes. It also seems to mean that various court decisions that protect the rights of suspects should be downplayed in favor of aiding the police in obtaining information and convictions. In its harshest form, law and order also seems to be a code directed against various forms of "lenient" penal practices: probation and parole, "coddling" of prisoners.

The crime issue raises perplexing problems that go to the heart of American society. At a simple, mechanical level, there is a great deal of dispute over the validity of various statistics, because FBI Uniform Crime Reports rely upon local police reports that are in turn widely varying in their accuracy. In addition, a 1965 public opinion survey for the President's Law Enforcement Commission found that certain kinds of crimes are widely unreported by the victims. Thus, virtually all murders get reported, but only about two thirds of all robberies and perhaps as few as one half of all assaults (perhaps because these often involve family disputes or people known to each other, or groups who prefer to "work things out" outside the law-enforcement structure). To further confuse the question of just how much crime there is, it is known that criminal activity is highest among young males, and the proportion of young men in our population has been increasing since World War II. On the other hand, the rate of increase of young men has not been as great as the rate of increase of violent crime.

Some propositions about street crime can be advanced with certainty. In 1960 there were 2,015,000 major reported crimes; in 1969, there were 4,990,000. The annual rate of increase is over 14 per cent, and there has been little decline since then. In some years, rates have gone up. Even adjusted for population growth, the crime rate has increased by over 12 per cent a year. This does not mean that every kind of crime has increased. There are fewer murders per 100,000 population in the 1970's than there were in the 1930's or in the exceptionally violent period that followed the Civil War. There are also fewer armed robberies per 100,000 population than in the 1930's. The risk of burglary, however, is substantially greater.

Different segments of the public bear different risks. Those most likely to be the victims of major crimes are poor blacks living in central cities. Victimization rates decline as one moves outward to suburbs and smaller cities from the central cities. The risk of violent crime in central cities is about five times as great as in smaller communities; the risk of burglary is about twice as great. Crime obviously has both a racial and a class impact. Poorer people and black people are more likely to be victims. Poorer people are also more likely to be perpetrators, because street crime is inextricably bound up with urban slum life.

There is very little evidence that standard schemes of deterring crime, such as harsh prison sentences, have any effect on overall crime rates. Saturation and visible stationing of policemen on every corner will reduce rates in the area affected. No one knows whether such a process also deflects criminals into other areas or deters them completely. The costs of saturation use of police are also very high. No one knows why crime rates vary so greatly among metropolitan areas either, as Table 15.1 shows, beyond the fact that smaller centers have less crime. Nor is it clear why

Table 15.1 *Crime rates per 100,000 population for different metropolitan areas (includes cities and suburbs)*

Metropolitan area (SMSA)	Total crime index * (rate per 100,000)	Violent crime †	Property crime ‡
Abilene, Tex.	1,828	123	1,705
Arkon, Ohio	2,954	291	2,662
Atlanta, Ga.	3,567	391	3,175
Baltimore, Md.	4,369	1,008	3,361
Boston, Mass	3,098	250	2,847
Detroit, Mich.	5,148	916	4,232
Fargo, N.D.	1,592	44	1,547
Houston, Tex.	3,592	562	3,030
Knoxville, Tenn.	2,009	254	1,755
Los Angeles, Calif.	5,063	737	4,326
Manchester, N.H.	1,031	57	973
New York, N.Y.	5,220	980	4,239
St. Louis, Mo.	3,565	531	3,034
San Francisco, Calif.	5,329	625	4,704
Seattle, Wash.	4,133	305	3,827

Source: Federal Bureau of Investigation, *Uniform Crime Reports, 1970* (Washington, D.C.: U.S. Government Printing Office, 1971), pp. 82–97.

* The total crime index = violent crimes + property crimes.

† Violent crimes = murder, forcible rape, robbery, and aggravated assault.

‡ Property crime = burglary, larceny of $50 and over, and auto theft.

particular cities have different rates for different kinds of crime. The rate of solution of crimes other than murder is relatively low, and the repeat rates (called recidivism) for those ultimately caught, convicted, and imprisoned, is very high. Some estimate that over 85 per cent of those with one arrest for a nontraffic offense will be arrested again.

The political impact of crime comes because people are very conscious of potential danger, even in high-priced suburban areas where the risk of physical assault is actually very small. In central cities, perhaps with good reason, people organize their lives around minimizing risk. The President's Law Enforcement Commission found that in high crime areas of two large cities, 43 per cent of the citizens said they stayed off the streets at night because of fear of crime, 35 per cent would not speak to strangers because of such fear, and 21 per cent used cars and cabs at night rather then walking because they were afraid. Whether one relies upon such quantitative data or the news reports of earlier theatre times in New York City (so patrons can be home by 10 P.M.), or the wild growth of the home security industry (burglar alarms, locks, private guards), the picture is clear. Millions of people live in fear of being victims of crime and this fear is as real as for the millions who actually are victims. At one point in 1968, crime was listed as the most important problem facing the country in the Gallup Poll.

Several factors complicate the political issue of crime. Certain kinds of crime, particularly robbery and burglary, appear to be tied to drug usage, especially heroin. That raises special emotional reactions. Some authorities suggest that over half of the urban robberies and burglaries are connected to heroin. Heroin habits are expensive to support and require addicts to steal and sell what they get through "fences" at well marked-down values. The goods—televisions, stereos, radios, clothes —then find their way into black-market distribution systems that exist in rather widespread form in many cities. Furthermore, the heroin trade itself is such an elaborate net that books could be devoted to it. Heroin is an opium derivative, refined from poppies grown in Asia Minor and Asia, largely refined in European countries, and smuggled into the United States in fantastic ways. Although members of organized crime control part of the trade here and abroad, there seems to be a lot of free-lancing. The reasons are easy to find: just a few successful years in the trade make millionaires.

Organized Crime Activities

Another complicating factor in crime as a political issue is that street crime is really only one part of the major crime in America. In fact, there are three partially separable aspects of American crime: street crime, organized crime, and white-collar crime. Street crime is what most people talk about, what gets most reported, and what generates fear. In dollar terms, however, it may or may not be the largest facet of crime. Organized crime consists of systematically organized conspirators, some who operate for brief periods and some of whom have seventy-year histories, who break laws in fairly clear ways: primarily they engage in providing illegal services for other Americans who want to buy them. Thus, one fundamental difference between street crime and organized crime is that a person who is robbed does not want a relationship with a criminal. A person who places an illegal bet, buys drugs, purchases a stolen car, patronizes a call girl, borrows money from a loanshark, or enters into an elaborate financial fraud, wants to do what he is doing.

Organized crime has received wide publicity, usually in its more lurid aspects, in books, on television, and in movies. Everyone has heard of Al Capone, the bootleg king of 1925 Chicago, and the "Mafia," the supposed national organization of criminals of Italian descent. The facts of organized crime are more complicated than the public image.

There have been organized criminal gangs in America since the nineteenth century. At all periods, the captains of these crews, and the crews themselves, come from those ethnic groups that are at the bottom of the American socioeconomic ladder and are most discriminated against: the Irish in the nineteenth century, the Jews at the turn of the century until the 1940's, the Italians beginning in the 1920's and continuing perhaps until the present, and, beginning in the 1960's, blacks,

Cubans, and Puerto Ricans. Participating in such criminal activities provides a channel of social mobility for those at the bottom. The incentives are the all-American incentives: wealth, status within one's own group, a better life for one's children.

Organized criminals usually begin in small-time neighborhood activities—loan-sharking (loaning money at illegally high rates such as 5 to 10 per cent a week, with the borrower's body as collateral), extortion, or gambling. Larger gangs successively branch out into citywide or regionwide illegal activities, providing whichever service is most in demand. Organizing such black markets takes skill and nerve, and the profits are high. Thus, around the turn of the century, prostitution was the main source of gang revenue; during Prohibition it was liquor; during the 1940's and 1950's it was gambling. Today, gambling, loansharking, and systematic financial fraud, along with the drug trade, are the main sources of funds.

Although some argue that organized criminals are linked in a single hierarchical syndicate, the evidence is more persuasive that they are regional "families" or gangs. There is communication across territories because of common enemies—particularly the Justice Department's Organized Crime Strike Task Forces—and common opportunities for investment. Within ethnic subgroups there is considerable inter-marriage and cohesion, but that is a common characteristic of American society, including upper-class Protestants. No one knows the annual "volume" of organized crime's business, but it is, cumulatively, surely a multi-billion-dollar operation. Organized criminals have been big-time financial magnates since the 1920's, when Prohibition was, in effect, their industrial revolution: it capitalized them. Then, with the stock-market crash in 1929, they were the only ones with large amounts of money to loan to businessmen, large and small. Subsequently they have systematically invested in legitimate businesses, which provide them with a financial cushion against disaster, with generational continuity, and with a continuing option of going straight at any time if they want to. Indeed, there is some evidence that large numbers of organized criminals function on either an occasional or part-time basis, rather than as a continuing career.

There are two paradoxes about organized crime. It would not continue to exist if our society did not demand the enactment into law of moral preferences that some people hold strongly but others reject: no gambling, no prostitution, no drugs, no high-priced loan money. In other words, organized crime exists to serve markets created by the law itself, which, by making what some people want illegal, provides a premium for those who will provide the services. The second paradox is that there could be no organized crime without political corruption. At a lower level, the street, corruption must involve the police, who sell territories to numbers runners and narcotics dealers in return for the right to operate. At higher levels, Alexander Heard has estimated that 15 per cent of all state and local campaign funds come from the underworld.[1] There is no way of knowing how much money for national campaigns comes from such sources. Above the street level, what organized crimi-

[1] Garden City, N.Y.: Anchor, 1962, p. 142.

nals seek most often is immunity from prosecution; failing that, they seek light sentences, paroles, and probation.

White-Collar Criminal Behavior

Finally, there are white-collar crimes. In this category, are the wide range of corporate crimes, most of which go undetected and unpunished, ranging from price-fixing to illegal pollution. In this category also are various forms of individual fraud and tax evasion. Further, certain kinds of political corruption involve taking percentages of contracts from perfectly legitimate businessmen, or getting an inside track on stock deals. Ours is a an era that has seen state party chairmen go to jail for trying to shake down night club operators, mayors convicted of extortion, and Governors and others involved in under-the-table secret purchases of race track stocks at low rates. Is this behavior, or the actions of the corporate executive who knowingly markets an unsafe product, or the bureaucrat who knowingly lets a harmful drug stay on the market, different at a moral level from street crime?

The question about the moral distinctions among types of crime is difficult, and no less so than the political aspects. Crime in the streets is a good political issue. There are evidences of widespread public revulsion against political corruption, going back some time in our history, and more recent opposition to illegal polluting and marketing procedures. But other white-collar crimes, and the service aspects of organized crime (apart from the violent aspects), do not seem to arouse the same response. Further, at various levels public officials are corrupted by organized crime and by certain kinds of white-collar crime. That is, they are connected to it, and some officials, at least, risk their own careers and certainly their own advantages if they take steps to stop such crime. In some crude way, one could almost say that there is a distinctive form of crime for different levels of our society: street crime for the poorest elements (and against them); organized crime for the aspiring middle class; and white-collar crime as upper-class crime.[2]

The punishments and the politics, however, do not fit the crimes. Crimes by individuals, especially violent ones, invoke heavy response. But neither the law nor the public seem equipped to deal with crime that results from *organizational* rather than individual behavior. The organized criminal acts rationally to achieve group ends, and conspires intelligently to do so. The corporate executive involved in price-fixing likewise is part of a national and profitable organizational conspiracy. There is no "criminal personality" involved. Behavior is, from the perspective of those concerned, quite sane and strategic: the risks are small and the rewards are likely to be large. Furthermore, oddly, both the organized-crime type of criminal and the corporate executive operate in a social and cultural milieu in which "taking care of one's own" and "getting away with it" against the outside world are encouraged.[3]

[2] For an analysis that points out that street crime is only one aspect of American criminal behavior, see Edwin M. Schur, *Our Criminal Society* (Englewood Cliffs, N.J.: Prentice-Hall, 1969).

[3] See the classic *White Collar Crime* by Edwin H. Sutherland, first published in 1949 and republished with a foreword by Donald R. Cressey by Holt (New York, 1961).

It is almost a cliché to say that the sources of street crime lie in the roots of our society—depending upon one's political views, on socioeconomic causes or a more general breakdown of morality. The sources of organized crime and white-collar crime lie in those roots as well. One can predict that all types of crime will be political issues more and more in the future without knowing how they will be resolved. Can any society, with crime rates of all kinds as high as ours, reverse the process? Perhaps we can and perhaps we cannot. There is some evidence that crime rates are cyclical. Can a system that tolerates white-collar crime and coexists with organized crime ever erase the cynicism that must pervade street society about "the system"?

Pollution as a Political Issue

Every industrialized society has created waste and noxious living conditions. Accounts of the dawn of the Industrial Revolution in England make that clear. Further, at various stages of our history, individuals and political leaders have worried about spoliation and the depletion of our natural environment. The Refuse Act of 1899 remains the strongest law against water pollution on our statute books, with $2,500 fines for each offense and jail sentences. Enforcement, from enactment until 1970, was virtually nonexistent. Rachel Carson wrote her prize-winning book *Silent Spring* in 1962, warning of the effects of pesticides upon crops, animals, and eventually humans and the entire life cycle.[4] Yet only those pesticides with the most persistent effects, such as DDT and 2-, 4-, and 5-T, have been regulated to such a degree that usage has dropped substantially. Likewise, automobile pollution was identified as the cause of petrochemical smog at least ten years before carmakers were forced by California state law to install antipollution devices, and a full twenty years before the strong federal clean air standards of 1975 were scheduled to go into effect.

Pollution as a political issue involves several separate questions.[5] Why, at some point in the late 1960's, did pollution suddenly become a political cause with sufficient support to generate considerable political response? And, perhaps more complicated, how much of the air, water, land, and natural resource pollution in our country can be improved by essentially regulatory political measures and how much is embedded in deeper structural aspects of our society or industrialization itself?

As the chapter on interest groups pointed out, any interest group or social movement has to begin with group consciousness and organization. The ecology movement did not begin with politicians; it was generated by middle- and upper-middle-class college students and housewives, and was carried to its next stages by media publicity, by old-line conservation groups, and by new ecology-action-oriented groups. The basic goal of a cleaner environment, with its presumption that there will have to be sacrifices in terms of production and consumption, or both,

---

[4] (Boston: Houghton.)

[5] A fine introductory treatment of various aspects of the pollution issue is the First Annual Report of the President's Council on Environmental Quality, *Environmental Quality* (Washington, D.C.: United States Government Printing Office, 1970).

does not meet with a uniform public enthusiasm. Concern for both air and water pollution is greater with more educated and higher-income groups.[6] Thus, an interesting side question is whether these supporters of antipollution measures see changes in their own standard of living, or as something to be undergone by those who are already less fortunate. The class aspect of the pollution issue has led lower-income groups in this country to be less enthusiastic about cleaner air than about factories that will give them jobs, despite the fact that the poor are in many ways the worst victims of dirty air, noise pollution, and the piling-up of debris in the inner city. Furthermore, outside of the United States, in the less developed nations, the pollution issue strikes an even dimmer note among the millions who have yet to achieve the most basic fundamentals of a decent standard of life.

Nonetheless, American political leaders have accepted the antipollution cause almost without exception, although with varying degrees of enthusiasm. Senator Edmund S. Muskie's legislative record rests on his sponsorship of an increasingly strong series of bills aimed at curbing auto exhausts, which have been responsible for 40 to 60 per cent of air pollution. President Richard M. Nixon presided over the creation of the Environmental Protection Agency in the Executive Office of the President. And the Congress passed legislation requiring all federal agencies to file a statement outlining the environmental impact before proceeding with any project. Further, federal courts have been increasingly sympathetic to lawsuits initiated by environmental groups and even to claims of ordinary citizens that they have the right to sue against polluters. Whether all of the political response will, in the end, lead to a cleaner environment, or merely a few spectacular symbolic victories, is not yet clear.

The reason the substantive outcome of the environmental issue cannot be judged has to do with the nature and causes of pollution. There are four major forms of pollution: air, water, solid waste, and noise. In addition, there are damages to natural systems from such man-made activities as weather modification and radiation, from X-rays in medical use, in nuclear power facilities, and in nuclear weapons production. Figure 15.1 shows the main air pollutants and where they originated for 1968, a good takeoff year for considering environmental politics. The impact of air pollution is severe: it increases the incidence of respiratory diseases of all kinds, damages crops and vegetation, interferes with visibility, and may, at some point in time, alter the global climate by raising the level of carbon monoxide and also the temperature level. The costs of air pollution have been variously estimated, but measurable damages must be in the billions of dollars every year, leaving aside aesthetic costs. The costs of the cleanup will also be high. The major cleanup steps are to reduce the emissions of power plants and automobiles. Figure 15.2 indicates that the 1970–1975 costs alone, to reach acceptable governmental air standards, would be $22.1 billion. Further, yearly maintenance costs on equipment would be $1.9 billion.

Water pollution results from dumping materials that use up the water's oxygen

---

[6] See J. Clarence [Davies] III, *The Politics of Pollution* (New York: Pegasus, 1970), p. 80.

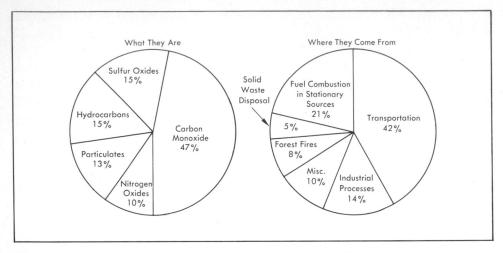

Figure 15.1. Air pollution emissions in the United States, 1968 (percentage by weight).

Source: Council on Environmental Quality, *Report.* U.S. Government Printing Office. Washington, D.C., 1970, p. 64.

supply, as measured by the BOD (biological oxygen demand) or COD (chemical oxygen demand), units indicating how much oxygen is required by each element. Dumping heated waters also interferes with the natural processes of lakes and rivers. The major sources of water pollution are industrial, municipal, and agricultural. There are more than 300,000 water-using factories in the United States, and their waste, often highly toxic chemicals, amounts to four times as much oxygen demand as all the sewered population of the country. Apparently half of all industrial water

Figure 15.2. Cumulative public and private expenditures for air and water pollution control, 1970–1975.

Source: Council on Environmental Quality, *Report.* U.S. Government Printing Office. Washington, D.C. 1970, p. 115.

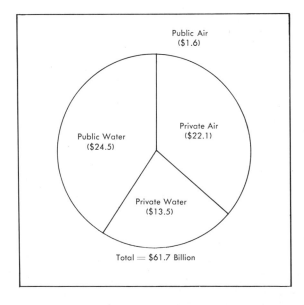

pollution results from processes in the production of four major materials: paper, organic chemicals, petroleum, and steel. Estimated private water cleanup costs are $13.5 billion for 1970–1975.

About 60 per cent of the population served by sewers and treatment plants is well served, but only one third of the nation was so equipped in 1970. Sewers carry not only solid wastes from homes and commercial establishments, but a large amount of industrial waste. The crucial problem with sewers, aside from building more and constructing both primary and secondary waste treatment plants, is that some of what they carry is only partially treatable. Thus, the phosphates commonly used in washing detergents add to the nitrate content of lakes and streams, speed up their aging, and cause their eventual death. Yet all home washing machines will operate only on detergents, not with soap, the alternative and prior product. Agricultural wastes come in two forms. Solid wastes from farm animals are a major problem, and, especially when the animals are contained in feedlots, wastes cannot be absorbed by the land but drain off, generally raw, into water supplies. Feedlot wastes may be as great as all of the municipal sewage of the country. In addition, fertilizers, especially nitrates, run off into ground waters.

Finally, a growing form of water pollution comes from oil spills into offshore waters, from tankers or from accidents in some of the thousands of offshore oil wells. Penalties for violators have so far been minimal. Worldwide, oil pollution of the oceans is becoming a major problem. The consequences of water pollution of all kinds are well known: water that is increasingly difficult to purify for drinking and is dangerous to health, reduction in commercial fish stocks and sport fishing, removal of once-safe waters from recreational use for boating and swimming, and, once again, aesthetic damage.

As for solid waste involving refuse or trash, the problem mounts steadily. Refuse collected in urban areas is now over five pounds per person per day and is expected to rise to eight pounds by 1980. Over three fourths of this debris is simply disposed of in open dumps and the available land for such use may someday be exhausted. The remainder goes into so-called sanitary landfills or is burned. Across the country, collection costs for the over 250 million tons of trash disposed of by residential, commercial, and institutional users *yearly* is over $18 per ton and rising rapidly. This figure does not include the debris of industrial and mining processes, which add close to 2 billion tons of waste—from used paper to slag heaps to mill tailings—each year.

Trash pollution has its obvious aesthetic costs, but some of its problems go deeper. Many of the consumer products eventually thrown away—especially plastics, non-returnable bottles, and aluminum cans—are virtually indestructable in nature. They do not degrade. If burnable, they pollute (some plastics when burned form poisonous phosgene gas). They last forever. A basic law of ecology is that everything must go somewhere. So far, trash-recycling processes are not at advanced stages of technology, and the tax laws give concessions to extractive industries, but not to recycling ones. As for noise pollution, although there is no way to cumulatively quantify American noise levels, it is certain that they have been rising constantly and are most severe in urban places and work environments. Some factories are exceptionally noisy. The millions who live near airports can testify to the impact of widespread jet travel. Excessive exposure to noise can damage hearing and may have psychological effects as well.

Theories as to the deeper, societal causes of pollution vary. Some think that pollution is an evitable by-product of a high standard of living coupled with rising population. Many economists argue that certain kinds of pollution are widespread because nature has been what they call "a free good." By that they mean that those who produce a product do not have to pay extra for polluting the river abutting their factory. Consumers who buy a beer can do not have to pay the cumulative disposal costs. Power companies that encourage the use of electric gadgets through advertising do not pay for the air they pollute, or for the damage to the water they heat through their generating processes. Treating air and water as inexhaustible natural resources to be had for free may have made some sense in the eighteenth century, when the United States was an underpopulated, agricultural country with abundant resources. It is obvious now that the air and the water are not "free," but that the public pays, and especially future generations pay, for each industrial or consumer usage.

These economic aspects of pollution have led many economists to propose use taxes on air and water, special fees for pollution. If this process extended to power plants and to consumers, a wide variety of products would become more expensive, or, more accurately, reflect their true costs. On the other hand, even if the economists' ideas were put into practice, it is by no means evident that exhaustion of of the natural environment would stop, for a variety of reasons.

For one thing, at present rates of growth, the American economy doubles every thirty to forty years. That would automatically mean more consumption, even if prices more accurately reflect air and water costs. This relationship has led many ecology-minded persons to call for a rejection of the traditional goals of industrialization: economic growth and mass consumption themselves. And it is probably true that, as a trade-off, a no-growth, zero-population-growth society could preserve its environment longer, especially if the hard sell for certain kinds of consumer products were abandoned. Those who feel that the West must make this choice make one particularly telling point: environmental problems seem to occur in all industrial countries, regardless of their economic system. Thus, the Soviet Union has suffered water pollution as severe as our own. Neither capitalism nor socialism appears to be the key independent variable. It is industrialization itself, in this view.

Professor Barry Commoner has advanced a somewhat different argument.[7] He maintains that in terms of the calories consumed, the fiber used and the beer drunk, America has not changed much since 1946. What has changed is that the agricultural, chemical, and packaging processes involved have meant exponentially more pollution. Likewise, he points out that the rise in automotive horsepower was not

---

[7] "A Reporter at Large (Ecology-II)," *New Yorker*, XLVII, No. 33 (October 2, 1971), pp. 44–91.

inevitable with the increased use of motorcars. Sales of detergents rather than soap are advertising-induced, not consumer-chosen. His point is that much pollution results from corporate behavior that may improve profits but does not add to the standard of living. Commoner's view is "that the present course of environmental degradation, at least in industrialized countries, represents such a serious challenge to essential ecological systems that if it is continued it will destroy the ability of the environment to support a reasonably civilized human society." [8]

Once again, the student will have to form his own conclusions. If some critics are correct, then governmental regulation and an alteration of economic incentives may reverse the deterioration of our environment. If those who think the roots lie in industrialization itself are correct, then no single governmental program, and probably no single government, can reverse the process. What these analysts are talking about is a change in Western values and culture, nothing less.

The Politics of Housing

Housing is important enough to affect everyone, yet not so important that it is at the top of national priorities. As a consequence, policy is, by and large, made at the congressional and bureaucratic level. Great debates over housing rarely intrude into presidential politics. Such has not always been the case. In the early 1930's with mortgage foreclosures reaching record highs, the forerunner of the FHA (Federal Housing Administration) was set up under President Roosevelt. In the face of a considerable housing shortage after World War II, President Truman did take the lead in a variety of ways. But today, with almost two thirds of all Americans as owners/occupiers of their own homes, housing is not usually on the political front-burner. Nonetheless, because of the myriad ways housing affects individuals and families, and the multiplicity of governmental involvements, housing remains a sort of permanent issue.

For most families, a house is their largest capital investment, the use to which they put the greatest part of their accumulated savings, and a symbol of their location in the social status hierarchy. Not only the size and quality of the housing, but location are crucial social indicators. Americans have used housing as a way of moving up and out of inner city slums. The suburbs are relatively rigidly stratified on an economic basis, with metropolitan location and the location within neighborhoods as the indicators. Every group has used housing-related aspects of local government, particularly in the suburbs, to protect his own position against newcomers or those beneath it on the social scale. Thus various local zoning, tax assessment, and construction policies can be devices of racial or economic discrimination. When housing is viewed in this framework, its potential for political controversy becomes evident.

Further, many of our existing patterns owe a great deal to the historical role of government. The federal government has guaranteed mortages since the 1930's.

[8] Ibid., p. 90.

Since the late 1930's, the federal government has constructed hundreds of thousands of units of public housing, all but a tiny number in the central cities. Most of this housing has been racially segregated by virtue of where it was built. Through urban renewal, Washington has constructed many commercial projects but at a net loss in demolished low-income housing. The federal highway program has also affected the housing market by destroying low-income housing. Federal tax policy benefits middle-income home owners by allowing them to deduct interest and local taxes on their federal taxes, and by not taxing the potential income of their homes.

Other levels of government and nongovernmental interests also enter into the housing picture. Local governments are virtually dependent upon property taxes for their revenues, and thus are silent part owners of everybody's house.[9] Home-building, in its various production, construction, financing, and furnishing phases, may be the country's largest sector employer. Thus the economic interests involved are vast, although the industry tends to be characterized by thousands of small firms rather than by standardization or large companies. There are over eight thousand local building codes, for example, which constitute a distinct disincentive for large national marketers to enter the field. The craft unions play a major part in setting local standards.

There are some paradoxes in the ways that housing is an "issue." To begin with, the supply of substandard housing (*substandard* defined most rigorously as lack of indoor toilets, lack of hot water, and unsafe facilities) has declined steadily, from 37 per cent of the housing stock in 1950 to less than 10 per cent in 1970. Furthermore, although some of the worst housing is in urban slums, overall the largest amount of substandard housing is in rural areas. The reality of living conditions is that the rural poor pay little but live in bad housing, whereas the urban poor pay a very large percentage of their available incomes but have increasingly been housed in minimally standard facilities. All of this leads to a key question for the future: Should the goal of government policy be to produce a certain minimal number of *new* units (through whatever mix of overall fiscal management and direct and indirect subsidies to builders in the private sector is likely to work best), or should it concentrate on underwriting the incomes of the poor to make up the difference between what they should be spending on housing and what they are forced to spend in high rents? In other words, should government stimulate housing construction or subsidize the housing costs of families?[10]

Present federal policy follows both paths. Under the Housing Act of 1968, a national goal of 25 million new units is set for the 1970–1980 decade. At the same time, various forms of indirect subsidies (including public housing programs and purchase and rental assistance for moderate-income families) amounted to $1.9 billion for 1972 alone.

The costs of governmental housing policy may be the least controversial aspects

[9] See Anthony Downs, "Home Ownership and American Free Enterprise," in *Urban Problems and Prospects* (Chicago: Markham, 1971), pp. 156–164.

[10] See Charles L. Schultze, et al., "Housing," in *Setting National Priorities: The 1972 Budget* (Washington, D.C.: The Brookings Institution, 1971), pp. 276–296.

in the 1970's. Many strategies, including those advocated by some in the Cabinet Department of Housing and Urban Development (HUD) call for using housing assistance to low- and moderate-income families to break the racial and economic segregation of the suburbs. In an economic sense, it is cheaper to build on vacant suburban land than to tear down and rebuild in the central cities. Yet suburban residents have bitterly resisted various low-income and even moderate-income programs in their communities. Such housing programs go beyond the physical aspects into all of the emotionally charged side features we mentioned before: status, race, education. Some questions are: Should housing policy be used as a device for getting at the deep-rooted class and racial barriers Americans have elaborately constructed against each other? If housing policy is used in this manner, what incentives might be constructed to persuade those in affected suburbs to cooperate (a bonus in other federal programs, extra school aid, tax breaks)? If housing policy is not used in this manner, are Americans prepared to live with the fulfillment of the prediction of the 1967 Kerner Commission Report, that ours would be a country with two separate societies, one black and one white? In other words, if the alternative to acting through housing policy is apartheid, what will be done and what should be done?

School Busing as a Political Issue

We have illustrated the relationship of housing, seemingly a second-rank political issue, to the more emotional questions of equity, race, class, and status. School busing is another good example of how what might be a technical problem encapsulizes a variety of values important to different Americans in different ways. In a simple physical sense, thousands of schoolchildren have used buses to get to and from school for many years. When the southern states maintained "dual" or racially separate school systems (not entirely eliminated until the early 1970's), black children were frequently bused long distances. In many urban communities, students at parochial schools are bused to class. Likewise, in the largest cities, students at the most expensive private preparatory schools are often bused. In addition, millions of children travel considerable distances by a variety of means, on their own, to school, especially at the secondary level. Why then the fuss about busing?

What busing means today is a potential final end to school segregation established by patterns of settlement. Thus busing is a device that can integrate individual schools within a community, or can integrate communities within a metropolitan area. But if and when busing is used to these ends, it means that moving to the suburbs or living in an expensive neighborhood will no longer serve to gurantee racial or class homogeneity for peoples' children. The impact of the busing upon those bused and those in the receiving communities is perceived as uncertain and threatening. Hence the resistance.

Whatever the outcome, the mutual perceptions of the high stakes involved are accurate. Education is a crucial variable in the carrying on of community values and in the life chances of children. As things are without busing, richer districts spend

more money on education than burdened urban systems, and the cultural homogeneity of suburban schools probably adds another plus in terms of traditional education for the individual child. Wide-scale busing would racially integrate schools,
mix children of widely varying cultural and class backgrounds. It would, for the
country, go a long way toward fulfilling the often-stated value of equality of opportunity. But although busing would fulfill a goal for the country, for individual
parents in the suburbs the cost of the national achievement is perceived as being
billed to them and their children personally. To add to the class hostility the issue
raises, it is well known that the very wealthy can opt out of the controversy by
placing their children in private schools.

Not only suburban whites perceive busing as a threat to the legal autonomy
they have created for their schools. Many black leaders feel that the only possible
route to a successful education of black children lies in decentralization or "community control" of schools. Community control means neighborhood schools controlled by the neighborhood racial or ethnic group in each case, black or white, poor
or middle-class. With commmunity control, unless there is greater residential integration, racial separation will be the order of the day and the future.

The essentially racial basis of busing is a problem, and the ethnic composition
of many of the groups resisting such policies in the North, suggest another emerging
issue area. Ethnic groups other than blacks, by the beginning of the 1970s, had
begun to make demands for more attention to their dissatisfactions. Often the Poles,
Italo-Americans, Slavs and other groups have felt that efforts to solve the problems
of racial minorities were being pressed at their direct or indirect expense. Straws in
the wind heralding a revolt among the "ethnics," with which policy makers will have
to cope, have been multiplying in the last year or two. Louis Harris found, for
example, that Italo-American voters, who as a group had backed Democrat Hubert
Humphrey 57 per cent, to 37 per cent for Richard Nixon in 1968, were recorded
in pre-election polls in 1972 as favoring the President 62 per cent to 27 per cent
for Senator McGovern.

School busing is likely to remain a heated issue throughout the 1970s. The
Supreme Court decisions of the 1950's and the Civil Rights Acts of the 1960's
largely settled the question of legal equality for blacks. There is no longer any basis
in law for discrimination against blacks in government or industry or education.
So what remains to be resolved is close to the core values of how people live, who
their children will grow up with, what their children's life chances will be. When
politics is the medium for deciding issues such as these, the intensity is inevitably
great. Few other predictions could safely be made.

The Future of Foreign Policy as a Political Issue

Although the bulk of this chapter is devoted to other future concerns, foreign policy
will continue to occupy the center stage of American politics. Foreign policy concerns will be with us through the 1970's in a variety of ways, although the argument

may take some different forms from the prior decade. For example, the 1960's were consumed with the *particular* case of Vietnam. In the 1970's, a major question will be whether our *general* foreign policy posture should be one of modified globalism or neoisolationism. Under a stance of modified globalism, we would continue the worldwide involvement of the post-World War II era, but put more reliance on various forms of military and economic aid and less upon direct use or stationing of our own troops. Under a neoisolationism, the country would turn back to some version of its pre-World War II stance, reducing its commitments and involvements overseas, turning inward toward domestic issues, while probably maintaining a heavy home-based defense structure. Which of these general postures the country is to adopt is certain to arouse political controversy.

Within the framework of a general issue over global postures, there will be some new versions of some familiar foreign policy struggles. If we opt for a modified globalism, then the question will arise as to whether we should use what chips we have in Europe, or in Asia. If there is a question of the general policy, or of emphasis within a policy, which branch of government will call the shots? Will it be the executive, ruling virtually unilaterally and often arbitrarily as in the 1960's? Or will the Congress somehow reassert its influence despite its fragmented organization, more limited sources of information, and diffused relationship with the public?

Furthermore, there are some possible outcomes, however unlikely, of foreign policy interactions that could have devastating impacts upon American politics. For example, although nuclear war is not probable, it is possible. A full-scale nuclear war or even a limited "nuclear exchange" would, if any Americans survived at all, certainly radically alter our country and its political systems. At a still different level, another Vietnam—in Cambodia, in South America, or somewhere else—would certainly put severe strains on the political system. These examples indicate that not only what Americans argue about in foreign policy, but how well whatever is chosen works will be important for our future.

In the world arena, influencing foreign policy outcomes will be more difficult for American policy-makers in the years ahead. From World War II until the mid-1960's, we enjoyed hegemony in a largely bipolar world. Both the hegemony and the bipolarity are now gone. Although the international environment is different from any time since World War II, it is not unique in our historical experience. Although conditions were different, the fact is we survived quite nicely as a nation for one hundred years as a minor state, fifty years as a regional power, and for at least twenty years a noninvolved major power prior to 1940. Thus, leaving aside the examples of other nations that have adjusted to changing world roles, there would seem to be within our own history a sufficient source of insights to help us adapt to whatever new international system evolves. That we survived before without hegemony suggests that we can do it again, and perhaps very well. In the excitement, conflict, and tension of the post-World War II era, both our history and our potential adaptability often have been lost sight of by decision-makers. Now that the choice of ignoring the long past or the long-term future is no longer ours to make alone, such a historical perspective may give us both comfort and aid.

America's Political Potential

What are the prospects that the American political system can cope with its vast, intractable problems? Or, alternatively, what are the prospects that the pressures, dissatisfactions, and frustrations generated by the perplexing issues of the 1970's will forceably alter the system in the direction of a less open society? In trying to supply tentative answers to these questions we will again be able to do no more than offer hunches that, hopefully, will be suggestive to the reader while inviting him to draw whatever conclusions seem most plausible or desirable. A few paragraphs of necessarily synoptic summary are necessary before any general appraisals or prognostications are attempted. We begin with the assumption that the system overall is at least structurally pluralistic. (This is not to say that all the apparently autonomous foci of semi-independent power are in fact fully autonomous, nor is it to say that the pluralism of the current system, or pluralism in general, is theoretically desirable.)

The framers of the Constitution presumably intended the Congress to be the heart of the scheme they were framing. They expected it to wield true legislative— policy-making—power, and to a unique degree among democratic legislatures it does, or tries to. Yet its internal structuring is almost a model of pluralistic decentralization of power and influence. Lack of party discipline in and out of Congress accounts for this in large part. Congress's decentralized structure is both its strength and its weakness. Many points of view thus secure representation and a measure of influence (recall the anti-Vietnam-war forces based in the Senate during the late 1960's and early 1970's). On the other hand, Congress is handicapped in policy-making by leaderlessness and inadequate access to expertise in the face of highly complex clusters of problems like the environment, crime, and, above all, foreign policy.

The obsolescence of the concept of congressional government during this century, pushed the executive to the fore. Presidents, massively backstopped by thousands of bureaucratic experts, have increasingly taken over policy leadership. Congress at first resisted, but has come to acquiesce grudgingly, and even criticize incoming Presidents for not supplying the legislative agenda their deliberations depend upon. This increasing reliance on executive initiative has raised severe but contradictory problems: frequent cases of presidential inability to force through a viable solution to a problem, or inordinate delays in congressional acceptance of such solutions, because the President lacks the clout to force decisions. These cases are balanced, especially in the foreign policy sphere, by enormous, at times dangerous, presidential authority to lead the nation down paths that the Congress and the nation come to find unacceptable but virtually irreversible.

Then there is the bureaucracy, often called the "fourth" branch of government. (We shall get to the courts, the "third" branch, momentarily.) The President sits uneasily atop an executive pyramid made up of some two and a half million federal civilian employees. Most of these men and women are far more loyal to their own department or agency and/or the programs they are charged with implementing than they are to their remote and transient political superior—and in some cases may be more loyal to their key congressional contacts than to the President. Thus the national bureaucracy is not one integrated mass of public servants, but a jungle of rival bureaucracies, each part of a political subsystem of some sort, and each with the power and incentive to resist any but the most determined efforts at coordination or central direction.

Let us pause at this point and pose again the first question listed at the head of this section. Clearly the prospects that the American system can cope with its vast problems depend on meshing the efforts of President, Congress, and bureaucracy. Each of these has institutional, clientele, and constituency incentives to resist meshing, to insist only on cooperation on its own terms, or to balk entirely. A major attack on the problem of air pollution, for instance, would have first to recommend itself as politically feasible to the President (read *feasible* to mean: likely to win more votes than it will lose, not likely to alienate major campaign donors, and so on). Pressed upon Congress, the antipollution package would again be weighed for its political impact by legislators whose constituencies are quite different from the President's, and who are more vulnerable to local organized interests. If passed, the new policy must either take its chances for implementation in the hands of a line agency staff that also has *its* constituency or be handed to a new (and because new, politically vulnerable) agency.

That these parts of the system, collectively, represent a something-less-than-ideal instrument for solving the problems of truly historic dimensions that face the nation is obvious. All too often, programs that seem to be the essence of common sense and urgently necessary in the national interest will not get through the obstacle course, or if they do, will emerge twisted, and with most of their teeth extracted. The system provides numerous opportunities for special-interest pressure. But, by the same token, it allows offended minorities to challenge ill-advised policies.

Now for the Court. The Supreme Court (and the lower fedreal courts too) represents, as is often said, a supplementary legislative arm as well as an adjudicating mechanism. Characteristically, it has offered a more-or-less independent avenue toward cherished goals for groups, like blacks, who in the past have found the Congress inhospitable and the President unwilling to spend his political capital. The landmark school desegregation decision of 1954 was but one among many instances during the life of the Warren Court when the judiciary made a political decision of incalculable ramifications. In the thirties, the twenties, and earlier, the Court played a similar role, at the other end of the liberal-conservative spectrum, with the captains of industry and finance rather than the NAACP as clients. In short, the judiciary has been a major alternative political resource and safety valve. It may well be that more will be done to solve the water pollution problem by bright young activist lawyers using the courts and the 1899 statute cited earlier, than by the Environmental Protection Agency.

Political parties and interest groups are part of the system, too. Our parties have always been election-winning machines, not creed carriers or policy generators. If parties could be made truly democratic, the reasoning goes, they could also become programmatic and fight campaigns on the basis of programs and ideologies rather than images and slogans. Intraparty democracy would ensure their broad representativeness of public desires and would enable them to wrest from the pressure groups the interest articulation role. Such parties could help the President work his will with Congress (when that will was his party's program), and would enable legislators to resist the policy-distorting pressures of both constituents and organized special interests. But parties resist in part because *their* constituencies too have been intensely pluralistic. Furthermore, our national mythology of classlessness, skepticism of ideology, and militant independence from binding political loyalties means that such reformed parties would probably not be welcomed.

While we are talking about the American mythology (or political culture), there is the vastly important impact of our reverence for decentralized power. The federal system, contrived as an expedient in the beginning, soon came to be clothed in the vestments of constitutional necessity. "States' rights" were at the heart of the liturgy, as was the myth of the town meeting at the local level. The closer to the people government can be kept, the more democratic and responsive it will be. Towns or counties have traditionally resisted state encroachment no less than states have resisted (or at least pretended to resist) federal bureaucracies. Yet in practice, it has almost invariably been the case that social progress, the solving of major problems of public policy, rarely comes until the issue has been bucked or forced up to a higher level of government. Local governments are more resistant and conservative than state governments, and state than federal. It is easier for a remote government with a broad constituency to override special-interest veto power than for a closer government to withstand locally potent pressure. The federal agents in the Department of Health, Education and Welfare could enforce busing when local or even state governments never would be able to.

The mass media do not figure in most accounts of the formal or even the informal parts of the governmental structure, but they are part of the overall political system. Radio first became a potent political force as early as the 1924 presidential campaign when President Calvin Coolidge used the medium to mount the first electronic campaign for the White House. Franklin Roosevelt, of course, raised the political and leadership potency of radio to the nth degree with his superb "fireside chat" style. Television has seemingly had a rather different impact. Its greatest effect seems to be felt via the continuous diet of news it carries to the public, with a vividness and immediacy that radio could never achieve. The half-hour evening network newscasts have become a national institution. The media provide the informational and opinion matrix in which policy problems are viewed and solutions appraised.

Thus the policy-making process, described earlier as centering on Congress, the President, the bureaucracy, and, at times, the Court, must be read against a broader background. The parties influence it far less than one might expect—either in Congress or via the electoral process. Their role is the recruitment of leadership, essentially, and little more. And of course they are not solely responsible for recruitment, as we saw in an earlier chapter in the discussion of the nominating machinery. Interest groups play a considerably more potent policy role.

The Limits of Politics

The American system has both the strengths and the weaknesses of its complex and seemingly indirect, illogical mode of operation. The weaknesses lie, as implied earlier, in the fact that for most major decisions to be made and implemented a series of two or more partially autonomous subsystems must be meshed in cooperative effort. Opponents of the action contemplated can often block cooperation by one or another of these subsystems, thereby short-circuiting the whole policy effort. For this reason, it is often said that the American government stacks the deck in favor of opponents and against proponents of social change.

On the other hand, multiple access can be an advantage to those who want to get government to do something. The most obvious example has already been noted: recourse to the courts on behalf of civil rights causes when Congress and/or the Executive were unresponsive. To some extent the bureaucracy also represents an independent access point. The various levels of government have often provided independent access points both for securing and for blocking action. More often than not, bucking a problem up from the state to the national level has made it possible to bypass intransigence. If the only recourse for blacks in attempting to secure their right to register as voters in the Deep South had been the state authorities, little could have been done. Even the courts, unassisted, could do no more than establish the legal right. Direct intervention by the national government in the actual process of registration was necessary to solve the problem and bypass the local political logjam.

The ultimate question, however, is: How responsive *is* the system in overall terms, in face of the enormously perplexing problems that confront the nation? What *are* the limits of politics in America? It would probably be impossible to design a study that could provide quantitatively verifiable answers to these questions, and certainly no such study exists at the moment. The best that can be done is to offer some rather impressionistic generalizations. And the first generalization probably should be that system effectiveness, like the attractiveness of human beings for one another, is to a considerable extent in the eye of the beholder. Assuming it were desirable to secure a "value-free" measure of the effectiveness of the American system, no such measure could really be contrived on which all would agree. Roughly speaking, the higher the level of dissatisfaction with the present state of national policy, and the greater the sense of urgency about change, the more one is likely to rate the system as ineffective. Even the three authors of this book come to somewhat different appraisals on this basis.

With all this in mind, the best one-sentence evaluation of system effectiveness that we can offer is that, by and large, the system moves more slowly than it should, encounters very serious difficulties in producing problem solutions undistorted by special interests, and may well, at least partially, fail to meet the challenges posed during the next decade. For reasons that have already been suggested the system moves exasperatingly slowly in regard to most policy innovations. And the more potentially disruptive the innovation to the established order, and to the existing pattern of distribution of the loaves and fishes of society, the more booby traps will be strewn in its path. In Lowi's terms (see Chapter 2) redistributive policies are the most disruptive and hence the most politically accident-prone.

One must, however, qualify any sweeping generalization that the American system is always slow moving, because striking exceptions come to mind. There are two especially good examples of the ability of the system to move, on occasion, more swiftly through even its most difficult political process for ratifying a major innovation: the process of constitutional amendment. In this respect, recall the case study relating to the eighteen-year-old vote. Despite the fact that both houses of Congress had to approve the proposed amendment by two-thirds majorities, and that it had to be ratified by three fourths of the states, it found its way into the Constitution in the surprisingly short time of three months and seven days. The other constitutional amendment that exemplifies a similarly major policy shift, and yet was adopted very speedily, within fourteen months, was the Eighteenth, prohibiting the use of alcoholic beverages. (Whatever one's views of the importance of this rather foolish experiment, at the time it was seen as a vastly important social reform.) Repeal of prohibition via the Twenty-first Amendment was accomplished even faster, in about nine months.

On the legislative front, one could cite the speed with which the Poverty Program was put together and passed by Congress (see Chapter 12), or an extreme case: the Emergency Banking Act of 1933, which went through all the legislative stages in just one day! Why, if the system is generally slow to enact major change, can one find this kind of striking exception? The answer seems to be that the system can and often will move quickly when some combination of the following factors is present:

1. The issue (like prohibition) is highly moralistic, to the extent that opponents are intimidated by the difficulties of opposing a righteous cause.
2. Questions of justice and equity of a very obvious sort seem to be the prime considerations (as in the case of the eighteen-year-old vote).
3. There are potentially disruptive political ramifications, but the program or its methods of implementation are so novel and unprecedented that the stakes of prospective opponents are not immediately recognized (the Poverty Program).
4. Crisis or emergency (peacetime or otherwise) can cause America's essentially unideological politics to be suspended for the duration (the Emergency Banking Act, and to a degree, some of the early Johnson Administration enactments passed under the shadow of the Kennedy assassination).

Our generally negative appraisal of system effectiveness raises again the pluralistic quality of the American political system and of the community it serves. That is to say, the impact of organized interests and competing, semiautonomous institutions is almost completely unmitigated by programmatic parties, widely held unifying ideologies, or broad-based self-conscious classes. Such unmediated pluralism is bound to manifest itself in a policy-making system that is incremental, that relies on finding least common denominators rather than logical solutions, and that must wait until enough gears can be meshed by negotiation to allow limited forward motion.

Furthermore, democracy itself, and particularly the American pluralist version, is basically conservative as a form of government. The authors of the *Federalist Papers,* and the framers in general, were said to have feared the mob as a radical force bent, unless checked, on using its majority power to despoil the wealthy minority of their property. However likely this may have been in the late-eighteenth-century America, precisely the reverse is the case today. The unprecedentedly long period of affluence that much of the population—though by no means all—has enjoyed since World War II has given most voters a stake in the status quo. Recall that nearly two thirds of Americans own their own homes. When one sees white backlash, resistance to school busing, taxpayer revolts, waves of unsuccessful bond referenda, resistance to low-income housing in the suburbs, and so forth, one is seeing the conservative aspect of democracy in action.

Seemingly short-sighted or inhumane or even immoral action by the voter may appear to be a perfectly justifiable use of his vote for self-protection from the point of view of the citizen involved. Innovation, especially redistributive innovation, however reasonable, just, and indeed essential it may seem to its supporters, may look quite different to the local voter asked for his ratification. Much of the immobilism of American—or any—democracy stems from this sort of cause. Highly financed and organized vested capitalistic interests are not the only roadblocks on the path toward a better society. Moreover, citizen resistance poses more difficult theoretical if not practical problems. The selfish vested interest can be exposed and condemned, and perhaps thus circumvented. The right of such a selfish minority to veto power is highly questionable in a democratic context. But how does one cope with hostile citizen majorities?

One might hope that education and persuasion would often be the answer. But so simple an answer is not likely to be adequate where divisions are deep-seated and stakes are perceived to be high. The political party mechanism theoretically should be available to solve these kinds of problems of popular support. If, for instance, we had programmatic parties to which voters were loyal, it would be less necessary to cater to every aroused local group. Voters could then be persuaded to put their generalized party support above their special concerns in one policy area. Ideological commitment to a party cause should help to ensure this ordering of voter priorities. (On the other hand, the British Labor Party has lost otherwise loyal voters because of blue-collar hostility to "coloreds.")

Another approach is, as noted earlier, to buck the problem up to a higher level of government. This means either that the voter no longer has a direct voice in the decision (e.g., through a bond referendum to build a new school), but only an indirect voice (through his state legislator) in controlling the state-level agency that now has jurisdiction over the problem. In other words, voter obstruction in the path of reform can, within limits, be circumvented either by dilution or by insulation of the program from it. Current taxpayer concern with rising welfare costs has provoked local and state efforts to institute residency requirements, cut benefits, or force the able-bodied to accept jobs. Many of these expedients have been struck down by the courts on grounds that they violate federal regulations, statutes, or constitutional guarantees. Thus this citizen opposition will have to become so widespread, articulate, and powerful that Congress itself is moved to act and change the rules.

The final recourse in the face of voter intransigence is confrontation politics, or, in the eyes of extreme radicals, revolution. The former tactic, starting with lunch-counter sit-ins has proved very effective. Resisting publics have been either frightened or shamed into accepting change. This tactic always runs the risk, however, that too much induced fear will bring a backlash and generate an issue analogous to "crime in the streets" with all the potential danger to individual rights that such reactions involve.

In short, all that we have been saying in this summary description and evaluation of the American system underscores beyond dispute that structurally decision-making is fragmented, and that there are multiple veto and access points. This pattern matches and doubtless enhances the tendency for the community at large to be similarly pluralistic. There are few policy areas in which a comprehensive "public interest" can be asserted without some group or groups' insisting that their contrary point of view is the true public interest, and the prior assertion is in reality partial, prejudiced, or selfish.

None of this is to say that pluralism as observable fact should be transmuted, as many commentators on the system have in recent years, into a positive value. The fact that we make public policy in an incremental way through a process that is sensitive to the demands of the most vocal and best-financed special interests should hardly be taken as meaning that this is the best way or the only way in which such decisions can be made or should be made. Certainly in theory there are better ways. The real question centers on how the current system can be induced to change.

Alternative Scenarios for the Future

Many feel that change must come, that the present American system is nonviable and hence unstable in the sense that it cannot continue in its present form and mode of operation. Much of the case that such observers make has already been summarized. One of the distinguishing characteristics of current critics is, however, their vagueness about specific cures. Aside from the call for more democratic and ideological parties already discussed, future prognoses and prescriptions seem to follow one or the other of two general lines. Some insist that they see a fascist future for America. This is, of course, not a prescription, but a diagnosis based on despair of salutary change. This group of forecasters is convinced that in fact the system cannot change, cannot cure itself, and that the pressures exerted by the blacks, the urban poor, and the dispossessed generally will eventually provoke such a repressive reaction that the result can only be called fascism.

Presumably the image of the future they would conjure up would include massive police efforts to curb crime, harsh reforms in welfare policies to curb rising tax burdens, bloody repression of all activist leaders and groups among minority groups (blacks especially), the virtual walling off of inner city ghettos to contain their sources of infection and prevent them from spreading into the suburbs, a bowing to the needs of capitalist enterprise through only ineffective efforts to improve the environment and a continuation of high levels of defense expenditure on new weapons systems, and foreign military entanglements as the least difficult means of maintaining economic prosperity.

Prophecy about a nation's future is no more a scientific venture than any other kind of prophecy. For every piece of apparent evidence than can be adduced to show a fascist trend, some other piece of evidence can usually be cited that appears to argue the opposite. For example, police brutality in tracking down and even killing Black Panthers can be balanced against the fact that Panther trials in New Haven, New York, and elsewhere have resulted in far more acquittals than convictions. Or, at a more general level, repeated instances of antiblack backlash and prejudice can in some cases be matched by instances of the election of black mayors in Cleveland, Gary, and Newark. Furthermore, the general blue-collar and lower-middle-class revolt against coddling blacks and welfare recipients seems to be balanced by a liberal trend among upper-middle-class and upper-income Americans.

In short, if fascism does come to America, it will be a rather peculiar version of that pre-World War II aberration. True, German and Italian fascism did draw substantial support from the blue-collar and lower-middle-class segments of society. Yet it is a bit hard to imagine an American version growing up in the face of an increasingly liberal upper-middle-income stratum. It is, after all, these latter who, presumably, are among the chief beneficiaries of the incipient "techno-urban fascism" that Bertram Gross described.[11] In Europe, Germany especially, the coming of fascism was paced by a polarization of the electorate with the upper-income and middle-class voters drifting toward right-wing parties and working-class people toward the left. A contemporary American alliance of blacks, ghetto dwellers, welfare recipients, and portions of the economic elite against the lower-middle class and organized labor is something else again.

Yet, to insist that all forms or aspects of fascism are impossible to imagine in the United States of the 1970's would be foolhardy indeed. Perhaps the best guess that can be made is that the nation *will* generate some forms of heightened repression of groups that become particularly threatening or frustrating. One suspects that such trends will be more in line with past instances of similar behavior than they will be comparable with the European-style fascism. (The very word has become so prevalent as an epithet that it has lost most of the definitional precision it may once have had.) From the Alien and Sedition Acts, through the Know-Nothing era, the Ku Klux Klan of Reconstruction and its revival in the 1920's, and McCarthyite witch-

---

[11] "A New Style Fascism in America?" *Current*, February, 1971, No. 126, pp. 13–25.

hunting, America has had a tradition of periodic repression, or "majority tyranny" as Tocqueville called it. Each time in the past, the pendulum has swung back to a more liberal and tolerant position. True, history teaches no final lessons, but it does create some presumptions of rough continuity and argues against major, sharp discontinuities.

If fascism in any meaningful sense of the term seems to be at worst a problematical and vague possibility, perhaps there is hope for reform. The more sanguine observers, who feel reform is possible, appear to feel that socialism, or in any event planning, is the answer. Democratic socialism, like so many theoretical reforms, is attractive largely for what it promises to replace than for any clear-cut notion of how it would function in practice. Generations of socialists have wanted to replace capitalism and its accompanying private control of the means of production by an owning-and-managing elite, with public ownership and control. But quite aside from the question of whether acceptance could be gained for such a general proposition, there is no thoroughgoing and viable model available upon which American socialism could be patterned.

British nationalization is the most likely model, and an uncertain guide it is. Ailing industries like coal mining undoubtedly benefited, but true planning and industrial rationalization in the public interest came painfully slowly. The workers had merely exchanged one set of masters for another—and often the same people turned up as "bosses" who had been bosses before. The unions took up the battle with the Coal Board where they had left off their age-old battle with the private owners. And Parliament got in the act as a new participant, as pressures were exerted to block the closing of uneconomic pits. The case of steel nationalization—a seriocomic sequence of nationalization, denationalization, renationalization, redenationalization, as Laborites and Tories alternated in office—is hardly one to be emulated, but it was the almost inevitable result of the clash between socialist dogma and the vagaries of democratic politics.

There are, of course, limited versions of public control that might be modeled on European practices of placing public members on corporate boards, or the use of regulatory agencies, but none thus far devised promises the millenium. Actually, it could be argued that the problem is less the formalistic one of where technical ownership is vested than the need for coordinated planning of major sectors of public and private activity in conjunction with one another. Planning and socialism are obviously related, but are not necessarily linked.

One can cite many policy areas in which planning could theoretically bring vast improvement in the texture and rationality of policy outputs—fuels and energy, for one example. If some central authority could allocate functions and markets among electricity, coal, petroleum products, natural gas, and so on, with due regard to which is most efficient for each purpose; to what would represent the most balanced program for resource development or facility construction in relation to each; to the solution of the problems of pollution, economy for the user, and other considerations, the result would have obvious advantages over the present jungle of competition and partial, contradictory regulation. The same could be said of the field of transportation, both intraurban and long-distance, passenger in particular, but the transport of goods as well. But what kind of planning mechanism could possibly be devised that would be able to cope with the enormous concentration of pressures such planning efforts would generate?

The most pressing area for possible planning in the early 1970's is the Gordian knot of problems best typified by chronic inflation. Here some kind of overall planning seems mandatory. Partial planning of sorts exists here too and is causing the most serious disequilibrium, apparently. For example, there is "planning" in the form of managed prices in major sectors of the economy, and planning in the form of generous pay increases won by members of powerful unions. Wages and prices spiral upward, placing elements of the economy that have no such concerted power at a serious disadvantage. Governments have in the recent past encouraged mild inflation —in order to avoid politically unacceptable levels of unemployment—through monetary policies, and, some would allege, by pyramiding new weapons systems or engaging in overseas ventures like Vietnam.

Surely, because partial planning is already involved, the logical answer is to introduce a measure of overall government planning that can mesh or curb the self-interested efforts of economic power blocs into a pattern that is in the general public interest. But logical as this may sound, it is doubtful that we yet have either the economic theory *or* the political technique to make such comprehensive planning workable. Soviet economic planning has been only partially successful over the years where no democratic niceties had to be observed. What hope is there for democratic planning?

Unfortunately the prospects are not encouraging. If America had a highly disciplined two-party system, at least it would be theoretically possible for each party to "plan" during its term in office: that is, mute the contradictory pressures sufficiently to come out with some kind of overall policy rationality. We do not have such parties, however. Furthermore, even the British parties, so often held up as a model, have stood nearly helpless in the face of the thrust and counterthrust of major economic power blocs.

In practice, the price and wage control efforts of World War II are the closest America has come to attempting overall economic planning. And this experience, even in the face of the demands and the unifying impact of total war, was at best minimally successful. Powerful sectors of the economy, like agriculture, labor, and individual industries, were all too often able to bend the rules to their advantage, or insert special provisions to give themselves preferential treatment. The Phase I and Phase II effort at curbing inflation launched by President Nixon in August, 1971, was the first attempt to institute a degree of economic planning in peacetime. Predictably the pluralistic pressures for special consideration built up quickly.

Twist and turn as we might, we may find ourselves stuck over the next couple of decades with a political system that remains very much like the one described in the foregoing chapters. Modest incremental reforms may be just as frustrating to pursue as incremental policy outputs are to tolerate, but that too may be our only choice. Strewn throughout this volume, and especially in this last chapter, are numerous targets for incremental reform, all of which will be difficult to put into effect, modest as they may be, and none of which, nor any combination thereof, will bring the golden age. But each is likely to help a bit, and be worth the effort it takes. The system may still come apart at the seams. But if politics teaches any lesson at all, it teaches that there are no magic formulae and no unconditional guarantees in this uncertain world.

suggested additional readings

Amundsen, Kirsten. *The Silenced Majority: Woman and American Democracy*. Englewood Cliffs, N.J.: Prentice-Hall, Inc., 1971.*

Beyle, Thad L. *Planning and Politics: Uneasy Partnership*. New York: Odyssey Press, 1970.*

Cater, Douglass. *Power in Washington*. New York: Random House, Inc., 1964.*

Commoner, Barry. *The Closing Circle: Nature, Man and Technology*. New York: Alfred A. Knopf, Inc., 1971.

Council on Environmental Quality. *Environmental Quality: The First Annual Report*. Washington, D.C.: U.S. Government Printing Office, 1971.*

———. *Environmental Quality: The Third Annual Report*. Washington, D.C.: U.S. Government Printing Office, 1972.*

Donovan, John C. *The Policy Makers*. New York: Pegasus, 1970.*

Golembiewski, Robert T., et al. *The New Politics*. New York: McGraw-Hill Book Company, 1970.*

Lipsky, Michael (ed.). *Police Encounters*. Chicago: Aldine Atherton, 1970, transaction book #13.*

National Commission on the Causes and Prevention of Violence. *To Establish Justice, to Insure Domestic Tranquility*. Washington, D.C.: U.S. Government Printing Office, 1969.*

Odum, Eugene P., et al. *The Crisis of Survival*. New York: Scott, Foresman and Company, 1970.*

President's Commission on Law Enforcement and the Administration of Justice. *The Challenge of Crime in a Free Society*. Washington, D.C.: U.S. Government Printing Office, 1967.*

Schiller, Herbert I. *Mass Communications and the American Empire*. Boston: Beacon Press, 1971.*

Schur, Edwin M., *Our Criminal Society*. Englewood Cliffs, N.J.: Prentice-Hall, Inc., 1969.*

Wolman, Harold. *Politics of Federal Housing*. New York: Dodd, Mead & Co., 1971.*

* Available in paperback.

APPENDIX
the constitution of the united states of america

Preamble

We the people of the United States, in order to form a more perfect union, establish justice, insure domestic tranquillity, provide for the common defense, promote the general welfare, and secure the blessings of liberty to ourselves and our posterity, do ordain and establish this Constitution for the United States of America.

Article I

Section 1

All legislative powers herein granted shall be vested in a Congress of the United States, which shall consist of a Senate and House of Representatives.

Section 2

(1) The House of Representatives shall be composed of members chosen every second year by the people of the several States, and the electors in each State shall have the qualifications requisite for electors of the most numerous branch of the State legislature.

(2) No person shall be a Representative who shall not have attained to the age of twenty five years, and been seven years a citizen of the United States, and who shall not, when elected, be an inhabitant of the State in which he shall be chosen.

(3) Representatives and direct taxes [1] shall be apportioned among the several States which may be included within this Union, according to their respective numbers, which shall be determined by adding to the whole number of free persons, including those bound to service for a term of years, and excluding Indians not

Adopted September 17, 1787; became effective on March 4, 1789.

[1] Modified as to income taxes by the 16th Amendment.

taxed, three fifths of all other persons.[2] The actual enumeration shall be made within three years after the first meeting of the Congress of the United States, and within every subsequent term of ten years, in such manner as they shall by law direct. The number of Representatives shall not exceed one for every thirty thousand, but each State shall have at least one Representative; and until such enumeration shall be made, the State of New Hampshire shall be entitled to choose three, Massachusetts eight, Rhode Island and Providence Plantations one, Connecticut five, New York six, New Jersey four, Pennsylvania eight, Delaware one, Maryland six, Virginia ten, North Carolina five, South Carolina five, and Georgia three.

(4) When vacancies happen in the representation from any State, the executive authority thereof shall issue writs of election to fill such vacancies.

(5) The House of Representatives shall choose their Speaker and other officers; and shall have the sole power of impeachment.

Section 3

(1) The Senate of the United States shall be composed of two Senators from each State, chosen by the Legislature thereof,[3] for six years; and each Senator shall have one vote.

(2) Immediately after they shall be assembled in consequence of the first election, they shall be divided as equally as may be into three classes. The seats of the Senators of the first class shall be vacated at the expiration of the second year, of the second class at the expiration of the fourth year, and of the third class at the expiration of the sixth year, so that one third may be chosen every second year; and if vacancies happen by resignation, or otherwise, during the recess of the legislature of any State, the executive thereof may make temporary appointments until the next meeting of the legislature, which shall then fill such vacancies.[4]

(3) No person shall be a Senator who shall not have attained to the age of thirty years, and been nine years a citizen of the United States, and who shall not, when elected, be an inhabitant of that State for which he shall be chosen.

(4) The Vice President of the United States shall be president of the Senate, but shall have no vote, unless they be equally divided.

(5) The Senate shall choose their other officers, and also a president pro tempore, in the absence of the Vice President, or when he shall exercise the office of President of the United States.

(6) The Senate shall have the sole power to try all impeachments. When sitting for that purpose, they shall be on oath or affirmation. When the President of the United States is tried, the Chief Justice shall preside: and no person shall be convicted without the concurrence of two thirds of the members present.

(7) Judgment in cases of impeachment shall not extend further than to removal

---

[2] Replaced by the 14th Amendment.
[3] Modified by the 17th Amendment.
[4] Modified by the 17th Amendment.

from office, and disqualification to hold and enjoy any office of honor, trust or profit under the United States: but the party convicted shall nevertheless be liable and subject to indictment, trial, judgment and punishment, according to law.

Section 4

(1) The times, places and manner of holding elections for Senators and Representatives, shall be prescribed in each State by the legislature thereof; but the Congress may at any time by law make or alter such regulations, except as to the places of choosing Senators.

(2) The Congress shall assemble at least once in every year, and such meeting shall be on the first Monday in December, unless they shall by law appoint a different day.[5]

Section 5

(1) Each House shall be the judge of the elections, returns and qualifications of its own members, and a majority of each shall constitute a quorum to do business; but a smaller number may adjourn from day to day, and may be authorized to compel the attendance of absent members, in such manner, and under such penalties as each House may provide.

(2) Each House may determine the rules of its proceedings, punish its members for disorderly behavior, and, with the concurrence of two thirds, expel a member.

(3) Each House shall keep a journal of its proceedings, and from time to time publish the same, excepting such parts as may in their judgment require secrecy; and the yeas and nays of the members of either House on any question shall, at the desire of one fifth of those present, be entered on the journal.

(4) Neither House, during the session of Congress, shall, without the consent of the other, adjourn for more than three days, nor to any other place than that in which the two Houses shall be sitting.

Section 6

(1) The Senators and Representatives shall receive a compensation for their services, to be ascertained by law, and paid out of the Treasury of the United States. They shall in all cases, except treason, felony and breach of the peace, be privileged from arrest during their attendance at the session of their respective Houses, and in going to and returning from the same; and for any speech or debate in either House, they shall not be questioned in any other place.

(2) No Senator or Representative shall, during the time for which he was elected, be appointed to any civil office under the authority of the United States, which shall have been created, or the emoluments whereof shall have been increased during such time; and no person holding any office under the United States, shall be a member of either House during his continuance in office.

[5] Modified by the 20th Amendment.

Section 7

(1) All bills for raising revenue shall originate in the House of Representatives; but the Senate may propose or concur with amendments as on other bills.

(2) Every bill which shall have passed the House of Representatives and the Senate, shall, before it become a law, be presented to the President of the United States; if he approve he shall sign it, but if not he shall return it, with his objections to that House in which it shall have originated, who shall enter the objections at large on their journal, and proceed to reconsider it. If after such reconsideration two thirds of that House shall agree to pass the bill, it shall be sent, together with the objections, to the other House, by which it shall likewise be reconsidered, and if approved by two thirds of that House, it shall become a law. But in all such cases the votes of both Houses shall be determined by yeas and nays, and the names of the persons voting for and against the bill shall be entered on the journal of each House respectively. If any bill shall not be returned by the President within ten days (Sundays excepted) after it shall have been presented to him, the same shall be a law, in like manner as if he had signed it, unless the Congress by their adjournment prevent its return, in which case it shall not be a law.

(3) Every order, resolution, or vote to which the concurrence of the Senate and House of Representatives may be neccessary (except on a question of adjournment) shall be presented to the President of the United States; and before the same shall take effect, shall be approved by him, or being disapproved by him, shall be repassed by two thirds of the Senate and House of Representatives, according to the rules and limitations prescribed in the case of a bill.

Section 8

The Congress shall have power (1) to lay and collect taxes, duties, imposts and excises, to pay the debts and provide for the common defense and general welfare of the United States; but all duties, imposts and excises shall be uniform throughout the United States;

(2) To borrow money on the credit of the United States;

(3) To regulate commerce with foreign nations, and among the several States, and with the Indian tribes;

(4) To establish a uniform rule of naturalization, and uniform laws on the subject of bankruptcies throughout the United States;

(5) To coin money, regulate the value thereof, and a foreign coin, and fix the standard of weights and measures;

(6) To provide for the punishment of counterfeiting the securities and current coin of the United States;

(7) To establish post offices and post roads;

(8) To promote the progress of science and useful arts, by securing for limited times to authors and inventors the exclusive right to their respective writings and discoveries;

(9) To constitute tribunals inferior to the Supreme Court;

(10) To define and punish piracies and felonies committed on the high seas, and offenses against the law of nations;

(11) To declare war, grant letters of marque and reprisal, and make rules concerning captures on land and water;

(12) To raise and support armies, but no appropriation of money to that use shall be for a longer term than two years;

(13) To provide and maintain a navy;

(14) To make rules for the government and regulation of the land and naval forces;

(15) To provide for calling forth the militia to execute the laws of the Union, suppress insurrections and repel invasions;

(16) To provide for organizing, arming, and disciplining the militia, and for governing such part of them as may be employed in the service of the United States, reserving to the States respectively, the appointment of the officers, and the authority of training the militia according to the discipline prescribed by Congress;

(17) To exercise exclusive legislation in all cases whatsoever, over such district (not exceeding ten miles square) as may, by cession of particular States, and the acceptance of Congress, become the seat of the government of the United States, and to exercise like authority over all places purchased by the consent of the legislature of the State in which the same shall be, for the erection of forts, magazines, arsenals, dock-yards, and other needful buildings;—And

(18) To make all laws which shall be necessary and proper for carrying into execution the foregoing powers, and all other powers vested by this Constitution in the government of the United States, or in any department or officer thereof.

Section 9

(1) The migration or importance of such persons as any of the States now existing shall think proper to admit, shall not be prohibited by the Congress prior to the year one thousand eight hundred and eight, but a tax or duty may be imposed on such importation, not exceeding ten dollars for each person.

(2) The privilege of the writ of habeas corpus shall not be suspended, unless when in cases of rebellion or invasion the public safety may require it.

(3) No bill of attainder or ex post facto law shall be passed.

(4) No capitation, or other direct, tax shall be laid, unless in proportion to the census or enumeration herein before directed to be taken.[6]

(5) No tax or duty shall be laid on articles exported from any State.

(6) No preference shall be given by any regulation of commerce or revenue to the ports of one State over those of another: nor shall vessels bound to, or from, one State, be obliged to enter, clear, or pay duties in another.

(7) No money shall be drawn from the Treasury, but in consequence of appropriations made by law; and a regular statement and account of the receipts and expenditures of all public money shall be published from time to time.

---

[6] Modified by the 16th Amendment.

(8) No title of nobility shall be granted by the United States: And no person holding any office of profit or trust under them, shall, without the consent of the Congress, accept of any present, emolument, office, or title, of any kind whatever, from any king, prince, or foreign State.

Section 10

(1) No State shall enter into any treaty, alliance, or confederation; grant letters of marque and reprisal; coin money; emit bills of credit; make anything but gold and silver coin a tender in payment of debts; pass any bill of attainder, ex post facto law, or law impairing the obligation of contracts, or grant any title of nobility.

(2) No State shall, without the consent of the Congress, lay any imposts or duties on imports or exports, except what may be absolutely necessary for executing its inspection laws: and the net produce of all duties and imposts, laid by any State on imports or exports, shall be for the use of the Treasury of the United States; and all such laws shall be subject to the revision and control of the Congress.

(3) No State shall, without the consent of Congress, lay any duty of tonnage, keep troops, or ships of war in time of peace, enter into any agreement or compact with another State, or with a foreign power, or engage in war, unless actually invaded, or in such imminent danger as will not admit of delay.

Article II

Section 1

(1) The executive power shall be vested in a President of the United States of America. He shall hold his office during the term of four years,[7] and, together with the Vice President, chosen for the same term, be elected, as follows:

(2) Each State shall appoint, in such manner as the legislature thereof may direct, a number of electors, equal to the whole number of Senators and Representatives to which the State may be entitled in the Congress: but no Senator or Representative, or person holding an office of trust or profit under the United States, shall be appointed an elector.

The electors shall meet in their respective States,[8] and vote by ballot for two persons, of whom one at least shall not be an inhabitant of the same State with themselves. And they shall make a list of all the persons voted for, and of the number of votes for each; which list they shall sign and certify, and transmit sealed to the seat of the government of the United States, directed to the president of the Senate. The president of the Senate shall, in the presence of the Senate and House of Representatives, open all the certificates, and the votes shall then be counted. The person having the greatest number of votes shall be the President, if such number be a majority of the whole number of electors appointed; and if there be more than one who have such majority, and have an equal number of votes, then the House of Representatives

---

[7] Qualified, as to length of service, by the 22nd Amendment.

[8] The 12th Amendment (1804) superseded the provisions of this paragraph, and the 12th Amendment is modified by the 20th.

shall immediately choose by ballot one of them for President; and if no person have a majority, then from the five highest on the list the said House shall in like manner choose the President. But in choosing the President, the votes shall be taken by States, the representation from each State having one vote; a quorum for this purpose shall consist of a member or members from two thirds of the States, and a majority of all the States shall be necessary to a choice. In every case, after the choice of the President, the person having the greatest number of votes of the electors shall be the Vice President. But if there should remain two or more who have equal votes, the Senate shall choose from them by ballot the Vice President.

(3) The Congress may determine the time of choosing the electors, and the day on which they shall give their votes; which day shall be the same throughout the United States.

(4) No person except a natural born citizen, or a citizen of the United States, at the time of the adoption of this Constitution, shall be eligible to the office of President; neither shall any person be eligible to that office who shall not have attained to the age of thirty five years, and been fourteen years a resident within the United States.

(5) In case of the removal of the President from office,[9] or of his death, resignation, or inability to discharge the powers and duties of the said office, the same shall devolve on the Vice President, and the Congress may by law provide for the case of removal, death, resignation or inability, both of the President and Vice President, declaring what officer shall then act as President, and such officer shall act accordingly, until the disability be removed, or a President shall be elected.

(6) The President shall, at stated times, receive for his services, a compensation, which shall neither be increased nor diminished during the period for which he shall have been elected, and he shall not receive within that period any other emolument from the United States, or any of them.

(7) Before he enter on the execution of his office, he shall take the following oath or affirmation:—"I do solemnly swear (or affirm) that I will faithfully execute the office of President of the United States, and will to the best of my ability, preserve, protect and defend the Constitution of the United States."

Section 2

(1) The President shall be commander in chief of the army and navy of the United States, and of the militia of the several States, when called into the actual service of the United States; he may require the opinion, in writing, of the principal officer in each of the executive departments, upon any subject relating to the duties of their respective offices, and he shall have power to grant reprieves and pardons for offenses against the United States, except in cases of impeachment.

(2) He shall have power, by and with the advice and consent of the Senate, to make treaties, provided two thirds of the Senators present concur; and he shall nominate, and by and with the advice and consent of the Senate, shall appoint ambassadors, other public ministers and consuls, judges of the Supreme Court, and all

---

[9] The provisions of this paragraph are clarified by the 25th Amendment.

other officers of the United States, whose appointments are not herein otherwise provided for, and which shall be established by law: but the Congress may by law vest the appointment of such inferior officers, as they think proper, in the President alone, in the courts of law, or in the heads of departments.

(3) The President shall have power to fill up all vacancies that may happen during the recess of the Senate, by granting commissions which shall expire at the end of their next session.

Section 3

He shall from time to time give to the Congress information of the state of the Union, and recommend to their consideration such measures as he shall judge necessary and expedient; he may, on extraordinary occasions, convene both Houses, or either of them, and in case of disagreement between them, with respect to the time of adjournment, he may adjourn them to such time as he shall think proper; he shall receive ambassadors and other public ministers; he shall take care that the laws be faithfully executed, and shall commission all the officers of the United States.

Section 4

The President, Vice President and all civil officers of the United States, shall be removed from office on impeachment for, and conviction of, treason, bribery, or other high crimes and misdemeanors.

Article III

Section 1

The judicial power of the United States, shall be vested in one Supreme Court, and in such inferior courts as the Congress may from time to time ordain and establish. The judges, both of the Supreme and inferior courts, shall hold their offices during good behavior, and shall, at stated times, receive for their services, a compensation, which shall not be diminished during their continuance in office.

Section 2

(1) The judicial power shall extend to all cases, in law and equity, arising under this Constitution, the laws of the United States, and treaties made, or which shall be made, under their authority;—to all cases affecting ambassadors, other public ministers and consuls;—to all cases of admiralty and maritime jurisdiction;—to controversies to which the United States shall be a party;—to controversies between two or more States;—between a State and citizens of another State; [10]—between citizens of different States;—between citizens of the same State claiming lands under grants of different States, and between a State, or the citizens thereof, and foreign States, citizens or subjects.

(2) In all cases affecting ambassadors, other public ministers and consuls, and those in which a State shall be party, the Supreme Court shall have original juris-

[10] Changed by the 11th Amendment.

diction. In all the other cases before mentioned, the Supreme Court shall have appellate jurisdiction, both as to law and fact, with such exceptions, and under such regulations as the Congress shall make.

(3) The trial of all crimes, except in cases of impeachment, shall be by jury; and such trial shall be held in the State where the said crimes shall have been committed; but when not committed within any State, the trial shall be at such place or places as the Congress may by law have directed.

Section 3

(1) Treason against the United States, shall consist only in levying war against them, or in adhering to their enemies, giving them aid and comfort. No person shall be convicted of treason unless on the testimony of two witnesses to the same overt act, or on confession in open court.

(2) The Congress shall have power to declare the punishment of treason, but no attainder of treason shall work corruption of blood, or forfeiture except during the life of the person attainted.

Article IV

Section 1

Full faith and credit shall be given in each State to the public acts, records, and judicial proceedings of every other State. And the Congress may by general laws prescribe the manner in which such acts, records and proceedings shall be proved, and the effect thereof.

Section 2

(1) The citizens of each State shall be entitled to all privileges and immunities of citizens in the several States.

(2) A person charged in any State with treason, felony, or other crime, who shall flee from justice, and be found in another State, shall on demand of the executive authority of the State from which he fled, be delivered up, to be removed to the State having jurisdiction of the crime.

(3) No person held to service or labor in one State, under the laws thereof, escaping into another, shall, in consequence of any law or regulation therein, be discharged from such service or labor, but shall be delivered up on claim of the party to whom such service or labor may be due.[11]

Section 3

(1) New States may be admitted by the Congress into this Union; but no new State shall be formed or erected within the jurisdiction of any other State; nor any State be formed by the junction of two or more States, or parts of States, without the consent of the legislatures of the States concerned as well as of the Congress.

[11] Superseded by the 13th Amendment.

(2) The Congress shall have power to dispose of and make all needful rules and regulations respecting the territory or other property belonging to the United States; and nothing in this Constitution shall be so construed as to prejudice any claims of the United States, or of any particular State.

Section 4

The United States shall guarantee to every State in this Union a republican form of government, and shall protect each of them against invasion; and on application of the legislature, or of the executive (when the legislature cannot be convened) against domestic violence.

Article V

The Congress, whenever two thirds of both Houses shall deem it necessary, shall propose amendments to this Constitution, or, on the application of the legislatures of two thirds of the several States, shall call a convention for proposing amendments, which, in either case, shall be valid to all intents and purposes, as part of this Constitution, when ratified by the legislatures of three fourths of the several States, or by conventions in three fourths thereof, as the one or the other mode of ratification may be proposed by the Congress; Provided that no amendment which may be made prior to the year one thousand eight hundred and eight shall in any manner affect the first and fourth clauses in the ninth section of the first article; and that no State, without its consent, shall be deprived of its equal suffrage in the Senate.

Article VI

Section 1

All debts contracted and engagements entered into, before the adoption of this Constitution, shall be as valid against the United States under this Constitution, as under the Confederation.

Section 2

This Constitution, and the laws of the United States which shall be made in pursuance thereof; and all treaties made, or which shall be made, under the authority of the United States, shall be the supreme law of the land; and the judges in every State shall be bound thereby, anything in the constitution or laws of any State to the contrary notwithstanding.

Section 3

The Senators and Representatives before mentioned, and the members of the several State legislatures, and all executive and judicial officers, both of the United States and of the several States, shall be bound by oath or affirmation, to support this Constitution; but no religious test shall ever be required as a qualification to any office or public trust under the United States.

Article VII

The ratification of the conventions of nine States, shall be sufficient for the establishment of this Constitution between the States so ratifying the same.

Done in Convention by the unanimous consent of the States present the seventeenth day of September in the year of our Lord one thousand seven hundred and eighty-seven, and of the independence of the United States of America the twelfth. In witness whereof we have hereunto subscribed our names.

GO. WASHINGTON
Presidt. and Deputy from Virginia

Articles in addition to and amendment of the Constitution of the United States of America, proposed by Congress, and ratified by the legislatures of the several States, pursuant to the fifth article of the original Constitution.

Article 1 [12]

Congress shall make no law respecting an establishment of religion, or prohibiting the free exercise thereof; or abridging the freedom of speech, or of the press; or the right of the people peaceably to assemble, and to petition the government for a redress of grievances.

Article II

A well regulated militia, being necessary to the security of a free State, the right of the people to keep and bear arms, shall not be infringed.

Article III

No soldier shall, in time of peace be quartered in any house, without the consent of the owner, nor in time of war, but in a manner to be prescribed by law.

Article IV

The right of the people to be secure in their persons, houses, papers, and effects, against unreasonable searches and seizures, shall not be violated, and no warrants shall issue, but upon probable cause, supported by oath or affirmation, and particularly describing the place to be searched, and the persons or things to be seized.

[12] Amendments I–X were adopted in 1791.

Article V

No person shall be held to answer for a capital, or otherwise infamous crime, unless on a presentment or indictment of a grand jury, except in cases arising in the land or naval forces, or in the militia, when in actual service in time of war or public danger; nor shall any person be subject for the same offense to be twice put in jeopardy of life or limb; nor shall be compelled in any criminal case to be a witness against himself, nor be deprived of life, liberty, or property, without due process of law; nor shall private property be taken for public use, without just compensation.

Article VI

In all criminal prosecutions, the accused shall enjoy the right to a speedy and public trial, by an impartial jury of the State and district wherein the crime shall have been committed, which district shall have been previously ascertained by law, and to be informed of the nature and cause of the accusation; to be confronted with the witnesses against him; to have compulsory process for obtaining witnesses in his favor, and to have the assistance of counsel for his defense.

Article VII

In suits at common law, where the value in controversy shall exceed twenty dollars, the right of trial by jury shall be preserved, and no fact tried by a jury, shall be otherwise re-examined in any court of the United States, than according to the rules of the common law.

Article VIII

Excessive bail shall not be required, nor excessive fines imposed, nor cruel and unusual punishments inflicted.

Article IX

The enumeration in the Constitution, of certain rights, shall not be construed to deny or disparage others retained by the people.

Article X

The powers not delegated to the United States by the Constitution, nor prohibited by it to the States, are reserved to the States respectively, or to the people.

Article XI [13]

The judicial power of the United States shall not be construed to extend to any suit in law or equity, commenced or prosecuted against one of the United States by citizens of another State, or by citizens or subjects of any foreign State.

[13] Adopted in 1798.

Article XII [14]

The electors shall meet in their respective States and vote by ballot for President and Vice-President, one of whom, at least, shall not be an inhabitant of the same State with themselves; they shall name in their ballots the person voted for as President, and in distinct ballots the person voted for as Vice-President, and they shall make distinct lists of all persons voted for as President, and of all persons voted for as Vice-President, and of the number of votes for each, which lists they shall sign and certify, and transmit sealed to the seat of the government of the United States, directed to the president of the Senate;—The president of the Senate shall, in the presence of the Senate and House of Representatives, open all the certificates and the votes shall then be counted;—The person having the greatest number of votes for President, shall be the President, if such number be a majority of the whole number of electors appointed; and if no person have such majority, then from the persons having the highest numbers not exceeding three on the list of those voted for as President, the House of Representatives shall choose immediately, by ballot, the President. But in choosing the President, the votes shall be taken by States, the representation from each State having one vote; a quorum for this purpose shall consist of a member or members from two-thirds of the States, and a majority of all the States shall be necessary to a choice. And if the House of Representatives shall not choose a President whenever the right of choice shall devolve upon them, before the fourth day of March next following,[15] then the Vice-President shall act as President, as in the case of the death or other constitutional disability of the President.—The person having the greatest number of votes as Vice-President, shall be the Vice-President, if such number be a majority of the whole number of electors appointed, and if no person have a majority, then from the two highest numbers on the list, the Senate shall choose the Vice-President; a quorum for the purpose shall consist of two-thirds of the whole number of Senators, and a majority of the whole number shall be necessary to a choice. But no person constitutionally ineligible to the office of President shall be eligible to that of Vice-President of the United States.

Article XIII [16]

Section 1

Neither slavery nor involuntary servitude, except as a punishment for crime whereof the party shall have been duly convicted, shall exist within the United States, or any place subject to their jurisdiction.

Section 2

Congress shall have power to enforce this article by appropriate legislation.

[14] Adopted in 1804.
[15] Modified by the 20th Amendment.
[16] Adopted in 1865.

Article XIV [17]

Section 1

All persons born or naturalized in the United States, and subject to the jurisdiction thereof, are citizens of the United States and of the State wherein they reside. No State shall make or enforce any law which shall abridge the privileges or immunities of citizens of the United States; nor shall any State deprive any person of life, liberty, or property, without due process of law; nor deny to any person within its jurisdiction the equal protection of the laws.

Section 2

Representatives shall be apportioned among the several States according to their respective numbers, counting the whole number of persons in each State, excluding Indians not taxed. But when the right to vote at any election for the choice of electors for President and Vice President of the United States, Representatives in Congress, the executive and judicial officers of a State, or the members of the legislature thereof, is denied to any of the male inhabitants of such State, being twenty-one years of age, and citizens of the United States, or in any way abridged, except for participation in rebellion, or other crime, the basis of representation therein shall to reduced in the proportion which the number of such male citizens shall bear to the whole number of male citizens twenty-one years of age in such State.

Section 3

No person shall be a Senator or Representative in Congress, or elector of President and Vice President, or hold any office, civil or military, under the United States, or under any State, who, having previously taken an oath, as a member of Congress, or as an officer of the United States, or as a member of any State legislature, or as an executive or judicial officer of any State, to support the Constitution of the United States, shall have engaged in insurrection or rebellion against the same, or given aid or comfort to the enemies thereof. But Congress may by a vote of two-thirds of each House, remove such disability.

Section 4

The validity of the public debt of the United States, authorized by law, including debts incurred for payment of pensions and bounties for services in suppressing insurrection or rebellion, shall not be questioned. But neither the United States nor any State shall assume or pay any debt or obligation incurred in aid of insurrection or rebellion against the United States, or any claim for the loss or emancipation of any slave; but all such debts, obligations and claims shall be held illegal and void.

Section 5

The Congress shall have power to enforce, by appropriate legislation, the provisions of this article.

[17] Adopted in 1868.

Article XV [18]

Section 1

The right of citizens of the United States to vote shall not be denied or abridged by the United States or by any State on account of race, color, or previous condition of servitude.

Section 2

The Congress shall have power to enforce this article by appropriate legislation.

Article XVI [19]

The Congress shall have power to lay and collect taxes on incomes, from whatever source derived, without apportionment among the several States, and without regard to any census or enumeration.

Article XVII [20]

The Senate of the United States shall be composed of two Senators from each State, elected by the people thereof, for six years; and each Senator shall have one vote. The electors in each State shall have the qualifications requisite for electors of the most numerous branch of the State legislatures.

When vacancies happen in the representation of any State in the Senate, the executive authority of such State shall issue writs of election to fill such vacancies: *Provided,* That the legislature of any State may empower the executive thereof to make temporary appointments until the people fill the vacancies by election as the legislature may direct.

This amendment shall not be so construed as to affect the election or term of any Senator chosen before it becomes valid as part of the Constitution.

Article XVIII [21]

Section 1

After one year from the ratification of this article the manufacture, sale, or transportation of intoxicating liquors within, the importation thereof into, or the exportation thereof from the United States and all territory subject to the jurisdiction thereof for beverage purposes is hereby prohibited.

Section 2

The Congress and the several States shall have concurrent power to enforce this article by appropriate legislation.

[18] Adopted in 1870.
[19] Adopted in 1913.
[20] Adopted in 1913.
[21] Adopted in 1919. Repealed by Article XXI.

Section 3

This article shall be inoperative unless it shall have been ratified as an amendment to the Constitution by the legislatures of the several States, as provided in the Constitution, within seven years from the date of the submission hereof to the States by the Congress.

Article XIX [22]

The right of citizens of the United States to vote shall not be denied or abridged by the United States or by any State on account of sex.

The Congress shall have power to enforce this article by appropriate legislation.

Article XX [23]

Section 1

The terms of the President and Vice President shall end at noon on the 20th day of January, and the terms of Senators and Representatives at noon on the 3d day of January, of the years in which such terms would have ended if this article had not been ratified; and the terms of their successors shall then begin.

Section 2

The Congress shall assemble at least once in every year, and such meeting shall begin at noon on the 3d day of January, unless they shall by law appoint a different day.

Section 3

If, at the time fixed for the beginning of the term of the President, the President-elect shall have died, the Vice President-elect shall become President. If a President shall not have been chosen before the time fixed for the beginning of his term, or if the President-elect shall have failed to qualify, then the Vice President-elect shall act as President until a President shall have qualified; and the Congress may by law provide for the case wherein neither a President-elect nor a Vice President-elect shall have qualified, declaring who shall then act as President, or the manner in which one who is to act shall be selected, and such person shall act accordingly until a President or Vice President shall have qualified.

Section 4

The Congress may by law provide for the case of the death of any of the persons from whom the House of Representatives may choose a President whenever the right of choice shall have devolved upon them, and for the case of the death of any

[22] Adopted in 1920.
[23] Adopted in 1933.

of the persons from whom the Senate may choose a Vice President whenever the right of choice shall have devolved upon them.

Section 5

Sections 1 and 2 shall take effect on the 15th day of October following the ratification of this article.

Section 6

This article shall be inoperative unless it shall have been ratified as an amendment to the Constitution by the legislatures of three-fourths of the several States within seven years from the date of its submission.

Article XXI [24]

Section 1

The Eighteenth Article of Amendment to the Constitution of the United States is hereby repealed.

Section 2

The transportation or importation into any State, Territory or possession of the United States for delivery or use therein of intoxicating liquors, in violation of the laws thereof, is hereby prohibited.

Section 3

This article shall be inoperative unless it shall have been ratified as an amendment to the Constitution by conventions in the several States, as provided in the Constitution, within seven years from the date of the submission hereof to the States by the Congress.

Article XXII [25]

Section 1

No person shall be elected to the office of the President more than twice, and no person who has held the office of President, or acted as President, for more than two years of a term to which some other person was elected President shall be elected to the office of the President more than once. But this Article shall not apply to any person holding the office of President when this Article was proposed by the Congress, and shall not prevent any person who may be holding the office of President, or acting as President, during the term within which this Article becomes operative from holding the office of President or acting as President during the remainder of such term.

[24] Adopted in 1933.
[25] Adopted in 1951.

Section 2

This Article shall be inoperative unless it shall have been ratified as an amendment to the Constitution by the legislatures of three-fourths of the several States within seven years from the date of its submission to the States by the Congress.

Article XXIII [26]

Section 1

The District constituting the seat of Government of the United States shall appoint in such manner as the Congress may direct:

A number of electors of President and Vice President equal to the whole number of Senators and Representatives in Congress to which the District would be entitled if it were a State, but in no event more than the least populous State; they shall be in addition to those appointed by the States, but they shall be considered, for the purposes of the election of President and Vice President, to be electors appointed by a State; and they shall meet in the District and perform such duties as provided by the twelfth article of amendment.

Section 2

The Congress shall have power to enforce this article by appropriate legislation.

Article XXIV [27]

Section 1

The right of citizens of the United States to vote in any primary or other election for President or Vice President, for electors for President or Vice President, or for Senator or Representative in Congress, shall not be denied or abridged by the United States or any State by reason of failure to pay any poll tax or other tax.

Section 2

The Congress shall have power to enforce this article by appropriate legislation.

Article XXV [28]

Section 1

In case of the removal of the President from office or of his death or resignation, the Vice President shall become President.

[26] Adopted in 1961.
[27] Adopted in 1964.
[28] Adopted in 1967.

Section 2

Whenever there is a vacancy in the office of the Vice President, the President shall nominate a Vice President who shall take office upon confirmation by a majority vote of both Houses of Congress.

Section 3

Whenever the President transmits to the president pro tempore of the Senate and the Speaker of the House of Representatives his written declaration that he is unable to discharge the powers and duties of his office, and until he transmits to them a written declaration to the contrary, such powers and duties shall be discharged by the Vice President as Acting President.

Section 4

Whenever the Vice President and a majority of either the principal officers of the executive departments or of such other body as Congress may by law provide, transmit to the president pro tempore of the Senate and the Speaker of the House of Representatives their written declaration that the President is unable to discharge the powers and duties of his office, the Vice President shall immediately assume the powers and duties of the office as Acting President.

Thereafter, when the President transmits to the president pro tempore of the Senate and the Speaker of the House of Representatives his written declaration that no inability exists, he shall resume the powers and duties of his office unless the Vice President and a majority of either the principal officers of the executive department or of such other body as Congress may by law provide, transmit within four days to the president pro tempore of the Senate and the Speaker of the House of Representatives their written declaration that the President is unable to discharge the powers and duties of his office. Thereupon Congress shall decide the issue, assembling within forty-eight hours for that purpose if not in session. If the Congress, within twenty-one days after receipt of the latter written declaration, or, if Congress is not in session, within twenty-one days after Congress is required to assemble, determines by two-thirds vote of both Houses that the President is unable to discharge the powers and duties of his office, the Vice President shall continue to discharge the same as Acting President; otherwise, the President shall resume the powers and duties of his office.

Article XXVI [29]

Section 1

The right of citizens of the United States, who are eighteen years of age or older,

[29] Adopted in 1971.

to vote shall not be denied or abridged by the United States or by any State on account of age.

Section 2

The Congress shall have power to enforce this article by appropriate legislation.

Article XXVII [30]

Section 1

Equality of rights under the law shall not be denied or abridged by the United States or by any State on account of sex.

Section 2

The Congress shall have the power to enforce, by appropriate legislation, the provisions of this article.

Section 3

This amendment shall take effect two years after the date of ratification.

---

[30] Proposed to the states in 1972 and ratified by twenty-two states within that year; thirty-eight states must ratify if the Equal Rights Amendment is to become part of the Constitution.

INDEX